Systems Performance

Second Edition

Systems Performance

Enterprise and the Cloud

Second Edition

Brendan Gregg

♦Addison-Wesley

Boston • Columbus • New York • San Francisco • Amsterdam • Cape Town
Dubai • London • Madrid • Milan • Munich • Paris • Montreal • Toronto • Delhi • Mexico City
São Paulo • Sydney • Hong Kong • Seoul • Singapore • Taipei • Tokyo

Many of the designations used by manufacturers and sellers to distinguish their products are claimed as trademarks. Where those designations appear in this book, and the publisher was aware of a trademark claim, the designations have been printed with initial capital letters or in all capitals.

The author and publisher have taken care in the preparation of this book, but make no expressed or implied warranty of any kind and assume no responsibility for errors or omissions. No liability is assumed for incidental or consequential damages in connection with or arising out of the use of the information or programs contained herein.

For information about buying this title in bulk quantities, or for special sales opportunities (which may include electronic versions; custom cover designs; and content particular to your business, training goals, marketing focus, or branding interests), please contact our corporate sales department at corpsales@pearsoned.com or (800) 382-3419.

For government sales inquiries, please contact governmentsales@pearsoned.com.

For questions about sales outside the U.S., please contact intlcs@pearson.com.

Visit us on the Web: informit.com/aw

Library of Congress Control Number: 2020944455

Cover images by Brendan Gregg
Page 9, Figure 1.5: Screenshot of System metrics GUI (Grafana) © 2020 Grafana Labs
Page 84, Figure 2.32: Screenshot of Firefox timeline chart © Netflix
Page 164, Figure 4.7: Screenshot of sar(1) sadf(1) SVG output © 2010 W3C
Page 560, Figure 10.12: Screenshot of Wireshark screenshot © Wireshark
Page 740, Figure 14.3: Screenshot of KernelShark © KernelShark

ISBN-13: 978-0-13-682015-4
ISBN-10: 0-13-682015-8

1018 2024

Publisher
Mark L. Taub

Executive Editor
Greg Doench

Managing Producer
Sandra Schroeder

Sr. Content Producer
Julie B. Nahil

Project Manager
Rachel Paul

Copy Editor
Kim Wimpsett

Indexer
Ted Laux

Proofreader
Rachel Paul

Compositor
The CIP Group

For Deirdré Straughan,
an amazing person in technology,
and an amazing person—we did it.

Contents at a Glance

Contents

Preface

"There are known knowns; there are things we know we know. We also know there are known unknowns; that is to say we know there are some things we do not know. But there are also unknown unknowns—there are things we do not know we don't know."

—U.S. Secretary of Defense Donald Rumsfeld, February 12, 2002

While the previous statement was met with chuckles from those attending the press briefing, it summarizes an important principle that is as relevant in complex technical systems as it is in geopolitics: performance issues can originate from anywhere, including areas of the system that you know nothing about and you are therefore not checking (the unknown unknowns). This book may reveal many of these areas, while providing methodologies and tools for their analysis.

About This Edition

I wrote the first edition eight years ago and designed it to have a long shelf life. Chapters are structured to first cover durable skills (models, architecture, and methodologies) and then faster-changing skills (tools and tuning) as example implementations. While the example tools and tuning will go out of date, the durable skills show you how to stay updated.

There has been a large addition to Linux in the past eight years: Extended BPF, a kernel technology that powers a new generation of performance analysis tools, which is used by companies including Netflix and Facebook. I have included a BPF chapter and BPF tools in this new edition, and I have also published a deeper reference on the topic [Gregg 19]. The Linux perf and Ftrace tools have also seen many developments, and I have added separate chapters for them as well. The Linux kernel has gained many performance features and technologies, also covered. The hypervisors that drive cloud computing virtual machines, and container technologies, have also changed considerably; that content has been updated.

The first edition covered both Linux and Solaris equally. Solaris market share has shrunk considerably in the meantime [ITJobsWatch 20], so the Solaris content has been largely removed from this edition, making room for more Linux content to be included. However, your understanding of an operating system or kernel can be enhanced by considering an alternative, for perspective. For that reason, some mentions of Solaris and other operating systems are included in this edition.

For the past six years I have been a senior performance engineer at Netflix, applying the field of systems performance to the Netflix microservices environment. I've worked on the performance of hypervisors, containers, runtimes, kernels, databases, and applications. I've developed new methodologies and tools as needed, and worked with experts in cloud performance and Linux kernel engineering. These experiences have contributed to improving this edition.

About This Book

Welcome to *Systems Performance: Enterprise and the Cloud*, 2nd Edition! This book is about the performance of operating systems and of applications from the operating system context, and it is written for both enterprise server and cloud computing environments. Much of the material in this book can also aid your analysis of client devices and desktop operating systems. My aim is to help you get the most out of your systems, whatever they are.

When working with application software that is under constant development, you may be tempted to think of operating system performance—where the kernel has been developed and tuned for decades—as a solved problem. It isn't! The operating system is a complex body of software, managing a variety of ever-changing physical devices with new and different application workloads. The kernels are also in constant development, with features being added to improve the performance of particular workloads, and newly encountered bottlenecks being removed as systems continue to scale. Kernel changes such as the mitigations for the Meltdown vulnerability that were introduced in 2018 can also hurt performance. Analyzing and working to improve the performance of the operating system is an ongoing task that should lead to continual performance improvements. Application performance can also be analyzed from the operating system context to find more clues that might be missed using application-specific tools alone; I'll cover that here as well.

Operating System Coverage

The main focus of this book is the study of systems performance, using Linux-based operating systems on Intel processors as the primary example. The content is structured to help you study other kernels and processors as well.

Unless otherwise noted, the specific Linux distribution is not important in the examples used. The examples are mostly from the Ubuntu distribution and, when necessary, notes are included to explain differences for other distributions. The examples are also taken from a variety of system types: bare metal and virtualized, production and test, servers and client devices.

Across my career I've worked with a variety of different operating systems and kernels, and this has deepened my understanding of their design. To deepen your understanding as well, this book includes some mentions of Unix, BSD, Solaris, and Windows.

Other Content

Example screenshots from performance tools are included, not just for the data shown, but also to illustrate the types of data available. The tools often present the data in intuitive and self-explanatory ways, many in the familiar style of earlier Unix tools. This means that screenshots can be a powerful way to convey the purpose of these tools, some requiring little additional description. (If a tool does require laborious explanation, that may be a failure of design!)

Where it provides useful insight to deepen your understanding, I touch upon the history of certain technologies. It is also useful to learn a bit about the key people in this industry: you're likely to come across them or their work in performance and other contexts. A "who's who" list has been provided in Appendix E.

A handful of topics in this book were also covered in my prior book, *BPF Performance Tools* [Gregg 19]: in particular, BPF, BCC, bpftrace, tracepoints, kprobes, uprobes, and various BPF-based tools. You can refer to that book for more information. The summaries of these topics in this book are often based on that earlier book, and sometimes use the same text and examples.

What Isn't Covered

This book focuses on performance. To undertake all the example tasks given will require, at times, some system administration activities, including the installation or compilation of software (which is not covered here).

The content also summarizes operating system internals, which are covered in more detail in separate dedicated texts. Advanced performance analysis topics are summarized so that you are aware of their existence and can study them as needed from additional sources. See the Supplemental Material section at the end of this Preface.

How This Book Is Structured

Chapter 1, Introduction, is an introduction to systems performance analysis, summarizing key concepts and providing examples of performance activities.

Chapter 2, Methodologies, provides the background for performance analysis and tuning, including terminology, concepts, models, methodologies for observation and experimentation, capacity planning, analysis, and statistics.

Chapter 3, Operating Systems, summarizes kernel internals for the performance analyst. This is necessary background for interpreting and understanding what the operating system is doing.

Chapter 4, Observability Tools, introduces the types of system observability tools available, and the interfaces and frameworks upon which they are built.

Chapter 5, Applications, discusses application performance topics and observing them from the operating system.

Chapter 6, CPUs, covers processors, cores, hardware threads, CPU caches, CPU interconnects, device interconnects, and kernel scheduling.

Chapter 7, Memory, is about virtual memory, paging, swapping, memory architectures, buses, address spaces, and allocators.

Chapter 8, File Systems, is about file system I/O performance, including the different caches involved.

Chapter 9, Disks, covers storage devices, disk I/O workloads, storage controllers, RAID, and the kernel I/O subsystem.

Chapter 10, Network, is about network protocols, sockets, interfaces, and physical connections.

Chapter 11, Cloud Computing, introduces operating system– and hardware-based virtualization methods in common use for cloud computing, along with their performance overhead, isolation, and observability characteristics. This chapter covers hypervisors and containers.

Chapter 12, Benchmarking, shows how to benchmark accurately, and how to interpret others' benchmark results. This is a surprisingly tricky topic, and this chapter shows how you can avoid common mistakes and try to make sense of it.

Chapter 13, perf, summarizes the standard Linux profiler, perf(1), and its many capabilities. This is a reference to support perf(1)'s use throughout the book.

Chapter 14, Ftrace, summarizes the standard Linux tracer, Ftrace, which is especially suited for exploring kernel code execution.

Chapter 15, BPF, summarizes the standard BPF front ends: BCC and bpftrace.

Chapter 16, Case Study, contains a systems performance case study from Netflix, showing how a production performance puzzle was analyzed from beginning to end.

Chapters 1 to 4 provide essential background. After reading them, you can reference the remainder of the book as needed, in particular Chapters 5 to 12, which cover specific targets for analysis. Chapters 13 to 15 cover advanced profiling and tracing, and are optional reading for those who wish to learn one or more tracers in more detail.

Chapter 16 uses a storytelling approach to paint a bigger picture of a performance engineer's work. If you're new to performance analysis, you might want to read this first as an example of performance analysis using a variety of different tools, and then return to it when you've read the other chapters.

As a Future Reference

This book has been written to provide value for many years, by focusing on background and methodologies for the systems performance analyst.

To support this, many chapters have been separated into two parts. The first part consists of terms, concepts, and methodologies (often with those headings), which should stay relevant many years from now. The second provides examples of how the first part is implemented: architecture, analysis tools, and tunables, which, while they will become out-of-date, will still be useful as examples.

Tracing Examples

We frequently need to explore the operating system in depth, which can be done using tracing tools.

Since the first edition of this book, extended BPF has been developed and merged into the Linux kernel, powering a new generation of tracing tools that use the BCC and bpftrace front ends. This book focuses on BCC and bpftrace, and also the Linux kernel's built-in Ftrace tracer. BPF, BCC, and bpftrace, are covered in more depth in my prior book [Gregg 19].

Linux perf is also included in this book and is another tool that can do tracing. However, perf is usually included in chapters for its sampling and PMC analysis capabilities, rather than for tracing.

You may need or wish to use different tracing tools, which is fine. The tracing tools in this book are used to show the questions that you can ask of the system. It is often these questions, and the methodologies that pose them, that are the most difficult to know.

Intended Audience

The intended audience for this book is primarily systems administrators and operators of enterprise and cloud computing environments. It is also a reference for developers, database administrators, and web server administrators who need to understand operating system and application performance.

As a performance engineer at a company with a large compute environment (Netflix), I frequently work with SREs (site reliability engineers) and developers who are under enormous time pressure to solve multiple simultaneous performance issues. I have also been on the Netflix CORE SRE on-call rotation and have experienced this pressure firsthand. For many people, performance is not their primary job, and they need to know just enough to solve the current issues. Knowing that your time may be limited has encouraged me to keep this book as short as possible, and structure it to facilitate jumping ahead to specific chapters.

Another intended audience is students: this book is also suitable as a supporting text for a systems performance course. I have taught these classes before and learned which types of material work best in leading students to solve performance problems; that has guided my choice of content for this book.

Whether or not you are a student, the chapter exercises give you an opportunity to review and apply the material. These include some optional advanced exercises, which you are not expected to solve. (They may be impossible; they should at least be thought-provoking.)

In terms of company size, this book should contain enough detail to satisfy environments from small to large, including those with dozens of dedicated performance staff. For many smaller companies, the book may serve as a reference when needed, with only some portions of it used day to day.

Typographic Conventions

The following typographical conventions are used throughout this book:

Example	Description
netif_receive_skb()	Function name
iostat(1)	A command referenced by chapter 1 of its man page
read(2)	A system call referenced by its man page
malloc(3)	A C library function call referenced by its man page
vmstat(8)	An administration command referenced by its man page
Documentation/...	Linux documentation in the Linux kernel source tree
kernel/...	Linux kernel source code
fs/...	Linux kernel source code, file systems
CONFIG_...	Linux kernel configuration option (Kconfig)
r_await	Command line input and output

Example	Description
`mpstat 1`	Highlighting of a typed command or key detail
`#`	Superuser (root) shell prompt
`$`	User (non-root) shell prompt
`^C`	A command was interrupted (Ctrl-C)
`[...]`	Truncation

Supplemental Material, References, and Bibliography

References are listed are at the end of each chapter rather than in a single bibliography, allowing you to browse references related to each chapter's topic. The following selected texts can also be referenced for further background on operating systems and performance analysis:

[Jain 91] Jain, R., *The Art of Computer Systems Performance Analysis: Techniques for Experimental Design, Measurement, Simulation, and Modeling*, Wiley, 1991.

[Vahalia 96] Vahalia, U., *UNIX Internals: The New Frontiers*, Prentice Hall, 1996.

[Cockcroft 98] Cockcroft, A., and Pettit, R., *Sun Performance and Tuning: Java and the Internet*, Prentice Hall, 1998.

[Musumeci 02] Musumeci, G. D., and Loukides, M., *System Performance Tuning*, 2nd Edition, O'Reilly, 2002.

[Bovet 05] Bovet, D., and Cesati, M., *Understanding the Linux Kernel*, 3rd Edition, O'Reilly, 2005.

[McDougall 06a] McDougall, R., Mauro, J., and Gregg, B., *Solaris Performance and Tools: DTrace and MDB Techniques for Solaris 10 and OpenSolaris*, Prentice Hall, 2006.

[Gove 07] Gove, D., *Solaris Application Programming*, Prentice Hall, 2007.

[Love 10] Love, R., *Linux Kernel Development*, 3rd Edition, Addison-Wesley, 2010.

[Gregg 11a] Gregg, B., and Mauro, J., *DTrace: Dynamic Tracing in Oracle Solaris, Mac OS X and FreeBSD*, Prentice Hall, 2011.

[Gregg 13a] Gregg, B., *Systems Performance: Enterprise and the Cloud*, Prentice Hall, 2013 (first edition).

[Gregg 19] Gregg, B., *BPF Performance Tools: Linux System and Application Observability*, Addison-Wesley, 2019.

[ITJobsWatch 20] ITJobsWatch, "Solaris Jobs," https://www.itjobswatch.co.uk/jobs/uk/solaris.do#demand_trend, accessed 2020.

Acknowledgments

Thanks to all those who bought the first edition, especially those who made it recommended or required reading at their companies. Your support for the first edition has led to the creation of this second edition. Thank you.

This is the latest book on systems performance, but not the first. I'd like to thank prior authors for their work, work that I have built upon and referenced in this text. In particular I'd like to thank Adrian Cockcroft, Jim Mauro, Richard McDougall, Mike Loukides, and Raj Jain. As they have helped me, I hope to help you.

I'm grateful for everyone who provided feedback on this edition:

Deirdré Straughan has again supported me in various ways throughout this book, including using her years of experience in technical copy editing to improve every page. The words you read are from both of us. We enjoy not just spending time together (we are married now), but also working together. Thank you.

Philipp Marek is an IT forensics specialist, IT architect, and performance engineer at the Austrian Federal Computing Center. He provided early technical feedback on every topic in this book (an amazing feat) and even spotted problems in the first edition text. Philipp started programming in 1983 on a 6502, and has been looking for additional CPU cycles ever since. Thanks, Philipp, for your expertise and relentless work.

Dale Hamel (Shopify) also reviewed every chapter, providing important insights for various cloud technologies, and another consistent point of view across the entire book. Thanks for taking this on, Dale—right after helping with the BPF book!

Daniel Borkmann (Isovalent) provided deep technical feedback for a number of chapters, especially the networking chapter, helping me to better understand the complexities and technologies involved. Daniel is a Linux kernel maintainer with years of experience working on the kernel network stack and extended BPF. Thank you, Daniel, for the expertise and rigor.

I'm especially thankful that perf maintainer Arnaldo Carvalho de Melo (Red Hat) helped with Chapter 13, perf; and Ftrace creator Steven Rostedt (VMware) helped with Chapter 14, Ftrace, two topics that I had not covered well enough in the first edition. Apart from their help with this book, I also appreciate their excellent work on these advanced performance tools, tools that I've used to solve countless production issues at Netflix.

It has been a pleasure to have Dominic Kay pick through several chapters and find even more ways to improve their readability and technical accuracy. Dominic also helped with the first edition (and before that, was my colleague at Sun Microsystems working on performance). Thank you, Dominic.

My current performance colleague at Netflix, Amer Ather, provided excellent feedback on several chapters. Amer is a go-to engineer for understanding complex technologies. Zachary Jones (Verizon) also provided feedback for complex topics, and shared his performance expertise to improve the book. Thank you, Amer and Zachary.

A number of reviewers took on multiple chapters and engaged in discussion on specific topics: Alejandro Proaño (Amazon), Bikash Sharma (Facebook), Cory Lueninghoener (Los Alamos

National Laboratory), Greg Dunn (Amazon), John Arrasjid (Ottometric), Justin Garrison (Amazon), Michael Hausenblas (Amazon), and Patrick Cable (Threat Stack). Thanks, all, for your technical help and enthusiasm for the book.

Also thanks to Aditya Sarwade (Facebook), Andrew Gallatin (Netflix), Bas Smit, George Neville-Neil (JUUL Labs), Jens Axboe (Facebook), Joel Fernandes (Google), Randall Stewart (Netflix), Stephane Eranian (Google), and Toke Høiland-Jørgensen (Red Hat), for answering questions and timely technical feedback.

The contributors to my earlier book, *BPF Performance Tools*, have indirectly helped, as some material in this edition is based on that earlier book. That material was improved thanks to Alastair Robertson (Yellowbrick Data), Alexei Starovoitov (Facebook), Daniel Borkmann, Jason Koch (Netflix), Mary Marchini (Netflix), Masami Hiramatsu (Linaro), Mathieu Desnoyers (EfficiOS), Yonghong Song (Facebook), and more. See that book for the full acknowledgments.

This second edition builds upon the work in the first edition. The acknowledgments from the first edition thanked the many people who supported and contributed to that work; in summary, across multiple chapters I had technical feedback from Adam Leventhal, Carlos Cardenas, Darryl Gove, Dominic Kay, Jerry Jelinek, Jim Mauro, Max Bruning, Richard Lowe, and Robert Mustacchi. I also had feedback and support from Adrian Cockcroft, Bryan Cantrill, Dan McDonald, David Pacheco, Keith Wesolowski, Marsell Kukuljevic-Pearce, and Paul Eggleton. Roch Bourbonnais and Richard McDougall helped indirectly as I learned so much from their prior performance engineering work, and Jason Hoffman helped behind the scenes to make the first edition possible.

The Linux kernel is complicated and ever-changing, and I appreciate the stellar work by Jonathan Corbet and Jake Edge of lwn.net for summarizing so many deep topics. Many of their articles are referenced in this book.

A special thanks to Greg Doench, executive editor at Pearson, for his help, encouragement, and flexibility in making this process more efficient than ever. Thanks to content producer Julie Nahil (Pearson) and project manager Rachel Paul, for their attention to detail and help in delivering a quality book. Thanks to copy editor Kim Wimpsett for the working through another one of my lengthy and deeply technical books, finding many ways to improve the text.

And thanks, Mitchell, for your patience and understanding.

Since the first edition, I've continued to work as a performance engineer, debugging issues everywhere in the stack, from applications to metal. I now have many new experiences with performance tuning hypervisors, analyzing runtimes including the JVM, using tracers including Ftrace and BPF in production, and coping with the fast pace of changes in the Netflix microservices environment and the Linux kernel. So much of this is not well documented, and it had been daunting to consider what I needed to do for this edition. But I like a challenge.

About the Author

Brendan Gregg is an industry expert in computing performance and cloud computing. He is a senior performance architect at Netflix, where he does performance design, evaluation, analysis, and tuning. The author of multiple technical books, including *BPF Performance Tools*, he received the USENIX LISA Award for Outstanding Achievement in System Administration. He has also been a kernel engineer, performance lead, and professional technical trainer, and was program co-chair for the USENIX LISA 2018 conference. He has created performance tools included in multiple operating systems, along with visualizations and methodologies for performance analysis, including flame graphs.

Chapter 1

Introduction

Computer performance is an exciting, varied, and challenging discipline. This chapter introduces you to the field of systems performance. The learning objectives of this chapter are:

- Understand systems performance, roles, activities, and challenges.

- Understand the difference between observability and experimental tools.

- Develop a basic understanding of performance observability: statistics, profiling, flame graphs, tracing, static instrumentation, and dynamic instrumentation.

- Learn the role of methodologies and the Linux 60-second checklist.

References to later chapters are included so that this works as an introduction both to systems performance and to this book. This chapter finishes with case studies to show how systems performance works in practice.

1.1   Systems Performance

Systems performance studies the performance of an entire computer system, including all major software and hardware components. Anything in the data path, from storage devices to application software, is included, because it can affect performance. For distributed systems this means multiple servers and applications. If you don't have a diagram of your environment showing the data path, find one or draw it yourself; this will help you understand the relationships between components and ensure that you don't overlook entire areas.

The typical goals of systems performance are to improve the end-user experience by reducing latency and to reduce computing cost. Reducing cost can be achieved by eliminating inefficiencies, improving system throughput, and general tuning.

Figure 1.1 shows a generic system software stack on a single server, including the operating system (OS) kernel, with example database and application tiers. The term *full stack* is sometimes used to describe only the application environment, including databases, applications, and web servers. When speaking of systems performance, however, we use *full stack* to mean the entire software stack from the application down to metal (the hardware), including system libraries, the kernel, and the hardware itself. Systems performance studies the full stack.

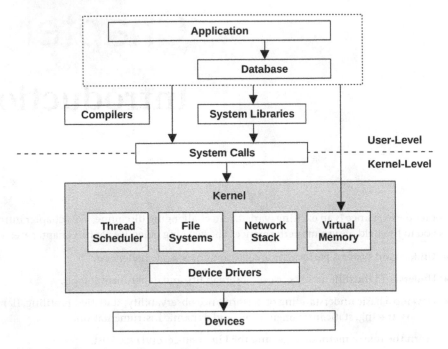

Figure 1.1   Generic system software stack

Compilers are included in Figure 1.1 because they play a role in systems performance. This stack is discussed in Chapter 3, Operating Systems, and investigated in more detail in later chapters. The following sections describe systems performance in more detail.

1.2   Roles

Systems performance is done by a variety of job roles, including system administrators, site reliability engineers, application developers, network engineers, database administrators, web administrators, and other support staff. For many of these roles, performance is only part of the job, and performance analysis focuses on that role's area of responsibility: the network team checks the network, the database team checks the database, and so on. For some performance issues, finding the root cause or contributing factors requires a cooperative effort from more than one team.

Some companies employ *performance engineers*, whose primary activity is performance. They can work with multiple teams to perform a holistic study of the environment, an approach that may be vital in resolving complex performance issues. They can also act as a central resource to find and develop better tooling for performance analysis and capacity planning across the whole environment.

For example, Netflix has a cloud performance team, of which I am a member. We assist the microservice and SRE teams with performance analysis and build performance tools for everyone to use.

Companies that hire multiple performance engineers can allow individuals to specialize in one or more areas, providing deeper levels of support. For example, a large performance engineering team may include specialists in kernel performance, client performance, language performance (e.g., Java), runtime performance (e.g., the JVM), performance tooling, and more.

1.3 Activities

Systems performance involves a variety of activities. The following is a list of activities that are also ideal steps in the life cycle of a software project from conception through development to production deployment. Methodologies and tools to help perform these activities are covered in this book.

1. Setting performance objectives and performance modeling for a future product.
2. Performance characterization of prototype software and hardware.
3. Performance analysis of in-development products in a test environment.
4. Non-regression testing for new product versions.
5. Benchmarking product releases.
6. Proof-of-concept testing in the target production environment.
7. Performance tuning in production.
8. Monitoring of running production software.
9. Performance analysis of production issues.
10. Incident reviews for production issues.
11. Performance tool development to enhance production analysis.

Steps 1 to 5 comprise traditional product development, whether for a product sold to customers or a company-internal service. The product is then launched, perhaps first with proof-of-concept testing in the target environment (customer or local), or it may go straight to deployment and configuration. If an issue is encountered in the target environment (steps 6 to 9), it means that the issue was not detected or fixed during the development stages.

Performance engineering should ideally begin before any hardware is chosen or software is written: the first step should be to set objectives and create a performance model. However, products are often developed without this step, deferring performance engineering work to a later time, after a problem arises. With each step of the development process it can become progressively harder to fix performance issues that arise due to architectural decisions made earlier.

Cloud computing provides new techniques for proof-of-concept testing (step 6) that encourage skipping the earlier steps (steps 1 to 5). One such technique is testing new software on a single instance with a fraction of the production workload: this is known as *canary testing*. Another technique makes this a normal step in software deployment: traffic is gradually moved to a new pool of instances while leaving the old pool online as a backup; this is known as *blue-green deployment.*[1] With such safe-to-fail options available, new software is often tested in production without any prior performance analysis, and quickly reverted if need be. I recommend that, when practical, you also perform the earlier activities so that the best performance can be achieved (although there may be time-to-market reasons for moving to production sooner).

The term *capacity planning* can refer to a number of the preceding activities. During design, it includes studying the resource footprint of development software to see how well the design can meet the target needs. After deployment, it includes monitoring resource usage to predict problems before they occur.

The performance analysis of production issues (step 9) may also involve site reliability engineers (SREs); this step is followed by incident review meetings (step 10) to analyze what happened, share debugging techniques, and look for ways to avoid the same incident in the future. Such meetings are similar to developer *retrospectives* (see [Corry 20] for retrospectives and their anti-patterns).

Environments and activities vary from company to company and product to product, and in many cases not all ten steps are performed. Your job may also focus on only some or just one of these activities.

1.4 Perspectives

Apart from a focus on different activities, performance roles can be viewed from different perspectives. Two perspectives for performance analysis are labeled in Figure 1.2: *workload analysis* and *resource analysis*, which approach the software stack from different directions.

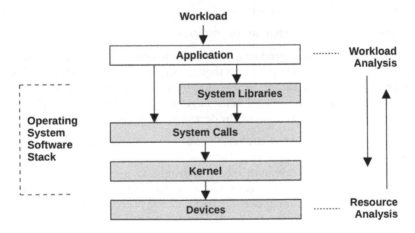

Figure 1.2   Analysis perspectives

The resource analysis perspective is commonly employed by system administrators, who are responsible for the system resources. Application developers, who are responsible for the

---

[1] Netflix uses the terminology *red-black deployments*.

delivered performance of the workload, commonly focus on the workload analysis perspective. Each perspective has its own strengths, discussed in detail in Chapter 2, Methodologies. For challenging issues, it helps to try analyzing from both perspectives.

1.5 Performance Is Challenging

Systems performance engineering is a challenging field for a number of reasons, including that it is subjective, it is complex, there may not be a single root cause, and it often involves multiple issues.

1.5.1 Subjectivity

Technology disciplines tend to be *objective*, so much so that people in the industry are known for seeing things in black and white. This can be true of software troubleshooting, where a bug is either present or absent and is either fixed or not fixed. Such bugs often manifest as error messages that can be easily interpreted and understood to mean the presence of an error.

Performance, on the other hand, is often *subjective*. With performance issues, it can be unclear whether there is an issue to begin with, and if so, when it has been fixed. What may be considered "bad" performance for one user, and therefore an issue, may be considered "good" performance for another.

Consider the following information:

The average disk I/O response time is 1 ms.

Is this "good" or "bad"? While response time, or latency, is one of the best metrics available, interpreting latency information is difficult. To some degree, whether a given metric is "good" or "bad" may depend on the performance expectations of the application developers and end users.

Subjective performance can be made objective by defining clear goals, such as having a target average response time, or requiring a percentage of requests to fall within a certain latency range. Other ways to deal with this subjectivity are introduced in Chapter 2, Methodologies, including latency analysis.

1.5.2 Complexity

In addition to subjectivity, performance can be a challenging discipline due to the complexity of systems and the lack of an obvious starting point for analysis. In cloud computing environments you may not even know which server instance to look at first. Sometimes we begin with a hypothesis, such as blaming the network or a database, and the performance analyst must figure out if this is the right direction.

Performance issues may also originate from complex interactions between subsystems that perform well when analyzed in isolation. This can occur due to a *cascading failure*, when one failed component causes performance issues in others. To understand the resulting issue, you must untangle the relationships between components and understand how they contribute.

Bottlenecks can also be complex and related in unexpected ways; fixing one may simply move the bottleneck elsewhere in the system, with overall performance not improving as much as hoped.

Apart from the complexity of the system, performance issues may also be caused by a complex characteristic of the production workload. These cases may never be reproducible in a lab environment, or only intermittently so.

Solving complex performance issues often requires a holistic approach. The whole system—both its internals and its external interactions—may need to be investigated. This requires a wide range of skills, and can make performance engineering a varied and intellectually challenging line of work.

Different methodologies can be used to guide us through these complexities, as introduced in Chapter 2; Chapters 6 to 10 include specific methodologies for specific system resources: CPUs, Memory, File Systems, Disks, and Network. (The analysis of complex systems in general, including oil spills and the collapse of financial systems, has been studied by [Dekker 18].)

In some cases, a performance issue can be caused by the interaction of these resources.

1.5.3 Multiple Causes

Some performance issues do not have a single root cause, but instead have multiple contributing factors. Imagine a scenario where three normal events occur simultaneously and combine to cause a performance issue: each is a normal event that in isolation is not the root cause.

Apart from multiple causes, there can also be multiple performance issues.

1.5.4 Multiple Performance Issues

Finding *a* performance issue is usually not the problem; in complex software there are often many. To illustrate this, try finding the bug database for your operating system or applications and search for the word *performance*. You might be surprised! Typically, there will be a number of performance issues that are known but not yet fixed, even in mature software that is considered to have high performance. This poses yet another difficulty when analyzing performance: the real task isn't finding an issue; it's identifying which issue or issues matter *the most*.

To do this, the performance analyst must *quantify* the magnitude of issues. Some performance issues may not apply to your workload, or may apply only to a very small degree. Ideally, you will not just quantify the issues but also estimate the potential speedup to be gained for each one. This information can be valuable when management looks for justification for spending engineering or operations resources.

A metric well suited to performance quantification, when available, is *latency*.

1.6 Latency

Latency is a measure of time spent waiting, and is an essential performance metric. Used broadly, it can mean the time for any operation to complete, such as an application request, a database query, a file system operation, and so forth. For example, latency can express the time for a website to load completely, from link click to screen paint. This is an important metric for both the customer and the website provider: high latency can cause frustration, and customers may take their business elsewhere.

As a metric, latency can allow maximum speedup to be estimated. For example, Figure 1.3 depicts a database query that takes 100 ms (which is the latency) during which it spends 80 ms blocked waiting for disk reads. The maximum performance improvement by eliminating disk reads (e.g., by caching) can be calculated: from 100 ms to 20 ms (100 – 80) is five times (5x) faster. This is the estimated *speedup*, and the calculation has also quantified the performance issue: disk reads are causing the query to run up to 5x more slowly.

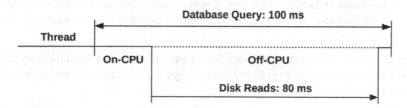

Figure 1.3   Disk I/O latency example

Such a calculation is not possible when using other metrics. I/O operations per second (IOPS), for example, depend on the type of I/O and are often not directly comparable. If a change were to reduce the IOPS rate by 80%, it is difficult to know what the performance impact would be. There might be 5x fewer IOPS, but what if each of these I/O increased in size (bytes) by 10x?

Latency can also be ambiguous without qualifying terms. For example, in networking, latency can mean the time for a connection to be established but not the data transfer time; or it can mean the total duration of a connection, including the data transfer (e.g., DNS latency is commonly measured this way). Throughout this book I will use clarifying terms where possible: those examples would be better described as *connection* latency and *request* latency. Latency terminology is also summarized at the beginning of each chapter.

While latency is a useful metric, it hasn't always been available when and where needed. Some system areas provide average latency only; some provide no latency measurements at all. With the availability of new BPF[2]-based observability tools, latency can now be measured from custom arbitrary points of interest and can provide data showing the full distribution of latency.

1.7   Observability

Observability refers to understanding a system through observation, and classifies the tools that accomplish this. This includes tools that use counters, profiling, and tracing. It does not include benchmark tools, which modify the state of the system by performing a workload *experiment*. For production environments, observability tools should be tried first wherever possible, as experimental tools may perturb production workloads through resource contention. For test environments that are idle, you may wish to begin with benchmarking tools to determine hardware performance.

---

[2] BPF is now a name and no longer an acronym (originally Berkeley Packet Filter).

In this section I'll introduce counters, metrics, profiling, and tracing. I'll explain observability in more detail in Chapter 4, covering system-wide versus per-process observability, Linux observability tools, and their internals. Chapters 5 to 11 include chapter-specific sections on observability, for example, Section 6.6 for CPU observability tools.

1.7.1   Counters, Statistics, and Metrics

Applications and the kernel typically provide data on their state and activity: operation counts, byte counts, latency measurements, resource utilization, and error rates. They are typically implemented as integer variables called *counters* that are hard-coded in the software, some of which are cumulative and always increment. These cumulative counters can be read at different times by performance tools for calculating *statistics*: the rate of change over time, the average, percentiles, etc.

For example, the vmstat(8) utility prints a system-wide summary of virtual memory statistics and more, based on kernel counters in the /proc file system. This example vmstat(8) output is from a 48-CPU production API server:

```
$ vmstat 1 5
procs -----------memory---------- ---swap-- -----io---- -system-- ------cpu-----
 r  b   swpd   free   buff  cache   si   so    bi    bo   in   cs us sy id wa st
19  0      0 6531592  42656 1672040    0    0     1     7   21    33 51  4 46  0  0
26  0      0 6533412  42656 1672064    0    0     0     0 81262 188942 54  4 43  0  0
62  0      0 6533856  42656 1672088    0    0     0     8 80865 180514 53  4 43  0  0
34  0      0 6532972  42656 1672088    0    0     0     0 81250 180651 53  4 43  0  0
31  0      0 6534876  42656 1672088    0    0     0     0 74389 168210 46  3 51  0  0
```

This shows a system-wide CPU utilization of around 57% (cpu us + sy columns). The columns are explained in detail in Chapters 6 and 7.

A *metric* is a statistic that has been selected to evaluate or monitor a target. Most companies use monitoring agents to record selected statistics (metrics) at regular intervals, and chart them in a graphical interface to see changes over time. Monitoring software can also support creating custom *alerts* from these metrics, such as sending emails to notify staff when problems are detected.

This hierarchy from counters to alerts is depicted in Figure 1.4. Figure 1.4 is provided as a guide to help you understand these terms, but their use in the industry is not rigid. The terms *counters*, *statistics*, and *metrics* are often used interchangeably. Also, alerts may be generated by any layer, and not just a dedicated alerting system.

As an example of graphing metrics, Figure 1.5 is a screenshot of a Grafana-based tool observing the same server as the earlier vmstat(8) output.

These line graphs are useful for capacity planning, helping you predict when resources will become exhausted.

Your interpretation of performance statistics will improve with an understanding of how they are calculated. Statistics, including averages, distributions, modes, and outliers, are summarized in Chapter 2, Methodologies, Section 2.8, Statistics.

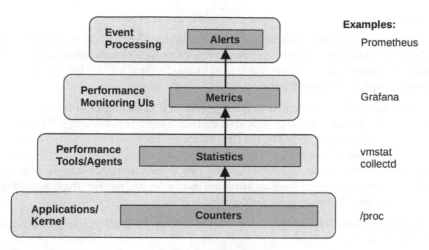

Figure 1.4   Performance instrumentation terminology

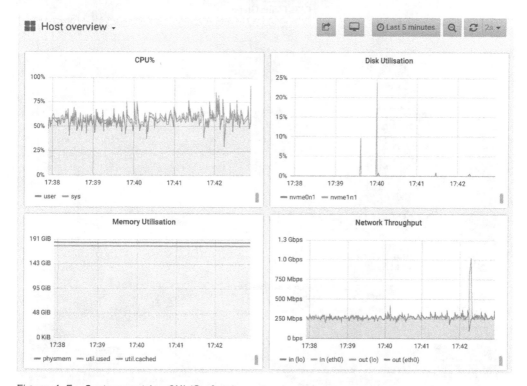

Figure 1.5   System metrics GUI (Grafana)

Sometimes, time-series metrics are all that is needed to resolve a performance issue. Knowing the exact time a problem began may correlate with a known software or configuration change, which can be reverted. Other times, metrics only point in a direction, suggesting that there is a CPU or disk issue, but without explaining why. Profiling or tracing tools are necessary to dig deeper and find the cause.

1.7.2 Profiling

In systems performance, the term *profiling* usually refers to the use of tools that perform sampling: taking a subset (a sample) of measurements to paint a coarse picture of the target. CPUs are a common profiling target. The commonly used method to profile CPUs involves taking timed-interval samples of the on-CPU code paths.

An effective visualization of CPU profiles is *flame graphs*. CPU flame graphs can help you find more performance wins than any other tool, after metrics. They reveal not only CPU issues, but other types of issues as well, found by the CPU footprints they leave behind. Issues of lock contention can be found by looking for CPU time in spin paths; memory issues can be analyzed by finding excessive CPU time in memory allocation functions (malloc()), along with the code paths that led to them; performance issues involving misconfigured networking may be discovered by seeing CPU time in slow or legacy codepaths; and so on.

Figure 1.6 is an example CPU flame graph showing the CPU cycles spent by the iperf(1) network micro-benchmark tool.

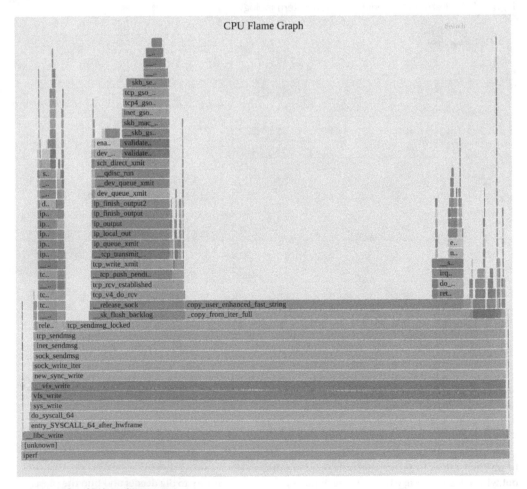

Figure 1.6   CPU profiling using flame graphs

This flame graph shows how much CPU time is spent copying bytes (the path that ends in copy_user_enhanced_fast_string()) versus TCP transmission (the tower on the left that includes tcp_write_xmit()). The widths are proportional to the CPU time spent, and the vertical axis shows the code path.

Profilers are explained in Chapters 4, 5, and 6, and the flame graph visualization is explained in Chapter 6, CPUs, Section 6.7.3, Flame Graphs.

1.7.3 Tracing

Tracing is event-based recording, where event data is captured and saved for later analysis or consumed on-the-fly for custom summaries and other actions. There are special-purpose tracing tools for system calls (e.g., Linux strace(1)) and network packets (e.g., Linux tcpdump(8)); and general-purpose tracing tools that can analyze the execution of all software and hardware events (e.g., Linux Ftrace, BCC, and bpftrace). These all-seeing tracers use a variety of event sources, in particular, static and dynamic instrumentation, and BPF for programmability.

Static Instrumentation

Static instrumentation describes hard-coded software instrumentation points added to the source code. There are hundreds of these points in the Linux kernel that instrument disk I/O, scheduler events, system calls, and more. The Linux technology for kernel static instrumentation is called *tracepoints*. There is also a static instrumentation technology for user-space software called *user statically defined tracing* (USDT). USDT is used by libraries (e.g., libc) for instrumenting library calls and by many applications for instrumenting service requests.

As an example tool that uses static instrumentation, execsnoop(8) prints new processes created while it is tracing (running) by instrumenting a tracepoint for the execve(2) system call. The following shows execsnoop(8) tracing an SSH login:

```
# execsnoop
PCOMM          PID    PPID   RET ARGS
ssh            30656  20063    0 /usr/bin/ssh 0
sshd           30657   1401    0 /usr/sbin/sshd -D -R
sh             30660  30657    0
env            30661  30660    0 /usr/bin/env -i PATH=/usr/local/sbin:/usr/local...
run-parts      30661  30660    0 /bin/run-parts --lsbsysinit /etc/update-motd.d
00-header      30662  30661    0 /etc/update-motd.d/00-header
uname          30663  30662    0 /bin/uname -o
uname          30664  30662    0 /bin/uname -r
uname          30665  30662    0 /bin/uname -m
10-help-text   30666  30661    0 /etc/update-motd.d/10-help-text
50-motd-news   30667  30661    0 /etc/update-motd.d/50-motd-news
cat            30668  30667    0 /bin/cat /var/cache/motd-news
cut            30671  30667    0 /usr/bin/cut -c -80
tr             30670  30667    0 /usr/bin/tr -d \000-\011\013\014\016-\037
head           30669  30667    0 /usr/bin/head -n 10
```

```
80-esm          30672  30661     0 /etc/update-motd.d/80-esm
lsb_release     30673  30672     0 /usr/bin/lsb_release -cs
[...]
```

This is especially useful for revealing short-lived processes that may be missed by other observability tools such as top(1). These short-lived processes can be a source of performance issues.

See Chapter 4 for more information about tracepoints and USDT probes.

Dynamic Instrumentation

Dynamic instrumentation creates instrumentation points after the software is running, by modifying in-memory instructions to insert instrumentation routines. This is similar to how debuggers can insert a breakpoint on any function in running software. Debuggers pass execution flow to an interactive debugger when the breakpoint is hit, whereas dynamic instrumentation runs a routine and then continues the target software. This capability allows custom performance statistics to be created from any running software. Issues that were previously impossible or prohibitively difficult to solve due to a lack of observability can now be fixed.

Dynamic instrumentation is so different from traditional observation that it can be difficult, at first, to grasp its role. Consider an operating system kernel: analyzing kernel internals can be like venturing into a dark room, with candles (system counters) placed where the kernel engineers thought they were needed. Dynamic instrumentation is like having a flashlight that you can point anywhere.

Dynamic instrumentation was first created in the 1990s [Hollingsworth 94], along with tools that use it called *dynamic tracers* (e.g., kerninst [Tamches 99]). For Linux, dynamic instrumentation was first developed in 2000 [Kleen 08] and began merging into the kernel in 2004 (kprobes). However, these technologies were not well known and were difficult to use. This changed when Sun Microsystems launched their own version in 2005, DTrace, which was easy to use and production-safe. I developed many DTrace-based tools that showed how important it was for systems performance, tools that saw widespread use and helped make DTrace and dynamic instrumentation well-known.

BPF

BPF, which originally stood for Berkeley Packet Filter, is powering the latest dynamic tracing tools for Linux. BPF originated as a mini in-kernel virtual machine for speeding up the execution of tcpdump(8) expressions. Since 2013 it has been extended (hence is sometimes called eBPF[3]) to become a generic in-kernel execution environment, one that provides safety and fast access to resources. Among its many new uses are tracing tools, where it provides programmability for the BPF Compiler Collection (BCC) and bpftrace front ends. execsnoop(8), shown earlier, is a BCC tool.[4]

---

[3] eBPF was initially used to describe this extended BPF; however, the technology is now referred to as just BPF.

[4] I first developed it for DTrace, and I have since developed it for other tracers including BCC and bpftrace.

Chapter 3 explains BPF, and Chapter 15 introduces the BPF tracing front ends: BCC and bpf-trace. Other chapters introduce many BPF-based tracing tools in their observability sections; for example, CPU tracing tools are included in Chapter 6, CPUs, Section 6.6, Observability Tools. I have also published prior books on tracing tools (for DTrace [Gregg 11a] and BPF [Gregg 19]).

Both perf(1) and Ftrace are also tracers with some similar capabilities to the BPF front ends. perf(1) and Ftrace are covered in Chapters 13 and 14.

1.8 Experimentation

Apart from observability tools there are also *experimentation* tools, most of which are bench-marking tools. These perform an experiment by applying a synthetic workload to the system and measuring its performance. This must be done carefully, because experimental tools can perturb the performance of systems under test.

There are *macro-benchmark* tools that simulate a real-world workload such as clients making application requests; and there are *micro-benchmark* tools that test a specific component, such as CPUs, disks, or networks. As an analogy: a car's lap time at Laguna Seca Raceway could be considered a macro-benchmark, whereas its top speed and 0 to 60mph time could be considered micro-benchmarks. Both benchmark types are important, although micro-benchmarks are typically easier to debug, repeat, and understand, and are more stable.

The following example uses iperf(1) on an idle server to perform a TCP network throughput micro-benchmark with a remote idle server. This benchmark ran for ten seconds (-t 10) and produces per-second averages (-i 1):

```
# iperf -c 100.65.33.90 -i 1 -t 10
------------------------------------------------------------
Client connecting to 100.65.33.90, TCP port 5001
TCP window size: 12.0 MByte (default)
------------------------------------------------------------
[  3] local 100.65.170.28 port 39570 connected with 100.65.33.90 port 5001
[ ID] Interval        Transfer      Bandwidth
[  3]  0.0- 1.0 sec    582 MBytes   4.88 Gbits/sec
[  3]  1.0- 2.0 sec    568 MBytes   4.77 Gbits/sec
[  3]  2.0- 3.0 sec    574 MBytes   4.82 Gbits/sec
[  3]  3.0- 4.0 sec    571 MBytes   4.79 Gbits/sec
[  3]  4.0- 5.0 sec    571 MBytes   4.79 Gbits/sec
[  3]  5.0- 6.0 sec    432 MBytes   3.63 Gbits/sec
[  3]  6.0- 7.0 sec    383 MBytes   3.21 Gbits/sec
[  3]  7.0- 8.0 sec    388 MBytes   3.26 Gbits/sec
[  3]  8.0- 9.0 sec    390 MBytes   3.28 Gbits/sec
[  3]  9.0-10.0 sec    383 MBytes   3.22 Gbits/sec
[  3]  0.0-10.0 sec   4.73 GBytes   4.06 Gbits/sec
```

The output shows a throughput[5] of around 4.8 Gbits for the first five seconds, which drops to around 3.2 Gbits/sec. This is an interesting result that shows bi-modal throughput. To improve performance, one might focus on the 3.2 Gbits/sec mode, and search for other metrics that can explain it.

Consider the drawbacks of debugging this performance issue on a production server using observability tools alone. Network throughput can vary from second to second because of natural variance in the client workload, and the underlying bi-modal behavior of the network might not be apparent. By using iperf(1) with a fixed workload, you eliminate client variance, revealing the variance due to other factors (e.g., external network throttling, buffer utilization, and so on).

As I recommended earlier, on production systems you should first try observability tools. However, there are so many observability tools that you might spend hours working through them when an experimental tool would lead to quicker results. An analogy taught to me by a senior performance engineer (Roch Bourbonnais) many years ago was this: you have two hands, observability and experimentation. Only using one type of tool is like trying to solve a problem one-handed.

Chapters 6 to 10 include sections on experimental tools; for example, CPU experimental tools are covered in Chapter 6, CPUs, Section 6.8, Experimentation.

1.9 Cloud Computing

Cloud computing, a way to deploy computing resources on demand, has enabled rapid scaling of applications by supporting their deployment across an increasing number of small virtual systems called *instances*. This has decreased the need for rigorous capacity planning, as more capacity can be added from the cloud at short notice. In some cases it has also increased the desire for performance analysis, because using fewer resources can mean fewer systems. Since cloud usage is typically charged by the minute or hour, a performance win resulting in fewer systems can mean immediate cost savings. Compare this scenario to an enterprise data center, where you may be locked into a fixed support contract for years, unable to realize cost savings until the contract has ended.

New difficulties caused by cloud computing and virtualization include the management of performance effects from other tenants (sometimes called *performance isolation*) and physical system observability from each tenant. For example, unless managed properly by the system, disk I/O performance may be poor due to contention with a neighbor. In some environments, the true usage of the physical disks may not be observable by each tenant, making identification of this issue difficult.

These topics are covered in Chapter 11, Cloud Computing.

---

[5] The output uses the term "Bandwidth," a common misuse. Bandwidth refers to the maximum possible throughput, which iperf(1) is not measuring. iperf(1) is measuring the current rate of its network workload: its *throughput*.

1.10   Methodologies

Methodologies are a way to document the recommended steps for performing various tasks in systems performance. Without a methodology, a performance investigation can turn into a fishing expedition: trying random things in the hope of catching a win. This can be time-consuming and ineffective, while allowing important areas to be overlooked. Chapter 2, Methodologies, includes a library of methodologies for systems performance. The following is the first I use for any performance issue: a tool-based checklist.

1.10.1   Linux Perf Analysis in 60 Seconds

This is a Linux tool-based checklist that can be executed in the first 60 seconds of a performance issue investigation, using traditional tools that should be available for most Linux distributions [Gregg 15a]. Table 1.1 shows the commands, what to check for, and the section in this book that covers the command in more detail.

Table 1.1   Linux 60-second analysis checklist

#	Tool	Check	Section
1	uptime	Load averages to identify if load is increasing or decreasing (compare 1-, 5-, and 15-minute averages).	6.6.1
2	dmesg -T | tail	Kernel errors including OOM events.	7.5.11
3	vmstat -SM 1	System-wide statistics: run queue length, swapping, overall CPU usage.	7.5.1
4	mpstat -P ALL 1	Per-CPU balance: a single busy CPU can indicate poor thread scaling.	6.6.3
5	pidstat 1	Per-process CPU usage: identify unexpected CPU consumers, and user/system CPU time for each process.	6.6.7
6	iostat -sxz 1	Disk I/O statistics: IOPS and throughput, average wait time, percent busy.	9.6.1
7	free -m	Memory usage including the file system cache.	8.6.2
8	sar -n DEV 1	Network device I/O: packets and throughput.	10.6.6
9	sar -n TCP,ETCP 1	TCP statistics: connection rates, retransmits.	10.6.6
10	top	Check overview.	6.6.6

This checklist can also be followed using a monitoring GUI, provided the same metrics are available.[6]

---

[6]You could even make a custom dashboard for this checklist; however, bear in mind that this checklist was designed to make the most of readily available CLI tools, and monitoring products may have more (and better) metrics available. I'd be more inclined to make custom dashboards for the USE method and other methodologies.

Chapter 2, Methodologies, as well as later chapters, contain many more methodologies for performance analysis, including the USE method, workload characterization, latency analysis, and more.

1.11 Case Studies

If you are new to systems performance, case studies showing when and why various activities are performed can help you relate them to your current environment. Two hypothetical examples are summarized here; one is a performance issue involving disk I/O, and one is performance testing of a software change.

These case studies describe activities that are explained in other chapters of this book. The approaches described here are also intended to show not the right way or the only way, but rather *a* way that these performance activities can be conducted, for your critical consideration.

1.11.1 Slow Disks

Sumit is a system administrator at a medium-size company. The database team has filed a support ticket complaining of "slow disks" on one of their database servers.

Sumit's first task is to learn more about the issue, gathering details to form a problem statement. The ticket claims that the disks are slow, but it doesn't explain whether this is causing a database issue or not. Sumit responds by asking these questions:

- Is there currently a database performance issue? How is it measured?

- How long has this issue been present?

- Has anything changed with the database recently?

- Why were the disks suspected?

The database team replies: "We have a log for queries slower than 1,000 milliseconds. These usually don't happen, but during the past week they have been growing to dozens per hour. AcmeMon showed that the disks were busy."

This confirms that there is a real database issue, but it also shows that the disk hypothesis is likely a guess. Sumit wants to check the disks, but he also wants to check other resources quickly in case that guess was wrong.

AcmeMon is the company's basic server monitoring system, providing historical performance graphs based on standard operating system metrics, the same metrics printed by mpstat(1), iostat(1), and system utilities. Sumit logs in to AcmeMon to see for himself.

Sumit begins with a methodology called the USE method (defined in Chapter 2, Methodologies, Section 2.5.9) to quickly check for resource bottlenecks. As the database team reported, utilization for the disks is high, around 80%, while for the other resources (CPU, network) utilization is much lower. The historical data shows that disk utilization has been steadily increasing during the past week, while CPU utilization has been steady. AcmeMon doesn't provide saturation or error statistics for the disks, so to complete the USE method Sumit must log in to the server and run some commands.

He checks disk error counters from /sys; they are zero. He runs iostat(1) with an interval of one second and watches utilization and saturation metrics over time. AcmeMon reported 80% utilization but uses a one-minute interval. At one-second granularity, Sumit can see that disk utilization fluctuates, often hitting 100% and causing levels of saturation and increased disk I/O latency.

To further confirm that this is blocking the database—and isn't asynchronous with respect to the database queries—he uses a BCC/BPF tracing tool called offcputime(8) to capture stack traces whenever the database was descheduled by the kernel, along with the time spent off-CPU. The stack traces show that the database is often blocking during a file system read, during a query. This is enough evidence for Sumit.

The next question is why. The disk performance statistics appear to be consistent with high load. Sumit performs workload characterization to understand this further, using iostat(1) to measure IOPS, throughput, average disk I/O latency, and the read/write ratio. For more details, Sumit can use disk I/O tracing; however, he is satisfied that this already points to a case of high disk load, and not a problem with the disks.

Sumit adds more details to the ticket, stating what he checked and including screenshots of the commands used to study the disks. His summary so far is that the disks are under high load, which increases I/O latency and is slowing the queries. However, the disks appear to be acting normally for the load. He asks if there is a simple explanation: did the database load increase?

The database team responds that it did not, and that the rate of queries (which isn't reported by AcmeMon) has been steady. This sounds consistent with an earlier finding, that CPU utilization was also steady.

Sumit thinks about what else could cause higher disk I/O load without a noticeable increase in CPU and has a quick talk with his colleagues about it. One of them suggests file system fragmentation, which is expected when the file system approaches 100% capacity. Sumit finds that it is only at 30%.

Sumit knows he can perform drill-down analysis[7] to understand the exact causes of disk I/O, but this can be time-consuming. He tries to think of other easy explanations that he can check quickly first, based on his knowledge of the kernel I/O stack. He remembers that this disk I/O is largely caused by file system cache (page cache) misses.

Sumit checks the file system cache hit ratio using cachestat(8)[8] and finds it is currently at 91%. This sounds high (good), but he has no historical data to compare it to. He logs in to other database servers that serve similar workloads and finds their cache hit ratio to be over 98%. He also finds that the file system cache size is much larger on the other servers.

Turning his attention to the file system cache size and server memory usage, he finds something that had been overlooked: a development project has a prototype application that is consuming a growing amount of memory, even though it isn't under production load yet. This memory is taken from what is available for the file system cache, reducing its hit rate and causing more file system reads to become disk reads.

---

[7] This is covered in Chapter 2, Methodologies, Section 2.5.12, Drill-Down Analysis.

[8] A BCC tracing tool covered in Chapter 8, File Systems, Section 8.6.12, cachestat.

Sumit contacts the application development team and asks them to shut down the application and move it to a different server, referring to the database issue. After they do this, Sumit watches disk utilization creep downward in AcmeMon as the file system cache recovers to its original size. The slow queries return to zero, and he closes the ticket as resolved.

1.11.2   Software Change

Pamela is a performance and scalability engineer at a small company where she works on all performance-related activities. The application developers have developed a new core feature and are unsure whether its introduction could hurt performance. Pamela decides to perform non-regression testing[9] of the new application version, before it is deployed in production.

Pamela acquires an idle server for the purpose of testing and searches for a client workload simulator. The application team had written one a while ago, although it has various limitations and known bugs. She decides to try it but wants to confirm that it adequately resembles the current production workload.

She configures the server to match the current deployment configuration and runs the client workload simulator from a different system to the server. The client workload can be characterized by studying an access log, and there is already a company tool to do this, which she uses. She also runs the tool on a production server log for different times of day and compares workloads. It appears that the client simulator applies an average production workload but doesn't account for variance. She notes this and continues her analysis.

Pamela knows a number of approaches to use at this point. She picks the easiest: increasing load from the client simulator until a limit is reached (this is sometimes called *stress testing*). The client simulator can be configured to execute a target number of client requests per second, with a default of 1,000 that she had used earlier. She decides to increase load starting at 100 and adding increments of 100 until a limit is reached, each level being tested for one minute. She writes a shell script to perform the test, which collects results in a file for plotting by other tools.

With the load running, she performs active benchmarking to determine what the limiting factors are. The server resources and server threads seem largely idle. The client simulator shows that the request throughput levels off at around 700 per second.

She switches to the new software version and repeats the test. This also reaches the 700 mark and levels off. She also analyzes the server to look for limiting factors but again cannot see any.

She plots the results, showing completed request rate versus load, to visually identify the scalability profile. Both appear to reach an abrupt ceiling.

While it appears that the software versions have similar performance characteristics, Pamela is disappointed that she wasn't able to identify the limiting factor causing the scalability ceiling. She knows she checked only server resources, and the limiter could instead be an application logic issue. It could also be elsewhere: the network or the client simulator.

---

[9]Some call it *regression* testing, but it is an activity intended to confirm that a software or hardware change does not cause performance to regress, hence, *non*-regression testing.

Pamela wonders if a different approach may be needed, such as running a fixed rate of operations and then characterizing resource usage (CPU, disk I/O, network I/O), so that it can be expressed in terms of a single client request. She runs the simulator at a rate of 700 per second for the current and new software and measures resource consumption. The current software drove the 32 CPUs to an average of 20% utilization for the given load. The new software drove the same CPUs to 30% utilization, for the same load. It would appear that this is indeed a regression, one that consumes more CPU resources.

Curious to understand the 700 limit, Pamela launches a higher load and then investigates all components in the data path, including the network, the client system, and the client workload generator. She also performs drill-down analysis of the server and client software. She documents what she has checked, including screenshots, for reference.

To investigate the client software she performs thread state analysis and finds that it is single-threaded! That one thread is spending 100% of its time executing on-CPU. This convinces her that this is the limiter of the test.

As an experiment, she launches the client software in parallel on different client systems. In this way, she drives the server to 100% CPU utilization for both the current and new software. The current version reaches 3,500 requests/sec, and the new version 2,300 requests/sec, consistent with earlier findings of resource consumption.

Pamela informs the application developers that there is a regression with the new software version, and she begins to profile its CPU usage using a CPU flame graph to understand why: what code paths are contributing. She notes that an average production workload was tested and that varied workloads were not. She also files a bug to note that the client workload generator is single-threaded, which can become a bottleneck.

1.11.3   More Reading

A more detailed case study is provided as Chapter 16, Case Study, which documents how I resolved a particular cloud performance issue. The next chapter introduces the methodologies used for performance analysis, and the remaining chapters cover the necessary background and specifics.

1.12   References

[**Hollingsworth 94**] Hollingsworth, J., Miller, B., and Cargille, J., "Dynamic Program Instrumentation for Scalable Performance Tools," *Scalable High-Performance Computing Conference (SHPCC)*, May 1994.

[**Tamches 99**] Tamches, A., and Miller, B., "Fine-Grained Dynamic Instrumentation of Commodity Operating System Kernels," *Proceedings of the 3rd Symposium on Operating Systems Design and Implementation*, February 1999.

[**Kleen 08**] Kleen, A., "On Submitting Kernel Patches," *Intel Open Source Technology Center*, http://halobates.de/on-submitting-patches.pdf, 2008.

[Gregg 11a] Gregg, B., and Mauro, J., *DTrace: Dynamic Tracing in Oracle Solaris, Mac OS X and FreeBSD*, Prentice Hall, 2011.

[Gregg 15a] Gregg, B., "Linux Performance Analysis in 60,000 Milliseconds," *Netflix Technology Blog*, http://techblog.netflix.com/2015/11/linux-performance-analysis-in-60s.html, 2015.

[Dekker 18] Dekker, S., *Drift into Failure: From Hunting Broken Components to Understanding Complex Systems*, CRC Press, 2018.

[Gregg 19] Gregg, B., *BPF Performance Tools: Linux System and Application Observability*, Addison-Wesley, 2019.

[Corry 20] Corry, A., *Retrospectives Antipatterns*, Addison-Wesley, 2020.

Chapter 2

Methodologies

Give a man a fish and you feed him for a day.
Teach a man to fish and you feed him for a lifetime.

Chinese proverb (English equivalent)

I began my tech career as a junior system administrator, and I thought I could learn performance by studying command-line tools and metrics alone. I was wrong. I read man pages from top to bottom and learned the definitions for page faults, context switches, and various other system metrics, but I didn't know what to do with them: how to move from signals to solutions.

I noticed that, whenever there was a performance issue, the senior system administrators had their own mental procedures for moving quickly through tools and metrics to find the root cause. They understood which metrics were important and when they pointed to an issue, and how to use them to narrow down an investigation. It was this *know-how* that was missing from the man pages—it was typically learned by watching over the shoulder of a senior admin or engineer.

Since then I've collected, documented, shared, and developed performance *methodologies* of my own. This chapter includes these methodologies and other essential background for systems performance: concepts, terminology, statistics, and visualizations. This covers theory before later chapters dive into implementation.

The learning objectives of this chapter are:

- Understand key performance metrics: latency, utilization, and saturation.
- Develop a sense for the scale of measured time, down to nanoseconds.
- Learn tuning trade-offs, targets, and when to stop analysis.
- Identify problems of workload versus architecture.
- Consider resource versus workload analysis.
- Follow different performance methodologies, including: the USE method, workload characterization, latency analysis, static performance tuning, and performance mantras.
- Understand the basics of statistics and queueing theory.

Of all the chapters in this book, this one has changed the least since the first edition. Software, hardware, performance tools, and performance tunables have all changed over the course of my career. What have remained the same are the theory and methodologies: the durable skills covered in this chapter.

This chapter has three parts:

- **Background** introduces terminology, basic models, key performance concepts, and perspectives. Much of this will be assumed knowledge for the rest of this book.

- **Methodology** discusses performance analysis methodologies, both observational and experimental; modeling; and capacity planning.

- **Metrics** introduces performance statistics, monitoring, and visualizations.

Many of the methodologies introduced here are explored in more detail in later chapters, including the methodology sections in Chapters 5 through 10.

2.1   Terminology

The following are key terms for systems performance. Later chapters provide additional terms and describe some of these in different contexts.

- **IOPS:** Input/output operations per second is a measure of the rate of data transfer operations. For disk I/O, IOPS refers to reads and writes per second.

- **Throughput:** The rate of work performed. Especially in communications, the term is used to refer to the *data rate* (bytes per second or bits per second). In some contexts (e.g., databases) throughput can refer to the *operation rate* (operations per second or transactions per second).

- **Response time:** The time for an operation to complete. This includes any time spent waiting and time spent being serviced (*service time*), including the time to transfer the result.

- **Latency:** A measure of time an operation spends waiting to be serviced. In some contexts it can refer to the entire time for an operation, equivalent to response time. See Section 2.3, Concepts, for examples.

- **Utilization:** For resources that service requests, utilization is a measure of how busy a resource is, based on how much time in a given interval it was actively performing work. For resources that provide storage, utilization may refer to the capacity that is consumed (e.g., memory utilization).

- **Saturation:** The degree to which a resource has queued work it cannot service.

- **Bottleneck:** In systems performance, a bottleneck is a resource that limits the performance of the system. Identifying and removing systemic bottlenecks is a key activity of systems performance.

- **Workload:** The input to the system or the load applied is the workload. For a database, the workload consists of the database queries and commands sent by the clients.

- **Cache:** A fast storage area that can duplicate or buffer a limited amount of data, to avoid communicating directly with a slower tier of storage, thereby improving performance. For economic reasons, a cache is often smaller than the slower tier.

The Glossary includes more terminology for reference if needed.

2.2 Models

The following simple models illustrate some basic principles of system performance.

2.2.1 System Under Test

The performance of a system under test (SUT) is shown in Figure 2.1.

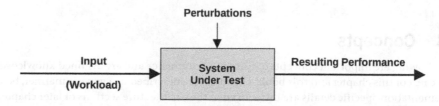

Figure 2.1 Block diagram of system under test

It is important to be aware that perturbations (interference) can affect results, including those caused by scheduled system activity, other users of the system, and other workloads. The origin of the perturbations may not be obvious, and careful study of system performance may be required to determine it. This can be particularly difficult in some cloud environments, where other activity (by guest tenants) on the physical host system may not be observable from within a guest SUT.

Another difficulty with modern environments is that they may be composed of several networked components servicing the input workload, including load balancers, proxy servers, web servers, caching servers, application servers, database servers, and storage systems. The mere act of mapping the environment may help to reveal previously overlooked sources of perturbations. The environment may also be modeled as a network of queueing systems, for analytical study.

2.2.2 Queueing System

Some components and resources can be modeled as a queueing system so that their performance under different situations can be predicted based on the model. Disks are commonly modeled as a queueing system, which can predict how response time degrades under load. Figure 2.2 shows a simple queueing system.

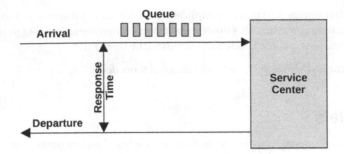

Figure 2.2 Simple queueing model

The field of queueing theory, introduced in Section 2.6, Modeling, studies queueing systems and networks of queueing systems.

2.3 Concepts

The following are important concepts of systems performance and are assumed knowledge for the rest of this chapter and this book. The topics are described in a generic manner, before implementation-specific details are introduced in the Architecture sections of later chapters.

2.3.1 Latency

For some environments, latency is the sole focus of performance. For others, it is the top one or two key metrics for analysis, along with throughput.

As an example of latency, Figure 2.3 shows a network transfer, such as an HTTP GET request, with the time split into latency and data transfer components.

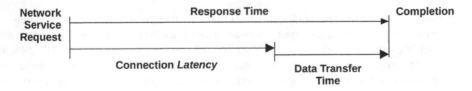

Figure 2.3 Network connection latency

The latency is the time spent waiting before an operation is performed. In this example, the operation is a network service request to transfer data. Before this operation can take place, the system must wait for a network connection to be established, which is latency for this operation. The *response time* spans this latency and the operation time.

Because latency can be measured from different locations, it is often expressed with the target of the measurement. For example, the load time for a website may be composed of three different times measured from different locations: *DNS latency*, *TCP connection latency*, and then *TCP data transfer time*. DNS latency refers to the entire DNS operation. TCP connection latency refers to the initialization only (TCP handshake).

At a higher level, all of these, including the TCP data transfer time, may be treated as latency of something else. For example, the time from when the user clicks a website link to when the resulting page is fully loaded may be termed *latency*, which includes the time for the browser to fetch a web page over a network and render it. Since the single word "latency" can be ambiguous, it is best to include qualifying terms to explain what it measures: request latency, TCP connection latency, etc.

As latency is a time-based metric, various calculations are possible. Performance issues can be quantified using latency and then ranked because they are expressed using the same units (time). Predicted speedup can also be calculated, by considering when latency can be reduced or removed. Neither of these can be accurately performed using an IOPS metric, for example.

For reference, time orders of magnitude and their abbreviations are listed in Table 2.1.

Table 2.1 **Units of time**

Unit	Abbreviation	Fraction of 1 Second
Minute	m	60
Second	s	1
Millisecond	ms	0.001 or 1/1000 or 1×10^{-3}
Microsecond	µs	0.000001 or 1/1000000 or 1×10^{-6}
Nanosecond	ns	0.000000001 or 1/1000000000 or 1×10^{-9}
Picosecond	ps	0.000000000001 or 1/1000000000000 or 1×10^{-12}

When possible, converting other metric types to latency or time allows them to be compared. If you had to choose between 100 network I/O or 50 disk I/O, how would you know which would perform better? It's a complicated question, involving many factors: network hops, rate of network drops and retransmits, I/O size, random or sequential I/O, disk types, and so on. But if you compare 100 ms of total network I/O and 50 ms of total disk I/O, the difference is clear.

2.3.2 Time Scales

While times can be compared numerically, it also helps to have an instinct about time, and reasonable expectations for latency from different sources. System components operate over vastly different time scales (orders of magnitude), to the extent that it can be difficult to grasp just how big those differences are. In Table 2.2, example latencies are provided, starting with CPU register access for a 3.5 GHz processor. To demonstrate the differences in time scales we're working with, the table shows an average time that each operation might take, scaled to an imaginary system in which a CPU cycle—0.3 ns (about one-third of one-billionth[1] of a second) in real life—takes one full second.

---

[1] US billionth: 1/1000,000,000

Table 2.2   **Example time scale of system latencies**

Event	Latency	Scaled
1 CPU cycle	0.3 ns	1 s
Level 1 cache access	0.9 ns	3 s
Level 2 cache access	3 ns	10 s
Level 3 cache access	10 ns	33 s
Main memory access (DRAM, from CPU)	100 ns	6 min
Solid-state disk I/O (flash memory)	10–100 µs	9–90 hours
Rotational disk I/O	1–10 ms	1–12 months
Internet: San Francisco to New York	40 ms	4 years
Internet: San Francisco to United Kingdom	81 ms	8 years
Lightweight hardware virtualization boot	100 ms	11 years
Internet: San Francisco to Australia	183 ms	19 years
OS virtualization system boot	< 1 s	105 years
TCP timer-based retransmit	1–3 s	105–317 years
SCSI command time-out	30 s	3 millennia
Hardware (HW) virtualization system boot	40 s	4 millennia
Physical system reboot	5 m	32 millennia

As you can see, the time scale for CPU cycles is tiny. The time it takes light to travel 0.5 m, per-haps the distance from your eyes to this page, is about 1.7 ns. During the same time, a modern CPU may have executed five CPU cycles and processed several instructions.

For more about CPU cycles and latency, see Chapter 6, CPUs, and for disk I/O latency, Chapter 9, Disks. The Internet latencies included are from Chapter 10, Network, which has more examples.

2.3.3   Trade-Offs

You should be aware of some common performance trade-offs. The good/fast/cheap "pick two" trade-off is shown in Figure 2.4, alongside the terminology adjusted for IT projects.

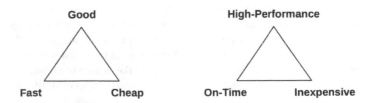

Figure 2.4   Trade-offs: pick two

Many IT projects choose on-time and inexpensive, leaving performance to be fixed later. This choice can become problematic when earlier decisions inhibit improving performance, such as choosing and populating a suboptimal storage architecture, using a programming language or operating system that is implemented inefficiently, or selecting a component that lacks comprehensive performance analysis tools.

A common trade-off in performance tuning is the one between CPU and memory, as memory can be used to cache results, reducing CPU usage. On modern systems with an abundance of CPU, the trade may work the other way: CPU time may be spent compressing data to reduce memory usage.

Tunable parameters often come with trade-offs. Here are a couple of examples:

- **File system record size** (or block size): Small record sizes, close to the application I/O size, will perform better for random I/O workloads and make more efficient use of the file system cache while the application is running. Large record sizes will improve streaming workloads, including file system backups.

- **Network buffer size:** Small buffer sizes will reduce the memory overhead per connection, helping the system scale. Large sizes will improve network throughput.

Look for such trade-offs when making changes to the system.

2.3.4 Tuning Efforts

Performance tuning is most effective when done closest to where the work is performed. For workloads driven by applications, this means within the application itself. Table 2.3 shows an example software stack with tuning possibilities.

By tuning at the application level, you may be able to eliminate or reduce database queries and improve performance by a large factor (e.g., 20x). Tuning down to the storage device level may eliminate or improve storage I/O, but a tax has already been paid in executing higher-level OS stack code, so this may improve resulting application performance only by percentages (e.g., 20%).

Table 2.3 Example targets of tuning

Layer	Example Tuning Targets
Application	Application logic, request queue sizes, database queries performed
Database	Database table layout, indexes, buffering
System calls	Memory-mapped or read/write, sync or async I/O flags
File system	Record size, cache size, file system tunables, journaling
Storage	RAID level, number and type of disks, storage tunables

There is another reason for finding large performance wins at the application level. Many of today's environments target rapid deployment for features and functionality, pushing software changes into production weekly or daily.[2] Application development and testing therefore tend to focus on correctness, leaving little or no time for performance measurement or optimization before production deployment. These activities are conducted later, when performance becomes a problem.

While the application can be the most effective level at which to tune, it isn't necessarily the most effective level from which to base observation. Slow queries may be best understood from their time spent on-CPU, or from the file system and disk I/O that they perform. These are observable from operating system tools.

In many environments (especially cloud computing) the application level is under constant development, pushing software changes into production weekly or daily. Large performance wins, including fixes for regressions, are frequently found as the application code changes. In these environments, tuning for the operating system and observability from the operating system can be easy to overlook. Remember that operating system performance analysis can also identify application-level issues, not just OS-level issues, in some cases more easily than from the application alone.

2.3.5 Level of Appropriateness

Different organizations and environments have different requirements for performance. You may have joined an organization where it is the norm to analyze much deeper than you've seen before, or even knew was possible. Or you may find that, in your new workplace, what you consider basic analysis is considered advanced and has never before been performed (good news: low-hanging fruit!).

This doesn't necessarily mean that some organizations are doing it right and some wrong. It depends on the return on investment (ROI) for performance expertise. Organizations with large data centers or large cloud environments may employ a team of performance engineers who analyze everything, including kernel internals and CPU performance counters, and make frequent use of a variety of tracing tools. They may also formally model performance and develop accurate predictions for future growth. For environments spending millions per year on computing, it can be easy to justify hiring such a performance team, as the wins they find are the ROI. Small startups with modest computing spend may only perform superficial checks, trusting third-party monitoring solutions to check their performance and provide alerts.

However, as introduced in Chapter 1, systems performance is not just about cost: it is also about the end-user experience. A startup may find it necessary to invest in performance engineering to improve website or application latency. The ROI here is not necessarily a reduction in cost, but happier customers instead of ex-customers.

The most extreme environments include stock exchanges and high-frequency traders, where performance and latency are critical and can justify intense effort and expense. As an example of this, a transatlantic cable between the New York and London exchanges was planned with a cost of $300 million, to reduce transmission latency by 6 ms [Williams 11].

---

[2] Examples of environments that change rapidly include the Netflix cloud and Shopify, which push multiple changes per day.

When doing performance analysis, the level of appropriateness also comes in to play in deciding when to stop analysis.

2.3.6   When to Stop Analysis

A challenge whenever doing performance analysis is knowing when to stop. There are so many tools, and so many things to examine!

When I teach performance classes (as I've begun to do again recently), I can give my students a performance issue that has three contributing reasons, and find that some students stop after finding one reason, others two, and others all three. Some students keep going, trying to find even more reasons for the performance issue. Who is doing it right? It might be easy to say you should stop after finding all three reasons, but for real-life issues you don't know the number of causes.

Here are three scenarios where you may consider stopping analysis, with some personal examples:

- **When you've explained the bulk of the performance problem**. A Java application was consuming three times more CPU than it had been. The first issue I found was one of exception stacks consuming CPU. I then quantified time in those stacks and found that they accounted for only 12% of the overall CPU footprint. If that figure had been closer to 66%, I could have stopped analysis—the 3x slowdown would have been accounted for. But in this case, at 12%, I needed to keep looking.

- **When the potential ROI is less than the cost of analysis**. Some performance issues I work on can deliver wins measured in tens of millions of dollars per year. For these I can justify spending months of my own time (engineering cost) on analysis. Other performance wins, say for tiny microservices, may be measured in hundreds of dollars: it may not be worth even an hour of engineering time to analyze them. Exceptions might include when I have nothing better to do with company time (which never happens in practice) or if I suspected that this might be a canary for a bigger issue later on, and therefore worth debugging before the problem grows.

- **When there are bigger ROIs elsewhere**. Even if the previous two scenarios have not been met, there may be larger ROIs elsewhere that take priority.

If you are working full-time as a performance engineer, prioritizing the analysis of different issues based on their potential ROI is likely a daily task.

2.3.7   Point-in-Time Recommendations

The performance characteristics of environments change over time, due to the addition of more users, newer hardware, and updated software or firmware. An environment currently limited by a 10 Gbit/s network infrastructure may start to experience a bottleneck in disk or CPU performance after an upgrade to 100 Gbits/s.

Performance recommendations, especially the values of tunable parameters, are valid only at a specific *point in time*. What may have been the best advice from a performance expert one week may become invalid a week later after a software or hardware upgrade, or after adding more users.

Tunable parameter values found by searching on the Internet can provide quick wins—in *some* cases. They can also cripple performance if they are not appropriate for your system or workload, were appropriate once but are not now, or are appropriate only as a temporary workaround for a software bug that is fixed properly in a later software upgrade. It is akin to raiding someone else's medicine cabinet and taking drugs that may not be appropriate for you, may have expired, or were supposed to be taken only for a short duration.

It can be useful to browse such recommendations just to see which tunable parameters exist and have needed changing in the past. Your task then becomes to see whether and how these should be tuned for your system and workload. But you may still miss an important parameter if others have not needed to tune that one before, or have tuned it but haven't shared their experience anywhere.

When changing tunable parameters, it can be helpful to store them in a version control system with a detailed history. (You may already do something similar when using configuration management tools such as Puppet, Salt, Chef, etc.) That way the times and reasons that tunables were changed can be examined later on.

2.3.8 Load vs. Architecture

An application can perform badly due to an issue with the software configuration and hardware on which it is running: its architecture and implementation. However, an application can also perform badly simply due to too much load being applied, resulting in queueing and long latencies. Load and architecture are pictured in Figure 2.5.

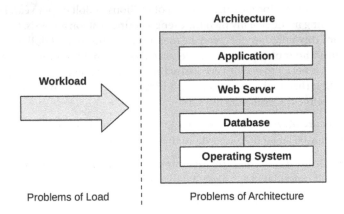

Figure 2.5 Load versus architecture

If analysis of the architecture shows queueing of work but no problems with how the work is performed, the issue may be too much load applied. In a cloud computing environment, this is the point where more server instances can be introduced on demand to handle the work.

For example, an issue of architecture may be a single-threaded application that is busy on-CPU, with requests queueing while other CPUs are available and idle. In this case, performance is limited by the application's single-threaded architecture. Another issue of architecture may be a multi-threaded program that contends for a single lock, such that only one thread can make forward progress while others wait.

An issue of load may be a multithreaded application that is busy on all available CPUs, with requests still queueing. In this case, performance is limited by the available CPU capacity, or put differently, by there being more load than the CPUs can handle.

2.3.9 Scalability

The performance of the system under increasing load is its *scalability*. Figure 2.6 shows a typical throughput profile as a system's load increases.

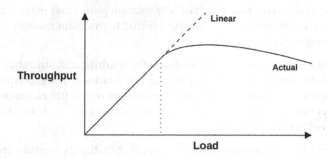

Figure 2.6 Throughput versus load

For some period, linear scalability is observed. A point is then reached, marked with a dotted line, where contention for a resource begins to degrade throughput. This point can be described as a *knee point*, as it is the boundary between two functions. Beyond this point, the throughput profile departs from linear scalability, as contention for the resource increases. Eventually the overheads for increased contention and coherency cause less work to be completed and throughput to decrease.

This point may occur when a component reaches 100% utilization: the *saturation point*. It may also occur when a component approaches 100% utilization and queueing begins to be frequent and significant.

An example system that may exhibit this profile is an application that performs heavy computation, with more load added as additional threads. As the CPUs approach 100% utilization, response time begins to degrade as CPU scheduler latency increases. After peak performance, at 100% utilization, throughput begins to decrease as more threads are added, causing more context switches, which consume CPU resources and cause less actual work to be completed.

The same curve can be seen if you replace "load" on the x-axis with a resource such as CPU cores. For more on this topic, see Section 2.6, Modeling.

The degradation of performance for nonlinear scalability, in terms of average response time or latency, is graphed in Figure 2.7 [Cockcroft 95].

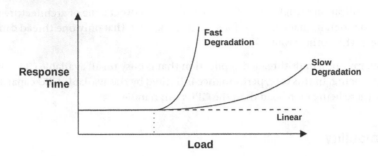

Figure 2.7 Performance degradation

Higher response time is, of course, bad. The "fast" degradation profile may occur for memory load, when the system begins moving memory pages to disk to free main memory. The "slow" degradation profile may occur for CPU load.

Another "fast" profile example is disk I/O. As load (and the resulting disk utilization) increases, I/O becomes more likely to queue behind other I/O. An idle rotational (not solid state) disk may serve I/O with a response time of about 1 ms, but when load increases, this can approach 10 ms. This is modeled in Section 2.6.5, Queueing Theory, under M/D/1 and 60% Utilization, and disk performance is covered in Chapter 9, Disks.

Linear scalability of response time could occur if the application begins to return errors when resources are unavailable, instead of queueing work. For example, a web server may return 503 "Service Unavailable" instead of adding requests to a queue, so that those requests that are served can be performed with a consistent response time.

2.3.10 Metrics

Performance metrics are selected statistics generated by the system, applications, or additional tools that measure activity of interest. They are studied for performance analysis and monitoring, either numerically at the command line or graphically using visualizations.

Common types of system performance metrics include:

- **Throughput:** Either operations or data volume per second
- **IOPS:** I/O operations per second
- **Utilization:** How busy a resource is, as a percentage
- **Latency:** Operation time, as an average or percentile

The usage of throughput depends on its context. Database throughput is usually a measure of queries or requests (operations) per second. Network throughput is a measure of bits or bytes (volume) per second.

IOPS is a throughput measurement for I/O operations only (reads and writes). Again, context matters, and definitions can vary.

Overhead

Performance metrics are not free; at some point, CPU cycles must be spent to gather and store them. This causes overhead, which can negatively affect the performance of the target of measurement. This is called the *observer effect*. (It is often confused with Heisenberg's Uncertainty Principle, which describes the limit of precision at which pairs of physical properties, such as position and momentum, may be known.)

Issues

You might assume that a software vendor has provided metrics that are well chosen, are bug-free, and provide complete visibility. In reality, metrics can be confusing, complicated, unreliable, inaccurate, and even plain wrong (due to bugs). Sometimes a metric was correct in one software version but did not get updated to reflect the addition of new code and code paths.

For more about problems with metrics, see Chapter 4, Observability Tools, Section 4.6, Observing Observability.

2.3.11 Utilization

The term *utilization*[3] is often used for operating systems to describe device usage, such as for the CPU and disk devices. Utilization can be time-based or capacity-based.

Time-Based

Time-based utilization is formally defined in queueing theory. For example [Gunther 97]:

> the average amount of time the server or resource was busy

along with the ratio

$$U = B/T$$

where U = utilization, B = total time the system was busy during T, the observation period.

This is also the "utilization" most readily available from operating system performance tools. The disk monitoring tool iostat(1) calls this metric %b for *percent busy*, a term that better conveys the underlying metric: B/T.

This utilization metric tells us how busy a component is: when a component approaches 100% utilization, performance can seriously degrade when there is contention for the resource. Other metrics can be checked to confirm and to see if the component has therefore become a system bottleneck.

Some components can service multiple operations in parallel. For them, performance may not degrade much at 100% utilization as they can accept more work. To understand this, consider a

---

[3] Spelled *utilisation* in some parts of the world.

building elevator. It may be considered utilized when it is moving between floors, and not utilized when it is idle waiting. However, the elevator may be able to accept more passengers even when it is busy 100% of the time responding to calls—that is, it is at 100% utilization.

A disk that is 100% busy may also be able to accept and process more work, for example, by buffering writes in the on-disk cache to be completed later. Storage arrays frequently run at 100% utilization because *some* disk is busy 100% of the time, but the array has plenty of idle disks and can accept more work.

Capacity-Based

The other definition of utilization is used by IT professionals in the context of capacity planning [Wong 97]:

> A system or component (such as a disk drive) is able to deliver a certain amount of throughput. At any level of performance, the system or component is working at some proportion of its capacity. That proportion is called the utilization.

This defines utilization in terms of capacity instead of time. It implies that a disk at 100% utilization *cannot* accept any more work. With the time-based definition, 100% utilization only means it is busy 100% of the time.

> 100% busy does not mean 100% capacity.

For the elevator example, 100% capacity may mean the elevator is at its maximum payload capacity and cannot accept more passengers.

In an ideal world, we would be able to measure both types of utilization for a device, so that, for example, you would know when a disk is 100% busy and performance begins to degrade due to contention, and also when it is at 100% capacity and cannot accept more work. Unfortunately, this usually isn't possible. For a disk, it would require knowledge of what the disk's on-board controller was doing and a prediction of capacity. Disks do not currently provide this information.

In this book, *utilization* usually refers to the time-based version, which you could also call *non-idle time*. The capacity version is used for some volume-based metrics, such as memory usage.

2.3.12   Saturation

The degree to which more work is requested of a resource than it can process is *saturation*. Saturation begins to occur at 100% utilization (capacity-based), as extra work cannot be processed and begins to queue. This is pictured in Figure 2.8.

The figure pictures saturation increasing linearly beyond the 100% capacity-based utilization mark as load continues to increase. Any degree of saturation is a performance issue, as time is spent waiting (latency). For time-based utilization (percent busy), queueing and therefore saturation may not begin at the 100% utilization mark, depending on the degree to which the resource can operate on work in parallel.

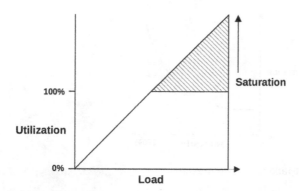

Figure 2.8   Utilization versus saturation

2.3.13   Profiling

Profiling builds a picture of a target that can be studied and understood. In the field of computing performance, profiling is typically performed by *sampling* the state of the system at timed intervals and then studying the set of samples.

Unlike the previous metrics covered, including IOPS and throughput, the use of sampling provides a *coarse* view of the target's activity. How coarse depends on the rate of sampling.

As an example of profiling, CPU usage can be understood in reasonable detail by sampling the CPU instruction pointer or stack trace at frequent intervals to gather statistics on the code paths that are consuming CPU resources. This topic is covered in Chapter 6, CPUs.

2.3.14   Caching

Caching is frequently used to improve performance. A cache stores results from a slower storage tier in a faster storage tier, for reference. An example is caching disk blocks in main memory (RAM).

Multiple tiers of caches may be used. CPUs commonly employ multiple hardware caches for main memory (Levels 1, 2, and 3), beginning with a very fast but small cache (Level 1) and increasing in both storage size and access latency. This is an economic trade-off between density and latency; levels and sizes are chosen for the best performance for the on-chip space available. These caches are covered in Chapter 6, CPUs.

There are many other caches present in a system, many of them implemented in software using main memory for storage. See Chapter 3, Operating Systems, Section 3.2.11, Caching, for a list of caching layers.

One metric for understanding cache performance is each cache's *hit ratio*—the number of times the needed data was found in the cache (hits) versus the total accesses (hits + misses):

hit ratio = hits / (hits + misses)

The higher, the better, as a higher ratio reflects more data successfully accessed from faster media. Figure 2.9 shows the expected performance improvement for increasing cache hit ratios.

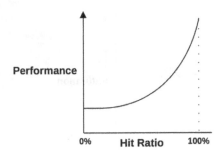

Figure 2.9   Cache hit ratio and performance

The performance difference between 98% and 99% is much greater than that between 10% and 11%. This is a nonlinear profile because of the difference in speed between cache hits and misses—the two storage tiers at play. The greater the difference, the steeper the slope becomes.

Another metric for understanding cache performance is the *cache miss rate*, in terms of misses per second. This is proportional (linear) to the performance penalty of each miss and can be easier to interpret.

For example, workloads A and B perform the same task using different algorithms and use a main memory cache to avoid reading from disk. Workload A has a cache hit ratio of 90%, and workload B has a cache hit ratio of 80%. This information alone suggests workload A performs better. What if workload A had a miss rate of 200/s and workload B, 20/s? In those terms, workload B performs 10x *fewer* disk reads, which may complete the task much sooner than A. To be certain, the total runtime for each workload can be calculated as

runtime = (hit rate × hit latency) + (miss rate × miss latency)

This calculation uses the average hit and miss latencies and assumes the work is serialized.

Algorithms

Cache management algorithms and policies determine what to store in the limited space available for a cache.

Most recently used (MRU) refers to a cache *retention policy*, which decides what to favor keeping in the cache: the objects that have been used most recently. *Least recently used* (LRU) can refer to an equivalent cache *eviction policy*, deciding what objects to remove from the cache when more space is needed. There are also *most frequently used* (MFU) and *least frequently used* (LFU) policies.

You may encounter *not frequently used* (NFU), which may be an inexpensive but less thorough version of LRU.

Hot, Cold, and Warm Caches

These words are commonly used to describe the state of the cache:

- **Cold:** A *cold cache* is empty, or populated with unwanted data. The hit ratio for a cold cache is zero (or near zero as it begins to warm up).

- **Warm:** A *warm cache* is one that is populated with useful data but doesn't have a high enough hit ratio to be considered hot.

- **Hot:** A *hot cache* is populated with commonly requested data and has a high hit ratio, for example, over 99%.

- **Warmth:** Cache warmth describes how hot or cold a cache is. An activity that improves cache warmth is one that aims to improve the cache hit ratio.

When caches are first initialized, they begin cold and then warm up over time. When the cache is large or the next-level storage is slow (or both), the cache can take a long time to become populated and warm.

For example, I worked on a storage appliance that had 128 Gbytes of DRAM as a file system cache, 600 Gbytes of flash memory as a second-level cache, and rotational disks for storage. With a random read workload, the disks delivered around 2,000 reads/s. With an 8 Kbyte I/O size, this meant that the caches could warm up at a rate of only 16 Mbytes/s (2,000 × 8 Kbytes). When both caches began cold, it took more than 2 hours for the DRAM cache to warm up, and more than 10 hours for the flash memory cache to warm up.

2.3.15 Known-Unknowns

Introduced in the Preface, the notion of *known-knowns*, *known-unknowns*, and *unknown-unknowns* is important for the field of performance. The breakdown is as follows, with examples for systems performance analysis:

- **Known-knowns:** These are things you know. You know you should be checking a performance metric, and you know its current value. For example, you know you should be checking CPU utilization, and you also know that the value is 10% on average.

- **Known-unknowns:** These are things you know that you do not know. You know you can check a metric or the existence of a subsystem, but you haven't yet observed it. For example, you know you could use profiling to check what is making the CPUs busy, but have yet to do so.

- **Unknown-unknowns:** These are things you do not know that you do not know. For example, you may not know that device interrupts can become heavy CPU consumers, so you are not checking them.

Performance is a field where "the more you know, the more you don't know." The more you learn about systems, the more unknown-unknowns you become aware of, which are then known-unknowns that you can check on.

2.4 Perspectives

There are two common perspectives for performance analysis, each with different audiences, metrics, and approaches. They are *workload analysis* and *resource analysis*. They can be thought of as either top-down or bottom-up analysis of the operating system software stack, as shown in Figure 2.10.

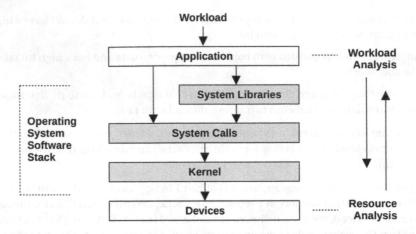

Figure 2.10   Analysis perspectives

Section 2.5, Methodology, provides specific strategies to apply for each. These perspectives are introduced here in more detail.

2.4.1   Resource Analysis

Resource analysis begins with analysis of the system resources: CPUs, memory, disks, network interfaces, buses, and interconnects. It is most likely performed by system administrators—those responsible for the physical resources. Activities include

- **Performance issue investigations:** To see if a particular type of resource is responsible

- **Capacity planning:** For information to help size new systems, and to see when existing system resources may become exhausted

This perspective focuses on utilization, to identify when resources are at or approaching their limit. Some resource types, such as CPUs, have utilization metrics readily available. Utilization for other resources can be estimated based on available metrics, for example, estimating network interface utilization by comparing the send and receive megabits per second (throughput) with the known or expected maximum bandwidth.

Metrics best suited for resource analysis include:

- IOPS

- Throughput

- Utilization

- Saturation

These measure what the resource is being asked to do, and how utilized or saturated it is for a given load. Other types of metrics, including latency, are also useful to see how well the resource is responding for the given workload.

Resource analysis is a common approach to performance analysis, in part thanks to the widely available documentation on the topic. Such documentation focuses on the operating system "stat" tools: vmstat(8), iostat(1), mpstat(1). It's important when you read such documentation to understand that this is one perspective, but not the only perspective.

2.4.2 Workload Analysis

Workload analysis (see Figure 2.11) examines the performance of applications: the workload applied and how the application is responding. It is most commonly used by application developers and support staff—those responsible for the application software and configuration.

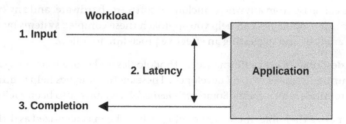

Figure 2.11   Workload analysis

The targets for workload analysis are:

- **Requests**: The workload applied
- **Latency**: The response time of the application
- **Completion**: Looking for errors

Studying workload requests typically involves checking and summarizing their attributes: this is the process of *workload characterization* (described in more detail in Section 2.5, Methodology). For databases, these attributes may include the client host, database name, tables, and query string. This data may help identify unnecessary work, or unbalanced work. Even when a system is performing its current workload well (low latency), examining these attributes may identify ways to reduce or eliminate the work applied. Keep in mind that the fastest query is the one you don't do at all.

Latency (response time) is the most important metric for expressing application performance. For a MySQL database, it's query latency; for Apache, it's HTTP request latency; and so on. In these contexts, the term *latency* is used to mean the same as response time (refer to Section 2.3.1, Latency, for more about context).

The tasks of workload analysis include identifying and confirming issues—for example, by looking for latency beyond an acceptable threshold—then finding the source of the latency and confirming that the latency is improved after applying a fix. Note that the starting point is the application. Investigating latency usually involves drilling down deeper into the application, libraries, and the operating system (kernel).

System issues may be identified by studying characteristics related to the completion of an event, including its error status. While a request may complete quickly, it may do so with an error status that causes the request to be retried, accumulating latency.

Metrics best suited for workload analysis include:

- Throughput (transactions per second)
- Latency

These measure the rate of requests and the resulting performance.

2.5 Methodology

When faced with an underperforming and complicated system environment, the first challenge can be knowing where to begin your analysis and how to proceed. As I said in Chapter 1, performance issues can arise from anywhere, including software, hardware, and any component along the data path. Methodologies can help you approach these complex systems by showing where to start your analysis and suggesting an effective procedure to follow.

This section describes many performance methodologies and procedures for system performance and tuning, some of which I developed. These methodologies help beginners get started and serve as reminders for experts. Some *anti-methodologies* have also been included.

To help summarize their role, these methodologies have been categorized as different types, such as observational analysis and experimental analysis, as shown in Table 2.4.

Table 2.4 **Generic system performance methodologies**

Section	Methodology	Type
2.5.1	Streetlight anti-method	Observational analysis
2.5.2	Random change anti-method	Experimental analysis
2.5.3	Blame-someone-else anti-method	Hypothetical analysis
2.5.4	Ad hoc checklist method	Observational and experimental analysis
2.5.5	Problem statement	Information gathering
2.5.6	Scientific method	Observational analysis
2.5.7	Diagnosis cycle	Analysis life cycle
2.5.8	Tools method	Observational analysis
2.5.9	USE method	Observational analysis
2.5.10	RED method	Observational analysis
2.5.11	Workload characterization	Observational analysis, capacity planning
2.5.12	Drill-down analysis	Observational analysis
2.5.13	Latency analysis	Observational analysis
2.5.14	Method R	Observational analysis
2.5.15	Event tracing	Observational analysis
2.5.16	Baseline statistics	Observational analysis
2.5.17	Static performance tuning	Observational analysis, capacity planning

Section	Methodology	Type
2.5.18	Cache tuning	Observational analysis, tuning
2.5.19	Micro-benchmarking	Experimental analysis
2.5.20	Performance mantras	Tuning
2.6.5	Queueing theory	Statistical analysis, capacity planning
2.7	Capacity planning	Capacity planning, tuning
2.8.1	Quantifying performance gains	Statistical analysis
2.9	Performance monitoring	Observational analysis, capacity planning

Performance monitoring, queueing theory, and capacity planning are covered later in this chapter. Other chapters also recast some of these methodologies in different contexts and provide some additional methodologies for specific targets of performance analysis. Table 2.5 lists these additional methodologies.

Table 2.5 **Additional performance methodologies**

Section	Methodology	Type
1.10.1	Linux performance analysis in 60s	Observational analysis
5.4.1	CPU profiling	Observational analysis
5.4.2	Off-CPU analysis	Observational analysis
6.5.5	Cycle analysis	Observational analysis
6.5.8	Priority tuning	Tuning
6.5.8	Resource controls	Tuning
6.5.9	CPU binding	Tuning
7.4.6	Leak detection	Observational analysis
7.4.10	Memory shrinking	Experimental analysis
8.5.1	Disk analysis	Observational analysis
8.5.7	Workload separation	Tuning
9.5.10	Scaling	Capacity planning, tuning
10.5.6	Packet sniffing	Observational analysis
10.5.7	TCP analysis	Observational analysis
12.3.1	Passive benchmarking	Experimental analysis
12.3.2	Active benchmarking	Observational analysis
12.3.6	Custom benchmarks	Software development
12.3.7	Ramping load	Experimental analysis
12.3.8	Sanity check	Observational analysis

The following sections begin with commonly used but weaker methodologies for comparison, including the anti-methodologies. For the analysis of performance issues, the first methodology you should attempt is the problem statement method, before moving on to others.

2.5.1 Streetlight Anti-Method

This method is actually the *absence* of a deliberate methodology. The user analyzes performance by choosing observability tools that are familiar, found on the Internet, or just at random to see if anything obvious shows up. This approach is hit or miss and can overlook many types of issues.

Tuning performance may be attempted in a similar trial-and-error fashion, setting whatever tunable parameters are known and familiar to different values to see if that helps.

Even when this method reveals an issue, it can be slow as tools or tunings unrelated to the issue are found and tried, just because they're familiar. This methodology is therefore named after an observational bias called the *streetlight effect*, illustrated by this parable:

> One night a police officer sees a drunk searching the ground beneath a streetlight and asks what he is looking for. The drunk says he has lost his keys. The police officer can't find them either and asks: "Are you sure you lost them here, under the streetlight?" The drunk replies: "No, but this is where the light is best."

The performance equivalent would be looking at top(1), not because it makes sense, but because the user doesn't know how to read other tools.

An issue that this methodology does find may be *an* issue but not *the* issue. Other methodologies quantify findings, so that false positives can be ruled out more quickly, and bigger issues prioritized.

2.5.2 Random Change Anti-Method

This is an experimental anti-methodology. The user randomly guesses where the problem may be and then changes things until it goes away. To determine whether performance has improved or not as a result of each change, a metric is studied, such as application runtime, operation time, latency, operation rate (operations per second), or throughput (bytes per second). The approach is as follows:

1. Pick a random item to change (e.g., a tunable parameter).
2. Change it in one direction.
3. Measure performance.
4. Change it in the other direction.
5. Measure performance.
6. Were the results in step 3 or step 5 better than the baseline? If so, keep the change and go back to step 1.

While this process may eventually unearth tuning that works for the tested workload, it is very time-consuming and can also result in tuning that doesn't make sense in the long term. For example, an application change may improve performance because it works around a database or operating system bug that is later fixed. But the application will still have that tuning that no longer makes sense, and that no one understood properly in the first place.

Another risk is where a change that isn't properly understood causes a worse problem during peak production load, and a need to back out the change.

2.5.3 Blame-Someone-Else Anti-Method

This anti-methodology follows these steps:

1. Find a system or environment component for which you are not responsible.
2. Hypothesize that the issue is with that component.
3. Redirect the issue to the team responsible for that component.
4. When proven wrong, go back to step 1.

"Maybe it's the network. Can you check with the network team if they've had dropped packets or something?"

Instead of investigating performance issues, the user of this methodology makes them someone else's problem, which can be wasteful of other teams' resources when it turns out not to be their problem after all. This anti-methodology can be identified by a lack of data leading to the hypothesis.

To avoid becoming a victim of blame-someone-else, ask the accuser for screenshots showing which tools were run and how the output was interpreted. You can take these screenshots and interpretations to someone else for a second opinion.

2.5.4 Ad Hoc Checklist Method

Stepping through a canned checklist is a common methodology used by support professionals when asked to check and tune a system, often in a short time frame. A typical scenario involves the deployment of a new server or application in production, and a support professional spending half a day checking for common issues now that the system is under real load. These checklists are ad hoc and are built from recent experience and issues for that system type.

Here is an example checklist entry:

Run `iostat -x 1` and check the r_await column. If this is consistently over 10 (ms) during load, then either disk reads are slow or the disk is overloaded.

A checklist may be composed of a dozen or so such checks.

While these checklists can provide the most value in the shortest time frame, they are point-in-time recommendations (see Section 2.3, Concepts) and need to be frequently refreshed to stay current. They also tend to focus on issues for which there are known fixes that can be easily documented, such as the setting of tunable parameters, but not custom fixes to the source code or environment.

If you are managing a team of support professionals, an ad hoc checklist can be an effective way to ensure that everyone knows how to check for common issues. A checklist can be written to be clear and prescriptive, showing how to identify each issue and what the fix is. But bear in mind that this list must be constantly updated.

2.5.5 Problem Statement

Defining the problem statement is a routine task for support staff when first responding to issues. It's done by asking the customer the following questions:

1. What makes you think there is a performance problem?
2. Has this system ever performed well?
3. What changed recently? Software? Hardware? Load?
4. Can the problem be expressed in terms of latency or runtime?
5. Does the problem affect other people or applications (or is it just you)?
6. What is the environment? What software and hardware are used? Versions? Configuration?

Just asking and answering these questions often points to an immediate cause and solution. The problem statement has therefore been included here as its own methodology and should be the first approach you use when tackling a new issue.

I have solved performance issues over the phone by using the problem statement method alone, and without needing to log in to any server or look at any metrics.

2.5.6 Scientific Method

The scientific method studies the unknown by making hypotheses and then testing them. It can be summarized by the following steps:

1. Question
2. Hypothesis
3. Prediction
4. Test
5. Analysis

The question is the performance problem statement. From this you can hypothesize what the cause of poor performance may be. Then you construct a test, which may be observational or experimental, that tests a prediction based on the hypothesis. You finish with analysis of the test data collected.

For example, you may find that application performance is degraded after migrating to a system with less main memory, and you hypothesize that the cause of poor performance is a smaller file system cache. You might use an *observational test* to measure the cache miss rate on both systems, predicting that cache misses will be higher on the smaller system. An *experimental test* would be to increase the cache size (adding RAM), predicting that performance will improve. Another, perhaps easier, experimental test is to artificially reduce the cache size (using tunable parameters), predicting that performance will be worse.

The following are some more examples.

Example (Observational)

1. Question: What is causing slow database queries?

2. Hypothesis: Noisy neighbors (other cloud computing tenants) are performing disk I/O, contending with database disk I/O (via the file system).

3. Prediction: If file system I/O latency is measured during a query, it will show that the file system is responsible for the slow queries.

4. Test: Tracing of database file system latency as a ratio of query latency shows that less than 5% of the time is spent waiting for the file system.

5. Analysis: The file system and disks are not responsible for slow queries.

Although the issue is still unsolved, some large components of the environment have been ruled out. The person conducting this investigation can return to step 2 and develop a new hypothesis.

Example (Experimental)

1. Question: Why do HTTP requests take longer from host A to host C than from host B to host C?

2. Hypothesis: Host A and host B are in different data centers.

3. Prediction: Moving host A to the same data center as host B will fix the problem.

4. Test: Move host A and measure performance.

5. Analysis: Performance has been fixed—consistent with the hypothesis.

If the problem wasn't fixed, reverse the experimental change (move host A back, in this case) before beginning a new hypothesis—changing multiple factors at once makes it harder to identify which one mattered!

Example (Experimental)

1. Question: Why did file system performance degrade as the file system cache grew in size?

2. Hypothesis: A larger cache stores more records, and more compute is required to manage a larger cache than a smaller one.

3. Prediction: Making the record size progressively smaller, and therefore causing more records to be used to store the same amount of data, will make performance progressively *worse*.

4. Test: Test the same workload with progressively smaller record sizes.

5. Analysis: Results are graphed and are consistent with the prediction. Drill-down analysis is now performed on the cache management routines.

This is an example of a *negative test*—deliberately hurting performance to learn more about the target system.

2.5.7   Diagnosis Cycle

Similar to the scientific method is the *diagnosis cycle*:

hypothesis → instrumentation → data → hypothesis

Like the scientific method, this method also deliberately tests a hypothesis through the collection of data. The cycle emphasizes that the data can lead quickly to a new hypothesis, which is tested and refined, and so on. This is similar to a doctor making a series of small tests to diagnose a patient and refining the hypothesis based on the result of each test.

Both of these approaches have a good balance of theory and data. Try to move from hypothesis to data quickly, so that bad theories can be identified early and discarded, and better ones developed.

2.5.8   Tools Method

A tools-oriented approach is as follows:

1. List available performance tools (optionally, install or purchase more).

2. For each tool, list useful metrics it provides.

3. For each metric, list possible ways to interpret it.

The result of this is a prescriptive checklist showing which tool to run, which metrics to read, and how to interpret them. While this can be fairly effective, it relies exclusively on available (or known) tools, which can provide an incomplete view of the system, similar to the streetlight anti-method. Worse, the user is unaware that they have an incomplete view—and may remain unaware. Issues that require custom tooling (e.g., dynamic tracing) may never be identified and solved.

In practice, the tools method does identify certain resource bottlenecks, errors, and other types of problems, though it may not do this efficiently.

When a large number of tools and metrics are available, it can be time-consuming to iterate through them. The situation gets worse when multiple tools appear to have the same functionality and you spend additional time trying to understand the pros and cons of each. In some cases, such as file system micro-benchmark tools, there are over a dozen tools to choose from, when you may need only one.[4]

---

[4] As an aside, an argument I've encountered to support multiple overlapping tools is that "competition is good." I would be cautious about this: while it can be helpful to have overlapping tools for cross-checking results (and I frequently cross-check BPF tools using Ftrace), multiple overlapping tools can become a waste of developer time that could be more effectively used elsewhere, as well as a waste of time for end users who must evaluate each choice.

2.5.9 The USE Method

The utilization, saturation, and errors (USE) method should be used early in a performance investigation to identify systemic bottlenecks [Gregg 13b]. It is a methodology that focuses on system resources and can be summarized as:

> For every resource, check utilization, saturation, and errors.

These terms are defined as follows:

- **Resources**: All physical server functional components (CPUs, buses, . . .). Some software resources can also be examined, provided that the metrics make sense.

- **Utilization**: For a set time interval, the percentage of time that the resource was busy servicing work. While busy, the resource may still be able to accept more work; the degree to which it cannot do so is identified by saturation.

- **Saturation**: The degree to which the resource has extra work that it can't service, often waiting on a queue. Another term for this is *pressure*.

- **Errors**: The count of error events.

For some resource types, including main memory, utilization is the *capacity* of the resource that is used. This is different from the time-based definition and was explained earlier in Section 2.3.11, Utilization. Once a capacity resource reaches 100% utilization, more work cannot be accepted, and the resource either queues the work (saturation) or returns errors, which are also identified using the USE method.

Errors should be investigated because they can degrade performance but may not be immediately noticed when the failure mode is recoverable. This includes operations that fail and are retried, and devices that fail in a pool of redundant devices.

In contrast with the tools method, the USE method involves iterating over system resources instead of tools. This helps you create a complete list of questions to ask, and only then do you search for tools to answer them. Even when tools cannot be found to answer some questions, the knowledge that these questions are unanswered can be extremely useful for the performance analyst: they are now "known-unknowns."

The USE method also directs analysis to a limited number of key metrics, so that all system resources are checked as quickly as possible. After this, if no issues have been found, other methodologies can be used.

Procedure

The USE method is pictured as the flowchart in Figure 2.12. Errors are checked first because they are usually quick to interpret (they are usually an objective and not subjective metric), and it can be time-efficient to rule them out before investigating the other metrics. Saturation is checked second because it is quicker to interpret than utilization: any level of saturation can be an issue.

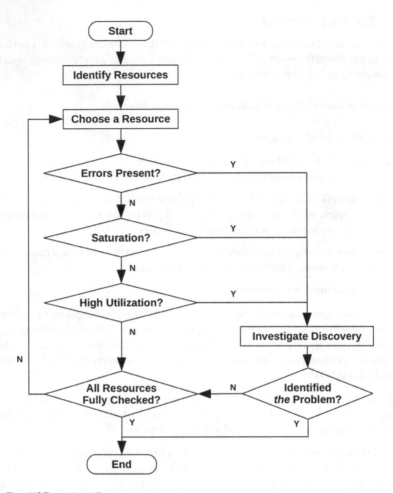

Figure 2.12   The USE method flow

This method identifies problems that are likely to be system bottlenecks. Unfortunately, a system may be suffering from more than one performance problem, so the first thing you find may be *a* problem but not *the* problem. Each discovery can be investigated using further methodologies, before returning to the USE method as needed to iterate over more resources.

Expressing Metrics

The USE method metrics are usually expressed as follows:

- **Utilization:** As a percent over a time interval (e.g., "One CPU is running at 90% utilization")
- **Saturation:** As a wait-queue length (e.g., "The CPUs have an average run-queue length of four")
- **Errors:** Number of errors reported (e.g., "This disk drive has had 50 errors")

Though it may seem counterintuitive, a short burst of high utilization can cause saturation and performance issues, even though the overall utilization is *low* over a long interval. Some monitoring tools report utilization over 5-minute averages. CPU utilization, for example, can vary dramatically from second to second, so a 5-minute average may disguise short periods of 100% utilization and, therefore, saturation.

Consider a toll plaza on a highway. Utilization can be defined as how many tollbooths were busy servicing a car. Utilization at 100% means you can't find an empty booth and must queue behind someone (saturation). If I told you the booths were at 40% utilization across the entire day, could you tell me whether any cars had queued at any time during that day? They probably did during rush hour, when utilization was at 100%, but that isn't visible in the daily average.

Resource List

The first step in the USE method is to create a list of resources. Try to be as complete as possible. Here is a generic list of server hardware resources, along with specific examples:

- **CPUs:** Sockets, cores, hardware threads (virtual CPUs)
- **Main memory:** DRAM
- **Network interfaces:** Ethernet ports, Infiniband
- **Storage devices:** Disks, storage adapters
- **Accelerators:** GPUs, TPUs, FPGAs, etc., if in use
- **Controllers:** Storage, network
- **Interconnects:** CPU, memory, I/O

Each component typically acts as a single resource type. For example, main memory is a *capacity* resource, and network interfaces are an *I/O* resource (which can mean either IOPS or throughput). Some components can behave as multiple resource types: for example, a storage device is both an I/O resource and a capacity resource. Consider all types that can lead to performance bottlenecks. Also note that I/O resources can be further studied as *queueing systems*, which queue and then service these requests.

Some physical components, such as hardware caches (e.g., CPU caches), can be left out of your checklist. The USE method is most effective for resources that suffer performance degradation under high utilization or saturation, leading to bottlenecks, while caches *improve* performance under high utilization. These can be checked using other methodologies. If you are unsure whether to include a resource, include it, and then see how well the metrics work in practice.

Functional Block Diagram

Another way to iterate over resources is to find or draw a functional block diagram for the system, such as the one shown in Figure 2.13. Such a diagram also shows relationships, which can be very useful when looking for bottlenecks in the flow of data.

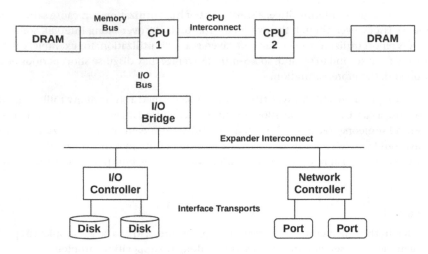

Figure 2.13   Example two-processor functional block diagram

CPU, memory, and I/O interconnects and buses are often overlooked. Fortunately, they are not common system bottlenecks, as they are typically designed to provide an excess of throughput. Unfortunately, if they are, the problem can be difficult to solve. Maybe you can upgrade the main board, or reduce load; for example, "zero copy" software techniques lighten memory bus load.

To investigate interconnects, see CPU Performance Counters in Chapter 6, CPUs, Section 6.4.1, Hardware.

Metrics

Once you have your list of resources, consider the metric types appropriate to each: utilization, saturation, and errors. Table 2.6 shows some example resources and metric types, along with possible metrics (generic OS).

Table 2.6   **Example USE method metrics**

Resource	Type	Metric
CPU	Utilization	CPU utilization (either per CPU or a system-wide average)
CPU	Saturation	Run queue length, scheduler latency, CPU pressure (Linux PSI)
Memory	Utilization	Available free memory (system-wide)
Memory	Saturation	Swapping (anonymous paging), page scanning, out-of-memory events, memory pressure (Linux PSI)
Network interface	Utilization	Receive throughput/max bandwidth, transmit throughput/max bandwidth
Storage device I/O	Utilization	Device busy percent

Resource	Type	Metric
Storage device I/O	Saturation	Wait queue length, I/O pressure (Linux PSI)
Storage device I/O	Errors	Device errors ("soft," "hard")

These metrics can be either averages per interval or counts.

Repeat for all combinations, and include instructions for fetching each metric. Take note of metrics that are not currently available; these are the known-unknowns. You'll end up with a list of about 30 metrics, some of which are difficult to measure, and some of which can't be measured at all. Fortunately, the most common issues are usually found with the easier metrics (e.g., CPU saturation, memory capacity saturation, network interface utilization, disk utilization), so these can be checked first.

Some examples of harder combinations are provided in Table 2.7.

Table 2.7 **Example USE method advanced metrics**

Resource	Type	Metric
CPU	Errors	For example, machine check exceptions, CPU cache errors[5]
Memory	Errors	For example, failed malloc()s (although a default Linux kernel configuration makes this rare due to overcommit)
Network	Saturation	Saturation-related network interface or OS errors, e.g., Linux "overruns"
Storage controller	Utilization	Depends on the controller; it may have a maximum IOPS or throughput that can be checked against current activity
CPU interconnect	Utilization	Per-port throughput/maximum bandwidth (CPU performance counters)
Memory interconnect	Saturation	Memory stall cycles, high cycles per instruction (CPU performance counters)
I/O interconnect	Utilization	Bus throughput/maximum bandwidth (performance counters may exist on your HW, e.g., Intel "uncore" events)

Some of these may not be available from standard operating system tools and may require the use of dynamic tracing or CPU performance monitoring counters.

Appendix A is an example USE method checklist for Linux systems, iterating over all combinations for hardware resources with the Linux observability toolset, and includes some software resources, such as those described in the next section.

---

[5] For example, recoverable error-correcting code (ECC) errors for CPU cache lines (if supported). Some kernels will offline a CPU if an increase in these is detected.

Software Resources

Some software resources can be similarly examined. This usually applies to smaller components of software (not entire applications), for example:

- **Mutex locks:** Utilization may be defined as the time the lock was held, saturation by those threads queued waiting on the lock.

- **Thread pools:** Utilization may be defined as the time threads were busy processing work, saturation by the number of requests waiting to be serviced by the thread pool.

- **Process/thread capacity:** The system may have a limited number of processes or threads, whose current usage may be defined as utilization; waiting on allocation may be saturation; and errors are when the allocation failed (e.g., "cannot fork").

- **File descriptor capacity:** Similar to process/thread capacity, but for file descriptors.

If the metrics work well in your case, use them; otherwise, alternative methodologies such as latency analysis can be applied.

Suggested Interpretations

Here are some general suggestions for interpreting the metric types:

- **Utilization:** Utilization at 100% is usually a sign of a bottleneck (check saturation and its effect to confirm). Utilization beyond 60% can be a problem for a couple of reasons: depending on the interval, it can hide short bursts of 100% utilization. Also, some resources such as hard disks (but not CPUs) usually cannot be interrupted during an operation, even for higher-priority work. As utilization increases, queueing delays become more frequent and noticeable. See Section 2.6.5, Queueing Theory, for more about 60% utilization.

- **Saturation:** Any degree of saturation (non-zero) can be a problem. It may be measured as the length of a wait queue, or as time spent waiting on the queue.

- **Errors:** Non-zero error counters are worth investigating, especially if they are increasing while performance is poor.

It's easy to interpret the negative cases: low utilization, no saturation, no errors. This is more useful than it sounds—narrowing down the scope of an investigation can help you focus quickly on the problem area, having identified that it is likely *not* a resource problem. This is the process of elimination.

Resource Controls

In cloud computing and container environments, software resource controls may be in place to limit or throttle tenants who are sharing one system. These may limit memory, CPU, disk I/O, and network I/O. For example, Linux containers use cgroups to limit resource usage. Each of these resource limits can be examined with the USE method, similarly to examining the physical resources.

For example, "memory capacity utilization" can be the tenant's memory usage versus its memory cap. "Memory capacity saturation" can be seen by limit-imposed allocation errors or swapping for that tenant, even if the host system is not experiencing memory pressure. These limits are discussed in Chapter 11, Cloud Computing.

Microservices

A microservice architecture presents a similar problem to that of too many resource metrics: there can be so many metrics for each service that it is laborious to check them all, and they can overlook areas where metrics do not yet exist. The USE method can address these problems with microservices as well. For example, for a typical Netflix microservice, the USE metrics are:

- **Utilization:** The average CPU utilization across the entire instance cluster.

- **Saturation:** An approximation is the difference between the 99th latency percentile and the average latency (assumes the 99th is saturation-driven).

- **Errors:** Request errors.

These three metrics are already examined for each microservice at Netflix using the Atlas cloud-wide monitoring tool [Harrington 14].

There is a similar methodology that has been designed specifically for services: the RED method.

2.5.10   The RED Method

The focus of this methodology is services, typically cloud services in a microservice architecture. It identifies three metrics for monitoring health from a user perspective and can be summarized as [Wilkie 18]:

> For every service, check the request rate, errors, and duration.

The metrics are:

- **Request rate:** The number of service requests per second

- **Errors:** The number of requests that failed

- **Duration:** The time for requests to complete (consider distribution statistics such as percentiles in addition to the average: see Section 2.8, Statistics)

Your task is to draw a diagram of your microservice architecture and ensure that these three metrics are monitored for each service. (Distributed tracing tools may provide such diagrams for you.) The advantages are similar to the USE method: the RED method is fast and easy to follow, and comprehensive.

The RED method was created by Tom Wilkie, who has also developed implementations of the USE and RED method metrics for Prometheus with dashboards using Grafana [Wilkie 18]. These methodologies are complementary: the USE method for machine health, and the RED method for user health.

The inclusion of the request rate provides an important early clue in an investigation: whether a performance problem is one of load versus architecture (see Section 2.3.8, Load vs. Architecture). If the request rate has been steady but the request duration has increased, it points to a problem with the architecture: the service itself. If both the request rate and duration have increased, then the problem may be one of the load applied. This can be further investigated using workload characterization.

2.5.11   Workload Characterization

Workload characterization is a simple and effective method for identifying a class of issues: those due to the load applied. It focuses on the *input* to the system, rather than the resulting performance. Your system may have no architectural, implementation, or configuration issues present, but be experiencing more load than it can reasonably handle.

Workloads can be characterized by answering the following questions:

- **Who** is causing the load? Process ID, user ID, remote IP address?

- **Why** is the load being called? Code path, stack trace?

- **What** are the load characteristics? IOPS, throughput, direction (read/write), type? Include variance (standard deviation) where appropriate.

- **How** is the load changing over time? Is there a daily pattern?

It can be useful to check all of these, even when you have strong expectations about what the answers will be, because you may be surprised.

Consider this scenario: You have a performance issue with a database whose clients are a pool of web servers. Should you check the IP addresses of who is using the database? You already expect them to be the web servers, as per the configuration. You check anyway and discover that the entire Internet appears to be throwing load at the databases, destroying their performance. You are actually under a denial-of-service (DoS) attack!

The best performance wins are the result of *eliminating unnecessary work*. Sometimes unnecessary work is caused by applications malfunctioning, for example, a thread stuck in a loop creating unnecessary CPU work. It can also be caused by bad configurations—for example, system-wide backups that run during peak hours—or even a DoS attack as described previously. Characterizing the workload can identify these issues, and with maintenance or reconfiguration they may be eliminated.

If the identified workload cannot be eliminated, another approach may be to use system resource controls to throttle it. For example, a system backup task may be interfering with a production database by consuming CPU resources to compress the backup, and then network resources to transfer it. This CPU and network usage may be throttled using resource controls (if the system supports them) so that the backup runs more slowly without hurting the database.

Apart from identifying issues, workload characterization can also be input for the design of simulation benchmarks. If the workload measurement is an average, ideally you will also collect details of the distribution and variation. This can be important for simulating the variety of workloads expected, rather than testing only an average workload. See Section 2.8, Statistics, for more about averages and variation (standard deviation), and Chapter 12, Benchmarking.

Analysis of the workload also helps separate problems of load from problems of architecture, by identifying the former. Load versus architecture was introduced in Section 2.3.8, Load vs. Architecture.

The specific tools and metrics for performing workload characterization depend on the target. Some applications record detailed logs of client activity, which can be the source for statistical analysis. They may also already provide daily or monthly reports of client usage, which can be mined for details.

2.5.12   Drill-Down Analysis

Drill-down analysis starts with examining an issue at a high level, then narrowing the focus based on the previous findings, discarding areas that seem uninteresting, and digging deeper into the interesting ones. The process can involve digging down through deeper layers of the software stack, to hardware if necessary, to find the root cause of the issue.

The following is a three-stage drill-down analysis methodology for system performance [McDougall 06a]:

1. **Monitoring:** This is used for continually recording high-level statistics over time, and identifying or alerting if a problem may be present.

2. **Identification:** Given a suspected problem, this narrows the investigation to particular resources or areas of interest, identifying possible bottlenecks.

3. **Analysis:** Further examination of particular system areas is done to attempt to root-cause and quantify the issue.

Monitoring may be performed company-wide and the results of all servers or cloud instances aggregated. A historical technology to do this is the Simple Network Monitoring Protocol (SNMP), which can be used to monitor any network-attached device that supports it. Modern monitoring systems use *exporters*: software agents that run on each system to collect and publish metrics. The resulting data is recorded by a monitoring system and visualized by front-end GUIs. This may reveal long-term patterns that can be missed when using command-line tools over short durations. Many monitoring solutions provide alerts if a problem is suspected, prompting analysis to move to the next stage.

Identification is performed by analyzing a server directly and checking system components: CPUs, disks, memory, and so on. It has historically been performed using command-line tools such as vmstat(8), iostat(1), and mpstat(1). Today there are many GUI dashboards that expose the same metrics to allow faster analysis.

Analysis tools include those based on tracing or profiling, for deeper inspection of suspect areas. Such deeper analysis may involve the creation of custom tools and inspection of source code (if available). Here is where most of the drilling down takes place, peeling away layers of the software stack as necessary to find the root cause. Tools for performing this on Linux include strace(1), perf(1), BCC tools, bpftrace, and Ftrace.

As an example implementation of this three-stage methodology, the following are the technologies used for the Netflix cloud:

1. **Monitoring:** Netflix Atlas: an open-source cloud-wide monitoring platform [Harrington 14].

2. **Identification:** Netflix perfdash (formally Netflix Vector): a GUI for analyzing a single instance with dashboards, including USE method metrics.

3. **Analysis:** Netflix FlameCommander, for generating different types of flame graphs; and command-line tools over an SSH session, including Ftrace-based tools, BCC tools, and bpftrace.

As an example of how we use this sequence at Netflix: Atlas may identify a problem microservice, perfdash may then narrow the problem to a resource, and then FlameCommander shows the code paths consuming that resource, which can then be instrumented using BCC tools and custom bpftrace tools.

Five Whys

An additional methodology you can use during the drill-down analysis stage is the *Five Whys* technique [Wikipedia 20]: ask yourself "why?" then answer the question, and repeat five times in total (or more). Here is an example procedure:

1. A database has begun to perform poorly for many queries. Why?

2. It is delayed by disk I/O due to memory paging. Why?

3. Database memory usage has grown too large. Why?

4. The allocator is consuming more memory than it should. Why?

5. The allocator has a memory fragmentation issue.

This is a real-world example that unexpectedly led to a fix in a system memory allocation library. It was the persistent questioning and drilling down to the core issue that led to the fix.

2.5.13 Latency Analysis

Latency analysis examines the time taken to complete an operation and then breaks it into smaller components, continuing to subdivide the components with the highest latency so that the root cause can be identified and quantified. Similarly to drill-down analysis, latency analysis may drill down through layers of the software stack to find the origin of latency issues.

Analysis can begin with the workload applied, examining how that workload was processed in the application, and then drill down into the operating system libraries, system calls, the kernel, and device drivers.

For example, analysis of MySQL query latency could involve answering the following questions (example answers are given here):

1. Is there a query latency issue? (yes)

2. Is the query time largely spent on-CPU or waiting off-CPU? (off-CPU)

3. What is the off-CPU time spent waiting for? (file system I/O)

4. Is the file system I/O time due to disk I/O or lock contention? (disk I/O)

5. Is the disk I/O time mostly spent queueing or servicing the I/O? (servicing)

6. Is the disk service time mostly I/O initialization or data transfer? (data transfer)

For this example, each step of the process posed a question that divided the latency into two parts and then proceeded to analyze the larger part: a binary search of latency, if you will. The process is pictured in Figure 2.14.

As the slower of A or B is identified, it is then further split into A or B, analyzed, and so on.

Latency analysis of database queries is the target of method R.

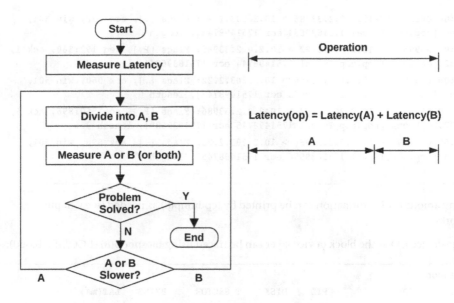

Figure 2.14 Latency analysis procedure

2.5.14 Method R

Method R is a performance analysis methodology developed for Oracle databases that focuses on finding the origin of latency, based on Oracle trace events [Millsap 03]. It is described as "a response time-based performance improvement method that yields maximum economic value to your business" and focuses on identifying and quantifying where time is spent during queries. While this is used for the study of databases, its approach could be applied to any system and is worth mentioning here as an avenue of possible study.

2.5.15 Event Tracing

Systems operate by processing discrete events. These include CPU instructions, disk I/O and other disk commands, network packets, system calls, library calls, application transactions, database queries, and so on. Performance analysis usually studies summaries of these events, such as operations per second, bytes per second, or average latency. Sometimes important detail is lost in the summary, and the events are best understood when inspected individually.

Network troubleshooting often requires packet-by-packet inspection, with tools such as tcpdump(8). This example summarizes packets as single lines of text:

```
# tcpdump -ni eth4 -ttt
tcpdump: verbose output suppressed, use -v or -vv for full protocol decode
listening on eth4, link-type EN10MB (Ethernet), capture size 65535 bytes
00:00:00.000000 IP 10.2.203.2.22 > 10.2.0.2.33986: Flags [P.], seq
1182098726:1182098918, ack 4234203806, win 132, options [nop,nop,TS val 1751498743
ecr 1751639660], length 192
```

```
00:00:00.000392 IP 10.2.0.2.33986 > 10.2.203.2.22: Flags [.], ack 192, win 501,
options [nop,nop,TS val 1751639684 ecr 1751498743], length 0
00:00:00.009561 IP 10.2.203.2.22 > 10.2.0.2.33986: Flags [P.], seq 192:560, ack 1,
win 132, options [nop,nop,TS val 1751498744 ecr 1751639684], length 368
00:00:00.000351 IP 10.2.0.2.33986 > 10.2.203.2.22: Flags [.], ack 560, win 501,
options [nop,nop,TS val 1751639685 ecr 1751498744], length 0
00:00:00.010489 IP 10.2.203.2.22 > 10.2.0.2.33986: Flags [P.], seq 560:896, ack 1,
win 132, options [nop,nop,TS val 1751498745 ecr 1751639685], length 336
00:00:00.000369 IP 10.2.0.2.33986 > 10.2.203.2.22: Flags [.], ack 896, win 501,
options [nop,nop,TS val 1751639686 ecr 1751498745], length 0
[...]
```

Varying amounts of information can be printed by tcpdump(8) as needed (see Chapter 10, Network).

Storage device I/O at the block device layer can be traced using biosnoop(8) (BCC/BPF-based):

```
# biosnoop
TIME(s)     COMM         PID    DISK    T SECTOR     BYTES    LAT(ms)
0.000004    supervise    1950   xvda1   W 13092560   4096      0.74
0.000178    supervise    1950   xvda1   W 13092432   4096      0.61
0.001469    supervise    1956   xvda1   W 13092440   4096      1.24
0.001588    supervise    1956   xvda1   W 13115128   4096      1.09
1.022346    supervise    1950   xvda1   W 13115272   4096      0.98
[...]
```

This biosnoop(8) output includes the I/O completion time (TIME(s)), initiating process details (COMM, PID), disk device (DISK), type of I/O (T), size (BYTES), and I/O duration (LAT(ms)). See Chapter 9, Disks, for more information about this tool.

The system call layer is another common location for tracing. On Linux, it can be traced using strace(1) and perf(1)'s trace subcommand (see Chapter 5, Applications). These tools also have options to print timestamps.

When performing event tracing, look for the following information:

- **Input:** All attributes of an event request: type, direction, size, and so on
- **Times:** Start time, end time, latency (difference)
- **Result:** Error status, result of event (e.g., successful transfer size)

Sometimes performance issues can be understood by examining attributes of the event, for either the request or the result. Event timestamps are particularly useful for analyzing latency and can often be included by using event tracing tools. The preceding tcpdump(8) output included delta timestamps, measuring the time between packets, using -ttt.

The study of prior events provides more information. An uncommonly high latency event, known as a *latency outlier*, may be caused by previous events rather than the event itself. For example, the event at the tail of a queue may have high latency but be caused by the previously queued events, not its own properties. This case can be identified from the traced events.

2.5.16   Baseline Statistics

Environments commonly use monitoring solutions to record server performance metrics and to visualize them as line charts, with time on the x-axis (see Section 2.9, Monitoring). These line charts can show whether a metric has changed recently, and if so, how it is now different, simply by examining changes in the line. Sometimes additional lines are added to include more historical data, such as historical averages or simply historical time ranges for comparison with the current range. Many Netflix dashboards, for example, draw an extra line to show the same time range but for the previous week, so that behavior at 3 p.m. on a Tuesday can be directly compared with 3 p.m. on the previous Tuesday.

These approaches work well with already-monitored metrics and a GUI to visualize them. However, there are many more system metrics and details available at the command line that may not be monitored. You may be faced with unfamiliar system statistics and wonder if they are "normal" for the server, or if they are evidence of an issue.

This is not a new problem, and there is a methodology to solve it that predates the widespread use of monitoring solutions using line charts. It is the collection of *baseline statistics*. This can involve collecting all the system metrics when the system is under "normal" load and recording them in a text file or database for later reference. The baseline software can be a shell script that runs observability tools and gathers other sources (cat(1) of /proc files). Profilers and tracing tools can be included in the baseline, providing far more detail than is typically recorded by monitoring products (but be careful with the overhead of those tools, so as not to perturb production). These baselines may be collected at regular intervals (daily), as well as before and after system or application changes, so that performance differences can be analyzed.

If baselines have not been collected and monitoring is not available, some observability tools (those based on kernel counters) can show summary-since-boot averages, for comparison with current activity. This is coarse, but better than nothing.

2.5.17   Static Performance Tuning

Static performance tuning focuses on issues of the configured architecture. Other methodologies focus on the performance of the applied load: the *dynamic performance* [Elling 00]. Static performance analysis can be performed when the system is at rest and no load is applied.

For static performance analysis and tuning, step through all the components of the system and check the following:

- Does the component make sense? (outdated, underpowered, etc.)

- Does the configuration make sense for the intended workload?

- Was the component autoconfigured in the best state for the intended workload?

- Has the component experienced an error such that it is now in a degraded state?

Here are some examples of issues that may be found using static performance tuning:

- Network interface negotiation: selecting 1 Gbits/s instead of 10 Gbit/s

- Failed disk in a RAID pool

- Older version of the operating system, applications, or firmware used

- File system nearly full (can cause performance issues)
- Mismatched file system record size compared to workload I/O size
- Application running with a costly debug mode accidentally left enabled
- Server accidentally configured as a network router (IP forwarding enabled)
- Server configured to use resources, such as authentication, from a remote data center instead of locally

Fortunately, these types of issues are easy to check for; the hard part is remembering to do it!

2.5.18   Cache Tuning

Applications and operating systems may employ multiple caches to improve I/O performance, from the application down to the disks. See Chapter 3, Operating Systems, Section 3.2.11, Caching, for a full list. Here is a general strategy for tuning each cache level:

1. Aim to cache as high in the stack as possible, closer to where the work is performed, reducing the operational overhead of cache hits. This location should also have more metadata available, which can be used to improve the cache retention policy.

2. Check that the cache is enabled and working.

3. Check the cache hit/miss ratios and miss rate.

4. If the cache size is dynamic, check its current size.

5. Tune the cache for the workload. This task depends on available cache tunable parameters.

6. Tune the workload for the cache. Doing this includes reducing unnecessary consumers of the cache, which frees up more space for the target workload.

Look out for double caching—for example, two different caches that consume main memory and cache the same data twice.

Also consider the overall performance gain of each level of cache tuning. Tuning the CPU Level 1 cache may save nanoseconds, as cache misses may then be served by Level 2. But improving CPU Level 3 cache may avoid much slower DRAM accesses and result in a greater overall performance gain. (These CPU caches are described in Chapter 6, CPUs.)

2.5.19   Micro-Benchmarking

Micro-benchmarking tests the performance of simple and artificial workloads. This differs from *macro-benchmarking* (or *industry benchmarking*), which typically aims to test a real-world and natural workload. Macro-benchmarking is performed by running workload simulations and can become complex to conduct and understand.

With fewer factors in play, micro-benchmarking is less complicated to conduct and understand. A commonly used micro-benchmark is Linux iperf(1), which performs a TCP throughput test: this can identify external network bottlenecks (which would otherwise be difficult to spot) by examining TCP counters during a production workload.

Micro-benchmarking can be performed by a *micro-benchmark tool* that applies the workload and measures its performance, or you can use a *load generator* tool that just applies the workload, leaving measurements of performance to other observability tools (example load generators are in Chapter 12, Benchmarking, Section 12.2.2, Simulation). Either approach is fine, but it can be safest to use a micro-benchmark tool *and* to double-check performance using other tools.

Some example targets of micro-benchmarks, including a second dimension for the tests, are:

- **Syscall time**: For fork(2), execve(2), open(2), read(2), close(2)
- **File system reads**: From a cached file, varying the read size from one byte to one Mbyte
- **Network throughput**: Transferring data between TCP endpoints, for varying socket buffer sizes

Micro-benchmarking typically conducts the target operation as quickly as possible and measures the time for a large number of these operations to complete. The average time can then be calculated (average time = runtime/operation count).

Later chapters include specific micro-benchmarking methodologies, listing the targets and attributes to test. The topic of benchmarking is covered in more detail in Chapter 12, Benchmarking.

2.5.20 Performance Mantras

This is a tuning methodology that shows how best to improve performance, listing actionable items in order from most to least effective. It is:

1. Don't do it.
2. Do it, but don't do it again.
3. Do it less.
4. Do it later.
5. Do it when they're not looking.
6. Do it concurrently.
7. Do it more cheaply.

Here are some examples for each of these:

1. Don't do it: Eliminate unnecessary work.
2. Do it, but don't do it again: Caching.
3. Do it less: Tune refreshes, polling, or updates to be less frequent.
4. Do it later: Write-back caching.
5. Do it when they're not looking: Schedule work to run during off-peak hours.
6. Do it concurrently: Switch from single-threaded to multi-threaded.
7. Do it more cheaply: Buy faster hardware.

This is one of my favorite methodologies, which I learned from Scott Emmons at Netflix. He attributes it to Craig Hanson and Pat Crain (though I've yet to find a published reference).

2.6 Modeling

Analytical modeling of a system can be used for various purposes, in particular *scalability analysis*: studying how performance scales as load or resources increase. Resources may be hardware (such as CPU cores) or software (processes or threads).

Analytical modeling can be considered the third type of performance evaluation activity, along with observability of a production system ("measurement") and experimental testing ("simulation") [Jain 91]. Performance is best understood when at least two of these activities are performed: analytical modeling and simulation, or simulation and measurement.

If the analysis is for an existing system, you can begin with measurement: characterizing the load and resulting performance. Experimental analysis, by testing a workload simulation, can be used if the system does not yet have production load, or in order to test workloads beyond what is seen in production. Analytical modeling can be used to predict performance and can be based on the results of measurement or simulation.

Scalability analysis may reveal that performance stops scaling linearly at a particular point due to a resource constraint. This is referred to as a *knee point*: when one function switches to another, in this case, from linear scaling to contention. Finding whether these points exist, and where, can direct an investigation to performance issues that inhibit scalability so that they can be fixed before they are encountered in production.

See Section 2.5.11, Workload Characterization, and Section 2.5.19, Micro-Benchmarking, for more on those steps.

2.6.1 Enterprise vs. Cloud

While modeling allows us to simulate large-scale enterprise systems without the expense of owning one, the performance of large-scale environments is often complex and difficult to model accurately.

With cloud computing, environments of any scale can be rented for short durations—the length of a benchmark test. Instead of creating a mathematical model from which to predict performance, the workload can be characterized, simulated, and then tested on clouds of different scales. Some of the findings, such as knee points, may be the same but will now be based on measured data rather than theoretical models, and by testing a real environment you may discover limiters that were not included in your model.

2.6.2 Visual Identification

When enough results can be collected experimentally, plotting them as delivered performance versus a scaling parameter may reveal a pattern.

Figure 2.15 shows the throughput of an application as the number of threads is scaled. There appears to be a knee point around eight threads, where the slope changes. This can now be investigated, for example by looking at the application and system configuration for any setting around the value of eight.

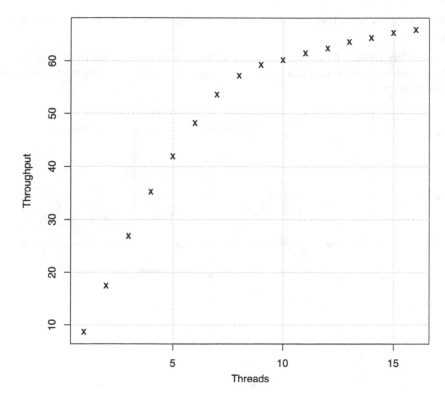

Figure 2.15   Scalability test results

In this case, the system was an eight-core system, each core having two hardware threads. To further confirm that this is related to the CPU core count, the CPU effects at fewer than and more than eight threads can be investigated and compared (e.g., IPC; see Chapter 6, CPUs). Or, this can be investigated experimentally by repeating the scaling test on a system with a different core count and confirming that the knee point moves as expected.

There are a number of scalability profiles to look for that may be identified visually, without using a formal model. These are shown in Figure 2.16.

For each of these, the x-axis is the scalability dimension, and the y-axis is the resulting performance (throughput, transactions per second, etc.). The patterns are:

- **Linear scalability**: Performance increases proportionally as the resource is scaled. This may not continue forever and may instead be the early stages of another scalability pattern.

- **Contention**: Some components of the architecture are shared and can be used only serially, and contention for these shared resources begins to reduce the effectiveness of scaling.

- **Coherence**: The tax to maintain data coherency including propagation of changes begins to outweigh the benefits of scaling.

- **Knee point:** A factor is encountered at a scalability point that changes the scalability profile.

- **Scalability ceiling:** A hard limit is reached. This may be a device bottleneck, such as a bus or interconnect reaching maximum throughput, or a software-imposed limit (system resource control).

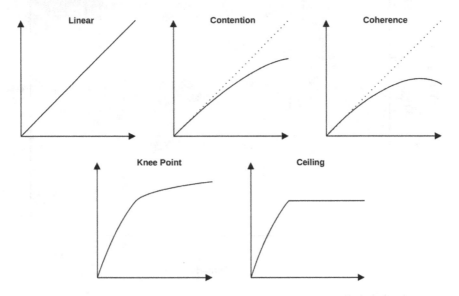

Figure 2.16   Scalability profiles

While visual identification can be easy and effective, you can learn more about system scalability by using a mathematical model. The model may deviate from the data in an unexpected way, which can be useful to investigate: either there is a problem with the model, and hence with your understanding of the system, or the problem is in the real scalability of the system. The next sections introduce Amdahl's Law of Scalability, the Universal Scalability Law, and queueing theory.

2.6.3   Amdahl's Law of Scalability

Named after computer architect Gene Amdahl [Amdahl 67], this law models system scalability, accounting for serial components of workloads that do not scale in parallel. It can be used to study the scaling of CPUs, threads, workloads, and more.

Amdahl's Law of Scalability was shown in the earlier scalability profiles as contention, which describes contention for the serial resource or workload component. It can be defined as [Gunther 97]:

$$C(N) = N/(1 + \alpha(N - 1))$$

The relative capacity is $C(N)$, and N is the scaling dimension, such as the CPU count or user load. The α parameter (where $0 <= \alpha <= 1$) represents the degree of seriality and is how this deviates from linear scalability.

Amdahl's Law of Scalability can be applied by taking the following steps:

1. Collect data for a range of N, either by observation of an existing system or experimentally using micro-benchmarking or load generators.

2. Perform regression analysis to determine the Amdahl parameter (α); this may be done using statistical software, such as gnuplot or R.

3. Present the results for analysis. The collected data points can be plotted along with the model function to predict scaling and reveal differences between the data and the model. This may also be done using gnuplot or R.

The following is example gnuplot code for Amdahl's Law of Scalability regression analysis, to provide a sense of how this step can be performed:

```
inputN = 10                    # rows to include as model input
alpha = 0.1                    # starting point (seed)
amdahl(N) = N1 * N/(1 + alpha * (N - 1))
# regression analysis (non-linear least squares fitting)
fit amdahl(x) filename every ::1::inputN using 1:2 via alpha
```

A similar amount of code is required to process this in R, involving the nls() function for non-linear least squares fitting to calculate the coefficients, which are then used during plotting. See the Performance Scalability Models toolkit in the references at the end of this chapter for the full code in both gnuplot and R [Gregg 14a].

An example Amdahl's Law of Scalability function is shown in the next section.

2.6.4 Universal Scalability Law

The Universal Scalability Law (USL), previously called the *super-serial model* [Gunther 97], was developed by Dr. Neil Gunther to include a parameter for coherency delay. This was pictured earlier as the coherence scalability profile, which includes the effects of contention.

USL can be defined as:

$$C(N) = N/(1 + \alpha(N - 1) + \beta N(N - 1))$$

$C(N)$, N, and α are as with Amdahl's Law of Scalability. β is the coherence parameter. When $\beta == 0$, this becomes Amdahl's Law of Scalability.

Examples of both USL and Amdahl's Law of Scalability analysis are graphed in Figure 2.17.

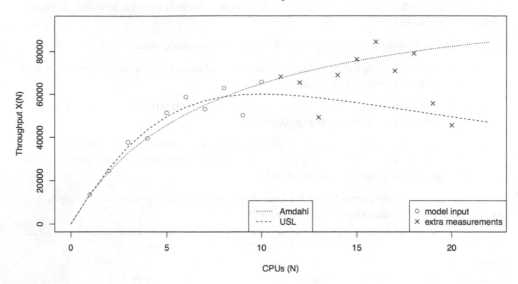

Figure 2.17   Scalability models

The input dataset has a high degree of variance, making it difficult to visually determine the scalability profile. The first ten data points, drawn as circles, were provided to the models. An additional ten data points are also plotted, drawn as crosses, which check the model prediction against reality.

For more on USL analysis, see [Gunther 97] and [Gunther 07].

2.6.5   Queueing Theory

Queueing theory is the mathematical study of systems with queues, providing ways to analyze their queue length, wait time (latency), and utilization (time-based). Many components in computing, both software and hardware, can be modeled as *queueing systems*. The modeling of multiple queueing systems is called *queueing networks*.

This section summarizes the role of queueing theory and provides an example to help you understand that role. It is a large field of study, covered in detail in other texts [Jain 91][Gunther 97].

Queueing theory builds upon various areas of mathematics and statistics, including probability distributions, stochastic processes, Erlang's C formula (Agner Krarup Erlang invented queueing theory), and Little's Law. Little's Law can be expressed as

$$L = \lambda W$$

which determines the average number of requests in a system, L, as the average arrival rate, λ, multiplied by the average request time in the system, W. This can be applied to a queue, such that L is the number of requests in the queue, and W is the average wait time on the queue.

Queueing systems can be used to answer a variety of questions, including the following:

- What will the mean response time be if the load doubles?
- What will be the effect on mean response time after adding an additional processor?
- Can the system provide a 90th percentile response time of under 100 ms when the load doubles?

Apart from response time, other factors, including utilization, queue lengths, and number of resident jobs, can be studied.

A simple queueing system model is shown in Figure 2.18.

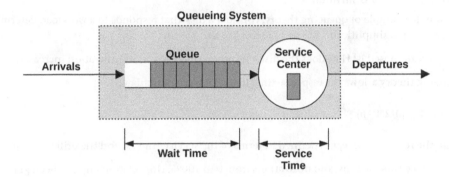

Figure 2.18   Queueing model

This has a single service center that processes jobs from the queue. Queueing systems can have multiple service centers that process work in parallel. In queueing theory, the service centers are often called *servers*.

Queueing systems can be categorized by three factors:

- **Arrival process:** This describes the inter-arrival time for requests to the queueing system, which may be random, fixed-time, or a process such as Poisson (which uses an exponential distribution for arrival time).
- **Service time distribution:** This describes the service times for the service center. They may be fixed (deterministic), exponential, or of another distribution type.
- **Number of service centers:** One or many.

These factors can be written in Kendall's notation.

Kendall's Notation

This notation assigns codes for each attribute. It has the form

$A/S/m$

These are the arrival process (A), service time distribution (S), and number of service centers (m). There is also an extended form of Kendall's notation that includes more factors: number of buffers in the system, population size, and service discipline.

Examples of commonly studied queueing systems are

- **M/M/1**: Markovian arrivals (exponentially distributed arrival times), Markovian service times (exponential distribution), one service center
- **M/M/c**: same as M/M/1, but multiserver
- **M/G/1**: Markovian arrivals, general distribution of service times (any), one service center
- **M/D/1**: Markovian arrivals, deterministic service times (fixed), one service center

M/G/1 is commonly applied to study the performance of rotational hard disks.

M/D/1 and 60% Utilization

As a simple example of queueing theory, consider a disk that responds to a workload deterministically (this is a simplification). The model is M/D/1.

The question posed is: How does the disk's response time vary as its utilization increases?

Queueing theory allows the response time for M/D/1 to be calculated:

$$r = s(2 - \rho)/2(1 - \rho)$$

where the response time, r, is defined in terms of the service time, s, and the utilization, ρ.

For a service time of 1 ms, and utilizations from 0 to 100%, this relationship has been graphed in Figure 2.19.

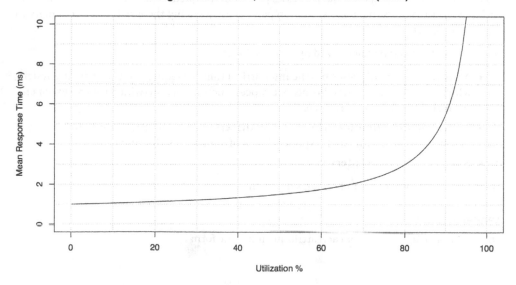

Figure 2.19   M/D/1 mean response time versus utilization

Beyond 60% utilization, the average response time doubles. By 80%, it has tripled. As disk I/O latency is often the bounding resource for an application, increasing the average latency by double or higher can have a significant negative effect on application performance. This is why disk utilization can become a problem well before it reaches 100%, as it is a queueing system where requests (typically) cannot be interrupted and must wait their turn. This is different from CPUs, for example, where higher-priority work can preempt.

This graph can visually answer an earlier question—what will the mean response time be if the load doubles?—when utilization is relative to load.

This model is simple, and in some ways it shows the best case. Variations in service time can drive the mean response time higher (e.g., using M/G/1 or M/M/1). There is also a distribution of response times, not pictured in Figure 2.19, such that the 90th and 99th percentiles degrade much faster beyond 60% utilization.

As with the earlier gnuplot example for Amdahl's Law of Scalability, it may be illustrative to show some actual code, for a sense of what may be involved. This time the R statistics software was used [R Project 20]:

```
svc_ms <- 1                 # average disk I/O service time, ms
util_min <- 0               # range to plot
util_max <- 100             # "
ms_min <- 0                 # "
ms_max <- 10                # "
# Plot mean response time vs utilization (M/D/1)
plot(x <- c(util_min:util_max), svc_ms * (2 - x/100) / (2 * (1 - x/100)),
    type="l", lty=1, lwd=1,
    xlim=c(util_min, util_max), ylim=c(ms_min, ms_max),
    xlab="Utilization %", ylab="Mean Response Time (ms)")
```

The earlier M/D/1 equation has been passed to the plot() function. Much of this code specifies limits to the graph, line properties, and axis labels.

2.7 Capacity Planning

Capacity planning examines how well the system will handle load and how it will scale as load scales. It can be performed in a number of ways, including studying resource limits and factor analysis, which are described here, and modeling, as introduced previously. This section also includes solutions for scaling, including load balancers and sharding. For more on this topic, see *The Art of Capacity Planning* [Allspaw 08].

For capacity planning of a particular application, it helps to have a quantified performance objective to plan for. Determining this is discussed early on in Chapter 5, Applications.

2.7.1   Resource Limits

This method is a search for the resource that will become the bottleneck under load. For containers, a resource may encounter a software-imposed limit that becomes the bottleneck. The steps for this method are:

1. Measure the rate of server requests, and monitor this rate over time.

2. Measure hardware and software resource usage. Monitor this rate over time.

3. Express server requests in terms of resources used.

4. Extrapolate server requests to known (or experimentally determined) limits for each resource.

Begin by identifying the role of the server and the type of requests it serves. For example, a web server serves HTTP requests, a Network File System (NFS) server serves NFS protocol requests (operations), and a database server serves query requests (or command requests, for which queries are a subset).

The next step is to determine the system resource consumption per request. For an existing system, the current rate of requests along with resource utilization can be measured. Extrapolation can then be used to see which resource will hit 100% utilization first, and what the rate of requests will be.

For a future system, micro-benchmarking or load generation tools can be used to simulate the intended requests in a test environment, while measuring resource utilization. Given sufficient client load, you may be able to find the limit experimentally.

The resources to monitor include:

- **Hardware:** CPU utilization, memory usage, disk IOPS, disk throughput, disk capacity (volume used), network throughput

- **Software:** Virtual memory usage, processes/tasks/threads, file descriptors

Let's say you're looking at an existing system currently performing 1,000 requests/s. The busiest resources are the 16 CPUs, which are averaging 40% utilization; you predict that they will become the bottleneck for this workload once they become 100% utilized. The question becomes: What will the requests-per-second rate be at that point?

CPU% per request = total CPU%/requests = 16 × 40%/1,000 = 0.64% CPU per request

max requests/s = 100% × 16 CPUs/CPU% per request = 1,600 / 0.64 = 2,500 requests/s

The prediction is 2,500 requests/s, at which point the CPUs will be 100% busy. This is a rough best-case estimate of capacity, as some other limiting factor may be encountered before the requests reach that rate.

This exercise used only one data point: application throughput (requests per second) of 1,000 versus device utilization of 40%. If monitoring over time is enabled, multiple data points at different throughput and utilization rates can be included, to improve the accuracy of the estimation. Figure 2.20 illustrates a visual method for processing these and extrapolating the maximum application throughput.

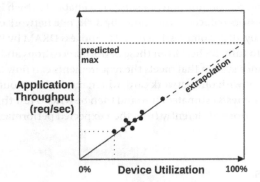

Figure 2.20 Resource limit analysis

Is 2,500 requests/s enough? Answering this question requires understanding what the peak workload will be, which shows up in daily access patterns. For an existing system that you have monitored over time, you may already have an idea of what the peak will look like.

Consider a web server that is processing 100,000 website hits per day. This may sound like many, but as an average is only one request/s—not much. However, it may be that most of the 100,000 website hits occur in the seconds after new content is posted, so the peak is significant.

2.7.2 Factor Analysis

When purchasing and deploying new systems, there are often many factors that can be changed to achieve the desired performance. These may include varying the number of disks and CPUs, the amount of RAM, the use of flash devices, RAID configurations, file system settings, and so forth. The task is usually to achieve the performance required for the minimum cost.

Testing all combinations would determine which has the best price/performance ratio; however, this can quickly get out of hand: eight binary factors would require 256 tests.

A solution is to test a limited set of combinations. Here is an approach based on knowing the maximum system configuration:

1. Test performance with all factors configured to maximum.

2. Change factors one by one, testing performance (it should drop for each).

3. Attribute a percentage performance drop to each factor, based on measurements, along with the cost savings.

4. Starting with maximum performance (and cost), choose factors to save cost, while maintaining the required requests per second based on their combined performance drop.

5. Retest the calculated configuration for confirmation of delivered performance.

For an eight-factor system, this approach may require only ten tests.

As an example, consider capacity planning for a new storage system, with a requirement of 1 Gbyte/s read throughput and a 200 Gbyte working set size. The maximum configuration achieves 2 Gbytes/s and includes four processors, 256 Gbytes of DRAM, 2 dual-port 10 GbE network cards, jumbo frames, and no compression or encryption enabled (which is costly to activate). Switching to two processors reduces performance by 30%, one network card by 25%, non-jumbo by 35%, encryption by 10%, compression by 40%, and less DRAM by 90% as the workload is no longer expected to fully cache. Given these performance drops and their known savings, the best price/performance system that meets the requirements can now be calculated; it might be a two-processor system with one network card, which meets the throughput needed: $2 \times (1 - 0.30) \times (1 - 0.25) = 1.04$ Gbytes/s estimated. It would then be wise to test this configuration, in case these components perform differently from their expected performance when used together.

2.7.3   Scaling Solutions

Meeting higher performance demands has often meant larger systems, a strategy called *vertical scaling*. Spreading load across numerous systems, usually fronted by systems called *load balancers* that make them all appear as one, is called *horizontal scaling*.

Cloud computing takes horizontal scaling further, by building upon smaller virtualized systems rather than entire systems. This provides finer granularity when purchasing compute to process the required load and allows scaling in small, efficient increments. Since no initial large purchase is required, as with enterprise mainframes (including a support contract commitment), there is less need for rigorous capacity planning in the early stages of a project.

There are technologies to automate cloud scaling based on a performance metric. The AWS technology for this is called an *auto scaling group (ASG)*. A custom scaling policy can be created to increase and decrease the number of instances based on a usage metric. This is pictured in Figure 2.21.

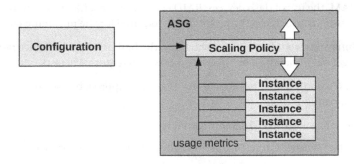

Figure 2.21   Auto scaling group

Netflix commonly uses ASGs that target a CPU utilization of 60%, and will scale up and down with the load to maintain that target.

Container orchestration systems may also provide support for automatic scaling. For example, Kubernetes provides horizontal pod autoscalers (HPAs) that can scale the number of Pods (containers) based on CPU utilization or another custom metric [Kubernetes 20a].

For databases, a common scaling strategy is *sharding*, where data is split into logical components, each managed by its own database (or redundant group of databases). For example, a customer database may be split into parts by splitting the customer names into alphabetical ranges. Picking an effective sharding key is crucial to evenly spread the load across the databases.

2.8 Statistics

It's important to have a good understanding of how to use statistics and what their limitations are. This section discusses quantifying performance issues using statistics (metrics) and statistical types including averages, standard deviations, and percentiles.

2.8.1 Quantifying Performance Gains

Quantifying issues and the potential performance improvement for fixing them allows them to be compared and prioritized. This task may be performed using observation or experiments.

Observation-Based

To quantify performance issues using observation:

1. Choose a reliable metric.

2. Estimate the performance gain from resolving the issue.

For example:

- Observed: Application request takes 10 ms.

- Observed: Of that, 9 ms is disk I/O.

- Suggestion: Configure the application to cache I/O in memory, with expected DRAM latency around ~10 μs.

- Estimated gain: 10 ms → 1.01 ms (10 ms - 9 ms + 10 μs) = ~9x gain.

As introduced in Section 2.3, Concepts, latency (time) is well suited for this, as it can be directly compared between components, which makes calculations like this possible.

When using latency, ensure that it is measured as a synchronous component of the application request. Some events occur asynchronously, such as background disk I/O (write flush to disk), and do not directly affect application performance.

Experimentation-Based

To quantify performance issues experimentally:

1. Apply the fix.

2. Quantify before versus after using a reliable metric.

For example:

- Observed: Application transaction latency averages 10 ms.

- Experiment: Increase the application thread count to allow more concurrency instead of queueing.

- Observed: Application transaction latency averages 2 ms.

- Gain: 10 ms → 2 ms = 5x.

This approach may not be appropriate if the fix is expensive to attempt in the production environment! For that case, observation-based should be used.

2.8.2 Averages

An average represents a dataset by a single value: an index of central tendency. The most common type of average used is an *arithmetic mean* (or *mean* for short), which is a sum of values divided by the count of values. Other types include the geometric mean and harmonic mean.

Geometric Mean

The *geometric mean* is the nth root (where n is the count of values) of multiplied values. This is described in [Jain 91], which includes an example of using it for network performance analysis: if the performance improvement of each layer of the kernel network stack is measured individually, what is the average performance improvement? Since the layers work together on the same packet, performance improvements have a "multiplicative" effect, which can be best summarized by the geometric mean.

Harmonic Mean

The *harmonic mean* is the count of values divided by the sum of their reciprocals. It is more appropriate for taking the average of rates, for example, calculating the average transfer rate for 800 Mbytes of data, when the first 100 Mbytes will be sent at 50 Mbytes/s and the remaining 700 Mbytes at a throttled rate of 10 Mbytes/s. The answer, using the harmonic mean, is 800/(100/50 + 700/10) = 11.1 Mbytes/s.

Averages over Time

With performance, many metrics we study are averages over time. A CPU is never "at 50% utilization"; it has been utilized during 50% of some interval, which could be a second, minute, or hour. It is important to check for intervals whenever considering averages.

For example, I had an issue where a customer had performance problems caused by CPU saturation (scheduler latency) even though their monitoring tools showed CPU utilization was never higher than 80%. The monitoring tool was reporting *5-minute averages*, which masked periods in which CPU utilization hit 100% for seconds at a time.

Decayed Average

A *decayed average* is sometimes used in systems performance. An example is the system "load averages" reported by various tools including uptime(1).

A decayed average is still measured over a time interval, but recent time is weighted more heavily than time further past. This reduces (dampens) short-term fluctuations in the average.

See Load Averages in Chapter 6, CPUs, Section 6.6, Observability Tools, for more on this.

Limitations

Averages are a summary statistic that hides details. I've analyzed many cases of occasional disk I/O latency outliers exceeding 100 ms, while the average latency was close to 1 ms. To better understand the data, you can use additional statistics covered in Section 2.8.3, Standard Deviation, Percentiles, Median (the next section), and visualizations covered in Section 2.10, Visualizations.

2.8.3 Standard Deviation, Percentiles, Median

Standard deviations and percentiles (e.g., 99th percentile) are statistical techniques to provide information on the *distribution* of data. The standard deviation is a measure of *variance*, with larger values indicating greater variance from the average (mean). The 99th percentile shows the point in the distribution that includes 99% of the values. Figure 2.22 pictures these for a *normal distribution*, along with the minimum and maximum.

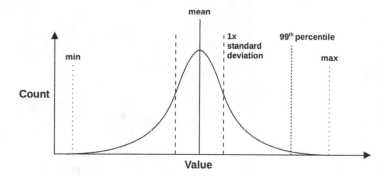

Figure 2.22   Statistical values

Percentiles such as 90th, 95th, 99th, and 99.9th are used in performance monitoring of request latency to quantify the slowest in the population. These may also be specified in service-level agreements (SLAs) as a way to measure that performance is acceptable for most users.

The 50th percentile, called the *median*, can be examined to show where the bulk of the data is.

2.8.4   Coefficient of Variation

Since standard deviation is relative to the mean, variance can be understood only when considering both standard deviation and mean. A standard deviation of 50 alone tells us little. That plus a mean of 200 tells us a lot.

There is a way to express variation as a single metric: the ratio of the standard deviation to the mean, which is called the *coefficient of variation* (CoV or CV). For this example, the CV is 25%. Lower CVs mean less variance.

Another expression of variance as a single metric is the z value, which is how many standard deviations a value is from the mean.

2.8.5   Multimodal Distributions

There is a problem with means, standard deviations, and percentiles, which may be obvious from the previous chart: they are intended for *normal*-like or unimodal distributions. System performance is often *bimodal*, returning low latencies for a fast code path and high latencies for a slow one, or low latencies for cache hits and high latencies for cache misses. There may also be more than two modes.

Figure 2.23 shows the distribution of disk I/O latency for a mixed workload of reads and writes, which includes random and sequential I/O.

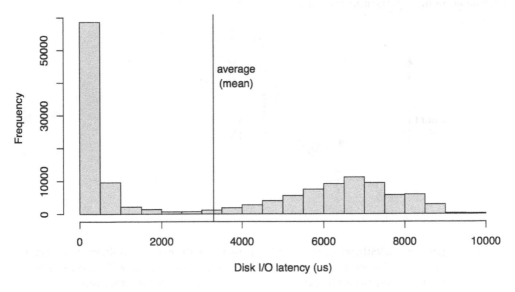

Figure 2.23   Latency distribution

This is presented as a histogram, which shows two modes. The mode on the left shows latencies of less than 1 ms, which is for on-disk cache hits. The right, with a peak around 7 ms, is for on-disk cache misses: random reads. The average (mean) I/O latency is 3.3 ms, which is plotted as a vertical line. This average is not the index of central tendency (as described earlier); in fact, it is almost the opposite. As a metric, the average for this distribution is seriously misleading.

> Then there was the man who drowned crossing a stream with an average depth of six inches. —W. I. E. Gates

Every time you see an average used as a performance metric, especially an average latency, ask: What is the distribution? Section 2.10, Visualizations, provides another example and shows how effective different visualizations and metrics are at showing this distribution.

2.8.6 Outliers

Another statistical problem is the presence of *outliers*: a very small number of extremely high or low values that don't appear to fit the expected distribution (single- or multimode).

Disk I/O latency outliers are an example—very occasional disk I/O that can take over 1,000 ms, when the majority of disk I/O is between 0 and 10 ms. Latency outliers like these can cause serious performance problems, but their presence can be difficult to identify from most metric types, other than as a maximum. Another example is network I/O latency outliers caused by TCP timer-based retransmits.

For a normal distribution, the presence of outliers is likely to shift the mean by a little, but not the median (which may be useful to consider). The standard deviation and 99th percentile have a better chance of identifying outliers, but this is still dependent on their frequency.

To better understand multimodal distributions, outliers, and other complex yet common behaviors, inspect the full distribution, for example by using a histogram. See Section 2.10, Visualizations, for more ways to do this.

2.9 Monitoring

System performance monitoring records performance statistics over time (a *time series*) so that the past can be compared to the present and time-based usage patterns can be identified. This is useful for capacity planning, quantifying growth, and showing peak usage. Historic values can also provide context for understanding the current value of performance metrics, by showing what the "normal" range and average have been in the past.

2.9.1 Time-Based Patterns

Examples of time-based patterns are shown in Figures 2.24, 2.25, and 2.26, which plot file system reads from a cloud computing server over different time intervals.

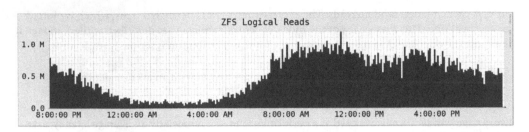

Figure 2.24   Monitoring activity: one day

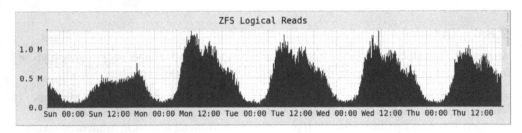

Figure 2.25   Monitoring activity: five days

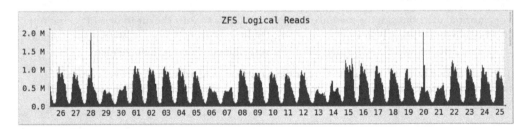

Figure 2.26   Monitoring activity: 30 days

These graphs show a daily pattern that begins to ramp up around 8 a.m., dips a little in the afternoon, and then decays during the night. The longer-scale charts show that activity is lower on the weekend days. A couple of short spikes are also visible in the 30-day chart.

Various cycles of behavior including those shown in the figures can commonly be seen in historic data, including:

- **Hourly**: Activity may occur every hour from the application environment, such as monitoring and reporting tasks. It's also common for these to execute with a 5- or 10-minute cycle.

- **Daily**: There may be a daily pattern of usage that coincides with work hours (9 a.m. to 5 p.m.), which may be stretched if the server is for multiple time zones. For Internet servers, the pattern may follow when worldwide users are active. Other daily activity may include nightly log rotation and backups.

- **Weekly**: As well as a daily pattern, there may be a weekly pattern present based on work-days and weekends.

- **Quarterly**: Financial reports are done on a quarterly schedule.

- **Yearly**: Yearly patterns of load may be due to school schedules and vacations.

Irregular increases in load may occur with other activities, such as releasing new content on a website, and sales (Black Friday/Cyber Monday in the US). Irregular decreases in load can occur due to external activities, such as widespread power or internet outages, and sports finals (where everyone watches the game instead of using your product).[6]

2.9.2 Monitoring Products

There are many third-party products for system performance monitoring. Typical features include archiving data and presenting it as browser-based interactive graphs, and providing configurable alerts.

Some of these operate by running *agents* (also known as *exporters*) on the system to gather their statistics. These agents either execute operating system observability tools (such as iostat(1) or sar(1)) and parse the text of the output (which is considered inefficient) or read directly from operating system libraries and kernel interfaces. Monitoring products support a collection of custom agents for exporting statistics from specific targets: web servers, databases, and language runtimes.

As systems become more distributed and the usage of cloud computing continues to grow, you will more often need to monitor numerous systems: hundreds, thousands, or more. This is where a centralized monitoring product can be especially useful, allowing an entire environment to be monitored from one interface.

As a specific example: the Netflix cloud is composed of over 200,000 instances and is monitored using the Atlas cloud-wide monitoring tool, which was custom built by Netflix to operate at this scale and is open source [Harrington 14]. Other monitoring products are discussed in Chapter 4, Observability Tools, Section 4.2.4, Monitoring.

2.9.3 Summary-Since-Boot

If monitoring has not been performed, check whether at least *summary-since-boot* values are available from the operating system, which can be used to compare with the current values.

2.10 Visualizations

Visualizations allow more data to be examined than can be easily understood (or sometimes even displayed) as text. They also enable pattern recognition and pattern matching. This can be an effective way to identify correlations between different metric sources, which may be difficult to accomplish programmatically, but easy to do visually.

---

[6]When I was on the Netflix SRE on-call rotation, I learned some non-traditional analysis tools for these cases: to check social media for suspected power outages and to ask in team chatrooms if anyone knew of a sports final.

2.10.1   Line Chart

A line chart (also called *line graph*) is a well-known, basic visualization. It is commonly used for examining performance metrics over time, showing the passage of time on the x-axis.

Figure 2.27 is an example, showing the average (mean) disk I/O latency for a 20-second period. This was measured on a production cloud server running a MySQL database, where disk I/O latency was suspected to be causing slow queries.

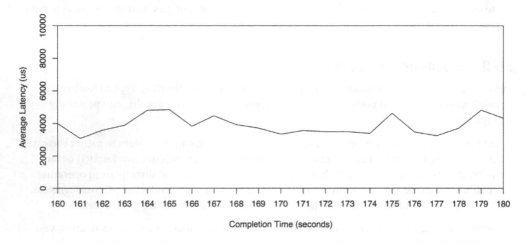

Figure 2.27   Line chart of average latency

This line chart shows fairly consistent average read latency of around 4 ms, which is higher than expected for these disks.

Multiple lines can be plotted, showing related data on the same set of axes. With this example, a separate line may be plotted for each disk, showing whether they exhibit similar performance.

Statistical values can also be plotted, providing more information on the distribution of data. Figure 2.28 shows the same range of disk I/O events, with lines added for the per-second median, standard deviation, and percentiles. Note that the y-axis now has a much greater range than the previous line chart (by a factor of 8).

This shows why the average is higher than expected: the distribution includes higher-latency I/O. Specifically, 1% of the I/O is over 20 ms, as shown by the 99th percentile. The median also shows where I/O latency was expected, around 1 ms.

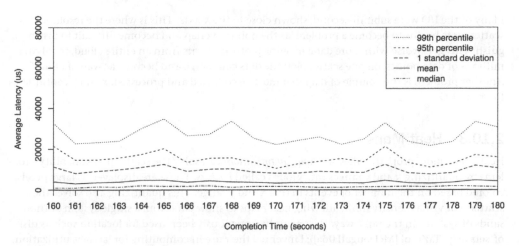

Figure 2.28 Median, mean, standard deviation, percentiles

2.10.2 Scatter Plots

Figure 2.29 shows disk I/O events for the same time range as a scatter plot, which enables all data to be seen. Each disk I/O is drawn as a point, with its completion time on the x-axis and latency on the y-axis.

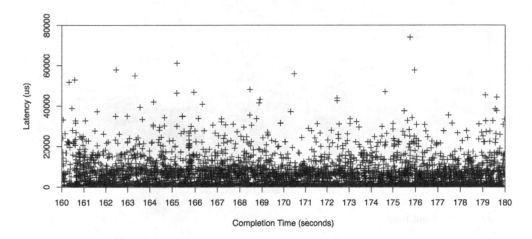

Figure 2.29 Scatter plot

Now the source of the higher-than-expected average latency can be understood fully: there are many disk I/O with latencies of 10 ms, 20 ms, even over 50 ms. The scatter plot has shown all the data, revealing the presence of these outliers.

Many of the I/O were submillisecond, shown close to the x-axis. This is where the resolution of scatter plots begins to become a problem, as the points overlap and become difficult to distinguish. This gets worse with more data: imagine plotting events from an entire cloud, involving millions of data points, on one scatter plot: the dots can merge and become a "wall of paint." Another problem is the volume of data that must be collected and processed: x and y coordinates for every I/O.

2.10.3 Heat Maps

Heat maps (more properly called a *column quantization*) can solve the scatter plot scalability problems by quantizing x and y ranges into groups called *buckets*. These are displayed as large pixels, colored based on the number of events in that x and y range. This quantizing also solves the scatter plot visual density limit, allowing heat maps to show data from a single system or thousands of systems in the same way. Heat maps had previously been used for location such as disk offsets (e.g., TazTool [McDougall 06a]); I invented their use in computing for latency, utilization, and other metrics. Latency heat maps were first included in Analytics for the Sun Microsystems ZFS Storage appliance, released in 2008 [Gregg 10a][Gregg 10b], and are now commonplace in performance monitoring products such as Grafana [Grafana 20].

The same dataset as plotted earlier is shown in Figure 2.30 as a heat map.

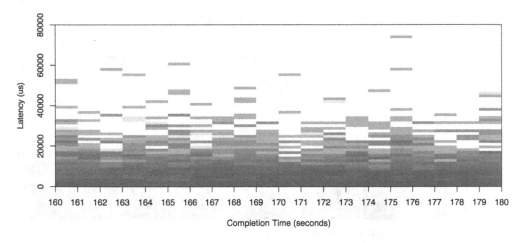

Figure 2.30   Heat map

High-latency outliers can be identified as blocks that are high in the heat map, usually of light colors as they span few I/O (often a single I/O). Patterns in the bulk of the data begin to emerge, which may be impossible to see with a scatter plot.

The full range of seconds for this disk I/O trace (not shown earlier) is shown in the Figure 2.31 heat map.

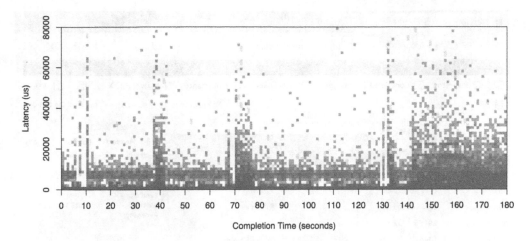

Figure 2.31   Heat map: full range

Despite spanning nine times the range, the visualization is still very readable. A bimodal distribution can be seen for much of the range, with some I/O returning with near-zero latency (likely a disk cache hit), and others with a little less than 1 ms (likely a disk cache miss).

There are other examples of heat maps later in this book, including in Chapter 6, CPUs, Section 6.7, Visualizations; Chapter 8, File Systems, Section 8.6.18, Visualizations; and Chapter 9, Disks, Section 9.7.3, Latency Heat Maps. My website also has examples of latency, utilization, and subsecond-offset heat maps [Gregg 15b].

2.10.4 Timeline Charts

A timeline chart shows a set of activities as bars on a timeline. These are commonly used for front-end performance analysis (web browsers), where they are also called *waterfall charts*, and show the timing of network requests. An example from the Firefox web browser is shown in Figure 2.32.

In Figure 2.32, the first network request is highlighted: apart from showing its duration as a horizontal bar, components of this duration are also shown as colored bars. These are also explained in the right panel: the slowest component for the first request is "Waiting," which is waiting for the HTTP response from the server. Requests two to six begin after the first request begins receiving data, and are likely dependent on that data. If explicit dependency arrows are included in the chart, it becomes a type of Gantt chart.

For back-end performance analysis (servers), similar charts are used to show timelines for threads or CPUs. Example software includes KernelShark [KernelShark 20] and Trace Compass [Eclipse 20]. For an example KernelShark screenshot, see Chapter 14, Ftrace, Section 14.11.5, KernelShark. Trace Compass also draws arrows showing dependencies, where one thread has woken up another.

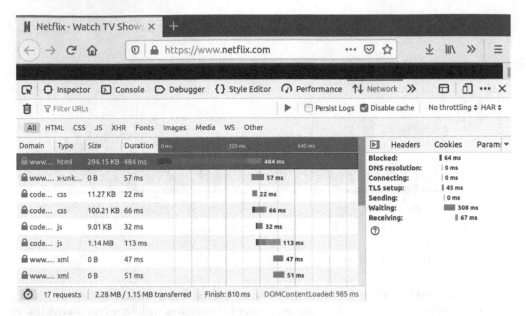

Figure 2.32   Firefox timeline chart

2.10.5 Surface Plot

This is a representation of three dimensions, rendered as a three-dimensional surface. It works best when the third-dimension value does not frequently change dramatically from one point to the next, producing a surface resembling rolling hills. A surface plot is often rendered as a *wireframe model*.

Figure 2.33 shows a wireframe surface plot of per-CPU utilization. It contains 60 seconds of per-second values from many servers (this is cropped from an image that spanned a data center of over 300 physical servers and 5,312 CPUs) [Gregg 11b].

Each server is represented by plotting its 16 CPUs as rows on the surface, the 60 per-second utilization measurements as columns, and then setting the height of the surface to the utilization value. Color is also set to reflect the utilization value. Both hue and saturation could be used, if desired, to add fourth and fifth dimensions of data to the visualization. (With sufficient resolution, a pattern could be used to indicate a sixth dimension.)

These 16 × 60 server rectangles are then mapped across the surface as a checkerboard. Even without markings, some server rectangles can be clearly seen in the image. One that appears as an elevated plateau on the right shows that its CPUs are almost always at 100%.

The use of grid lines highlights subtle changes in elevation. Some faint lines are visible, which indicate a single CPU constantly running at low utilization (a few percent).

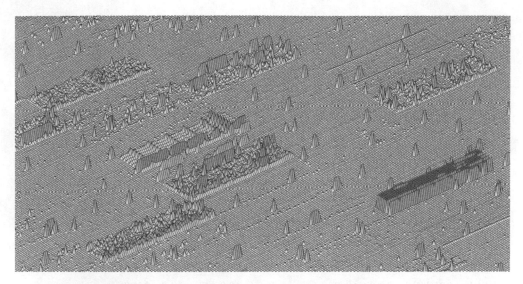

Figure 2.33 Wireframe surface plot: data center CPU utilization

2.10.6 Visualization Tools

Unix performance analysis has historically focused on the use of text-based tools, due in part to limited graphical support. Such tools can be executed quickly over a login session and report data in real time. Visualizations have been more time-consuming to access and often require a trace-and-report cycle. When working urgent performance issues, the speed at which you can access metrics can be critical.

Modern visualization tools provide real-time views of system performance, accessible from the browser and mobile devices. There are numerous products that do this, including many that can monitor your entire cloud. Chapter 1, Introduction, Section 1.7.1, Counters, Statistics, and Metrics, includes an example screenshot from one such product, Grafana, and other monitoring products are discussed in Chapter 4, Observability Tools, Section 4.2.4, Monitoring.

2.11 Exercises

1. Answer the following questions about key performance terminology:

   - What are IOPS?
   - What is utilization?
   - What is saturation?
   - What is latency?
   - What is micro-benchmarking?

2. Choose five methodologies to use for your (or a hypothetical) environment. Select the order in which they can be conducted, and explain the reason for choosing each.

3. Summarize problems when using average latency as a sole performance metric. Can these problems be solved by including the 99th percentile?

2.12   References

[**Amdahl 67**] Amdahl, G., "Validity of the Single Processor Approach to Achieving Large Scale Computing Capabilities," *AFIPS*, 1967.

[**Jain 91**] Jain, R., *The Art of Computer Systems Performance Analysis: Techniques for Experimental Design, Measurement, Simulation and Modeling*, Wiley, 1991.

[**Cockcroft 95**] Cockcroft, A., *Sun Performance and Tuning*, Prentice Hall, 1995.

[**Gunther 97**] Gunther, N., *The Practical Performance Analyst*, McGraw-Hill, 1997.

[**Wong 97**] Wong, B., *Configuration and Capacity Planning for Solaris Servers*, Prentice Hall, 1997.

[**Elling 00**] Elling, R., "Static Performance Tuning," *Sun Blueprints*, 2000.

[**Millsap 03**] Millsap, C., and J. Holt., *Optimizing Oracle Performance*, O'Reilly, 2003.

[**McDougall 06a**] McDougall, R., Mauro, J., and Gregg, B., *Solaris Performance and Tools: DTrace and MDB Techniques for Solaris 10 and OpenSolaris*, Prentice Hall, 2006.

[**Gunther 07**] Gunther, N., *Guerrilla Capacity Planning*, Springer, 2007.

[**Allspaw 08**] Allspaw, J., *The Art of Capacity Planning*, O'Reilly, 2008.

[**Gregg 10a**] Gregg, B., "Visualizing System Latency," *Communications of the ACM*, July 2010.

[**Gregg 10b**] Gregg, B., "Visualizations for Performance Analysis (and More)," *USENIX LISA*, https://www.usenix.org/legacy/events/lisa10/tech/#gregg, 2010.

[**Gregg 11b**] Gregg, B., "Utilization Heat Maps," http://www.brendangregg.com/HeatMaps/utilization.html, published 2011.

[**Williams 11**] Williams, C., "The $300m Cable That Will Save Traders Milliseconds," *The Telegraph*, https://www.telegraph.co.uk/technology/news/8753784/The-300m-cable-that-will-save-traders-milliseconds.html, 2011.

[**Gregg 13b**] Gregg, B., "Thinking Methodically about Performance," *Communications of the ACM*, February 2013.

[**Gregg 14a**] Gregg, B., "Performance Scalability Models," https://github.com/brendangregg/PerfModels, 2014.

[**Harrington 14**] Harrington, B., and Rapoport, R., "Introducing Atlas: Netflix's Primary Telemetry Platform," *Netflix Technology Blog*, https://medium.com/netflix-techblog/introducing-atlas-netflixs-primary-telemetry-platform-bd31f4d8ed9a, 2014.

[**Gregg 15b**] Gregg, B., "Heatmaps," http://www.brendangregg.com/heatmaps.html, 2015.

[Wilkie 18] Wilkie, T., "The RED Method: Patterns for Instrumentation & Monitoring," *Grafana Labs*, https://www.slideshare.net/grafana/the-red-method-how-to-monitoring-your-microservices, 2018.

[Eclipse 20] Eclipse Foundation, "Trace Compass," https://www.eclipse.org/tracecompass, accessed 2020.

[Wikipedia 20] Wikipedia, "Five Whys," https://en.wikipedia.org/wiki/Five_whys, accessed 2020.

[Grafana 20] Grafana Labs, "Heatmap," https://grafana.com/docs/grafana/latest/features/panels/heatmap, accessed 2020.

[KernelShark 20] "KernelShark," https://www.kernelshark.org, accessed 2020.

[Kubernetes 20a] Kubernetes, "Horizontal Pod Autoscaler," https://kubernetes.io/docs/tasks/run-application/horizontal-pod-autoscale, accessed 2020.

[R Project 20] R Project, "The R Project for Statistical Computing," https://www.r-project.org, accessed 2020.

Chapter 3

Operating Systems

An understanding of the operating system and its kernel is essential for systems performance analysis. You will frequently need to develop and then test hypotheses about system behavior, such as how system calls are being performed, how the kernel schedules threads on CPUs, how limited memory could be affecting performance, or how a file system processes I/O. These activities will require you to apply your knowledge of the operating system and the kernel.

The learning objectives of this chapter are:

- Learn kernel terminology: context switches, swapping, paging, preemption, etc.
- Understand the role of the kernel and system calls.
- Gain a working knowledge of kernel internals, including: interrupts, schedulers, virtual memory, and the I/O stack.
- See how kernel performance features have been added from Unix to Linux.
- Develop a basic understanding of extended BPF.

This chapter provides an overview of operating systems and kernels and is assumed knowledge for the rest of the book. If you missed operating systems class, you can treat this as a crash course. Keep an eye out for any gaps in your knowledge, as there will be an exam at the end (I'm kidding; it's just a quiz). For more on kernel internals, see the references at the end of this chapter.

This chapter has three sections:

- **Terminology** lists essential terms.
- **Background** summarizes key operating system and kernel concepts.
- **Kernels** summarizes implementation specifics of Linux and other kernels.

Areas related to performance, including CPU scheduling, memory, disks, file systems, networking, and many specific performance tools, are covered in more detail in the chapters that follow.

3.1   Terminology

For reference, here is the core operating system terminology used in this book. Many of these are also concepts that are explained in more detail in this and later chapters.

- **Operating system:** This refers to the software and files that are installed on a system so that it can boot and execute programs. It includes the kernel, administration tools, and system libraries.

- **Kernel:** The kernel is the program that manages the system, including (depending on the kernel model) hardware devices, memory, and CPU scheduling. It runs in a privileged CPU mode that allows direct access to hardware, called *kernel mode*.

- **Process:** An OS abstraction and environment for executing a program. The program runs in *user mode*, with access to kernel mode (e.g., for performing device I/O) via system calls or traps into the kernel.

- **Thread:** An executable context that can be scheduled to run on a CPU. The kernel has multiple threads, and a process contains one or more.

- **Task:** A Linux runnable entity, which can refer to a process (with a single thread), a thread from a multithreaded process, or kernel threads.

- **BPF program:** A kernel-mode program running in the BPF[1] execution environment.

- **Main memory:** The physical memory of the system (e.g., RAM).

- **Virtual memory:** An abstraction of main memory that supports multitasking and over-subscription. It is, practically, an infinite resource.

- **Kernel space:** The virtual memory address space for the kernel.

- **User space:** The virtual memory address space for processes.

- **User land:** User-level programs and libraries (/usr/bin, /usr/lib...).

- **Context switch:** A switch from running one thread or process to another. This is a normal function of the kernel CPU scheduler, and involves switching the set of running CPU registers (the thread context) to a new set.

- **Mode switch:** A switch between kernel and user modes.

- **System call (syscall):** A well-defined protocol for user programs to request the kernel to perform privileged operations, including device I/O.

- **Processor:** Not to be confused with *process*, a processor is a physical chip containing one or more CPUs.

- **Trap:** A signal sent to the kernel to request a system routine (privileged action). Trap types include system calls, processor exceptions, and interrupts.

---

[1] BPF originally stood for Berkeley Packet Filter, but the technology today has so little to do with Berkeley, packets, or filtering that BPF has become a name in itself rather than an acronym.

- **Hardware interrupt**: A signal sent by physical devices to the kernel, usually to request servicing of I/O. An interrupt is a type of trap.

The Glossary includes more terminology for reference if needed for this chapter, including *address space*, *buffer*, *CPU*, *file descriptor*, *POSIX*, and *registers*.

3.2 Background

The following sections describe generic operating system and kernel concepts, and will help you understand any operating system. To aid your comprehension, this section includes some Linux implementation details. The next sections, 3.3 Kernels, and 3.4 Linux, focus on Unix, BSD, and Linux kernel implementation specifics.

3.2.1 Kernel

The kernel is the core software of the operating system. What it does depends on the kernel model: Unix-like operating systems including Linux and BSD have a *monolithic* kernel that manages CPU scheduling, memory, file systems, network protocols, and system devices (disks, network interfaces, etc.). This kernel model is shown in Figure 3.1.

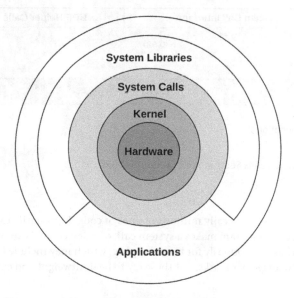

Figure 3.1   Role of a monolithic operating system kernel

Also shown are system libraries, which are often used to provide a richer and easier programming interface than the system calls alone. Applications include all running user-level software, including databases, web servers, administration tools, and operating system shells.

System libraries are pictured here as a broken ring to show that applications can call system calls (*syscalls*) directly.[2] For example, the Golang runtime has its own syscall layer that doesn't require the system library, libc. Traditionally, this diagram is drawn with complete rings, which reflect decreasing levels of privilege starting with the kernel at the center (a model that originated in Multics [Graham 68], the predecessor of Unix).

Other kernel models also exist: *microkernels* employ a small kernel with functionality moved to user-mode programs; and *unikernels* compile kernel and application code together as a single program. There are also *hybrid kernels*, such as the Windows NT kernel, which use approaches from both monolithic kernels and microkernels together. These are summarized in Section 3.5, Other Topics.

Linux has recently changed its model by allowing a new software type: Extended BPF, which enables secure kernel-mode applications along with its own kernel API: BPF helpers. This allows some applications and system functions to be rewritten in BPF, providing higher levels of security and performance. This is pictured in Figure 3.2.

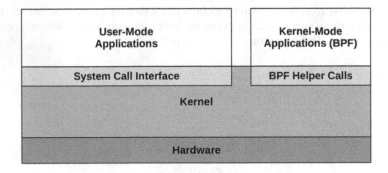

Figure 3.2   BPF applications

Extended BPF is summarized is Section 3.4.4, Extended BPF.

Kernel Execution

The kernel is a large program, typically millions of lines of code. It primarily executes on demand, when a user-level program makes a system call, or a device sends an interrupt. Some kernel threads operate asynchronously for housekeeping, which may include the kernel clock routine and memory management tasks, but these try to be lightweight and consume very little CPU resources.

---

[2]There are some exceptions to this model. Kernel bypass technologies, sometimes used for networking, allow user-level to access hardware directly (see Chapter 10, Network, Section 10.4.3, Software, heading Kernel Bypass). I/O to hardware may also be submitted without the expense of the syscall interface (although syscalls are required for initialization), for example, with memory-mapped I/O, major faults (see Chapter 7, Memory, Section 7.2.3, Demand Paging), sendfile(2), and Linux io_uring (see Chapter 5, Applications, Section 5.2.6, Non-Blocking I/O).

Workloads that perform frequent I/O, such as web servers, execute mostly in kernel context. Workloads that are compute-intensive usually run in user mode, uninterrupted by the kernel. It may be tempting to think that the kernel cannot affect the performance of these compute-intensive workloads, but there are many cases where it does. The most obvious is CPU contention, when other threads are competing for CPU resources and the kernel scheduler needs to decide which will run and which will wait. The kernel also chooses which CPU a thread will run on and can choose CPUs with warmer hardware caches or better memory locality for the process, to significantly improve performance.

3.2.2 Kernel and User Modes

The kernel runs in a special CPU mode called *kernel mode*, allowing full access to devices and the execution of privileged instructions. The kernel arbitrates device access to support multitasking, preventing processes and users from accessing each other's data unless explicitly allowed.

User programs (processes) run in *user mode*, where they request privileged operations from the kernel via system calls, such as for I/O.

Kernel and user mode are implemented on processors using *privilege rings* (or *protection rings*) following the model in Figure 3.1. For example, x86 processors support four privilege rings, numbered 0 to 3. Typically only two or three are used: for user mode, kernel mode, and the hypervisor if present. Privileged instructions for accessing devices are only allowed in kernel mode; executing them in user mode causes *exceptions*, which are then handled by the kernel (e.g., to generate a permission denied error).

In a traditional kernel, a system call is performed by switching to kernel mode and then executing the system call code. This is shown in Figure 3.3.

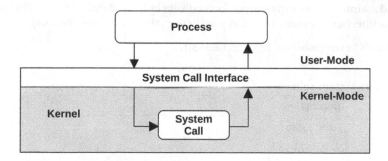

Figure 3.3 System call execution modes

Switching between user and kernel modes is a *mode switch*.

All system calls mode switch. Some system calls also *context switch*: those that are blocking, such as for disk and network I/O, will context switch so that another thread can run while the first is blocked.

Since mode and context switches cost a small amount of overhead (CPU cycles),[3] there are various optimizations to avoid them, including:

- **User-mode syscalls:** It is possible to implement some syscalls in a user-mode library alone. The Linux kernel does this by exporting a virtual dynamic shared object (vDSO) that is mapped into the process address space, which contains syscalls such as gettimeofday(2) and getcpu(2) [Drysdale 14].

- **Memory mappings:** Used for demand paging (see Chapter 7, Memory, Section 7.2.3, Demand Paging), it can also be used for data stores and other I/O, avoiding syscall overheads.

- **Kernel bypass:** This allows user-mode programs to access devices directly, bypassing syscalls and the typical kernel code path. For example, DPDK for networking: the Data Plane Development Kit.

- **Kernel-mode applications:** These include the TUX web server [Lever 00], implemented in-kernel, and more recently the extended BPF technology pictured in Figure 3.2.

Kernel and user mode have their own software execution contexts, including a stack and registers. Some processor architectures (e.g., SPARC) use a separate address space for the kernel, which means the mode switch must also change the virtual memory context.

3.2.3 System Calls

System calls request the kernel to perform privileged system routines. There are hundreds of system calls available, but some effort is made by kernel maintainers to keep that number as small as possible, to keep the kernel simple (Unix philosophy; [Thompson 78]). More sophisticated interfaces can be built upon them in user-land as system libraries, where they are easier to develop and maintain. Operating systems generally include a C standard library that provides easier-to-use interfaces for many common syscalls (e.g., the libc or glibc libraries).

Key system calls to remember are listed in Table 3.1.

Table 3.1 **Key system calls**

System Call	Description
read(2)	Read bytes
write(2)	Write bytes
open(2)	Open a file
close(2)	Close a file
fork(2)	Create a new process
clone(2)	Create a new process or thread
exec(2)	Execute a new program

---

[3]With the current mitigation for the Meltdown vulnerability, context switches are now more expensive. See Section 3.4.3 KPTI (Meltdown).

System Call	Description
connect(2)	Connect to a network host
accept(2)	Accept a network connection
stat(2)	Fetch file statistics
ioctl(2)	Set I/O properties, or other miscellaneous functions
mmap(2)	Map a file to the memory address space
brk(2)	Extend the heap pointer
futex(2)	Fast user-space mutex

System calls are well documented, each having a man page that is usually shipped with the operating system. They also have a generally simple and consistent interface and use error codes to describe errors when needed (e.g., ENOENT for "no such file or directory").[4]

Many of these system calls have an obvious purpose. Here are a few whose common usage may be less obvious:

- **ioctl(2):** This is commonly used to request miscellaneous actions from the kernel, especially for system administration tools, where another (more obvious) system call isn't suitable. See the example that follows.

- **mmap(2):** This is commonly used to map executables and libraries to the process address space, and for memory-mapped files. It is sometimes used to allocate the working memory of a process, instead of the brk(2)-based malloc(2), to reduce the syscall rate and improve performance (which doesn't always work due to the trade-off involved: memory-mapping management).

- **brk(2):** This is used to extend the heap pointer, which defines the size of the working memory of the process. It is typically performed by a system memory allocation library, when a malloc(3) (memory allocate) call cannot be satisfied from the existing space in the heap. See Chapter 7, Memory.

- **futex(2):** This syscall is used to handle part of a user space lock: the part that is likely to block.

If a system call is unfamiliar, you can learn more in its man page (these are in section 2 of the man pages: syscalls).

The ioctl(2) syscall may be the most difficult to learn, due to its ambiguous nature. As an example of its usage, the Linux perf(1) tool (introduced in Chapter 6, CPUs) performs privileged actions to coordinate performance instrumentation. Instead of system calls being added for each action, a single system call is added: perf_event_open(2), which returns a file descriptor for use with ioctl(2). This ioctl(2) can then be called using different arguments to perform the different desired actions. For example, ioctl(fd, PERF_EVENT_IOC_ENABLE) enables instrumentation. The arguments, in this example PERF_EVENT_IOC_ENABLE, can be more easily added and changed by the developer.

---

[4]glibc provides these errors in an errno (error number) integer variable.

3.2.4 Interrupts

An *interrupt* is a signal to the processor that some event has occurred that needs processing, and interrupts the current execution of the processor to handle it. It typically causes the processor to enter kernel mode if it isn't already, save the current thread state, and then run an *interrupt service routine* (ISR) to process the event.

There are asynchronous interrupts generated by external hardware and synchronous interrupts generated by software instructions. These are pictured in Figure 3.4.

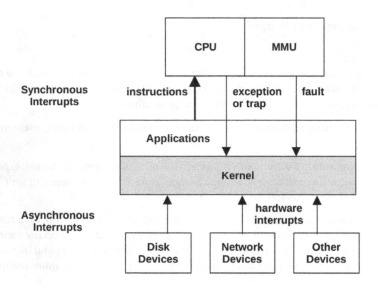

Figure 3.4   Interrupt types

For simplicity Figure 3.4 shows all interrupts sent to the kernel for processing; these are sent to the CPU first, which selects the ISR in the kernel to run the event.

Asynchronous Interrupts

Hardware devices can send *interrupt service requests* (IRQs) to the processor, which arrive asynchronously to the currently running software. Examples of hardware interrupts include:

- Disk devices signaling the completion of disk I/O
- Hardware indicating a failure condition
- Network interfaces signaling the arrival of a packet
- Input devices: keyboard and mouse input

To explain the concept of asynchronous interrupts, an example scenario is pictured in Figure 3.5 showing the passage of time as a database (MySQL) running on CPU 0 reads from a file system. The file system contents must be fetched from disk, so the scheduler context switches to another thread (a Java application) while the database is waiting. Sometime later, the disk I/O completes, but at this point the database is no longer running on CPU 0. The completion interrupt has occurred asynchronously to the database, showed by a dotted line in Figure 3.5.

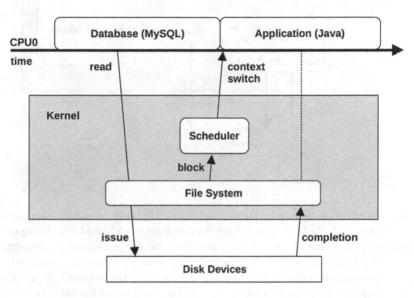

Figure 3.5 Asynchronous interrupt example

Synchronous Interrupts

Synchronous interrupts are generated by software instructions. The following describes different types of software interrupts using the terms *traps*, *exceptions*, and *faults*; however, these terms are often used interchangeably.

- **Traps**: A deliberate call into the kernel, such as by the int (interrupt) instruction. One implementation of syscalls involves calling the int instruction with a vector for a syscall handler (e.g., int 0x80 on Linux x86). int raises a software interrupt.

- **Exceptions**: A exceptional condition, such as by an instruction performing a divide by zero.

- **Faults**: A term often used for memory events, such as *page faults* triggered by accessing a memory location without an MMU mapping. See Chapter 7, Memory.

For these interrupts, the responsible software and instruction are still on CPU.

Interrupt Threads

Interrupt service routines (ISRs) are designed to operate as quickly as possible, to reduce the effects of interrupting active threads. If an interrupt needs to perform more than a little work, especially if it may block on locks, it can be processed by an interrupt thread that can be scheduled by the kernel. This is pictured in Figure 3.6.

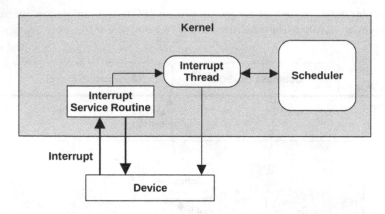

Figure 3.6   Interrupt processing

How this is implemented depends on the kernel version. On Linux, device drivers can be modeled as two halves, with the top half handling the interrupt quickly, and scheduling work to a bottom half to be processed later [Corbet 05]. Handling the interrupt quickly is important as the top half runs in *interrupt-disabled* mode to postpone the delivery of new interrupts, which can cause latency problems for other threads if it runs for too long. The bottom half can be either *tasklets* or *work queues*; the latter are threads that can be scheduled by the kernel and can sleep when necessary.

Linux network drivers, for example, have a top half to handle IRQs for inbound packets, which calls the bottom half to push the packet up the network stack. The bottom half is implemented as a *softirq* (software interrupt).

The time from an interrupt's arrival to when it is serviced is the *interrupt latency*, which is dependent on the hardware and implementation. This is a subject of study for real-time or low-latency systems.

Interrupt Masking

Some code paths in the kernel cannot be interrupted safely. An example is kernel code that acquires a spin lock during a system call, for a spin lock that might also be needed by an interrupt. Taking an interrupt with such a lock held could cause a deadlock. To prevent such a situation, the kernel can temporarily mask interrupts by setting the CPU's *interrupt mask* register. The interrupt disabled time should be as short as possible, as it can perturb the timely execution of applications that are woken up by other interrupts. This is an important factor for *real-time* systems—those that have strict response time requirements. Interrupt disabled time is also a target of performance analysis (such analysis is supported directly by the Ftrace irqsoff tracer, mentioned in Chapter 14, Ftrace).

Some high-priority events should not be ignored, and so are implemented as *non-maskable interrupts* (NMIs). For example, Linux can use an Intelligent Platform Management Interface (IPMI) watchdog timer that checks if the kernel appears to have locked up based on a lack of interrupts during a period of time. If so, the watchdog can issue an NMI interrupt to reboot the system.[5]

3.2.5 Clock and Idle

A core component of the original Unix kernel is the clock() routine, executed from a timer interrupt. It has historically been executed at 60, 100, or 1,000 times per second[6] (often expressed in Hertz: cycles per second), and each execution is called a *tick*.[7] Its functions have included updating the system time, expiring timers and time slices for thread scheduling, maintaining CPU statistics, and executing scheduled kernel routines.

There have been performance issues with the clock, improved in later kernels, including:

- **Tick latency:** For 100 Hertz clocks, up to 10 ms of additional latency may be encountered for a timer as it waits to be processed on the next tick. This has been fixed using high-resolution real-time interrupts so that execution occurs immediately.

- **Tick overhead:** Ticks consume CPU cycles and slightly perturb applications, and are one cause of what is known as *operating system jitter*. Modern processors also have dynamic power features, which can power down parts during idle periods. The clock routine interrupts this idle time, which can consume power needlessly.

Modern kernels have moved much functionality out of the clock routine to on-demand interrupts, in an effort to create a *tickless kernel*. This reduces overhead and improves power efficiency by allowing processors to remain in sleep states for longer.

The Linux clock routine is scheduler_tick(), and Linux has ways to omit calling the clock while there isn't any CPU load. The clock itself typically runs at 250 Hertz (configured by the CONFIG_HZ Kconfig option and variants), and its calls are reduced by the NO_HZ functionality (configured by CONFIG_NO_HZ and variants), which is now commonly enabled [Linux 20a].

Idle Thread

When there is no work for the CPUs to perform, the kernel schedules a placeholder thread that waits for work, called the *idle thread*. A simple implementation would check for the availability of new work in a loop. In modern Linux the *idle task* can call the hlt (halt) instruction to power down the CPU until the next interrupt is received, saving power.

3.2.6 Processes

A process is an environment for executing a user-level program. It consists of a memory address space, file descriptors, thread stacks, and registers. In some ways, a process is like a virtual early computer, where only one program is executing with its own registers and stacks.

---

[5] Linux also has a software NMI watchdog for detecting lockups [Linux 20d].

[6] Other rates include 250 for Linux 2.6.13, 256 for Ultrix, and 1,024 for OSF/1 [Mills 94].

[7] Linux also tracks *jiffies*, a unit of time similar to ticks.

Processes are multitasked by the kernel, which typically supports the execution of thousands of processes on a single system. They are individually identified by their *process ID* (PID), which is a unique numeric identifier.

A process contains one or more *threads*, which operate in the process address space and share the same file descriptors. A thread is an executable context consisting of a stack, registers, and an instruction pointer (also called a *program counter*). Multiple threads allow a single process to execute in parallel across multiple CPUs. On Linux, threads and processes are both *tasks*.

The first process launched by the kernel is called "init," from /sbin/init (by default), with PID 1, which launches user space services. In Unix this involved running start scripts from /etc, a method now referred to as SysV (after Unix System V). Linux distributions now commonly use the systemd software to start services and track their dependencies.

Process Creation

Processes are normally created using the fork(2) system call on Unix systems. On Linux, C libraries typically implement the fork function by wrapping around the versatile clone(2) syscall. These syscalls create a duplicate of the process, with its own process ID. The exec(2) system call (or a variant, such as execve(2)) can then be called to begin execution of a different program.

Figure 3.7 shows an example process creation for a bash shell (bash) executing the ls command.

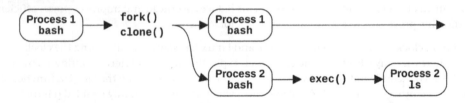

Figure 3.7   Process creation

The fork(2) or clone(2) syscall may use a copy-on-write (COW) strategy to improve performance. This adds references to the previous address space rather than copying all of the contents. Once either process modifies the multiple-referenced memory, a separate copy is then made for the modifications. This strategy either defers or eliminates the need to copy memory, reducing memory and CPU usage.

Process Life Cycle

The life cycle of a process is shown in Figure 3.8. This is a simplified diagram; for modern multithreaded operating systems it is the threads that are scheduled and run, and there are some additional implementation details regarding how these map to process states (see Figures 5.6 and 5.7 in Chapter 5 for more detailed diagrams).

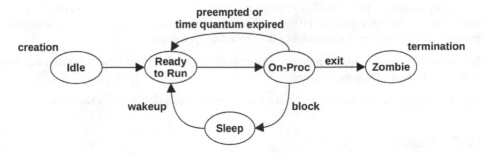

Figure 3.8 Process life cycle

The on-proc state is for running on a processor (CPU). The ready-to-run state is when the process is runnable but is waiting on a CPU run queue for its turn on a CPU. Most I/O will block, putting the process in the sleep state until the I/O completes and the process is woken up. The zombie state occurs during process termination, when the process waits until its process status has been reaped by the parent process or until it is removed by the kernel.

Process Environment

The process environment is shown in Figure 3.9; it consists of data in the address space of the process and metadata (context) in the kernel.

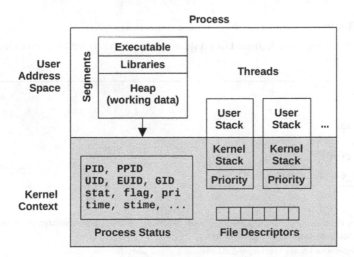

Figure 3.9 Process environment

The kernel context consists of various process properties and statistics: its process ID (PID), the owner's user ID (UID), and various times. These are commonly examined via the ps(1) and top(1) commands. It also has a set of file descriptors, which refer to open files and which are (usually) shared between threads.

This example pictures two threads, each containing some metadata, including a priority in kernel context[8] and user stack in the user address space. The diagram is not drawn to scale; the kernel context is very small compared to the process address space.

The user address space contains memory segments of the process: executable, libraries, and heap. For more details, see Chapter 7, Memory.

On Linux, each thread has its own user stack and a kernel exception stack[9] [Owens 20].

3.2.7 Stacks

A stack is a memory storage area for temporary data, organized as a last-in, first-out (LIFO) list. It is used to store less important data than that which fits in the CPU register set. When a function is called, the return address is saved to the stack. Some registers may be saved to the stack as well if their values are needed after the call.[10] When the called function has finished, it restores any required registers and, by fetching the return address from the stack, passes execution to the calling function. The stack can also be used for passing parameters to functions. The set of data on a stack related to a function's execution is called a *stack frame*.

The call path to the currently executing function can be seen by examining the saved return addresses across all the stack frames in the thread's stack (a process called *stack walking*).[11] This call path is referred to as a *stack back trace* or a *stack trace*. In performance engineering it is often called just a "stack" for short. These stacks can answer *why* something is executing, and are an invaluable tool for debugging and performance analysis.

How to Read a Stack

The following example kernel stack (from Linux) shows the path taken for TCP transmission, as printed by a tracing tool:

```
tcp_sendmsg+1
sock_sendmsg+62
SYSC_sendto+319
sys_sendto+14
do_syscall_64+115
entry_SYSCALL_64_after_hwframe+61
```

---

[8] The kernel context may be its own full address space (as with SPARC processors) or a restricted range that does not overlap with user addresses (as with x86 processors).

[9] There are also special-purpose kernel stacks per-CPU, including those used for interrupts.

[10] The calling convention from the processor ABI specifies which registers should retain their values after a function call (they are *non-volatile*) and are saved to the stack by the called function ("callee-saves"). Other registers are *volatile* and may be clobbered by the called function; if the caller wishes to retain their values, it must save them to the stack ("caller-saves").

[11] For more detail on stack walking and the different possible techniques (which include: frame-pointer based, debuginfo, last branch record, and ORC) see Chapter 2, Tech, Section 2.4, Stack Trace Walking, of *BPF Performance Tools* [Gregg 19].

Stacks are usually printed in leaf-to-root order, so the first line printed is the function currently executing, and beneath it is its parent, then its grandparent, and so on. In this example, the tcp_sendmsg() function was executing, called by sock_sendmsg(). In this stack example, to the right of the function name is the instruction offset, showing the location within a function. The first line shows tcp_sendmsg() offset 1 (which would be the second instruction), called by sock_sendmsg() offset 62. This offset is only useful if you desire a low-level understanding of the code path taken, down to the instruction level.

By reading down the stack, the full ancestry can be seen: function, parent, grandparent, and so on. Or, by reading bottom-up, you can follow the path of execution to the current function: how we got here.

Since stacks expose the internal path taken through source code, there is typically no documentation for these functions other than the code itself. For this example stack, this is the Linux kernel source code. An exception to this is where functions are part of an API and are documented.

User and Kernel Stacks

While executing a system call, a process thread has two stacks: a user-level stack and a kernel-level stack. Their scope is pictured in Figure 3.10.

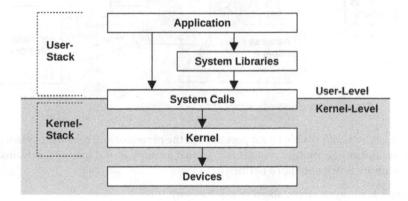

Figure 3.10   User and kernel stacks

The user-level stack of the blocked thread does not change for the duration of a system call, as the thread is using a separate kernel-level stack while executing in kernel context. (An exception to this may be signal handlers, which may borrow a user-level stack depending on their configuration.)

On Linux, there are multiple kernel stacks for different purposes. Syscalls use a kernel exception stack associated with each thread, and there are also stacks associated with soft and hard interrupts (IRQs) [Bovet 05].

3.2.8   Virtual Memory

Virtual memory is an abstraction of main memory, providing processes and the kernel with their own, almost infinite,[12] private view of main memory. It supports multitasking, allowing processes and the kernel to operate on their own private address spaces without worrying about contention. It also supports oversubscription of main memory, allowing the operating system to transparently map virtual memory between main memory and secondary storage (disks) as needed.

The role of virtual memory is shown in Figure 3.11. Primary memory is main memory (RAM), and secondary memory is the storage devices (disks).

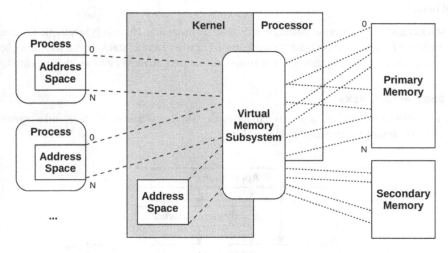

Figure 3.11   Virtual memory address spaces[13]

Virtual memory is made possible by support in both the processor and operating system. It is not real memory, and most operating systems map virtual memory to real memory only on demand, when the memory is first populated (written).

See Chapter 7, Memory, for more about virtual memory.

Memory Management

While virtual memory allows main memory to be extended using secondary storage, the kernel strives to keep the most active data in main memory. There are two kernel schemes for this:

- **Process swapping** moves entire processes between main memory and secondary storage.

- **Paging** moves small units of memory called *pages* (e.g., 4 Kbytes).

---

[12] On 64-bit processors, anyway. For 32-bit processors, virtual memory is limited to 4 Gbytes due to the limits of a 32-bit address (and the kernel may limit it to an even smaller amount).

[13] Process virtual memory is shown as starting from 0 as a simplification. Kernels today commonly begin a process's virtual address space at some offset such as 0x10000 or a random address. One benefit is that a common programming error of dereferencing a NULL (0) pointer will then cause the program to crash (SIGSEGV) as the 0 address is invalid. This is generally preferable to dereferencing data at address 0 by mistake, as the program would continue to run with corrupt data.

Process swapping is the original Unix method and can cause severe performance loss. Paging is more efficient and was added to BSD with the introduction of paged virtual memory. In both cases, least recently used (or not recently used) memory is moved to secondary storage and moved back to main memory only when needed again.

In Linux, the term *swapping* is used to refer to *paging*. The Linux kernel does not support the (older) Unix-style process swapping of entire threads and processes.

For more on paging and swapping, see Chapter 7, Memory.

3.2.9 Schedulers

Unix and its derivatives are time-sharing systems, allowing multiple processes to run at the same time by dividing execution time among them. The scheduling of processes on processors and individual CPUs is performed by the *scheduler*, a key component of the operating system kernel. The role of the scheduler is pictured in Figure 3.12, which shows that the scheduler operates on threads (in Linux, *tasks*), mapping them to CPUs.

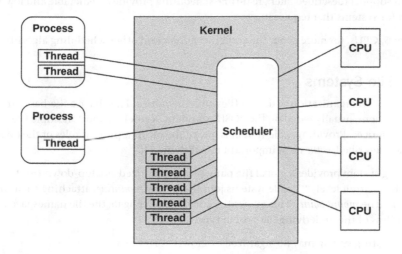

Figure 3.12 Kernel scheduler

The basic intent is to divide CPU time among the active processes and threads, and to maintain a notion of *priority* so that more important work can execute sooner. The scheduler keeps track of all threads in the ready-to-run state, traditionally on per-priority queues called *run queues* [Bach 86]. Modern kernels may implement these queues per CPU and may also use other data structures, apart from queues, to track the threads. When more threads want to run than there are available CPUs, the lower-priority threads wait their turn. Most kernel threads run with a higher priority than user-level processes.

Process priority can be modified dynamically by the scheduler to improve the performance of certain workloads. Workloads can be categorized as either:

- **CPU-bound**: Applications that perform heavy compute, for example, scientific and mathematical analysis, which are expected to have long runtimes (seconds, minutes, hours, days, or even longer). These become limited by CPU resources.
- **I/O-bound**: Applications that perform I/O, with little compute, for example, web servers, file servers, and interactive shells, where low-latency responses are desirable. When their load increases, they are limited by I/O to storage or network resources.

A commonly used scheduling policy dating back to UNIX identifies CPU-bound workloads and decreases their priority, allowing I/O-bound workloads—where low-latency responses are more desirable—to run sooner. This can be achieved by calculating the ratio of recent compute time (time executing on-CPU) to real time (elapsed time) and decreasing the priority of processes with a high (compute) ratio [Thompson 78]. This mechanism gives preference to shorter-running processes, which are usually those performing I/O, including human interactive processes.

Modern kernels support multiple *scheduling classes* or *scheduling policies* (Linux) that apply different algorithms for managing priority and runnable threads. These may include *real-time scheduling*, which uses a priority higher than all noncritical work, including kernel threads. Along with preemption support (described later), real-time scheduling provides predictable and low-latency scheduling for systems that require it.

See Chapter 6, CPUs, for more about the kernel scheduler and other scheduling algorithms.

3.2.10   File Systems

File systems are an organization of data as files and directories. They have a file-based interface for accessing them, usually based on the POSIX standard. Kernels support multiple file system types and instances. Providing a file system is one of the most important roles of the operating system, once described as *the* most important role [Ritchie 74].

The operating system provides a global file namespace, organized as a top-down tree topology starting with the root level ("/"). File systems join the tree by *mounting*, attaching their own tree to a directory (the *mount point*). This allows the end user to navigate the file namespace transparently, regardless of the underlying file system type.

A typical operating system may be organized as shown in Figure 3.13.

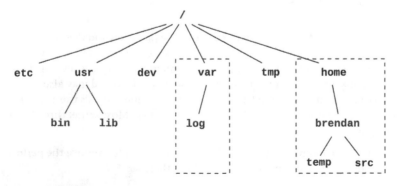

Figure 3.13   Operating system file hierarchy

The top-level directories include etc for system configuration files, usr for system-supplied user-level programs and libraries, dev for device nodes, var for varying files including system logs, tmp for temporary files, and home for user home directories. In the example pictured, var and home may reside on their own file system instances and separate storage devices; however, they can be accessed like any other component of the tree.

Most file system types use storage devices (disks) to store their contents. Some file system types are dynamically created by the kernel, such as /proc and /dev.

Kernels typically provide different ways to isolate processes to a portion of the file namespace, including chroot(8), and, on Linux, mount namespaces, commonly used for containers (see Chapter 11, Cloud Computing).

VFS

The virtual file system (VFS) is a kernel interface to abstract file system types, originally developed by Sun Microsystems so that the Unix file system (UFS) and the Network file system (NFS) could more easily coexist. Its role is pictured in Figure 3.14.

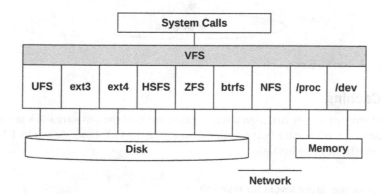

Figure 3.14   Virtual file system

The VFS interface makes it easier to add new file system types to the kernel. It also supports providing the global file namespace, pictured earlier, so that user programs and applications can access various file system types transparently.

I/O Stack

For storage-device-based file systems, the path from user-level software to the storage device is called the *I/O stack*. This is a subset of the entire software stack shown earlier. A generic I/O stack is shown in Figure 3.15.

Figure 3.15 shows a direct path to block devices on the left, bypassing the file system. This path is sometimes used by administrative tools and databases.

File systems and their performance are covered in detail in Chapter 8, File Systems, and the storage devices they are built upon are covered in Chapter 9, Disks.

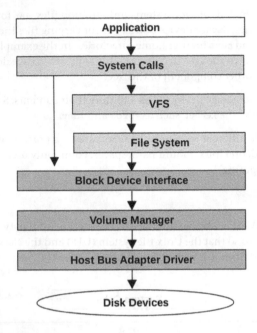

Figure 3.15   Generic I/O stack

3.2.11 Caching

Since disk I/O has historically had high latency, many layers of the software stack attempt to avoid it by caching reads and buffering writes. Caches may include those shown in Table 3.2 (in the order in which they are checked).

Table 3.2   **Example cache layers for disk I/O**

	Cache	Examples
1	Client cache	Web browser cache
2	Application cache	—
3	Web server cache	Apache cache
4	Caching server	memcached
5	Database cache	MySQL buffer cache
6	Directory cache	dcache
7	File metadata cache	inode cache
8	Operating system buffer cache	Buffer cache
9	File system primary cache	Page cache, ZFS ARC
10	File system secondary cache	ZFS L2ARC
11	Device cache	ZFS vdev

	Cache	Examples
12	Block cache	Buffer cache
13	Disk controller cache	RAID card cache
14	Storage array cache	—
15	On-disk cache	—

For example, the buffer cache is an area of main memory that stores recently used disk blocks. Disk reads may be served immediately from the cache if the requested block is present, avoiding the high latency of disk I/O.

The types of caches present will vary based on the system and environment.

3.2.12 Networking

Modern kernels provide a stack of built-in network protocols, allowing the system to communicate via the network and take part in distributed system environments. This is referred to as the *networking stack* or the *TCP/IP stack*, after the commonly used TCP and IP protocols. User-level applications access the network through programmable endpoints called *sockets*.

The physical device that connects to the network is the *network interface* and is usually provided on a *network interface card* (NIC). A historical duty of the system administrator was to associate an IP address with a network interface, so that it can communicate with the network; these mappings are now typically automated via the dynamic host configuration protocol (DHCP).

Network protocols do not change often, but there is a new transport protocol seeing growing adoption: QUIC (summarized in Chapter 10, Network). Protocol enhancements and options change more often, such as newer TCP options and TCP congestion control algorithms. Newer protocols and enhancements typically require kernel support (with the exception of user-space protocol implementations). Another change is support for different network interface cards, which require new device drivers for the kernel.

For more on networking and network performance, see Chapter 10, Network.

3.2.13 Device Drivers

A kernel must communicate with a wide variety of physical devices. Such communication is achieved using *device drivers*: kernel software for device management and I/O. Device drivers are often provided by the vendors who develop the hardware devices. Some kernels support *pluggable* device drivers, which can be loaded and unloaded without requiring a system restart.

Device drivers can provide *character* and/or *block* interfaces to their devices. Character devices, also called *raw devices*, provide unbuffered sequential access of any I/O size down to a single character, depending on the device. Such devices include keyboards and serial ports (and in original Unix, paper tape and line printer devices).

Block devices perform I/O in units of blocks, which have historically been 512 bytes each. These can be accessed randomly based on their block offset, which begins at 0 at the start of the block device. In original Unix, the block device interface also provided caching of block device buffers to improve performance, in an area of main memory called the *buffer cache*. In Linux, this buffer cache is now part of the page cache.

3.2.14   Multiprocessor

Multiprocessor support allows the operating system to use multiple CPU instances to execute work in parallel. It is usually implemented as *symmetric multiprocessing* (SMP) where all CPUs are treated equally. This was technically difficult to accomplish, posing problems for accessing and sharing memory and CPUs among threads running in parallel. On multiprocessor systems there may also be banks of main memory connected to different sockets (physical processors) in a *non-uniform memory access* (NUMA) architecture, which also pose performance challenges. See Chapter 6, CPUs, for details, including scheduling and thread synchronization, and Chapter 7, Memory, for details on memory access and architectures.

IPIs

For a multiprocessor system, there are times when CPUs need to coordinate, such as for cache coherency of memory translation entries (informing other CPUs that an entry, if cached, is now stale). A CPU can request other CPUs, or all CPUs, to immediately perform such work using an inter-processor interrupt (IPI) (also known as an *SMP call* or a *CPU cross call*). IPIs are processor interrupts designed to be executed quickly, to minimize interruption of other threads.

IPIs can also be used by preemption.

3.2.15   Preemption

Kernel preemption support allows high-priority user-level threads to interrupt the kernel and execute. This enables real-time systems that can execute work within a given time constraint, including systems in use by aircraft and medical devices. A kernel that supports preemption is said to be *fully preemptible*, although practically it will still have some small critical code paths that cannot be interrupted.

Another approach supported by Linux is *voluntary kernel preemption*, where logical stopping points in the kernel code can check and perform preemption. This avoids some of the complexity of supporting a fully preemptive kernel and provides low-latency preemption for common workloads. Voluntary kernel preemption is commonly enabled in Linux via the CONFIG_PREEMPT_ VOLUNTARY Kconfig option; there is also CONFIG_PREEMPT to allow all kernel code (except critical sections) to be preemptible, and CONFIG_PREEMPT_NONE to disable preemption, improving throughput at the cost of higher latencies.

3.2.16   Resource Management

The operating system may provide various configurable controls for fine-tuning access to system resources, such as CPUs, memory, disk, and the network. These are *resource controls* and can be used to manage performance on systems that run different applications or host multiple tenants (cloud computing). Such controls may impose fixed limits per process (or groups of processes) for resource usage, or a more flexible approach—allowing spare usage to be shared among them.

Early versions of Unix and BSD had basic per-process resource controls, including CPU priorities with nice(1), and some resource limits with ulimit(1).

For Linux, control groups (cgroups) have been developed and integrated in Linux 2.6.24 (2008), and various additional controls have been added since then. These are documented in the kernel source under Documentation/cgroups. There is also an improved unified hierarchical scheme called *cgroup v2*, made available in Linux 4.5 (2016) and documented in Documentation/admin-guide/cgroup-v2.rst.

Specific resource controls are mentioned in later chapters as appropriate. An example use case is described in Chapter 11, Cloud Computing, for managing the performance of OS-virtualized tenants.

3.2.17 Observability

The operating system consists of the kernel, libraries, and programs. These programs include tools to observe system activity and analyze performance, typically installed in /usr/bin and /usr/sbin. Third-party tools may also be installed on the system to provide additional observability.

Observability tools, and the operating system components upon which they are built, are introduced in Chapter 4.

3.3 Kernels

The following sections discuss Unix-like kernel implementation details with a focus on performance. As background, the performance features of earlier kernels are discussed: Unix, BSD, and Solaris. The Linux kernel is discussed in more detail in Section 3.4, Linux.

Kernel differences can include the file systems they support (see Chapter 8, File Systems), the system call (syscall) interfaces, network stack architecture, real-time support, and scheduling algorithms for CPUs, disk I/O, and networking.

Table 3.3 shows Linux and other kernel versions for comparison, with syscall counts based on the number of entries in section 2 of the OS man pages. This is a crude comparison, but enough to see some differences.

Table 3.3 **Kernel versions with documented syscall counts**

Kernel Version	Syscalls
UNIX Version 7	48
SunOS (Solaris) 5.11	142
FreeBSD 12.0	222
Linux 2.6.32-21-server	408
Linux 2.6.32-220.el6.x86_64	427
Linux 3.2.6-3.fc16.x86_64	431
Linux 4.15.0-66-generic	480
Linux 5.3.0-1010-aws	493

These are just the syscalls with documentation; more are usually provided by the kernel for private use by operating system software.

> UNIX had twenty system calls at the very first, and today Linux—which is a direct descendant—has over a thousand . . . I just worry about the complexity and the size of things that grow.

Ken Thompson, ACM Turing Centenary Celebration, 2012

Linux is growing in complexity and exposing this complexity to user-land by adding new system calls or through other kernel interfaces. Extra complexity makes learning, programming, and debugging more time-consuming.

3.3.1   Unix

Unix was developed by Ken Thompson, Dennis Ritchie, and others at AT&T Bell Labs during 1969 and the years that followed. Its exact origin was described in *The UNIX Time-Sharing System* [Ritchie 74]:

> The first version was written when one of us (Thompson), dissatisfied with the available computer facilities, discovered a little-used PDP-7 and set out to create a more hospitable environment.

The developers of UNIX had previously worked on the Multiplexed Information and Computer Services (Multics) operating system. UNIX was developed as a *lightweight* multitasked operating system and kernel, originally named UNiplexed Information and Computing Service (UNICS), as a pun on Multics. From *UNIX Implementation* [Thompson 78]:

> The kernel is the only UNIX code that cannot be substituted by a user to his own liking. For this reason, the kernel should make as few real decisions as possible. This does not mean to allow the user a million options to do the same thing. Rather, it means to allow only one way to do one thing, but have that way be the least-common divisor of all the options that might have been provided.

While the kernel was small, it did provide some features for high performance. Processes had scheduler priorities, reducing run-queue latency for higher-priority work. Disk I/O was performed in large (512-byte) blocks for efficiency and cached in an in-memory per-device buffer cache. Idle processes could be swapped out to storage, allowing busier processes to run in main memory. And the system was, of course, multitasking—allowing multiple processes to run concurrently, improving job throughput.

To support networking, multiple file systems, paging, and other features we now consider standard, the kernel had to grow. And with multiple derivatives, including BSD, SunOS (Solaris), and later Linux, kernel performance became competitive, which drove the addition of more features and code.

3.3.2 BSD

The Berkeley Software Distribution (BSD) OS began as enhancements to Unix 6th Edition at the University of California, Berkeley, and was first released in 1978. As the original Unix code required an AT&T software license, by the early 1990s this Unix code had been rewritten in BSD under a new BSD license, allowing free distributions including FreeBSD.

Major BSD kernel developments, especially performance-related, include:

- **Paged virtual memory**: BSD brought paged virtual memory to Unix: instead of swapping out entire processes to free main memory, smaller least-recently-used chunks of memory could be moved (paged). See Chapter 7, Memory, Section 7.2.2, Paging.

- **Demand paging:** This defers the mapping of physical memory to virtual memory to when it is first written, avoiding an early and sometimes unnecessary performance and memory cost for pages that may never be used. Demand paging was brought to Unix by BSD. See Chapter 7, Memory, Section 7.2.2, Paging.

- **FFS:** The Berkeley Fast File System (FFS) grouped disk allocation into cylinder groups, greatly reducing fragmentation and improving performance on rotational disks, as well as supporting larger disks and other enhancements. FFS became the basis for many other file systems, including UFS. See Chapter 8, File Systems, Section 8.4.5, File System Types.

- **TCP/IP network stack**: BSD developed the first high-performance TCP/IP network stack for Unix, included in 4.2BSD (1983). BSD is still known for its performant network stack.

- **Sockets**: Berkeley sockets are an API for connection endpoints. Included in 4.2BSD, they have become a standard for networking. See Chapter 10, Network.

- **Jails**: Lightweight OS-level virtualization, allowing multiple guests to share one kernel. Jails were first released in FreeBSD 4.0.

- **Kernel TLS**: As transport layer security (TLS) is now commonly used on the Internet, kernel TLS moves much of TLS processing to the kernel, improving performance[14] [Stewart 15].

While not as popular as Linux, BSD is used for some performance-critical environments, including for the Netflix content delivery network (CDN), as well as file servers from NetApp, Isilon, and others. Netflix summarized FreeBSD performance on its CDN in 2019 as [Looney 19]:

> "Using FreeBSD and commodity parts, we achieve 90 Gb/s serving TLS-encrypted connections with ~55% CPU on a 16-core 2.6-GHz CPU."

There is an excellent reference on the internals of FreeBSD, from the same publisher that brings you this book: *The Design and Implementation of the FreeBSD Operating System,* 2nd Edition [McKusick 15].

---

[14] Developed to improve the performance of the Netflix FreeBSD open connect appliances (OCAs) that are the Netflix CDN.

3.3.3 Solaris

Solaris is a Unix and BSD-derived kernel and OS created by Sun Microsystems in 1982. It was originally named SunOS and optimized for Sun workstations. By the late 1980s, AT&T developed a new Unix standard, Unix System V Release 4 (SVR4) based on technologies from SVR3, SunOS, BSD, and Xenix. Sun created a new kernel based on SVR4, and rebranded the OS under the name Solaris.

Major Solaris kernel developments, especially performance-related, include:

- **VFS:** The virtual file system (VFS) is an abstraction and interface that allows multiple file systems to easily coexist. Sun initially created it so that NFS and UFS could coexist. VFS is covered in Chapter 8, File Systems.

- **Fully preemptible kernel:** This provided low latency for high-priority work, including real-time work.

- **Multiprocessor support:** In the early 1990s, Sun invested heavily in multiprocessor operating system support, developing kernel support for both asymmetric and symmetric multiprocessing (ASMP and SMP) [Mauro 01].

- **Slab allocator:** Replacing the SVR4 buddy allocator, the kernel slab memory allocator provided better performance via per-CPU caches of preallocated buffers that could be quickly reused. This allocator type, and its derivatives, has become the standard for kernels including Linux.

- **DTrace:** A static and dynamic tracing framework and tool providing virtually unlimited observability of the entire software stack, in real time and in production. Linux has BPF and bpftrace for this type of observability.

- **Zones:** An OS-based virtualization technology for creating OS instances that share one kernel, similar to the earlier FreeBSD jails technology. OS virtualization is now in widespread use as Linux containers. See Chapter 11, Cloud Computing.

- **ZFS:** A file system with enterprise-level features and performance. It is now available for other OSes, including Linux. See Chapter 8, File Systems.

Oracle purchased Sun Microsystems in 2010, and Solaris is now called Oracle Solaris. Solaris is covered in more detail in the first edition of this book.

3.4 Linux

Linux was created in 1991 by Linus Torvalds as a free operating system for Intel personal computers. He announced the project in a Usenet post:

> I'm doing a (free) operating system (just a hobby, won't be big and professional like gnu) for 386(486) AT clones. This has been brewing since April, and is starting to get ready. I'd like any feedback on things people like/dislike in minix, as my OS resembles it somewhat (same physical layout of the file-system (due to practical reasons) among other things).

This refers to the MINIX operating system, which was being developed as a free and small (mini) version of Unix for small computers. BSD was also aiming to provide a free Unix version although at the time it had legal troubles.

The Linux kernel was developed taking general ideas from many ancestors, including:

- **Unix (and Multics):** Operating system layers, system calls, multitasking, processes, process priorities, virtual memory, global file system, file system permissions, device nodes, buffer cache

- **BSD:** Paged virtual memory, demand paging, fast file system (FFS), TCP/IP network stack, sockets

- **Solaris:** VFS, NFS, page cache, unified page cache, slab allocator

- **Plan 9:** Resource forks (rfork), for creating different levels of sharing between processes and threads (*tasks*)

Linux now sees widespread use for servers, cloud instances, and embedded devices including mobile phones.

3.4.1 Linux Kernel Developments

Linux kernel developments, especially those related to performance, include the following (many of these descriptions include the Linux kernel version where they were first introduced):

- **CPU scheduling classes:** Various advanced CPU scheduling algorithms have been developed, including scheduling domains (2.6.7) to make better decisions regarding non-uniform memory access (NUMA). See Chapter 6, CPUs.

- **I/O scheduling classes:** Different block I/O scheduling algorithms have been developed, including deadline (2.5.39), anticipatory (2.5.75), and completely fair queueing (CFQ) (2.6.6). These are available in kernels up to Linux 5.0, which removed them to support only newer multi-queue I/O schedulers. See Chapter 9, Disks.

- **TCP congestion algorithms:** Linux allows different TCP congestion control algorithms to be configured, and supports Reno, Cubic, and more in later kernels mentioned in this list. See also Chapter 10, Network.

- **Overcommit:** Along with the out-of-memory (OOM) killer, this is a strategy for doing more with less main memory. See Chapter 7, Memory.

- **Futex** (2.5.7): Short for *fast user-space mutex*, this is used to provide high-performing user-level synchronization primitives.

- **Huge pages** (2.5.36): This provides support for preallocated large memory pages by the kernel and the memory management unit (MMU). See Chapter 7, Memory.

- **OProfile** (2.5.43): A system profiler for studying CPU usage and other events, for both the kernel and applications.

- **RCU** (2.5.43): The kernel provides a read-copy update synchronization mechanism that allows multiple reads to occur concurrently with updates, improving performance and scalability for data that is mostly read.

- **epoll** (2.5.46): A system call for efficiently waiting for I/O across many open file descriptors, which improves the performance of server applications.

- **Modular I/O scheduling** (2.6.10): Linux provides pluggable scheduling algorithms for scheduling block device I/O. See Chapter 9, Disks.

- **DebugFS** (2.6.11): A simple unstructured interface for the kernel to expose data to user level, which is used by some performance tools.

- **Cpusets** (2.6.12): exclusive CPU grouping for processes.

- **Voluntary kernel preemption** (2.6.13): This process provides low-latency scheduling without the complexity of full preemption.

- **inotify** (2.6.13): A framework for monitoring file system events.

- **blktrace** (2.6.17): A framework and tool for tracing block I/O events (later migrated into tracepoints).

- **splice** (2.6.17): A system call to move data quickly between file descriptors and pipes, without a trip through user-space. (The sendfile(2) syscall, which efficiently moves data between file descriptors, is now a wrapper to splice(2).)

- **Delay accounting** (2.6.18): Tracks per-task delay states. See Chapter 4, Observability Tools.

- **IO accounting** (2.6.20): Measures various storage I/O statistics per process.

- **DynTicks** (2.6.21): Dynamic ticks allow the kernel timer interrupt (clock) to not fire during idle, saving CPU resources and power.

- **SLUB** (2.6.22): A new and simplified version of the slab memory allocator.

- **CFS** (2.6.23): Completely fair scheduler. See Chapter 6, CPUs.

- **cgroups** (2.6.24): Control groups allow resource usage to be measured and limited for groups of processes.

- **TCP LRO** (2.6.24): TCP Large Receive Offload (LRO) allows network drivers and hardware to aggregate packets into larger sizes before sending them to the network stack. Linux also supports Large Send Offload (LSO) for the send path.

- **latencytop** (2.6.25): Instrumentation and a tool for observing sources of latency in the operating system.

- **Tracepoints** (2.6.28): Static kernel tracepoints (aka *static probes*) that instrument logical execution points in the kernel, for use by tracing tools (previously called *kernel markers*). Tracing tools are introduced in Chapter 4, Observability Tools.

- **perf** (2.6.31): Linux Performance Events (perf) is a set of tools for performance observability, including CPU performance counter profiling and static and dynamic tracing. See Chapter 6, CPUs, for an introduction.

- **No BKL** (2.6.37): Final removal of the big kernel lock (BKL) performance bottleneck.

- **Transparent huge pages** (2.6.38): This is a framework to allow easy use of huge (large) memory pages. See Chapter 7, Memory.

- **KVM**: The Kernel-based Virtual Machine (KVM) technology was developed for Linux by Qumranet, which was purchased by Red Hat in 2008. KVM allows virtual operating system instances to be created, running their own kernel. See Chapter 11, Cloud Computing.

- **BPF JIT** (3.0): A Just-In-Time (JIT) compiler for the Berkeley Packet Filter (BPF) to improve packet filtering performance by compiling BPF bytecode to native instructions.

- **CFS bandwidth control** (3.2): A CPU scheduling algorithm that supports CPU quotas and throttling.

- **TCP anti-bufferbloat** (3.3+): Various enhancements were made from Linux 3.3 onwards to combat the bufferbloat problem, including Byte Queue Limits (BQL) for the transmission of packet data (3.3), CoDel queue management (3.5), TCP small queues (3.6), and the Proportional Integral controller Enhanced (PIE) packet scheduler (3.14).

- **uprobes** (3.5): The infrastructure for dynamic tracing of user-level software, used by other tools (perf, SystemTap, etc.).

- **TCP early retransmit** (3.5): RFC 5827 for reducing duplicate acknowledgments required to trigger fast retransmit.

- **TFO** (3.6, 3.7, 3.13): TCP Fast Open (TFO) can reduce the TCP three-way handshake to a single SYN packet with a TFO cookie, improving performance. It was made the default in 3.13.

- **NUMA balancing** (3.8+): This added ways for the kernel to automatically balance memory locations on multi-NUMA systems, reducing CPU interconnect traffic and improving performance.

- **SO_REUSEPORT** (3.9): A socket option to allow multiple listener sockets to bind to the same port, improving multi-threaded scalability.

- **SSD cache devices** (3.9): Device mapper support for an SSD device to be used as a cache for a slower rotating disk.

- **bcache** (3.10): An SSD cache technology for the block interface.

- **TCP TLP** (3.10): TCP Tail Loss Probe (TLP) is a scheme to avoid costly timer-based retransmits by sending new data or the last unacknowledged segment after a shorter probe timeout, to trigger faster recovery.

- **NO_HZ_FULL** (3.10, 3.12): Also known as *timerless multitasking* or a *tickless kernel*, this allows non-idle threads to run without clock ticks, avoiding workload perturbations [Corbet 13a].

- **Multiqueue block I/O** (3.13): This provides per-CPU I/O submission queues rather than a single request queue, improving scalability especially for high IOPS SSD devices [Corbet 13b].

- **SCHED_DEADLINE** (3.14): An optional scheduling policy that implements earliest deadline first (EDF) scheduling [Linux 20b].

- **TCP autocorking** (3.14): This allows the kernel to coalesce small writes, reducing the sent packets. An automatic version of the TCP_CORK setsockopt(2).

- **MCS locks and qspinlocks** (3.15): Efficient kernel locks, using techniques such as per-CPU structures. MCS is named after the original lock inventors (Mellor-Crummey and Scott) [Mellor-Crummey 91][Corbet 14].

- **Extended BPF** (3.18+): An in-kernel execution environment for running secure kernel-mode programs. The bulk of extended BPF was added in the 4.x series. Support for attached to kprobes was added in 3.19, to tracepoints in 4.7, to software and hardware events in 4.9, and to cgroups in 4.10. Bounded loops were added in 5.3, which also increased the instruction limit to allow complex applications. See Section 3.4.4, Extended BPF.

- **Overlayfs** (3.18): A union mount file system included in Linux. It creates virtual file systems on top of others, which can also be modified without changing the first. Often used for containers.

- **DCTCP** (3.18): The Data Center TCP (DCTCP) congestion control algorithm, which aims to provide high burst tolerance, low latency, and high throughput [Borkmann 14a].

- **DAX** (4.0): Direct Access (DAX) allows user space to read from persistent-memory storage devices directly, without buffer overheads. ext4 can use DAX.

- **Queued spinlocks** (4.2): Offering better performance under contention, these became the default spinlock kernel implementation in 4.2.

- **TCP lockless listener** (4.4): The TCP listener fast path became lockless, improving performance.

- **cgroup v2** (4.5, 4.15): A unified hierarchy for cgroups was in earlier kernels, and considered stable and exposed in 4.5, named cgroup v2 [Heo 15]. The cgroup v2 CPU controller was added in 4.15.

- **epoll scalability** (4.5): For multithreaded scalability, epoll(7) avoids waking up all threads that are waiting on the same file descriptors for each event, which caused a thundering-herd performance issue [Corbet 15].

- **KCM** (4.6): The Kernel Connection Multiplexor (KCM) provides an efficient message-based interface over TCP.

- **TCP NV** (4.8): New Vegas (NV) is a new TCP congestion control algorithm suited for high-bandwidth networks (those that run at 10+ Gbps).

- **XDP** (4.8, 4.18): eXpress Data Path (XDP) is a BPF-based programmable fast path for high-performance networking [Herbert 16]. An AF_XDP socket address family that can bypass much of the network stack was added in 4.18.

- **TCP BBR** (4.9): Bottleneck Bandwidth and RTT (BBR) is a TCP congestion control algorithm that provides improved latency and throughput over networks suffering packet loss and bufferbloat [Cardwell 16].

- **Hardware latency tracer** (4.9): An Ftrace tracer that can detect system latency caused by hardware and firmware, including system management interrupts (SMIs).

- **perf c2c** (4.10): The cache-to-cache (c2c) perf subcommand can help identify CPU cache performance issues, including false sharing.

- **Intel CAT** (4.10): Support for Intel Cache Allocation Technology (CAT) allowing tasks to have dedicated CPU cache space. This can be used by containers to help with the noisy neighbor problem.

- **Multiqueue I/O schedulers: BPQ, Kyber** (4.12): The Budget Fair Queueing (BFQ) multi-queue I/O scheduler provides low latency I/O for interactive applications, especially for slower storage devices. BFQ was significantly improved in 5.2. The Kyber I/O scheduler is suited for fast multiqueue devices [Corbet 17].

- **Kernel TLS** (4.13, 4.17): Linux version of kernel TLS [Edge 15].

- **MSG_ZEROCOPY** (4.14): A send(2) flag to avoid extra copies of packet bytes between an application and the network interface [Linux 20c].

- **PCID** (4.14): Linux added support for process-context ID (PCID), a processor MMU feature to help avoid TLB flushes on context switches. This reduced the performance cost of the kernel page table isolation (KPTI) patches needed to mitigate the meltdown vulnerability. See Section 3.4.3, KPTI (Meltdown).

- **PSI** (4.20, 5.2): Pressure stall information (PSI) is a set of new metrics to show time spent stalled on CPU, memory, or I/O. PSI threshold notifications were added in 5.2 to support PSI monitoring.

- **TCP EDT** (4.20): The TCP stack switched to Early Departure Time (EDT): This uses a timing-wheel scheduler for sending packets, providing better CPU efficiency and smaller queues [Jacobson 18].

- **Multi-queue I/O** (5.0): Multi-queue block I/O schedulers became the default in 5.0, and classic schedulers were removed.

- **UDP GRO** (5.0): UDP Generic Receive Offload (GRO) improves performance by allowing packets to be aggregated by the driver and card and passed up stack.

- **io_uring** (5.1): A generic asynchronous interface for fast communication between applications and the kernel, making use of shared ring buffers. Primary uses include fast disk and network I/O.

- **MADV_COLD, MADV_PAGEOUT** (5.4): These madvise(2) flags are hints to the kernel that memory is needed but not anytime soon. MADV_PAGEOUT is also a hint that memory can be reclaimed immediately. These are especially useful for memory-constrained embedded Linux devices.

- **MultiPath TCP** (5.6): Multiple network links (e.g., 3G and WiFi) can be used to improve the performance and reliability of a single TCP connection.

- **Boot-time tracing** (5.6): Allows Ftrace to trace the early boot process. (systemd can provide timing information on the late boot process: see Section 3.4.2, systemd.)

- **Thermal pressure** (5.7): The scheduler accounts for thermal throttling to make better placement decisions.

- **perf flame graphs** (5.8): perf(1) support for the flame graph visualization.

Not listed here are the many small performance improvements for locking, drivers, VFS, file systems, asynchronous I/O, memory allocators, NUMA, new processor instruction support, GPUs, and the performance tools perf(1) and Ftrace. System boot time has also been improved by the adoption of systemd.

The following sections describe in more detail three Linux topics important to performance: systemd, KPTI, and extended BPF.

3.4.2   systemd

systemd is a commonly used service manager for Linux, developed as a replacement for the original UNIX init system. systemd has various features including dependency-aware service startup and service time statistics.

An occasional task in systems performance is to tune the system's boot time, and the systemd time statistics can show where to tune. The overall boot time can be reported using systemd-analyze(1):

```
# systemd-analyze
Startup finished in 1.657s (kernel) + 10.272s (userspace) = 11.930s
graphical.target reached after 9.663s in userspace
```

This output shows that the system booted (reached the graphical.target in this case) in 9.663 seconds. More information can be seen using the `critical-chain` subcommand:

```
# systemd-analyze critical-chain
The time when unit became active or started is printed after the "@" character.
The time the unit took to start is printed after the "+" character.

graphical.target @9.663s
└─multi-user.target @9.661s
  └─snapd.seeded.service @9.062s +62ms
    └─basic.target @6.336s
      └─sockets.target @6.334s
        └─snapd.socket @6.316s +16ms
          └─sysinit.target @6.281s
            └─cloud-init.service @5.361s +905ms
              └─systemd-networkd-wait-online.service @3.498s +1.860s
                └─systemd-networkd.service @3.254s +235ms
                  └─network-pre.target @3.251s
                    └─cloud-init-local.service @2.107s +1.141s
                      └─systemd-remount-fs.service @391ms +81ms
                        └─systemd-journald.socket @387ms
                          └─system.slice @366ms
                            └─-.slice @366ms
```

This output shows the *critical path*: the sequence of steps (in this case, services) that causes the latency. The slowest service was `systemd-networkd-wait-online.service`, taking 1.86 seconds to start.

There are other useful subcommands: `blame` shows the slowest initialization times, and `plot` produces an SVG diagram. See the man page for systemd-analyze(1) for more information.

3.4.3 KPTI (Meltdown)

The kernel page table isolation (KPTI) patches added to Linux 4.14 in 2018 are a mitigation for the Intel processor vulnerability called "meltdown." Older Linux kernel versions had KAISER patches for a similar purpose, and other kernels have employed mitigations as well. While these work around the security issue, they also reduce processor performance due to extra CPU cycles and additional TLB flushing on context switches and syscalls. Linux added process-context ID (PCID) support in the same release, which allows some TLB flushes to be avoided, provided the processor supports pcid.

 I evaluated the performance impact of KPTI as between 0.1% and 6% for Netflix cloud production workloads, depending on the workload's syscall rate (higher costs more) [Gregg 18a]. Additional tuning will further reduce the cost: the use of huge pages so that a flushed TLB warms up faster, and using tracing tools to examine syscalls to identify ways to reduce their rate. A number of such tracing tools are implemented using extended BPF.

3.4.4 Extended BPF

BPF stands for Berkeley Packet Filter, an obscure technology first developed in 1992 that improved the performance of packet capture tools [McCanne 92]. In 2013, Alexei Starovoitov proposed a major rewrite of BPF [Starovoitov 13], which was further developed by himself and Daniel Borkmann and included in the Linux kernel in 2014 [Borkmann 14b]. This turned BPF into a general-purpose execution engine that can be used for a variety of things, including networking, observability, and security.

BPF itself is a flexible and efficient technology composed of an instruction set, storage objects (maps), and helper functions. It can be considered a virtual machine due to its virtual instruction set specification. BPF programs run in kernel mode (as pictured earlier in Figure 3.2) and are configured to run on events: socket events, tracepoints, USDT probes, kprobes, uprobes, and perf_events. These are shown in Figure 3.16.

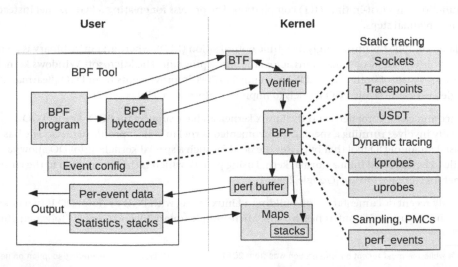

Figure 3.16 BPF components

BPF bytecode must first pass through a verifier that checks for safety, ensuring that the BPF program will not crash or corrupt the kernel. It may also use a BPF Type Format (BTF) system for understanding data types and structures. BPF programs can output data via a perf ring buffer, an efficient way to emit per-event data, or via maps, which are suited for statistics.

Because it is powering a new generation of efficient, safe, and advanced tracing tools, BPF is important for systems performance analysis. It provides programmability to existing kernel event sources: tracepoints, kprobes, uprobes, and perf_events. A BPF program can, for example, record a timestamp on the start and end of I/O to time its duration, and record this in a custom histogram. This book contains many BPF-based programs using the BCC and bpftrace front-ends. These front-ends are covered in Chapter 15.

3.5   Other Topics

Some additional kernel and operating system topics worth summarizing are PGO kernels, Unikernels, microkernels, hybrid kernels, and distributed operating systems.

3.5.1   PGO Kernels

Profile-guided optimization (PGO), also known as feedback-directed optimization (FDO), uses CPU profile information to improve compiler decisions [Yuan 14a]. This can be applied to kernel builds, where the procedure is:

1. While in production, take a CPU profile.

2. Recompile the kernel based on that CPU profile.

3. Deploy the new kernel in production.

This creates a kernel with improved performance for a specific workload. Runtimes such as the JVM do this automatically, recompiling Java methods based on their runtime performance, in conjunction with just-in-time (JIT) compilation. The process for creating a PGO kernel instead involves manual steps.

A related compile optimization is link-time optimization (LTO), where an entire binary is compiled at once to allow optimizations across the entire program. The Microsoft Windows kernel makes heavy use of both LTO and PGO, seeing 5 to 20% improvements from PGO [Bearman 20]. Google also use LTO and PGO kernels to improve performance [Tolvanen 20].

The gcc and clang compilers, and the Linux kernel, all have support for PGO. Kernel PGO typically involves running a specially instrumented kernel to collect profile data. Google has released an AutoFDO tool that bypasses the need for such a special kernel: AutoFDO allows a profile to be collected from a normal kernel using perf(1), which is then converted to the correct format for compilers to use [Google 20a].

The only recent documentation on building a Linux kernel with PGO or AutoFDO is two talks from Linux Plumber's Conference 2020 by Microsoft [Bearman 20] and Google [Tolvanen 20].[15]

---

[15] For a while the most recent documentation was from 2014 for Linux 3.13 [Yuan 14b], hindering adoption on newer kernels.

3.5.2 Unikernels

A unikernel is a single-application machine image that combines kernel, library, and application software together, and can typically run this in a single address space in either a hardware VM or on bare metal. This potentially has performance and security benefits: less instruction text means higher CPU cache hit ratios and fewer security vulnerabilities. This also creates a problem: there may be no SSH, shells, or performance tools available for you to log in and debug the system, nor any way to add them.

For unikernels to be performance tuned in production, new performance tooling and metrics must be built to support them. As a proof of concept, I built a rudimentary CPU profiler that ran from Xen dom0 to profile a domU unikernel guest and then built a CPU flame graph, just to show that it was possible [Gregg 16a].

Examples of unikernels include MirageOS [MirageOS 20].

3.5.3 Microkernels and Hybrid Kernels

Most of this chapter discusses Unix-like kernels, also described as *monolithic kernels*, where all the code that manages devices runs together as a single large kernel program. For the *microkernel* model, kernel software is kept to a minimum. A microkernel supports essentials such as memory management, thread management, and inter-process communication (IPC). File systems, the network stack, and drivers are implemented as user-mode software, which allows those user-mode components to be more easily modified and replaced. Imagine not only choosing which database or web server to install, but also choosing which network stack to install. The microkernel is also more fault-tolerant: a crash in a driver does not crash the entire kernel. Examples of microkernels include QNX and Minix 3.

A disadvantage with microkernels is that there are additional IPC steps for performing I/O and other functions, reducing performance. One solution for this is *hybrid kernels*, which combine the benefits of microkernels and monolithic kernels. Hybrid kernels move performance-critical services back into kernel space (with direct function calls instead of IPC) as they are with a monolithic kernel, but retains the modular design and fault tolerance of a micro kernel. Examples of hybrid kernels include the Windows NT kernel and the Plan 9 kernel.

3.5.4 Distributed Operating Systems

A distributed operating system runs a single operating system instance across a set of separate computer nodes, networked together. A microkernel is commonly used on each of the nodes. Examples of distributed operating systems include Plan 9 from Bell Labs, and the Inferno operating system.

While an innovative design, this model has not seen widespread use. Rob Pike, co-creator of Plan 9 and Inferno, has described various reasons for this, including [Pike 00]:

> "There was a claim in the late 1970s and early 1980s that Unix had killed operating systems research because no one would try anything else. At the time, I didn't believe it. Today, I grudgingly accept that the claim may be true (Microsoft notwithstanding)."

On the cloud, today's common model for scaling compute nodes is to load-balance across a group of identical OS instances, which may scale in response to load (see Chapter 11, Cloud Computing, Section 11.1.3, Capacity Planning).

3.6 Kernel Comparisons

Which kernel is fastest? This will depend partly on the OS configuration and workload and how much the kernel is involved. In general, I expect that Linux will outperform other kernels due to its extensive work on performance improvements, application and driver support, and widespread use and the large community who discover and report performance issues. The top 500 supercomputers, as tracked by the TOP500 list since 1993, became 100% Linux in 2017 [TOP500 17]. There will be some exceptions; for example, Netflix uses Linux on the cloud and FreeBSD for its CDN.[16]

Kernel performance is commonly compared using micro-benchmarks, and this is error-prone. Such benchmarks may discover that one kernel is much faster at a particular syscall, but that syscall is not used in the production workload. (Or it is used, but with certain flags not tested by the microbenchmark, which greatly affect performance.) Comparing kernel performance accurately is a task for a senior performance engineer—a task that can take weeks. See Chapter 12, Benchmarking, Section 12.3.2, Active Benchmarking, as a methodology to follow.

In the first edition of this book, I concluded this section by noting that Linux did not have a mature dynamic tracer, without which you might miss out on large performance wins. Since that first edition, I have moved to a full-time Linux performance role, and I helped develop the dynamic tracers that Linux was missing: BCC and bpftrace, based on extended BPF. These are covered in Chapter 15 and in my previous book [Gregg 19].

Section 3.4.1, Linux Kernel Developments, lists many other Linux performance developments that have occurred in the time between the first edition and this edition, spanning kernel versions 3.1 and 5.8. A major development not listed earlier is that OpenZFS now supports Linux as its primary kernel, providing a high-performance and mature file system option on Linux.

With all this Linux development, however, comes complexity. There are so many performance features and tunables on Linux that it has become laborious to configure and tune them for each workload. I have seen many deployments running untuned. Bear this in mind when comparing kernel performance: has each kernel been tuned? Later chapters of this book, and their tuning sections, can help you remedy this.

3.7 Exercises

1. Answer the following questions about OS terminology:

   - What is the difference between a process, a thread, and a task?

   - What is a mode switch and a context switch?

---

[16] FreeBSD delivers higher performance for the Netflix CDN workload, especially due to kernel improvements made by the Netflix OCA team. This is routinely tested, most recently during 2019 with a production comparison of Linux 5.0 versus FreeBSD, which I helped analyze.

- What is the difference between paging and process swapping?
- What is the difference between I/O-bound and CPU-bound workloads?

2. Answer the following conceptual questions:

- Describe the role of the kernel.
- Describe the role of system calls.
- Describe the role of VFS and its location in the I/O stack.

3. Answer the following deeper questions:

- List the reasons why a thread would leave the current CPU.
- Describe the advantages of virtual memory and demand paging.

3.8 References

[Graham 68] Graham, B., "Protection in an Information Processing Utility," *Communications of the ACM*, May 1968.

[Ritchie 74] Ritchie, D. M., and Thompson, K., "The UNIX Time-Sharing System," *Communications of the ACM* 17, no. 7, pp. 365–75, July 1974.

[Thompson 78] Thompson, K., *UNIX Implementation*, Bell Laboratories, 1978.

[Bach 86] Bach, M. J., *The Design of the UNIX Operating System*, Prentice Hall, 1986.

[Mellor-Crummey 91] Mellor-Crummey, J. M., and Scott, M., "Algorithms for Scalable Synchronization on Shared-Memory Multiprocessors," *ACM Transactions on Computing Systems*, Vol. 9, No. 1, https://www.cs.rochester.edu/u/scott/papers/1991_TOCS_synch.pdf, 1991.

[McCanne 92] McCanne, S., and Jacobson, V., "The BSD Packet Filter: A New Architecture for User-Level Packet Capture", *USENIX Winter Conference*, 1993.

[Mills 94] Mills, D., "RFC 1589: A Kernel Model for Precision Timekeeping," *Network Working Group*, 1994.

[Lever 00] Lever, C., Eriksen, M. A., and Molloy, S. P., "An Analysis of the TUX Web Server," *CITI Technical Report 00-8*, http://www.citi.umich.edu/techreports/reports/citi-tr-00-8.pdf, 2000.

[Pike 00] Pike, R., "Systems Software Research Is Irrelevant," http://doc.cat-v.org/bell_labs/utah2000/utah2000.pdf, 2000.

[Mauro 01] Mauro, J., and McDougall, R., *Solaris Internals: Core Kernel Architecture*, Prentice Hall, 2001.

[Bovet 05] Bovet, D., and Cesati, M., *Understanding the Linux Kernel*, 3rd Edition, O'Reilly, 2005.

[Corbet 05] Corbet, J., Rubini, A., and Kroah-Hartman, G., *Linux Device Drivers*, 3rd Edition, O'Reilly, 2005.

[Corbet 13a] Corbet, J., "Is the whole system idle?" *LWN.net*, https://lwn.net/Articles/558284, 2013.

[Corbet 13b] Corbet, J., "The multiqueue block layer," *LWN.net*, https://lwn.net/Articles/552904, 2013.

[Starovoitov 13] Starovoitov, A., "[PATCH net-next] extended BPF," *Linux kernel mailing list*, https://lkml.org/lkml/2013/9/30/627, 2013.

[Borkmann 14a] Borkmann, D., "net: tcp: add DCTCP congestion control algorithm," https://git.kernel.org/pub/scm/linux/kernel/git/torvalds/linux.git/commit/?id=e3118e8359bb7c59555aca60c725106e6d78c5ce, 2014.

[Borkmann 14b] Borkmann, D., "[PATCH net-next 1/9] net: filter: add jited flag to indicate jit compiled filters," *netdev mailing list*, https://lore.kernel.org/netdev/1395404418-25376-1-git-send-email-dborkman@redhat.com/T, 2014.

[Corbet 14] Corbet, J., "MCS locks and qspinlocks," *LWN.net*, https://lwn.net/Articles/590243, 2014.

[Drysdale 14] Drysdale, D., "Anatomy of a system call, part 2," *LWN.net*, https://lwn.net/Articles/604515, 2014.

[Yuan 14a] Yuan, P., Guo, Y., and Chen, X., "Experiences in Profile-Guided Operating System Kernel Optimization," *APSys*, 2014.

[Yuan 14b] Yuan P., Guo, Y., and Chen, X., "Profile-Guided Operating System Kernel Optimization," http://coolypf.com, 2014.

[Corbet 15] Corbet, J., "Epoll evolving," LWN.*net*, https://lwn.net/Articles/633422, 2015.

[Edge 15] Edge, J., "TLS in the kernel," *LWN.net*, https://lwn.net/Articles/666509, 2015.

[Heo 15] Heo, T., "Control Group v2," *Linux documentation*, https://www.kernel.org/doc/Documentation/cgroup-v2.txt, 2015.

[McKusick 15] McKusick, M. K., Neville-Neil, G. V., and Watson, R. N. M., *The Design and Implementation of the FreeBSD Operating System*, 2nd Edition, Addison-Wesley, 2015.

[Stewart 15] Stewart, R., Gurney, J. M., and Long, S., "Optimizing TLS for High-Bandwidth Applicationsin FreeBSD," *AsiaBSDCon*, https://people.freebsd.org/~rrs/asiabsd_2015_tls.pdf, 2015.

[Cardwell 16] Cardwell, N., Cheng, Y., Stephen Gunn, C., Hassas Yeganeh, S., and Jacobson, V., "BBR: Congestion-Based Congestion Control," *ACM queue*, https://queue.acm.org/detail.cfm?id=3022184, 2016.

[Gregg 16a] Gregg, B., "Unikernel Profiling: Flame Graphs from dom0," http://www.brendangregg.com/blog/2016-01-27/unikernel-profiling-from-dom0.html, 2016.

[Herbert 16] Herbert, T., and Starovoitov, A., "eXpress Data Path (XDP): Programmable and High Performance Networking Data Path," https://github.com/iovisor/bpf-docs/raw/master/Express_Data_Path.pdf, 2016.

[Corbet 17] Corbet, J., "Two new block I/O schedulers for 4.12," *LWN.net*, https://lwn.net/Articles/720675, 2017.

[TOP500 17] TOP500, "List Statistics," https://www.top500.org/statistics/list, 2017.

[Gregg 18a] Gregg, B., "KPTI/KAISER Meltdown Initial Performance Regressions," http://www.brendangregg.com/blog/2018-02-09/kpti-kaiser-meltdown-performance.html, 2018.

[Jacobson 18] Jacobson, V., "Evolving from AFAP: Teaching NICs about Time," *netdev 0x12*, https://netdevconf.info/0x12/session.html?evolving-from-afap-teaching-nics-about-time, 2018.

[Gregg 19] Gregg, B., *BPF Performance Tools: Linux System and Application Observability*, Addison-Wesley, 2019.

[Looney 19] Looney, J., "Netflix and FreeBSD: Using Open Source to Deliver Streaming Video," *FOSDEM*, https://papers.freebsd.org/2019/fosdem/looney-netflix_and_freebsd, 2019.

[Bearman 20] Bearman, I., "Exploring Profile Guided Optimization of the Linux Kernel," *Linux Plumber's Conference*, https://linuxplumbersconf.org/event/7/contributions/771, 2020.

[Google 20a] Google, "AutoFDO," https://github.com/google/autofdo, accessed 2020.

[Linux 20a] "NO_HZ: Reducing Scheduling-Clock Ticks," *Linux documentation*, https://www.kernel.org/doc/html/latest/timers/no_hz.html, accessed 2020.

[Linux 20b] "Deadline Task Scheduling," *Linux documentation*, https://www.kernel.org/doc/Documentation/scheduler/sched-deadline.rst, accessed 2020.

[Linux 20c] "MSG_ZEROCOPY," *Linux documentation*, https://www.kernel.org/doc/html/latest/networking/msg_zerocopy.html, accessed 2020.

[Linux 20d] "Softlockup Detector and Hardlockup Detector (aka nmi_watchdog)," *Linux documentation*, https://www.kernel.org/doc/html/latest/admin-guide/lockup-watchdogs.html, accessed 2020.

[MirageOS 20] MirageOS, "Mirage OS," https://mirage.io, accessed 2020.

[Owens 20] Owens, K., et al., "4. Kernel Stacks," *Linux documentation*, https://www.kernel.org/doc/html/latest/x86/kernel-stacks.html, accessed 2020.

[Tolvanen 20] Tolvanen, S., Wendling, B., and Desaulniers, N., "LTO, PGO, and AutoFDO in the Kernel," *Linux Plumber's Conference*, https://linuxplumbersconf.org/event/7/contributions/798, 2020.

3.8.1 Additional Reading

Operating systems and their kernels is a fascinating and extensive topic. This chapter summarized only the essentials. In addition to the sources mentioned in this chapter, the following are also excellent references, applicable to Linux-based operating systems and others:

[Goodheart 94] Goodheart, B., and Cox J., *The Magic Garden Explained: The Internals of UNIX System V Release 4, an Open Systems Design*, Prentice Hall, 1994.

[Vahalia 96] Vahalia, U., *UNIX Internals: The New Frontiers*, Prentice Hall, 1996.

[Singh 06] Singh, A., *Mac OS X Internals: A Systems Approach*, Addison-Wesley, 2006.

[McDougall 06b] McDougall, R., and Mauro, J., *Solaris Internals: Solaris 10 and OpenSolaris Kernel Architecture*, Prentice Hall, 2006.

[Love 10] Love, R., *Linux Kernel Development*, 3rd Edition, Addison-Wesley, 2010.

[Tanenbaum 14] Tanenbaum, A., and Bos, H., *Modern Operating Systems*, 4th Edition, Pearson, 2014.

[Yosifovich 17] Yosifovich, P., Ionescu, A., Russinovich, M. E., and Solomon, D. A., *Windows Internals, Part 1 (Developer Reference)*, 7th Edition, Microsoft Press, 2017.

Chapter 4

Observability Tools

Operating systems have historically provided many tools for observing system software and hardware components. To the newcomer, the wide range of available tools and metrics suggested that everything—or at least everything important—could be observed. In reality there were many gaps, and systems performance experts became skilled in the art of inference and interpretation: figuring out activity from indirect tools and statistics. For example, network packets could be examined individually (sniffing), but disk I/O could not (at least, not easily).

Observability has greatly improved in Linux thanks to the rise of dynamic tracing tools, including the BPF-based BCC and bpftrace. Dark corners are now illuminated, including individual disk I/O using biosnoop(8). However, many companies and commercial monitoring products have not yet adopted system tracing, and are missing out on the insight it brings. I have led the way by developing, publishing, and explaining new tracing tools, tools already in use by companies such as Netflix and Facebook.

The learning objectives of this chapter are:

- Identify static performance tools and crisis tools.

- Understand tool types and their overhead: counters, profiling, and tracing.

- Learn about observability sources, including: /proc, /sys, tracepoints, kprobes, uprobes, USDT, and PMCs.

- Learn how to configure sar(1) for archiving statistics.

In Chapter 1 I introduced different types of observability: counters, profiling, and tracing, as well as static and dynamic instrumentation. This chapter explains observability tools and their data sources in detail, including a summary of sar(1), the system activity reporter, and an introduction to tracing tools. This gives you the essentials for understanding Linux observability; later chapters (6 to 11) use these tools and sources to solve specific issues. Chapters 13 to 15 cover the tracers in depth.

This chapter uses the Ubuntu Linux distribution as an example; most of these tools are the same across other Linux distributions, and some similar tools exist for other kernels and operating systems where these tools originated.

4.1 Tool Coverage

Figure 4.1 shows an operating system diagram that I have annotated with the Linux workload observability tools[1] relevant to each component.

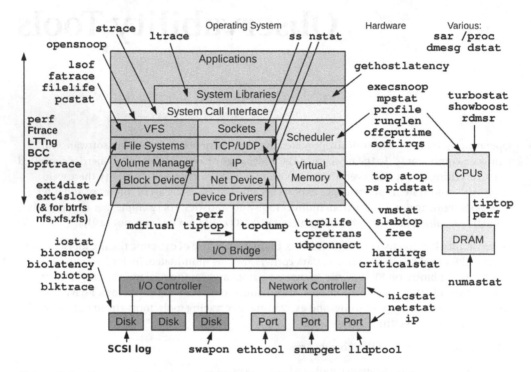

Figure 4.1   Linux workload observability tools

Most of these tools focus on a particular resource, such as CPU, memory, or disks, and are covered in a later chapter dedicated to that resource. There are some multi-tools that can analyze many areas, and they are introduced later in this chapter: perf, Ftrace, BCC, and bpftrace.

4.1.1 Static Performance Tools

There is another type of observability that examines attributes of the system at rest rather than under active workload. This was described as the *static performance tuning* methodology in Chapter 2, Methodologies, Section 2.5.17, Static Performance Tuning, and these tools are shown in Figure 4.2.

---

[1]When teaching performance classes in the mid-2000s, I would draw my own kernel diagram on a whiteboard and annotate it with the different performance tools and what they observed. I found it an effective way for explaining tool coverage as a form of mental map. I've since published digital versions of these, which adorn cubicle walls around the world. You can download them on my website [Gregg 20a].

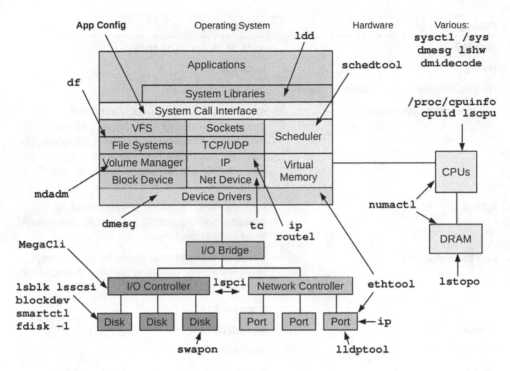

Figure 4.2   Linux static performance tuning tools

Remember to use the tools in Figure 4.2 to check for issues with configuration and components. Sometimes performance issues are simply due to a misconfiguration.

4.1.2   Crisis Tools

When you have a production performance crisis that requires various performance tools to debug it, you might find that none of them are installed. Worse, since the server is suffering a performance issue, installing the tools may take much longer than usual, prolonging the crisis.

For Linux, Table 4.1 lists the recommended installation packages or source repositories that provide these *crisis tools*. Package names for Ubuntu/Debian are shown in this table (these package names may vary for different Linux distributions).

Table 4.1   **Linux crisis tool packages**

Package	Provides
procps	ps(1), vmstat(8), uptime(1), top(1)
util-linux	dmesg(1), lsblk(1), lscpu(1)
sysstat	iostat(1), mpstat(1), pidstat(1), sar(1)

Package	Provides
iproute2	ip(8), ss(8), nstat(8), tc(8)
numactl	numastat(8)
linux-tools-common linux-tools-$(uname -r)	perf(1), turbostat(8)
bcc-tools (aka bpfcc-tools)	opensnoop(8), execsnoop(8), runqlat(8), runqlen(8), softirqs(8), hardirqs(8), ext4slower(8), ext4dist(8), biotop(8), biosnoop(8), biolatency(8), tcptop(8), tcplife(8), trace(8), argdist(8), funccount(8), stackcount(8), profile(8), and many more
bpftrace	bpftrace, basic versions of opensnoop(8), execsnoop(8), runqlat(8), runqlen(8), biosnoop(8), biolatency(8), and more
perf-tools-unstable	Ftrace versions of opensnoop(8), execsnoop(8), iolatency(8), iosnoop(8), bitesize(8), funccount(8), kprobe(8)
trace-cmd	trace-cmd(1)
nicstat	nicstat(1)
ethtool	ethtool(8)
tiptop	tiptop(1)
msr-tools	rdmsr(8), wrmsr(8)
github.com/brendangregg/msr-cloud-tools	showboost(8), cpuhot(8), cputemp(8)
github.com/brendangregg/pmc-cloud-tools	pmcarch(8), cpucache(8), icache(8), tlbstat(8), resstalls(8)

Large companies, such as Netflix, have OS and performance teams who ensure that production systems have all of these packages installed. A default Linux distribution may only have procps and util-linux installed, so all the others must be added.

In container environments, it may be desirable to create a privileged debugging container that has full access to the system[2] and all tools installed. The image for this container can be installed on container hosts and deployed when needed.

Adding tool packages is often not enough: kernel and user-space software may also need to be configured to support these tools. Tracing tools typically require certain kernel CONFIG options to be enabled, such as CONFIG_FTRACE and CONFIG_BPF. Profiling tools typically require software to be configured to support stack walking, either by using frame-pointer compiled versions of all software (including system libraries: libc, libpthread, etc.) or debuginfo packages installed

---

[2] It could also be configured to share namespaces with a target container to analyze.

to support dwarf stack walking. If your company has yet to do this, you should check that each performance tool works and fix those that do not before they are urgently needed in a crisis.

The following sections explain performance observability tools in more detail.

4.2 Tool Types

A useful categorization for observability tools is whether they provide *system-wide* or *per-process* observability, and whether they are based on counters or *events*. These attributes are shown in Figure 4.3, along with Linux tool examples.

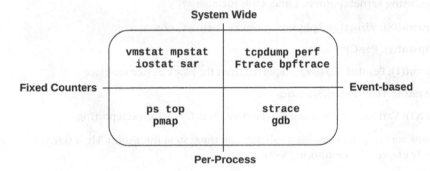

Figure 4.3 Observability tool types

Some tools fit in more than one quadrant; for example, top(1) also has a system-wide summary, and system-wide event tools can often filter for a particular process (-p PID).

Event-based tools include profilers and tracers. Profilers observe activity by taking a series of snapshots on events, painting a coarse picture of the target. Tracers instrument every event of interest, and may perform processing on them, for example to generate customized counters. Counters, tracing, and profiling were introduced in Chapter 1.

The following sections describe Linux tools that use fixed counters, tracing, and profiling, as well as those that perform monitoring (metrics).

4.2.1 Fixed Counters

Kernels maintain various counters for providing system statistics. They are usually implemented as unsigned integers that are incremented when events occur. For example, there are counters for the number of network packets received, disk I/O issued, and interrupts that occurred. These are exposed by monitoring software as *metrics* (see Section 4.2.4, Monitoring).

A common kernel approach is to maintain a pair of cumulative counters: one to count events and the other to record the total time in the event. These provide the count of events directly and the average time (or latency) in the event, by dividing the total time by the count. Since they are cumulative, by reading the pair at a time interval (e.g., one second) the delta can be calculated, and from that the per-second count and average latency. This is how many system statistics are calculated.

Performance-wise, counters are considered "free" to use since they are enabled by default and maintained continually by the kernel. The only additional cost when using them is the act of reading their values from user-space (which should be negligible). The following example tools read these system-wide or per process.

System-Wide

These tools examine system-wide activity in the context of system software or hardware resources, using kernel counters. Linux tools include:

- **vmstat(8)**: Virtual and physical memory statistics, system-wide
- **mpstat(1)**: Per-CPU usage
- **iostat(1)**: Per-disk I/O usage, reported from the block device interface
- **nstat(8)**: TCP/IP stack statistics
- **sar(1)**: Various statistics; can also archive them for historical reporting

These tools are typically viewable by all users on the system (non-root). Their statistics are also commonly graphed by monitoring software.

Many follow a usage convention where they accept an optional *interval* and *count*, for example, vmstat(8) with an interval of one second and an output count of three:

```
$ vmstat 1 3
procs -----------memory---------- ---swap-- -----io---- -system-- ------cpu-----
 r  b   swpd   free   buff  cache   si   so    bi    bo   in   cs us sy id wa st
 4  0 1446428 662012 142100 5644676  1    4    28   152   33    1 29  8 63  0  0
 4  0 1446428 665988 142116 5642272  0    0     0   284 4957 4969 51  0 48  0  0
 4  0 1446428 685116 142116 5623676  0    0     0     0 4488 5507 52  0 48  0  0
```

The first line of output is the summary-since-boot, which shows averages for the entire time the system has been up. The subsequent lines are the one-second interval summaries, showing current activity. At least, this is the intent: this Linux version mixes summary-since-boot and current values for the first line (the memory columns are current values; vmstat(8) is explained in Chapter 7).

Per-Process

These tools are process-oriented and use counters that the kernel maintains for each process. Linux tools include:

- **ps(1)**: Shows process status, shows various process statistics, including memory and CPU usage.

- **top(1):** Shows top processes, sorted by CPU usage or another statistic.

- **pmap(1):** Lists process memory segments with usage statistics.

These tools typically read statistics from the /proc file system.

4.2.2 Profiling

Profiling characterizes the target by collecting a set of samples or snapshots of its behavior. CPU usage is a common target of profiling, where timer-based samples are taken of the instruction pointer or stack trace to characterize CPU-consuming code paths. These samples are usually collected at a fixed rate, such as 100 Hz (cycles per second) across all CPUs, and for a short duration such as one minute. Profiling tools, or *profilers*, often use 99 Hz instead of 100 Hz to avoid sampling in lockstep with target activity, which could lead to over- or undercounting.

Profiling can also be based on untimed hardware events, such as CPU hardware cache misses or bus activity. It can show which code paths are responsible, information that can especially help developers optimize their code for memory usage.

Unlike fixed counters, profiling (and tracing) are typically only enabled on an as-needed basis, since they can cost some CPU overhead to collect, and storage overhead to store. The magnitudes of these overheads depend on the tool and the rate of events it instruments. Timer-based profilers are generally safer: the event rate is known, so its overhead can be predicted, and the event rate can be selected to have negligible overhead.

System-Wide

System-wide Linux profilers include:

- **perf(1):** The standard Linux profiler, which includes profiling subcommands.

- **profile(8):** A BPF-based CPU profiler from the BCC repository (covered in Chapter 15, BPF) that frequency counts stack traces in kernel context.

- **Intel VTune Amplifier XE:** Linux and Windows profiling, with a graphical interface including source browsing.

These can also be used to target a single process.

Per-Process

Process-oriented profilers include:

- **gprof(1):** The GNU profiling tool, which analyzes profiling information added by compilers (e.g., gcc –pg).

- **cachegrind:** A tool from the valgrind toolkit, can profile hardware cache usage (and more) and visualize profiles using kcachegrind.

- **Java Flight Recorder (JFR):** Programming languages often have their own special-purpose profilers that can inspect language context. For example, JFR for Java.

See Chapter 6, CPUs, and Chapter 13, perf, for more about profiling tools.

4.2.3   Tracing

Tracing instruments every occurrence of an event, and can store event-based details for later analysis or produce a summary. This is similar to profiling, but the intent is to collect or inspect all events, not just a sample. Tracing can incur higher CPU and storage overheads than profiling, which can slow the target of tracing. This should be taken into consideration, as it may negatively affect the production workload, and measured timestamps may also be skewed by the tracer. As with profiling, tracing is typically only used as needed.

Logging, where infrequent events such as errors and warnings are written to a log file for later reading, can be thought of as low-frequency tracing that *is* enabled by default. Logs include the system log.

The following are examples of system-wide and per-process tracing tools.

System-Wide

These tracing tools examine system-wide activity in the context of system software or hardware resources, using kernel tracing facilities. Linux tools include:

- **tcpdump(8)**: Network packet tracing (uses libpcap)
- **biosnoop(8)**: Block I/O tracing (uses BCC or bpftrace)
- **execsnoop(8)**: New processes tracing (uses BCC or bpftrace)
- **perf(1)**: The standard Linux profiler, can also trace events
- **perf trace**: A special perf subcommand that traces system calls system-wide
- **Ftrace**: The Linux built-in tracer
- **BCC**: A BPF-based tracing library and toolkit
- **bpftrace**: A BPF-based tracer (bpftrace(8)) and toolkit

perf(1), Ftrace, BCC, and bpftrace are introduced in Section 4.5, Tracing Tools, and covered in detail in Chapters 13 to 15. There are over one hundred tracing tools built using BCC and bpftrace, including biosnoop(8) and execsnoop(8) from this list. More examples are provided throughout this book.

Per-Process

These tracing tools are process-oriented, as are the operating system frameworks on which they are based. Linux tools include:

- **strace(1)**: System call tracing
- **gdb(1)**: A source-level debugger

The debuggers can examine per-event data, but they must do so by stopping and starting the execution of the target. This can come with an enormous overhead cost, making them unsuitable for production use.

System-wide tracing tools such as perf(1) and bpftrace support filters for examining a single process and can operate with much lower overhead, making them preferred where available.

4.2.4 Monitoring

Monitoring was introduced in Chapter 2, Methodologies. Unlike the tool types covered previously, monitoring records statistics continuously in case they are later needed.

sar(1)

A traditional tool for monitoring a single operating system host is the System Activity Reporter, sar(1), originating from AT&T Unix. sar(1) is counter-based and has an agent that executes at scheduled times (via cron) to record the state of system-wide counters. The sar(1) tool allows these to be viewed at the command line, for example:

```
# sar
Linux 4.15.0-66-generic (bgregg)   12/21/2019     _x86_64_        (8 CPU)

12:00:01 AM     CPU     %user    %nice    %system   %iowait   %steal    %idle
12:05:01 AM     all     3.34     0.00     0.95      0.04      0.00      95.66
12:10:01 AM     all     2.93     0.00     0.87      0.04      0.00      96.16
12:15:01 AM     all     3.05     0.00     1.38      0.18      0.00      95.40
12:20:01 AM     all     3.02     0.00     0.88      0.03      0.00      96.06
[...]
Average:        all     0.00     0.00     0.00      0.00      0.00      0.00
```

By default, sar(1) reads its statistics archive (if enabled) to print recent historical statistics. You can specify an optional interval and count for it to examine current activity at the rate specified.

sar(1) can record dozens of different statistics to provide insight into CPU, memory, disks, networking, interrupts, power usage, and more. It is covered in more detail in Section 4.4, sar.

Third-party monitoring products are often built on sar(1) or the same observability statistics it uses, and expose these metrics over the network.

SNMP

The traditional technology for network monitoring is the Simple Network Management Protocol (SNMP). Devices and operating systems can support SNMP and in some cases provide it by default, avoiding the need to install third-party agents or exporters. SNMP includes many basic OS metrics, although it has not been extended to cover modern applications. Most environments have been switching to custom agent-based monitoring instead.

Agents

Modern monitoring software runs agents (also known as *exporters* or *plugins*) on each system to record kernel and application metrics. These can include agents for specific applications and targets, for example, the MySQL database server, the Apache Web Server, and the Memcached caching system. Such agents can provide detailed application request metrics that are not available from system counters alone.

Monitoring software and agents for Linux include:

- **Performance Co-Pilot (PCP)**: PCP supports dozens of different agents (called Performance Metric Domain Agents: PMDAs), including for BPF-based metrics [PCP 20].

- **Prometheus**: The Prometheus monitoring software supports dozens of different exporters, for databases, hardware, messaging, storage, HTTP, APIs, and logging [Prometheus 20].

- **collectd**: Supports dozens of different plugins.

An example monitoring architecture is pictured in Figure 4.4 involving a monitoring database server for archiving metrics, and a monitoring web server for providing a client UI. The metrics are sent (or made available) by agents to the database server and then made available to client UIs for display in as line graphs and in dashboards. For example, Graphite Carbon is a monitoring database server, and Grafana is a monitoring web server/dashboard.

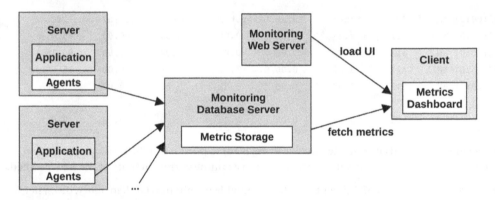

Figure 4.4 Example monitoring architecture

There are dozens of monitoring products, and hundreds of different agents for different target types. Covering them is beyond the scope of this book. There is, however, one common denominator that is covered here: system statistics (based on kernel counters). The system statistics shown by monitoring products are typically the same as those shown by system tools: vmstat(8), iostat(1), etc. Learning these will help you understand monitoring products, even if you never use the command-line tools. These tools are covered in later chapters.

Some monitoring products read their system metrics by running the system tools and parsing the text output, which is inefficient. Better monitoring products use library and kernel interfaces to read the metrics directly—the same interfaces as used by the command-line tools. These sources are covered in the next section, focusing on the most common denominator: the kernel interfaces.

4.3 Observability Sources

The sections that follow describe various interfaces that provide the data for observability tools on Linux. They are summarized in Table 4.2.

Table 4.2 **Linux observability sources**

Type	Source
Per-process counters	/proc
System-wide counters	/proc, /sys
Device configuration and counters	/sys
Cgroup statistics	/sys/fs/cgroup
Per-process tracing	ptrace
Hardware counters (PMCs)	perf_event
Network statistics	netlink
Network packet capture	libpcap
Per-thread latency metrics	Delay accounting
System-wide tracing	Function profiling (Ftrace), tracepoints, software events, kprobes, uprobes, perf_event

The main sources of systems performance statistics are covered next: /proc and /sys. Then other Linux sources are covered: delay accounting, netlink, tracepoints, kprobes, USDT, uprobes, PMCs, and more.

The tracers covered in Chapter 13 perf, Chapter 14 Ftrace, and Chapter 15 BPF utilize many of these sources, especially system-wide tracing. The scope of these tracing sources is pictured in Figure 4.5, along with event and group names: for example, block: is for all the block I/O tracepoints, including block:block_rq_issue.

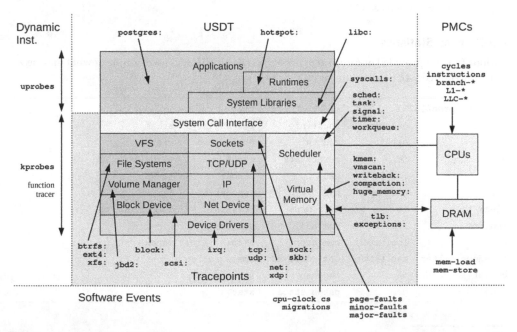

Figure 4.5   Linux tracing sources

Only a few example USDT sources are pictured in Figure 4.5, for the PostgreSQL database (`postgres:`), the JVM hotspot compiler (`hotspot:`), and libc (`libc:`). You may have many more depending on your user-level software.

For more information on how tracepoints, kprobes, and uprobes work, their internals are documented in Chapter 2 of *BPF Performance Tools* [Gregg 19].

4.3.1 /proc

This is a file system interface for kernel statistics. /proc contains a number of directories, where each directory is named after the process ID for the process it represents. In each of these directories is a number of files containing information and statistics about each process, mapped from kernel data structures. There are additional files in /proc for system-wide statistics.

/proc is dynamically created by the kernel and is not backed by storage devices (it runs in-memory). It is mostly read-only, providing statistics for observability tools. Some files are writeable, for controlling process and kernel behavior.

The file system interface is convenient: it's an intuitive framework for exposing kernel statistics to user-land via the directory tree, and has a well-known programming interface via the POSIX file system calls: open(), read(), close(). You can also explore it at the command line using cd, cat(1), grep(1), and awk(1). The file system also provides user-level security through use of file access permissions. In rare cases where the typical process observability tools (ps(1), top(1), etc.) cannot be executed, some process debugging can still be performed by shell built-ins from the /proc directory.

The overhead of reading most /proc files is negligible; exceptions include some memory-map related files that walk page tables.

Per-Process Statistics

Various files are provided in /proc for per-process statistics. Here is an example of what may be available (Linux 5.4), here looking at PID 18733[3]:

```
$ ls -F /proc/18733
arch_status      environ      mountinfo       personality    statm
attr/            exe@         mounts          projid_map     status
autogroup        fd/          mountstats      root@          syscall
auxv             fdinfo/      net/            sched          task/
cgroup           gid_map      ns/             schedstat      timers
clear_refs       io           numa_maps       sessionid      timerslack_ns
cmdline          limits       oom_adj         setgroups      uid_map
comm             loginuid     oom_score       smaps          wchan
coredump_filter  map_files/   oom_score_adj   smaps_rollup
cpuset           maps         pagemap         stack
cwd@             mem          patch_state     stat
```

---

[3] You can also examine /proc/self for your current process (shell).

The exact list of files available depends on the kernel version and CONFIG options.

Those related to per-process performance observability include:

- **limits**: In-effect resource limits
- **maps**: Mapped memory regions
- **sched**: Various CPU scheduler statistics
- **schedstat**: CPU runtime, latency, and time slices
- **smaps**: Mapped memory regions with usage statistics
- **stat**: Process status and statistics, including total CPU and memory usage
- **statm**: Memory usage summary in units of pages
- **status**: stat and statm information, labeled
- **fd**: Directory of file descriptor symlinks (also see fdinfo)
- **cgroup**: Cgroup membership information
- **task**: Directory of per-task (thread) statistics

The following shows how per-process statistics are read by top(1), traced using strace(1):

```
stat("/proc/14704", {st_mode=S_IFDIR|0555, st_size=0, ...}) = 0
open("/proc/14704/stat", O_RDONLY)       = 4
read(4, "14704 (sshd) S 1 14704 14704 0 -"..., 1023) = 232
close(4)
```

This has opened a file called "stat" in a directory named after the process ID (14704), and then read the file contents.

top(1) repeats this for all active processes on the system. On some systems, especially those with many processes, the overhead from performing these can become noticeable, especially for versions of top(1) that repeat this sequence for every process on every screen update. This can lead to situations where top(1) reports that top itself is the highest CPU consumer!

System-Wide Statistics

Linux has also extended /proc to include system-wide statistics, contained in these additional files and directories:

```
$ cd /proc; ls -Fd [a-z]*
acpi/       dma           kallsyms      mdstat        schedstat     thread-self@
buddyinfo   driver/       kcore         meminfo       scsi/         timer_list
bus/        execdomains   keys          misc          self@         tty/
cgroups     fb            key-users     modules       slabinfo      uptime
cmdline     filesystems   kmsg          mounts@       softirqs      version
consoles    fs/           kpagecgroup   mtrr          stat          vmallocinfo
cpuinfo     interrupts    kpagecount    net@          swaps         vmstat
```

crypto	iomem	kpageflags	pagetypeinfo	sys/	zoneinfo
devices	ioports	loadavg	partitions	sysrq-trigger	
diskstats	irq/	locks	sched_debug	sysvipc/	

System-wide files related to performance observability include:

- **cpuinfo**: Physical processor information, including every virtual CPU, model name, clock speed, and cache sizes.

- **diskstats**: Disk I/O statistics for all disk devices

- **interrupts**: Interrupt counters per CPU

- **loadavg**: Load averages

- **meminfo**: System memory usage breakdowns

- **net/dev**: Network interface statistics

- **net/netstat**: System-wide networking statistics

- **net/tcp**: Active TCP socket information

- **pressure/**: Pressure stall information (PSI) files

- **schedstat**: System-wide CPU scheduler statistics

- **self**: A symlink to the current process ID directory, for convenience

- **slabinfo**: Kernel slab allocator cache statistics

- **stat**: A summary of kernel and system resource statistics: CPUs, disks, paging, swap, processes

- **zoneinfo**: Memory zone information

These are read by system-wide tools. For example, here's vmstat(8) reading /proc, as traced by strace(1):

```
open("/proc/meminfo", O_RDONLY)          = 3
lseek(3, 0, SEEK_SET)                     = 0
read(3, "MemTotal:         889484 kB\nMemF"..., 2047) = 1170
open("/proc/stat", O_RDONLY)              = 4
read(4, "cpu  14901 0 18094 102149804 131"..., 65535) = 804
open("/proc/vmstat", O_RDONLY)            = 5
lseek(5, 0, SEEK_SET)                     = 0
read(5, "nr_free_pages 160568\nnr_inactive"..., 2047) = 1998
```

This output shows that vmstat(8) was reading meminfo, stat, and vmstat.

CPU Statistic Accuracy

The /proc/stat file provides system-wide CPU utilization statistics and is used by many tools (vmstat(8), mpstat(1), sar(1), monitoring agents). The accuracy of these statistics depends on the kernel configuration. The default configuration (CONFIG_TICK_CPU_ACCOUNTING) measures CPU utilization with a granularity of clock ticks [Weisbecker 13], which may be four milliseconds (depending on CONFIG_HZ). This is generally sufficient. There are options to improve accuracy by using higher-resolution counters, though with a small performance cost (VIRT_CPU_ACCOUNTING_NATIVE and VIRT_CPU_ACCOUTING_GEN), as well an option to for more accurate IRQ time (IRQ_TIME_ACCOUNTING). A different approach to obtaining accurate CPU utilization measurements is to use MSRs or PMCs.

File Contents

/proc files are usually text formatted, allowing them to be read easily from the command line and processed by shell scripting tools. For example:

```
$ cat /proc/meminfo
MemTotal:       15923672 kB
MemFree:        10919912 kB
MemAvailable:   15407564 kB
Buffers:           94536 kB
Cached:          2512040 kB
SwapCached:            0 kB
Active:          1671088 kB
[...]
$ grep Mem /proc/meminfo
MemTotal:       15923672 kB
MemFree:        10918292 kB
MemAvailable:   15405968 kB
```

While this is convenient, it does add a small amount of overhead for the kernel to encode the statistics as text, and for any user-land tool that then parses the text. netlink, covered in Section 4.3.4, netlink, is a more efficient binary interface.

The contents of /proc are documented in the proc(5) man page and in the Linux kernel documentation: Documentation/filesystems/proc.txt [Bowden 20]. Some parts have extended documentation, such as diskstats in Documentation/iostats.txt and scheduler stats in Documentation/scheduler/sched-stats.txt. Apart from the documentation, you can also study the kernel source code to understand the exact origin of all items in /proc. It can also be helpful to read the source to the tools that consume them.

Some of the /proc entries depend on CONFIG options: schedstats is enabled with CONFIG_SCHEDSTATS, sched with CONFIG_SCHED_DEBUG, and pressure with CONFIG_PSI.

4.3.2   /sys

Linux provides a sysfs file system, mounted on /sys, which was introduced with the 2.6 kernel to provide a directory-based structure for kernel statistics. This differs from /proc, which has evolved over time and had various system statistics mostly added to the top-level directory. sysfs was originally designed to provide device driver statistics but has been extended to include any statistic type.

For example, the following lists /sys files for CPU 0 (truncated):

```
$ find /sys/devices/system/cpu/cpu0 -type f
/sys/devices/system/cpu/cpu0/uevent
/sys/devices/system/cpu/cpu0/hotplug/target
/sys/devices/system/cpu/cpu0/hotplug/state
/sys/devices/system/cpu/cpu0/hotplug/fail
/sys/devices/system/cpu/cpu0/crash_notes_size
/sys/devices/system/cpu/cpu0/power/runtime_active_time
/sys/devices/system/cpu/cpu0/power/runtime_active_kids
/sys/devices/system/cpu/cpu0/power/pm_qos_resume_latency_us
/sys/devices/system/cpu/cpu0/power/runtime_usage
[...]
/sys/devices/system/cpu/cpu0/topology/die_id
/sys/devices/system/cpu/cpu0/topology/physical_package_id
/sys/devices/system/cpu/cpu0/topology/core_cpus_list
/sys/devices/system/cpu/cpu0/topology/die_cpus_list
/sys/devices/system/cpu/cpu0/topology/core_siblings
[...]
```

Many of the listed files provide information about the CPU hardware caches. The following output shows their contents (using grep(1) so that the file name is included with the output):

```
$ grep . /sys/devices/system/cpu/cpu0/cache/index*/level
/sys/devices/system/cpu/cpu0/cache/index0/level:1
/sys/devices/system/cpu/cpu0/cache/index1/level:1
/sys/devices/system/cpu/cpu0/cache/index2/level:2
/sys/devices/system/cpu/cpu0/cache/index3/level:3
$ grep . /sys/devices/system/cpu/cpu0/cache/index*/size
/sys/devices/system/cpu/cpu0/cache/index0/size:32K
/sys/devices/system/cpu/cpu0/cache/index1/size:32K
/sys/devices/system/cpu/cpu0/cache/index2/size:1024K
/sys/devices/system/cpu/cpu0/cache/index3/size:33792K
```

This shows that CPU 0 has access to two Level 1 caches, each 32 Kbytes, a Level 2 cache of 1 Mbyte, and a Level 3 cache of 33 Mbytes.

The /sys file system typically has tens of thousands of statistics in read-only files, as well as many writeable files for changing kernel state. For example, CPUs can be set to online or offline by writing "1" or "0" to a file named "online." As with reading statistics, some state settings can be made by using text strings at the command line (echo 1 > filename), rather than a binary interface.

4.3.3 Delay Accounting

Linux systems with the CONFIG_TASK_DELAY_ACCT option track time per task in the following states:

- **Scheduler latency:** Waiting for a turn on-CPU
- **Block I/O:** Waiting for a block I/O to complete
- **Swapping:** Waiting for paging (memory pressure)
- **Memory reclaim:** Waiting for the memory reclaim routine

Technically, the scheduler latency statistic is sourced from schedstats (mentioned earlier, in /proc) but is exposed with the other delay accounting states. (It is in struct sched_info, not struct task_delay_info.)

These statistics can be read by user-level tools using taskstats, which is a netlink-based interface for fetching per-task and process statistics. In the kernel source there is:

- Documentation/accounting/delay-accounting.txt: the documentation
- tools/accounting/getdelays.c: an example consumer

The following is some output from getdelays.c:

```
$ ./getdelays -dp 17451
print delayacct stats ON
PID     17451

CPU           count     real total  virtual total   delay total  delay average
              386       3452475144  31387115236      1253300657         3.247ms
IO            count     delay total  delay average
              302       1535758266               5ms
SWAP          count     delay total  delay average
              0                  0               0ms
RECLAIM       count     delay total  delay average
              0                  0               0ms
```

Times are given in nanoseconds unless otherwise specified. This example was taken from a heavily CPU-loaded system, and the process inspected was suffering scheduler latency.

4.3.4 netlink

netlink is a special socket address family (AF_NETLINK) for fetching kernel information. Use of netlink involves opening a networking socket with the AF_NETLINK address family and then using a series of send(2) and recv(2) calls to pass requests and receiving information in binary structs. While this is a more complicated interface to use than /proc, it is more efficient, and also supports notifications. The libnetlink library helps with usage.

As with earlier tools, strace(1) can be used to show where the kernel information is coming from. Inspecting the socket statistics tool ss(8):

```
# strace ss
[...]
socket(AF_NETLINK, SOCK_RAW|SOCK_CLOEXEC, NETLINK_SOCK_DIAG) = 3
[...]
```

This is opening an AF_NETLINK socket for the group NETLINK_SOCK_DIAG, which returns information about sockets. It is documented in the sock_diag(7) man page. netlink groups include:

- **NETLINK_ROUTE**: Route information (there is also /proc/net/route)
- **NETLINK_SOCK_DIAG**: Socket information
- **NETLINK_SELINUX**: SELinux event notifications
- **NETLINK_AUDIT**: Auditing (security)
- **NETLINK_SCSITRANSPORT**: SCSI transports
- **NETLINK_CRYPTO**: Kernel crypto information

Commands that use netlink include ip(8), ss(8), routel(8), and the older ifconfig(8) and netstat(8).

4.3.5 Tracepoints

Tracepoints are a Linux kernel event source based on *static instrumentation*, a term introduced in Chapter 1, Introduction, Section 1.7.3, Tracing. Tracepoints are hard-coded instrumentation points placed at logical locations in kernel code. For example, there are tracepoints at the start and end of system calls, scheduler events, file system operations, and disk I/O.[4] The tracepoint infrastructure was developed by Mathieu Desnoyers and first made available in the Linux 2.6.32 release in 2009. Tracepoints are a stable API[5] and are limited in number.

Tracepoints are an important resource for performance analysis as they power advanced tracing tools that go beyond summary statistics, providing deeper insight into kernel behavior. While function-based tracing can provide a similar power (e.g., Section 4.3.6, kprobes), only tracepoints provide a stable interface, allowing robust tools to be developed.

This section explains tracepoints. These can be used by the tracers introduced in Section 4.5, Tracing Tools, and are covered in depth in Chapters 13 to 15.

---

[4] Some are gated by Kconfig options and may not be available if the kernel is compiled without them; e.g., rcu tracepoints and CONFIG_RCU_TRACE.

[5] I'd call it "best-effort stable." It is rare, but I have seen tracepoints change.

Tracepoints Example

Available tracepoints can be listed using the `perf list` command (the syntax for perf(1) syntax is covered in Chapter 14):

```
# perf list tracepoint

List of pre-defined events (to be used in -e):
[...]
  block:block_rq_complete                       [Tracepoint event]
  block:block_rq_insert                         [Tracepoint event]
  block:block_rq_issue                          [Tracepoint event]
[...]
  sched:sched_wakeup                            [Tracepoint event]
  sched:sched_wakeup_new                        [Tracepoint event]
  sched:sched_waking                            [Tracepoint event]
  scsi:scsi_dispatch_cmd_done                   [Tracepoint event]
  scsi:scsi_dispatch_cmd_error                  [Tracepoint event]
  scsi:scsi_dispatch_cmd_start                  [Tracepoint event]
  scsi:scsi_dispatch_cmd_timeout                [Tracepoint event]
[...]
  skb:consume_skb                               [Tracepoint event]
  skb:kfree_skb                                 [Tracepoint event]
[...]
```

I have truncated the output to show a dozen example tracepoints from the block device layer, the scheduler, and SCSI. On my system there are 1808 different tracepoints, 634 of which are for instrumenting syscalls.

Apart from showing when an event happened, tracepoints can also provide contextual data about the event. As an example, the following perf(1) command traces the block:block_rq_issue tracepoint and prints events live:

```
# perf trace -e block:block_rq_issue
[...]
     0.000 kworker/u4:1-e/20962 block:block_rq_issue:259,0 W 8192 () 875216 + 16
[kworker/u4:1]
   255.945 :22696/22696 block:block_rq_issue:259,0 RA 4096 () 4459152 + 8 [bash]
   256.957 :22705/22705 block:block_rq_issue:259,0 RA 16384 () 367936 + 32 [bash]
[...]
```

The first three fields are a timestamp (seconds), process details (name/thread ID), and event description (followed by a colon separator instead of a space). The remaining fields are *arguments* for the tracepoint and are generated by a *format string* explained next; for the specific block:block_rq_issue format string, see Chapter 9, Disks, Section 9.6.5, perf.

A note about terminology: *tracepoints* (or *trace points*) are technically the tracing functions (also called tracing *hooks*) placed in the kernel source. For example, trace_sched_wakeup() is a trace-point, and you will find it called from kernel/sched/core.c. This tracepoint may be instrumented via tracers using the name "sched:sched_wakeup"; however, that is technically a *trace event*, defined by the TRACE_EVENT macro. TRACE_EVENT also defines and formats its arguments, auto-generates the trace_sched_wakeup() code, and places the trace event in the tracefs and perf_event_open(2) interfaces [Ts'o 20]. Tracing tools primarily instrument trace events, although they may refer to them as "tracepoints." perf(1) calls trace events "Tracepoint event," which is confusing since kprobe- and uprobe-based trace events are also labeled "Tracepoint event."

Tracepoints Arguments and Format String

Each tracepoint has a format string that contains event arguments: extra context about the event. The structure of this format string can be seen in a "format" file under /sys/kernel/debug/tracing/events. For example:

```
# cat /sys/kernel/debug/tracing/events/block/block_rq_issue/format
name: block_rq_issue
ID: 1080
format:
        field:unsigned short common_type;  offset:0;  size:2;  signed:0;
        field:unsigned char common_flags;  offset:2;  size:1;  signed:0;
        field:unsigned char common_preempt_count;  offset:3;  size:1;  signed:0;
        field:int common_pid;    offset:4;  size:4;  signed:1;

        field:dev_t dev;         offset:8;  size:4;  signed:0;
        field:sector_t sector;  offset:16;  size:8;  signed:0;
        field:unsigned int nr_sector;  offset:24;  size:4;  signed:0;
        field:unsigned int bytes;    offset:28;  size:4;  signed:0;
        field:char rwbs[8];    offset:32;  size:8;  signed:1;
        field:char comm[16];  offset:40;  size:16;  signed:1;
        field:__data_loc char[] cmd;  offset:56;  size:4;  signed:1;

print fmt: "%d,%d %s %u (%s) %llu + %u [%s]", ((unsigned int) ((REC->dev) >> 20)),
((unsigned int) ((REC->dev) & ((1U << 20) - 1))), REC->rwbs, REC->bytes,
__get_str(cmd), (unsigned long long)REC->sector, REC->nr_sector, REC->comm
```

The final line shows the string format and arguments. The following shows the format string formatting from this output, followed by an example format string from the previous `perf` `script` output:

```
%d,%d %s %u (%s) %llu + %u [%s]
259,0 W 8192 () 875216 + 16 [kworker/u4:1]
```

These match up.

Tracers can typically access the arguments from format strings via their names. For example, the following uses perf(1) to trace block I/O issue events only when the size (bytes argument) is larger than 65536[6]:

```
# perf trace -e block:block_rq_issue --filter 'bytes > 65536'
    0.000 jbd2/nvme0n1p1/174 block:block_rq_issue:259,0 WS 77824 () 2192856 + 152
[jbd2/nvme0n1p1-]
    5.784 jbd2/nvme0n1p1/174 block:block_rq_issue:259,0 WS 94208 () 2193152 + 184
[jbd2/nvme0n1p1-]
[...]
```

As an example of a different tracer, the following uses bpftrace to print the bytes argument only for this tracepoint (bpftrace syntax is covered in Chapter 15, BPF; I'll use bpftrace for subsequent examples as it is concise to use, requiring fewer commands):

```
# bpftrace -e 't:block:block_rq_issue { printf("size: %d bytes\n", args->bytes); }'
Attaching 1 probe...
size: 4096 bytes
size: 49152 bytes
size: 40960 bytes
[...]
```

The output is one line for each I/O issue, showing its size.

Tracepoints are a stable API that consists of the tracepoint name, format string, and arguments.

Tracepoints Interface

Tracing tools can use tracepoints via their trace event files in tracefs (typically mounted at /sys/kernel/debug/tracing) or the perf_event_open(2) syscall. As an example, my Ftrace-based iosnoop(8) tool uses the tracefs files:

```
# strace -e openat ~/Git/perf-tools/bin/iosnoop
chdir("/sys/kernel/debug/tracing")       = 0
openat(AT_FDCWD, "/var/tmp/.ftrace-lock", O_WRONLY|O_CREAT|O_TRUNC, 0666) = 3
[...]
openat(AT_FDCWD, "events/block/block_rq_issue/enable", O_WRONLY|O_CREAT|O_TRUNC,
0666) = 3
openat(AT_FDCWD, "events/block/block_rq_complete/enable", O_WRONLY|O_CREAT|O_TRUNC,
0666) = 3
[...]
```

---

[6]The --filter argument for perf trace was added in Linux 5.5. On older kernels, you can accomplish this using:
perf trace -e block:block_rq_issue --filter 'bytes > 65536' -a; perf script

The output includes a chdir(2) to the tracefs directory and the opening of "enable" files for block tracepoints. It also includes a /var/tmp/.ftrace-lock: this is a precaution I coded that blocks concurrent tool users, which the tracefs interface does not easily support. The perf_event_open(2) interface does support concurrent users and is preferred where possible. It is used by my newer BCC version of the same tool:

```
# strace -e perf_event_open /usr/share/bcc/tools/biosnoop
perf_event_open({type=PERF_TYPE_TRACEPOINT, size=0 /* PERF_ATTR_SIZE_??? */,
config=2323, ...}, -1, 0, -1, PERF_FLAG_FD_CLOEXEC) = 8
perf_event_open({type=PERF_TYPE_TRACEPOINT, size=0 /* PERF_ATTR_SIZE_??? */,
config=2324, ...}, -1, 0, -1, PERF_FLAG_FD_CLOEXEC) = 10
[...]
```

perf_event_open(2) is the interface to the kernel perf_events subsystem, which provides various profiling and tracing capabilities. See its man page for more details, as well as the perf(1) front end in Chapter 13.

Tracepoints Overhead

When tracepoints are activated, they add a small amount of CPU overhead to each event. The tracing tool may also add CPU overhead to post-process events, plus file system overheads to record them. Whether the overheads are high enough to perturb production applications depends on the rate of events and the number of CPUs, and is something you will need to consider when using tracepoints.

On typical systems of today (4 to 128 CPUs), I find that event rates of less than 10,000 per second cost negligible overhead, and only over 100,000 does the overhead begin to become measurable. As event examples, you may find that disk events are typically fewer than 10,000 per second, but scheduler events can be well over 100,000 per second and therefore can be expensive to trace.

I've previously analyzed overheads for a particular system and found the minimum tracepoint overhead to be 96 nanoseconds of CPU time [Gregg 19]. There is a new type of tracepoint called *raw tracepoints*, added to Linux 4.7 in 2018, which avoids the cost of creating stable tracepoint arguments, reducing this overhead.

Apart from the enabled overhead while tracepoints are in use, there is also the disabled overhead for making them available. A disabled tracepoint becomes a small number of instructions: for x86_64 it is a 5-byte no-operation (nop) instruction. There is also a tracepoint handler added to the end of the function, which increases its text size a little. While these overheads are very small, they are something you should analyze and understand when adding tracepoints to the kernel.

Tracepoint Documentation

The tracepoints technology is documented in the kernel source under Documentation/trace/tracepoints.rst. The tracepoints themselves are (sometimes) documented in the header files that define them, found in the Linux source under include/trace/events. I summarized advanced tracepoint topics in *BPF Performance Tools*, Chapter 2 [Gregg 19]: how they are added to kernel code, and how they work at the instruction level.

Sometimes you may wish to trace software execution for which there are no tracepoints: for that you can try the unstable kprobes interface.

4.3.6   kprobes

kprobes (short for kernel probes) is a Linux kernel event source for tracers based on *dynamic instrumentation*, a term introduced in Chapter 1, Introduction, Section 1.7.3, Tracing. kprobes can trace any kernel function or instruction, and were made available in Linux 2.6.9, released in 2004. They are considered an unstable API because they expose raw kernel functions and arguments that may change between kernel versions.

kprobes can work in different ways internally. The standard method is to modify the instruction text of running kernel code to insert instrumentation where needed. When instrumenting the entry of functions, an optimization may be used where kprobes make use of existing Ftrace function tracing, as it has lower overhead.[7]

kprobes are important because they are a last-resort[8] source of virtually unlimited information about kernel behavior in production, which can be crucial for observing performance issues that are invisible to other tools. They can be used by the tracers introduced in Section 4.5, Tracing Tools, and are covered in depth in Chapters 13 to 15.

kprobes and tracepoints are compared in Table 4.3.

Table 4.3 **kprobes to tracepoints comparison**

Detail	kprobes	Tracepoints
Type	Dynamic	Static
Rough Number of Events	50,000+	1,000+
Kernel Maintenance	None	Required
Disabled Overhead	None	Tiny (NOPs + metadata)
Stable API	No	Yes

kprobes can trace the entry to functions as well as instruction offsets within functions. The use of kprobes creates *kprobe events* (a kprobe-based trace event). These kprobe events only exist when a tracer creates them: by default, the kernel code runs unmodified.

---

[7] It can also be enabled/disabled via the debug.kprobes-optimization sysctl(8).

[8] Without kprobes, the last resort option would be to modify the kernel code to add instrumentation where needed, recompile, and redeploy.

kprobes Example

As an example of using kprobes, the following bpftrace command instruments the do_nanosleep() kernel function and prints the on-CPU process:

```
# bpftrace -e 'kprobe:do_nanosleep { printf("sleep by: %s\n", comm); }'
Attaching 1 probe...
sleep by: mysqld
sleep by: mysqld
sleep by: sleep
^C
#
```

The output shows a couple of sleeps by a process named "mysqld", and one by "sleep" (likely /bin/sleep). The kprobe event for do_nanosleep() is created when the bpftrace program begins running and is removed when bpftrace terminates (Ctrl-C).

kprobes Arguments

As kprobes can trace kernel function calls, it is often desirable to inspect the arguments to the function for more context. Each tracing tool exposes them in its own way and is covered in later sections. For example, using bpftrace to print the second argument to do_nanosleep(), which is the hrtimer_mode:

```
# bpftrace -e 'kprobe:do_nanosleep { printf("mode: %d\n", arg1); }'
Attaching 1 probe...
mode: 1
mode: 1
mode: 1
[...]
```

Function arguments are available in bpftrace using the arg0..argN built-in variable.

kretprobes

The return from kernel functions and their return value can be traced using *kretprobes* (short for kernel return probes), which are similar to kprobes. kretprobes are implemented using a kprobe for the function entry, which inserts a trampoline function to instrument the return.

When paired with kprobes and a tracer that records timestamps, the duration of a kernel function can be measured. For example, measuring the duration of do_nanosleep() using bpftrace:

```
# bpftrace -e 'kprobe:do_nanosleep { @ts[tid] = nsecs; }
    kretprobe:do_nanosleep /@ts[tid]/ {
    @sleep_ms = hist((nsecs - @ts[tid]) / 1000000); delete(@ts[tid]); }
    END { clear(@ts); }'
Attaching 3 probes...
```

```
^C

@sleep_ms:
[0]                    1280 |@@@@@@@@@@@@@@@@@@@@@@@@@@@@@@@@@@@@@@@@@@@@@@@@@@@@|
[1]                       1 |                                                  |
[2, 4)                    1 |                                                  |
[4, 8)                    0 |                                                  |
[8, 16)                   0 |                                                  |
[16, 32)                  0 |                                                  |
[32, 64)                  0 |                                                  |
[64, 128)                 0 |                                                  |
[128, 256)                0 |                                                  |
[256, 512)                0 |                                                  |
[512, 1K)                 2 |                                                  |
```

The output shows that do_nanosleep() was usually a fast function, returning in zero milliseconds (rounded down) 1,280 times. Two occurrences reached the 512 to 1024 millisecond range.

bpftrace syntax is explained in Chapter 15, BPF, which includes a similar example for timing vfs_read().

kprobes Interface and Overhead

The kprobes interface is similar to tracepoints. There is a way to instrument them via /sys files, via the perf_event_open(2) syscall (which is preferred), and also via the register_kprobe() kernel API. The overhead is similar to that of tracepoints when the entries to functions are traced (Ftrace method, if available), and higher when function offsets are traced (breakpoint method) or when kretprobes are used (trampoline method). For a particular system I measured the minimum kprobe CPU cost to be 76 nanoseconds, and the minimum kretprobe CPU cost to be 212 nanoseconds [Gregg 19].

kprobes Documentation

kprobes are documented in the Linux source under Documentation/kprobes.txt. The kernel functions they instrument are typically not documented outside of the kernel source (since most are not an API, they don't need to be). I summarized advanced kprobe topics in *BPF Performance Tools*, Chapter 2 [Gregg 19]: how they work at the instruction level.

4.3.7   uprobes

uprobes (user-space probes) are similar to kprobes, but for user-space. They can dynamically instrument functions in applications and libraries, and provide an unstable API for diving deep into software internals beyond the scope of other tools. uprobes were made available in Linux 3.5, released in 2012.

uprobes can be used by the tracers introduced in Section 4.5, Tracing Tools, and covered in depth in Chapters 13 to 15.

uprobes Example

As an example of uprobes, the following bpftrace command lists possible uprobe function entry locations in the bash(1) shell:

```
# bpftrace -l 'uprobe:/bin/bash:*'
uprobe:/bin/bash:rl_old_menu_complete
uprobe:/bin/bash:maybe_make_export_env
uprobe:/bin/bash:initialize_shell_builtins
uprobe:/bin/bash:extglob_pattern_p
uprobe:/bin/bash:dispose_cond_node
uprobe:/bin/bash:decode_prompt_string
[..]
```

The full output showed 1,507 possible uprobes. uprobes instrument code and create *uprobe events* when needed (a uprobe-based trace event): the user-space code runs unmodified by default. This is similar to using a debugger to add a breakpoint to a function: before the breakpoint is added, the function is running unmodified.

uprobes Arguments

Arguments to user functions are made available by uprobes. As an example, the following uses bpftrace to instrument the decode_prompt_string() bash function and print the first argument as a string:

```
# bpftrace -e 'uprobe:/bin/bash:decode_prompt_string { printf("%s\n", str(arg0)); }'
Attaching 1 probe...
\[\e[31;1m\]\u@\h:\w>\[\e[0m\]
\[\e[31;1m\]\u@\h:\w>\[\e[0m\]
^C
```

The output shows the bash(1) prompt string on this system. The uprobe for decode_prompt_string() is created when the bpftrace program begins running, and is removed when bpftrace terminates (Ctrl-C).

uretprobes

The return from user functions and their return value can be traced using *uretprobes* (short for user-level return probes), which are similar to uprobes. When paired with uprobes and a tracer that records timestamps, the duration of a user-level function can be measured. Be aware that the overhead of uretprobes can significantly skew such measurements of fast functions.

uprobes Interface and Overhead

The uprobes interface is similar to kprobes. There is a way to instrument them via /sys files and also (preferably) via the perf_event_open(2) syscall.

uprobes currently work by trapping into the kernel. This costs much higher CPU overheads than kprobes or tracepoints. For a particular system I measured, the minimum uprobe cost 1,287 nanoseconds, and the minimum uretprobe cost 1,931 nanoseconds [Gregg 19]. The uretprobe overhead is higher because it is a uprobe plus a trampoline function.

uprobe Documentation

uprobes are documented in the Linux source under Documentation/trace/uprobetracer.rst. I summarized advanced uprobe topics in *BPF Performance Tools*, Chapter 2 [Gregg 19]: how they work at the instruction level. The user functions they instrument are typically not documented outside of the application source (since most are unlikely to be an API, they don't need to be). For documented user-space tracing, use USDT.

4.3.8   USDT

User-level statically-defined tracing (USDT) is the user-space version of tracepoints. USDT is to uprobes as tracepoints is to kprobes. Some applications and libraries have added USDT probes to their code, providing a stable (and documented) API for tracing application-level events. For example, there are USDT probes in the Java JDK, in the PostgreSQL database, and in libc. The following lists OpenJDK USDT probes using bpftrace:

```
# bpftrace -lv 'usdt:/usr/lib/jvm/openjdk/libjvm.so:*'
usdt:/usr/lib/jvm/openjdk/libjvm.so:hotspot:class__loaded
usdt:/usr/lib/jvm/openjdk/libjvm.so:hotspot:class__unloaded
usdt:/usr/lib/jvm/openjdk/libjvm.so:hotspot:method__compile__begin
usdt:/usr/lib/jvm/openjdk/libjvm.so:hotspot:method__compile__end
usdt:/usr/lib/jvm/openjdk/libjvm.so:hotspot:gc__begin
usdt:/usr/lib/jvm/openjdk/libjvm.so:hotspot:gc__end
[...]
```

This lists USDT probes for Java class loading and unloading, method compilation, and garbage collection. Many more were truncated: the full listing shows 524 USDT probes for this JDK version.

Many applications already have custom event logs that can be enabled and configured, and are useful for performance analysis. What makes USDT probes different is that they can be used from various tracers that can combine application context with kernel events such as disk and network I/O. An application-level logger may tell you that a database query was slow due to file system I/O, but a tracer can reveal more information: e.g., the query was slow due to lock contention in the file system, and not disk I/O as you might have assumed.

Some applications contain USDT probes, but they are not currently enabled in the packaged version of the application (this is the case with OpenJDK). Using them requires rebuilding the application from source with the appropriate config option. That option may be called --enable-dtrace-probes after the DTrace tracer, which drove adoption of USDT in applications.

USDT probes must be compiled into the executable they instrument. This is not possible for JIT-compiled languages such as Java, which usually compiles on the fly. A solution to this is *dynamic USDT*, which precompiles probes as a shared library, and provides an interface to call them from the JIT-compiled language. Dynamic USDT libraries exist for Java, Node.js, and other languages. Interpreted languages have a similar problem and need for dynamic USDT.

USDT probes are implemented in Linux using uprobes: see the previous section for a description of uprobes and their overhead. In addition to the enabled overhead, USDT probes place nop instructions in the code, as do tracepoints.

USDT probes can be used by the tracers introduced in Section 4.5, Tracing Tools, covered in depth in Chapters 13 to 15 (although using USDT with Ftrace requires some extra work).

USDT Documentation

If an application makes USDT probes available, they should be documented in the application's documentation. I summarized advanced USDT topics in *BPF Performance Tools*, Chapter 2 [Gregg 19]: how USDT probes can be added to application code, how they work internally, and dynamic USDT.

4.3.9 Hardware Counters (PMCs)

The processor and other devices commonly support hardware counters for observing activity. The main source are the processors, where they are commonly called *performance monitoring counters* (PMCs). They are known by other names as well: *CPU performance counters* (CPCs), *performance instrumentation counters* (PICs), and *performance monitoring unit events* (PMU events). These all refer to the same thing: programmable hardware registers on the processor that provide low-level performance information at the CPU cycle level.

PMCs are a vital resource for performance analysis. Only through PMCs can you measure the efficiency of CPU instructions, the hit ratios of CPU caches, the utilization of memory and device buses, interconnect utilization, stall cycles, and so on. Using these to analyze performance can lead to various performance optimizations.

PMC Examples

While there are many PMCs, Intel have selected seven as an "architectural set," which provide a high-level overview of some core functions [Intel 16]. The presence of these architectural set PMCs can be checked using the cpuid instruction. Table 4.4 shows this set, which serves as an example set of useful PMCs.

Table 4.4 **Intel architectural PMCs**

Event Name	UMask	Event Select	Example Event Mask Mnemonic
UnHalted Core Cycles	00H	3CH	CPU_CLK_UNHALTED.THREAD_P
Instruction Retired	00H	C0H	INST_RETIRED.ANY_P
UnHalted Reference Cycles	01H	3CH	CPU_CLK_THREAD_UNHALTED.REF_XCLK
LLC References	4FH	2EH	LONGEST_LAT_CACHE.REFERENCE

Event Name	UMask	Event Select	Example Event Mask Mnemonic
LLC Misses	41H	2EH	LONGEST_LAT_CACHE.MISS
Branch Instruction Retired	00H	C4H	BR_INST_RETIRED.ALL_BRANCHES
Branch Misses Retired	00H	C5H	BR_MISP_RETIRED.ALL_BRANCHES

As an example of PMCs, if you run the perf stat command without specifying events (no -e), it defaults to instrumenting the architectural PMCs. For example, the following runs perf stat on the gzip(1) command:

```
# perf stat gzip words

Performance counter stats for 'gzip words':

     156.927428      task-clock (msec)        #    0.987 CPUs utilized
              1      context-switches         #    0.006 K/sec
              0      cpu-migrations           #    0.000 K/sec
            131      page-faults              #    0.835 K/sec
    209,911,358      cycles                   #    1.338 GHz
    288,321,441      instructions             #    1.37  insn per cycle
     66,240,624      branches                 #  422.110 M/sec
      1,382,627      branch-misses            #    2.09% of all branches

    0.159065542 seconds time elapsed
```

The raw counts are the first column; after a hash are some statistics, including an important performance metric: instructions per cycle (insn per cycle). This shows how efficiently the CPUs are executing instructions—the higher, the better. This metric is explained in the Chapter 6, CPUs, Section 6.3.7, IPC, CPI.

PMC Interface

On Linux PMCs are accessed via the perf_event_open(2) syscall and are consumed by tools including perf(1).

While there are hundreds of PMCs available, there is only a fixed number of registers available in the CPUs to measure them at the same time, perhaps as few as six. You need to choose which PMCs you'd like to measure on those six registers, or cycle through different PMC sets as a way of sampling them (Linux perf(1) supports this automatically). Other software counters do not suffer from these constraints.

PMCs can be used in different modes: *counting*, where they count events with practically zero overhead; and *overflow sampling*, where an interrupt is raised for one in every configurable number of events, so that state can be captured. Counting can be used to quantify problems; overflow sampling can be used to show the code path responsible.

perf(1) can perform counting using the stat subcommand, and sampling using the record sub-command; see Chapter 13, perf.

PMC Challenges

Two common challenges when using PMCs are their accuracy for overflow sampling and their availability in cloud environments.

Overflow sampling may not record the correct instruction pointer that triggered the event, due to interrupt latency (often called "skid") or out-of-order instruction execution. For CPU cycle profiling, such skid may not be a problem, and some profilers deliberately introduce jitter to avoid lockstep sampling (or use an offset sampling rate such as 99 Hertz). But for measuring other events, such as LLC misses, the sampled instruction pointer needs to be accurate.

The solution is processor support for what are known as *precise events*. On Intel, precise events use a technology called precise event-based sampling (PEBS),[9] which uses hardware buffers to record a more accurate ("precise") instruction pointer at the time of the PMC event. On AMD, precise events use instruction-based sampling (IBS) [Drongowski 07]. The Linux perf(1) command supports precise events (see Chapter 13, perf, Section 13.9.2, CPU Profiling).

Another challenge is cloud computing, as many cloud environments disable PMC access for their guests. It is technically possible to enable it: for example, the Xen hypervisor has the vpmu command line option, which allows different sets of PMCs to be exposed to guests[10] [Xenbits 20]. Amazon have enabled many PMCs for their Nitro hypervisor guests.[11] Also, some cloud providers offer "bare-metal instances" where the guest has full processor access, and therefore full PMC access.

PMCs Documentation

PMCs are processor-specific and documented in the appropriate processor software developer's manual. Examples by processor manufacturer:

- **Intel**: Chapter 19, "Performance Monitoring Events," of *Intel® 64 and IA-32 Architectures Software Developer's Manual Volume 3* [Intel 16].

- **AMD**: Section 2.1.1, "Performance Monitor Counters," of *Open-Source Register Reference For AMD Family 17h Processors Models 00h-2Fh* [AMD 18]

- **ARM**: Section D7.10, "PMU Events and Event Numbers," of *Arm® Architecture Reference Manual Armv8, for Armv8-A architecture profile* [ARM 19]

There has been work to develop a standard naming scheme for PMCs that could be supported across all processors, called the *performance application programming interface* (PAPI) [UTK 20]. Operating system support for PAPI has been mixed: it requires frequent updates to map PAPI names to vendor PMC codes.

Chapter 6, CPUs, Section 6.4.1, Hardware, subsection Hardware Counters (PMCs), describes their implementation in more detail and provides additional PMC examples.

---

[9] Some of Intel's documentation expands PEBS differently, as: *processor* event-based sampling.

[10] I wrote the Xen code that allows different PMC modes: "ipc" for instructions-per-cycle PMCs only, and "arch" for the Intel architectural set. My code was just a firewall on the existing vpmu support in Xen.

[11] Currently only for larger Nitro instances where the VM owns a full processor socket (or more).

4.3.10   Other Observability Sources

Other observability sources include:

- **MSRs:** PMCs are implemented using model-specific registers (MSRs). There are other MSRs for showing the configuration and health of the system, including the CPU clock rate, usage, temperatures, and power consumption. The available MSRs are dependent on the processor type (model-specific), BIOS version and settings, and hypervisor settings. One use is an accurate cycle-based measurement of CPU utilization.

- **ptrace(2):** This syscall controls process tracing, which is used by gdb(1) for process debugging and strace(1) for tracing syscalls. It is breakpoint-based and can slow the target over one hundred-fold. Linux also has tracepoints, introduced in Section 4.3.5, Tracepoints, for more efficient syscall tracing.

- **Function profiling:** Profiling function calls (mcount() or __fentry__()) are added to the start of all non-inlined kernel functions on x86 for efficient Ftrace function tracing. They are converted to nop instructions until needed. See Chapter 14, Ftrace.

- **Network sniffing (libpcap):** These interfaces provide a way to capture packets from network devices for detailed investigations into packet and protocol performance. On Linux, sniffing is provided via the libpcap library and /proc/net/dev and is consumed by the tcpdump(8) tool. There are overheads, both CPU and storage, for capturing and examining all packets. See Chapter 10 for more about network sniffing.

- **netfilter conntrack:** The Linux netfilter technology allows custom handlers to be executed on events, not just for firewall, but also for connection tracking (conntrack). This allows logs to be created of network flows [Ayuso 12].

- **Process accounting:** This dates back to mainframes and the need to bill departments and users for their computer usage, based on the execution and runtime of processes. It exists in some form for Linux and other systems and can sometimes be helpful for performance analysis at the process level. For example, the Linux atop(1) tool uses process accounting to catch and display information from short-lived processes that would otherwise be missed when taking snapshots of /proc [Atoptool 20].

- **Software events:** These are related to hardware events but are instrumented in software. Page faults are an example. Software events are made available via the perf_event_open(2) interface and are used by perf(1) and bpftrace. They are pictured in Figure 4.5.

- **System calls:** Some system or library calls may be available to provide some performance metrics. These include getrusage(2), a system call for processes to get their own resource usage statistics, including user- and system-time, faults, messages, and context switches.

If you are interested in how each of these works, you will find that documentation is usually available, intended for the developer who is building tools upon these interfaces.

And More

Depending on your kernel version and enabled options, even more observability sources may be available. Some are mentioned in later chapters of this book. For Linux these include I/O accounting, blktrace, timer_stats, lockstat, and debugfs.

One way to find such sources is to read the kernel code you are interested in observing and see what statistics or tracepoints have been placed there.

In some cases there may be no kernel statistics for what you are after. Beyond dynamic instrumentation (Linux kprobes and uprobes), you may find that debuggers such as gdb(1) and lldb(1) can fetch kernel and application variables to shed some light on an investigation.

Solaris Kstat

As an example of a different way to provide system statistics, Solaris-based systems use a kernel statistics (Kstat) framework that provides a consistent hierarchical structure of kernel statistics, each named using the following four-tuple:

```
module:instance:name:statistic
```

These are

- **module**: This usually refers to the kernel module that created the statistic, such as sd for the SCSI disk driver, or zfs for the ZFS file system.
- **instance**: Some modules exist as multiple instances, such as an sd module for each SCSI disk. The instance is an enumeration.
- **name**: This is a name for the group of statistics.
- **statistic**: This is the individual statistic name.

Kstats are accessed using a binary kernel interface, and various libraries exist.

As an example Kstat, the following reads the "nproc" statistic using kstat(1M) and specifying the full four-tuple:

```
$ kstat -p unix:0:system_misc:nproc
unix:0:system_misc:nproc        94
```

This statistic shows the currently running number of processes.

In comparison, the /proc/stat-style sources on Linux have inconsistent formatting and usually require text parsing to process, costing some CPU cycles.

4.4 sar

sar(1) was introduced in Section 4.2.4, Monitoring, as a key monitoring facility. While there has been much excitement recently with BPF tracing superpowers (and I'm partly responsible), you should not overlook the utility of sar(1)—it's an essential systems performance tool that can solve many performance issues on its own. The Linux version of sar(1) is also well-designed, having self-descriptive column headings, network metric groups, and detailed documentation (man pages).

sar(1) is provided via the sysstat package.

4.4.1 sar(1) Coverage

Figure 4.6 shows the observability coverage from the different sar(1) command line options.

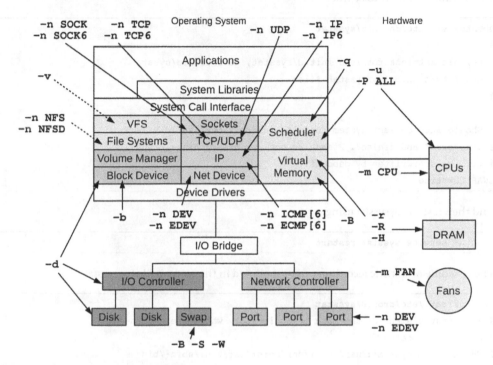

Figure 4.6   Linux sar(1) observability

This figure shows that sar(1) provides broad coverage of the kernel and devices, and even has observability for fans. The -m (power management) option also supports other arguments not shown in this figure, including IN for voltage inputs, TEMP for device temperatures, and USB for USB device power statistics.

4.4.2 sar(1) Monitoring

You may find that sar(1) data collecting (monitoring) is already enabled for your Linux systems. If it isn't, you need to enable it. To check, simply run sar without options. For example:

```
$ sar
Cannot open /var/log/sysstat/sa19: No such file or directory
Please check if data collecting is enabled
```

The output shows that sar(1) data collecting is not yet enabled on this system (the sa19 file refers to the daily archive for the 19th of the month). The steps to enable it may vary based on your distribution.

Configuration (Ubuntu)

On this Ubuntu system, I can enable sar(1) data collecting by editing the /etc/default/sysstat file and setting ENABLED to be true:

```
ubuntu# vi /etc/default/sysstat
#
# Default settings for /etc/init.d/sysstat, /etc/cron.d/sysstat
# and /etc/cron.daily/sysstat files
#

# Should sadc collect system activity informations? Valid values
# are "true" and "false". Please do not put other values, they
# will be overwritten by debconf!
ENABLED="true"
```

And then restarting sysstat using:

```
ubuntu# service sysstat restart
```

The schedule of statistic recording can be modified in the crontab file for sysstat:

```
ubuntu# cat /etc/cron.d/sysstat
# The first element of the path is a directory where the debian-sa1
# script is located
PATH=/usr/lib/sysstat:/usr/sbin:/usr/sbin:/usr/bin:/sbin:/bin

# Activity reports every 10 minutes everyday
5-55/10 * * * * root command -v debian-sa1 > /dev/null && debian-sa1 1 1

# Additional run at 23:59 to rotate the statistics file
59 23 * * * root command -v debian-sa1 > /dev/null && debian-sa1 60 2
```

The syntax 5-55/10 means it will record every 10 minutes for the minute range 5 to 55 minutes past the hour. You can adjust this to suit the resolution desired: the syntax is documented in the crontab(5) man page. More frequent data collection will increase the size of the sar(1) archive files, which can be found in /var/log/sysstat.

I often change data collection to:

```
*/5 * * * * root command -v debian-sa1 > /dev/null && debian-sa1 1 1 -S ALL
```

The */5 will record every five minutes, and the -S ALL will record all statistics. By default sar(1) will record most (but not all) statistic groups. The -S ALL option is used to record all statistic groups—it is passed to sadc(1), and documented in the man page for sadc(1). There is also an extended version, -S XALL, which records additional breakdowns of statistics.

Reporting

sar(1) can be executed with any of the options shown in Figure 4.6 to report the selected statistic group. Multiple options can be specified. For example, the following reports CPU statistics (-u), TCP (-n TCP), and TCP errors (-n ETCP):

```
$ sar -u -n TCP,ETCP
Linux 4.15.0-66-generic (bgregg)    01/19/2020        _x86_64_        (8 CPU)

10:40:01 AM      CPU     %user     %nice   %system   %iowait    %steal     %idle
10:45:01 AM      all      6.87      0.00      2.84      0.18      0.00     90.12
10:50:01 AM      all      6.87      0.00      2.49      0.06      0.00     90.58
[...]
10:40:01 AM  active/s passive/s    iseg/s    oseg/s
10:45:01 AM      0.16      0.00     10.98      9.27
10:50:01 AM      0.20      0.00     10.40      8.93
[...]
10:40:01 AM  atmptf/s  estres/s retrans/s isegerr/s   orsts/s
10:45:01 AM      0.04      0.02      0.46      0.00      0.03
10:50:01 AM      0.03      0.02      0.53      0.00      0.03
[...]
```

The first line of output is a system summary, showing the kernel type and version, the hostname, the date, processor architecture, and number of CPUs.

Running sar -A will dump all statistics.

Output Formats

The sysstat package comes with an sadf(1) command for viewing sar(1) statistics in different formats, including JSON, SVG, and CSV. The following examples emit the TCP (-n TCP) statistics in these formats.

JSON (-j):

JavaScript Object Notation (JSON) can be easily parsed and imported by many programming languages, making it a suitable output format when building other software upon sar(1).

```
$ sadf -j -- -n TCP
{"sysstat": {
  "hosts": [
    {
      "nodename": "bgregg",
      "sysname": "Linux",
      "release": "4.15.0-66-generic",
      "machine": "x86_64",
      "number-of-cpus": 8,
```

```
      "file-date": "2020-01-19",
      "file-utc-time": "18:40:01",
      "statistics": [
        {
          "timestamp": {"date": "2020-01-19", "time": "18:45:01", "utc": 1,
"interval": 300},
          "network": {
            "net-tcp": {"active": 0.16, "passive": 0.00, "iseg": 10.98, "oseg": 9.27}
          }
        },
[...]
```

You can process the JSON output at the command line using the jq(1) tool.

SVG (-g):

sadf(1) can emit Scalable Vector Graphics (SVG) files that can be viewed in web browsers.
Figure 4.7 shows an example. You can use this output format to build rudimentary dashboards.

Linux 4.15.0-66-generic (bgregg) 01/19/2020 _x86_64_ (8 CPU)

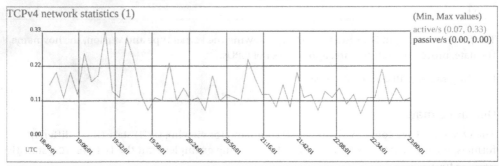

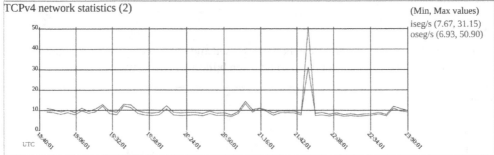

Figure 4.7   sar(1) sadf(1) SVG output[12]

---

[12] Note that I edited the SVG file to make this figure more legible, changing colors and increasing font sizes.

CSV (-d):

The comma-separated values (CSV) format is intended for import by databases (and uses a semicolon):

```
$ sadf -d -- -n TCP
# hostname;interval;timestamp;active/s;passive/s;iseg/s;oseg/s
bgregg;300;2020-01-19 18:45:01 UTC;0.16;0.00;10.98;9.27
bgregg;299;2020-01-19 18:50:01 UTC;0.20;0.00;10.40;8.93
bgregg;300;2020-01-19 18:55:01 UTC;0.12;0.00;9.27;8.07
[...]
```

4.4.3 sar(1) Live

When executed with an interval and optional count, sar(1) does live reporting. This mode can be used even when data collection is not enabled.

For example, showing the TCP statistics with an interval of one second and a count of five:

```
$ sar -n TCP 1 5
Linux 4.15.0-66-generic (bgregg)    01/19/2020      _x86_64_      (8 CPU)

03:09:04 PM  active/s passive/s    iseg/s    oseg/s
03:09:05 PM    1.00      0.00      33.00     42.00
03:09:06 PM    0.00      0.00     109.00     86.00
03:09:07 PM    0.00      0.00     107.00     67.00
03:09:08 PM    0.00      0.00     104.00    119.00
03:09:09 PM    0.00      0.00      70.00     70.00
Average:       0.20      0.00      84.60     76.80
```

Data collecting is intended for long intervals, such as five or ten minutes, whereas live reporting allows you to look at per-second variation.

Later chapters include various examples of live sar(1) statistics.

4.4.4 sar(1) Documentation

The sar(1) man page documents the individual statistics and includes SNMP names in square brackets. For example:

```
$ man sar
[...]
            active/s
                The number of times TCP connections have made a direct
                transition to the SYN-SENT state from the CLOSED state
                per second [tcpActiveOpens].
```

```
        passive/s
                The number of times TCP connections have  made  a  direct
                transition  to  the  SYN-RCVD state from the LISTEN state
                per second [tcpPassiveOpens].

        iseg/s
                The total number of segments received per second, includ-
                ing  those  received  in  error  [tcpInSegs].  This count
                includes segments received on currently established  con-
                nections.
[...]
```

Specific uses of sar(1) are described later in this book; see Chapters 6 to 10. Appendix C is a summary of the sar(1) options and metrics.

4.5   Tracing Tools

Linux tracing tools use the previously described events interfaces (tracepoints, kprobes, uprobes, USDT) for advanced performance analysis. The main tracing tools are:

- **perf(1)**: The official Linux profiler. It is excellent for CPU profiling (sampling of stack traces) and PMC analysis, and can instrument other events, typically recording to an output file for post-processing.

- **Ftrace**: The official Linux tracer, it is a multi-tool composed of different tracing utilities. It is suited for kernel code path analysis and resource-constrained systems, as it can be used without dependencies.

- **BPF (BCC, bpftrace)**: Extended BPF was introduced in Chapter 3, Operating Systems, Section 3.4.4, Extended BPF. It powers advanced tracing tools, the main ones being BCC and bpftrace. BCC provides powerful tools, and bpftrace provides a high-level language for custom one-liners and short programs.

- **SystemTap**: A high-level language and tracer with many tapsets (libraries) for tracing different targets [Eigler 05][Sourceware 20]. It has recently been developing a BPF backend, which I recommend (see the stapbpf(8) man page).

- **LTTng**: A tracer optimized for black-box recording: optimally recording many events for later analysis [LTTng 20].

The first three tracers are covered in Chapter 13, perf; Chapter 14, Ftrace; and Chapter 15, BPF. The chapters that now follow (5 to 12) include various uses of these tracers, showing the commands to type and how to interpret the output. This ordering is deliberate, focusing on uses and performance wins first, and then covering the tracers in more detail later if and as needed.

At Netflix, I use perf(1) for CPU analysis, Ftrace for kernel code digging, and BCC/bpftrace for everything else (memory, file systems, disks, networking, and application tracing).

4.6   Observing Observability

Observability tools and the statistics upon which they are built are implemented in software, and all software has the potential for bugs. The same is true for the documentation that describes the software. Regard with a healthy skepticism any statistics that are new to you, questioning what they really mean and whether they are really correct.

Metrics may be subject to any of the following problems:

- Tools and measurements are sometimes wrong.

- Man pages are not always right.

- Available metrics may be incomplete.

- Available metrics may be poorly designed and confusing.

- Metric collectors (e.g., that parse tool output) can have bugs.[13]

- Metric processing (algorithms/spreadsheets) can also introduce errors.

When multiple observability tools have overlapping coverage, you can use them to cross-check each other. Ideally, they will source different instrumentation frameworks to check for bugs in the frameworks as well. Dynamic instrumentation is especially useful for this purpose, as custom tools can be created to double-check metrics.

Another verification technique is to apply *known workloads* and then to check that the observability tools agree with the results you expect. This can involve the use of micro-benchmarking tools that report their own statistics for comparison.

Sometimes it isn't the tool or statistic that is in error, but the documentation that describes it, including man pages. The software may have evolved without the documentation being updated.

Realistically, you may not have time to double-check every performance measurement you use and will do this only if you encounter unusual results or a result that is company critical. Even if you do not double-check, it can be valuable to be aware that you didn't and that you assumed the tools were correct.

Metrics can also be incomplete. When faced with a large number of tools and metrics, it may be tempting to assume that they provide complete and effective coverage. This is often not the case: metrics may have been added by programmers to debug their own code, and later built into observability tools without much study of real customer needs. Some programmers may not have added any at all to new subsystems.

---

[13] In this case the tool and measurement are correct, but an automated collector has introduced errors. At Surge 2013 I gave a lightning talk on an astonishing case [Gregg 13c]: a benchmarking company reported poor metrics for a product I was supporting, and I dug in. It turned out the shell script they used to automate the benchmark had two bugs. First, when processing output from fio(1), it would take a result such as "100KB/s" and use a regular expression to elide nun-numeric characters, including "KB/s" to turn this into "100". Since fio(1) reported results with different units (bytes, Kbytes, Mbytes), this introduced massive (1024x) errors. Second, they also elided decimal places, so a result of "1.6" became "16".

An absence of metrics can be more difficult to identify than the presence of poor metrics. Chapter 2, Methodologies, can help you find these missing metrics by studying the questions you need answered for performance analysis.

4.7   Exercises

Answer the following questions about observability tools (you may wish to revisit the introduction to some of these terms in Chapter 1):

1. List some static performance tools.

2. What is profiling?

3. Why would profilers use 99 Hertz instead of 100 Hertz?

4. What is tracing?

5. What is static instrumentation?

6. Describe why dynamic instrumentation is important.

7. What is the difference between tracepoints and kprobes?

8. Describe the expected CPU overhead (low/medium/high) from the following:

   - Disk IOPS counters (as seen by iostat(1))

   - Tracing per-event disk I/O via tracepoints or kprobes

   - Tracing per-event context switches (tracepoints/kprobes)

   - Tracing per-event process execution (execve(2)) (tracepoints/kprobes)

   - Tracing per-event libc malloc() via uprobes

9. Describe why PMCs are valuable for performance analysis.

10. Given an observability tool, describe how you could determine what instrumentation sources it uses.

4.8   References

[**Eigler 05**] Eigler, F. Ch., et al. "Architecture of SystemTap: A Linux Trace/Probe Tool," http://sourceware.org/systemtap/archpaper.pdf, 2005.

[**Drongowski 07**] Drongowski, P., "Instruction-Based Sampling: A New Performance Analysis Technique for AMD Family 10h Processors," AMD (Whitepaper), 2007.

[**Ayuso 12**] Ayuso, P., "The Conntrack-Tools User Manual," http://conntrack-tools.netfilter.org/manual.html, 2012.

[**Gregg 13c**] Gregg, B., "Benchmarking Gone Wrong," *Surge 2013: Lightning Talks*, https://www.youtube.com/watch?v=vm1GJMp0QN4#t=17m48s, 2013.

[Weisbecker 13] Weisbecker, F., "Status of Linux dynticks," *OSPERT,*
http://www.ertl.jp/~shinpei/conf/ospert13/slides/FredericWeisbecker.pdf, 2013.

[Intel 16] *Intel 64 and IA-32 Architectures Software Developer's Manual Volume 3B: System
Programming Guide, Part 2, September 2016,* https://www.intel.com/content/www/us/en/
architecture-and-technology/64-ia-32-architectures-software-developer-vol-3b-part-2-
manual.html, 2016.

[AMD 18] *Open-Source Register Reference for AMD Family 17h Processors Models 00h-2Fh,*
https://developer.amd.com/resources/developer-guides-manuals, 2018.

[ARM 19] *Arm® Architecture Reference Manual Armv8, for Armv8-A architecture profile,*
https://developer.arm.com/architectures/cpu-architecture/a-profile/docs?_
ga=2.78191124.1893781712.1575908489-930650904.1559325573, 2019.

[Gregg 19] Gregg, B., *BPF Performance Tools: Linux System and Application Observability,*
Addison-Wesley, 2019.

[Atoptool 20] "Atop," www.atoptool.nl/index.php, accessed 2020.

[Bowden 20] Bowden, T., Bauer, B., et al., "The /proc Filesystem," *Linux documentation,*
https://www.kernel.org/doc/html/latest/filesystems/proc.html, accessed 2020.

[Gregg 20a] Gregg, B., "Linux Performance," http://www.brendangregg.com/
linuxperf.html, accessed 2020.

[LTTng 20] "LTTng," https://lttng.org, accessed 2020.

[PCP 20] "Performance Co-Pilot," https://pcp.io, accessed 2020.

[Prometheus 20] "Exporters and Integrations," https://prometheus.io/docs/instrumenting/
exporters, accessed 2020.

[Sourceware 20] "SystemTap," https://sourceware.org/systemtap, accessed 2020.

[Ts'o 20] Ts'o, T., Zefan, L., and Zanussi, T., "Event Tracing," *Linux documentation,*
https://www.kernel.org/doc/html/latest/trace/events.html, accessed 2020.

[Xenbits 20] "Xen Hypervisor Command Line Options," https://xenbits.xen.org/docs/
4.11-testing/misc/xen-command-line.html, accessed 2020.

[UTK 20] "Performance Application Programming Interface," http://icl.cs.utk.edu/papi,
accessed 2020.

Chapter 5
Applications

Performance is best tuned closest to where the work is performed: in the applications. These include databases, web servers, application servers, load balancers, file servers, and more. The chapters that follow approach applications from the perspectives of the resources they consume: CPUs, memory, file systems, disks, and the network. This chapter addresses the application level.

Applications themselves can become extremely complex, especially in distributed environments involving many components. The study of application internals is usually the domain of the application developer and can include the use of third-party tools for introspection. For those studying systems performance, application performance analysis includes configuration of the application to make best use of system resources, characterization of how the application is using the system, and analysis of common pathologies.

The learning objectives of this chapter are:

- Describe performance tuning objectives.
- Become familiar with performance improving techniques, including multithreaded programming, hash tables, and non-blocking I/O.
- Understand common locking and synchronization primitives.
- Understand challenges posed by different programming languages.
- Follow a thread state analysis methodology.
- Perform CPU and off-CPU profiling.
- Perform syscall analysis, including tracing process execution.
- Become aware of stack trace gotchas: missing symbols and stacks.

This chapter discusses application basics, fundamentals for application performance, programming languages and compilers, strategies for generic application performance analysis, and system-based application observability tools.

5.1 Application Basics

Before diving into application performance, you should familiarize yourself with the role of the application, its basic characteristics, and its ecosystem in the industry. This forms the context within which you can understand application activity. It also gives you opportunities to learn about common performance issues and tuning and provides avenues for further study. To learn this context, try answering the following questions:

- **Function:** What is the role of the application? Is it a database server, web server, load balancer, file server, object store?

- **Operation:** What requests does the application serve, or what operations does it perform? Databases serve *queries* (and *commands*), web servers serve *HTTP requests*, and so on. This can be measured as a rate, to gauge load and for capacity planning.

- **Performance requirements:** Does the company running the application have a service level objective (SLO) (e.g., 99.9% of requests at < 100 ms latency)?

- **CPU mode:** Is the application implemented as user-level or kernel-level software? Most applications are user-level, executing as one or more processes, but some are implemented as kernel services (for example, NFS), and BPF programs are also kernel-level.

- **Configuration:** How is the application configured, and why? This information may be found in a configuration file or via administration tools. Check if any tunable parameters related to performance have been changed, including buffer sizes, cache sizes, parallelism (processes or threads), and other options.

- **Host:** What hosts the application? A server or cloud instance? What are the CPUs, memory topology, storage devices, etc.? What are their limits?

- **Metrics:** Are application metrics provided, such as an operation rate? They may be provided by bundled tools or third-party tools, via API requests, or by processing operation logs.

- **Logs:** What operation logs does the application create? What logs can be enabled? What performance metrics, including latency, are available from the logs? For example, MySQL supports a *slow query log*, providing valuable performance details for each query slower than a certain threshold.

- **Version:** Is the application the latest version? Have performance fixes or improvements been noted in the release notes for recent versions?

- **Bugs:** Is there a bug database for the application? What are the "performance" bugs for your version of the application? If you have a current performance issue, search the bug database to see if anything like it has happened before, how it was investigated, and what else was involved.

- **Source code:** Is the application open source? If so, code paths identified by profilers and tracers can be studied, potentially leading to performance wins. You may be able to modify the application code yourself to improve performance, and submit your improvements upstream for inclusion in the official application.

- **Community:** Is there a community for the application where performance findings are shared? Communities may include forums, blogs, Internet Relay Chat (IRC) channels, other chat channels (e.g., Slack), meetups, and conferences. Meetups and conferences often post slides and videos online, which are useful resources for years afterward. They may also have a community manager who shares community updates and news.

- **Books:** Are there books about the application and/or its performance? Are they good books (e.g., written by an expert, practical/actionable, makes good use of reader's time, up to date, etc.)?

- **Experts:** Who are the recognized performance experts for the application? Learning their names can help you find material they have authored.

Regardless of the source, you are aiming to understand the application at a high level—what it does, how it operates, and how it performs. An immensely useful resource, if you can find one, is a *functional diagram* illustrating application internals.

The next sections cover other application basics: setting objectives, optimizing the common case, observability, and big O notation.

5.1.1 Objectives

A performance goal provides direction for your performance analysis work and helps you select which activities to perform. Without a clear goal, performance analysis risks turning into a random "fishing expedition."

For application performance, you can start with what operations the application performs (as described earlier) and what the goal for performance is. The goal may be:

- **Latency:** A low or consistent application response time
- **Throughput:** A high application operation rate or data transfer rate
- **Resource utilization:** Efficiency for a given application workload
- **Price:** Improving the performance/price ratio, lowering computing costs

It is better if these can be quantified using metrics that may be derived from business or quality-of-service requirements. Examples are:

- An average application request latency of 5 ms
- 95% of requests completed with a latency of 100 ms or less
- Elimination of latency outliers: zero requests beyond 1,000 ms
- A maximum throughput of at least 10,000 application requests per second per server of a given size[1]
- Average disk utilization under 50% for 10,000 application requests per second

Once a goal has been chosen, you can work on the limiters for that goal. For latency, the limiter may be disk or network I/O; for throughput, it may be CPU usage. The strategies in this and other chapters will help you identify them.

---

[1] If the server size is variable (as with cloud instances). This may be better expressed in terms of the bounding resource: e.g., a maximum 1,000 application requests per second per CPU, for a CPU-bound workload.

For throughput-based goals, note that not all operations are equal in terms of performance or cost. If the goal is a certain rate of operations, it may be important to also specify what type of operations they are. This may be a distribution based on expected or measured workloads.

Section 5.2, Application Performance Techniques, describes common methods for improving application performance. Some of these may make sense for one goal but not another; for example, selecting a larger I/O size may improve throughput at the expense of latency. Remember the goal that you are pursuing as you determine which topics are most applicable.

Apdex

Some companies use a target application performance index (ApDex or Apdex) as an objective and as a metric to monitor. It can better convey customer experience and involves first classifying customer events as to whether they are "satisfactory," "tolerable," or "frustrating." The Apdex is then calculated using [Apdex 20]:

Apdex = (satisfactory + 0.5 × tolerable + 0 × frustrating) / total events

The resulting Apdex ranges from 0 (no satisfied customers) to 1 (all satisfied customers).

5.1.2   Optimize the Common Case

Software internals can be complex, with many different code paths and behaviors. This may be especially evident if you browse the source code: applications are commonly tens of thousands of lines of code, while operating system kernels are upward of hundreds of thousands. Picking areas to optimize at random may involve a great deal of work for not much gain.

One way to efficiently improve application performance is to find the most common code path for the production workload and begin by improving that. If the application is CPU-bound, that may mean the code paths that are frequently on-CPU. If the application is I/O-bound, you should be looking at the code paths that frequently lead to I/O. These can be determined by analysis and profiling of the application, including studying stack traces and flame graphs, as covered in later chapters. A higher level of context for understanding the common case may also be provided by application observability tools.

5.1.3   Observability

As I reiterate in many chapters of this book, the biggest performance wins can come from *eliminating unnecessary work*.

This fact sometimes gets overlooked when an application is being selected based on performance. If benchmarking showed application A to be 10% faster than application B, it may be tempting to choose application A. However, if application A is opaque and application B provides a rich set of observability tools, it's very likely that application B will be the better choice in the long run. Those observability tools make it possible to see and eliminate unnecessary work and to better understand and tune active work. The performance wins gained through enhanced observability may dwarf the initial 10% performance difference. The same is true for the selection of languages and runtimes: such as choosing Java or C, which are mature and have many observability tools, versus choosing a new language.

5.1.4 Big O Notation

Big O notation, commonly taught as a computer science subject, is used to analyze the complexity of algorithms and to model how they will perform as the input dataset scales. The O refers to the *order* of the function, describing its growth rate. This notation helps programmers pick more efficient and performant algorithms when developing applications [Knuth 76][Knuth 97].

Common big O notations and algorithm examples are listed in Table 5.1.

Table 5.1 **Example big O notations**

Notation	Examples
O(1)	Boolean test
O(log n)	Binary search of a sorted array
O(n)	Linear search of a linked list
O(n log n)	Quick sort (average case)
O(n^2)	Bubble sort (average case)
O(2^n)	Factoring numbers; exponential growth
O(n!)	Brute force of traveling salesman problem

The notation allows programmers to estimate speedup of different algorithms, determining which areas of code will lead to the greatest improvements. For example, for searching a sorted array of 100 items, the difference between linear search and binary search is a factor of 21 (100/log(100)).

The performance of these algorithms is pictured in Figure 5.1, showing their trend as they scale.

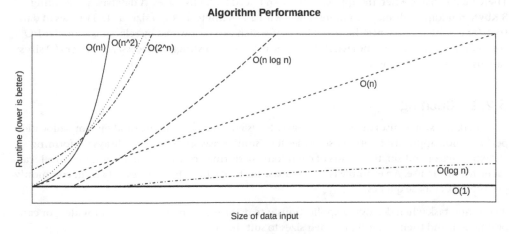

Figure 5.1 Runtime versus input size for different algorithms

This classification helps the systems performance analyst to understand that some algorithms will perform very poorly at scale. Performance problems may show up when applications are pushed to service more users or data objects than they ever have before, at which point algorithms such as O(n^2) may begin to be pathological. The fix may be for the developer to use a more efficient algorithm or to partition the population differently.

Big O notation does ignore some constant computation costs incurred for each algorithm. For cases where n (the input data size) is small, these costs may dominate.

5.2   Application Performance Techniques

This section describes some commonly used techniques by which application performance can be improved: selecting an I/O size, caching, buffering, polling, concurrency and parallelism, non-blocking I/O, and processor binding. Refer to the application documentation to see which of these are used, and for any additional application-specific features.

5.2.1   Selecting an I/O Size

Costs associated with performing I/O can include initializing buffers, making a system call, mode or context switching, allocating kernel metadata, checking process privileges and limits, mapping addresses to devices, executing kernel and driver code to deliver the I/O, and, finally, freeing metadata and buffers. "Initialization tax" is paid for small and large I/O alike. For efficiency, the more data transferred by each I/O, the better.

Increasing the I/O size is a common strategy used by applications to improve throughput. It's usually much more efficient to transfer 128 Kbytes as a single I/O than as 128 × 1 Kbyte I/O, considering any fixed per-I/O costs. Rotational disk I/O, in particular, has historically had a high per-I/O cost due to seek time.

There's a downside when the application doesn't need larger I/O sizes. A database performing 8 Kbyte random reads may run more slowly with a 128 Kbyte disk I/O size, as 120 Kbytes of data transfer is wasted. This introduces I/O latency, which can be lowered by selecting a smaller I/O size that more closely matches what the application is requesting. Unnecessarily larger I/O sizes can also waste cache space.

5.2.2   Caching

The operating system uses caches to improve file system read performance and memory allocation performance; applications often use caches for a similar reason. Instead of always performing an expensive operation, the results of commonly performed operations may be stored in a local cache for future use. An example is the database buffer cache, which stores data from commonly performed database queries.

A common task when deploying applications is to determine which caches are provided, or can be enabled, and then to configure their sizes to suit the system.

While caches improve read performance, their storage is often used as buffers to improve write performance.

5.2.3 Buffering

To improve write performance, data may be coalesced in a buffer before being sent to the next level. This increases the I/O size and efficiency of the operation. Depending on the type of writes, it may also increase write latency, as the first write to a buffer waits for subsequent writes before being sent.

A ring buffer (or *circular buffer*) is a type of fixed buffer that can be used for continuous transfer between components, which act upon the buffer asynchronously. It may be implemented using start and end pointers, which can be moved by each component as data is appended or removed.

5.2.4 Polling

Polling is a technique in which the system waits for an event to occur by checking the status of the event in a loop, with pauses between checks. There are some potential performance problems with polling when there is little work to do:

- Costly CPU overhead of repeated checks
- High latency between the occurrence of the event and the next polled check

Where this is a performance problem, applications may be able to change their behavior to listen for the event to occur, which immediately notifies the application and executes the desired routine.

poll() System Call

There is a poll(2) syscall to check for the status of file descriptors, which serves a similar function to polling, although it is event-based so it doesn't suffer the performance cost of polling.

The poll(2) interface supports multiple file descriptors as an array, which requires the application to scan the array when events occur to find the related file descriptors. This scanning is O(n) (see Section 5.1.4, Big O Notation), whose overhead can become a performance problem at scale. An alternative on Linux is epoll(2), which can avoid the scan and therefore be O(1). On BSD, the equivalent is kqueue(2).

5.2.5 Concurrency and Parallelism

Time-sharing systems (including all derived from Unix) provide program *concurrency*: the ability to load and begin executing multiple runnable programs. While their runtimes may overlap, they do not necessarily execute on-CPU at the same instant. Each of these programs may be an application process.

To take advantage of a multiprocessor system, an application must execute on multiple CPUs at the same time. This is *parallelism*, which an application may accomplish by using multiple processes (*multiprocess*) or multiple threads (*multithreaded*), each performing its own task. For reasons explained in Chapter 6, CPUs, Section 6.3.13, Multiprocess, Multithreading, multiple threads (or the equivalent tasks) are more efficient and are therefore the preferred approach.

Apart from increased throughput of CPU work, multiple threads (or processes) is one way to allow I/O to be performed concurrently, as other threads can execute while a thread blocked on I/O waits. (The other way is asynchronous I/O.)

The use of multiprocess or multithreaded architectures means allowing the kernel to decide who to run, via the CPU scheduler, and with the cost of context-switch overheads. A different approach is for the user-mode application to implement its own scheduling mechanism and program model so that it can service different application requests (or programs) in the same OS thread. Mechanisms include:

- **Fibers:** Also called *lightweight threads*, these are a user-mode version of threads where each fiber represents a schedulable program. The application can use its own scheduling logic to choose which fiber to run. These can be used, for example, to allocate a fiber to handle each application request, with less overhead than doing the same with OS threads. Microsoft Windows, for example, supports fibers.[2]

- **Co-routines:** More lightweight than a fiber, a co-routine is a subroutine that can be scheduled by the user-mode application, providing a mechanism for concurrency.

- **Event-based concurrency:** Programs are broken down into a series of event handlers, and runnable events can be planned on and executed from a queue. These can be used, for example, by allocating metadata for each application request, which is referenced by event handlers. For example, the Node.js runtime uses event-based concurrency using a single *event worker thread* (which can become a bottleneck, as it can only execute on one CPU).

With all of these mechanisms, I/O must still be handled by the kernel, so OS thread switching is typically inevitable.[3] Also, for parallelism, multiple OS threads must be used so they can be scheduled across multiple CPUs.

Some runtimes use both co-routines for lightweight concurrency and multiple OS threads for parallelism. An example is the Golang runtime, which uses *goroutines* (co-routines) on a pool of OS threads. To improve performance, when a goroutine makes a blocking call, Golang's scheduler automatically moves other goroutines on the blocking thread to other threads to run [Golang 20].

Three common models of multithreaded programming are:

- **Service thread pool:** A pool of threads services network requests, where each thread services one client connection at a time.

- **CPU thread pool:** One thread is created per CPU. This is commonly used by long-duration batch processing, such as video encoding.

- **Staged event-driven architecture (SEDA):** Application requests are decomposed into stages that may be processed by pools of one or more threads.

---

[2]The official Microsoft documentation warns about problems that fibers can pose: e.g., thread-local storage is shared between fibers, so programmers must switch to fiber-local storage, and any routine that exits a thread will exit all fibers on that thread. The documentation states: "In general, fibers do not provide advantages over a well-designed multithreaded application" [Microsoft 18].

[3]With some exceptions, such as using sendfile(2) to avoid I/O syscalls, and Linux io_uring, which allows user-space to schedule I/O by writing and reading from io_uring queues (these are summarized in Section 5.2.6, Non-Blocking I/O).

Since multithreaded programming shares the same address space as the process, threads can read and write the same memory directly, without the need for more expensive interfaces (such as inter-process communication [IPC] for multiprocess programming). For integrity, synchronization primitives are used so that data does not become corrupted by multiple threads reading and writing simultaneously.

Synchronization Primitives

Synchronization primitives manage access to memory to ensure integrity, and can operate similarly to traffic lights regulating access to an intersection. And, like traffic lights, they can halt the flow of traffic, causing wait time (latency). The three commonly used types for applications are:

- **Mutex (MUTually EXclusive) locks:** Only the holder of the lock can operate. Others block and wait off-CPU.

- **Spin locks:** Spin locks allow the holder to operate, while others *spin* on-CPU in a tight loop, checking for the lock to be released. While these can provide low-latency access—the blocked thread never leaves CPU and is ready to run in a matter of cycles once the lock is available—they also waste CPU resources while threads spin, waiting.

- **RW locks:** Reader/writer locks ensure integrity by allowing either multiple readers or one writer only and no readers.

- **Semaphores:** This is a variable type that can be counting to allow a given number of parallel operations, or binary to allow only one (effectively a mutex lock).

Mutex locks may be implemented by the library or kernel as a hybrid of spin and mutex locks, which spin if the holder is currently running on another CPU and block if it isn't (or if a spin threshold is reached). They were initially implemented for Linux in 2009 [Zijlstra 09] and now have three paths depending on the state of the lock (as described in Documentation/locking/mutex-design.rst [Molnar 20]):

1. **fastpath:** Attempts to acquire the lock using the cmpxchg instruction to set the owner. This only succeeds if the lock is not held.

2. **midpath:** Also known as *optimistic spinning*, this spins on CPU while the lock holder is also running, hoping that it is soon released and can be acquired without blocking.

3. **slowpath:** This blocks and deschedules the thread, to be woken up later when the lock is available.

The Linux read-copy-update (RCU) mechanism is another synchronization mechanism in heavy use for kernel code. It allows read operations without needing to acquire a lock, improving performance over other lock types. With RCUs, writes create a copy of the protected data and update the copy while in-flight reads can still access the original. It can detect when there are no longer any readers (based on various per-CPU conditions) and then replace the original with the updated copy [Linux 20e].

Investigating performance issues involving locks can be time-consuming and often requires familiarity with the application source code. This is usually an activity for the developer.

Hash Tables

A hash table of locks can be used to employ the optimum number of locks for a large number of data structures. While hash tables are summarized here, this is an advanced topic that assumes a programming background.

Picture the following two approaches:

- A single global mutex lock for all data structures. While this solution is simple, concurrent access will encounter contention for the lock and latency while waiting for it. Multiple threads that need the lock will *serialize*—execute in sequence, rather than concurrently.

- A mutex lock for every data structure. While this reduces contention to only the times it is really needed—concurrent access to the same data structure—there are storage overheads for the lock, and CPU overheads for the creation and destruction of the lock for every data structure.

A hash table of locks is an in-between solution and is suitable when lock contention is expected to be light. A fixed number of locks is created, and a hashing algorithm is used to select which lock is used for which data structure. This avoids the creation and destruction cost with the data structure and also avoids the problem of having only a single lock.

The example hash table shown in Figure 5.2 has four entries, called *buckets*, each of which contains its own lock.

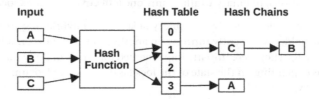

Figure 5.2   Example hash table

This example also shows one approach for solving *hash collisions*, where two or more input data structures hash to the same bucket. Here, a chain of data structures is created to store them all under the same bucket, where they will be found again by the hashing function. These hash chains can be a performance problem if they become too long and are walked serially, because they are protected by only one lock that can begin to have long hold times. The hash function and table size can be selected with the goal of uniformly spreading data structures over many buckets, to keep hash chain length to a minimum. Hash chain length should be checked for production workloads, in case the hashing algorithm is not working as intended and is instead creating long hash chains that perform poorly.

Ideally, the number of hash table buckets should be equal to or greater than the CPU count, for the potential of maximum parallelism. The hashing algorithm may be as simple as taking low-order bits[4] of the data structure address and using this as an index into a power-of-two-size array of locks. Such simple algorithms are also fast, allowing data structures to be located quickly.

---

[4] Or middle bits. The lowest-order bits for addresses to an array of structs may have too many collisions.

With an array of adjacent locks in memory, a performance problem can arise when locks fall within the same cache line. Two CPUs updating different locks in the same cache line will encounter cache coherency overhead, with each CPU invalidating the cache line in the other's cache. This situation is called *false sharing* and is commonly solved by *padding* locks with unused bytes so that only one lock exists in each cache line in memory.

5.2.6 Non-Blocking I/O

The Unix process life cycle, pictured in Chapter 3, Operating Systems, shows processes blocking and entering the sleep state during I/O. There are a couple of performance problems with this model:

- Each I/O operation consumes a thread (or process) while it is blocked. In order to support many concurrent I/O, the application must create many threads (typically one for each client), which have a cost associated with thread creation and destruction, as well as stack space required to keep them.

- For frequent short-lived I/O, the overhead of frequent context switching can consume CPU resources and add application latency.

The *non-blocking I/O* model issues I/O asynchronously, without blocking the current thread, which can then perform other work. This has been a key feature of Node.js [Node.js 20], a server-side JavaScript application environment that directs code to be developed in non-blocking ways.

There are a number of mechanisms to perform non-blocking or asynchronous I/O, including:

- **open(2)**: Via the O_ASYNC flag. The process is notified using a signal when I/O becomes possible on the file descriptor.

- **io_submit(2)**: Linux asynchronous I/O (AIO).

- **sendfile(2)**: This copies data from one file descriptor to the other, deferring I/O to the kernel instead of user-level I/O.[5]

- **io_uring_enter(2)**: Linux io_uring allows asynchronous I/O to be submitted using a ring buffer that is shared between user and kernel space [Axboe 19].

Check your operating system documentation for other methods.

5.2.7 Processor Binding

For NUMA environments, it can be advantageous for a process or thread to remain running on a single CPU and to run on the same CPU as it did previously after performing I/O. This can improve the memory locality of the application, reducing the cycles for memory I/O and improving overall application performance. Operating systems are well aware of this and are designed to keep application threads on the same CPUs (*CPU affinity*). These topics are introduced in Chapter 7, Memory.

---

[5]This is used by the Netflix CDN for sending video assets to customers without user-level I/O overheads.

Some applications force this behavior by *binding* themselves to CPUs. This can significantly improve performance for some systems. It can also reduce performance when the bindings conflict with other CPU bindings, such as device interrupt mappings to CPUs.

Be especially careful about the risks of CPU binding when there are other tenants or applications running on the same system. This is a problem I've encountered in OS virtualization (container) environments, where an application can see all the CPUs and then bind to some, on the assumption that it is the only application on the server. When a server is shared by other tenant applications that are also binding, multiple tenants may unknowingly bind to the same CPUs, causing CPU contention and scheduler latency even though other CPUs are idle.

Over the lifespan of an application the host system may also change, and bindings that are not updated may hurt instead of help performance, for example when they needlessly bind to CPUs across multiple sockets.

5.2.8 Performance Mantras

For more techniques for improving application performance, see the Performance Mantras methodology from Chapter 2. In summary:

1. Don't do it.

2. Do it, but don't do it again.

3. Do it less.

4. Do it later.

5. Do it when they're not looking.

6. Do it concurrently.

7. Do it cheaper.

The first item, "Don't do it," is eliminating unnecessary work. For more detail on this methodology see Chapter 2, Methodologies, Section 2.5.20, Performance Mantras.

5.3 Programming Languages

Programming languages may be compiled or interpreted and may also be executed via a virtual machine. Many languages list "performance optimizations" as features, but, strictly speaking, these are usually features of the software that *executes* the language, not the language itself. For example, the Java HotSpot Virtual Machine software includes a just-in-time (JIT) compiler to dynamically improve performance.

Interpreters and language virtual machines also provide different levels of performance observability support via their own specific tools. For the system performance analyst, basic profiling using these tools can lead to some quick wins. For example, high CPU usage may be identified as a result of garbage collection (GC) and then fixed via some commonly used tunables. Or it may be caused by a code path that can be found as a known bug in a bug database and fixed by upgrading the software version (this happens a lot).

The following sections describe basic performance characteristics per programming language type. For more about individual language performance, look for texts about that language.

5.3.1 Compiled Languages

Compilation takes a program and generates machine instructions in advance of runtime that are stored in binary executable files called *binaries*, which commonly use the Executable and Linking Format (ELF) on Linux and other Unix derivatives, and the Portable Executable (PE) format on Windows. These can be run at any time without compiling again. Compiled languages include C, C++, and assembly. Some languages may have both interpreters and compilers.

Compiled code is generally high-performing as it does not require further translation before execution by the CPUs. A common example of compiled code is the Linux kernel, which is written mostly in C, with some critical paths written in assembly.

Performance analysis of compiled languages is usually straightforward, as the executed machine code usually maps closely to the original program (although this depends on compilation optimizations). During compilation, a symbol table can be generated that maps addresses to program functions and object names. Later profiling and tracing of CPU execution can then be mapped directly to these program names, allowing the analyst to study program execution. Stack traces, and the numerical addresses they contain, can also be mapped and translated to function names to provide code path ancestry.

Compilers can improve performance by use of *compiler optimizations*—routines that optimize the choice and placement of CPU instructions.

Compiler Optimizations

The gcc(1) compiler offers seven levels of optimization: 0, 1, 2, 3, s, fast, and g. The numbers are a range where 0 uses the least optimizations and 3 uses the most. There are also "s" to optimize for size, "g" for debugging, and "fast" to use all optimizations plus extras that disregard standards compliance. You can query gcc(1) to show which optimizations it uses for different levels. For example:

```
$ gcc -Q -O3 --help=optimizers
The following options control optimizations:
  -O<number>
  -Ofast
  -Og
  -Os
  -faggressive-loop-optimizations       [enabled]
  -falign-functions                     [disabled]
  -falign-jumps                         [disabled]
  -falign-label                         [enabled]
  -falign-loops                         [disabled]
  -fassociative-math                    [disabled]
  -fasynchronous-unwind-tables          [enabled]
```

```
  -fauto-inc-dec                        [enabled]
  -fbranch-count-reg                    [enabled]
  -fbranch-probabilities                [disabled]
  -fbranch-target-load-optimize         [disabled]
[...]
  -fomit-frame-pointer                  [enabled]
[...]
```

The full list for gcc version 7.4.0 includes about 230 options, some of which are enabled even at −O0. As an example of what one of these options does, the `-fomit-frame-pointer` option, seen in this list, is described in the gcc(1) man page:

> Don't keep the frame pointer in a register for functions that don't need one. This avoids the instructions to save, set up and restore frame pointers; it also makes an extra register available in many functions. **It also makes debugging impossible on some machines.**

This is an example of a trade-off: omitting the frame pointer typically breaks the operation of analyzers that profile stack traces.

Given the usefulness of stack profilers, this option may sacrifice much in terms of later performance wins that can no longer be easily found, which may far outweigh the performance gains that this option initially offers. A solution, in this case, can be to compile with `-fno-omit-frame-pointer` to avoid this optimization.[6] Another recommended option is `-g` to include debuginfo, to aid later debugging. Debuginfo can be removed or stripped later if need be.[7]

Should performance issues arise, it may be tempting to simply recompile the application with a reduced optimization level (from −O3 to −O2, for example) in the hope that any debugging needs could then be met. This turns out not to be simple: the changes to the compiler output can be massive and important, and may affect the behavior of the issue you were originally trying to analyze.

5.3.2   Interpreted Languages

Interpreted languages execute a program by translating it into actions during runtime, a process that adds execution overhead. Interpreted languages are not expected to exhibit high performance and are used for situations where other factors are more important, such as ease of programming and debugging. *Shell scripting* is an example of an interpreted language.

Unless observability tools are provided, performance analysis of interpreted languages can be difficult. CPU profiling can show the operation of the interpreter—including parsing, translating, and performing actions—but it may not show the original program function names, leaving

---

[6] Depending on the profiler, there may be other solutions available for stack walking, such as using debuginfo, LBR, BTS, and more. For the perf(1) profiler, ways to use different stack walkers are described in Chapter 13, perf, Section 13.9, perf record.

[7] If you do distribute stripped binaries, consider making debuginfo packages so that the debug information can be installed when needed.

essential program context a mystery. This interpreter analysis may not be totally fruitless, as there can be performance issues with the interpreter itself, even when the code it is executing appears to be well designed.

Depending on the interpreter, program context may be available as arguments to interpreter functions, which can be seen using dynamic instrumentation. Another approach is examine the process's memory, given knowledge of program layout (e.g., using the Linux process_vm_readv(2) syscall).

Often these programs are studied by simply adding print statements and timestamps. More rigorous performance analysis is uncommon, since interpreted languages are not commonly selected for high-performance applications in the first place.

5.3.3 Virtual Machines

A *language virtual machine* (also called a *process virtual machine*) is software that simulates a computer. Some programming languages, including Java and Erlang, are commonly executed using virtual machines (VMs) that provide them with a platform-independent programming environment. The application program is compiled to the virtual machine instruction set (*bytecode*) and then executed by the virtual machine. This allows portability of the compiled objects, provided a virtual machine is available to run them on the target platform.

The bytecode can be executed by the language virtual machine in different ways. The Java HotSpot Virtual Machine supports execution via interpretation and also JIT compilation, which compiles bytecode to machine code for direct execution by the processor. This provides the performance advantages of compiled code, together with the portability of a virtual machine.

Virtual machines are typically the most difficult of the language types to observe. By the time the program is executing on-CPU, multiple stages of compilation or interpretation may have passed, and information about the original program may not be readily available. Performance analysis usually focuses on the toolset provided with the language virtual machine, many of which provide USDT probes, and on third-party tools.

5.3.4 Garbage Collection

Some languages use automatic memory management, where allocated memory does not need to be explicitly freed, leaving that to an asynchronous garbage collection process. While this makes programs easier to write, there can be disadvantages:

- **Memory growth:** There is less control of the application's memory usage, which may grow when objects are not identified automatically as eligible to be freed. If the application grows too large, it may either hit its own limits or encounter system paging (Linux swapping), severely harming performance.

- **CPU cost:** GC will typically run intermittently and involves searching or scanning objects in memory. This consumes CPU resources, reducing what is available to the application for short periods. As the memory of the application grows, CPU consumption by GC may also grow. In some cases this can reach the point where GC continually consumes an entire CPU.

- **Latency outliers:** Application execution may be paused while GC executes, causing occasional application responses with high latency that were interrupted by GC.[8] This depends on the GC type: stop-the-world, incremental, or concurrent.

GC is a common target for performance tuning to reduce CPU cost and occurrence of latency outliers. For example, the Java VM provides many tunable parameters to set the GC type, number of GC threads, maximum heap size, target heap free ratio, and more.

If tuning is not effective, the problem may be the application creating too much garbage, or leaking references. These are issues for the application developer to resolve. One approach is to allocate fewer objects, when possible, to reduce the GC load. Observability tools that show object allocations and their code paths can be used to find potential targets for elimination.

5.4 Methodology

This section describes methodologies for application analysis and tuning. The tools used for analysis are either introduced here or are referenced from other chapters. The methodologies are summarized in Table 5.2.

Table 5.2 **Application performance methodologies**

Section	Methodology	Type
5.4.1	CPU profiling	Observational analysis
5.4.2	Off-CPU profiling	Observational analysis
5.4.3	Syscall analysis	Observational analysis
5.4.4	USE method	Observational analysis
5.4.5	Thread state analysis	Observational analysis
5.4.6	Lock analysis	Observational analysis
5.4.7	Static performance tuning	Observational analysis, tuning
5.4.8	Distributed tracing	Observational analysis

See Chapter 2, Methodologies, for the introduction to some of these, and also additional general methodologies: for applications, in particular consider CPU profiling, workload characterization, and drill-down analysis. Also see the chapters that follow for the analysis of system resources and virtualization.

These methodologies may be followed individually or used in combination. My suggestion is to try them in the order listed in the table.

---

[8]There has been much work on techniques to reduce GC time or application interrupts from GC. One example uses system and application metrics to determine when best to call GC [Schwartz 18].

In addition to these, look for custom analysis techniques for the specific application and the programming language in which it is developed. These may consider logical behavior of the application, including known issues, and lead to some quick performance wins.

5.4.1   CPU Profiling

CPU profiling is an essential activity for application performance analysis and is explained in Chapter 6, CPUs, beginning with Section 6.5.4, Profiling. This section summarizes CPU profiling and CPU flame graphs, and describes how CPU profiling can be used for some off-CPU analysis.

There are many CPU profilers for Linux, including perf(1) and profile(8), summarized in Section 5.5, Observability Tools, both of which used timed sampling. These profilers run in kernel mode and can capture both the kernel and user stacks, producing a *mixed-mode* profile. This provides (almost) complete visibility for CPU usage.

Applications and runtimes sometimes provide their own profiler that runs in user mode, which cannot show kernel CPU usage. These user-based profilers may have a skewed notion of CPU time as they may be unaware of when the kernel has descheduled the application, and do not account for it. I always start with kernel-based profilers (perf(1) and profile(8)) and use user-based ones as a last resort.

Sample-based profilers produce many samples: a typical CPU profile at Netflix collects stack traces at 49 Hertz across (around) 32 CPUs for 30 seconds: this produces a total of 47,040 samples. To make sense of these, profilers typically provide different ways to summarize or visualize them. A commonly used visualization for sampled stack traces is called *flame graphs*, which I invented.

CPU Flame Graphs

A CPU flame graph was shown in Chapter 1, and a different example excerpt is shown as Figure 2.15. The Figure 5.3 example includes an ext4 annotation for later reference. These are *mixed-mode* flame graphs, showing both user and kernel stacks.

In a flame graph, each rectangle is a frame from a stack trace, and the y-axis shows the code flow: top-down shows the current function and then its ancestry. The frame width is proportional to its presence in the profile, and the x-axis ordering has no meaning (it is an alphabetical sort). You look for the big "plateaus" or "towers"—that's where the bulk of the CPU time is spent. See Chapter 6, CPUs, Section 6.7.3, Flame Graphs, for more detail about flame graphs.

In Figure 5.3, crc32_z() is the function that is on-CPU the most, spanning about 40% of this excerpt (the center plateau). A tower on the left shows a syscall write(2) path into the kernel, spanning about 30% of CPU time in total. With a quick glance, we've identified these two as possible low-level targets for optimization. Browsing the code-path ancestry (downwards) can reveal high-level targets: in this case, all the CPU usage is from the MYSQL_BIN_LOG::commit() function.

I do not know what crc32_z() or MYSQL_BIN_LOG::commit() do (although I can probably guess). CPU profiles expose the inner workings of applications, and unless you are the application developer, you are not expected to know what any of these functions are. You will need to research them to develop actionable performance improvements.

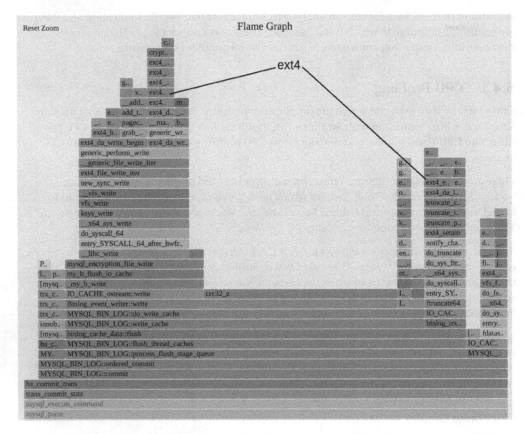

Figure 5.3   CPU flame graph excerpt

As an example, I performed an internet search for MYSQL_BIN_LOG::commit() and quickly found articles describing MySQL binary logging, used for database restoration and replication, and how it can be tuned or disabled entirely. A quick search for crc32_z() shows it is a checksumming function from zlib. Perhaps there is a newer and faster version of zlib? Does the processor have the optimized CRC instruction, and is zlib using it? Does MySQL even need to calculate the CRC, or can it be turned off? See Chapter 2, Methodologies, Section 2.5.20, Performance Mantras, for more on this style of thinking.

Section 5.5.1, perf, summarizes instructions for generating CPU flame graphs using perf(1).

Off-CPU Footprints

CPU profiles can show more than just CPU usage. You can look for evidence of other off-CPU issue types. Disk I/O, for example, can be seen to some extent by its CPU usage for file system access and block I/O initialization. This is like finding the footprints of a bear: you don't see the bear, but you've discovered that one exists.

By browsing the CPU flame graph you may find evidence of file system I/O, disk I/O, network I/O, lock contention, and more. Figure 5.3 highlights the ext4 file system I/O as an example. If you browse enough flame graphs, you'll become familiar with the function names to look for: "tcp_*" for kernel TCP functions, "blk_*" for kernel block I/O functions, etc. Here are some suggested search terms for Linux systems:

- **"ext4"** (or **"btrfs"**, **"xfs"**, **"zfs"**): to find file system operations.
- **"blk"**: to find block I/O.
- **"tcp"**: to find network I/O.
- **"utex"**: to show lock contention ("mutex" or "futex").
- **"alloc"** or **"object"**: to show code paths doing memory allocation.

This method only identifies the presence of these activities, not their magnitude. The CPU flame graph shows the magnitude of CPU usage, not the time spent blocked off-CPU. To measure off-CPU time directly, you can use off-CPU analysis, covered next, although it typically costs greater overhead to measure.

5.4.2 Off-CPU Analysis

Off-CPU analysis is the study of threads that are not currently running on a CPU: This state is called *off-CPU*. It includes all the reasons that threads block: disk I/O, network I/O, lock contention, explicit sleeps, scheduler preemption, etc. The analysis of these reasons and the performance issues they cause typically involves a wide variety of tools. Off-CPU analysis is one method to analyze them all, and can be supported by a single off-CPU profiling tool.

Off-CPU profiling can be performed in different ways, including:

- **Sampling**: Collecting timer-based samples of threads that are off-CPU, or simply all threads (called *wallclock sampling*).

- **Scheduler tracing**: Instrumenting the kernel CPU scheduler to time the duration that threads are off-CPU, and recording these times with the off-CPU stack trace. Stack traces do not change when a thread is off-CPU (because it is not running to change it), so the stack trace only needs to be read once for each blocking event.

- **Application instrumentation**: Some applications have built-in instrumentation for commonly blocking code paths, such as disk I/O. Such instrumentation may include application-specific context. While convenient and useful, this approach is typically blind to off-CPU events (scheduler preemption, page faults, etc.).

The first two approaches are preferable as they work for all applications and can see all off-CPU events; however, they come with major overhead. Sampling at 49 Hertz should cost negligible overhead on, say, an 8-CPU system, but off-CPU sampling must sample the pool of threads rather than the pool of CPUs. The same system may have 10,000 threads, most of which are idle, so sampling them increases the overhead by 1,000x[9] (imagine CPU-profiling a 10,000-CPU system). Scheduler tracing can also cost significant overhead, as the same system may have 100,000 scheduler events or more per second.

---

[9] Likely higher, as it would require sampling stack traces for threads that are off-CPU, and their stack is unlikely to be CPU-cached (unlike with CPU profiling). Restricting it to a single application should help reduce the thread count, though the profile will be incomplete.

Scheduler tracing is the technique now commonly used, based on my own tools such as offcputime(8) (Section 5.5.3, offcputime). An optimization I use is to record only off-CPU events that exceed a tiny duration, which reduces the number of samples.[10] I also use BPF to aggregate stacks in kernel context, rather than emitting all samples to user space, reducing overhead even further. Much as these techniques help, you should be careful with off-CPU rofiling in production, and evaluate the overhead in a test environment before use.

Off-CPU Time Flame Graphs

Off-CPU profiles can be visualized as an *off-CPU time flame graph*. Figure 5.4 shows a 30-second system-wide off-CPU profile, where I have zoomed in to show a MySQL server thread handling commands (queries).

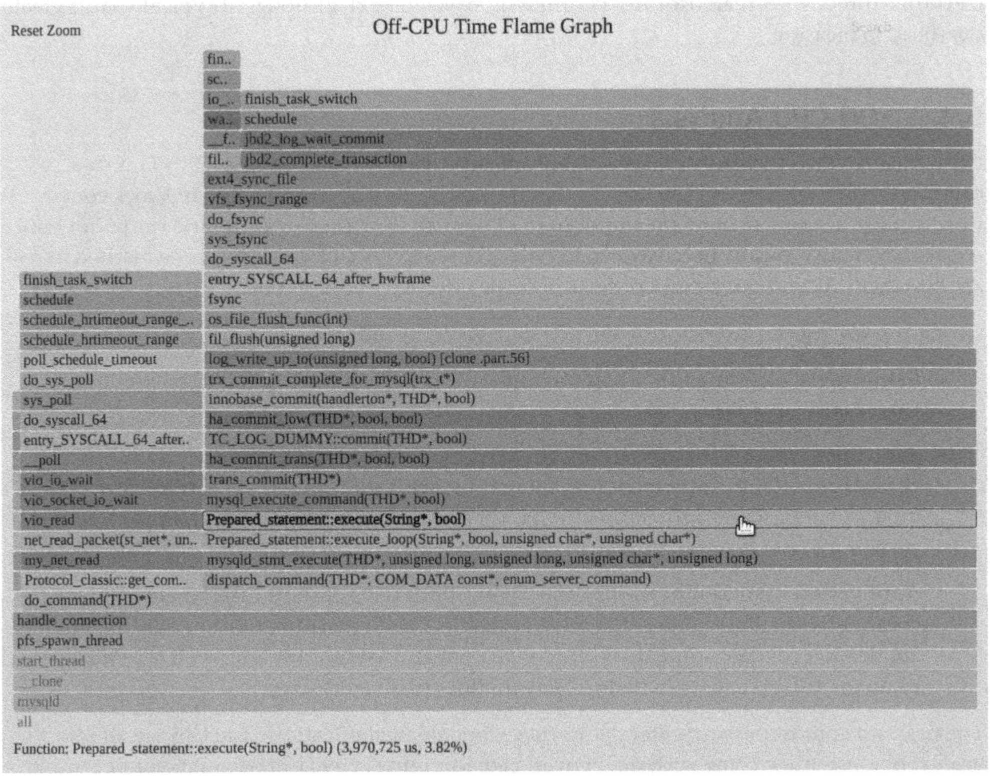

Figure 5.4   Off-CPU time flame graph, zoomed

The bulk of the off-CPU time is in a fsync() code path and the ext4 file system. The mouse pointer is over one function, Prepared_statement::execute(), to demonstrate that the information line

---

[10] Before you say "what if there is an avalanche of tiny sleep durations that are excluded by this optimization?"—you should see evidence of it in a CPU profile due to calling the scheduler so frequently, prompting you to turn off this optimization.

at the bottom shows the off-CPU time in this function: 3.97 seconds in total. Interpretation is similar as for CPU flame graphs: look for the widest towers and investigate those first.

By using both on- and off-CPU flame graphs, you have a complete view of on- and off-CPU time by code path: a powerful tool. I typically show them as separate flame graphs. It is possible to combine them into a single flame graph, which I've called *hot/cold flame graphs*. It doesn't work well: the CPU time gets squeezed into a thin tower as the bulk of the hot/cold flame graph is displaying wait time. This is because the off-CPU thread count can outweigh the running on-CPU count by two orders of magnitude, causing the hold/cold flame graph to consist of 99% off-CPU time, which (unless filtered) is mostly wait time.

Wait Time

Apart from the overheads of collecting off-CPU profiles, another issue is interpreting them: they can be dominated by wait time. This is time spent by threads waiting for work. Figure 5.5 shows the same off-CPU time flame graph, but not zoomed in to an interesting thread.

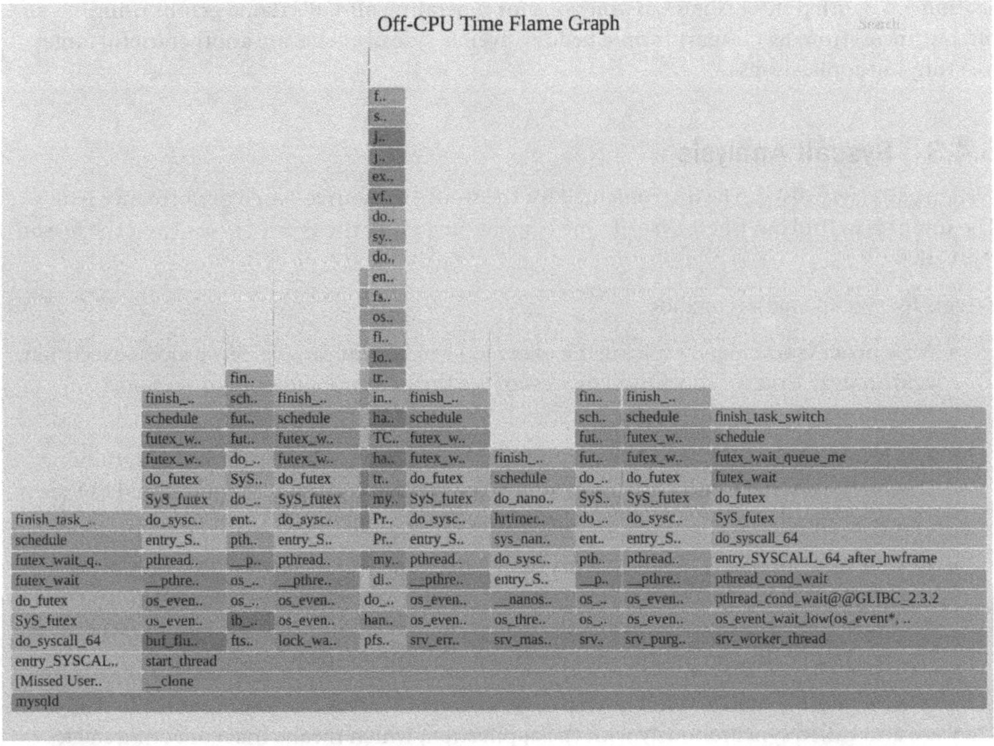

Off-CPU Time Flame Graph

Figure 5.5 Off-CPU time flame graph, full

Most of the time in this flame graph is now in a similar pthread_cond_wait() and futex() code path: these are threads waiting for work. The thread functions can be seen in the flame graph: from right to left, there is srv_worker_thread(), srv_purge_coordinator_thread(), srv_monitor_thread(), and so on.

There are a couple of techniques for finding the off-CPU time that matters:

- Zoom into (or filter by) the application request handling function(s), since we care most about off-CPU time during the handling of an application request. For MySQL server this is the do_command() function. A search for do_command() and then zooming in produces a similar flame graph to Figure 5.4. While this approach is effective, you will need to know what function to search for in your specific application.

- Use a kernel filter during collection to exclude uninteresting thread states. The effectiveness is dependent on the kernel; on Linux, matching on TASK_UNINTERRUPTIBLE focuses on many interesting off-CPU events, but does exclude some as well.

You will sometimes find application-blocking code paths that are waiting on something else, such as a lock. To drill down further, you need to know why the holder of the lock took so long to release it. Apart from lock analysis, described in Section 5.4.7, Static Performance Tuning, a generic technique is to instrument the waker event. This is an advanced activity: see Chapter 14 of *BPF Performance Tools* [Gregg 19], and the tools wakeuptime(8) and offwaketime(8) from BCC.

Section 5.5.3, offcputime, shows instructions for generating off-CPU flame graphs using offcputime(8) from BCC. Apart from scheduler events, syscall events are another useful target for studying applications.

5.4.3   Syscall Analysis

System calls (syscalls) can be instrumented for the study of resource-based performance issues. The intent is to find out where syscall time is spent, including the type of syscall and the reason it is called.

Targets for syscall analysis include:

- **New process tracing:** By tracing the execve(2) syscall you can log new process execution, and analyze issues of short-lived processes. See the execsnoop(8) tool in Section 5.5.5, execsnoop.

- **I/O profiling:** Tracing read(2)/write(2)/send(2)/recv(2) and their variants, and studying their I/O sizes, flags, and code paths, will help you identify issues of suboptimal I/O, such as a large number of small I/O. See the bpftrace tool in Section 5.5.7, bpftrace.

- **Kernel time analysis:** When systems show a high amount of kernel CPU time, often reported as "%sys," instrumenting syscalls can locate the cause. See the syscount(8) tool in Section 5.5.6, syscount. Syscalls explain most but not all of kernel CPU time; exceptions include page faults, asynchronous kernel threads, and interrupts.

Syscalls are a well-documented API (man pages), making them an easy event source to study. They are also called synchronously with the application, which means that collecting stack traces from syscalls will show the application code path responsible. Such stack traces can be visualized as a flame graph.

5.4.4 USE Method

As introduced in Chapter 2, Methodologies, and applied in later chapters, the USE method checks the utilization, saturation, and errors of all hardware resources. Many application performance issues may be solved this way, by showing that a resource has become a bottleneck.

The USE method can also be applied to software resources. If you can find a functional diagram showing the internal components of an application, consider the utilization, saturation, and error metrics for each software resource and see what makes sense.

For example, the application may use a pool of worker threads to process requests, with a queue for requests waiting their turn. Treating this as a resource, the three metrics could then be defined in this way:

- **Utilization:** Average number of threads busy processing requests during an interval, as a percentage of the total threads. For example, 50% would mean that, on average, half the threads were busy working on requests.

- **Saturation:** Average length of the request queue during an interval. This shows how many requests have backed up waiting for a worker thread.

- **Errors:** Requests denied or failed for any reason.

Your task is then to find how these metrics can be measured. They may already be provided by the application somewhere, or they may need to be added or measured using another tool, such as dynamic tracing.

Queueing systems, like this example, can also be studied using queueing theory (see Chapter 2, Methodologies).

For a different example, consider file descriptors. The system may impose a limit, such that these are a finite resource. The three metrics could be as follows:

- **Utilization:** Number of in-use file descriptors, as a percentage of the limit

- **Saturation:** Depends on the OS behavior: if threads block waiting for file descriptors, this can be the number of blocked threads waiting for this resource

- **Errors:** Allocation error, such as EFILE, "Too many open files"

Repeat this exercise for the components of your application, and skip any metrics that don't make sense. This process may help you develop a short checklist for checking application health before moving on to other methodologies.

5.4.5 Thread State Analysis

This is the first methodology I use for every performance issue, but it is also an advanced activity on Linux. The goal is to identify at a high level where application threads are spending their time, which solves some issues immediately, and directs the investigation of others. You can do this by dividing each application's thread time into a number of meaningful states.

At a minimum, there are two thread states: on-CPU and off-CPU. You can identify if threads are in the on-CPU state using standard metrics and tools (e.g., top(1)), and follow with CPU profiling or off-CPU analysis as appropriate (see Sections 5.4.1, CPU Profiling, and 5.4.2, Off-CPU Analysis). This methodology is more effective with more states.

Nine States

This is a list of nine thread states I've chosen to give better starting points for analysis than the two earlier states (on-CPU and off-CPU):

- **User:** On-CPU in user mode
- **Kernel:** On-CPU in kernel mode
- **Runnable:** And off-CPU waiting for a turn on-CPU
- **Swapping** (anonymous paging): Runnable, but blocked for anonymous page-ins
- **Disk I/O:** Waiting for block device I/O: reads/writes, data/text page-ins
- **Net I/O:** Waiting for network device I/O: socket reads/writes
- **Sleeping:** A voluntary sleep
- **Lock:** Waiting to acquire a synchronization lock (waiting on someone else)
- **Idle:** Waiting for work

This nine-state model is pictured in Figure 5.6.

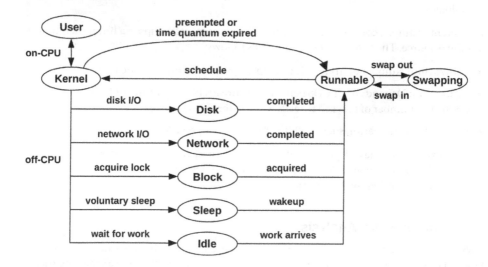

Figure 5.6   Nine-state thread model

Performance for an application request is improved by reducing the time in every state except idle. Other things being equal, this would mean that application requests have lower latency, and the application can handle more load.

Once you've established in which states the threads are spending their time, you can investigate them further:

- **User or Kernel:** Profiling can determine which code paths are consuming CPU, including time spent spinning on locks. See Section 5.4.1, CPU Profiling.

- **Runnable:** Time in this state means the application wants more CPU resources. Examine CPU load for the entire system, and any CPU limits present for the application (e.g., resource controls).

- **Swapping** (anonymous paging): A lack of available main memory for the application can cause swapping delays. Examine memory usage for the entire system and any memory limits present. See Chapter 7, Memory, for details.

- **Disk:** This state includes direct disk I/O and page faults. To analyze, see Section 5.4.3, Syscall Analysis, Chapter 8, File Systems, and Chapter 9, Disks. Workload characterization can help solve many disk I/O problems; examine file names, I/O sizes, and I/O types.

- **Network:** This state is for time blocked during network I/O (send/receive), but not listening for new connections (that's idle time). To analyze, see Section 5.4.3, Syscall Analysis; Section 5.5.7, bpftrace and the I/O Profiling heading; and Chapter 10, Network. Workload characterization can also be useful for network I/O problems; examine hostnames, protocols, and throughput.

- **Sleeping:** Analyze the reason (code path) and duration of the sleeps.

- **Lock:** Identify the lock, the thread holding it, and the reason why the holder held it for so long. The reason may be that the holder was blocked on another lock, which requires further unwinding. This is an advanced activity, usually performed by the software developer who has intimate knowledge of the application and its locking hierarchy. I have developed a BCC tool to aid this type of analysis: offwaketime(8) (included in BCC), which shows the blocking stack trace along with the waker.

Because of how applications typically wait for work, you will often find that time in the network I/O and lock states is actually idle time. An application worker thread may implement idle by waiting on network I/O for the next request (e.g., HTTP keep-alive) or by waiting on a conditional variable (lock state) to be woken up to process work.

The following summarizes how these thread states may be measured on Linux.

Linux

Figure 5.7 shows a Linux thread state model based on kernel thread state.

The kernel thread state is based on the kernel task_struct state member: Runnable is TASK_RUNNING, Disk is TASK_UNINTERRUPTIBLE, and Sleep is TASK_INTERRUPTIBLE. These states are shown by tools including ps(1) and top(1) using single-letter codes: R, D, and S, respectively. (There are more states, such as stopped by a debugger, that I did not include here.)

While this provides some clues for further analysis, it is far from dividing time into the nine states described earlier. More information is required: for example, Runnable can be split into user and kernel time using /proc or getrusage(2) statistics.

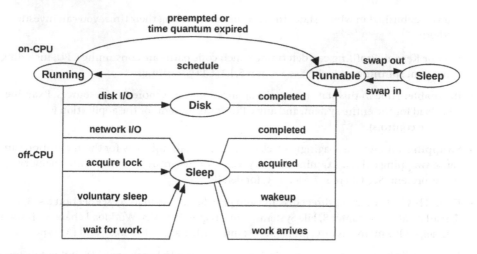

Figure 5.7   Linux thread states

Other kernels typically provide more states, making this methodology easier to apply. I originally developed and used this methodology on the Solaris kernel, inspired by its microstate accounting feature, which recorded thread time in eight different states: user, system, trap, text fault, data fault, lock, sleep, and run queue (scheduler latency). These don't match my ideal states, but are a better starting point.

I'll discuss three approaches that I use on Linux: clue-based, off-CPU analysis, and direct measurement.

Clue-Based

You can start by using common OS tools, such as pidstat(1) and vmstat(8), to suggest where thread state time may be spent. The tools and column of interest are:

- **User:** pidstat(1) "%usr" (this state is measured directly)
- **Kernel:** pidstat(1) "%system" (this state is measured directly)
- **Runnable:** vmstat(8) "r" (system-wide)
- **Swapping:** vmstat(8) "si" and "so" (system-wide)
- **Disk I/O:** pidstat(1) ‑d "iodelay" (includes the swapping state)
- **Network I/O:** sar(1) ‑n DEV "rxkB/s" and "txkB/s" (system-wide)
- **Sleeping:** Not easily available
- **Lock:** perf(1) top (may identify spin lock time directly)
- **Idle:** Not easily available

Some of these statistics are system-wide. If you find via vmstat(8) that there is a system-wide rate of swapping, you could investigate that state using deeper tools to confirm that the application is affected. These tools are covered in the following sections and chapters.

Off-CPU Analysis

As many of the states are off-CPU (everything except User and Kernel), you can apply off-CPU analysis to determine the thread state. See Section 5.4.2, Off-CPU Analysis.

Direct Measurement

Measure thread time accurately by thread state as follows:

User: User-mode CPU is available from a number of tools and in /proc/PID/stat and getrusage(2). pidstat(1) reports this as `%usr`.

Kernel: Kernel-mode CPU is also in /proc/PID/stat and getrusage(2). pidstat(1) reports this as `%system`.

Runnable: This is tracked by the kernel *schedstats* feature in nanoseconds and is exposed via /proc/PID/schedstat. It can also be measured, at the cost of some overhead, using tracing tools including the perf(1) `sched` subcommand and BCC runqlat(8), both covered in Chapter 6, CPUs.

Swapping: Time swapping (anonymous paging) in nanoseconds can be measured by *delay accounting*, introduced in Chapter 4, Observability Tools, Section 4.3.3, Delay Accounting, which included an example tool: getdelays.c. Tracing tools can also be used to instrument swapping latency.

Disk: pidstat(1) -d shows "iodelay" as the number of clock ticks during which a process was delayed by block I/O and swapping; if there was no system-wide swapping (as reported by vmstat(8)), you could conclude that any iodelay was the I/O state. Delay accounting and other accounting features, if enabled, also provide block I/O time, as used by iotop(8). You can also use tracing tools such as biotop(8) from BCC.

Network: Network I/O can be investigated using tracing tools such as BCC and bpftrace, including the tcptop(8) tool for TCP network I/O. The application may also have instrumentation to track time in I/O (network and disk).

Sleeping: Time entering voluntary sleep can be examined using tracers and events including the syscalls:sys_enter_nanosleep tracepoint. My naptime.bt tool traces these sleeps and prints the PID and duration [Gregg 19][Gregg 20b].

Lock: Lock time can be investigated using tracing tools, including klockstat(8) from BCC and, from the bpf-perf-tools-book repository, pmlock.bt and pmheld.bt for pthread mutex locks, and mlock.bt and mheld.bt for kernel mutexes.

Idle: Tracing tools can be used to instrument the application code paths that handle waiting for work.

Sometimes applications can appear to be completely asleep: they remain blocked off-CPU without a rate of I/O or other events. To determine what state the application threads are in, it may be necessary to use a debugger such as pstack(1) or gdb(1) to inspect thread stack traces, or to read them from the /proc/PID/stack files. Note that debuggers like these can pause the target application and cause performance problems of their own: understand how to use them and their risks before trying them in production.

5.4.6   Lock Analysis

For multithreaded applications, locks can become a bottleneck, inhibiting parallelism and scalability. Single-threaded applications can be inhibited by kernel locks (e.g., file system locks). Locks can be analyzed by:

- Checking for contention
- Checking for excessive hold times

The first identifies whether there is a problem *now*. Excessive hold times are not necessarily an immediate problem, but they may become so in the future with more parallel load. For each, try to identify the name of the lock (if it exists) and the code path that led to using it.

While there are special-purpose tools for lock analysis, you can sometimes solve issues from CPU profiling alone. For *spin locks*, contention shows up as CPU usage and can easily be identified using CPU profiling of stack traces. For *adaptive mutex locks*, contention often involves some spinning, which can also be identified by CPU profiling of stack traces. In that case, be aware that the CPU profile gives only a part of the story, as threads may have blocked and slept while waiting for the locks. See Section 5.4.1, CPU Profiling.

For specific lock analysis tools on Linux, see Section 5.5.7, bpftrace.

5.4.7   Static Performance Tuning

Static performance tuning focuses on issues of the configured environment. For application performance, examine the following aspects of the static configuration:

- What version of the application is running, and what are its dependencies? Are there newer versions? Do their release notes mention performance improvements?
- Are there known performance issues? Is there a bug database that lists them?
- How is the application configured?
- If it was configured or tuned differently from the defaults, what was the reason? (Was it based on measurements and analysis, or guesswork?)
- Does the application employ a cache of objects? How is it sized?
- Does the application run concurrently? How is that configured (e.g., thread pool sizing)?
- Is the application running in a special mode? (For example, debug mode may have been enabled and be reducing performance, or the application may be a debug build instead of a release build.)
- What system libraries does the application use? What versions are they?
- What memory allocator does the application use?
- Is the application configured to use large pages for its heap?
- Is the application compiled? What version of the compiler? What compiler options and optimizations? 64-bit?

- Does the native code include advanced instructions? (Should it?) (For example, SIMD/vector instructions including Intel SSE.)

- Has the application encountered an error, and is it now in a degraded mode? Or is it misconfigured and always running in a degraded mode?

- Are there system-imposed limits or resource controls for CPU, memory, file system, disk, or network usage? (These are common with cloud computing.)

Answering these questions may reveal configuration choices that have been overlooked.

5.4.8 Distributed Tracing

In a distributed environment, an application may be composed of services that run on separate systems. While each service can be studied as though it is its own mini-application, it is also necessary to study the distributed application as a whole. This requires new methodologies and tools, and is commonly performed using distributed tracing.

Distributed tracing involves logging information on each service request and then later combining this information for study. Each application request that spans multiple services can then be broken down into its dependency requests, and the service responsible for high application latency or errors can be identified.

Collected information can include:

- A unique identifier for the application request (external request ID)

- Information about its location in the dependency hierarchy

- Start and end times

- Error status

A challenge with distributed tracing is the amount of log data generated: multiple entries for every application request. One solution is to perform *head-based sampling* where at the start ("head") of the request, a decision is made whether to sample ("trace") it: for example, to trace one in every ten thousands requests. This is sufficient to analyze the performance of the bulk of the requests, but it may make the analysis of intermittent errors or outliers difficult due to limited data. Some distributed tracers are *tail-based*, where all events are first captured and then a decision is made as to what to keep, perhaps based on latency and errors.

Once a problematic service has been identified, it can be analyzed in more detail using other methodologies and tools.

5.5 Observability Tools

This section introduces application performance observability tools for Linux-based operating systems. See the previous section for strategies to follow when using them.

The tools in this section are listed in Table 5.3 along with a description of how these tools are used in this chapter.

Table 5.3 **Linux application observability tools**

Section	Tool	Description
5.5.1	perf	CPU profiling, CPU flame graphs, syscall tracing
5.5.2	profile	CPU profiling using timed sampling
5.5.3	offcputime	Off-CPU profiling using scheduler tracing
5.5.4	strace	Syscall tracing
5.5.5	execsnoop	New process tracing
5.5.6	syscount	Syscall counting
5.5.7	bpftrace	Signal tracing, I/O profiling, lock analysis

These begin with CPU profiling tools then tracing tools. Many of the tracing tools are BPF-based, and use the BCC and bpftrace frontends (Chapter 15); they are: profile(8), offcputime(8), execsnoop(8), and syscount(8). See the documentation for each tool, including its man pages, for full references of its features.

Also look for application-specific performance tools not listed in this table. Later chapters cover resource-oriented tools: CPUs, memory, disks, etc., which are also useful for application analysis.

Many of the following tools collect application stack traces. If you find your stack trace contains "[unknown]" frames or appears impossibly short, see Section 5.6, Gotchas, which describes common problems and summarizes methods to fix them.

5.5.1 perf

perf(1) is the standard Linux profiler, a multi-tool with many uses. It is explained in Chapter 13, perf. As CPU profiling is critical for application analysis, a summary of CPU profiling using perf(1) is included here. Chapter 6, CPUs, covers CPU profiling and flame graphs in more detail.

CPU Profiling

The following uses perf(1) to sample stack traces (-g) across all CPUs (-a) at 49 Hertz (-F 49: samples per second) for 30 seconds, and then to list the samples:

```
# perf record -F 49 -a -g -- sleep 30
[ perf record: Woken up 1 times to write data ]
[ perf record: Captured and wrote 0.560 MB perf.data (2940 samples) ]
# perf script
mysqld 10441 [000] 64918.205722:   10101010 cpu-clock:pppH:
        5587b59bf2f0 row_mysql_store_col_in_innobase_format+0x270 (/usr/sbin/mysqld)
        5587b59c3951 [unknown] (/usr/sbin/mysqld)
        5587b58803b3 ha_innobase::write_row+0x1d3 (/usr/sbin/mysqld)
        5587b47e10c8 handler::ha_write_row+0x1a8 (/usr/sbin/mysqld)
        5587b49ec13d write_record+0x64d (/usr/sbin/mysqld)
```

```
      5587b49ed219 Sql_cmd_insert_values::execute_inner+0x7f9 (/usr/sbin/mysqld)
      5587b45dfd06 Sql_cmd_dml::execute+0x426 (/usr/sbin/mysqld)
      5587b458c3ed mysql_execute_command+0xb0d (/usr/sbin/mysqld)
      5587b4591067 mysql_parse+0x377 (/usr/sbin/mysqld)
      5587b459388d dispatch_command+0x22cd (/usr/sbin/mysqld)
      5587b45943b4 do_command+0x1a4 (/usr/sbin/mysqld)
      5587b46b22c0 [unknown] (/usr/sbin/mysqld)
      5587b5cfff0a [unknown] (/usr/sbin/mysqld)
      7fbdf66a9669 start_thread+0xd9 (/usr/lib/x86_64-linux-gnu/libpthread-2.30.so)
[...]
```

There are 2,940 stack samples in this profile; only one stack has been included here. The perf(1) script subcommand prints each stack sample in a previously recorded profile (the perf.data file). perf(1) also has a report subcommand for summarizing the profile as a code-path hierarchy. The profile can also be visualized as a CPU flame graph.

CPU Flame Graphs

CPU flame graphs have been automated at Netflix so that operators and developers can request them from a browser-based UI. They can be built entirely using open-source software, including from the GitHub repository in the following commands. For the Figure 5.3 CPU flame graph shown earlier, the commands were:

```
# perf record -F 49 -a -g -- sleep 10; perf script --header > out.stacks
# git clone https://github.com/brendangregg/FlameGraph; cd FlameGraph
# ./stackcollapse-perf.pl < ../out.stacks | ./flamegraph.pl --hash > out.svg
```

The out.svg file can then be loaded in a web browser.

flamegraph.pl provides custom color palettes for different languages: for example, for Java applications, try --color=java. Run flamegraph.pl -h for all options.

Syscall Tracing

The perf(1) trace subcommand traces system calls by default, and is perf(1)'s version of strace(1) (Section 5.5.4, strace). For example, tracing a MySQL server process:

```
# perf trace -p $(pgrep mysqld)
         ? (             ): mysqld/10120  ... [continued]: futex())
= -1 ETIMEDOUT (Connection timed out)
     0.014 ( 0.002 ms): mysqld/10120 futex(uaddr: 0x7fbddc37ed48, op: WAKE|
PRIVATE_FLAG, val: 1)          = 0
     0.023 (10.103 ms): mysqld/10120 futex(uaddr: 0x7fbddc37ed98, op: WAIT_BITSET|
PRIVATE_FLAG, utime: 0x7fbdc9cfcbc0, val3: MATCH_ANY) = -1 ETIMEDOUT (Connection
timed out)
[...]
```

Only a few output lines are included, showing futex(2) calls as various MySQL threads wait for work (these dominated the off-CPU time flame graph in Figure 5.5).

The advantage of perf(1) is that it uses per-CPU buffers to reduce the overhead, making it much safer to use than the current implementation of strace(1). It can also trace system-wide, whereas strace(1) is limited to a set of processes (typically a single process), and it can trace events other than syscalls. perf(1), however, does not have as many syscall argument translations as strace(1); here is a single line from strace(1) for comparison:

```
[pid 10120] futex(0x7fbddc37ed98, FUTEX_WAIT_BITSET_PRIVATE, 0, {tv_sec=445110,
tv_nsec=427289364}, FUTEX_BITSET_MATCH_ANY) = -1 ETIMEDOUT (Connection timed out)
```

The strace(1) version has expanded the utime struct. There is work underway for perf(1) trace to use BPF for improved argument "beautification." As an end goal, perf(1) trace could ultimately be a swap-in replacement for strace(1). (For more on strace(1), see Section 5.5.4, strace.)

Kernel Time Analysis

As perf(1) trace shows time in syscalls, it helps explain the system CPU time commonly shown by monitoring tools, although it is easier to start with a summary than the event-by-event output. perf(1) trace summarizes syscalls with -s:

```
# perf trace -s -p $(pgrep mysqld)
 mysqld (14169), 225186 events, 99.1%

   syscall            calls     total       min       avg       max     stddev
                                (msec)    (msec)    (msec)    (msec)       (%)

   ---------------   --------  --------  ---------  ---------  ---------   ------
   sendto             27239   267.904     0.002     0.010     0.109      0.28%
   recvfrom           69861   212.213     0.001     0.003     0.069      0.23%
   ppoll              15478   201.183     0.002     0.013     0.412      0.75%

[...]
```

The output shows syscall counts and timing for each thread.

The earlier output showing futex(2) calls is not very interesting in isolation, and running perf(1) trace on any busy application will produce an avalanche of output. It helps to start with this summary first, and then to use perf(1) trace with a filter to inspect only the syscall types of interest.

I/O Profiling

I/O syscalls are particularly interesting, and some were seen in the previous output. Tracing the sendto(2) calls using a filter (-e):

```
# perf trace -e sendto -p $(pgrep mysqld)
     0.000 ( 0.015 ms): mysqld/14097 sendto(fd: 37<socket:[833323]>, buff:
0x7fbdac072040, len: 12664, flags: DONTWAIT) = 12664
     0.451 ( 0.019 ms): mysqld/14097 sendto(fd: 37<socket:[833323]>, buff:
0x7fbdac072040, len: 12664, flags: DONTWAIT) = 12664
     0.624 ( 0.011 ms): mysqld/14097 sendto(fd: 37<socket:[833323]>, buff:
0x7fbdac072040, len: 11, flags: DONTWAIT) = 11
     0.788 ( 0.010 ms): mysqld/14097 sendto(fd: 37<socket:[833323]>, buff:
0x7fbdac072040, len: 11, flags: DONTWAIT) = 11
[...]
```

The output shows two 12664-byte sends followed by two 11-byte sends, all with the DONTWAIT flag. If I saw a flood of small sends, I might wonder if performance could be improved by coalescing them, or avoiding the DONTWAIT flag.

While perf(1) trace can be used for some I/O profiling, I often wish to dig further into the arguments and summarize them in custom ways. For example, this sendto(2) trace shows the file descriptor (37) and socket number (833323), but I'd rather see the socket type, IP addresses, and ports. For such custom tracing, you can switch to bpftrace in Section 5.5.7, bpftrace.

5.5.2   profile

profile(8)[11] is timer-based CPU profiler from BCC (Chapter 15). It uses BPF to reduce overhead by aggregating stack traces in kernel context, and only passes unique stacks and their counts to user space.

The following profile(8) example samples at 49 Hertz across all CPUs, for 10 seconds:

```
# profile -F 49 10
Sampling at 49 Hertz of all threads by user + kernel stack for 10 secs.
[...]

    SELECT_LEX::prepare(THD*)
    Sql_cmd_select::prepare_inner(THD*)
    Sql_cmd_dml::prepare(THD*)
    Sql_cmd_dml::execute(THD*)
    mysql_execute_command(THD*, bool)
    Prepared_statement::execute(String*, bool)
    Prepared_statement::execute_loop(String*, bool)
    mysqld_stmt_execute(THD*, Prepared_statement*, bool, unsigned long, PS_PARAM*)
    dispatch_command(THD*, COM_DATA const*, enum_server_command)
    do_command(THD*)
    [unknown]
```

---

[11]Origin: I developed profile(8) for BCC on 15-Jul-2016, based on code from Sasha Goldshtein, Andrew Birchall, Evgeny Vereshchagin, and Teng Qin.

```
[unknown]
start_thread
-
                mysqld (10106)
    13
```

[...]

Only one stack trace is included in this output, showing that SELECT_LEX::prepare() was sampled on-CPU with that ancestry 13 times.

profile(8) is further discussed in Chapter 6, CPUs, Section 6.6.14, profile, which lists its various options and includes instructions for generating CPU flame graphs from its output.

5.5.3   offcputime

offcputime(8)[12] is a BCC and bpftrace tool (Chapter 15) to summarize time spent by threads blocked and off-CPU, showing stack traces to explain why. It supports Off-CPU analysis (Section 5.4.2, Off-CPU Analysis). offcputime(8) is the counterpart to profile(8): between them, they show the entire time spent by threads on the system.

The following shows offcputime(8) from BCC, tracing for 5 seconds:

```
# offcputime 5
Tracing off-CPU time (us) of all threads by user + kernel stack for 5 secs.
[...]

    finish_task_switch
    schedule
    jbd2_log_wait_commit
    jbd2_complete_transaction
    ext4_sync_file
    vfs_fsync_range
    do_fsync
    __x64_sys_fdatasync
    do_syscall_64
    entry_SYSCALL_64_after_hwframe
    fdatasync
    IO_CACHE_ostream::sync()
    MYSQL_BIN_LOG::sync_binlog_file(bool)
    MYSQL_BIN_LOG::ordered_commit(THD*, bool, bool)
    MYSQL_BIN_LOG::commit(THD*, bool)
    ha_commit_trans(THD*, bool, bool)
    trans_commit(THD*, bool)
```

---

[12] Origin: I created off-CPU analysis as a methodology, along with tools for performing it, in 2005; I developed this offcputime(8) BCC tool on 13-Jan-2016.

```
mysql_execute_command(THD*, bool)
Prepared_statement::execute(String*, bool)
Prepared_statement::execute_loop(String*, bool)
mysqld_stmt_execute(THD*, Prepared_statement*, bool, unsigned long, PS_PARAM*)
dispatch_command(THD*, COM_DATA const*, enum_server_command)
do_command(THD*)
[unknown]
[unknown]
start_thread
-                mysqld (10441)
    352107
```

[...]

The output shows unique stack traces and their time spent off-CPU in microseconds. This particular stack shows ext4 file system sync operations via a code path through MYSQL_BIN_LOG::sync_binlog_file(), totaling 352 milliseconds during this trace.

For efficiency, offcputime(8) aggregates these stacks in kernel context, and emits only unique stacks to user space. It also only records stack traces for off-CPU durations that exceed a threshold, one microsecond by default, which can be tuned using the -m option.

There is also a -M option to set the maximum time for recording stacks. Why would we want to exclude long-duration stacks? This can be an effective way to filter out uninteresting stacks: threads waiting for work and blocking for one or more seconds in a loop. Try using -M 900000, to exclude durations longer than 900 ms.

Off-CPU Time Flame Graphs

Despite only showing unique stacks, the full output from the previous example was still over 200,000 lines. To make sense of it, it can be visualized as an off-CPU time flame graph. An example was shown in Figure 5.4. The commands to generate these are similar to those with profile(8):

```
# git clone https://github.com/brendangregg/FlameGraph; cd FlameGraph
# offcputime -f 5 | ./flamegraph.pl --bgcolors=blue \
    --title="Off-CPU Time Flame Graph"> out.svg
```

This time I've set the background color to blue, as a visual reminder that this is an off-CPU flame graph rather than the commonly-used CPU flame graphs.

5.5.4 strace

The strace(1) command is the Linux system call tracer.[13] It can trace syscalls, printing a one-line summary for each, and can also count syscalls and print a report.

---

[13] Syscall tracers for other operating systems are: BSD has ktrace(1), Solaris has truss(1), OS X has dtruss(1) (a tool I originally developed), and Windows has a number of options including logger.exe and ProcMon.

For example, tracing syscalls by PID 1884:

```
$ strace -ttt -T -p 1884
1356982510.395542 close(3)                 = 0 <0.000267>
1356982510.396064 close(4)                 = 0 <0.000293>
1356982510.396617 ioctl(255, TIOCGPGRP, [1975]) = 0 <0.000019>
1356982510.396980 rt_sigprocmask(SIG_SETMASK, [], NULL, 8) = 0 <0.000024>
1356982510.397288 rt_sigprocmask(SIG_BLOCK, [CHLD], [], 8) = 0 <0.000014>
1356982510.397365 wait4(-1, [{WIFEXITED(s) && WEXITSTATUS(s) == 0}], WSTOPPED|
WCONTINUED, NULL) = 1975 <0.018187>
[...]
```

The options in this invocation were (see the strace(1) man page for all):

- **-ttt**: Prints the first column of time-since-epoch, in units of seconds with microsecond resolution.

- **-T**: Prints the last field (<$time$>), which is the duration of the system call, in units of seconds with microsecond resolution.

- **-p PID**: Trace this process ID. A command can also be specified so that strace(1) launches and traces it.

Other options not used here include **-f** to follow child threads, and **-o** *filename* to write the strace(1) output to the given file name.

A feature of strace(1) can be seen in the output—translation of syscall arguments into a human-readable form. This is especially useful for understanding ioctl(2) calls.

The **-c** option can be used to summarize system call activity. The following example also invokes and traces a command (dd(1)) rather than attaching to a PID:

```
$ strace -c dd if=/dev/zero of=/dev/null bs=1k count=5000k
5120000+0 records in
5120000+0 records out
5242880000 bytes (5.2 GB) copied, 140.722 s, 37.3 MB/s
% time     seconds  usecs/call     calls    errors syscall
------ ----------- ----------- --------- --------- ----------------
 51.46    0.008030           0   5120005           read
 48.54    0.007574           0   5120003           write
  0.00    0.000000           0        20        13 open
[...]
------ ----------- ----------- --------- --------- ----------------
100.00    0.015604              10240092        19 total
```

The output begins with three lines from dd(1) followed by the strace(1) summary. The columns are:

- **time**: Percentage showing where system CPU time was spent
- **seconds**: Total system CPU time, in seconds
- **usecs/call**: Average system CPU time per call, in microseconds
- **calls**: Number of system calls
- **syscall**: System call name

strace Overhead

WARNING: The current version of strace(1) employs breakpoint-based tracing via the Linux ptrace(2) interface. This sets breakpoints for the entry and return of all syscalls (even if the -e option is used to select only some). This is invasive, and applications with high syscall rates may find their performance worsened by an order of magnitude. To illustrate this, here is the same dd(1) command without strace(1):

```
$ dd if=/dev/zero of=/dev/null bs=1k count=5000k
5120000+0 records in
5120000+0 records out
5242880000 bytes (5.2 GB) copied, 1.91247 s, 2.7 GB/s
```

dd(1) includes throughput statistics on the final line: by comparing them, we can conclude that strace(1) slowed dd(1) by a factor of 73. This is a particularly severe case, as dd(1) performs a high rate of system calls.

Depending on application requirements, this style of tracing may be acceptable to use for short durations to determine the syscall types being called. strace(1) would be of greater use if the overhead was not such a problem. Other tracers, including perf(1), Ftrace, BCC, and bpftrace, greatly reduce tracing overhead by using buffered tracing, where events are written to a shared kernel ring buffer and the user-level tracer periodically reads the buffer. This reduces context switching between user and kernel context, lowering overhead.

A future version of strace(1) may solve its overhead problem by becoming an alias to the perf(1) trace subcommand (described earlier in Section 5.5.1, perf). Other higher-performing syscall tracers for Linux, based on BPF, include: vltrace by Intel [Intel 18], and a Linux version of the Windows ProcMon tool by Microsoft [Microsoft 20].

5.5.5   execsnoop

execsnoop(8)[14] is a BCC and bpftrace tool that traces new process execution system-wide. It can find issues of short-lived processes that consume CPU resources and can also be used to debug software execution, including application start scripts.

---

[14] Origin: I created the first execsnoop on 24-Mar-2004; I developed the Linux BCC version on 07-Feb-2016 and the bpftrace version on 15-Nov-2017. See [Gregg 19] for more origin details.

Example output from the BCC version:

```
# execsnoop
PCOMM          PID    PPID   RET ARGS
oltp_read_write 13044 18184   0 /usr/share/sysbench/oltp_read_write.lua --db-
driver=mysql --mysql-password=... --table-size=100000 run
oltp_read_write 13047 18184   0 /usr/share/sysbench/oltp_read_write.lua --db-
driver=mysql --mysql-password=... --table-size=100000 run
sh             13050  13049   0 /bin/sh -c command -v debian-sa1 > /dev/null &&
debian-sa1 1 1 -S XALL
debian-sa1     13051  13050   0 /usr/lib/sysstat/debian-sa1 1 1 -S XALL
sa1            13051  13050   0 /usr/lib/sysstat/sa1 1 1 -S XALL
sadc           13051  13050   0 /usr/lib/sysstat/sadc -F -L -S DISK 1 1 -S XALL
/var/log/sysstat
[...]
```

I ran this on my database system in case it would find anything interesting, and it did: the first
two lines show that a read/write microbenchmark was still running, launching oltp_read_write
commands in a loop—I had accidentally left this running for days! Since the database is handling a different workload, it wasn't obvious from other system metrics that showed CPU and
disk load. The lines after oltp_read_write show sar(1) collecting system metrics.

execsnoop(8) works by tracing the execve(2) system call, and prints a one-line summary for
each. The tool supports some options, including -t for timestamps.

Chapter 1 shows another example of execsnoop(8). I have also published a threadsnoop(8) tool
for bpftrace to trace the creation of threads via libpthread pthread_create().

5.5.6   syscount

syscount(8)[15] is a BCC and bpftrace tool to count system calls system-wide.

Example output from the BCC version:

```
# syscount
Tracing syscalls, printing top 10... Ctrl+C to quit.
^C[05:01:28]
SYSCALL             COUNT
recvfrom            114746
sendto              57395
ppoll               28654
futex                 953
io_getevents           55
bpf                    33
```

---

[15] Origin: I first created this using Ftrace and perf(1) for the perf-tools collection on 07-Jul-2014, and Sasha
Goldshtein developed the BCC version on 15-Feb-2017.

```
rt_sigprocmask          12
epoll_wait              11
select                   7
nanosleep                6

Detaching...
```

This shows the most frequent syscall was recvfrom(2), which was called 114,746 times while tracing. You can explore further using other tracing tools to examine the syscall arguments, latency, and calling stack trace. For example, you can use perf(1) `trace` with a `-e recvfrom` filter, or use bpftrace to instrument the syscalls:sys_enter_recvfrom tracepoint. See the tracers in Chapters 13 to 15.

syscount(8) can also count by process using -P:

```
# syscount -P
Tracing syscalls, printing top 10... Ctrl+C to quit.
^C[05:03:49]
PID    COMM            COUNT
10106  mysqld          155463
13202  oltp_read_only.  61779
9618   sshd                36
344    multipathd          13
13204  syscount-bpfcc      12
519    accounts-daemon      5
```

The output shows the processes and syscall counts.

5.5.7 bpftrace

bpftrace is a BPF-based tracer that provides a high-level programming language, allowing the creation of powerful one-liners and short scripts. It is well suited for custom application analysis based on clues from other tools.

bpftrace is explained in Chapter 15. This section shows some examples for application analysis.

Signal Tracing

This bpftrace one-liner traces process signals (via the kill(2) syscall) showing the source PID and process name, and destination PID and signal number:

```
# bpftrace -e 't:syscalls:sys_enter_kill { time("%H:%M:%S ");
    printf("%s (PID %d) send a SIG %d to PID %d\n",
    comm, pid, args->sig, args->pid); }'
Attaching 1 probe...
09:07:59 bash (PID 9723) send a SIG 2 to PID 9723
```

```
09:08:00 systemd-journal (PID 214) send a SIG 0 to PID 501
09:08:00 systemd-journal (PID 214) send a SIG 0 to PID 550
09:08:00 systemd-journal (PID 214) send a SIG 0 to PID 392
...
```

The output shows a bash shell sending a signal 2 (Ctrl-C) to itself, followed by systemd-journal sending signal 0 to other PIDs. Signal 0 does nothing: it is typically used to check if another process still exists based on the syscall return value.

This one-liner can be useful for debugging strange application issues, such as early terminations. Timestamps are included for cross-checking with performance issues in monitoring software. Tracing signals is also available as the standalone killsnoop(8) tool in BCC and bpftrace.

I/O Profiling

bpftrace can be used to analyze I/O in various ways: examining sizes, latency, return values, and stack traces.[16] For example, the recvfrom(2) syscall was frequently called in previous examples, and can be examined further using bpftrace.

Showing recvfrom(2) buffer sizes as a histogram:

```
# bpftrace -e 't:syscalls:sys_enter_recvfrom { @bytes = hist(args->size); }'
Attaching 1 probe...
^C

@bytes:
[4, 8)             40142 |@@@@@@@@@@@@@@@@@@@@@@@@@@@@@@@@@@@@@@@@@@@@@@@@@@@@|
[8, 16)             1218 |@                                                 |
[16, 32)           17042 |@@@@@@@@@@@@@@@@@@@@@@                             |
[32, 64)               0 |                                                  |
[64, 128)              0 |                                                  |
[128, 256)             0 |                                                  |
[256, 512)             0 |                                                  |
[512, 1K)              0 |                                                  |
[1K, 2K)               0 |                                                  |
[2K, 4K)               0 |                                                  |
[4K, 8K)               0 |                                                  |
[8K, 16K)              0 |                                                  |
[16K, 32K)         19477 |@@@@@@@@@@@@@@@@@@@@@@@@@                          |
```

The output shows that about half of the sizes were very small, between 4 and 7 bytes, and the largest sizes were in the 16 to 32 Kbyte range. It may also be useful to compare this buffer size histogram to the actual bytes received, by tracing the syscall exit tracepoint:

---

[16] E.g., ioprofile(8) from [Gregg 19], although in practice this often fails to capture full stacks due to glibc by default missing the frame pointer; see Section 5.3.1, Compiled Languages.

```
# bpftrace -e 't:syscalls:sys_exit_recvfrom { @bytes = hist(args->ret); }'
```

A large mismatch may show an application is allocating larger buffers that it needs to. (Note that this exit one-liner will include syscall errors in the histogram as a size of -1.)

If the received sizes also show some small and some large I/O, this may also affect the latency of the syscall, with larger I/O taking longer. To measure recvfrom(2) latency, both the start and end of the syscall can be traced at the same time, as shown by the following bpftrace program. The syntax is explained in Chapter 15, BPF, Section 15.2.4, Programming, which ends with a similar latency histogram for a kernel function.

```
# bpftrace -e 't:syscalls:sys_enter_recvfrom { @ts[tid] = nsecs; }
    t:syscalls:sys_exit_recvfrom /@ts[tid]/ {
    @usecs = hist((nsecs - @ts[tid]) / 1000); delete(@ts[tid]); }'
Attaching 2 probes...
^C
@usecs:
[0]               23280 |@@@@@@@@@@@@@@@@@@@@@@@@@@@@@           |
[1]               40468 |@@@@@@@@@@@@@@@@@@@@@@@@@@@@@@@@@@@@@@@@@@@@@@@@@@@@@@|
[2, 4)              144 |                                       |
[4, 8)            31612 |@@@@@@@@@@@@@@@@@@@@@@@@@@@@@@@@@@@@@@@@@ |
[8, 16)              98 |                                       |
[16, 32)             98 |                                       |
[32, 64)          20297 |@@@@@@@@@@@@@@@@@@@@@@@@@@@       |
[64, 128)          5365 |@@@@@@                                 |
[128, 256)         5871 |@@@@@@@                                |
[256, 512)          384 |                                       |
[512, 1K)            16 |                                       |
[1K, 2K)             14 |                                       |
[2K, 4K)              8 |                                       |
[4K, 8K)              0 |                                       |
[8K, 16K)             1 |                                       |
```

The output shows that recvfrom(2) was often less than 8 microseconds, with a slower mode between 32 and 256 microseconds. Some latency outliers are present, the slowest reaching the 8 to 16 millisecond range.

You can continue to drill down further. For example, the output map declaration (@usecs = ...) can be changed to:

- **@usecs[args->ret]**: To break down by syscall return value, showing a histogram for each. Since the return value is the number of bytes received, or -1 for error, this breakdown will confirm if larger I/O sizes caused higher latency.

- **@usecs[ustack]**: To break down by user stack trace, showing a latency histogram for each code path.

I would also consider adding a filter after the first tracepoint so that this showed the MySQL server only, and not other processes:

```
# bpftrace -e 't:syscalls:sys_enter_recvfrom /comm == "mysqld"/ { ...
```

You could also add filters to match on latency outliers or slow modes only.

Lock Tracing

bpftrace can be used to investigate application lock contention in a number of ways. For a typical pthread mutex lock, uprobes can be used to trace the pthread library functions: pthread_mutex_lock(), etc.; and tracepoints can be used to trace the futex(2) syscall that manages lock blocking.

I previously developed the pmlock(8) and pmheld(8) bpftrace tools for instrumenting the pthread library functions, and have published these as open source [Gregg 20b] (also see Chapter 13 of [Gregg 19]). For example, tracing the pthread_mutex_lock() function duration:

```
# pmlock.bt $(pgrep mysqld)
Attaching 4 probes...
Tracing libpthread mutex lock latency, Ctrl-C to end.
^C
[...]

@lock_latency_ns[0x7f37280019f0,
    pthread_mutex_lock+36
    THD::set_query(st_mysql_const_lex_string const&)+94
    Prepared_statement::execute(String*, bool)+336
    Prepared_statement::execute_loop(String*, bool, unsigned char*, unsigned char*...
    mysqld_stmt_execute(THD*, unsigned long, unsigned long, unsigned char*, unsign...
, mysqld]:
[1K, 2K)              47 |                                                         |
[2K, 4K)             945 |@@@@@@@@                                                 |
[4K, 8K)            3290 |@@@@@@@@@@@@@@@@@@@@@@@@@@@@@@                            |
[8K, 16K)           5702 |@@@@@@@@@@@@@@@@@@@@@@@@@@@@@@@@@@@@@@@@@@@@@@@@@@@@@@@@@@@@|
```

This output has been truncated to show only one of the many stacks printed. This stack shows that lock address 0x7f37280019f0 was acquired via the THD::setquery() codepath, and acquisition was often in the 8 to 16 microsecond range.

Why did this lock take this long? pmheld.bt shows the stack trace of the holder, by tracing the lock to unlock duration:

```
# pmheld.bt $(pgrep mysqld)
Attaching 5 probes...
Tracing libpthread mutex held times, Ctrl-C to end.
^C
[...]
```

```
@held_time_ns[0x7f37280019f0,
    __pthread_mutex_unlock+0
    THD::set_query(st_mysql_const_lex_string const&)+147
    dispatch_command(THD*, COM_DATA const*, enum_server_command)+1045
    do_command(THD*)+544
    handle_connection+680
, mysqld]:
[2K, 4K)            3848 |@@@@@@@@@@@@@@@@@@@@@@@@@@@@@@@@@@@@@@@@@@@      |
[4K, 8K)            5038 |@@@@@@@@@@@@@@@@@@@@@@@@@@@@@@@@@@@@@@@@@@@@@@@@@@@@|
[8K, 16K)             0 |                                                 |
[16K, 32K)            0 |                                                 |
[32K, 64K)            1 |                                                 |
```

This shows a different code path for the holder.

If the lock has a symbol name, it is printed instead of the address. Without the symbol name, you can identify the lock from the stack trace: this is a lock in THD::set_query() at instruction offset 147. The source code to that function shows it only acquires one lock: LOCK_thd_query.

Tracing of locks does add overhead, and lock events can be frequent. See the uprobes overhead details in Chapter 4, Observability Tools, Section 4.3.7, uprobes. It may be possible to develop similar tools based on kprobes of kernel futex functions, reducing the overhead somewhat. An alternate approach with negligible overhead is to use CPU profiling instead. CPU profiling typically costs little overhead as it is bounded by the sample rate, and heavy lock contention can use enough CPU cycles to show up in a CPU profile.

Application Internals

If needed, you can develop custom tools to summarize application internals. Start by checking whether USDT probes are available, or can be made available (usually by recompilation with an option). If these cannot be made available or are insufficient, consider using uprobes. For examples of bpftrace and uprobes and USDT, see Chapter 4, Observability Tools, Sections 4.3.7, uprobes, and 4.3.8, USDT. Section 4.3.8 also describes dynamic USDT, which may be necessary for insight into JIT-compiled software, which uprobes may be unable to instrument.

A complex example is Java: uprobes can instrument the JVM runtime (C++ code) and OS libraries, USDT can instrument high-level JVM events, and dynamic USDT can be placed in the Java code to provide insight for method execution.

5.6 Gotchas

The following sections describe common problems with application performance analysis, specifically missing symbols and stack traces. You may first encounter these problems when examining a CPU profile, such as a flame graph, and find that it is missing function names and stack traces.

These problems are an advanced topic that I cover in more detail in Chapters 2, 12, and 18 of *BPF Performance Tools*, and have summarized here.

5.6.1   Missing Symbols

When a profiler or tracer cannot resolve an application instruction address to its function name (symbol), it may print it as a hexadecimal number or the string "[unknown]" instead. The fix for this depends on the application's compiler, runtime, and tuning, and the profiler itself.

ELF Binaries (C, C++, ...)

Symbols may be missing from compiled binaries, especially those that are packaged and distributed, as they have been processed using strip(1) to reduce their file size. One fix is to adjust the build process to avoid stripping symbols; another is to use a different source of symbol information, such as debuginfo or BPF Type Format (BTF). Linux profiling via perf(1), BCC, and bpftrace support debuginfo symbols.

JIT Runtimes (Java, Node.js, ...)

Missing symbols commonly occur for just-in-time (JIT) compiler runtimes like Java and Node. js. In those cases, the JIT compiler has its own symbol table that is changing at runtime and is not part of the pre-compiled symbol tables in the binary. The common fix is to use supplemental symbol tables generated by the runtime, which are placed in /tmp/perf-<PID>.map files read by both perf(1) and BCC.

For example, Netflix uses perf-map-agent [Rudolph 18], which can attach to a live Java process and dump a supplemental symbol file. I have automated its use with another tool called jmaps [Gregg 20c], which should be run immediately after the profile and before symbol translation. For example, using perf(1) (Chapter 13):

```
# perf record -F 49 -a -g -- sleep 10; jmaps
# perf script --header > out.stacks
# [...]
```

And using bpftrace (Chapter 15):

```
# bpftrace --unsafe -e 'profile:hz:49 { @[ustack] = count(); }
    interval:s:10 { exit(); } END { system("jmaps"); }'
```

A symbol mapping may change between the profile sample and the symbol table dump, producing invalid function names in the profile. This is called *symbol churn*, and running jmaps immediately after perf record reduces it. It has so far not been a serious problem; if it was, a symbol dump could be taken before and after the profile to look for changes.

There are other approaches for resolving JIT symbols. One is to use symbol-timestamp logging, which is supported by perf(1) and solves the symbol churn problem, albeit with higher overhead while enabled. Another is for perf(1) to call into the runtime's own stack walker (which typically exists for exception stacks). This approach is sometimes called using *stack helpers*, and for Java it has been implemented by the async-profiler [Pangin 20].

Note that JIT runtimes also also have precompiled components: the JVM also uses libjvm and libc. See the previous ELF binaries section for addressing those components.

5.6.2 Missing Stacks

Another common problem is missing or incomplete stack traces, perhaps as short as one or two frames. For example, from an off-CPU profile of MySQL server:

```
finish_task_switch
schedule
futex_wait_queue_me
futex_wait
do_futex
__x64_sys_futex
do_syscall_64
entry_SYSCALL_64_after_hwframe
pthread_cond_timedwait@@GLIBC_2.3.2
[unknown]
```

This stack is incomplete: after pthread_cond_timedwait() is a single "[unknown]" frame. It's missing the MySQL functions beneath this point, and it's those MySQL functions we really need to understand application context.

Sometimes the stack is a single frame:

```
send
```

In flame graphs this can appear as "grass": many thin single frames at the bottom of the profile.

Incomplete stack traces are unfortunately common, and are usually caused by a confluence of two factors: 1) the observability tool using a frame pointer-based approach for reading the stack trace, and 2) the target binary not reserving a register (RBP on x86_64) for the frame pointer, instead reusing it as a general-purpose register as a compiler performance optimization. The observability tool reads this register expecting it to be a frame pointer, but in fact it could now contain anything: numbers, object address, pointers to strings, etc. The observability tool tries to resolve this number in the symbol table and, if it is lucky, it doesn't find it and can print "[unknown]". If it is unlucky, that random number resolves to an unrelated symbol, and now the printed stack trace has a function name that is wrong, confusing you, the end user.

Since the libc library is typically compiled without frame pointers, broken stacks are common in any path through libc, including the two examples earlier: pthread_cond_timedwait() and send().[17]

The easiest solution is usually to fix the frame pointer register:

- **For C/C++ software, and others compiled with gcc(1) or LLVM:** Recompile the software with -fno-omit-frame-pointer.
- **For Java:** Run java(1) with -XX:+PreserveFramePointer.

---

[17] I've sent build instructions to package maintainers asking for a libc with frame pointers to be packaged.

This may come with a performance cost, but it has often been measured at less than 1%; the benefits of being able to use stack traces to find performance wins usually far outweigh this cost.

The other approach is to switch to a stack walking technique that is not frame pointer-based. perf(1) supports DWARF-based stack walking, ORC, and last branch record (LBR). Other stack walking methods are mentioned in Chapter 13, perf, Section 13.9, perf record.

At the time of writing, DWARF-based and LBR stack walking are not available from BPF, and ORC is not yet available for user-level software.

5.7   Exercises

1. Answer the following questions about terminology:

   - What is a cache?

   - What is a ring buffer?

   - What is a spin lock?

   - What is an adaptive mutex lock?

   - What is the difference between concurrency and parallelism?

   - What is CPU affinity?

2. Answer the following conceptual questions:

   - What are the general pros and cons of using a large I/O size?

   - What is a hash table of locks used for?

   - Describe general performance characteristics of the runtime of compiled languages, interpreted languages, and those using virtual machines.

   - Explain the role of garbage collection and how it can affect performance.

3. Choose an application, and answer the following basic questions about it:

   - What is the role of the application?

   - What discrete operation does the application perform?

   - Does the application run in user mode or kernel mode?

   - How is the application configured? What key options are available regarding performance?

   - What performance metrics are provided by the application?

   - What logs does the application create? Do they contain performance information?

   - Has the most recent version of the application fixed performance issues?

   - Are there known performance bugs for the application?

   - Does the application have a community (e.g., IRC, meetups)? A performance community?

   - Are there books about the application? Performance books?

   - Are there well-known performance experts for the application? Who are they?

4. Choose an application that is under load, and perform these tasks (many of which may require the use of dynamic tracing):

   - Before taking any measurements, do you expect the application to be CPU-bound or I/O-bound? Explain your reasoning.

   - Determine using observability tools if it is CPU-bound or I/O-bound.

   - Generate a CPU flame graph for the application. You may need to fix symbols and stack traces for this to work. What is the hottest CPU code path?

   - Generate an off-CPU flame graph for the application. What is the longest blocking event during the application's request (ignore idle stacks)?

   - Characterize the size of I/O it performs (e.g., file system reads/writes, network sends/receives).

   - Does the application have caches? Identify their size and hit rate.

   - Measure the latency (response time) for the operation that the application serves. Show the average, minimum, maximum, and full distribution.

   - Perform drill-down analysis of the operation, investigating the origin of the bulk of the latency.

   - Characterize the workload applied to the application (especially who and what).

   - Step through the static performance tuning checklist.

   - Does the application run concurrently? Investigate its use of synchronization primitives.

5. (optional, advanced) Develop a tool for Linux called tsastat(8) that prints columns for multiple thread state analysis states, with time spent in each. This can behave similarly to pidstat(1) and produce a rolling output.[18]

5.8 References

[**Knuth 76**] Knuth, D., "Big Omicron and Big Omega and Big Theta," *ACM SIGACT News*, 1976.

[**Knuth 97**] Knuth, D., *The Art of Computer Programming, Volume 1: Fundamental Algorithms*, 3rd Edition, Addison-Wesley, 1997.

[**Zijlstra 09**] Zijlstra, P., "mutex: implement adaptive spinning," http://lwn.net/Articles/314512, 2009.

[**Gregg 17a**] Gregg, B., "EuroBSDcon: System Performance Analysis Methodologies," *EuroBSDcon*, http://www.brendangregg.com/blog/2017-10-28/bsd-performance-analysis-methodologies.html, 2017.

---

[18] Trivia: since the first edition I'm not aware of anyone solving this. I proposed a thread state analysis talk (TSA) for OSCON, and planned to develop a Linux TSA tool for the talk; however, my talk was rejected (my fault: my abstract was lousy), and I have yet to develop the tool. EuroBSDcon invited me to give a keynote, for which I covered TSA, and I did develop a tool for it: tstates.d, for FreeBSD [Gregg 17a].

[Intel 18] "Tool tracing syscalls in a fast way using eBPF linux kernel feature," https://github.com/pmem/vltrace, last updated 2018.

[Microsoft 18] "Fibers," *Windows Dev Center,* https://docs.microsoft.com/en-us/windows/win32/procthread/fibers, 2018.

[Rudolph 18] Rudolph, J., "perf-map-agent," https://github.com/jvm-profiling-tools/perf-map-agent, last updated 2018.

[Schwartz 18] Schwartz, E., "Dynamic Optimizations for SBCL Garbage Collection," *11th European Lisp Symposium*, https://european-lisp-symposium.org/static/proceedings/2018.pdf, 2018.

[Axboe 19] Axboe, J., "Efficient IO with io_uring," https://kernel.dk/io_uring.pdf, 2019.

[Gregg 19] Gregg, B., *BPF Performance Tools: Linux System and Application Observability*, Addison-Wesley, 2019.

[Apdex 20] Apdex Alliance, "Apdex," https://www.apdex.org, accessed 2020.

[Golang 20] "Why goroutines instead of threads?" *Golang documentation,* https://golang.org/doc/faq#goroutines, accessed 2020.

[Gregg 20b] Gregg, B., "BPF Performance Tools," https://github.com/brendangregg/bpf-perf-tools-book, last updated 2020.

[Gregg 20c] Gregg, B., "jmaps," https://github.com/brendangregg/FlameGraph/blob/master/jmaps, last updated 2020.

[Linux 20e] "RCU Concepts," *Linux documentation*, https://www.kernel.org/doc/html/latest/RCU/rcu.html, accessed 2020.

[Microsoft 20] "Procmon Is a Linux Reimagining of the Classic Procmon Tool from the Sysinternals Suite of Tools for Windows," https://github.com/microsoft/ProcMon-for-Linux, last updated 2020.

[Molnar 20] Molnar, I., and Bueso, D., "Generic Mutex Subsystem," *Linux documentation,* https://www.kernel.org/doc/Documentation/locking/mutex-design.rst, accessed 2020.

[Node.js 20] "Node.js," http://nodejs.org, accessed 2020.

[Pangin 20] Pangin, A., "async-profiler," https://github.com/jvm-profiling-tools/async-profiler, last updated 2020.

Chapter 6

CPUs

CPUs drive all software and are often the first target for systems performance analysis. This chapter explains CPU hardware and software, and shows how CPU usage can be examined in detail to look for performance improvements.

At a high level, system-wide CPU utilization can be monitored, and usage by process or thread can be examined. At a lower level, the code paths within applications and the kernel can be profiled and studied, as well as CPU usage by interrupts. At the lowest level, CPU instruction execution and cycle behavior can be analyzed. Other behaviors can also be investigated, including scheduler latency as tasks wait their turn on CPUs, which degrades performance.

The learning objectives of this chapter are:

- Understand CPU models and concepts.
- Become familiar with CPU hardware internals.
- Become familiar with CPU scheduler internals.
- Follow different methodologies for CPU analysis.
- Interpret load averages and PSI.
- Characterize system-wide and per-CPU utilization.
- Identify and quantify issues of scheduler latency.
- Perform CPU cycle analysis to identify inefficiencies.
- Investigate CPU usage using profilers and CPU flame graphs.
- Identify soft and hard IRQ CPU consumers.
- Interpret CPU flame graphs and other CPU visualizations.
- Become aware of CPU tunable parameters.

This chapter has six parts. The first three provide the basis for CPU analysis, and the last three show its practical application to Linux-based systems. The parts are:

- **Background** introduces CPU-related terminology, basic models of CPUs, and key CPU performance concepts.

- **Architecture** introduces processor and kernel scheduler architecture.

- **Methodology** describes performance analysis methodologies, both observational and experimental.

- **Observability Tools** describes CPU performance analysis tools on Linux-based systems, including profiling, tracing, and visualizations.

- **Experimentation** summarizes CPU benchmark tools.

- **Tuning** includes examples of tunable parameters.

The effects of memory I/O on CPU performance are covered, including CPU cycles stalled on memory and the performance of CPU caches. Chapter 7, Memory, continues the discussion of memory I/O, including MMU, NUMA/UMA, system interconnects, and memory buses.

6.1   Terminology

For reference, CPU-related terminology used in this chapter includes the following:

- **Processor:** The physical chip that plugs into a socket on the system or processor board and contains one or more CPUs implemented as cores or hardware threads.

- **Core:** An independent CPU instance on a *multicore processor*. The use of cores is a way to scale processors, called *chip-level multiprocessing* (CMP).

- **Hardware thread:** A CPU architecture that supports executing multiple threads in parallel on a single core (including Intel's Hyper-Threading Technology), where each thread is an independent CPU instance. This scaling approach is called *simultaneous multithreading* (SMT).

- **CPU instruction:** A single CPU operation, from its *instruction set*. There are instructions for arithmetic operations, memory I/O, and control logic.

- **Logical CPU:** Also called a *virtual processor,*[1] an operating system CPU instance (a schedulable CPU entity). This may be implemented by the processor as a hardware thread (in which case it may also be called a *virtual core*), a core, or a single-core processor.

- **Scheduler:** The kernel subsystem that assigns threads to run on CPUs.

- **Run queue:** A queue of runnable threads that are waiting to be serviced by CPUs. Modern kernels may use some other data structure (e.g., a red-black tree) to store runnable threads, but we still often use the term run queue.

Other terms are introduced throughout this chapter. The Glossary includes basic terminology for reference, including *CPU*, *CPU cycle*, and *stack*. Also see the terminology sections in Chapters 2 and 3.

---

[1] It is also sometimes called a *virtual CPU*; however, that term is more commonly used to refer to virtual CPU instances provided by a virtualization technology. See Chapter 11, Cloud Computing.

6.2 Models

The following simple models illustrate some basic principles of CPUs and CPU performance. Section 6.4, Architecture, digs much deeper and includes implementation-specific details.

6.2.1 CPU Architecture

Figure 6.1 shows an example CPU architecture, for a single processor with four cores and eight hardware threads in total. The physical architecture is pictured, along with how it is seen by the operating system.[2]

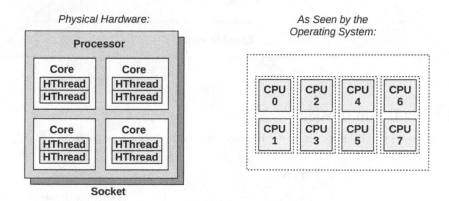

Figure 6.1   CPU architecture

Each hardware thread is addressable as a *logical CPU*, so this processor appears as eight CPUs. The operating system may have some additional knowledge of topology to improve its scheduling decisions, such as which CPUs are on the same core and how CPU caches are shared.

6.2.2 CPU Memory Caches

Processors provide various hardware caches for improving memory I/O performance. Figure 6.2 shows the relationship of cache sizes, which become smaller and faster (a trade-off) the closer they are to the CPU.

The caches that are present, and whether they are on the processor (integrated) or external to the processor, depends on the processor type. Earlier processors provided fewer levels of integrated cache.

---

[2]There is a tool for Linux, lstopo(1), that can generate diagrams similar to this figure for the current system, an example is in Section 6.6.21, Other Tools.

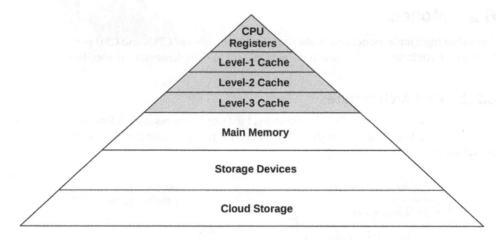

Figure 6.2   CPU cache sizes

6.2.3   CPU Run Queues

Figure 6.3 shows a CPU run queue, which is managed by the kernel scheduler.

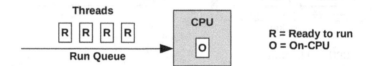

Figure 6.3   CPU run queue

The thread states shown in the figure, ready to run and on-CPU, are covered in Figure 3.8 in Chapter 3, Operating Systems.

The number of software threads that are queued and ready to run is an important performance metric indicating CPU saturation. In this figure (at this instant) there are four, with an additional thread running on-CPU. The time spent waiting on a CPU run queue is sometimes called *run-queue latency* or *dispatcher-queue latency*. In this book, the term *scheduler latency* is often used, as it is appropriate for all schedulers, including those that do not use queues (see the discussion of CFS in Section 6.4.2, Software).

For multiprocessor systems, the kernel typically provides a run queue for each CPU, and aims to keep threads on the same run queue. This means that threads are more likely to keep running on the same CPUs where the CPU caches have cached their data. These caches are described as having *cache warmth*, and this strategy to keep threads running on the same CPUs is called *CPU affinity*. On NUMA systems, per-CPU run queues also improve *memory locality*. This improves performance by keeping threads running on the same memory node (as described in Chapter 7, Memory), and avoids the cost of thread synchronization (mutex locks) for queue operations, which would hurt scalability if the run queue was global and shared among all CPUs.

6.3   Concepts

The following are a selection of important concepts regarding CPU performance, beginning with a summary of processor internals: the CPU clock rate and how instructions are executed. This is background for later performance analysis, particularly for understanding the instructions-per-cycle (IPC) metric.

6.3.1   Clock Rate

The clock is a digital signal that drives all processor logic. Each CPU instruction may take one or more cycles of the clock (called *CPU cycles*) to execute. CPUs execute at a particular clock rate; for example, a 4 GHz CPU performs 4 billion clock cycles per second.

Some processors are able to vary their clock rate, increasing it to improve performance or decreasing it to reduce power consumption. The rate may be varied on request by the operating system, or dynamically by the processor itself. The kernel idle thread, for example, can request the CPU to throttle down to save power.

Clock rate is often marketed as the primary feature of a processor, but this can be a little misleading. Even if the CPU in your system appears to be fully utilized (a bottleneck), a faster clock rate may not speed up performance—it depends on what those fast CPU cycles are actually doing. If they are mostly stall cycles while waiting on memory access, executing them more quickly doesn't actually increase the CPU instruction rate or workload throughput.

6.3.2   Instructions

CPUs execute instructions chosen from their instruction set. An instruction includes the following steps, each processed by a component of the CPU called a *functional unit*:

1. Instruction fetch

2. Instruction decode

3. Execute

4. Memory access

5. Register write-back

The last two steps are optional, depending on the instruction. Many instructions operate on registers only and do not require the memory access step.

Each of these steps takes at least a single clock cycle to be executed. Memory access is often the slowest, as it may take dozens of clock cycles to read or write to main memory, during which instruction execution has *stalled* (and these cycles while stalled are called *stall cycles*). This is why CPU caching is important, as described in Section 6.4.1, Hardware: it can dramatically reduce the number of cycles needed for memory access.

6.3.3   Instruction Pipeline

The instruction pipeline is a CPU architecture that can execute multiple instructions in parallel by executing different components of different instructions at the same time. It is similar to a factory assembly line, where stages of production can be executed in parallel, increasing throughput.

Consider the instruction steps previously listed. If each were to take a single clock cycle, it would take five cycles to complete the instruction. At each step of this instruction, only one functional unit is active and four are idle. By use of pipelining, multiple functional units can be active at the same time, processing different instructions in the pipeline. Ideally, the processor can then complete one instruction with every clock cycle.

Instruction pipelining may involve breaking down an instruction into multiple simple steps for execution in parallel. (Depending on the processor, these steps may become simple operations called *micro-operations* (uOps) for execution by a processor area called the *back-end*. The *front-end* of such a processor is responsible for fetching instructions and branch prediction.)

Branch Prediction

Modern processors can perform out-of-order execution of the pipeline, where later instructions can be completed while earlier instructions are stalled, improving instruction throughput. However, conditional branch instructions pose a problem. Branch instructions jump execution to a different instruction, and conditional branches do so based on a test. With conditional branches, the processor does not know what the later instructions will be. As an optimization, processors often implement *branch prediction*, where they will guess the outcome of the test and begin processing the outcome instructions. If the guess later proves to be wrong, the progress in the instruction pipeline must be discarded, hurting performance. To improve the chances of guessing correctly, programmers can place hints in the code (e.g., likely() and unlikely() macros in the Linux Kernel sources).

6.3.4   Instruction Width

But we can go faster still. Multiple functional units of the same type can be included, so that even more instructions can make forward progress with each clock cycle. This CPU architecture is called *superscalar* and is typically used with pipelining to achieve a high instruction throughput.

The instruction *width* describes the target number of instructions to process in parallel. Modern processors are *3-wide* or *4-wide*, meaning they can complete up to three or four instructions per cycle. How this works depends on the processor, as there may be different numbers of functional units for each stage.

6.3.5   Instruction Size

Another instruction characteristic is the instruction *size*: for some processor architectures it is variable: For example, x86, which is classified as a *complex instruction set computer* (CISC), allows up to 15-byte instructions. ARM, which is a *reduced instruction set computer* (RISC), has 4 byte instructions with 4-byte alignment for AArch32/A32, and 2- or 4-byte instructions for ARM Thumb.

6.3.6 SMT

Simultaneous multithreading makes use of a superscalar architecture and hardware multi-threading support (by the processor) to improve parallelism. It allows a CPU core to run more than one thread, effectively scheduling between them during instructions, e.g., when one instruction stalls on memory I/O. The kernel presents these hardware threads as virtual CPUs, and schedules threads and processes on them as usual. This was introduced and pictured in Section 6.2.1, CPU Architecture.

An example implementation is Intel's Hyper-Threading Technology, where each core often has two hardware threads. Another example is POWER8, which has eight hardware threads per core.

The performance of each hardware thread is not the same as a separate CPU core, and depends on the workload. To avoid performance problems, kernels may spread out CPU load across cores so that only one hardware thread on each core is busy, avoiding hardware thread contention. Workloads that are stall cycle-heavy (low IPC) may also have better performance than those that are instruction-heavy (high IPC) because stall cycles reduce core contention.

6.3.7 IPC, CPI

Instructions per cycle (IPC) is an important high-level metric for describing how a CPU is spending its clock cycles and for understanding the nature of CPU utilization. This metric may also be expressed as *cycles per instruction* (CPI), the inverse of IPC. IPC is more often used by the Linux community and by the Linux perf(1) profiler, and CPI more often used by Intel and elsewhere.[3]

A low IPC indicates that CPUs are often stalled, typically for memory access. A high IPC indicates that CPUs are often not stalled and have a high instruction throughput. These metrics suggest where performance tuning efforts may be best spent.

Memory-intensive workloads, for example, may be improved by installing faster memory (DRAM), improving memory locality (software configuration), or reducing the amount of memory I/O. Installing CPUs with a higher clock rate may not improve performance to the degree expected, as the CPUs may need to wait the same amount of time for memory I/O to complete. Put differently, a faster CPU may mean more stall cycles but the same rate of completed instructions per second.

The actual values for high or low IPC are dependent on the processor and processor features and can be determined experimentally by running known workloads. As an example, you may find that low-IPC workloads run with an IPC at 0.2 or lower, and high IPC workloads run with an IPC of over 1.0 (which is possible due to instruction pipelining and width, described earlier). At Netflix, cloud workloads range from an IPC of 0.2 (considered slow) to 1.5 (considered good). Expressed as CPI, this range is 5.0 to 0.66.

It should be noted that IPC shows the efficiency of instruction *processing*, but not of the instructions themselves. Consider a software change that added an inefficient software loop, which operates mostly on CPU registers (no stall cycles): such a change may result in a higher overall IPC, but also higher CPU usage and utilization.

---

[3] In the first edition of this book I used CPI; I've since switched to working more on Linux, including switching to IPC.

6.3.8   Utilization

CPU utilization is measured by the time a CPU instance is busy performing work during an interval, expressed as a percentage. It can be measured as the time a CPU is not running the kernel idle thread but is instead running user-level application threads or other kernel threads, or processing interrupts.

High CPU utilization may not necessarily be a problem, but rather a sign that the system is doing work. Some people also consider this a return of investment (ROI) indicator: a highly utilized system is considered to have good ROI, whereas an idle system is considered wasted. Unlike with other resource types (disks), performance does not degrade steeply under high utilization, as the kernel supports priorities, preemption, and time sharing. These together allow the kernel to understand what has higher priority, and to ensure that it runs first.

The measure of CPU utilization spans all clock cycles for eligible activities, including memory stall cycles. This can be misleading: a CPU may be highly utilized because it is often stalled waiting for memory I/O, not just executing instructions, as described in the previous section. This is the case for the Netflix cloud, where the CPU utilization is mostly memory stall cycles [Gregg 17b].

CPU utilization is often split into separate kernel- and user-time metrics.

6.3.9   User Time/Kernel Time

The CPU time spent executing user-level software is called *user time*, and kernel-level software is *kernel time*. Kernel time includes time during system calls, kernel threads, and interrupts. When measured across the entire system, the user time/kernel time ratio indicates the type of workload performed.

Applications that are computation-intensive may spend almost all their time executing user-level code and have a user/kernel ratio approaching 99/1. Examples include image processing, machine learning, genomics, and data analysis.

Applications that are I/O-intensive have a high rate of system calls, which execute kernel code to perform the I/O. For example, a web server performing network I/O may have a user/kernel ratio of around 70/30.

These numbers are dependent on many factors and are included to express the kinds of ratios expected.

6.3.10   Saturation

A CPU at 100% utilization is *saturated*, and threads will encounter *scheduler latency* as they wait to run on-CPU, decreasing overall performance. This latency is the time spent waiting on the CPU run queue or other structure used to manage threads.

Another form of CPU saturation involves CPU resource controls, as may be imposed in a multi-tenant cloud computing environment. While the CPU may not be 100% utilized, the imposed limit has been reached, and threads that are runnable must wait their turn. How visible this is to users of the system depends on the type of virtualization in use; see Chapter 11, Cloud Computing.

A CPU running at saturation is less of a problem than other resource types, as higher-priority work can preempt the current thread.

6.3.11   Preemption

Preemption, introduced in Chapter 3, Operating Systems, allows a higher-priority thread to preempt the currently running thread and begin its own execution instead. This eliminates the run-queue latency for higher-priority work, improving its performance.

6.3.12   Priority Inversion

Priority inversion occurs when a lower-priority thread holds a resource and blocks a higher-priority thread from running. This reduces the performance of the higher-priority work, as it is blocked waiting.

This can be solved using a *priority inheritance* scheme. Here is an example of how this can work (based on a real-world case):

1. Thread A performs monitoring and has a low priority. It acquires an address space lock for a production database, to check memory usage.

2. Thread B, a routine task to perform compression of system logs, begins running.

3. There is insufficient CPU to run both. Thread B preempts A and runs.

4. Thread C is from the production database, has a high priority, and has been sleeping waiting for I/O. This I/O now completes, putting thread C back into the runnable state.

5. Thread C preempts B, runs, but then blocks on the address space lock held by thread A. Thread C leaves CPU.

6. The scheduler picks the next-highest-priority thread to run: B.

7. With thread B running, a high-priority thread, C, is effectively blocked on a lower-priority thread, B. This is priority inversion.

8. Priority inheritance gives thread A thread C's high priority, preempting B, until it releases the lock. Thread C can now run.

Linux since 2.6.18 has provided a user-level mutex that supports priority inheritance, intended for real-time workloads [Corbet 06a].

6.3.13   Multiprocess, Multithreading

Most processors provide multiple CPUs of some form. For application to make use of them, it needs separate threads of execution so that it can run in parallel. For a 64-CPU system, for example, this may mean that an application can execute up to 64 times faster if it can make use of all CPUs in parallel, or handle 64 times the load. The degree to which the application can effectively scale with an increase in CPU count is a measure of *scalability*.

The two techniques to scale applications across CPUs are *multiprocess* and *multithreading*, which are pictured in Figure 6.4. (Note that this is software multithreading, and not the hardware-based SMT mentioned earlier.)

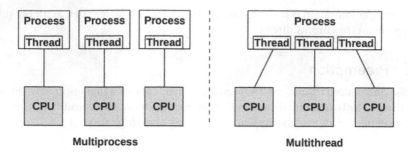

Figure 6.4 Software CPU scalability techniques

On Linux both the multiprocess and multithread models may be used, and both are implemented by tasks.

Differences between multiprocess and multithreading are shown in Table 6.1.

Table 6.1   Multiprocess and multithreading attributes

Attribute	Multiprocess	Multithreading
Development	Can be easier. Use of fork(2) or clone(2).	Use of threads API (pthreads).
Memory overhead	Separate address space per process consumes some memory resources (reduced to some degree by page-level copy-on-write).	Small. Requires only extra stack and register space, and space for thread-local data.
CPU overhead	Cost of fork(2)/clone(2)/exit(2), which includes MMU work to manage address spaces.	Small. API calls.
Communication	Via IPC. This incurs CPU cost including context switching for moving data between address spaces, unless shared memory regions are used.	Fastest. Direct access to shared memory. Integrity via synchronization primitives (e.g., mutex locks).
Crash resilience	High, processes are independent.	Low, any bug can crash the entire application.
Memory Usage	While some memory may be duplicated, separate processes can exit(2) and return all memory back to the system.	Via system allocator. This may incur some CPU contention from multiple threads, and fragmentation before memory is reused.

With all the advantages shown in the table, multithreading is generally considered superior, although more complicated for the developer to implement. Multithreaded programming is covered in [Stevens 13].

Whichever technique is used, it is important that enough processes or threads be created to span the desired number of CPUs—which, for maximum performance, may be all of the CPUs available. Some applications may perform better when running on fewer CPUs, when the cost of thread synchronization and reduced memory locality (NUMA) outweighs the benefit of running across more CPUs.

Parallel architectures are also discussed in Chapter 5, Applications, Section 5.2.5, Concurrency and Parallelism, which also summarizes co-routines.

6.3.14 Word Size

Processors are designed around a maximum *word size*—32-bit or 64-bit—which is the integer size and register size. Word size is also commonly used, depending on the processor, for the address space size and data path width (where it is sometimes called the *bit width*).

Larger sizes can mean better performance, although it's not as simple as it sounds. Larger sizes may cause memory overheads for unused bits in some data types. The data footprint also increases when the size of pointers (word size) increases, which can require more memory I/O. For the x86 64-bit architecture, these overheads are compensated by an increase in registers and a more efficient register calling convention, so 64-bit applications will likely be faster than their 32-bit versions.

Processors and operating systems can support multiple word sizes and can run applications compiled for different word sizes simultaneously. If software has been compiled for the smaller word size, it may execute successfully but perform relatively poorly.

6.3.15 Compiler Optimization

The CPU runtime of applications can be significantly improved through compiler options (including setting the word size) and optimizations. Compilers are also frequently updated to take advantage of the latest CPU instruction sets and to implement other optimizations. Sometimes application performance can be significantly improved simply by using a newer compiler.

This topic is covered in more detail in Chapter 5, Applications, Section 5.3.1, Compiled Languages.

6.4   Architecture

This section introduces CPU architecture and implementation, for both hardware and software. Simple CPU models were introduced in Section 6.2, Models, and generic concepts in the previous section.

Here I summarize these topics as background for performance analysis. For more details, see vendor processor manuals and documentation on operating system internals. Some are listed at the end of this chapter.

6.4.1 Hardware

CPU hardware includes the processor and its subsystems, and the CPU interconnect for multiprocessor systems.

Processor

Components of a generic two-core processor are shown in Figure 6.5.

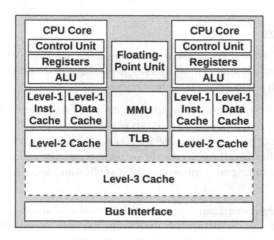

Figure 6.5   Generic two-core processor components

The *control unit* is the heart of the CPU, performing instruction fetch, decoding, managing execution, and storing results.

This example processor depicts a shared floating-point unit and (optional) shared Level 3 cache. The actual components in your processor will vary depending on its type and model. Other performance-related components that may be present include:

- **P-cache:** Prefetch cache (per CPU core)
- **W-cache:** Write cache (per CPU core)
- **Clock:** Signal generator for the CPU clock (or provided externally)
- **Timestamp counter:** For high-resolution time, incremented by the clock
- **Microcode ROM:** Quickly converts instructions to circuit signals
- **Temperature sensors:** For thermal monitoring
- **Network interfaces:** If present on-chip (for high performance)

Some processor types use the temperature sensors as input for dynamic overclocking of individual cores (including Intel Turbo Boost technology), increasing the clock rate while the core remains in its temperature envelope. The possible clock rates can be defined by P-states.

P-States and C-States

The *advanced configuration and power interface* (ACPI) standard, in use by Intel processors, defines *processor performance states* (P-states) and *processor power states* (C-states) [ACPI 17].

P-states provide different levels of performance during normal execution by varying the CPU frequency: P0 is the highest frequency (for some Intel CPUs this is the highest "turbo boost" level) and P1...N are lower-frequency states. These states can be controlled by both hardware (e.g., based on the processor temperature) or via software (e.g., kernel power saving modes). The current operating frequency and available states can be observed using model-specific registers (MSRs) (e.g., using the showboost(8) tool in Section 6.6.10, showboost).

C-states provide different idle states for when execution is halted, saving power. The C-states are shown in Table 6.2: C0 is for normal operation, and C1 and above are for idle states: the higher the number, the deeper the state.

Table 6.2 **Processor power states (C-states)**

C-state	Description
C0	Executing. The CPU is fully on, processing instructions.
C1	Halts execution. Entered by the hlt instruction. Caches are maintained. Wakeup latency is the lowest from this state.
C1E	Enhanced halt with lower power consumption (supported by some processors).
C2	Halts execution. Entered by a hardware signal. This is a deeper sleep state with higher wakeup latency.
C3	A deeper sleep state with improved power savings over C1 and C2. The caches may maintain state, but stop snooping (cache coherency), deferring it to the OS.

Processor manufacturers can define additional states beyond C3. Some Intel processors define additional levels up to C10 where more processor functionality is powered down, including cache contents.

CPU Caches

Various hardware caches are usually included in the processor (where they are referred to as *on-chip*, *on-die*, *embedded*, or *integrated*) or with the processor (*external*). These improve memory performance by using faster memory types for caching reads and buffering writes. The levels of cache access for a generic processor are shown in Figure 6.6.

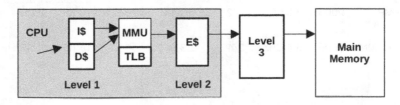

Figure 6.6 CPU cache hierarchy

They include:

- **Level 1 instruction cache** (I$)
- **Level 1 data cache** (D$)
- **Translation lookaside buffer** (TLB)
- **Level 2 cache** (E$)
- **Level 3 cache** (optional)

The *E* in E$ originally stood for *external* cache, but with the integration of Level 2 caches it has since been cleverly referred to as *embedded* cache. The "Level" terminology is used nowadays instead of the "E$"-style notation, which avoids such confusion.

It is often desirable to refer to the last cache before main memory, which may or may not be level 3. Intel uses the term *last-level cache* (LLC) for this, also described as the *longest-latency cache*.

The caches available on each processor depend on its type and model. Over time, the number and sizes of these caches have been increasing. This is illustrated in Table 6.3, which lists example Intel processors since 1978, including advances in caches [Intel 19a][Intel 20a].

Table 6.3   **Example Intel processor cache sizes from 1978 to 2019**

Processor	Year	Max Clock	Cores/ Threads	Transistors	Data Bus (bits)	Level 1	Level 2	Level 3
8086	1978	8 MHz	1/1	29 K	16	—		
Intel 286	1982	12.5 MHz	1/1	134 K	16	—		
Intel 386 DX	1985	20 MHz	1/1	275 K	32	—	—	—
Intel 486 DX	1989	25 MHz	1/1	1.2 M	32	8 KB	—	—
Pentium	1993	60 MHz	1/1	3.1 M	64	16 KB	—	
Pentium Pro	1995	200 MHz	1/1	5.5 M	64	16 KB	256/ 512 KB	—
Pentium II	1997	266 MHz	1/1	7 M	64	32 KB	256/ 512 KB	—
Pentium III	1999	500 MHz	1/1	8.2 M	64	32 KB	512 KB	—
Intel Xeon	2001	1.7 GHz	1/1	42 M	64	8 KB	512 KB	—
Pentium M	2003	1.6 GHz	1/1	77 M	64	64 KB	1 MB	—
Intel Xeon MP 3.33	2005	3.33 GHz	1/2	675 M	64	16 KB	1 MB	8 MB
Intel Xeon 7140M	2006	3.4 GHz	2/4	1.3 B	64	16 KB	1 MB	16 MB

Processor	Year	Max Clock	Cores/ Threads	Transistors	Data Bus (bits)	Level 1	Level 2	Level 3
Intel Xeon 7460	2008	2.67 GHz	6/6	1.9 B	64	64 KB	3 MB	16 MB
Intel Xeon 7560	2010	2.26 GHz	8/16	2.3 B	64	64 KB	256 KB	24 MB
Intel Xeon E7-8870	2011	2.4 GHz	10/20	2.2 B	64	64 KB	256 KB	30 MB
Intel Xeon E7-8870v2	2014	3.1 GHz	15/30	4.3 B	64	64 KB	256 KB	37.5 MB
Intel Xeon E7-8870v3	2015	2.9 GHz	18/36	5.6 B	64	64 KB	256 KB	45 MB
Intel Xeon E7-8870v4	2016	3.0 GHz	20/40	7.2 B	64	64 KB	256 KB	50 MB
Intel Platinum 8180	2017	3.8 GHz	28/56	8.0 B	64	64 KB	1 MB	38.5 MB
Intel Xeon Platinum 9282	2019	3.8 GHz	56/112	8.0 B	64	64 KB	1 MB	77 MB

For multicore and multithreading processors, some caches may be shared between cores and threads. For the examples in Table 6.3, all processors since the Intel Xeon 7460 (2008) have multiple Level 1 and Level 2 caches, typically one for each core (the sizes in the table refer to the per-core cache, not the total size).

Apart from the increasing number and sizes of CPU caches, there is also a trend toward providing these on-chip, where access latency can be minimized, instead of providing them externally to the processor.

Latency

Multiple levels of cache are used to deliver the optimum configuration of size and latency. The access time for the Level 1 cache is typically a few CPU clock cycles, and for the larger Level 2 cache around a dozen clock cycles. Main memory access can take around 60 ns (around 240 cycles for a 4 GHz processor), and address translation by the MMU also adds latency.

The CPU cache latency characteristics for your processor can be determined experimentally using micro-benchmarking [Ruggiero 08]. Figure 6.7 shows the result of this, plotting memory access latency for an Intel Xeon E5620 2.4 GHz tested over increasing ranges of memory using LMbench [McVoy 12].

Both axes are logarithmic. The steps in the graphs show when a cache level was exceeded, and access latency becomes a result of the next (slower) cache level.

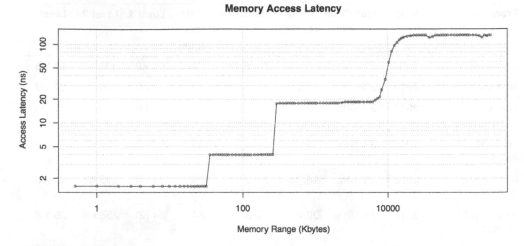

Figure 6.7   Memory access latency testing

Associativity

Associativity is a cache characteristic describing a constraint for locating new entries in the cache. Types are:

- **Fully associative**: The cache can locate new entries anywhere. For example, a least recently used (LRU) algorithm could be used for eviction across the entire cache.

- **Direct mapped**: Each entry has only one valid location in the cache, for example, a hash of the memory address, using a subset of the address bits to form an address in the cache.

- **Set associative**: A subset of the cache is identified by mapping (e.g., hashing) from within which another algorithm (e.g., LRU) may be performed. It is described in terms of the subset size; for example, *four-way set associative* maps an address to four possible locations, and then picks the best from those four (e.g., the least recently used location).

CPU caches often use set associativity as a balance between fully associative (which is expensive to perform) and direct mapped (which has poor hit rates).

Cache Line

Another characteristic of CPU caches is their *cache line* size. This is a range of bytes that are stored and transferred as a unit, improving memory throughput. A typical cache line size for x86 processors is 64 bytes. Compilers take this into account when optimizing for performance. Programmers sometimes do as well; see Hash Tables in Chapter 5, Applications, Section 5.2.5, Concurrency and Parallelism.

Cache Coherency

Memory may be cached in multiple CPU caches on different processors at the same time. When one CPU modifies memory, all caches need to be aware that their cached copy is now *stale* and should be discarded, so that any future reads will retrieve the newly modified copy. This process, called *cache coherency*, ensures that CPUs are always accessing the correct state of memory.

One of the effects of cache coherency is LLC access penalties. The following examples are provided as a rough guide (these are from [Levinthal 09]):

- LLC hit, line unshared: ~40 CPU cycles
- LLC hit, line shared in another core: ~65 CPU cycles
- LLC hit, line modified in another core: ~75 CPU cycles

Cache coherency is one of the greatest challenges in designing scalable multiprocessor systems, as memory can be modified rapidly.

MMU

The memory management unit (MMU) is responsible for virtual-to-physical address translation.

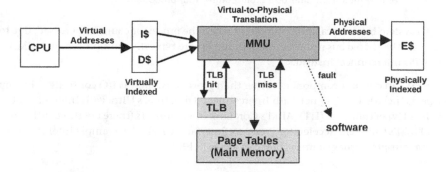

Figure 6.8   Memory management unit and CPU caches

A generic MMU is pictured in Figure 6.8, along with CPU cache types. This MMU uses an on-chip translation lookaside buffer (TLB) to cache address translations. Cache misses are satisfied by translation tables in main memory (DRAM), called *page tables*, which are read directly by the MMU (hardware) and maintained by the kernel.

These factors are processor-dependent. Some (older) processors handle TLB misses using kernel software to walk the page tables, and then populate the TLB with the requested mappings. Such software may maintain its own, larger, in-memory cache of translations, called the *translation storage buffer* (TSB). Newer processors can service TLB misses in hardware, greatly reducing their cost.

Interconnects

For multiprocessor architectures, processors are connected using either a shared system bus or a dedicated interconnect. This is related to the memory architecture of the system, uniform memory access (UMA) or NUMA, as discussed in Chapter 7, Memory.

A shared system bus, called the *front-side bus*, used by earlier Intel processors is illustrated by the four-processor example in Figure 6.9.

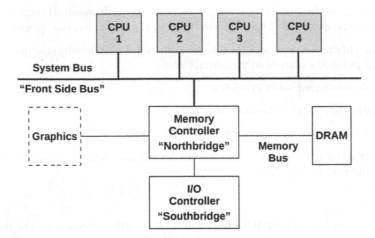

Figure 6.9   Example Intel front-side bus architecture, four-processor

The use of a system bus has scalability problems when the processor count is increased, due to contention for the shared bus resource. Modern servers are typically multiprocessor, NUMA, and use a CPU interconnect instead.

Interconnects can connect components other than processors, such as I/O controllers. Example interconnects include Intel's Quick Path Interconnect (QPI), Intel's Ultra Path Interconnect (UPI), AMD's HyperTransport (HT), ARM's CoreLink Interconnects (there are three different types), and IBM's Coherent Accelerator Processor Interface (CAPI). An example Intel QPI architecture for a four-processor system is shown in Figure 6.10.

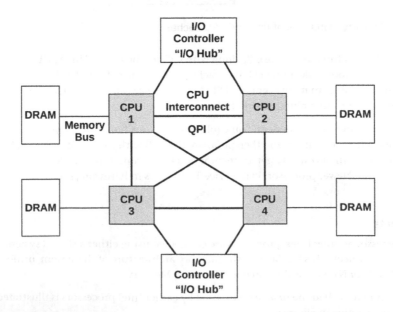

Figure 6.10   Example Intel QPI architecture, four-processor

The private connections between processors allow for non-contended access and also allow higher bandwidths than the shared system bus. Some example speeds for Intel FSB and QPI are shown in Table 6.4 [Intel 09][Mulnix 17].

Table 6.4   Intel CPU interconnect example bandwidths

Intel	Transfer Rate	Width	Bandwidth
FSB (2007)	1.6 GT/s	8 bytes	12.8 Gbytes/s
QPI (2008)	6.4 GT/s	2 bytes	25.6 Gbytes/s
UPI (2017)	10.4 GT/s	2 bytes	41.6 Gbytes/s

To explain how transfer rates can relate to bandwidth, I will explain the QPI example, which is for a 3.2 GHz clock. QPI is *double-pumped*, performing a data transfer on both rising and falling edges of the clock.[4] This doubles the transfer rate (3.2 GHz × 2 = 6.4 GT/s). The final bandwidth of 25.6 Gbytes/s is for both send and receive directions (6.4 GT/s × 2 byte width × 2 directions = 25.6 Gbytes/s).

An interesting detail of QPI is that its cache coherency mode could be tuned in the BIOS, with options including Home Snoop to optimize for memory bandwidth, Early Snoop to optimize for memory latency, and Directory Snoop to improve scalability (it involves tracking what is shared). UPI, which is replacing QPI, only supports Directory Snoop.

Apart from external interconnects, processors have internal interconnects for core communication.

Interconnects are typically designed for high bandwidth, so that they do not become a systemic bottleneck. If they do, performance will degrade as CPU instructions encounter stall cycles for operations that involve the interconnect, such as remote memory I/O. A key indicator for this is a drop in IPC. CPU instructions, cycles, IPC, stall cycles, and memory I/O can be analyzed using CPU performance counters.

Hardware Counters (PMCs)

Performance monitoring counters (PMCs) were summarized as a source of observability statistics in Chapter 4, Observability Tools, Section 4.3.9, Hardware Counters (PMCs). This section describes their CPU implementation in more detail, and provides additional examples.

PMCs are processor registers implemented in hardware that can be programmed to count low-level CPU activity. They typically include counters for the following:

- **CPU cycles:** Including stall cycles and types of stall cycles
- **CPU instructions:** Retired (executed)
- **Level 1, 2, 3 cache accesses:** Hits, misses

---

[4] There is also *quad-pumped*, where data is transferred on the rising edge, peak, falling edge, and trough of the clock cycle. Quad pumping is used by the Intel FSB.

- **Floating-point unit:** Operations

- **Memory I/O:** Reads, writes, stall cycles

- **Resource I/O:** Reads, writes, stall cycles

Each CPU has a small number of registers, usually between two and eight, that can be pro-grammed to record events like these. Those available depend on the processor type and model and are documented in the processor manual.

As a relatively simple example, the Intel P6 family of processors provide performance counters via four model-specific registers (MSRs). Two MSRs are the counters and are read-only. The other two MSRs, called *event-select* MSRs, are used to program the counters and are read-write. The performance counters are 40-bit registers, and the event-select MSRs are 32-bit. The format of the event-select MSRs is shown in Figure 6.11.

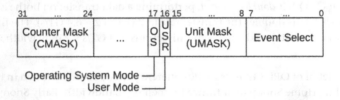

Figure 6.11 Example Intel performance event-select MSR

The counter is identified by the event select and the UMASK. The event select identifies the type of event to count, and the UMASK identifies subtypes or groups of subtypes. The OS and USR bits can be set so that the counter is incremented only while in kernel mode (OS) or user mode (USR), based on the processor protection rings. The CMASK can be set to a threshold of events that must be reached before the counter is incremented.

The Intel processor manual (volume 3B [Intel 19b]) lists the dozens of events that can be counted by their event-select and UMASK values. The selected examples in Table 6.5 provide an *idea* of the different targets (processor functional units) that may be observable, including descriptions from the manual. You will need to refer to your current processor manual to see what you actu-ally have.

Table 6.5 **Selected examples of Intel CPU performance counters**

Event Select	UMASK	Unit	Name	Description
0x43	0x00	Data cache	DATA_MEM_REFS	All loads from any memory type. All stores to any memory type. Each part of a split is counted separately. ... Does not include I/O accesses or other non-memory accesses.

Event Select	UMASK	Unit	Name	Description
0x48	0x00	Data cache	DCU_MISS_ OUTSTANDING	Weighted number of cycles while a DCU miss is outstanding, incremented by the number of outstanding cache misses at any particular time. Cacheable read requests only are considered. ...
0x80	0x00	Instruction fetch unit	IFU_IFETCH	Number of instruction fetches, both cacheable and noncacheable, including UC (uncacheable) fetches.
0x28	0x0F	L2 cache	L2_IFETCH	Number of L2 instruction fetches. ...
0xC1	0x00	Floating-point unit	FLOPS	Number of computational floating-point operations retired. ...
0x7E	0x00	External bus logic	BUS_SNOOP_ STALL	Number of clock cycles during which the bus is snoop stalled.
0xC0	0x00	Instruction decoding and retirement	INST_RETIRED	Number of instructions retired.
0xC8	0x00	Interrupts	HW_INT_RX	Number of hardware interrupts received.
0xC5	0x00	Branches	BR_MISS_PRED_ RETIRED	Number of mis-predicted branches retired.
0xA2	0x00	Stalls	RESOURCE_ STALLS	Incremented by one during every cycle for which there is a resource-related stall. ...
0x79	0x00	Clocks	CPU_CLK_UNHALTED	Number of cycles during which the processor is not halted.

There are many, many more counters, especially for newer processors.

Another processor detail to be aware of is how many hardware counter registers it provides. For example, the Intel Skylake microarchitecture provides three fixed counters per hardware thread, and an additional eight programmable counters per core ("general-purpose"). These are 48-bit counters when read.

For more examples of PMCs, see Table 4.4 in Section 4.3.9 for the Intel architectural set. Section 4.3.9 also provides PMC references for AMD and ARM processor vendors.

GPUs

Graphics processing units (GPUs) were created to support graphical displays, and are now finding use in other workloads including artificial intelligence, machine learning, analytics, image processing, and cryptocurrency mining. For servers and cloud instances, a GPU is a processor-like resource that can execute a portion of a workload, called the *compute kernel*, that is suited to highly parallel data processing such as matrix transformations. General-purpose GPUs from Nvidia using its Compute Unified Device Architecture (CUDA) have seen widespread adoption. CUDA provides APIs and software libraries for using Nvidia GPUs.

While a processor (CPU) may contain a dozen cores, a GPU may contain hundreds or thousands of smaller cores called *streaming processors* (SPs),[5] which each can execute a thread. Since GPU workloads are highly parallel, threads that can execute in parallel are grouped into *thread blocks,* where they may cooperate among themselves. These thread blocks may be executed by groups of SPs called *streaming multiprocessors* (SMs) that also provide other resources including a memory cache. Table 6.6 further compares processors (CPUs) with GPUs [Ather 19].

Table 6.6 **CPUs versus GPUs**

Attribute	CPU	GPU
Package	A processor package plugs into a socket on the system board, connected directly to the system bus or CPU interconnect.	A GPU is typically provided as an expansion card and connected via an expansion bus (e.g., PCIe). They may also be embedded on a system board or in a processor package (on-chip).
Package scalability	Multi-socket configurations, connected via a CPU interconnect (e.g., Intel UPI).	Multi-GPU configurations are possible, connected via a GPU-to-GPU interconnect (e.g., NVIDIA's NVLink).
Cores	A typical processor of today contains 2 to 64 cores.	A GPU may have a similar number of streaming multiprocessors (SMs).
Threads	A typical core may execute two hardware threads (or more, depending on the processor).	An SM may contain dozens or hundreds of streaming processors (SPs). Each SP can only execute one thread.
Caches	Each core has L2 and L2 caches, and may share an L3 cache.	Each SM has a cache, and may share an L2 cache between them.
Clock	High (e.g., 3.4 GHz).	Relatively lower (e.g., 1.0 GHz).

Custom tools must be used for GPU observability. Possible GPU performance metrics include the instructions per cycle, cache hit ratios, and memory bus utilization.

Other Accelerators

Apart from GPUs, be aware that other accelerators may exist for offloading CPU work to faster application-specific integrated circuits. These include field-programmable gate arrays (FPGAs)

---

[5] Nvidia also calls these *CUDA cores* [Verma 20].

and tensor processing units (TPUs). If in use, their usage and performance should be analyzed alongside CPUs, although they typically require custom tooling.

GPUs and FPGAs are used to improve the performance of cryptocurrency mining.

6.4.2 Software

Kernel software to support CPUs includes the scheduler, scheduling classes, and the idle thread.

Scheduler

Key functions of the kernel CPU scheduler are shown in Figure 6.12.

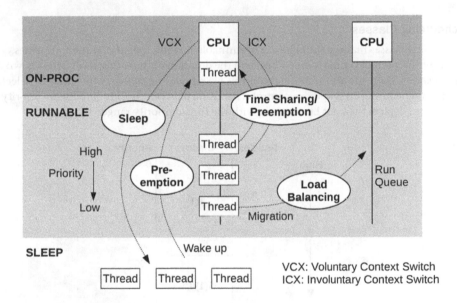

Figure 6.12 Kernel CPU scheduler functions

These functions are:

- **Time sharing:** Multitasking between runnable threads, executing those with the highest priority first.

- **Preemption:** For threads that have become runnable at a high priority, the scheduler can preempt the currently running thread, so that execution of the higher-priority thread can begin immediately.

- **Load balancing:** Moving runnable threads to the run queues of idle or less-busy CPUs.

Figure 6.12 shows run queues, which is how scheduling was originally implemented. The term and mental model are still used to describe waiting tasks. However, the Linux CFS scheduler actually uses a red/black tree of future task execution.

In Linux, time sharing is driven by the system timer interrupt by calling scheduler_tick(), which calls scheduler class functions to manage priorities and the expiration of units of CPU time called *time slices*. Preemption is triggered when threads become runnable and the scheduler class check_preempt_curr() function is called. Thread switching is managed by __schedule(), which selects the highest-priority thread via pick_next_task() for running. Load balancing is performed by the load_balance() function.

The Linux scheduler also uses logic to avoid migrations when the cost is expected to exceed the benefit, preferring to leave busy threads running on the same CPU where the CPU caches should still be warm (CPU affinity). In the Linux source, see the idle_balance() and task_hot() functions.

Note that all these function names may change; refer to the Linux source code, including documentation in the Documentation directory, for more detail.

Scheduling Classes

Scheduling classes manage the behavior of runnable threads, specifically their priorities, whether their on-CPU time is *time-sliced*, and the duration of those *time slices* (also known as *time quanta*). There are also additional controls via scheduling *policies*, which may be selected within a scheduling class and can control scheduling between threads of the same priority. Figure 6.13 depicts them for Linux along with the thread priority range.

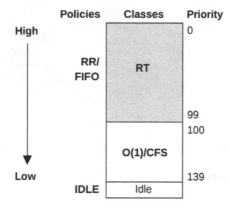

Figure 6.13   Linux thread scheduler priorities

The priority of user-level threads is affected by a user-defined *nice* value, which can be set to lower the priority of unimportant work (so as to be *nice* to other system users). In Linux, the nice value sets the *static priority* of the thread, which is separate from the *dynamic priority* that the scheduler calculates.

For Linux kernels, the scheduling classes are:

- **RT:** Provides fixed and high priorities for real-time workloads. The kernel supports both user- and kernel-level preemption, allowing RT tasks to be dispatched with low latency. The priority range is 0–99 (MAX_RT_PRIO-1).

- **O(1):** The O(1) scheduler was introduced in Linux 2.6 as the default time-sharing scheduler for user processes. The name comes from the algorithm complexity of O(1) (see Chapter 5, Applications, for a summary of big O notation). The prior scheduler contained routines that iterated over all tasks, making it O(n), which became a scalability issue. The O(1) scheduler dynamically improved the priority of I/O-bound over CPU-bound workloads, to reduce the latency of interactive and I/O workloads.

- **CFS:** Completely fair scheduling was added to the Linux 2.6.23 kernel as the default time-sharing scheduler for user processes. The scheduler manages tasks on a red-black tree keyed from the task CPU time, instead of traditional run queues. This allows low CPU consumers to be easily found and executed in preference to CPU-bound workloads, improving the performance of interactive and I/O-bound workloads.

- **Idle:** Runs threads with the lowest possible priority.

- **Deadline:** Added to Linux 3.14, applies earliest deadline first (EDF) scheduling using three parameters: *runtime*, *period*, and *deadline*. A task should receive runtime microseconds of CPU time every period microseconds, and do so within the deadline.

To select a scheduling class, user-level processes select a *scheduling policy* that maps to a class, using either the sched_setscheduler(2) syscall or the chrt(1) tool.

Scheduler policies are:

- **RR:** SCHED_RR is round-robin scheduling. Once a thread has used its time quantum, it is moved to the end of the run queue for that priority level, allowing others of the same priority to run. Uses the RT scheduling class.

- **FIFO:** SCHED_FIFO is first-in, first-out scheduling, which continues running the thread at the head of the run queue until it voluntarily leaves, or until a higher-priority thread arrives. The thread continues to run, even if other threads of the same priority are on the run queue. Uses the RT class.

- **NORMAL:** SCHED_NORMAL (previously known as SCHED_OTHER) is time-sharing scheduling and is the default for user processes. The scheduler dynamically adjusts priority based on the scheduling class. For O(1), the time slice duration is set based on the static priority: longer durations for higher-priority work. For CFS, the time slice is dynamic. Uses the CFS scheduling class.

- **BATCH:** SCHED_BATCH is similar to SCHED_NORMAL, but with the expectation that the thread will be CPU-bound and should not be scheduled to interrupt other I/O-bound interactive work. Uses the CFS scheduling class.

- **IDLE:** SCHED_IDLE uses the Idle scheduling class.

- **DEADLINE:** SCHED_DEADLINE uses the Deadline scheduling class.

Other classes and policies may be added over time. Scheduling algorithms have been researched that are *hyperthreading-aware* [Bulpin 05] and *temperature-aware* [Otto 06], which optimize performance by accounting for additional processor factors.

When there is no thread to run, a special *idle task* (also called *idle thread*) is executed as a placeholder until another thread is runnable.

Idle Thread

Introduced in Chapter 3, the kernel "idle" thread (or *idle task*) runs on-CPU when there is no other runnable thread and has the lowest possible priority. It is usually programmed to inform the processor that CPU execution may either be halted (halt instruction) or throttled down to conserve power. The CPU will wake up on the next hardware interrupt.

NUMA Grouping

Performance on NUMA systems can be significantly improved by making the kernel *NUMA-aware*, so that it can make better scheduling and memory placement decisions. This can automatically detect and create groups of localized CPU and memory resources and organize them in a topology to reflect the NUMA architecture. This topology allows the cost of any memory access to be estimated.

On Linux systems, these are called *scheduling domains*, which are in a topology beginning with the *root domain*.

A manual form of grouping can be performed by the system administrator, either by binding processes to run on one or more CPUs only, or by creating an exclusive set of CPUs for processes to run on. See Section 6.5.10, CPU Binding.

Processor Resource-Aware

The CPU resource topology can also be understood by the kernel so that it can make better scheduling decisions for power management, hardware cache usage, and load balancing.

6.5   Methodology

This section describes various methodologies and exercises for CPU analysis and tuning. Table 6.7 summarizes the topics.

Table 6.7   **CPU performance methodologies**

Section	Methodology	Types
6.5.1	Tools method	Observational analysis
6.5.2	USE method	Observational analysis
6.5.3	Workload characterization	Observational analysis, capacity planning
6.5.4	Profiling	Observational analysis
6.5.5	Cycle analysis	Observational analysis
6.5.6	Performance monitoring	Observational analysis, capacity planning
6.5.7	Static performance tuning	Observational analysis, capacity planning
6.5.8	Priority tuning	Tuning
6.5.9	Resource controls	Tuning
6.5.10	CPU binding	Tuning
6.5.11	Micro-benchmarking	Experimental analysis

See Chapter 2, Methodologies, for more methodologies and the introduction to many of these. You are not expected to use them all; treat this as a cookbook of recipes that may be followed individually or used in combination.

My suggestion is to use the following, in this order: performance monitoring, the USE method, profiling, micro-benchmarking, and static performance tuning.

Section 6.6, Observability Tools, and later sections, show the operating system tools for applying these methodologies.

6.5.1 Tools Method

The tools method is a process of iterating over available tools, examining key metrics that they provide. While this is a simple methodology, it can overlook issues for which the tools provide poor or no visibility, and it can be time-consuming to perform.

For CPUs, the tools method can involve checking the following (Linux):

- **uptime/top**: Check the load averages to see if load is increasing or decreasing over time. Bear this in mind when using the following tools, as load may be changing during your analysis.
- **vmstat**: Run vmstat(1) with a one-second interval and check the system-wide CPU utilization ("us" + "sy"). Utilization approaching 100% increases the likelihood of scheduler latency.
- **mpstat**: Examine statistics per-CPU and check for individual hot (busy) CPUs, identifying a possible thread scalability problem.
- **top**: See which processes and users are the top CPU consumers.
- **pidstat**: Break down the top CPU consumers into user- and system-time.
- **perf/profile**: Profile CPU usage stack traces for both user- or kernel-time, to identify why the CPUs are in use.
- **perf**: Measure IPC as an indicator of cycle-based inefficiencies.
- **showboost/turboboost**: Check the current CPU clock rates, in case they are unusually low.
- **dmesg**: Check for CPU temperature stall messages ("cpu clock throttled").

If an issue is found, examine all fields from the available tools to learn more context. See Section 6.6, Observability Tools, for more about each tool.

6.5.2 USE Method

The USE method can be used to identify bottlenecks and errors across all components early in a performance investigation, before trying deeper and more time-consuming strategies.

For each CPU, check for:

- **Utilization:** The time the CPU was busy (not in the idle thread)
- **Saturation:** The degree to which runnable threads are queued waiting their turn on-CPU
- **Errors:** CPU errors, including correctable errors

You can check errors first since they are typically quick to check and the easiest to interpret. Some processors and operating systems will sense an increase in correctable errors (error-correction code, ECC) and will offline a CPU as a precaution, before an uncorrectable error causes a CPU failure. Checking for these errors can be a matter of checking that all CPUs are still online.

Utilization is usually readily available from operating system tools as *percent busy*. This metric should be examined per CPU, to check for scalability issues. High CPU and core utilization can be understood by using profiling and cycle analysis.

For environments that implement CPU limits or quotas (resource controls; e.g., Linux tasksets and cgroups), as is common in cloud computing environments, CPU utilization should be measured in terms of the imposed limit, in addition to the physical limit. Your system may exhaust its CPU quota well before the physical CPUs reach 100% utilization, encountering saturation earlier than expected.

Saturation metrics are commonly provided system-wide, including as part of load averages. This metric quantifies the degree to which the CPUs are overloaded, or a CPU quota, if present, is used up.

You can follow a similar process for checking the health of GPUs and other accelerators, if in use, depending on available metrics.

6.5.3   Workload Characterization

Characterizing the load applied is important in capacity planning, benchmarking, and simulating workloads. It can also lead to some of the largest performance gains by identifying unnecessary work that can be eliminated.

Basic attributes for characterizing CPU workload are:

- CPU load averages (utilization + saturation)
- User-time to system-time ratio
- Syscall rate
- Voluntary context switch rate
- Interrupt rate

The intent is to characterize the applied load, not the delivered performance. The load averages on some operating systems (e.g., Solaris) show CPU demand only, making them a primary metric for CPU workload characterization. On Linux, however, load averages include other load types. See the example and further explanation in Section 6.6.1, uptime.

The rate metrics are a little harder to interpret, as they reflect both the applied load and to some degree the delivered performance, which can throttle their rate.[6]

The user-time to system-time ratio shows the type of load applied, as introduced earlier in Section 6.3.9, User Time/Kernel Time. High user time rates are due to applications spending time

---

[6] E.g., imagine finding that a given batch computing workload has higher syscall rates when run on faster CPUs, even though the workload is the same. It completes sooner!

performing their own compute. High system time shows time spent in the kernel instead, which may be further understood by the syscall and interrupt rate. I/O-bound workloads have higher system time, syscalls, and higher voluntary context switches than CPU-bound workloads as threads block waiting for I/O.

Here is an example workload description, designed to show how these attributes can be expressed together:

> On an average 48-CPU application server, the load average varies between 30 and 40 during the day. The user/system ratio is 95/5, as this is a CPU-intensive workload. There are around 325 K syscalls/s, and around 80 K voluntary context switches/s.

These characteristics can vary over time as different load is encountered.

Advanced Workload Characterization/Checklist

Additional details may be included to characterize the workload. These are listed here as questions for consideration, which may also serve as a checklist when studying CPU issues thoroughly:

- What is the CPU utilization system-wide? Per CPU? Per core?
- How parallel is the CPU load? Is it single-threaded? How many threads?
- Which applications or users are using the CPUs? How much?
- Which kernel threads are using the CPUs? How much?
- What is the CPU usage of interrupts?
- What is the CPU interconnect utilization?
- Why are the CPUs being used (user- and kernel-level call paths)?
- What types of stall cycles are encountered?

See Chapter 2, Methodologies, for a higher-level summary of this methodology and the characteristics to measure (who, why, what, how). The sections that follow expand upon the last two questions in this list: how call paths can be analyzed using profiling, and stall cycles using cycle analysis.

6.5.4 Profiling

Profiling builds a picture of the target for study. CPU profiling can be performed in different ways, typically either:

- **Timer-based sampling:** Collecting timer-based samples of the currently running function or stack trace. A typical rate used is 99 Hertz (samples per second) per CPU. This provides a coarse view of CPU usage, with enough detail for large and small issues. 99 is used to avoid lock-step sampling that may occur at 100 Hertz, which would produce a skewed profile. If needed, the timer rate can be lowered and the time span enlarged until the overhead is negligible and suitable for production use.

- **Function tracing**: Instrumenting all or some function calls to measure their duration. This provides a fine-level view, but the overhead can be prohibitive for production use, often 10% or more, because function tracing adds instrumentation to every function call.

Most profilers used in production, and those in this book, use timer-based sampling. This is pictured in Figure 6.14, where an application calls function A(), which calls function B(), and so on, while stack trace samples are collected. See Chapter 3, Operating Systems, Section 3.2.7, Stacks, for an explanation of stack traces and how to read them.

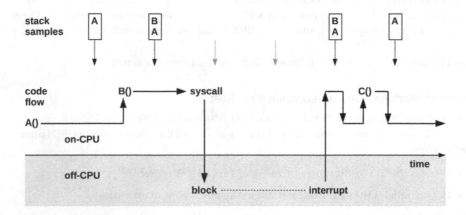

Figure 6.14 Sample-based CPU profiling

Figure 6.14 shows how samples are only collected when the process is on-CPU: two samples show function A() on-CPU, and two samples show function B() on-CPU called by A(). The time off-CPU during a syscall was not sampled. Also, the short-lived function C() was entirely missed by sampling.

Kernels typically maintain two stack traces for processes: a user-level stack and a kernel stack when in kernel context (e.g., syscalls). For a complete CPU profile, the profiler must record both stacks when available.

Apart from sampling stack traces, profilers can also record just the instruction pointer, which shows the on-CPU function and instruction offset. Sometimes this is sufficient for solving issues, without the extra overhead of collecting stack traces.

Sample Processing

As described in Chapter 5, a typical CPU profile at Netflix collects user and kernel stack traces at 49 Hertz across (around) 32 CPUs for 30 seconds: this produces a total of 47,040 samples, and presents two challenges:

1. **Storage I/O**: Profilers typically write samples to a profile file, which can then be read and examined in different ways. However, writing so many samples to the file system can generate storage I/O that perturbs the performance of the production application. The

BPF-based profile(8) tool solves the storage I/O problem by summarizing the samples in kernel memory, and only emitting the summary. No intermediate profile file is used.

2. **Comprehension**: It is impractical to read 47,040 multi-line stack traces one by one: summaries and visualizations must be used to make sense of the profile. A commonly used stack trace visualization is *flame graphs*, some examples of which are shown in earlier chapters (1 and 5); and there are more examples in this chapter.

Figure 6.15 shows the overall steps to generate CPU flame graphs from perf(1) and profile, solving the comprehension problem. It also shows how the storage I/O problem is solved: profile(8) does not use an intermediate file, saving overhead. The exact commands used are listed in Section 6.6.13, perf.

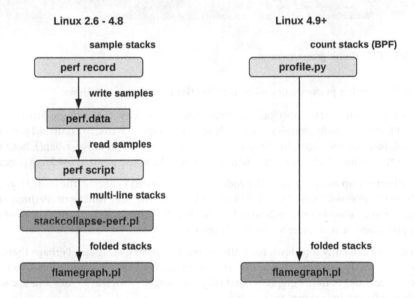

Figure 6.15   CPU flame graph generation

While the BPF-based approach has lower overhead, the perf(1) approach saves the raw samples (with timestamps), which can be reprocessed using different tools, including FlameScope (Section 6.7.4).

Profile Interpretation

Once you have collected and summarized or visualized a CPU profile, your next task is to understand it and search for performance problems. A CPU flame graph excerpt is shown in Figure 6.16, and the instructions for reading this visualization are in Section 6.7.3, Flame Graphs. How would you summarize the profile?

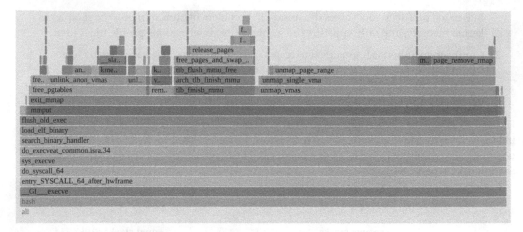

Figure 6.16   CPU flame graph excerpt

My method for finding performance wins in a CPU flame graphs is as follows:

1. Look top-down (leaf to root) for large "plateaus." These show that a single function is on-CPU during many samples, and can lead to some quick wins. In Figure 6.16, there are two plateaus on the right, in unmap_page_range() and page_remove_rmap(), both related to memory pages. Perhaps a quick win is to switch the application to use large pages.

2. Look bottom-up to understand the code hierarchy. In this example, the bash(1) shell was calling the execve(2) syscall, which eventually called the page functions. Perhaps an even bigger win is to avoid execve(2) somehow, such as by using bash builtins instead of external processes, or switching to another language.

3. Look more carefully top-down for scattered but common CPU usage. Perhaps there are many small frames related to the same problem, such as lock contention. Inverting the merge order of flame graphs so that they are merged from leaf to root and become *icicle graphs* can help reveal these cases.

Another example of interpreting a CPU flame graph is provided in Chapter 5, Applications, Section 5.4.1, CPU Profiling.

Further Information

The commands for CPU profiling and flame graphs are provided in Section 6.6, Observability Tools. Also see Section 5.4.1 on CPU analysis of applications, and Section 5.6, Gotchas, which describes common profiling problems with missing stack traces and symbols.

For the usage of specific CPU resources, such as caches and interconnects, profiling can use PMC-based event triggers instead of timed intervals. This is described in the next section.

6.5.5 Cycle Analysis

You can use Performance Monitoring Counters (PMCs) to understand CPU utilization at the cycle level. This may reveal that cycles are spent stalled on Level 1, 2, or 3 cache misses, memory or resource I/O, or spent on floating-point operations or other activity. This information may show performance wins you can achieve by adjusting compiler options or changing the code.

Begin cycle analysis by measuring IPC (inverse of CPI). If IPC is low, continue to investigate types of stall cycles. If IPC is high, look for ways in the code to reduce instructions performed. The values for "high" or "low" IPC depend on your processor: low could be less than 0.2, and high could be greater than 1. You can get a sense of these values by performing known workloads that are either memory I/O-intensive or instruction-intensive, and measuring the resulting IPC for each.

Apart from measuring counter values, PMCs can be configured to interrupt the kernel on the overflow of a given value. For example, at every 10,000 Level 3 cache misses, the kernel could be interrupted to gather a stack backtrace. Over time, the kernel builds a profile of the code paths that are causing Level 3 cache misses, without the prohibitive overhead of measuring every single miss. This is typically used by integrated developer environment (IDE) software, to annotate code with the locations that are causing memory I/O and stall cycles.

As described in Chapter 4, Observability Tools, Section 4.3.9 under PMC Challenges, overflow sampling can miss recording the correct instruction due to skid and out-of-order execution. On Intel the solution is PEBS, which is supported by the Linux perf(1) tool.

Cycle analysis is an advanced activity that can take days to perform with command-line tools, as demonstrated in Section 6.6, Observability Tools. You should also expect to spend some quality time with your CPU vendor's processor manuals. Performance analyzers such as Intel vTune [Intel 20b] and AMD uprof [AMD 20] can save time as they are programmed to find the PMCs of interest to you.

6.5.6 Performance Monitoring

Performance monitoring can identify active issues and patterns of behavior over time. Key metrics for CPUs are:

- **Utilization**: Percent busy
- **Saturation**: Either run-queue length or scheduler latency

Utilization should be monitored on a per-CPU basis to identify thread scalability issues. For environments that implement CPU limits or quotas (resource controls), such as cloud computing environments, CPU usage compared to these limits should also be recorded.

Choosing the right interval to measure and archive is a challenge in monitoring CPU usage. Some monitoring tools use five-minute intervals, which can hide the existence of shorter bursts of CPU utilization. Per-second measurements are preferable, but you should be aware that there can be bursts even within one second. These can be identified from saturation, and examined using FlameScope (Section 6.7.4), which was created for subsecond analysis.

6.5.7 Static Performance Tuning

Static performance tuning focuses on issues of the configured environment. For CPU perfor-mance, examine the following aspects of the static configuration:

- How many CPUs are available for use? Are they cores? Hardware threads?
- Are GPUs or other accelerators available and in use?
- Is the CPU architecture single- or multiprocessor?
- What is the size of the CPU caches? Are they shared?
- What is the CPU clock speed? Is it dynamic (e.g., Intel Turbo Boost and SpeedStep)? Are those dynamic features enabled in the BIOS?
- What other CPU-related features are enabled or disabled in the BIOS? E.g., turboboost, bus settings, power saving settings?
- Are there performance issues (bugs) with this processor model? Are they listed in the processor errata sheet?
- What is the microcode version? Does it include performance-impacting mitigations for security vulnerabilities (e.g., Spectre/Meltdown)?
- Are there performance issues (bugs) with this BIOS firmware version?
- Are there software-imposed CPU usage limits (resource controls) present? What are they?

The answers to these questions may reveal previously overlooked configuration choices.

The last question is especially true for cloud computing environments, where CPU usage is commonly limited.

6.5.8 Priority Tuning

Unix has always provided a nice(2) system call for adjusting process priority, which sets a nice-ness value. Positive nice values result in lower process priority (nicer), and negative values—which can be set only by the superuser (root)[7]—result in higher priority. A nice(1) command became available to launch programs with nice values, and a renice(1M) command was later added (in BSD) to adjust the nice value of already running processes. The man page from Unix 4th edition provides this example [TUHS 73]:

> The value of 16 is recommended to users who wish to execute long-running programs without flak from the administration.

The nice value is still useful today for adjusting process priority. This is most effective when there is contention for CPUs, causing scheduler latency for high-priority work. Your task is to identify low-priority work, which may include monitoring agents and scheduled backups, that can be modified to start with a nice value. Analysis may also be performed to check that the tuning is effective, and that the scheduler latency remains low for high-priority work.

---

[7] Since Linux 2.6.12, a "nice ceiling" can be modified per process, allowing non-root processes to have lower nice values. E.g., using: `prlimit --nice=-19 -p PID`.

Beyond nice, the operating system may provide more advanced controls for process priority such as changing the scheduler class and scheduler policy, and tunable parameters. Linux includes a *real-time scheduling class*, which can allow processes to preempt all other work. While this can eliminate scheduler latency (other than for other real-time processes and interrupts), make sure that you understand the consequences. If the real-time application encounters a bug where multiple threads enter an infinite loop, it can cause all CPUs to become unavailable for all other work—including the administrative shell required to manually fix the problem.[8]

6.5.9 Resource Controls

The operating system may provide fine-grained controls for allocating CPU cycles to processes or groups of processes. These may include fixed limits for CPU utilization and shares for a more flexible approach—allowing idle CPU cycles to be consumed based on a share value. How these work is implementation-specific and discussed in Section 6.9, Tuning.

6.5.10 CPU Binding

Another way to tune CPU performance involves binding processes and threads to individual CPUs, or collections of CPUs. This can increase CPU cache warmth for the process, improving its memory I/O performance. For NUMA systems it also improves memory locality, further improving performance.

There are generally two ways this is performed:

- **CPU binding**: Configuring a process to run only on a single CPU, or only on one CPU from a defined set.

- **Exclusive CPU sets**: Partitioning a set of CPUs that can be used only by the process(es) assigned to them. This can further improve CPU cache warmth, as when the process is idle other processes cannot use those CPUs.

On Linux-based systems, the exclusive CPU sets approach can be implemented using *cpusets*. Configuration examples are provided in Section 6.9, Tuning.

6.5.11 Micro-Benchmarking

Tools for CPU micro-benchmarking typically measure the time taken to perform a simple operation many times. The operation may be based on:

- **CPU instructions**: Integer arithmetic, floating-point operations, memory loads and stores, branch and other instructions

- **Memory access**: To investigate latency of different CPU caches and main memory throughput

- **Higher-level languages**: Similar to CPU instruction testing, but written in a higher-level interpreted or compiled language

---

[8] Linux has a solution since 2.6.25 for this problem: RLIMIT_RTTIME, which sets a limit in microseconds of CPU time a real-time thread may consume before making a blocking syscall.

- **Operating system operations:** Testing system library and system call functions that are CPU-bound, such as getpid(2) and process creation

An early example of a CPU benchmark is Whetstone by the National Physical Laboratory, written in 1972 in Algol 60 and intended to simulate a scientific workload. The Dhrystone benchmark was developed in 1984 to simulate integer workloads of the time, and became a popular means to compare CPU performance. These, and various Unix benchmarks including process creation and pipe throughput, were included in a collection called *UnixBench*, originally from Monash University and published by *BYTE* magazine [Hinnant 84]. More recent CPU benchmarks have been created to test compression speeds, prime number calculation, encryption, and encoding.

Whichever benchmark you use, when comparing results between systems, it's important that you understand what is really being tested. Benchmarks like those listed earlier often end up testing differences in compiler optimizations between compiler versions, rather than the benchmark code or CPU speed. Many benchmarks execute single-threaded, and their results lose meaning in systems with multiple CPUs. (A four-CPU system may benchmark slightly faster than an eight-CPU system, but the latter is likely to deliver much greater throughput when given enough parallel runnable threads.)

For more on benchmarking, see Chapter 12, Benchmarking.

6.6   Observability Tools

This section introduces CPU performance observability tools for Linux-based operating systems. See the previous section for methodologies to follow when using them.

The tools in this section are listed in Table 6.8.

Table 6.8   **Linux CPU observability tools**

Section	Tool	Description
6.6.1	uptime	Load averages
6.6.2	vmstat	Includes system-wide CPU averages
6.6.3	mpstat	Per-CPU statistics
6.6.4	sar	Historical statistics
6.6.5	ps	Process status
6.6.6	top	Monitor per-process/thread CPU usage
6.6.7	pidstat	Per-process/thread CPU breakdowns
6.6.8	time, ptime	Time a command, with CPU breakdowns
6.6.9	turboboost	Show CPU clock rate and other states
6.6.10	showboost	Show CPU clock rate and turbo boost
6.6.11	pmcarch	Show high-level CPU cycle usage
6.6.12	tlbstat	Summarize TLB cycles

Section	Tool	Description
6.6.13	perf	CPU profiling and PMC analysis
6.6.14	profile	Sample CPU stack traces
6.6.15	cpudist	Summarize on-CPU time
6.6.16	runqlat	Summarize CPU run queue latency
6.6.17	runqlen	Summarize CPU run queue length
6.6.18	softirqs	Summarize soft interrupt time
6.6.19	hardirqs	Summarize hard interrupt time
6.6.20	bpftrace	Tracing programs for CPU analysis

This is a selection of tools and capabilities to support Section 6.5, Methodology. We begin with traditional tools for CPU statistics, then proceed to tools for deeper analysis using code-path profiling, CPU cycle analysis, and tracing tools. Some of the traditional tools are likely available on (and sometimes originated on) other Unix-like operating systems, including: uptime(1), vmstat(8), mpstat(1), sar(1), ps(1), top(1), and time(1). The tracing tools are based on BPF and the BCC and bpftrace frontends (Chapter 15), and are: profile(8), cpudist(8), runqlat(8), runqlen(8), softirqs(8), and hardirqs(8).

See the documentation for each tool, including its man pages, for full references for its features.

6.6.1   uptime

uptime(1) is one of several commands that print the system *load averages*:

```
$ uptime
  9:04pm  up 268 day(s), 10:16,  2 users,  load average: 7.76, 8.32, 8.60
```

The last three numbers are the 1-, 5-, and 15-minute load averages. By comparing the three numbers, you can determine if the load is increasing, decreasing, or steady during the last 15 minutes (or so). This can be useful to know: if you are responding to a production performance issue and find that the load is decreasing, you may have missed the issue; if the load is increasing, the issue may be getting worse!

The following sections explain load averages in more detail, but they are only a starting point, so you shouldn't spend more than five minutes considering them before moving on to other metrics.

Load Averages

The load averages indicate the demand for system resources: higher means more demand. On some operating systems (e.g., Solaris) the load averages show CPU demand, as did early versions of Linux. But in 1993, Linux changed load averages to show system-wide demand: CPUs, disks, and other resources.[9] This was implemented by including threads in the TASK_UNINTERRUPTIBLE thread state, shown by some tools as state "D" (this state was mentioned in Chapter 5, Applications, Section 5.4.5, Thread State Analysis).

The *load* is measured as the current resource usage (utilization) plus queued requests (saturation). Imagine a car toll plaza: you could measure the load at various points during the day by counting how many cars were being serviced (utilization) plus how many cars were queued (saturation).

The *average* is an exponentially damped moving average, which reflects load beyond the 1-, 5-, and 15-minute times (the times are actually constants used in the exponential moving sum [Myer 73]). Figure 6.17 shows the results of a simple experiment where a single CPU-bound thread was launched and the load averages plotted.

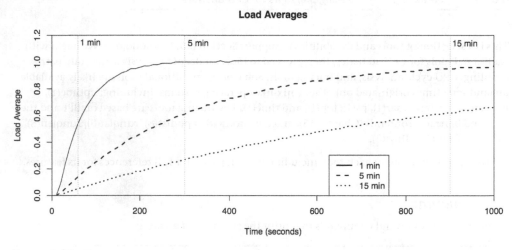

Figure 6.17   Exponentially damped load averages

By the 1-, 5-, and 15-minute marks, the load averages had reached about 61% of the known load of 1.0.

Load averages were introduced to Unix in early BSD and were based on scheduler average queue length and load averages commonly used by earlier operating systems (CTSS, Multics [Saltzer 70], TENEX [Bobrow 72]). They were described in RFC 546 [Thomas 73]:

> [1] The TENEX load average is a measure of CPU demand. The load average is an average of the number of runable processes over a given time period. For example, an hourly load average of 10 would mean that (for a single CPU system) at any time during that hour one could expect to see 1 process running and 9 others ready to run (i.e., not blocked for I/O) waiting for the CPU.

---

[9]The change happened so long ago that the reason for it had been forgotten and was undocumented, predating the Linux history in git and other resources; I eventually found the original patch in an online tarball from an old mail system archive. Matthias Urlichs made that change, pointing out that if demand moved from CPUs to disks, then the load averages should stay the same because the demand hadn't changed [Gregg 17c]. I emailed him (for the first time ever) about his 24-year old change, and got a reply in one hour!

As a modern example, consider a 64-CPU system with a load average of 128. If the load was CPU only, it would mean that on average there is always one thread running on each CPU, and one thread waiting for each CPU. The same system with a CPU load average of 20 would indicate significant headroom, as it could run another 44 CPU-bound threads before all CPUs are busy. (Some companies monitor a normalized load average metric, where it is automatically divided by the CPU count, allowing it to be interpreted without knowing the CPU count.)

Pressure Stall Information (PSI)

In the first edition of this book, I described how load averages could be provided for each resource type to aid interpretation. An interface has now been added in Linux 4.20 that provides such a breakdown: pressure stall information (PSI), which gives averages for CPU, memory, and I/O. The average shows the percent of time something was stalled on a resource (saturation only). This is compared with load averages in Table 6.9.

Table 6.9 **Linux load averages versus pressure stall information**

Attribute	Load Averages	Pressure Stall Information
Resources	System-wide	cpu, memory, io (each individually)
Metric	Number of busy and queued tasks	Percent of time stalled (waiting)
Times	1 min, 5 min, 15 min	10 s, 60 s, 300 s
Average	Exponentially damped moving sum	Exponentially damped moving sum

Table 6.10 shows what the metric shows for different scenarios:

Table 6.10 **Linux load average examples versus pressure stall information**

Example Scenario	Load Averages	Pressure Stall Information
2 CPUs, 1 busy thread	1.0	0.0
2 CPUs, 2 busy threads	2.0	0.0
2 CPUs, 3 busy threads	3.0	50.0
2 CPUs, 4 busy threads	4.0	100.0
2 CPUs, 5 busy threads	5.0	100.0

For example, showing the 2 CPU with 3 busy threads scenario:

```
$ uptime
 07:51:13 up 4 days,  9:56,  2 users,  load average: 3.00, 3.00, 2.55
$ cat /proc/pressure/cpu
some avg10=50.00 avg60=50.00 avg300=49.70 total=1031438206
```

This 50.0 value means a thread ("some") has stalled 50% of the time. The io and memory metrics include a second line for when all non-idle threads have stalled ("full"). PSI best answers the question: how likely is it that a task will have to wait on the resources?

Whether you use load averages or PSI, you should quickly move to more detailed metrics to understand load, such as those provided by vmstat(1) and mpstat(1).

6.6.2   vmstat

The virtual memory statistics command, vmstat(8), prints system-wide CPU averages in the last few columns, and a count of runnable threads in the first column. Here is example output from the Linux version:

```
$ vmstat 1
procs -----------memory---------- ---swap-- -----io---- -system-- ------cpu-----
 r  b   swpd   free   buff  cache   si   so    bi    bo   in   cs us sy id wa st
15  0      0 451732  70588 866628    0    0     1    10   43   38  2  1 97  0  0
15  0      0 450968  70588 866628    0    0     0   612 1064 2969 72 28  0  0  0
15  0      0 450660  70588 866632    0    0     0     0  961 2932 72 28  0  0  0
15  0      0 450952  70588 866632    0    0     0     0 1015 3238 74 26  0  0  0
[...]
```

The first line of output is supposed to be the summary-since-boot. However, on Linux the procs and memory columns begin by showing the current state. (Perhaps one day they will be fixed.) CPU-related columns are:

- **r**: Run-queue length—the total number of runnable threads
- **us**: User-time percent
- **sy**: System-time (kernel) percent
- **id**: Idle percent
- **wa**: Wait I/O percent, which measures CPU idle when threads are blocked on disk I/O
- **st**: Stolen percent, which for virtualized environments shows CPU time spent servicing other tenants

All of these values are system-wide averages across all CPUs, with the exception of r, which is the total.

On Linux, the r column is the total number of tasks waiting *plus* those running. For other operating systems (e.g., Solaris) the r column only shows tasks waiting, not those running. The original vmstat(1) by Bill Joy and Ozalp Babaoglu for 3BSD in 1979 begins with an RQ column for the number of runnable *and* running processes, as the Linux vmstat(8) currently does.

6.6.3 mpstat

The multiprocessor statistics tool, mpstat(1), can report statistics per CPU. Here is example output from the Linux version:

```
$ mpstat -P ALL 1
Linux 5.3.0-1009-aws (ip-10-0-239-218)   02/01/20      _x86_64_      (2 CPU)

18:00:32  CPU  %usr  %nice   %sys %iowait   %irq  %soft %steal %guest %gnice  %idle
18:00:33  all 32.16   0.00  61.81    0.00   0.00   0.00   0.00   0.00   0.00   6.03
18:00:33    0 32.00   0.00  64.00    0.00   0.00   0.00   0.00   0.00   0.00   4.00
18:00:33    1 32.32   0.00  59.60    0.00   0.00   0.00   0.00   0.00   0.00   8.08

18:00:33  CPU  %usr  %nice   %sys %iowait   %irq  %soft %steal %guest %gnice  %idle
18:00:34  all 33.83   0.00  61.19    0.00   0.00   0.00   0.00   0.00   0.00   4.98
18:00:34    0 34.00   0.00  62.00    0.00   0.00   0.00   0.00   0.00   0.00   4.00
18:00:34    1 33.66   0.00  60.40    0.00   0.00   0.00   0.00   0.00   0.00   5.94
[...]
```

The -P ALL option was used to print the per-CPU report. By default, mpstat(1) prints only the system-wide summary line (all). The columns are:

- **CPU**: Logical CPU ID, or all for summary
- **%usr**: User-time, excluding %nice
- **%nice**: User-time for processes with a nice'd priority
- **%sys**: System-time (kernel)
- **%iowait**: I/O wait
- **%irq**: Hardware interrupt CPU usage
- **%soft**: Software interrupt CPU usage
- **%steal**: Time spent servicing other tenants
- **%guest**: CPU time spent in guest virtual machines
- **%gnice**: CPU time to run a niced guest
- **%idle**: Idle

Key columns are %usr, %sys, and %idle. These identify CPU usage per CPU and show the user-time/kernel-time ratio (see Section 6.3.9, User-Time/Kernel-Time). This can also identify "hot" CPUs—those running at 100% utilization (%usr + %sys) while others are not—which can be caused by single-threaded application workloads or device interrupt mapping.

Note that the CPU times reported by this and other tools that source the same kernel statistics (/proc/stat etc.), and the accuracy of these statistics depends on the kernel configuration. See the CPU Statistic Accuracy heading in Chapter 4, Observability Tools, Section 4.3.1, /proc.

6.6.4   sar

The system activity reporter, sar(1), can be used to observe current activity and can be configured to archive and report historical statistics. It was introduced in Chapter 4, Observability Tools, Section 4.4, sar, and is mentioned in other chapters as appropriate.

The Linux version provides the following options for CPU analysis:

- **-P ALL**: Same as mpstat -P ALL
- **-u**: Same as mpstat(1)'s default output: system-wide average only
- **-q**: Includes run-queue size as runq-sz (waiting plus running, the same as vmstat(1)'s r) and load averages

sar(1) data collection may be enabled so that these metrics can be observed from the past. See Section 4.4, sar, for more detail.

6.6.5   ps

The process status command, ps(1), can list details on all processes, including CPU usage statistics. For example:

```
$ ps aux
USER        PID %CPU %MEM    VSZ   RSS TTY       STAT START   TIME COMMAND
root          1  0.0  0.0  23772  1948 ?         Ss   2012   0:04 /sbin/init
root          2  0.0  0.0      0     0 ?         S    2012   0:00 [kthreadd]
root          3  0.0  0.0      0     0 ?         S    2012   0:26 [ksoftirqd/0]
root          4  0.0  0.0      0     0 ?         S    2012   0:00 [migration/0]
root          5  0.0  0.0      0     0 ?         S    2012   0:00 [watchdog/0]
[...]
web       11715 11.3  0.0 632700 11540 pts/0     Sl   01:36  0:27 node indexer.js
web       11721 96.5  0.1 638116 52108 pts/1     Rl+  01:37  3:33 node proxy.js
[...]
```

This style of operation originated from BSD, as can be recognized by the lack of a dash before the aux options. These list all users (a), with extended user details (u), and include processes without a terminal (x). The terminal is shown in the teletype (TTY) column.

A different style, from SVR4, uses options preceded by a dash:

```
$ ps -ef
UID         PID  PPID  C STIME TTY           TIME CMD
root          1     0  0 Nov13 ?         00:00:04 /sbin/init
root          2     0  0 Nov13 ?         00:00:00 [kthreadd]
root          3     2  0 Nov13 ?         00:00:00 [ksoftirqd/0]
root          4     2  0 Nov13 ?         00:00:00 [migration/0]
root          5     2  0 Nov13 ?         00:00:00 [watchdog/0]
[...]
```

This lists every process (-e) with full details (-f). Various other options are available for ps(1) including -o to customize the output and columns shown.

Key columns for CPU usage are TIME and %CPU (earlier example).

The TIME column shows the total CPU time consumed by the process (user + system) since it was created, in hours:minutes:seconds.

On Linux, the %CPU column from the first example shows the average CPU utilization over the lifetime of the process, summed across all CPUs. A single-threaded process that has always been CPU-bound will report 100%. A two-thread CPU-bound process will report 200%. Other operating systems may normalize %CPU to the CPU count so that its maximum is 100%, and they may only show recent or current CPU usage rather than the average over the lifetime. On Linux, to see the current CPU usage of processes, you can use top(1).

6.6.6 top

top(1) was created by William LeFebvre in 1984 for BSD. He was inspired by the VMS command MONITOR PROCESS/TOPCPU, which showed the top CPU-consuming jobs with CPU percentages and an ASCII bar chart histogram (but not columns of data).

The top(1) command monitors top running processes, updating the screen at regular intervals. For example, on Linux:

```
$ top
top - 01:38:11 up 63 days,  1:17,  2 users,  load average: 1.57, 1.81, 1.77
Tasks: 256 total,   2 running, 254 sleeping,   0 stopped,   0 zombie
Cpu(s):  2.0%us,  3.6%sy,  0.0%ni, 94.2%id,  0.0%wa,  0.0%hi,  0.2%si,  0.0%st
Mem:  49548744k total, 16746572k used, 32802172k free,   182900k buffers
Swap: 100663292k total,       0k used, 100663292k free, 14925240k cached

  PID USER      PR  NI  VIRT  RES  SHR S %CPU %MEM    TIME+  COMMAND
11721 web       20   0  623m  50m 4984 R   93  0.1  0:59.50 node
11715 web       20   0  619m  20m 4916 S   25  0.0  0:07.52 node
   10 root      20   0     0    0    0 S    1  0.0 248:52.56 ksoftirqd/2
   51 root      20   0     0    0    0 S    0  0.0  0:35.66 events/0
11724 admin     20   0 19412 1444  960 R    0  0.0  0:00.07 top
    1 root      20   0 23772 1948 1296 S    0  0.0  0:04.35 init
```

A system-wide summary is at the top and a process/task listing at the bottom, sorted by the top CPU consumer by default. The system-wide summary includes the load averages and CPU states: %us, %sy, %ni, %id, %wa, %hi, %si, %st. These states are equivalent to those printed by mpstat(1), as described earlier, and are averaged across all CPUs.

CPU usage is shown by the TIME and %CPU columns. TIME is the total CPU time consumed by the process at a resolution of hundredths of a second. For example, "1:36.53" means 1 minute and 36.53 seconds of on-CPU time in total. Some versions of top(1) provide an optional "cumulative time" mode, which includes the CPU time from child processes that have exited.

The %CPU column shows the total CPU utilization for the current screen update interval. On Linux, this is not normalized by the CPU count, and so a two-thread CPU-bound process will report 200%; top(1) calls this "Irix mode," after its behavior on IRIX. This can be switched to "Solaris mode" (by pressing I to toggle the modes), which divides the CPU usage by the CPU count. In that case, the two-thread process on a 16-CPU server would report CPU as 12.5%.

Though top(1) is often a tool for beginning performance analysts, you should be aware that the CPU usage of top(1) itself can become significant and place top(1) as the top CPU-consuming process! This has been due to the system calls it uses to read /proc—open(2), read(2), close(2)— and calling these over many processes. Some versions of top(1) on other operating systems have reduced the overhead by leaving file descriptors open and calling pread(2).

There is a variant of top(1) called htop(1), which provides more interactive features, customizations, and ASCII bar charts for CPU usage. It also calls four times as many syscalls, perturbing the system even further. I rarely use it.

Since top(1) takes snapshots of /proc, it can miss short-lived processes that exit before a snapshot is taken. This commonly happens during software builds, where the CPUs can be heavily loaded by many short-lived tools from the build process. A variant of top(1) for Linux, called atop(1), uses process accounting to catch the presence of short-lived processes, which it includes in its display.

6.6.7 pidstat

The Linux pidstat(1) tool prints CPU usage by process or thread, including user- and system-time breakdowns. By default, a rolling output is printed of only active processes. For example:

```
$ pidstat 1
Linux 2.6.35-32-server (dev7)    11/12/12        _x86_64_       (16 CPU)

22:24:42         PID    %usr %system  %guest     %CPU   CPU  Command
22:24:43         7814   0.00    1.98    0.00     1.98     3  tar
22:24:43         7815  97.03    2.97    0.00   100.00    11  gzip

22:24:43         PID    %usr %system  %guest     %CPU   CPU  Command
22:24:44          448   0.00    1.00    0.00     1.00     0  kjournald
22:24:44         7814   0.00    2.00    0.00     2.00     3  tar
22:24:44         7815  97.00    3.00    0.00   100.00    11  gzip
22:24:44         7816   0.00    2.00    0.00     2.00     2  pidstat
[...]
```

This example captured a system backup, involving a tar(1) command to read files from the file system, and the gzip(1) command to compress them. The user-time for gzip(1) is high, as expected, as it becomes CPU-bound in compression code. The tar(1) command spends more time in the kernel, reading from the file system.

The -p ALL option can be used to print all processes, including those that are idle. -t prints per-thread statistics. Other pidstat(1) options are included in other chapters of this book.

6.6.8   time, ptime

The time(1) command can be used to run programs and report CPU usage. It is provided in the operating system under /usr/bin, and as a shell built-in.

This example runs time twice on a cksum(1) command, calculating the checksum of a large file:

```
$ time cksum ubuntu-19.10-live-server-amd64.iso
1044945083 883949568 ubuntu-19.10-live-server-amd64.iso

real    0m5.590s
user    0m2.776s
sys     0m0.359s
$ time cksum ubuntu-19.10-live-server-amd64.iso
1044945083 883949568 ubuntu-19.10-live-server-amd64.iso

real    0m2.857s
user    0m2.733s
sys     0m0.114s
```

The first run took 5.6 seconds, of which 2.8 seconds was in user mode, calculating the checksum. There was 0.4 seconds in system-time, spanning the system calls required to read the file. There is a missing 2.4 seconds (5.6 – 2.8 – 0.4), which is likely time spent blocked on disk I/O reads as this file was only partially cached. The second run completed more quickly, in 2.9 seconds, with almost no blocked time. This is expected, as the file may be fully cached in main memory for the second run.

On Linux, the /usr/bin/time version supports verbose details. For example:

```
$ /usr/bin/time -v cp fileA fileB
        Command being timed: "cp fileA fileB"
        User time (seconds): 0.00
        System time (seconds): 0.26
        Percent of CPU this job got: 24%
        Elapsed (wall clock) time (h:mm:ss or m:ss): 0:01.08
        Average shared text size (kbytes): 0
        Average unshared data size (kbytes): 0
        Average stack size (kbytes): 0
        Average total size (kbytes): 0
        Maximum resident set size (kbytes): 3792
        Average resident set size (kbytes): 0
        Major (requiring I/O) page faults: 0
        Minor (reclaiming a frame) page faults: 294
        Voluntary context switches: 1082
        Involuntary context switches: 1
        Swaps: 0
```

```
        File system inputs: 275432
        File system outputs: 275432
        Socket messages sent: 0
        Socket messages received: 0
        Signals delivered: 0
        Page size (bytes): 4096
        Exit status: 0
```

The –v option is not typically provided in the shell built-in version.

6.6.9   turbostat

turbostat(1) is a model-specific register (MSR)–based tool that shows the state of the CPUs, and is often available in a linux-tools-common package. MSRs were mentioned in Chapter 4, Observability Tools, Section 4.3.10, Other Observability Sources. Here is some sample output:

```
# turbostat
turbostat version 17.06.23 - Len Brown <lenb@kernel.org>
CPUID(0): GenuineIntel 22 CPUID levels; family:model:stepping 0x6:8e:a (6:142:10)
CPUID(1): SSE3 MONITOR SMX EIST TM2 TSC MSR ACPI-TM TM
CPUID(6): APERF, TURBO, DTS, PTM, HWP, HWPnotify, HWPwindow, HWPepp, No-HWPpkg, EPB
cpu0: MSR_IA32_MISC_ENABLE: 0x00850089 (TCC EIST No-MWAIT PREFETCH TURBO)
CPUID(7): SGX
cpu0: MSR_IA32_FEATURE_CONTROL: 0x00040005 (Locked SGX)
CPUID(0x15): eax_crystal: 2 ebx_tsc: 176 ecx_crystal_hz: 0
TSC: 2112 MHz (24000000 Hz * 176 / 2 / 1000000)
CPUID(0x16): base_mhz: 2100 max_mhz: 4200 bus_mhz: 100
[...]

Core    CPU     Avg_MHz Busy%   Bzy_MHz TSC_MHz IRQ     SMI     C1      C1E
        C3      C6      C7s     C8      C9      C10     C1%     C1E%    C3%
        C6%     C7s%    C8%     C9%     C10%    CPU%c1  CPU%c3  CPU%c6  CPU%c7
        CoreTmp PkgTmp  GFX%rc6 GFXMHz  Totl%C0 Any%C0  GFX%C0  CPUGFX% Pkg%pc2
        Pkg%pc3 Pkg%pc6 Pkg%pc7 Pkg%pc8 Pkg%pc9 Pk%pc10 PkgWatt CorWatt GFXWatt
        RAMWatt PKG_%   RAM_%
[...]
0       0       97      2.70    3609    2112    1370    0       41      293
        41      453     0       693     0       311     0.24    1.23    0.15
        5.35    0.00    39.33   0.00    50.97   7.50    0.18    6.26    83.37
        52      75      91.41   300     118.58  100.38  8.47    8.30    0.00
        0.00    0.00    0.00    0.00    0.00    0.00    17.69   14.84   0.65
        1.23    0.00    0.00
[...]
```

turbostat(8) begins by printing information about the CPU and MSRs, which can be over 50 lines of output, truncated here. It then prints interval summaries of metrics for all CPUs and per-CPU, at a default five-second interval. This interval summary output is 389 characters wide in this example, and the lines have wrapped five times, making it difficult to read. The columns include the CPU number (CPU), average clock rate in MHz (Avg_MHz), C-state information, temperatures (*Tmp), and power (*Watt).

6.6.10 showboost

Prior to the availability of turbostat(8) on the Netflix cloud, I developed showboost(1) to show the CPU clock rate with a per-interval summary. showboost(1) is short for "show turbo boost" and also uses MSRs. Some sample output:

```
# showboost
Base CPU MHz : 3000
Set CPU MHz  : 3000
Turbo MHz(s) : 3400 3500
Turbo Ratios : 113% 116%
CPU 0 summary every 1 seconds...

TIME        C0_MCYC         C0_ACYC         UTIL   RATIO   MHz
21:41:43    3021819807      3521745975      100%   116%    3496
21:41:44    3021682653      3521564103      100%   116%    3496
21:41:45    3021389796      3521576679      100%   116%    3496
[...]
```

This output shows a clock rate of 3496 MHz on CPU0. The base CPU frequency is 3000 MHz: it is reaching 3496 via Intel turbo boost. The possible turbo boost levels, or "steps," are also listed in the output: 3400 and 3500 MHz.

showboost(8) is in my msr-cloud-tools repository [Gregg 20d], so named as I developed these for use in the cloud. Because I only keep it working for the Netflix environment, it may not work elsewhere due to CPU differences, in which case try turboboost(1).

6.6.11 pmcarch

pmcarch(8) shows a high-level view of CPU cycle performance. It is a PMC-based tool based on the Intel "architectural set" of PMCs, hence the name (PMCs were explained in Chapter 4, Observability Tools, Section 4.3.9, Hardware Counters (PMCs)). In some cloud environments, these architectural PMCs are the only ones available (e.g., some AWS EC2 instances). Some sample output:

```
# pmcarch
K_CYCLES    K_INSTR     IPC  BR_RETIRED    BR_MISPRED   BMR%  LLCREF      LLCMISS     LLC%
96163187    87166313    0.91 19730994925   679187299    3.44  656597454   174313799   73.45
93988372    87205023    0.93 19669256586   724072315    3.68  666041693   169603955   74.54
```

```
93863787    86981089   0.93 19548779510   669172769    3.42 649844207 176100680   72.90
93739565    86349653   0.92 19339320671   634063527    3.28 642506778 181385553   71.77
[...]
```

The tool prints raw counters as well as some ratios as percents. Columns include:

- **K_CYCLES**: CPU Cycles x 1000
- **K_INSTR**: CPU Instructions x 1000
- **IPC**: Instructions-Per-Cycle
- **BMR%**: Branch Misprediction Ratio, as a percentage
- **LLC%**: Last Level Cache hit ratio, as a percentage

IPC was explained in Section 6.3.7, IPC, CPI, along with example values. The other ratios provided, BMR% and LLC%, provide some insight as to why IPC may be low and where the stall cycles may be.

I developed pmcarch(8) for my pmc-cloud-tools repository, which also has cpucache(8) for more CPU cache statistics [Gregg 20e]. These tools employ workarounds and use processor-specific PMCs so that they work on the AWS EC2 cloud, and may not work elsewhere. Even if this never works for you, it provides examples of useful PMCs that you can instrument using perf(1) directly (Section 6.6.13, perf).

6.6.12   tlbstat

tlbstat(8) is another tool from pmc-cloud-tools, which shows the TLB cache statistics. Example output:

```
# tlbstat -C0 1
K_CYCLES   K_INSTR      IPC DTLB_WALKS  ITLB_WALKS  K_DTLBCYC  K_ITLBCYC   DTLB% ITLB%
2875793    276051     0.10 89709496    65862302    787913     650834      27.40 22.63
2860557    273767     0.10 88829158    65213248    780301     644292      27.28 22.52
2885138    276533     0.10 89683045    65813992    787391     650494      27.29 22.55
2532843    243104     0.10 79055465    58023221    693910     573168      27.40 22.63
[...]
```

This particular output showed a worst-case scenario for the KPTI patches that work around the Meltdown CPU vulnerability (the KPTI performance impact was summarized in Chapter 3, Operating Systems, Section 3.4.3, KPTI (Meltdown)). KPTI flushes the TLB caches on syscalls and other events, causing stall cycles during TLB walks: this is shown in the last two columns. In this output, the CPU is spending roughly half its time on TLB walks, and would be expected to run the application workload roughly half as fast.

Columns include:

- **K_CYCLES**: CPU Cycles × 1000
- **K_INSTR**: CPU Instructions × 1000

- **IPC**: Instructions-Per-Cycle
- **DTLB_WALKS**: Data TLB walks (count)
- **ITLB_WALKS**: Instruction TLB walks (count)
- **K_DTLBCYC**: Cycles at least one PMH is active with data TLB walks × 1000
- **K_ITLBCYC**: Cycles at least one PMH is active with instr. TLB walks × 1000
- **DTLB%**: Data TLB active cycles as a ratio of total cycles
- **ITLB%**: Instruction TLB active cycles as a ratio of total cycles

As with pmcarch(8), this tool may not work for your environment due to processor differences. It is nonetheless a useful source of ideas.

6.6.13 perf

perf(1) is the official Linux profiler, a multi-tool with many capabilities. Chapter 13 provides a summary of perf(1). This section covers its usage for CPU analysis.

One-Liners

The following one-liners are both useful and demonstrate different perf(1) capabilities for CPU analysis. Some are explained in more detail in the following sections.

Sample on-CPU functions for the specified command, at 99 Hertz:

```
perf record -F 99 command
```

Sample CPU stack traces (via frame pointers) system-wide for 10 seconds:

```
perf record -F 99 -a -g -- sleep 10
```

Sample CPU stack traces for the PID, using dwarf (dbg info) to unwind stacks:

```
perf record -F 99 -p PID --call-graph dwarf -- sleep 10
```

Record new process events via exec:

```
perf record -e sched:sched_process_exec -a
```

Record context switch events for 10 seconds with stack traces:

```
perf record -e sched:sched_switch -a -g -- sleep 10
```

Sample CPU migrations for 10 seconds:

```
perf record -e migrations -a -- sleep 10
```

Record all CPU migrations for 10 seconds:

```
perf record -e migrations -a -c 1 -- sleep 10
```

Show perf.data as a text report, with data coalesced and counts and percentages:

```
perf report -n --stdio
```

List all perf.data events, with data header (recommended):

```
perf script --header
```

Show PMC statistics for the entire system, for 5 seconds:

```
perf stat -a -- sleep 5
```

Show CPU last level cache (LLC) statistics for the command:

```
perf stat -e LLC-loads,LLC-load-misses,LLC-stores,LLC-prefetches command
```

Show memory bus throughput system-wide every second:

```
perf stat -e uncore_imc/data_reads/,uncore_imc/data_writes/ -a -I 1000
```

Show the rate of context switches per-second:

```
perf stat -e sched:sched_switch -a -I 1000
```

Show the rate of involuntary context switches per-second (previous state was TASK_RUNNING):

```
perf stat -e sched:sched_switch --filter 'prev_state == 0' -a -I 1000
```

Show the rate of mode switches and context switches per second:

```
perf stat -e cpu_clk_unhalted.ring0_trans,cs -a -I 1000
```

Record a scheduler profile for 10 seconds:

```
perf sched record -- sleep 10
```

Show per-process scheduler latency from a scheduler profile:

```
perf sched latency
```

List per-event scheduler latency from a scheduler profile:

```
perf sched timehist
```

For more perf(1) one-liners see Chapter 13, perf, Section 13.2, One-Liners.

System-Wide CPU Profiling

perf(1) can be used to profile CPU call paths, summarizing where CPU time is spent in both kernel- and user-space. This is performed by the record command, which captures sample to a perf.data file. A report command can then be used to view the contents of the file. It works by using the most accurate timer available: CPU-cycle-based if available, otherwise software based (the cpu-clock event).

In the following example, all CPUs (-a[10]) are sampled with call stacks (-g) at 99 Hz (-F 99) for 10 seconds (sleep 10). The --stdio option for report is used to print all the output, instead of operating in interactive mode.

```
# perf record -a -g -F 99 -- sleep 10
[ perf record: Woken up 20 times to write data ]
[ perf record: Captured and wrote 5.155 MB perf.data (1980 samples) ]
# perf report --stdio
[...]
# Children      Self  Command          Shared Object            Symbol
# ........  ........  ...............  .......................  ..................
...........................................................
#
    29.49%     0.00%  mysqld           libpthread-2.30.so       [.] start_thread
           |
           ---start_thread
              0x55dadd7b473a
              0x55dadc140fe0
              |
              --29.44%--do_command
                       |
                       |--26.82%--dispatch_command
                       |         |
                       |          --25.51%--mysqld_stmt_execute
                       |                   |
                       |                    --25.05%--
Prepared_statement::execute_loop
                       |                            |
                       |                             --24.90%--
Prepared_statement::execute
                       |                                     |
                       |                                      --24.34%--
mysql_execute_command
                       |                                              |
[...]
```

The full output is many pages long, in descending sample count order. These sample counts are given as percentages, which show where the CPU time was spent. In this example, 29.44% of time was spent in the do_command() and its children, including mysql_execute_command(). These kernel and process symbols are available only if their debuginfo files are available; otherwise, hex addresses are shown.

---

[10] The -a option became the default in Linux 4.11.

The stack ordering changed in Linux 4.4 from callee (beginning with the on-CPU function and listing ancestry) to caller (beginning with the parent function and listing children). You can switch back to callee using -g:

```
# perf report -g callee --stdio
[...]
    19.75%    0.00%  mysqld            mysqld                    [.]
Sql_cmd_dml::execute_inner
           |
           ---Sql_cmd_dml::execute_inner
              Sql_cmd_dml::execute
              mysql_execute_command
              Prepared_statement::execute
              Prepared_statement::execute_loop
              mysqld_stmt_execute
              dispatch_command
              do_command
              0x55dadc140fe0
              0x55dadd7b473a
              start_thread
[...]
```

To understand a profile, you can try both orderings. If you are unable to make sense of it quickly at the command line, try a visualization such as flame graphs.

CPU Flame Graphs

CPU flame graphs can be generated from the same perf.data profile by using the flamegraph report added in Linux 5.8.[11] For example:

```
# perf record -F 99 -a -g -- sleep 10
# perf script report flamegraph
```

This creates a flamegraph using a d3-flame-graph template file in /usr/share/d3-flame-graph/d3-flamegraph-base.html (if you do not have this file, it can be built by the d3-flame-graph software [Spier 20b]). These can also be combined as one command:

```
# perf script flamegraph -a -F 99 sleep 10
```

For older versions of Linux, you can use my original flamegraph software to visualize the samples reported by perf script. The steps (also included in Chapter 5) are:

```
# perf record -F 99 -a -g -- sleep 10
# perf script --header > out.stacks
```

---

[11] Thanks to Andreas Gerstmayr for adding this option.

```
$ git clone https://github.com/brendangregg/FlameGraph; cd FlameGraph
$ ./stackcollapse-perf.pl < ../out.stacks | ./flamegraph.pl --hash > out.svg
```

The out.svg file is the CPU flame graph, which can be loaded in a web browser. It includes JavaScript for interactivity: click to zoom, and Ctrl-F to search. See Section 6.5.4, Profiling, which illustrates these steps in Figure 6.15.

You can modify these steps to pipe `perf script` directly to stackcollapse-perf.pl, avoiding the out.stacks file. However, I've found these files useful to archive for later reference and use with other tools (e.g., FlameScope).

Options

flamegraph.pl supports various options, including:

- **--title TEXT**: Set the title.
- **--subtitle TEXT**: Set a subtitle.
- **--width NUM**: Set the image width (default 1200 pixels).
- **--countname TEXT**: Change the count label (default "samples").
- **--colors PALETTE**: Set a palette for the frame colors. Some of these use search terms or annotations to use different color hues for different code paths. Options include hot (the default), mem, io, java, js, perl, red, green, blue, yellow.
- **--bgcolors COLOR**: Set the background color. Gradient choices are yellow (the default), blue, green, grey; for flat (non-gradient) colors use "#rrggbb".
- **--hash**: Colors are keyed by a function name hash for consistency.
- **--reverse**: Generate a stack-reversed flame graph, merging from leaf to root.
- **--inverted**: Flip the y-axis to generate an icicle graph.
- **--flamechart**: Generate a flame chart (time on the x-axis).

For example, this is the set of options I use for Java CPU flame graphs:

```
$ ./flamegraph.pl --colors=java --hash
    --title="CPU Flame Graph, $(hostname), $(date)" < ...
```

This includes the hostname and date in the flame graph.

See Section 6.7.3, Flame Graphs, for interpreting flame graphs.

Process CPU Profiling

Apart from profiling across all CPUs, individual processes can be targeted using -p PID, and perf(1) can execute a command directly and profile it:

```
# perf record -F 99 -g command
```

A "--" is often inserted before the command to stop perf(1) processing command line options from the command.

Scheduler Latency

The sched command records and reports scheduler statistics. For example:

```
# perf sched record -- sleep 10
[ perf record: Woken up 63 times to write data ]
[ perf record: Captured and wrote 125.873 MB perf.data (1117146 samples) ]
# perf sched latency

-----------------------------------------------------------------------------------------
  Task                 | Runtime ms  | Switches | Average delay ms | Maximum delay ms |
-----------------------------------------------------------------------------------------
  jbd2/nvme0n1p1-:175  |    0.209 ms |        3 | avg:    0.549 ms | max:    1.630 ms |
  kauditd:22           |    0.180 ms |        6 | avg:    0.463 ms | max:    2.300 ms |
  oltp_read_only.:(4)  | 3969.929 ms |   184629 | avg:    0.007 ms | max:    5.484 ms |
  mysqld:(27)          | 8759.265 ms |    96025 | avg:    0.007 ms | max:    4.133 ms |
  bash:21391           |    0.275 ms |        1 | avg:    0.007 ms | max:    0.007 ms |
  [...]

-----------------------------------------------------------------------------------------
  TOTAL:               | 12916.132 ms |  281395 |
-------------------------------------------------------
```

This latency report summarizes average and maximum scheduler latency (aka run queue latency) per process. While there were many context switches for the oltp_read_only and mysqld processes, their average and maximum scheduler latencies were still low. (To fit the output width here, I elided a final "Maximum delay at" column.)

Scheduler events are frequent, so this type of tracing incurs significant CPU and storage overhead. The perf.data file in this case was 125 Mbytes from only ten seconds of tracing. The rate of scheduler events may inundate perf(1)'s per-CPU ring buffers, causing events to be lost: the report will state this at the end if it happened. Be careful with this overhead, as it may perturb production applications.

perf(1) sched also has map and timehist reports for displaying the scheduler profile in different ways. The timehist report shows per-event details:

```
# perf sched timehist
Samples do not have callchains.
           time    cpu  task name              wait time  sch delay   run time
                        [tid/pid]               (msec)     (msec)      (msec)
  -------------- ------ --------------------------- --------- --------- ---------
  437752.840756 [0000] mysqld[11995/5187]            0.000     0.000      0.000
  437752.840810 [0000] oltp_read_only.[21483/21482]  0.000     0.000      0.054
```

```
437752.840845 [0000]   mysqld[11995/5187]              0.054    0.000    0.034
437752.840847 [0000]   oltp_read_only.[21483/21482]    0.034    0.002    0.002
[...]
437762.842139 [0001]   sleep[21487]                 10000.080    0.004    0.127
```

This report shows each context switch event with the time sleeping (wait time), scheduler latency (sch delay), and time spent on CPU (runtime), all in milliseconds. The final line shows the dummy sleep(1) command used to set the duration of perf record, which slept for 10 seconds.

PMCs (Hardware Events)

The stat subcommand counts events and produces a summary, rather than recording events to perf.data. By default, perf stat counts several PMCs to show a high-level summary of CPU cycles. For example, summarizing a gzip(1) command:

```
$ perf stat gzip ubuntu-19.10-live-server-amd64.iso

 Performance counter stats for 'gzip ubuntu-19.10-live-server-amd64.iso':

        25235.652299      task-clock (msec)         #    0.997 CPUs utilized
                 142      context-switches          #    0.006 K/sec
                  25      cpu-migrations            #    0.001 K/sec
                 128      page-faults               #    0.005 K/sec
      94,817,146,941      cycles                    #    3.757 GHz
     152,114,038,783      instructions              #    1.60  insn per cycle
      28,974,755,679      branches                  # 1148.167 M/sec
       1,020,287,443      branch-misses             #    3.52% of all branches

        25.312054797 seconds time elapsed
```

The statistics include the cycle and instruction count, and the IPC. As described earlier, this is an extremely useful high-level metric for determining the types of cycles occurring and how many of them are stall cycles. In this case, the IPC of 1.6 is "good."

Here is a system-wide example of measuring IPC, this time from a Shopify benchmark to investigate NUMA tuning, which ultimately improved application throughput by 20–30%. These commands measure on all CPUs for 30 seconds.

Before:

```
# perf stat -a -- sleep 30
[...]
     404,155,631,577      instructions              #    0.72  insns per cycle
[100.00%]
[...]
```

After NUMA tuning:

```
# perf stat -a -- sleep 30
[...]
   490,026,784,002      instructions            #   0.89  insns per cycle
[100.00%]
[...]
```

IPC improved from 0.72 to 0.89: 24%, matching the final win. (See Chapter 16, Case Study, for another production example of measuring IPC.)

Hardware Event Selection

There are many more hardware events that can be counted. You can list them using perf list:

```
# perf list
[...]
  branch-instructions OR branches          [Hardware event]
  branch-misses                            [Hardware event]
  bus-cycles                               [Hardware event]
  cache-misses                             [Hardware event]
  cache-references                         [Hardware event]
  cpu-cycles OR cycles                     [Hardware event]
  instructions                             [Hardware event]
  ref-cycles                               [Hardware event]
[...]
  LLC-load-misses                          [Hardware cache event]
  LLC-loads                                [Hardware cache event]
  LLC-store-misses                         [Hardware cache event]
  LLC-stores                               [Hardware cache event]
[...]
```

Look for both "Hardware event" and "Hardware cache event." For some processors you will find additional groups of PMCs; a longer example is provided in Chapter 13, perf, Section 13.3, perf Events. Those available depend on the processor architecture and are documented in the processor manuals (e.g., the Intel *Software Developer's Manual*).

These events can be specified using −e. For example (this is from an Intel Xeon):

```
$ perf stat -e instructions,cycles,L1-dcache-load-misses,LLC-load-misses,dTLB-load-
misses gzip ubuntu-19.10-live-server-amd64.iso

 Performance counter stats for 'gzip ubuntu-19.10-live-server-amd64.iso':

   152,226,453,131      instructions            #   1.61  insn per cycle
    94,697,951,648      cycles
```

```
   2,790,554,850      L1-dcache-load-misses
       9,612,234      LLC-load-misses
         357,906      dTLB-load-misses


   25.275276704 seconds time elapsed
```

Apart from instructions and cycles, this example also measured the following:

- **L1-dcache-load-misses**: Level 1 data cache load misses. This gives you a measure of the memory load caused by the application, after some loads have been returned from the Level 1 cache. It can be compared with other L1 event counters to determine cache hit ratio.

- **LLC-load-misses**: Last level cache load misses. After the last level, this accesses main memory, and so this is a measure of main memory load. The difference between this and L1-dcache-load-misses gives an idea of the effectiveness of the CPU caches beyond Level 1, but other counters are needed for completeness.

- **dTLB-load-misses**: Data translation lookaside buffer misses. This shows the effectiveness of the MMU to cache page mappings for the workload, and can measure the size of the memory workload (working set).

Many other counters can be inspected. perf(1) supports both descriptive names (like those used for this example) and hexadecimal values. The latter may be necessary for esoteric counters you find in processor manuals, for which a descriptive name isn't provided.

Software Tracing

perf can also record and count software events. Listing some CPU-related events:

```
# perf list
[...]
  context-switches OR cs                         [Software event]
  cpu-migrations OR migrations                   [Software event]
[...]
  sched:sched_kthread_stop                       [Tracepoint event]
  sched:sched_kthread_stop_ret                   [Tracepoint event]
  sched:sched_wakeup                             [Tracepoint event]
  sched:sched_wakeup_new                         [Tracepoint event]
  sched:sched_switch                             [Tracepoint event]
[...]
```

The following example uses the context switch software event to trace when applications leave the CPU, and collects call stacks for one second:

```
# perf record -e sched:sched_switch -a -g -- sleep 1
[ perf record: Woken up 46 times to write data ]
[ perf record: Captured and wrote 11.717 MB perf.data (50649 samples) ]
```

```
# perf report --stdio
[...]
    16.18%    16.18%  prev_comm=mysqld prev_pid=11995 prev_prio=120 prev_state=S ==>
next_comm=swapper/1 next_pid=0 next_prio=120
            |
            ---__sched_text_start
              schedule
              schedule_hrtimeout_range_clock
              schedule_hrtimeout_range
              poll_schedule_timeout.constprop.0
              do_sys_poll
              __x64_sys_ppoll
              do_syscall_64
              entry_SYSCALL_64_after_hwframe
              ppoll
              vio_socket_io_wait
              vio_read
              my_net_read
              Protocol_classic::read_packet
              Protocol_classic::get_command
              do_command
              start_thread
[...]
```

This truncated output shows mysql context switching to block on a socket via poll(2). To investigate further, see the Off-CPU analysis methodology in Chapter 5, Applications, Section 5.4.2, Off-CPU Analysis, and supporting tools in Section 5.5.3, offcputime.

Chapter 9, Disks, includes another example of static tracing with perf(1): block I/O tracepoints. Chapter 10, Network, includes an example of dynamic instrumentation with perf(1) for the tcp_sendmsg() kernel function.

Hardware Tracing

perf(1) is also able to use hardware tracing for per-instruction analysis, if supported by the processor. This is a low-level advanced activity not covered here, but is mentioned again in Chapter 13, perf, Section 13.13, Other Commands.

Documentation

For more on perf(1), see Chapter 13, perf. Also see its man pages, documentation in the Linux kernel source under tools/perf/Documentation, my "perf Examples" page [Gregg 20f], the "Perf Tutorial" [Perf 15], and "The Unofficial Linux Perf Events Web-Page" [Weaver 11].

6.6.14 profile

profile(8) is a BCC tool that samples stack traces at timed intervals and reports a frequency count. This is the most useful tool in BCC for understanding CPU consumption as it summarizes almost all code paths that are consuming CPU resources. (See the hardirqs(8) tool in Section 6.6.19 for more CPU consumers.) profile(8) has lower overhead than perf(1) as only the stack trace summary is passed to user space. This overhead difference is pictured in Figure 6.15. profile(8) is also summarized in Chapter 5, Applications, Section 5.5.2, profile, for its use as an application profiler.

By default, profile(8) samples both user and kernel stack traces at 49 Hertz across all CPUs. This can be customized using options, and the settings are printed at the start of the output. For example:

```
# profile
Sampling at 49 Hertz of all threads by user + kernel stack... Hit Ctrl-C to end.
^C
[...]

    finish_task_switch
    __sched_text_start
    schedule
    schedule_hrtimeout_range_clock
    schedule_hrtimeout_range
    poll_schedule_timeout.constprop.0
    do_sys_poll
    __x64_sys_ppoll
    do_syscall_64
    entry_SYSCALL_64_after_hwframe
    ppoll
    vio_socket_io_wait(Vio*, enum_vio_io_event)
    vio_read(Vio*, unsigned char*, unsigned long)
    my_net_read(NET*)
    Protocol_classic::read_packet()
    Protocol_classic::get_command(COM_DATA*, enum_server_command*)
    do_command(THD*)
    start_thread
    -                mysqld (5187)
        151
```

The output shows the stack traces as a list of functions, followed by a dash ("-") and the process name and PID in parentheses, and finally a count for that stack trace. The stack traces are printed in frequency count order, from least to most frequent.

The full output in this example was 8,261 lines long and has been truncated here to show only the last, most frequent, stack trace. It shows that scheduler functions were on-CPU, called from a poll(2) code path. This particular stack trace was sampled 151 times while tracing.

profile(8) supports various options, including:

- **-U**: Includes user-level stacks only
- **-K**: Includes kernel-level stacks only
- **-a**: Includes frame annotations (e.g., "_[k]" for kernel frames)
- **-d**: Includes delimiters between kernel/user stacks
- **-f**: Provides output in folded format
- **-p PID**: Profiles this process only
- **--stack-storage-size SIZE**: Number of unique stack traces (default 16,384)

If profile(8) prints this type of warning:

```
WARNING: 5 stack traces could not be displayed.
```

It means that the stack storage was exceeded. You can increase it using the `--stack-storage-size` option.

profile CPU Flame Graphs

The **-f** option provides output suitable for importing by my flame graph software. Example instructions:

```
# profile -af 10 > out.stacks
# git clone https://github.com/brendangregg/FlameGraph; cd FlameGraph
# ./flamegraph.pl --hash < out.stacks > out.svg
```

The out.svg file can then be loaded in a web browser.

profile(8) and the following tools (runqlat(8), runqlen(8), softirqs(8), hardirqs(8)) are BPF-based tools from the BCC repository, which is covered in Chapter 15.

6.6.15   cpudist

cpudist(8)[12] is a BCC tool for showing the distribution of on-CPU time for each thread wakeup. This can be used to help characterize CPU workloads, providing details for later tuning and design decisions. For example, from a 2-CPU database instance:

```
# cpudist 10 1
Tracing on-CPU time... Hit Ctrl-C to end.

     usecs               : count    distribution
        0 -> 1           : 0        |                                        |
        2 -> 3           : 135      |                                        |
```

---

[12] Origin: Sasha Goldshtein developed the BCC cpudist(8) on 29-Jun-2016. I developed a cpudists histogram tool for Solaris in 2005.

```
       4 -> 7          : 26961    |********                                 |
       8 -> 15         : 123341   |*****************************************|
      16 -> 31         : 55939    |******************                       |
      32 -> 63         : 70860    |**********************                   |
      64 -> 127        : 12622    |****                                     |
     128 -> 255        : 13044    |****                                     |
     256 -> 511        : 3090     |*                                        |
     512 -> 1023       : 2        |                                         |
    1024 -> 2047       : 6        |                                         |
    2048 -> 4095       : 1        |                                         |
    4096 -> 8191       : 2        |                                         |
```

The output shows that the database usually spent between 4 and 63 microseconds on-CPU. That's pretty short.

Options include:

- **-m**: Prints output in milliseconds
- **-o**: Shows off-CPU time instead of on-CPU time
- **-P**: Prints a histogram per process
- **-p PID**: Traces this process ID only

This can be used in conjunction with profile(8) to summarize how long an application ran on-CPU, and what it was doing.

6.6.16 runqlat

runqlat(8)[13] is a BCC and bpftrace tool for measuring CPU scheduler latency, often called run queue latency (even when no longer implemented using run queues). It is useful for identifying and quantifying issues of CPU saturation, where there is more demand for CPU resources than they can service. The metric measured by runqlat(8) is the time each thread (task) spends waiting for its turn on CPU.

The following shows BCC runqlat(8) running on a 2-CPU MySQL database cloud instance operating at about 15% CPU utilization system-wide. The arguments to runqlat(8) are "10 1" to set a 10-second interval and output only once:

```
# runqlat 10 1
Tracing run queue latency... Hit Ctrl-C to end.

     usecs             : count     distribution
         0 -> 1        : 9017      |*****                                    |
         2 -> 3        : 7188      |****                                     |
         4 -> 7        : 5250      |***                                      |
```

---

[13]Origin: I developed the BCC runqlat version on 7-Feb-2016, and bpftrace on 17-Sep-2018, inspired by my earlier Solaris dispqlat.d tool (dispatcher queue latency: Solaris terminology for run queue latency).

```
     8 -> 15      : 67668   |****************************************|
    16 -> 31      : 3529    |**                                      |
    32 -> 63      : 315     |                                        |
    64 -> 127     : 98      |                                        |
   128 -> 255     : 99      |                                        |
   256 -> 511     : 9       |                                        |
   512 -> 1023    : 15      |                                        |
  1024 -> 2047    : 6       |                                        |
  2048 -> 4095    : 2       |                                        |
  4096 -> 8191    : 3       |                                        |
  8192 -> 16383   : 1       |                                        |
 16384 -> 32767   : 1       |                                        |
 32768 -> 65535   : 2       |                                        |
 65536 -> 131071  : 88      |                                        |
```

The output may be surprising for such a lightly-loaded system: there appears to be a high sched-uler latency with 88 events in the 65 to 131 millisecond range. It turns out this instance was CPU throttled by the hypervisor, injecting scheduler latency.

Options include:

- **-m**: Prints output in milliseconds
- **-P**: Prints a histogram per process ID
- **--pidnss**: Prints a histogram per PID namespace
- **-p PID**: Traces this process ID only
- **-T**: Includes timestamps on output

runqlat(8) works by instrumenting scheduler wakeup and context switch events to determine the time from wakeup to running. These events can be very frequent on busy production systems, exceeding one million events per second. Even though BPF is optimized, at these rates even adding one microsecond per event can cause noticeable overhead. Use with caution, and consider using runqlen(8) instead.

6.6.17   runqlen

runqlen(8)[14] is a BCC and bpftrace tool for sampling the length of the CPU run queues, counting how many tasks are waiting their turn, and presenting this as a linear histogram. This can be used to further characterize issues of run queue latency, or as a cheaper approximation. Since it uses sampling at 99 Hertz across all CPUs, the overhead is typically negligible. runqlat(8), on the other hand, samples every context switch, which can become millions of events per second.

---

[14] Origin: I developed the BCC version on 12-Dec-2016 and the bpftrace version on 7-Oct-2018, inspired by my earlier dispqlen.d tool.

The following shows runqlen(8) from BCC running on a 2-CPU MySQL database instance that is at about 15% CPU utilization system-wide (the same instance shown earlier with runqlat(8)). The arguments to runqlen(8) are "10 1" to set a 10-second interval and output only once:

```
# runqlen 10 1
Sampling run queue length... Hit Ctrl-C to end.

     runqlen       : count    distribution
        0          : 1824     |****************************************|
        1          : 158      |***                                     |
```

This output shows that for much of the time the run queue length was zero, and about 8% of the time the run queue length was one, meaning that threads needed to wait their turn.

Options include:

- **-C**: Prints a histogram per CPU
- **-O**: Prints run queue occupancy
- **-T**: Includes timestamps on output

Run queue occupancy is a separate metric that shows the percentage of time that there were threads waiting. This is sometimes useful when a single metric is needed for monitoring, alerting, and graphing.

6.6.18   softIrqs

softirqs(8)[15] is a BCC tool that shows the time spent servicing soft IRQs (soft interrupts). The system-wide time in soft interrupts is readily available from different tools. For example, mpstat(1) shows it as %soft. There is also /proc/softirqs to show counts of soft IRQ events. The BCC softirqs(8) tool differs in that it can show time per soft IRQ rather than an event count.

For example, from a 2-CPU database instance and a 10-second trace:

```
# softirqs 10 1
Tracing soft irq event time... Hit Ctrl-C to end.

SOFTIRQ          TOTAL_usecs
net_tx                     9
rcu                      751
sched                   3431
timer                   5542
tasklet                11368
net_rx                 12225
```

---

[15] Origin: I developed the BCC version on 20-Oct-2015.

This output shows that the most time was spent in net_rx, totaling 12 milliseconds. This provides insight for CPU consumers that may not be visible in typical CPU profiles, since these routines may not be interruptible by CPU profilers.

Options include:

- **-d**: Shows IRQ time as histograms
- **-T**: Includes timestamps on output

The -d option can be used to show the distribution of time per IRQ event.

6.6.19   hardirqs

hardirqs(8)[16] is a BCC tool that shows time spent servicing hard IRQs (hard interrupts). The system-wide time in hard interrupts is readily available from different tools. For example, mpstat(1) shows it as %irq. There is also /proc/interrupts to show counts of hard IRQ events. The BCC hardirqs(8) tool differs in that it can show time per hard IRQ rather than an event count.

For example, from a 2-CPU database instance and a 10-second trace:

```
# hardirqs 10 1
Tracing hard irq event time... Hit Ctrl-C to end.

HARDIRQ                    TOTAL_usecs
nvme0q2                             35
ena-mgmnt@pci:0000:00:05.0          72
ens5-Tx-Rx-1                       326
nvme0q1                            878
ens5-Tx-Rx-0                      5922
```

The output shows that 5.9 milliseconds were spent servicing the ens5-Tx-Rx-0 IRQ (networking) while tracing. As with softirqs(8), this can show CPU consumers that are not typically included in CPU profiling.

hardirqs(8) has similar options to softirqs(8).

6.6.20   bpftrace

bpftrace is a BPF-based tracer that provides a high-level programming language, allowing the creation of powerful one-liners and short scripts. It is well suited for custom application analysis based on clues from other tools. There are bpftrace versions of the earlier tools runqlat(8) and runqlen(8) in the bpftrace repository [Iovisor 20a].

bpftrace is explained in Chapter 15. This section shows some example one-liners for CPU analysis.

---

[16] Origin: I developed the BCC version on 19-Oct-2015, inspired by my earlier inttimes.d tool, which itself was based on another intr.d tool.

One-liners

The following one-liners are useful and demonstrate different bpftrace capabilities.

Trace new processes with arguments:

```
bpftrace -e 'tracepoint:syscalls:sys_enter_execve { join(args->argv); }'
```

Count syscalls by process:

```
bpftrace -e 'tracepoint:raw_syscalls:sys_enter { @[pid, comm] = count(); }'
```

Count syscalls by syscall probe name:

```
bpftrace -e 'tracepoint:syscalls:sys_enter_* { @[probe] = count(); }'
```

Sample running process names at 99 Hertz:

```
bpftrace -e 'profile:hz:99 { @[comm] = count(); }'
```

Sample user and kernel stacks at 49 Hertz, system wide, with the process name:

```
bpftrace -e 'profile:hz:49 { @[kstack, ustack, comm] = count(); }'
```

Sample user-level stacks at 49 Hertz, for PID 189:

```
bpftrace -e 'profile:hz:49 /pid == 189/ { @[ustack] = count(); }'
```

Sample user-level stacks 5 frames deep at 49 Hertz, for PID 189:

```
bpftrace -e 'profile:hz:49 /pid == 189/ { @[ustack(5)] = count(); }'
```

Sample user-level stacks at 49 Hertz, for processes named "mysqld":

```
bpftrace -e 'profile:hz:49 /comm == "mysqld"/ { @[ustack] = count(); }'
```

Count kernel CPU scheduler tracepoints:

```
bpftrace -e 'tracepont:sched:* { @[probe] = count(); }'
```

Count off-CPU kernel stacks for context switch events:

```
bpftrace -e 'tracepont:sched:sched_switch { @[kstack] = count(); }'
```

Count kernel function calls beginning with "vfs_":

```
bpftrace -e 'kprobe:vfs_* { @[func] = count(); }'
```

Trace new threads via pthread_create():

```
bpftrace -e 'u:/lib/x86_64-linux-gnu/libpthread-2.27.so:pthread_create {
    printf("%s by %s (%d)\n", probe, comm, pid); }'
```

Examples

The following shows bpftrace profiling the MySQL database server at 49 Hertz, and collecting only the first three levels of the user stack:

```
# bpftrace -e 'profile:hz:49 /comm == "mysqld"/ { @[ustack(3)] = count(); }'
Attaching 1 probe...
^C
[...]
@[
    my_lengthsp_8bit(CHARSET_INFO const*, char const*, unsigned long)+32
    Field::send_to_protocol(Protocol*) const+194
    THD::send_result_set_row(List<Item>*)+203
]: 8
@[
    ppoll+166
    vio_socket_io_wait(Vio*, enum_vio_io_event)+22
    vio_read(Vio*, unsigned char*, unsigned long)+236
]: 10
[...]
```

The output was been truncated to only include two stacks, sampled 8 and 10 times. These both appear to show CPU time spent in networking.

Scheduling Internals

If needed, you can develop custom tools that show the behavior of the CPU scheduler. Start by trying the tracepoints. Listing them:

```
# bpftrace -l 'tracepoint:sched:*'
tracepoint:sched:sched_kthread_stop
tracepoint:sched:sched_kthread_stop_ret
tracepoint:sched:sched_waking
tracepoint:sched:sched_wakeup
tracepoint:sched:sched_wakeup_new
tracepoint:sched:sched_switch
tracepoint:sched:sched_migrate_task
tracepoint:sched:sched_process_free
[...]
```

Each of these has arguments that can be listed using -lv. If the tracepoints are insufficient, consider using dynamic instrumentation with kprobes. Listing kprobe targets for kernel functions beginning with "sched":

```
# bpftrace -lv 'kprobe:sched*'
kprobe:sched_itmt_update_handler
kprobe:sched_set_itmt_support
kprobe:sched_clear_itmt_support
kprobe:sched_set_itmt_core_prio
kprobe:schedule_on_each_cpu
kprobe:sched_copy_attr
kprobe:sched_free_group
[...]
```

On this kernel version (5.3) there are 24 sched tracepoints and 104 possible kprobes beginning with "sched."

Because scheduler events can be frequent, instrumenting them can consume significant overhead. Use caution and find ways to reduce this overhead: use maps to summarize statistics instead of printing per-event details, and trace the fewest possible events.

6.6.21   Other Tools

CPU observability tools included in other chapters of this book, and in *BPF Performance Tools* [Gregg 19], are listed in Table 6.11.

Table 6.11   **Other CPU observability tools**

Section	Tool	Description
5.5.3	offcputime	Off-CPU profiling using scheduler tracing
5.5.5	execsnoop	Lists new process execution
5.5.6	syscount	Counts system calls by type and process
[Gregg 19]	runqslower	Prints run queue waits slower than a threshold
[Gregg 19]	cpufreq	Samples CPU frequency by process
[Gregg 19]	smpcalls	Times SMP remote CPU calls
[Gregg 19]	llcstat	Summarizes LLC hit ratio by process

Other Linux CPU observability tools and sources include:

- **oprofile:** The original CPU profiling tool by John Levon.
- **atop:** Includes many more system-wide statistics and uses process accounting to catch the presence of short-lived processes.
- **/proc/cpuinfo:** This can be read to see processor details, including clock speed and feature flags.
- **lscpu:** Shows CPU architecture information.

- **lstopo**: Shows hardware topology (provided by the hwloc package).

- **cpupower**: Shows processor power states.

- **getdelays.c**: This is an example of delay accounting observability and includes CPU scheduler latency per process. It is demonstrated in Chapter 4, Observability Tools.

- **valgrind**: A memory debugging and profiling toolkit [Valgrind 20]. It contains callgrind, a tool to trace function calls and gather a call graph, which can be visualized using kcachegrind; and cachegrind for analysis of hardware cache usage by a given program.

An example lstopo(1) output as SVG is shown in Figure 6.18.

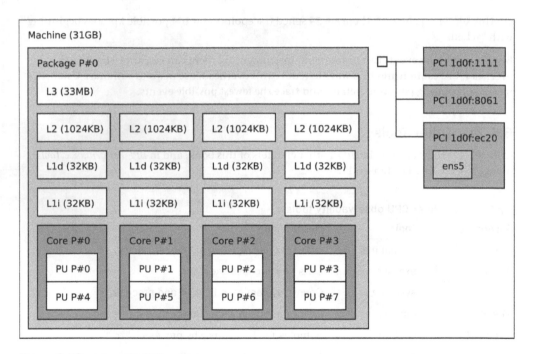

Figure 6.18   lstopo(1) SVG output

This lstopo(1) visualization shows which logical CPUs are mapped to which CPU cores (e.g., CPUs 0 and 4 are mapped to core 0).

Another tool worth showing is this output of cpupower(1):

```
# cpupower idle-info
CPUidle driver: intel_idle
CPUidle governor: menu
analyzing CPU 0:

Number of idle states: 9
Available idle states: POLL C1 C1E C3 C6 C7s C8 C9 C10
```

```
POLL:
Flags/Description: CPUIDLE CORE POLL IDLE
Latency: 0
Usage: 80442
Duration: 36139954
C1:
Flags/Description: MWAIT 0x00
Latency: 2
Usage: 3832139
Duration: 542192027
C1E:
Flags/Description: MWAIT 0x01
Latency: 10
Usage: 10701293
Duration: 1912665723
[...]
C10:
Flags/Description: MWAIT 0x60
Latency: 890
Usage: 7179306
Duration: 48777395993
```

This not only lists the processor power states, but also provides some statistics: `Usage` shows the number of times the state was entered, `Duration` is the time spent in the state in microseconds, and `Latency` is the exit latency in microseconds. This is only showing CPU 0: you can see all CPUs from their /sys files, for example, the durations can be read from /sys/devices/system/cpu/cpu*/cpuidle/state0/time [Wysocki 19].

There are also sophisticated products for CPU performance analysis, in particular Intel vTune [22] and AMD uprof [23].

GPUs

There is not yet a comprehensive set of standard tools for GPU analysis. GPU vendors typically release specific tools that only work for their own products. Examples include:

- **nvidia-smi, nvperf,** and **Nvidia Visual Profiler:** For Nvidia GPUs
- **intel_gpu_top** and **Intel vTune:** For Intel GPUs
- **radeontop:** For Radeon GPUs

These tools provide basic observability statistics such as instruction rates and GPU resource utilization. Other possible observability sources are PMCs and tracepoints (try `perf list | grep gpu`).

GPU profiling is different from CPU profiling, as GPUs do not have a stack trace showing code path ancestry. Profilers instead can instrument API and memory transfer calls and their timing.

6.7   Visualizations

CPU usage has historically been visualized as line graphs of utilization or load average, including the original X11 load tool (xload(1)). Such line graphs are an effective way to show variation, as magnitudes can be visually compared. They can also show patterns over time, as was shown in Chapter 2, Methodologies, Section 2.9, Monitoring.

However, line graphs of per-CPU utilization don't scale with the CPU counts we see today, especially for cloud computing environments involving tens of thousands of CPUs—a graph of 10,000 lines can become paint.

Other statistics plotted as line graphs, including averages, standard deviations, maximums, and percentiles, provide some value and do scale. However, CPU utilization is often *bimodal*—composed of some CPUs that are idle or near-idle, and some at 100% utilization—which is not effectively conveyed with these statistics. The full distribution often needs to be studied. A utilization heat map makes this possible.

The following sections introduce CPU utilization heat maps, CPU subsecond-offset heat maps, flame graphs, and FlameScope. I created these visualization types to solve problems in enterprise and cloud performance analysis.

6.7.1   Utilization Heat Map

Utilization versus time can be presented as a heat map, with the saturation (darkness) of each pixel showing the number of CPUs at that utilization and time range [Gregg 10a]. Heat maps were introduced in Chapter 2, Methodologies.

Figure 6.19 shows CPU utilization for an entire data center, running a public cloud environment. It includes over 300 physical servers and 5,312 CPUs.

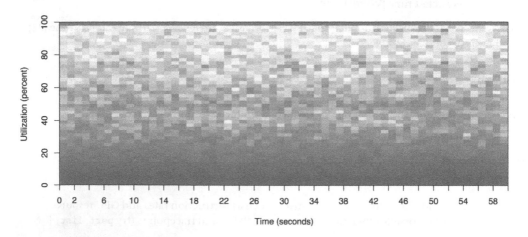

Figure 6.19   CPU utilization heat map, 5,312 CPUs

The darker shading at the bottom of this heat map shows that most CPUs are running between 0% and 30% utilization. However, the solid line at the top shows that, over time, there are also some CPUs at 100% utilization. The fact that the line is dark shows that multiple CPUs were at 100%, not just one.

6.7.2 Subsecond-Offset Heat Map

This heat map type allows activity within a second to be examined. CPU activity is typically measured in microseconds or milliseconds; reporting this data as averages over an entire second can wipe out useful information. The subsecond-offset heat map puts the subsecond offset on the y-axis, with the number of non-idle CPUs at each offset shown by the saturation. This visualizes each second as a column, "painting" it from bottom to top.

Figure 6.20 shows a CPU subsecond-offset heat map for a cloud database (Riak).

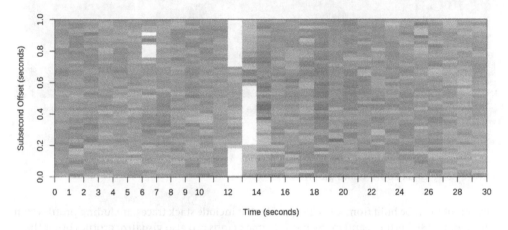

Figure 6.20 CPU subsecond-offset heat map

What is interesting about this heat map isn't the times that the CPUs were busy servicing the database, but the times that they were not, indicated by the white columns. The duration of these gaps was also interesting: hundreds of milliseconds during which none of the database threads were on-CPU. This led to the discovery of a locking issue where the entire database was blocked for hundreds of milliseconds at a time.

If we had examined this data using a line graph, a dip in per-second CPU utilization might have been dismissed as variable load and not investigated further.

6.7.3 Flame Graphs

Profiling stack traces is an effective way to explain CPU usage, showing which kernel- or user-level code paths are responsible. It can, however, produce thousands of pages of output. CPU flame graphs visualize the profile stack frames, so that CPU usage can be understood more quickly and more clearly [Gregg 16b]. The example in Figure 6.21 shows the Linux kernel profiled using perf(1) as a CPU flame graph.

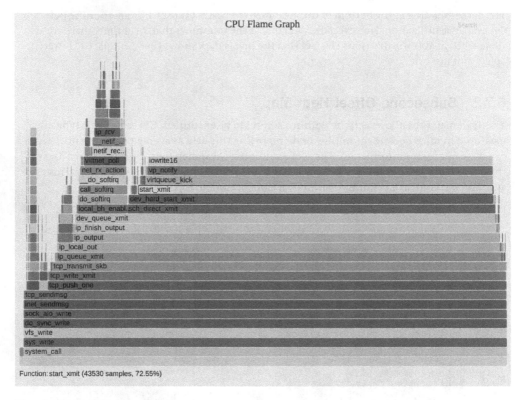

Figure 6.21   Linux kernel flame graph

Flame graphs can be built from any CPU profile that include stack traces, including profiles from perf(1), profile(8), bpftrace, and many more. Flame graphs can also visualize profiles other than CPU profiles. This section describes CPU flame graphs generated by flamegraph.pl [Gregg 20g]. (There are many other implementations, including d3 flame graphs created by my colleague Martin Spier [Spier 20a].)

Characteristics

A CPU flame graph has the following characteristics:

- Each box represents a function in the stack (a "stack frame").

- The **y-axis** shows stack depth (number of frames on the stack). The top-most box shows the function that was on-CPU. Everything beneath that is ancestry. The function beneath a function is its parent, just as in the stack traces shown earlier.

- The **x-axis** spans the sample population. It does not show the passing of time from left to right, as most graphs do. The left-to-right ordering has no meaning (it's sorted alphabetically).

- The **width** of the box shows the total time the function was on-CPU or part of an ancestry that was on-CPU (based on sample count). Wider box functions may be slower than narrow box functions, or they may simply be called more often. The call count is not shown (nor is it known via sampling).

The sample count can exceed elapsed time if multiple threads were running and sampled in parallel.

Colors

The frames can be colored based on different schemes. The default shown in Figure 6.21 uses random warm colors for each frame, which helps visually distinguish adjacent towers. Over the years I've added more color schemes. I've found the following to be most useful to flame graph end users:

- **Hue**: The hue indicates the code type.[17] For example, red can indicate native user-level code, orange for native kernel-level code, yellow for C++, green for interpreted functions, aqua for inlined functions, and so on depending on the languages you use. Magenta is used to highlight search matches. Some developers have customized flame graphs to always highlight their own code in a certain hue so that it stands out.

- **Saturation**: Saturation is hashed from the function name. It provides some color variance that helps differentiate adjacent towers, while preserving the same colors for function names to more easily compare multiple flame graphs.

- **Background color**: The background color provides a visual reminder of the flame graph type. For example, you might use yellow for CPU flame graphs, blue for off-CPU or I/O flame graphs, and green for memory flame graphs.

Another useful color scheme is one used for IPC (instructions per cycle) flame graphs, where an additional dimension, IPC, is visualized by coloring each frame using a gradient from blue to white to red.

Interactivity

Flame graphs are *interactive*. My original flamegraph.pl generates an SVG with an embedded JavaScript routine, that when opened in a browser allows you to mouse over elements to reveal details at the bottom, and other interactive functions. In the Figure 6.21 example, start_xmit() was highlighted, which shows that it was present in 72.55% of the sampled stacks.

You can also click to zoom[18] and Ctrl-F to search[19] for a term. When searching, a cumulative percentage is also shown to indicate how often a stack trace containing that search term was present. This makes it trivial to calculate how much of the profile was in particular code areas. For example, you can search for "tcp_" to show how much was in the kernel TCP code.

Interpretation

To explain how to interpret a flame graph in detail, consider the simple synthetic CPU flame graph shown in Figure 6.22.

---

[17] This was suggested to me by my colleague Amer Ather. My first version was a five-minute regex hack.
[18] Adrien Mahieux developed the horizontal zoom feature for flame graphs.
[19] Thorsten Lorenz first added a search feature to his flame graph implementation.

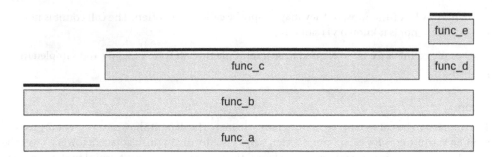

Figure 6.22   Synthetic CPU flame graph

The top edge has been highlighted with a line: this shows the functions that are directly running on-CPU. func_c() was directly on-CPU for 70% of the time, func_b() was on-CPU for 20% of the time, and func_e() was on-CPU for 10% of the time. The other functions, func_a() and func_d(), were never sampled on-CPU directly.

To read a flame graph, look for the widest towers and understand them first. In Figure 6.22, it is the code path func_a() -> func_b() -> func_c(). In the Figure 6.21 flame graph, it is the code path that ends in the iowrite16() plateau.

For large profiles of thousands of samples, there may be code paths that were sampled only a few times, and are printed in such a narrow tower that there is no room to include the function name. This turns out to be a benefit: Your attention is naturally drawn to the wider towers that have legible function names, and looking at them helps you understand the bulk of the profile first.

Note that for recursive functions, each level is shown by a separate frame.

Section 6.5.4, Profiling, includes more tips for interpretation, and Section 6.6.13, perf, shows how to create them using perf(1).

6.7.4   FlameScope

FlameScope is an open-source tool developed at Netflix that marries the previous two visualizations: subsecond-offset heat maps and flame graphs [Gregg 18b]. A subsecond-offset heat map shows a CPU profile, and ranges including subsecond ranges can be selected to show a flame graph just for that range. Figure 6.23 shows the FlameScope heat map with annotations and instructions.

FlameScope is suited for studying issues or perturbations and variance. These can be too small to see in a CPU profile, which shows the full profile at once: a 100 ms CPU perturbation during a 30-second profile will only span 0.3% of the width of a flame graph. In FlameScope, a 100 ms perturbation will show up as a vertical stripe 1/10th of the height of the heat map. Several such perturbations are visible in the Figure 6.23 example. When selected, a CPU flame graph is shown just for those time ranges, showing the code paths responsible.

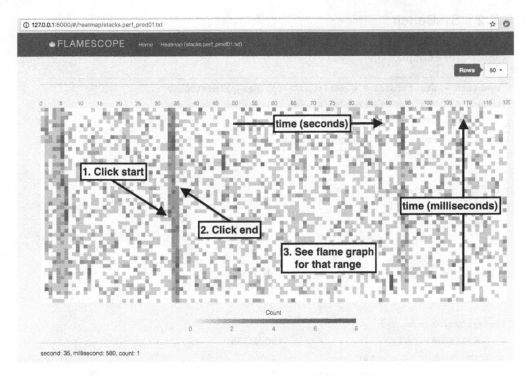

Figure 6.23 FlameScope

FlameScope is open source [Netflix 19] and has been used to find numerous performance wins at Netflix.

6.8 Experimentation

This section describes tools for actively testing CPU performance. See Section 6.5.11, Micro-Benchmarking, for background.

When using these tools, it's a good idea to leave mpstat(1) continually running to confirm CPU usage and parallelism.

6.8.1 Ad Hoc

While this is trivial and doesn't measure anything, it can be a useful known workload for confirming that observability tools show what they claim to show. This creates a single-threaded workload that is CPU-bound ("hot on one CPU"):

```
# while :; do :; done &
```

This is a Bourne shell program that performs an infinite loop in the background. It will need to be killed once you no longer need it.

6.8.2 SysBench

The SysBench system benchmark suite has a simple CPU benchmark tool that calculates prime numbers. For example:

```
# sysbench --num-threads=8 --test=cpu --cpu-max-prime=100000 run
sysbench 0.4.12:  multi-threaded system evaluation benchmark

Running the test with following options:
Number of threads: 8

Doing CPU performance benchmark

Threads started!
Done.

Maximum prime number checked in CPU test: 100000


Test execution summary:
    total time:                          30.4125s
    total number of events:              10000
    total time taken by event execution: 243.2310
    per-request statistics:
         min:                            24.31ms
         avg:                            24.32ms
         max:                            32.44ms
         approx.  95 percentile:         24.32ms

Threads fairness:
    events (avg/stddev):           1250.0000/1.22
    execution time (avg/stddev):   30.4039/0.01
```

This executed eight threads, with a maximum prime number of 100,000. The runtime was 30.4 s, which can be used for comparison with the results from other systems or configurations (assuming many things, such as that identical compiler options were used to build the software; see Chapter 12, Benchmarking).

6.9 Tuning

For CPUs, the biggest performance wins are typically those that eliminate unnecessary work, which is an effective form of tuning. Section 6.5, Methodology, and Section 6.6, Observability Tools, introduced many ways to analyze and identify the work performed, helping you find any unnecessary work. Other methodologies for tuning were also introduced: priority tuning and CPU binding. This section includes these and other tuning examples.

The specifics of tuning—the options available and what to set them to—depend on the processor type, the operating system version, and the intended workload. The following, organized by type, provide examples of what options may be available and how they are tuned. The earlier methodology sections provide guidance on when and why these tunables would be tuned.

6.9.1 Compiler Options

Compilers, and the options they provide for code optimization, can have a dramatic effect on CPU performance. Common options include compiling for 64-bit instead of 32-bit, and selecting a level of optimizations. Compiler optimization is discussed in Chapter 5, Applications.

6.9.2 Scheduling Priority and Class

The nice(1) command can be used to adjust process priority. Positive nice values decrease priority, and negative nice values (which only the superuser can set) *increase* priority. The range is from -20 to +19. For example:

```
$ nice -n 19 command
```

runs the command with a nice value of 19—the lowest priority that nice can set. To change the priority of an already running process, use renice(1).

On Linux, the chrt(1) command can show and set the scheduling priority directly, and the scheduling policy. For example:

```
$ chrt -b command
```

will run the command in SCHED_BATCH (see Scheduling Classes in Section 6.4.2, Software). Both nice(1) and chrt(1) can also be directed at a PID instead of launching a command (see their man pages).

Scheduling priority can also be set directly using the setpriority(2) syscall, and the priority and scheduling policy can be set using the sched_setscheduler(2) syscall.

6.9.3 Scheduler Options

Your kernel may provide tunable parameters to control scheduler behavior, although it is unlikely that these will need to be tuned.

On Linux systems, various CONFIG options control scheduler behavior at a high level, and can be set during kernel compilation. Table 6.12 shows examples from Ubuntu 19.10 and a Linux 5.3 kernel.

Table 6.12   **Example Linux scheduler CONFIG options**

Option	Default	Description
CONFIG_CGROUP_SCHED	y	Allows tasks to be grouped, allocating CPU time on a group basis
CONFIG_FAIR_GROUP_SCHED	y	Allows CFS tasks to be grouped
CONFIG_RT_GROUP_SCHED	n	Allows real-time tasks to be grouped
CONFIG_SCHED_AUTOGROUP	y	Automatically identifies and creates task groups (e.g., build jobs)
CONFIG_SCHED_SMT	y	Hyperthreading support
CONFIG_SCHED_MC	y	Multicore support
CONFIG_HZ	250	Sets kernel clock rate (timer interrupt)
CONFIG_NO_HZ	y	Tickless kernel behavior
CONFIG_SCHED_HRTICK	y	Use high-resolution timers
CONFIG_PREEMPT	n	Full kernel preemption (except spin lock regions and interrupts)
CONFIG_PREEMPT_NONE	n	No preemption
CONFIG_PREEMPT_VOLUNTARY	y	Preemption at voluntary kernel code points

There are also scheduler sysctl(8) tunables can be set live on a running system, including those listed in Table 6.13, with defaults from the same Ubuntu system.

Table 6.13   **Example Linux scheduler sysctl(8) tunables**

sysctl	Default	Description
kernel.sched_cfs_bandwidth_slice_us	5000	CPU time quanta used for CFS bandwidth calculations.
kernel.sched_latency_ns	12000000	Targeted preemption latency. Increasing this can increase a task's time on-CPU, at the cost of preemption latency.
kernel.sched_migration_cost_ns	500000	Task migration latency cost, used for affinity calculations. Tasks that have run more recently than this value are considered cache hot.
kernel.sched_nr_migrate	32	Sets how many tasks can be migrated at a time for load balancing.
kernel.sched_schedstats	0	Enables additional scheduler statistics, including sched:sched_stat* tracepoints.

These sysctl(8) tunables can also be set from /proc/sys/sched.

6.9.4   Scaling Governors

Linux supports different CPU scaling governors that control the CPU clock frequencies via software (the kernel). These can be set via /sys files. For example, for CPU 0:

```
# cat /sys/devices/system/cpu/cpufreq/policy0/scaling_available_governors
performance powersave
# cat /sys/devices/system/cpu/cpufreq/policy0/scaling_governor
powersave
```

This is an example of an untuned system: the current governor is "powersave," which will use lower CPU frequencies to save power. This can be set to "performance" to always use the maximum frequency. For example:

```
# echo performance > /sys/devices/system/cpu/cpufreq/policy0/scaling_governor
```

This must be done for all CPUs (policy0..N). This policy directory also contains files for setting the frequency directly (scaling_setspeed) and determining the range of possible frequencies (scaling_min_freq, scaling_max_freq).

Setting the CPUs to always run at maximum frequency may come with an enormous cost to the environment. If this setting does not provide a significant performance improvement, consider continuing to use the powersave setting for the sake of the planet. For hosts with the access to power MSRs (cloud guests may filter them), you can also use these MSRs to instrument the power consumed with and without a max CPU frequency setting, to quantify (part of[20]) the environmental cost.

6.9.5   Power States

Processor power states can be enabled and disabled using the cpupower(1) tool. As seen earlier in Section 6.6.21, Other Tools, deeper sleep states can have high exit latency (890 µs for C10 was shown). Individual states can be disabled using -d, and -D *latency* will disable all states with higher exit latency than that given (in microseconds). This allows you to fine-tune which lower-power states may be used, disabling those with excessive latency.

6.9.6   CPU Binding

A process may be bound to one or more CPUs, which may increase its performance by improving cache warmth and memory locality.

On Linux, this can be performed using the taskset(1) command, which uses a CPU mask or ranges to set CPU affinity. For example:

```
$ taskset -pc 7-10 10790
pid 10790's current affinity list: 0-15
pid 10790's new affinity list: 7-10
```

---

[20] Host-based power measurements do not account for the environmental costs of server air conditioning, server manufacturing and transportation, and other costs.

This sets PID 10790 to run only on CPUs 7 through 10.

The numactl(8) command can also set CPU binding as well as memory node binding (see Chapter 7, Memory, Section 7.6.4, NUMA Binding).

6.9.7 Exclusive CPU Sets

Linux provides *cpusets*, which allow CPUs to be grouped and processes assigned to them. This can improve performance similarly to CPU binding, but performance can be further improved by making the cpuset exclusive, preventing other processes from using it. The trade-off is a reduction in available CPU for the rest of the system.

The following commented example creates an exclusive set:

```
# mount -t cgroup -ocpuset cpuset /sys/fs/cgroup/cpuset  # may not be necessary
# cd /sys/fs/cgroup/cpuset
# mkdir prodset                      # create a cpuset called "prodset"
# cd prodset
# echo 7-10 > cpuset.cpus            # assign CPUs 7-10
# echo 1 > cpuset.cpu_exclusive      # make prodset exclusive
# echo 1159 > tasks        # assign PID 1159 to prodset
```

For reference, see the cpuset(7) man page.

When creating CPU sets, you may also wish to study which CPUs will continue to service interrupts. The irqbalance(1) daemon will attempt to distribute interrupts across CPUs to improve performance. You can manually set CPU affinity by IRQ via the /proc/irq/*IRQ*/smp_affinity files.

6.9.8 Resource Controls

Apart from associating processes with whole CPUs, modern operating systems provide resource controls for fine-grained allocation of CPU usage.

For Linux, there are control groups (cgroups), which can also control resource usage by processes or groups of processes. CPU usage can be controlled using shares, and the CFS scheduler allows fixed limits to be imposed (*CPU bandwidth*), in terms of allocating microseconds of CPU cycles per interval.

Chapter 11, Cloud Computing, describes a use case of managing the CPU usage of OS virtualized tenants, including how shares and limits can be used in concert.

6.9.9 Security Boot Options

Various kernel mitigations for the Meltdown and Spectre security vulnerabilities have the side effect of reducing performance. There may be some scenario where security is not a requirement but high performance is, and you wish to disable these mitigations. Because this is not recommended (due to the security risk), I will not include all the options here; but you should know that they exist. They are grub command line options that include nospectre_v1 and nospectre_v2. These are documented in Documentation/admin-guide/kernel-parameters.txt in the Linux source [Linux 20f]; an excerpt:

```
nospectre_v1    [PPC] Disable mitigations for Spectre Variant 1 (bounds
                check bypass). With this option data leaks are possible
                in the system.

nospectre_v2    [X86,PPC_FSL_BOOK3E,ARM64] Disable all mitigations for
                the Spectre variant 2 (indirect branch prediction)
                vulnerability. System may allow data leaks with this
                option.
```

There is also a website that lists them: https://make-linux-fast-again.com. This website lacks the warnings listed in the kernel documentation.

6.9.10 Processor Options (BIOS Tuning)

Processors typically provide settings to enable, disable, and tune processor-level features. On x86 systems, these are typically accessed via the BIOS settings menu at boot time.

The settings usually provide maximum performance by default and don't need to be adjusted. The most common reason I adjust these today is to disable Intel Turbo Boost, so that CPU benchmarks execute with a consistent clock rate (bearing in mind that, for production use, Turbo Boost should be enabled for slightly faster performance).

6.10 Exercises

1. Answer the following questions about CPU terminology:
   - What is the difference between a process and a processor?
   - What is a hardware thread?
   - What is the run queue?
   - What is the difference between user time and kernel time?

2. Answer the following conceptual questions:
   - Describe CPU utilization and saturation.
   - Describe how the instruction pipeline improves CPU throughput.
   - Describe how processor instruction width improves CPU throughput.
   - Describe the advantages of multiprocess and multithreaded models.

3. Answer the following deeper questions:
   - Describe what happens when the system CPUs are overloaded with runnable work, including the effect on application performance.

- When there is no runnable work to perform, what do the CPUs do?

- When handed a suspected CPU performance issue, name two methodologies you would use early during the investigation, and explain why.

4. Develop the following procedures for your environment:

- A USE method checklist for CPU resources. Include how to fetch each metric (e.g., which command to execute) and how to interpret the result. Try to use existing OS observability tools before installing or using additional software products.

- A workload characterization checklist for CPU resources. Include how to fetch each metric, and try to use existing OS observability tools first.

5. Perform these tasks:

- Calculate the load average for the following system, whose load is at steady state with no significant disk/lock load:

  □ The system has 64 CPUs.

  □ The system-wide CPU utilization is 50%.

  □ The system-wide CPU saturation, measured as the total number of runnable and queued threads on average, is 2.0.

- Choose an application, and profile its user-level CPU usage. Show which code paths are consuming the most CPU.

6. (optional, advanced) Develop bustop(1)—a tool that shows physical bus or interconnect utilization—with a presentation similar to iostat(1): a list of buses, columns for throughput in each direction, and utilization. Include saturation and error metrics if possible. This will require using PMCs.

6.11 References

[**Saltzer 70**] Saltzer, J., and Gintell, J., "The Instrumentation of Multics," *Communications of the ACM*, August 1970.

[**Bobrow 72**] Bobrow, D. G., Burchfiel, J. D., Murphy, D. L., and Tomlinson, R. S., "TENEX: A Paged Time Sharing System for the PDP-10*," *Communications of the ACM*, March 1972.

[**Myer 73**] Myer, T. H., Barnaby, J. R., and Plummer, W. W., *TENEX Executive Manual*, Bolt, Baranek and Newman, Inc., April 1973.

[**Thomas 73**] Thomas, B., "RFC 546: TENEX Load Averages for July 1973," *Network Working Group*, http://tools.ietf.org/html/rfc546, 1973.

[**TUHS 73**] "V4," *The Unix Heritage Society*, http://minnie.tuhs.org/cgi-bin/utree.pl?file=V4, materials from 1973.

[**Hinnant 84**] Hinnant, D., "Benchmarking UNIX Systems," *BYTE* magazine 9, no. 8, August 1984.

[**Bulpin 05**] Bulpin, J., and Pratt, I., "Hyper-Threading Aware Process Scheduling Heuristics," USENIX, 2005.

[**Corbet 06a**] Corbet, J., "Priority inheritance in the kernel," *LWN.net*, http://lwn.net/Articles/178253, 2006.

[**Otto 06**] Otto, E., "Temperature-Aware Operating System Scheduling," University of Virginia (Thesis), 2006.

[**Ruggiero 08**] Ruggiero, J., "Measuring Cache and Memory Latency and CPU to Memory Bandwidth," Intel (Whitepaper), 2008.

[**Intel 09**] "An Introduction to the Intel QuickPath Interconnect," Intel (Whitepaper), 2009.

[**Levinthal 09**] Levinthal, D., "Performance Analysis Guide for Intel® Core™ i7 Processor and Intel® Xeon™ 5500 Processors," Intel (Whitepaper), 2009.

[**Gregg 10a**] Gregg, B., "Visualizing System Latency," *Communications of the ACM*, July 2010.

[**Weaver 11**] Weaver, V., "The Unofficial Linux Perf Events Web-Page," http://web.eece.maine.edu/~vweaver/projects/perf_events, 2011.

[**McVoy 12**] McVoy, L., "LMbench - Tools for Performance Analysis," http://www.bitmover.com/lmbench, 2012.

[**Stevens 13**] Stevens, W. R., and Rago, S., *Advanced Programming in the UNIX Environment*, 3rd Edition, Addison-Wesley 2013.

[**Perf 15**] "Tutorial: Linux kernel profiling with perf," *perf wiki*, https://perf.wiki.kernel.org/index.php/Tutorial, last updated 2015.

[**Gregg 16b**] Gregg, B., "The Flame Graph," *Communications of the ACM,* Volume 59, Issue 6, pp. 48–57, June 2016.

[**ACPI 17**] *Advanced Configuration and Power Interface (ACPI) Specification*, https://uefi.org/sites/default/files/resources/ACPI%206_2_A_Sept29.pdf, 2017.

[**Gregg 17b**] Gregg, B., "CPU Utilization Is Wrong," http://www.brendangregg.com/blog/2017-05-09/cpu-utilization-is-wrong.html, 2017.

[**Gregg 17c**] Gregg, B., "Linux Load Averages: Solving the Mystery," http://www.brendangregg.com/blog/2017-08-08/linux-load-averages.html, 2017.

[**Mulnix 17**] Mulnix, D., "Intel® Xeon® Processor Scalable Family Technical Overview," https://software.intel.com/en-us/articles/intel-xeon-processor-scalable-family-technical-overview, 2017.

[**Gregg 18b**] Gregg, B., "Netflix FlameScope," *Netflix Technology Blog*, https://netflixtechblog.com/netflix-flamescope-a57ca19d47bb, 2018.

[**Ather 19**] Ather, A., "General Purpose GPU Computing," http://techblog.cloudperf.net/2019/12/general-purpose-gpu-computing.html, 2019.

[**Gregg 19**] Gregg, B., *BPF Performance Tools: Linux System and Application Observability*, Addison-Wesley, 2019.

[**Intel 19a**] *Intel 64 and IA-32 Architectures Software Developer's Manual*, Combined Volumes 1, 2A, 2B, 2C, 3A, 3B, and 3C. Intel, 2019.

[Intel 19b] *Intel 64 and IA-32 Architectures Software Developer's Manual,* Volume 3B, *System Programming Guide, Part 2.* Intel, 2019.

[Netflix 19] "FlameScope Is a Visualization Tool for Exploring Different Time Ranges as Flame Graphs," https://github.com/Netflix/flamescope, 2019.

[Wysocki 19] Wysocki, R., "CPU Idle Time Management," *Linux documentation,* https://www.kernel.org/doc/html/latest/driver-api/pm/cpuidle.html, 2019.

[AMD 20] "AMD μProf," https://developer.amd.com/amd-uprof, accessed 2020.

[Gregg 20d] Gregg, B., "MSR Cloud Tools," https://github.com/brendangregg/msr-cloud-tools, last updated 2020.

[Gregg 20e] Gregg, B., "PMC (Performance Monitoring Counter) Tools for the Cloud," https://github.com/brendangregg/pmc-cloud-tools, last updated 2020.

[Gregg 20f] Gregg, B., "perf Examples," http://www.brendangregg.com/perf.html, accessed 2020.

[Gregg 20g] Gregg, B., "FlameGraph: Stack Trace Visualizer," https://github.com/brendangregg/FlameGraph, last updated 2020.

[Intel 20a] "Product Specifications," https://ark.intel.com, accessed 2020.

[Intel 20b] "Intel® VTune™ Profiler," https://software.intel.com/content/www/us/en/develop/tools/vtune-profiler.html, accessed 2020.

[Iovisor 20a] "bpftrace: High-level Tracing Language for Linux eBPF," https://github.com/iovisor/bpftrace, last updated 2020.

[Linux 20f] "The Kernel's Command-Line Parameters," *Linux documentation,* https://www.kernel.org/doc/html/latest/admin-guide/kernel-parameters.html, accessed 2020.

[Spier 20a] Spier, M., "A D3.js Plugin That Produces Flame Graphs from Hierarchical Data," https://github.com/spiermar/d3-flame-graph, last updated 2020.

[Spier 20b] Spier, M., "Template," https://github.com/spiermar/d3-flame-graph#template, last updated 2020.

[Valgrind 20] "Valgrind Documentation," http://valgrind.org/docs/manual, May 2020.

[Verma 20] Verma, A., "CUDA Cores vs Stream Processors Explained," https://graphicscardhub.com/cuda-cores-vs-stream-processors, 2020.

Chapter 7

Memory

System main memory stores application and kernel instructions, their working data, and file system caches. The secondary storage for this data is typically the storage devices—the disks—which operate orders of magnitude more slowly. Once main memory has filled, the system may begin switching data between main memory and the storage devices. This is a slow process that will often become a system bottleneck, dramatically decreasing performance. The system may also terminate the largest memory-consuming process, causing application outages.

Other performance factors to consider include the CPU expense of allocating and freeing memory, copying memory, and managing memory address space mappings. On multisocket architectures, memory locality can become a factor, as memory attached to local sockets has lower access latency than remote sockets.

The learning objectives of this chapter are:

- Understand memory concepts.
- Become familiar with memory hardware internals.
- Become familiar with kernel and user allocator internals.
- Have a working knowledge of the MMU and TLB.
- Follow different methodologies for memory analysis.
- Characterize system-wide and per-process memory usage.
- Identify issues caused by low available memory.
- Locate memory usage in a process address space and kernel slabs.
- Investigate memory usage using profilers, tracers, and flame graphs.
- Become aware of tunable parameters for memory.

This chapter has five parts, the first three providing the basis for memory analysis, and the last two showing its practical application to Linux-based systems. The parts are as follows:

- **Background** introduces memory-related terminology and key memory performance concepts.
- **Architecture** provides generic descriptions of hardware and software memory architecture.

- **Methodology** explains performance analysis methodology.

- **Observability Tools** describes performance tools for memory analysis.

- **Tuning** explains tuning and example tunable parameters.

The on-CPU memory caches (Level 1/2/3, TLB) are covered in Chapter 6, CPUs.

7.1   Terminology

For reference, memory-related terminology used in this chapter includes the following:

- **Main memory**: Also referred to as *physical memory*, this describes the fast data storage area of a computer, commonly provided as DRAM.

- **Virtual memory**: An abstraction of main memory that is (almost) infinite and non-contended. Virtual memory is not real memory.

- **Resident memory**: Memory that currently resides in main memory.

- **Anonymous memory**: Memory with no file system location or path name. It includes the working data of a process address space, called the *heap*.

- **Address space**: A memory context. There are virtual address spaces for each process, and for the kernel.

- **Segment**: An area of virtual memory flagged for a particular purpose, such as for storing executable or writeable pages.

- **Instruction text**: Refers to CPU instructions in memory, usually in a segment.

- **OOM**: Out of memory, when the kernel detects low available memory.

- **Page**: A unit of memory, as used by the OS and CPUs. Historically it is either 4 or 8 Kbytes. Modern processors have *multiple page size support* for larger sizes.

- **Page fault**: An invalid memory access. These are normal occurrences when using on-demand virtual memory.

- **Paging**: The transfer of pages between main memory and the storage devices.

- **Swapping**: Linux uses the term *swapping* to refer to *anonymous paging* to the swap device (the transfer of *swap pages*). In Unix and other operating systems, swapping is the transfer of entire processes between main memory and the swap devices. This book uses the Linux version of the term.

- **Swap**: An on-disk area for paged anonymous data. It may be an area on a storage device, also called a *physical swap device*, or a file system file, called a *swap file*. Some tools use the term *swap* to refer to virtual memory (which is confusing and incorrect).

Other terms are introduced throughout this chapter. The Glossary includes basic terminology for reference if needed, including *address*, *buffer*, and *DRAM*. Also see the terminology sections in Chapters 2 and 3.

7.2 Concepts

The following are a selection of important concepts regarding memory and memory performance.

7.2.1 Virtual Memory

Virtual memory is an abstraction that provides each process and the kernel with its own large, linear, and private address space. It simplifies software development, leaving physical memory placement for the operating system to manage. It also supports multitasking (virtual address spaces are separated by design) and oversubscription (in-use memory can extend beyond main memory). Virtual memory was introduced in Chapter 3, Operating Systems, Section 3.2.8, Virtual Memory. For historical background, see [Denning 70].

Figure 7.1 shows the role of virtual memory for a process, on a system with a swap device (secondary storage). A page of memory is shown, as most virtual memory implementations are page-based.

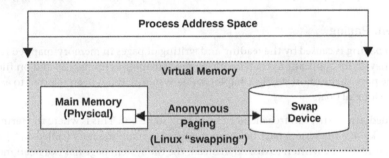

Figure 7.1   Process virtual memory

The process address space is mapped by the virtual memory subsystem to main memory and the physical swap device. Pages of memory can be moved between them by the kernel as needed, a process Linux calls *swapping* (and other OSes call *anonymous paging*). This allows the kernel to *oversubscribe* main memory.

The kernel may impose a limit to oversubscription. A commonly used limit is the size of main memory plus the physical swap devices. The kernel can fail allocations that try to exceed this limit. Such "out of virtual memory" errors can be confusing at first glance, since virtual memory itself is an abstract resource.

Linux also allows other behaviors, including placing *no* bounds on memory allocation. This is termed *overcommit* and is described after the following sections on paging and demand paging, which are necessary for overcommit to work.

7.2.2 Paging

Paging is the movement of pages in and out of main memory, which are referred to as *page-ins* and *page-outs*, respectively. It was first introduced by the Atlas Computer in 1962 [Corbató 68], allowing:

- Partially loaded programs to execute

- Programs larger than main memory to execute

- Efficient movement of programs between main memory and storage devices

These abilities are still true today. Unlike the earlier technique of swapping out entire programs, paging is a fine-grained approach to managing and freeing main memory, since the page size unit is relatively small (e.g., 4 Kbytes).

Paging with virtual memory (*paged virtual memory*) was introduced to Unix via BSD [Babaoglu 79] and became the standard.

With the later addition of the page cache for sharing file system pages (see Chapter 8, File Systems), two different types of paging became available: *file system paging* and *anonymous paging*.

File System Paging

File system paging is caused by the reading and writing of pages in memory-mapped files. This is normal behavior for applications that use file memory mappings (mmap(2)) and on file systems that use the page cache (most do; see Chapter 8, File Systems). It has been referred to as "good" paging [McDougall 06a].

When needed, the kernel can free memory by paging some out. This is where the terminology gets a bit tricky: if a file system page has been modified in main memory (called *dirty*), the page-out will require it to be written to disk. If, instead, the file system page has not been modified (called *clean*), the page-out merely frees the memory for immediate reuse, since a copy already exists on disk. Because of this, the term *page-out* means that a page was moved out of memory—which may or may not have included a write to a storage device (you may see the term page-out defined differently in other texts).

Anonymous Paging (Swapping)

Anonymous paging involves data that is private to processes: the process heap and stacks. It is termed *anonymous* because it has no named location in the operating system (i.e., no file system path name). Anonymous page-outs require moving the data to the physical swap devices or swap files. Linux uses the term *swapping* to refer to this type of paging.

Anonymous paging hurts performance and has therefore been referred to as "bad" paging [McDougall 06a]. When applications access memory pages that have been paged out, they block on the disk I/O required to read them back to main memory.[1] This is an *anonymous page-in*,

---

[1] If faster storage devices are used as swap devices, such as 3D XPoint with sub 10 μs latency, swapping may not be the same "bad" paging it once was, but rather become a simple way to intentionally extend main memory, one with mature kernel support.

which introduces synchronous latency to the application. Anonymous page-outs may not affect application performance directly, as they can be performed asynchronously by the kernel.

Performance is best when there is no anonymous paging (swapping). This can be achieved by configuring applications to remain within the main memory available and by monitoring page scanning, memory utilization, and anonymous paging, to ensure that there are no indicators of a memory shortage.

7.2.3 Demand Paging

Operating systems that support demand paging (most do) map pages of virtual memory to physical memory on demand, as shown in Figure 7.2. This defers the CPU overhead of creating the mappings until they are actually needed and accessed, instead of at the time a range of memory is first allocated.

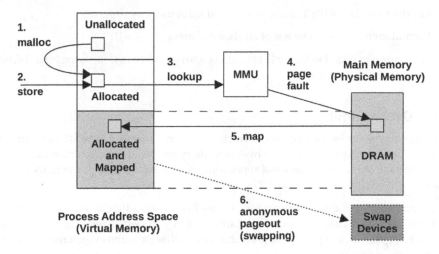

Figure 7.2   Page fault example

The sequence shown in Figure 7.2 begins with a malloc() (step 1) that provides allocated memory, and then a store instruction (step 2) to that newly allocated memory. For the MMU to determine the main memory location of the store, it performs a virtual to physical lookup (step 3) for the page of memory, which fails as there is not yet a mapping. This failure is termed a *page fault* (step 4), which triggers the kernel to create an on-demand mapping (step 5). Sometime later, the page of memory could be paged out to the swap devices to free up memory (step 6).

Step 2 could also be a load instruction in the case of a mapped file, which should contain data but isn't yet mapped to this process address space.

If the mapping can be satisfied from another page in memory, it is called a *minor fault*. This may occur for mapping a new page from available memory, during memory growth of the process (as pictured). It can also occur for mapping to another existing page, such as reading a page from a mapped shared library.

Page faults that require storage device access (not shown in this figure), such as accessing an uncached memory-mapped file, are called *major faults*.

The result of the virtual memory model and demand allocation is that any page of virtual memory may be in one of the following states:

A. Unallocated

B. Allocated, but unmapped (unpopulated and not yet faulted)

C. Allocated, and mapped to main memory (RAM)

D. Allocated, and mapped to the physical swap device (disk)

State (D) is reached if the page is paged out due to system memory pressure. A transition from (B) to (C) is a page fault. If it requires disk I/O, it is a major page fault; otherwise, a minor page fault.

From these states, two memory usage terms can also be defined:

- **Resident set size** (RSS): The size of allocated main memory pages (C)

- **Virtual memory size**: The size of all allocated areas (B + C + D)

Demand paging was added to Unix via BSD, along with paged virtual memory. It has become the standard and is used by Linux.

7.2.4 Overcommit

Linux supports the notion of *overcommit*, which allows more memory to be allocated than the system can possibly store—more than physical memory and swap devices combined. It relies on demand paging and the tendency of applications to not use much of the memory they have allocated.

With overcommit, application requests for memory (e.g., malloc(3)) will succeed when they would otherwise have failed. Instead of allocating memory conservatively to remain within virtual memory limits, an application programmer can allocate memory generously and later use it sparsely on demand.

On Linux, the behavior of overcommit can be configured with a tunable parameter. See Section 7.6, Tuning, for details. The consequences of overcommit depend on how the kernel manages memory pressure; see the discussion of the OOM killer in Section 7.3, Architecture.

7.2.5 Process Swapping

Process swapping is the movement of entire processes between main memory and the physical swap device or swap file. This is the original Unix technique for managing main memory and is the origin of the term *swap* [Thompson 78].

To swap out a process, all of its private data must be written to the swap device, including the process heap (anonymous data), its open file table, and other metadata that is only needed when the process is active. Data that originated from file systems and has not been modified can be dropped and read from the original locations again when needed.

Process swapping severely hurts performance, as a process that has been swapped out requires numerous disk I/O to run again. It made more sense on early Unix for the machines of the time, such as the PDP-11, which had a maximum process size of 64 Kbytes [Bach 86]. (Modern systems allow process sizes measured in the Gbytes.)

This description is provided for historical background. Linux systems do not swap processes at all and rely only on paging.

7.2.6   File System Cache Usage

It is normal for memory usage to grow after system boot as the operating system uses available memory to cache the file system, improving performance. The principle is: If there is spare main memory, use it for something useful. This can distress naïve users who see the available free memory shrink to near zero sometime after boot. But it does not pose a problem for applications, as the kernel should be able to quickly free memory from the file system cache when applications need it.

For more about the various file system caches that can consume main memory, see Chapter 8, File Systems.

7.2.7   Utilization and Saturation

Main memory utilization can be calculated as used memory versus total memory. Memory used by the file system cache can be treated as unused, as it is available for reuse by applications.

If demands for memory exceed the amount of main memory, main memory becomes *saturated*. The operating system may then free memory by employing paging, process swapping (if supported), and, on Linux, the OOM killer (described later). Any of these activities is an indicator of main memory saturation.

Virtual memory can also be studied in terms of capacity utilization, if the system imposes a limit on the amount of virtual memory it is willing to allocate (Linux overcommit does not). If so, once virtual memory is exhausted, the kernel will fail allocations; for example, malloc(3) fails with errno set to ENOMEM.

Note that the currently available virtual memory on a system is sometimes (confusingly) called *available swap*.

7.2.8   Allocators

While virtual memory handles multitasking of physical memory, the actual allocation and placement within a virtual address space are often handled by allocators. These are either userland libraries or kernel-based routines, which provide the software programmer with an easy interface for memory usage (e.g., malloc(3), free(3)).

Allocators can have a significant effect on performance, and a system may provide multiple user-level allocator libraries to pick from. They can improve performance by use of techniques including per-thread object caching, but they can also hurt performance if allocation becomes fragmented and wasteful. Specific examples are covered in Section 7.3, Architecture.

7.2.9   Shared Memory

Memory can be shared between processes. This is commonly used for system libraries to save memory by sharing one copy of their read-only instruction text with all processes that use it.

This presents difficulties for observability tools that show per-process main memory usage. Should shared memory be included when reporting the total memory size of a process? One technique in use by Linux is to provide an additional measure, the *proportional set size* (PSS), which includes private memory (not shared) plus shared memory divided by the number of users. See Section 7.5.9, pmap, for a tool that can show PSS.

7.2.10   Working Set Size

Working set size (WSS) is the amount of main memory a process frequently uses to perform work. It is a useful concept for memory performance tuning: performance should greatly improve if the WSS can fit into the CPU caches, rather than main memory. Also, performance will greatly degrade if the WSS exceeds the main memory size, and the application must swap to perform work.

While useful as a concept, it is difficult to measure in practice: there is no WSS statistic in observability tools (they commonly report RSS, not WSS). Section 7.4.10, Memory Shrinking, describes an experimental methodology for WSS estimation, and Section 7.5.12, wss, shows an experimental working set size estimation tool, wss(8).

7.2.11   Word Size

As introduced in Chapter 6, CPUs, processors may support multiple word sizes, such as 32-bit and 64-bit, allowing software for either to run. As the address space size is bounded by the addressable range from the word size, applications requiring more than 4 Gbytes of memory are too large for a 32-bit address space and need to be compiled for 64 bits or higher.[2]

Depending on the kernel and processor, some of the address space may be reserved for kernel addresses and is unavailable for application use. An extreme case is Windows with a 32-bit word size, where by default 2 Gbytes is reserved for the kernel, leaving only 2 Gbytes for the application [Hall 09]. On Linux (or Windows with the /3GB option enabled) the kernel reservation is 1 Gbyte. With a 64-bit word size (if the processor supports it) the address space is so much larger that the kernel reservation should not be an issue.

Depending on the CPU architecture, memory performance may also be improved by using larger bit widths, as instructions can operate on larger word sizes. A small amount of memory may be wasted, in cases where a data type has unused bits at the larger bit width.

---

[2]There is also the Physical Address Extension (PAE) feature (workaround) for x86 allowing 32-bit processors to access larger memory ranges (but not in a single process).

7.3   Architecture

This section introduces memory architecture, both hardware and software, including processor and operating system specifics.

These topics have been summarized as background for performance analysis and tuning. For more details, see the vendor processor manuals and texts on operating system internals listed at the end of this chapter.

7.3.1   Hardware

Memory hardware includes main memory, buses, CPU caches, and the MMU.

Main Memory

The common type of main memory in use today is *dynamic random-access memory* (DRAM). This is a type of volatile memory—its contents are lost when power is lost. DRAM provides high-density storage, as each bit is implemented using only two logical components: a capacitor and a transistor. The capacitor requires a periodic refresh to maintain charge.

Enterprise servers are configured with different amounts of DRAM depending on their purpose, typically ranging from one Gbyte to one Tbyte and larger. Cloud computing instances are typically smaller, ranging between 512 Mbytes and 256 Gbytes each.[3] However, cloud computing is designed to spread load over a pool of instances, so they can collectively bring much more DRAM online for a distributed application, although at a much higher coherency cost.

Latency

The access time of main memory can be measured as the *column address strobe* (CAS) latency: the time between sending a memory module the desired address (column) and when the data is available to be read. This varies depending on the type of memory (for DDR4 it is around 10 to 20ns [Crucial 18]). For memory I/O transfers, this latency may occur multiple times for a memory bus (e.g., 64 bits wide) to transfer a cache line (e.g., at 64 *bytes* wide). There are also other latencies involved with the CPU and MMU for then reading the newly available data. Read instructions avoid these latencies when they return from a CPU cache; write instructions may avoid them as well, if the processor supports write-back caching (e.g., Intel processors).

Main Memory Architecture

An example main memory architecture for a generic two-processor *uniform memory access* (UMA) system is shown in Figure 7.3.

Each CPU has uniform access latency to all of memory, via a shared system bus. When managed by a single operating system kernel instance that runs uniformly across all processors, this is also a symmetric multiprocessing (SMP) architecture.

---

[3] Exceptions include the AWS EC2 high memory instances, which reach 24 Tbytes of memory [Amazon 20].

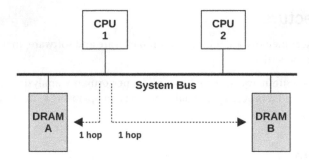

Figure 7.3   Example UMA main memory architecture, two-processor

For comparison, an example two-processor *non-uniform memory access* (NUMA) system is shown in Figure 7.4, which uses a CPU interconnect that becomes part of the memory architecture. For this architecture, the access time for main memory varies based on its location relative to the CPU.

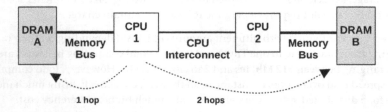

Figure 7.4   Example NUMA main memory architecture, two-processor

CPU 1 can perform I/O to DRAM A directly, via its memory bus. This is referred to as *local memory*. CPU 1 performs I/O to DRAM B via CPU 2 and the CPU interconnect (two hops). This is referred to as *remote memory* and has a higher access latency.

The banks of memory connected to each CPU are referred to as *memory nodes*, or just *nodes*. The operating system may be aware of the memory node topology based on information provided by the processor. This then allows it to assign memory and schedule threads based on *memory locality*, favoring local memory as much as possible to improve performance.

Buses

How main memory is physically connected to the system depends on the main memory architecture, as previously pictured. The actual implementation may involve additional controllers and buses between the CPUs and memory. Main memory may be accessed in one of the following ways:

- **Shared system bus**: Single or multiprocessor, via a shared system bus, a memory bridge controller, and finally a memory bus. This was pictured as the UMA example, Figure 7.3, and as the Intel front-side bus example, Figure 6.9 in Chapter 6, CPUs. The memory controller in that example was a Northbridge.

- **Direct:** Single processor with directly attached memory via a memory bus.

- **Interconnect:** Multiprocessor, each with directly attached memory via a memory bus, and processors connected via a CPU interconnect. This was pictured earlier as the NUMA example in Figure 7.4; CPU interconnects are discussed in Chapter 6, CPUs.

If you suspect your system is none of the above, find a system functional diagram and follow the data path between CPUs and memory, noting all components along the way.

DDR SDRAM

The speed of the memory bus, for any architecture, is often dictated by the memory interface standard supported by the processor and system board. A common standard in use since 1996 is *double data rate synchronous dynamic random-access memory* (DDR SDRAM). The term *double data rate* refers to the transfer of data on both the rise and fall of the clock signal (also called *double-pumped*). The term *synchronous* refers to the memory being clocked synchronously with the CPUs.

Example DDR SDRAM standards are shown in Table 7.1.

Table 7.1 **Example DDR bandwidths**

Standard	Specification Year	Memory Clock (MHz)	Data Rate (MT/s)	Peak Bandwidth (MB/s)
DDR-200	2000	100	200	1,600
DDR-333	2000	167	333	2,667
DDR2-667	2003	167	667	5,333
DDR2-800	2003	200	800	6,400
DDR3-1333	2007	167	1,333	10,667
DDR3-1600	2007	200	1,600	12,800
DDR4-3200	2012	200	3,200	25,600
DDR5-4800	2020	200	4,800	38,400
DDR5-6400	2020	200	6,400	51,200

The DDR5 standard is expected to be released during 2020 by the JEDEC Solid State Technology Association. These standards are also named using "PC-" followed by the data transfer rate in megabytes per second, for example, PC-1600.

Multichannel

System architectures may support the use of multiple memory buses in parallel, to improve bandwidth. Common multiples are dual-, triple-, and quad-channel. For example, the Intel Core i7 processors support up to quad-channel DDR3-1600, for a maximum memory bandwidth of 51.2 Gbytes/s.

CPU Caches

Processors typically include on-chip hardware caches to improve memory access performance. The caches may include the following levels, of decreasing speed and increasing size:

- **Level 1**: Usually split into a separate instruction cache and data cache
- **Level 2**: A cache for both instructions and data
- **Level 3**: Another larger level of cache

Depending on the processor, Level 1 is typically referenced by virtual memory addresses, and Level 2 onward by physical memory addresses.

These caches were discussed in more depth in Chapter 6, CPUs. An additional type of hardware cache, the TLB, is discussed in this chapter.

MMU

The MMU (memory management unit) is responsible for virtual-to-physical address translations. These are performed per page, and offsets within a page are mapped directly. The MMU was introduced in Chapter 6, CPUs, in the context of nearby CPU caches.

A generic MMU is pictured in Figure 7.5, with levels of CPU caches and main memory.

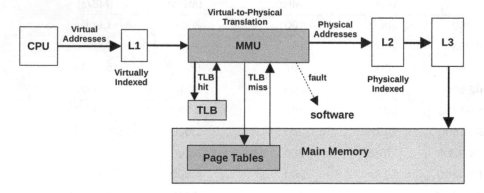

Figure 7.5   Memory management unit

Multiple Page Sizes

Modern processors support multiple page sizes, which allow different page sizes (e.g., 4 Kbytes, 2 Mbytes, 1 Gbyte) to be used by the operating system and the MMU. The Linux *huge pages* feature supports larger page sizes, such as 2 Mbytes or 1 Gbyte.

TLB

The MMU pictured in Figure 7.5 uses a TLB (translation lookaside buffer) as the first level of address translation cache, followed by the page tables in main memory. The TLB may be divided into separate caches for instruction and data pages.

Because the TLB has a limited number of entries for mappings, the use of larger page sizes increases the range of memory that can be translated from its cache (its *reach*), which reduces TLB misses and improves system performance. The TLB may be further divided into separate caches for each of these page sizes, improving the probability of retaining larger mappings in cache.

As an example of TLB sizes, a typical Intel Core i7 processor provides the four TLBs shown in Table 7.2 [Intel 19a].

Table 7.2 **TLBs for a typical Intel Core i7 processor**

Type	Page Size	Entrics
Instruction	4 K	64 per thread, 128 per core
Instruction	large	7 per thread
Data	4 K	64
Data	large	32

This processor has one level of data TLB. The Intel Core microarchitecture supports two levels, similar to the way CPUs provide multiple levels of main memory cache.

The exact makeup of the TLB is specific to the processor type. Refer to the vendor processor manuals for details on the TLBs in your processor and further information on their operation.

7.3.2 Software

Software for memory management includes the virtual memory system, address translation, swapping, paging, and allocation. The topics most related to performance are included in this section: freeing memory, the free list, page scanning, swapping, the process address space, and memory allocators.

Freeing Memory

When the available memory on the system becomes low, there are various methods that the kernel can use to free up memory, adding it to the *free list* of pages. These methods are pictured in Figure 7.6 for Linux, in the *general* order in which they are used as available memory decreases.

These methods are:

- **Free list:** A list of pages that are unused (also called *idle memory*) and available for immediate allocation. This is usually implemented as multiple *free page lists*, one for each locality group (NUMA).
- **Page cache:** The file system cache. A tunable parameter called *swappiness* sets the degree to which the system should favor freeing memory from the page cache instead of swapping.

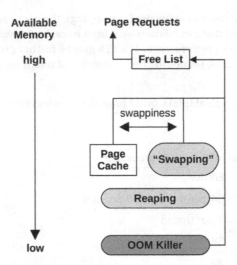

Figure 7.6   Linux memory availability management

- **Swapping**: This is paging by the page-out daemon, kswapd, which finds not recently used pages to add to the free list, including application memory. These are paged out, which may involve writing to either a file system-based swap file or a swap device. Naturally, this is available only if a swap file or device has been configured.

- **Reaping**: When a low-memory threshold is crossed, kernel modules and the kernel slab allocator can be instructed to immediately free any memory that can easily be freed. This is also known as *shrinking*.

- **OOM killer**: The out-of-memory killer will free memory by finding and killing a sacrificial process, found using select_bad_process() and then killed by calling oom_kill_process(). This may be logged in the system log (/var/log/messages) as an "Out of memory: Kill process" message.

The Linux swappiness parameter controls whether to favor freeing memory by paging applications or by reclaiming it from the page cache. It is a number between 0 and 100 (the default value is 60), where higher values favor freeing memory by paging. Controlling the balance between these memory freeing techniques allows system throughput to be improved by preserving warm file system cache while paging out cold application memory [Corbet 04].

It is also interesting to ask what happens if no swap device or swap file is configured. This limits virtual memory size, so if overcommit has been disabled, memory allocations will fail sooner. On Linux, this may also mean that the OOM killer is used sooner.

Consider an application with an issue of endless memory growth. With swap, this is likely to first become a performance issue due to paging, which is an opportunity to debug the issue live. Without swap, there is no paging grace period, so either the application hits an "Out of memory" error or the OOM killer terminates it. This may delay debugging the issue if it is seen only after hours of usage.

In the Netflix cloud, instances typically do not use swap, so applications are OOM killed if they exhaust memory. Applications are distributed across a large pool of instances, and having one

OOM killed causes traffic to be immediately redirected to other healthy instances. This is considered preferable to allowing one instance to run slowly due to swapping.

When memory cgroups are used, similar memory freeing techniques can be used as those shown in Figure 7.6 to manage cgroup memory. A system may have an abundance of free memory, but is swapping or encountering the OOM killer because a container has exhausted its cgroup-controlled limit [Evans 17]. For more on cgroups and containers, see Chapter 11, Cloud Computing.

The following sections describe free lists, reaping, and the page-out daemon.

Free List(s)

The original Unix memory allocator used a memory map and a first-fit scan. With the introduction of paged virtual memory in BSD, a *free list* and a *page-out daemon* were added [Babaoglu 79]. The free list, pictured in Figure 7.7, allows available memory to be located immediately.

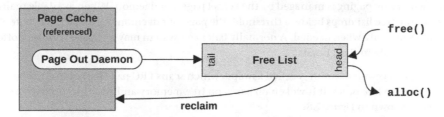

Figure 7.7   Free list operations

Memory freed is added to the head of the list for future allocations. Memory that is freed by the page-out daemon—and that may still contain useful cached file system pages—is added to the tail. Should a future request for one of these pages occur before the useful page has been reused, it can be *reclaimed* and removed from the free list.

A form of free list is still in use by Linux-based systems, as pictured in Figure 7.6. Free lists are typically consumed via allocators, such as the slab allocator for the kernel, and libc malloc() for user-space (which has its own free lists). These in turn consume pages and then expose them via their allocator API.

Linux uses the buddy allocator for managing pages. This provides multiple free lists for different-sized memory allocations, following a power-of-two scheme. The term *buddy* refers to finding neighboring pages of free memory so that they can be allocated together. For historical background, see [Peterson 77].

The buddy free lists are at the bottom of the following hierarchy, beginning with the per-memory node pg_data_t:

- **Nodes:** Banks of memory, NUMA-aware
- **Zones:** Ranges of memory for certain purposes (direct memory access [DMA],[4] normal, highmem)
- **Migration types:** Unmovable, reclaimable, movable, etc.
- **Sizes:** Power-of-two number of pages

---

[4] Although ZONE_DMA may be removed [Corbet 18a].

Allocating within the node free lists improves memory locality and performance. For the most common allocation, single pages, the buddy allocator keeps lists of single pages for each CPU to reduce CPU lock contention.

Reaping

Reaping mostly involves freeing memory from the kernel slab allocator caches. These caches contain unused memory in slab-size chunks, ready for reuse. Reaping returns this memory to the system for page allocations.

On Linux, kernel modules can also call register_shrinker() to register specific functions for reaping their own memory.

Page Scanning

Freeing memory by paging is managed by the kernel page-out daemon. When available main memory in the free list drops below a threshold, the page-out daemon begins *page scanning*. Page scanning occurs only when needed. A normally balanced system may not page scan very often and may do so only in short bursts.

On Linux, the page-out daemon is called kswapd, which scans LRU page lists of inactive and active memory to free pages. It is woken up based on free memory and two thresholds to provide hysteresis, as shown in Figure 7.8.

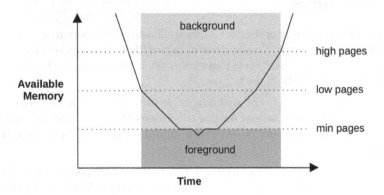

Figure 7.8   kswapd wake-ups and modes

Once free memory has reached the lowest threshold, kswapd runs in the foreground, synchronously freeing pages of memory as they are requested, a method sometimes known as *direct-reclaim* [Gorman 04]. This lowest threshold is tunable (vm.min_free_kbytes), and the others are scaled based on it (by 2x for low, 3x for high). For workloads with high allocation bursts that outpace kswap reclamation, Linux provides additional tunables for more aggressive scanning, vm.watermark_scale_factor and vm.watermark_boost_factor: see Section 7.6.1, Tunable Parameters.

The page cache has separate lists for *inactive pages* and *active pages*. These operate in an LRU fashion, allowing kswapd to find free pages quickly. They are shown in Figure 7.9.

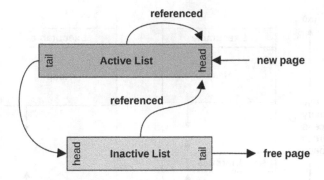

Figure 7.9   kswapd lists

kswapd scans the inactive list first, and then the active list, if needed. The term *scanning* refers to checking of pages as the list is walked: a page may be ineligible to be freed if it is locked/dirty. The term scanning as used by kswapd has a different meaning than the scanning done by the original UNIX page-out daemon, which scans all of memory.

7.3.3   Process Virtual Address Space

Managed by both hardware and software, the process virtual address space is a range of virtual pages that are mapped to physical pages as needed. The addresses are split into areas called *segments* for storing the thread stacks, process executable, libraries, and heap. Examples for 32-bit processes on Linux are shown in Figure 7.10, for both x86 and SPARC processors.

On SPARC the kernel resides in a separate full address space (which is not shown in Figure 7.10). Note that on SPARC it is not possible to distinguish between a user and kernel address based only on the pointer value; x86 employs a different scheme where the user and kernel addresses are non-overlapping.[5]

The program executable segment contains separate text and data segments. Libraries are also composed of separate executable text and data segments. These different segment types are:

- **Executable text**: Contains the executable CPU instructions for the process. This is mapped from the text segment of the binary program on the file system. It is read-only with the execute permission.

- **Executable data**: Contains initialized variables mapped from the data segment of the binary program. This has read/write permissions so that the variables can be modified while the program is running. It also has a private flag so that modifications are not flushed to disk.

- **Heap**: This is the working memory for the program and is anonymous memory (no file system location). It grows as needed and is allocated via malloc(3).

- **Stack**: Stacks of the running threads, mapped read/write.

---

[5] Note that for 64-bit addresses, the full 64-bit range may not be supported by the processor: the AMD specification allows implementations to only support 48-bit addresses, where the unused higher-order bits are set to the last bit: this creates two usable address ranges, called *canonical address*, of 0 to 0x00007fffffffffff, used for user space, and 0xffff800000000000 to 0xffffffffffffffff, used for kernel space. This is why x86 kernel addresses begin with 0xffff.

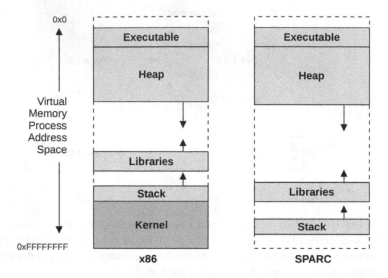

Figure 7.10   Example process virtual memory address space

The library text segments may be shared by other processes that use the same library, each of which has a private copy of the library data segment.

Heap Growth

A common source of confusion is the endless growth of heap. Is it a memory leak? For simple allocators, a free(3) does not return memory to the operating system; rather, memory is kept to serve future allocations. This means that the process resident memory can only grow, which is normal. Methods for processes to reduce system memory use include:

- **Re-exec**: Calling execve(2) to begin from an empty address space
- **Memory mapping**: Using mmap(2) and munmap(2), which will return memory to the system

Memory-mapped files are described in Chapter 8, File Systems, Section 8.3.10, Memory-Mapped Files.

Glibc, commonly used on Linux, is an advanced allocator that supports an mmap mode of operation, as well as a malloc_trim(3) function to release free memory to the system. malloc_trim(3) is automatically called by free(3) when the top-of-heap free memory becomes large,[6] and frees it using sbrk(2) syscalls.

Allocators

There are a variety of user- and kernel-level allocators for memory allocation. Figure 7.11 shows the role of allocators, including some common types.

---

[6] Larger than the M_TRIM_THRESHOLD mallopt(3) parameter, which is 128 Kbytes by default.

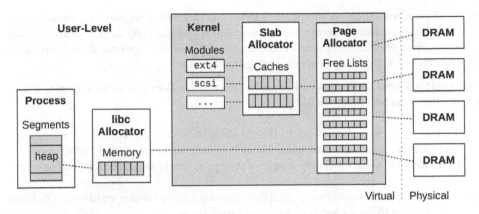

Figure 7.11   User- and kernel-level memory allocators

Page management was described earlier in Section 7.3.2, Software, under Free List(s).

Memory allocator features can include:

- **Simple API:** For example, malloc(3), free(3).

- **Efficient memory usage:** When servicing memory allocations of a variety of sizes, memory usage can become *fragmented*, where there are many unused regions that waste memory. Allocators can strive to coalesce the unused regions, so that larger allocations can make use of them, improving efficiency.

- **Performance:** Memory allocations can be frequent, and on multithreaded environments they can perform poorly due to contention for synchronization primitives. Allocators can be designed to use locks sparingly, and can also make use of per-thread or per-CPU caches to improve memory locality.

- **Observability:** An allocator may provide statistics and debug modes to show how it is being used, and which code paths are responsible for allocations.

The sections that follow describe kernel-level allocators—slab and SLUB—and user-level allocators—glibc, TCMalloc, and jemalloc.

Slab

The kernel slab allocator manages caches of objects of a specific size, allowing them to be recycled quickly without the overhead of page allocation. This is especially effective for kernel allocations, which are frequently for fixed-size structs.

As a kernel example, the following two lines are from ZFS arc.c[7]:

```
df = kmem_alloc(sizeof (l2arc_data_free_t), KM_SLEEP);
head = kmem_cache_alloc(hdr_cache, KM_PUSHPAGE);
```

---

[7] The only reason these came to mind as examples is because I developed the code.

The first, kmem_alloc(), shows a traditional-style kernel allocation whose size is passed as an argument. The kernel maps this to a slab cache based on that size (very large sizes are handled differently, by an *oversize arena*). The second, kmem_cache_alloc(), operates directly on a custom slab allocator cache, in this case (kmem_cache_t *)hdr_cache.

Developed for Solaris 2.4 [Bonwick 94], the slab allocator was later enhanced with per-CPU caches called *magazines* [Bonwick 01]:

> Our basic approach is to give each CPU an M-element cache of objects called a magazine, by analogy with automatic weapons. Each CPU's magazine can satisfy M allocations before the CPU needs to reload—that is, exchange its empty magazine for a full one.

Apart from high performance, the original slab allocator featured debug and analysis facilities including auditing to trace allocation details and stack traces.

Slab allocation has been adopted by various operating systems. BSD has a kernel slab allocator called the universal memory allocator (UMA), which is efficient and NUMA-aware. A slab allocator was also introduced to Linux in version 2.2, where it was the default option for many years. Linux has since moved to SLUB as an option or as the default.

SLUB

The Linux kernel SLUB allocator is based on the slab allocator and is designed to address various concerns, especially regarding the complexity of the slab allocator. Improvements include the removal of object queues, and per-CPU caches—leaving NUMA optimization to the page allocator (see the earlier Free List(s) section).

The SLUB allocator was made the default option in Linux 2.6.23 [Lameter 07].

glibc

The user-level GNU libc allocator is based on dlmalloc by Doug Lea. Its behavior depends on the allocation request size. Small allocations are served from bins of memory, containing units of a similar size, which can be coalesced using a buddy-like algorithm. Larger allocations can use a tree lookup to find space efficiently. Very large allocations switch to using mmap(2). The net result is a high-performing allocator that benefits from multiple allocation policies.

TCMalloc

TCMalloc is the user-level thread caching malloc, which uses a per-thread cache for small allocations, reducing lock contention and improving performance [Ghemawat 07]. Periodic garbage collection migrates memory back to a central heap for allocations.

jemalloc

Originating as the FreeBSD user-level libc allocator, libjemalloc is also available for Linux. It uses techniques such as multiple arenas, per-thread caching, and small object slabs to improve scalability and reduce memory fragmentation. It can use both mmap(2) and sbrk(2) to obtain system memory, preferring mmap(2). Facebook use jemalloc and have added profiling and other optimizations [Facebook 11].

7.4 Methodology

This section describes various methodologies and exercises for memory analysis and tuning. The topics are summarized in Table 7.3.

Table 7.3 **Memory performance methodologies**

Section	Methodology	Types
7.4.1	Tools method	Observational analysis
7.4.2	USE method	Observational analysis
7.4.3	Characterizing usage	Observational analysis, capacity planning
7.4.4	Cycle analysis	Observational analysis
7.4.5	Performance monitoring	Observational analysis, capacity planning
7.4.6	Leak detection	Observational analysis
7.4.7	Static performance tuning	Observational analysis, capacity planning
7.4.8	Resource controls	Tuning
7.4.9	Micro-benchmarking	Experimental analysis
7.4.10	Memory shrinking	Experimental analysis

See Chapter 2, Methodologies, for more strategies and an introduction to many of these.

These methods may be followed individually or used in combination. When troubleshooting memory issues, my suggestion is to start with the following strategies, in this order: performance monitoring, the USE method, and characterizing usage.

Section 7.5, Observability Tools, shows operating system tools for applying these methods.

7.4.1 Tools Method

The tools method is a process of iterating over available tools, examining key metrics they provide. This is a simple methodology that may overlook issues for which the tools you happen to have available provide poor or no visibility, and can be time-consuming to perform.

For memory, the tools method can involve checking the following for Linux:

- **Page scanning**: Look for continual page scanning (more than 10 seconds) as a sign of memory pressure. This can be done using sar -B and checking the pgscan columns.

- **Pressure stall information (PSI)**: cat /proc/pressure/memory (Linux 4.20+) to check memory pressure (saturation) statistics and how it is changing over time.

- **Swapping**: If swap is configured, the swapping of memory pages (Linux definition of swapping) is a further indication that the system is low on memory. You can use vmstat(8) and check the si and so columns.

- **vmstat**: Run vmstat 1 and check the free column for available memory.

- **OOM killer:** These events can be seen in the system log /var/log/messages, or from dmesg(1). Search for "Out of memory."

- **top:** See which processes and users are the top physical memory consumers (resident) and virtual memory consumers (see the man page for the names of the columns, which differ depending on version). top(1) also summarizes free memory.

- **perf(1)/BCC/bpftrace:** Trace memory allocations with stack traces, to identify the cause of memory usage. Note that this can cost considerable overhead. A cheaper, though coarse, solution is to perform CPU profiling (timed stack sampling) and search for allocation code paths.

See Section 7.5, Observability Tools, for more about each tool.

7.4.2   USE Method

The USE method is for identifying bottlenecks and errors across all components early in a performance investigation, before deeper and more time-consuming strategies are followed.

Check system-wide for:

- **Utilization:** How much memory is in use, and how much is available. Both physical memory and virtual memory should be checked.

- **Saturation:** The degree of page scanning, paging, swapping, and Linux OOM killer sacrifices performed, as measures to relieve memory pressure.

- **Errors:** Software or hardware errors.

You may want to check saturation first, as continual saturation is a sign of a memory issue. These metrics are usually readily available from operating system tools, including vmstat(8) and sar(1) for swapping statistics, and dmesg(1) for OOM killer sacrifices. For systems configured with a separate disk swap device, any activity to the swap device is another a sign of memory pressure. Linux also provides memory saturation statistics as part of pressure stall information (PSI).

Physical memory utilization can be reported differently by different tools, depending on whether they account for unreferenced file system cache pages or inactive pages. A system may report that it has only 10 Mbytes of available memory when it actually has 10 Gbytes of file system cache that can be reclaimed by applications immediately when needed. Check the tool documentation to see what is included.

Virtual memory utilization may also need to be checked, depending on whether the system performs overcommit. For systems that do not, memory allocations will fail once virtual memory is exhausted—a type of memory error.

Memory errors can be caused by software, such as failed memory allocations or the Linux OOM killer, or by hardware, such as ECC errors. Historically, memory allocation errors have been left for the applications to report, although not all applications do (and, with Linux overcommit, developers may not have felt it necessary). Hardware errors are also difficult to diagnose. Some tools can report ECC-correctable errors (e.g., on Linux, dmidecode(8), edac-utils, `ipmitool sel` when ECC memory is used. These correctable errors can be used as a USE method error metric, and can be a sign that uncorrectable errors may soon occur. With actual (uncorrectable) memory errors, you may experience unexplained, unreproducible crashes (including segfaults and bus error signals) of arbitrary applications.

For environments that implement memory limits or quotas (resource controls), as in some cloud computing environments, memory utilization and saturation may need to be measured differently. Your OS instance may be at its software memory limit and swapping, even though there is plenty of physical memory available on the host. See Chapter 11, Cloud Computing.

7.4.3 Characterizing Usage

Characterizing memory usage is an important exercise when capacity planning, benchmarking, and simulating workloads. It can also lead to some of the largest performance gains from finding and correcting misconfigurations. For example, a database cache may be configured too small and have low hit rates, or too large and cause system paging.

For memory, characterizing usage involves identifying where and how much memory is used:

- System-wide physical and virtual memory utilization
- Degree of saturation: swapping and OOM killing
- Kernel and file system cache memory usage
- Per-process physical and virtual memory usage
- Usage of memory resource controls, if present

This example description shows how these attributes can be expressed together:

> The system has 256 Gbytes of main memory, which has 1% in use (utilized) by processes and 30% in the file system cache. The largest process is a database, consuming 2 Gbytes of main memory (RSS), which is its configured limit from the previous system it was migrated from.

These characteristics can vary over time as more memory is used to cache working data. Kernel or application memory may also grow continually over time due to a memory leak—a software error—aside from regular cache growth.

Advanced Usage Analysis/Checklist

Additional characteristics are listed here as questions for consideration, which may also serve as a checklist when studying memory issues thoroughly:

- What is the working set size (WSS) for the applications?
- Where is the kernel memory used? Per slab?
- How much of the file system cache is active as opposed to inactive?
- Where is the process memory used (instructions, caches, buffers, objects, etc.)?
- Why are processes allocating memory (call paths)?
- Why is the kernel allocating memory (call paths)?

- Anything odd with process library mappings (e.g., changing over time)?
- What processes are actively being swapped out?
- What processes have previously been swapped out?
- Could processes or the kernel have memory leaks?
- In a NUMA system, how well is memory distributed across memory nodes?
- What are the IPC and memory stall cycle rates?
- How balanced are the memory buses?
- How much local memory I/O is performed as opposed to remote memory I/O?

The sections that follow can help answer some of these questions. See Chapter 2, Methodologies, for a higher-level summary of this methodology and the characteristics to measure (who, why, what, how).

7.4.4   Cycle Analysis

Memory bus load can be determined by inspecting the CPU performance monitoring counters (PMCs), which can be programmed to count memory stall cycles, memory bus usage, and more. A metric to begin with is the instructions per cycle (IPC), which reflects how memory-dependent the CPU load is. See Chapter 6, CPUs.

7.4.5   Performance Monitoring

Performance monitoring can identify active issues and patterns of behavior over time. Key metrics for memory are:

- **Utilization:** Percent used, which may be inferred from available memory
- **Saturation:** Swapping, OOM killing

For environments that implement memory limits or quotas (resource controls), statistics related to the imposed limits may also need to be collected.

Errors can also be monitored (if available), as described with utilization and saturation in Section 7.4.2, USE Method.

Monitoring memory usage over time, especially by process, can help identify the presence and rate of memory leaks.

7.4.6   Leak Detection

This problem occurs when an application or kernel module grows endlessly, consuming memory from the free lists, from the file system cache, and eventually from other processes. This may first be noticed because the system starts swapping or an application is OOM killed, in response to the endless memory pressure.

This type of issue is caused by either:

- **A memory leak:** A type of software bug where memory is no longer used but never freed. This is fixed by modifying the software code, or by applying patches or upgrades (which modify the code).

- **Memory growth:** The software is consuming memory normally, but at a much higher rate than is desirable for the system. This is fixed either by changing the software configuration, or by the software developer changing how the application consumes memory.

Memory growth issues are often misidentified as memory leaks. The first question to ask is: Is it supposed to do that? Check the memory usage, the configuration of your application, and the behavior of its allocators. An application may be configured to populate a memory cache, and the observed growth may be cache warmup.

How memory leaks can be analyzed depends on the software and language type. Some allocators provide debug modes for recording allocation details, which can then be analyzed postmortem for identifying the call path responsible. Some runtimes have methods for doing heap dump analysis, and other tools for doing memory leak investigations.

The Linux BCC tracing tools includes memleak(8) for growth and leak analysis: it tracks allocations and notes those that were not freed during an interval, along with the allocation code path. It cannot tell if these are leaks or normal growth, so your task is to analyze the code paths to determine which is the case. (Note that this tool also incurs high overhead with high allocation rates.) BCC is covered in Chapter 15, BPF, Section 15.1, BCC.

7.4.7   Static Performance Tuning

Static performance tuning focuses on issues of the configured environment. For memory performance, examine the following aspects of the static configuration:

- How much main memory is there in total?

- How much memory are applications configured to use (their own config)?

- Which memory allocators do the applications use?

- What is the speed of main memory? Is it the fastest type available (DDR5)?

- Has main memory ever been fully tested (e.g., using Linux memtester)?

- What is the system architecture? NUMA, UMA?

- Is the operating system NUMA-aware? Does it provide NUMA tunables?

- Is memory attached to the same socket, or split across sockets?

- How many memory buses are present?

- What are the number and size of the CPU caches? TLB?

- What are the BIOS settings?

- Are large pages configured and used?

- Is overcommit available and configured?

- What other system memory tunables are in use?

- Are there software-imposed memory limits (resource controls)?

Answering these questions may reveal configuration choices that have been overlooked.

7.4.8 Resource Controls

The operating system may provide fine-grained controls for the allocation of memory to processes or groups of processes. These controls may include fixed limits for main memory and virtual memory usage. How they work is implementation-specific and is discussed in Section 7.6, Tuning, and Chapter 11, Cloud Computing.

7.4.9 Micro-Benchmarking

Micro-benchmarking may be used to determine the speed of main memory and characteristics such as CPU cache and cache line sizes. It may be helpful when analyzing differences between systems, as the speed of memory access may have a greater effect on performance than CPU clock speed, depending on the application and workload.

In Chapter 6, CPUs, the Latency section under CPU Caches (in Section 6.4.1, Hardware) shows the result of micro-benchmarking memory access latency to determine characteristics of the CPU caches.

7.4.10 Memory Shrinking

This is a working set size (WSS) estimation method that uses a *negative* experiment, requiring swap devices to be configured to perform the experiment. Available main memory for an application is progressively reduced while measuring performance and swapping: the point where performance sharply degrades and swapping greatly increases shows when the WSS no longer fits into the available memory.

While worth mentioning as an example negative experiment, this is not recommended for production use as it deliberately harms performance. For other WSS estimation techniques, see the experimental wss(8) tool in Section 7.5.12, wss, and my website on WSS estimation [Gregg 18c].

7.5 Observability Tools

This section introduces memory observability tools for Linux-based operating systems. See the previous section for methodologies to follow when using them.

The tools in this section are shown in Table 7.4.

Table 7.4 **Linux memory observability tools**

Section	Tool	Description
7.5.1	vmstat	Virtual and physical memory statistics
7.5.2	PSI	Memory pressure stall information

Section	Tool	Description
7.5.3	swapon	Swap device usage
7.5.4	sar	Historical statistics
7.5.5	slabtop	Kernel slab allocator statistics
7.5.6	numastat	NUMA statistics
7.5.7	ps	Process status
7.5.8	top	Monitor per-process memory usage
7.5.9	pmap	Process address space statistics
7.5.10	perf	Memory PMC and tracepoint analysis
7.5.11	drsnoop	Direct reclaim tracing
7.5.12	wss	Working set size estimation
7.5.13	bpftrace	Tracing programs for memory analysis

This is a selection of tools and capabilities to support Section 7.4, Methodology. We begin with tools for system-wide memory usage statistics and then drill down to per-process and allocation tracing. Some of the traditional tools are likely available on other Unix-like operating systems where they originated, including: vmstat(8), sar(1), ps(1), top(1), and pmap(1). drsnoop(8) is a BPF tool from BCC (Chapter 15).

See the documentation for each tool, including its man pages, for full references on its features.

7.5.1 vmstat

The virtual memory statistics command, vmstat(8), provides a high-level view of system memory health, including current free memory and paging statistics. CPU statistics are also included, as described in Chapter 6, CPUs.

When it was introduced by Bill Joy and Ozalp Babaoglu in 1979 for BSD, the original man page included:

> BUGS: So many numbers print out that it's sometimes hard to figure out what to watch.

Here is example output from the Linux version:

```
$ vmstat 1
procs -----------memory---------- ---swap-- -----io---- -system-- ----cpu----
 r  b   swpd    free    buff  cache    si   so    bi    bo   in   cs us sy id wa
 4  0      0 34454064 111516 13438596    0    0     0     5    2    0  0  0 100  0
 4  0      0 34455208 111516 13438596    0    0     0     0 2262 15303 16 12 73  0
 5  0      0 34455588 111516 13438596    0    0     0     0 1961 15221 15 11 74  0
 4  0      0 34456300 111516 13438596    0    0     0     0 2343 15294 15 11 73  0
[...]
```

This version of vmstat(8) does not print summary-since-boot values for the procs or memory columns on the first line of output, instead showing current status immediately. The columns are in kilobytes by default and are:

- **swpd**: Amount of swapped-out memory
- **free**: Free available memory
- **buff**: Memory in the buffer cache
- **cache**: Memory in the page cache
- **si**: Memory swapped in (paging)
- **so**: Memory swapped out (paging)

The buffer and page caches are described in Chapter 8, File Systems. It is normal for the free memory in the system to drop after boot and be used by these caches to improve performance. It can be released for application use when needed.

If the si and so columns are continually nonzero, the system is under memory pressure and is swapping to a swap device or file (see swapon(8)). Other tools, including those that show memory by process (e.g., top(1), ps(1)), can be used to investigate what is consuming memory.

On systems with large amounts of memory, the columns can become unaligned and a little difficult to read. You can try changing the output units to megabytes using the -S option (use m for 1000000, and M for 1048576):

```
$ vmstat -Sm 1
procs -----------memory---------- ---swap-- -----io---- -system-- ----cpu----
 r  b   swpd   free   buff  cache   si   so    bi    bo   in   cs us sy id wa
 4  0      0  35280    114 13761    0    0     0     5    2    1  0  0 100  0
 4  0      0  35281    114 13761    0    0     0     0 2027 15146 16 13 70  0
[...]
```

There is also a -a option to print a breakdown of *inactive* and *active* memory from the page cache:

```
$ vmstat -a 1
procs -----------memory---------- ---swap-- -----io---- -system-- ----cpu----
 r  b   swpd     free   inact active   si   so    bi    bo   in   cs us sy id wa
 5  0      0 34453536 10358040 3201540    0    0     0     5    2    0  0  0 100  0
 4  0      0 34453228 10358040 3200648    0    0     0     0 2464 15261 16 12 71  0
[...]
```

These memory statistics can be printed as a list using the lowercase -s option.

7.5.2   PSI

Linux pressure stall information (PSI), added in Linux 4.20, includes statistics for memory saturation. These not only show if there is memory pressure, but how it is changing in the last five minutes. Example output:

```
# cat /proc/pressure/memory
some avg10=2.84 avg60=1.23 avg300=0.32 total=1468344
full avg10=1.85 avg60=0.66 avg300=0.16 total=702578
```

This output shows that memory pressure is increasing, with a higher 10-second average (2.84) than the 300-second average (0.32). These averages are percentages of time that a task was memory stalled. The `some` line shows when some tasks (threads) were affected, and the `full` line shows when all runnable tasks were affected.

PSI statistics are also tracked per cgroup2 (cgroups are covered in Chapter 11, Cloud Computing) [Facebook 19].

7.5.3 swapon

swapon(1) can show whether swap devices have been configured and how much of their volume is in use. For example:

```
$ swapon
NAME       TYPE      SIZE   USED PRIO
/dev/dm-2 partition 980M 611.6M   -2
/swap1     file       30G  10.9M   -3
```

This output shows two swap devices: a physical disk partition of 980 Mbytes, and a file named /swap1 of 30 Gbytes. The output also shows how much both are in use. Many systems nowadays do not have swap configured; in this case, swapon(1) will not print any output.

If a swap device has active I/O, that can be seen in the `si` and `so` columns in vmstat(1), and as device I/O in iostat(1) (Chapter 9).

7.5.4 sar

The system activity reporter, sar(1), can be used to observe current activity and can be configured to archive and report historical statistics. It is mentioned in various chapters in this book for the different statistics it provides, and was introduced in Chapter 4, Observability Tools, Section 4.4, sar.

The Linux version provides memory statistics via the following options:

- **-B**: Paging statistics
- **-H**: Huge pages statistics
- **-r**: Memory utilization
- **-S**: Swap space statistics
- **-W**: Swapping statistics

These span memory usage, activity of the page-out daemon, and huge pages usage. See Section 7.3, Architecture, for background on these topics.

Statistics provided include those in Table 7.5.

Table 7.5 **Linux sar memory statistics**

Option	Statistic	Description	Units
-B	pgpgin/s	Page-ins	Kbytes/s
-B	pgpgout/s	Page-outs	Kbytes/s
-B	fault/s	Both major and minor faults	Count/s
-B	majflt/s	Major faults	Count/s
-B	pgfree/s	Pages added to free list	Count/s
-B	pgscank/s	Pages scanned by background page-out daemon (kswapd)	Count/s
-B	pgscand/s	Direct page scans	Count/s
-B	pgsteal/s	Page and swap cache reclaims	Count/s
-B	%vmeff	Ratio of page steal/page scan, which shows page reclaim efficiency	Percent
-H	hbhugfree	Free huge pages memory (large page size)	Kbytes
-H	hbhugused	Used huge pages memory	Kbytes
-H	%hugused	Huge page usage	Percent
-r	kbmemfree	Free memory (completely unused)	Kbytes
-r	kbavail	Available memory, including pages that can be readily freed from the page cache	Kbytes
-r	kbmemused	Used memory (excluding the kernel)	Kbytes
-r	%memused	Memory usage	Percent
-r	kbbuffers	Buffer cache size	Kbytes
-r	kbcached	Page cache size	Kbytes
-r	kbcommit	Main memory committed: an estimate of the amount needed to serve the current workload	Kbytes
-r	%commit	Main memory committed for current workload, estimate	Percent
-r	kbactive	Active list memory size	Kbytes
-r	kbinact	Inactive list memory size	Kbytes
-r	kbdirtyw	Modified memory to be written to disk	Kbytes
-r ALL	kbanonpg	Process anonymous memory	Kbytes
-r ALL	kbslab	Kernel slab cache size	Kbytes
-r ALL	kbkstack	Kernel stack space size	Kbytes
-r ALL	kbpgtbl	Lowest-level page table size	Kbytes

Option	Statistic	Description	Units
-r ALL	kbvmused	Used virtual address space	Kbytes
-S	kbswpfree	Free swap space	Kbytes
-S	kbswpused	Used swap space	Kbytes
-S	%swpused	Used swap space	Percent
-S	kbswpcad	Cached swap space: this resides in both main memory and the swap device and so can be paged out without disk I/O	Kbytes
-S	%swpcad	Ratio of cached swap versus used swap	Percent
-W	pswpin/s	Page-ins (Linux "swap-ins")	Pages/s
-W	pswpout/s	Page-outs (Linux "swap-outs")	Pages/s

Many of the statistic names include the units measured: pg for pages, kb for kilobytes, % for a percentage, and /s for per second. See the man page for the full list, which includes some additional percentage-based statistics.

It is important to remember that this much detail is available, when needed, on the usage and operation of high-level memory subsystems. To understand these in deeper detail, you may need to use tracers to instrument memory tracepoints and kernel functions, such as perf(1) and bpftrace in the following sections. You can also browse the source code in mm, specifically mm/vmscan.c. There are many posts to the linux-mm mailing list that provide further insight, as the developers discuss what the statistics should be.

The %vmeff metric is a useful measure of page reclaim efficiency. High means pages are successfully stolen from the inactive list (healthy); low means the system is struggling. The man page describes near 100% as high, and less than 30% as low.

Another useful metric is pgscand, which effectively shows the rate at which an application is blocking on memory allocations and entering direct reclaim (higher is bad). To see the time spent by applications during direct reclaim events, you can use tracing tools: see Section 7.5.11, drsnoop.

7.5.5   slabtop

The Linux slabtop(1) command prints kernel slab cache usage from the slab allocator. Like top(1), it refreshes the screen in real time.

Here is some example output:

```
# slabtop -sc
 Active / Total Objects (% used)    : 686110 / 867574 (79.1%)
 Active / Total Slabs (% used)      : 30948 / 30948 (100.0%)
 Active / Total Caches (% used)     : 99 / 164 (60.4%)
 Active / Total Size (% used)       : 157680.28K / 200462.06K (78.7%)
 Minimum / Average / Maximum Object : 0.01K / 0.23K / 12.00K
```

OBJS	ACTIVE	USE	OBJ SIZE	SLABS	OBJ/SLAB	CACHE SIZE	NAME
45450	33712	74%	1.05K	3030	15	48480K	ext4_inode_cache
161091	81681	50%	0.19K	7671	21	30684K	dentry
222963	196779	88%	0.10K	5717	39	22868K	buffer_head
35763	35471	99%	0.58K	2751	13	22008K	inode_cache
26033	13859	53%	0.57K	1860	14	14880K	radix_tree_node
93330	80502	86%	0.13K	3111	30	12444K	kernfs_node_cache
2104	2081	98%	4.00K	263	8	8416K	kmalloc-4k
528	431	81%	7.50K	132	4	4224K	task_struct

[...]

The output has a summary at the top and a list of slabs, including their object count (OBJS), how many are active (ACTIVE), percent used (USE), the size of the objects (OBJ SIZE, bytes), and the total size of the cache (CACHE SIZE, bytes). In this example, the -sc option was used to sort by cache size, with the largest at the top: ext4_inode_cache.

The slab statistics are from /proc/slabinfo and can also be printed by vmstat -m.

7.5.6   numastat

The numastat(8)[8] tool provides statistics for non-uniform memory access (NUMA) systems, typically those with multiple CPU sockets. Here is some example output from a two-socket system:

```
# numastat
                         node0          node1
numa_hit          210057224016    151287435161
numa_miss            9377491084       291611562
numa_foreign          291611562      9377491084
interleave_hit            36476           36665
local_node        210056887752    151286964112
other_node           9377827348       292082611
```

This system has two NUMA nodes, one for each memory bank attached to each socket. Linux tries to allocate memory on the nearest NUMA node, and numastat(8) shows how successful this is. Key statistics are:

- **numa_hit**: Memory allocations on the intended NUMA node.

- **numa_miss** + **numa_foreign**: Memory allocations not on the preferred NUMA node. (numa_miss shows local allocations that should have been elsewhere, and numa_foreign shows remote allocations that should have been local.)

- **other_node**: Memory allocations on this node while the process was running elsewhere.

---

[8]Origin: Andi Kleen wrote the original numastat tool as a perl script around 2003; Bill Gray wrote the current version in 2012.

The example output shows the NUMA allocation policy performing well: a high number of hits compared to other statistics. If the hit ratio is much lower, you may consider adjusting NUMA tunables in sysctl(8), or using other approaches to improve memory locality (e.g., partitioning workloads or the system, or choosing a different system with fewer NUMA nodes). If there is no way to improve NUMA, numastat(8) does at least help explain poor memory I/O performance.

numastat(8) supports -n to print statistics in Mbytes, and -m to print the output in the style of /proc/meminfo. Depending on your Linux distribution, numastat(8) may be available in a numactl package.

7.5.7 ps

The process status command, ps(1), lists details on all processes, including memory usage statistics. Its usage was introduced in Chapter 6, CPUs.

For example, using the BSD-style options:

```
$ ps aux
USER       PID %CPU %MEM    VSZ    RSS TTY   STAT START   TIME COMMAND
[...]
bind      1152  0.0  0.4 348916 39568 ?     Ssl  Mar27  20:17 /usr/sbin/named -u bind
root      1371  0.0  0.0  39004  2652 ?     Ss   Mar27  11:04 /usr/lib/postfix/master
root      1386  0.0  0.6 207564 50684 ?     Sl   Mar27   1:57 /usr/sbin/console-kit-
daemon --no-daemon
rabbitmq  1469  0.0  0.0  10708   172 ?     S    Mar27   0:49 /usr/lib/erlang/erts-
5.7.4/bin/epmd -daemon
rabbitmq  1486  0.1  0.0 150208  2884 ?     Ssl  Mar27 453:29 /usr/lib/erlang/erts-
5.7.4/bin/beam.smp -W w -K true -A30 ...
```

This output includes the following columns:

- **%MEM**: Main memory usage (physical memory, RSS) as a percentage of the total in the system

- **RSS**: Resident set size (Kbytes)

- **VSZ**: Virtual memory size (Kbytes)

While RSS shows main memory usage, it includes shared memory segments such as system libraries, which may be mapped by dozens of processes. If you were to sum the RSS column, you might find that it exceeds the memory available in the system, due to overcounting of this shared memory. See Section 7.2.9, Shared Memory, for background on shared memory, and the later pmap(1) command for analysis of shared memory usage.

These columns may be selected using the SVR4-style -o option, for example:

```
# ps -eo pid,pmem,vsz,rss,comm
  PID %MEM  VSZ  RSS COMMAND
[...]
13419  0.0 5176 1796 /opt/local/sbin/nginx
```

```
13879   0.1 31060 22880 /opt/local/bin/ruby19
13418   0.0 4984 1456 /opt/local/sbin/nginx
15101   0.0 4580   32 /opt/riak/lib/os_mon-2.2.6/priv/bin/memsup
10933   0.0 3124 2212 /usr/sbin/rsyslogd
[...]
```

The Linux version can also print columns for major and minor faults (`maj_flt`, `min_flt`).

The output of ps(1) can be post-sorted on the memory columns so that the highest consumers can be quickly identified. Or, try top(1), which provides interactive sorting.

7.5.8   top

The top(1) command monitors top running processes and includes memory usage statistics. It was introduced in Chapter 6, CPUs. For example, on Linux:

```
$ top -o %MEM
top - 00:53:33 up 242 days,  2:38,  7 users,  load average: 1.48, 1.64, 2.10
Tasks: 261 total,   1 running, 260 sleeping,   0 stopped,   0 zombie
Cpu(s):  0.0%us,  0.0%sy,  0.0%ni, 99.9%id,  0.0%wa,  0.0%hi,  0.0%si,  0.0%st
Mem:   8181740k total,  6658640k used,  1523100k free,   404744k buffers
Swap:  2932728k total,   120508k used,  2812220k free,  2893684k cached
```

PID	USER	PR	NI	VIRT	RES	SHR	S	%CPU	%MEM	TIME+	COMMAND
29625	scott	20	0	2983m	2.2g	1232	S	45	28.7	81:11.31	node
5121	joshw	20	0	222m	193m	804	S	0	2.4	260:13.40	tmux
1386	root	20	0	202m	49m	1224	S	0	0.6	1:57.70	console-kit-dae
6371	stu	20	0	65196	38m	292	S	0	0.5	23:11.13	screen
1152	bind	20	0	340m	38m	1700	S	0	0.5	20:17.36	named
15841	joshw	20	0	67144	23m	908	S	0	0.3	201:37.91	mosh-server
18496	root	20	0	57384	16m	1972	S	3	0.2	2:59.99	python
1258	root	20	0	125m	8684	8264	S	0	0.1	2052:01	l2tpns
16295	wesolows	20	0	95752	7396	944	S	0	0.1	4:46.07	sshd
23783	brendan	20	0	22204	5036	1676	S	0	0.1	0:00.15	bash

```
[...]
```

The summary at the top shows total, used, and free for both main memory (`Mem`) and virtual memory (`Swap`). The sizes of the buffer cache (`buffers`) and page cache (`cached`) are also shown.

In this example, the per-process output has been sorted on `%MEM` using `-o` to set the sort column. The largest process in this example is node, using 2.2 Gbytes of main memory and almost 3 Gbytes of virtual memory.

The main memory percentage column (`%MEM`), virtual memory size (`VIRT`), and resident set size (`RES`) have the same meanings as the equivalent columns from ps(1) described earlier. For more details on top(1) memory statistics, see the section "Linux Memory Types" in the top(1) man page, which explains what type of memory is shown by each of the possible memory columns. You can also type "?" when using top(1) to see its built-in summary of interactive commands.

7.5.9 pmap

The pmap(1) command lists the memory mappings of a process, showing their sizes, permissions, and mapped objects. This allows process memory usage to be examined in more detail, and shared memory to be quantified.

For example, on a Linux-based system:

```
# pmap -x 5187
5187:   /usr/sbin/mysqld
Address           Kbytes     RSS   Dirty Mode  Mapping
000055dadb0dd000   58284   10748       0 r-x-- mysqld
000055dade9c8000    1316    1316    1316 r---- mysqld
000055dadeb11000    3592     816     764 rw--- mysqld
000055dadee93000    1168    1080    1080 rw--- [ anon ]
000055dae08b5000    5168    4836    4836 rw--- [ anon ]
00007f018c000000    4704    4696    4696 rw--- [ anon ]
00007f018c498000   60832       0       0 ----- [ anon ]
00007f0190000000     132      24      24 rw--- [ anon ]
[...]
00007f01f99da000       4       4       0 r---- ld-2.30.so
00007f01f99db000     136     136       0 r-x-- ld-2.30.so
00007f01f99fd000      32      32       0 r---- ld-2.30.so
00007f01f9a05000       4       0       0 rw-s- [aio] (deleted)
00007f01f9a06000       4       4       4 r---- ld-2.30.so
00007f01f9a07000       4       4       4 rw--- ld-2.30.so
00007f01f9a08000       4       4       4 rw--- [ anon ]
00007ffd2c528000     132      52      52 rw--- [ stack ]
00007ffd2c5b3000      12       0       0 r---- [ anon ]
00007ffd2c5b6000       4       4       0 r-x-- [ anon ]
ffffffffff600000       4       0       0 --x-- [ anon ]
---------------- ------- ------- -------
total kB         1828228  450388  434200
```

This shows the memory mappings of a MySQL database server, including virtual memory (Kbytes), main memory (RSS), private anonymous memory (Anon), and permissions (Mode). For many of the mappings, very little memory is anonymous, and many mappings are read-only (r-...), allowing those pages to be shared with other processes. This is especially the case for system libraries. The bulk of the memory consumed in this example is in the heap, shown as the first wave of [anon] segments (truncated in this output).

The **-x** option prints extended fields. There is also **-X** for even more details, and **-XX** for "everything" the kernel provides. Just showing the headers for these modes:

```
# pmap -X $(pgrep mysqld) | head -2
5187:   /usr/sbin/mysqld
        Address Perm   Offset Device   Inode    Size    Rss    Pss Referenced
Anonymous LazyFree ShmemPmdMapped Shared_Hugetlb Private_Hugetlb Swap SwapPss Locked
THPeligible ProtectionKey Mapping
[...]
# pmap -XX  $(pgrep mysqld) | head -2
5187:   /usr/sbin/mysqld
        Address Perm   Offset Device   Inode    Size KernelPageSize MMUPageSize
Rss    Pss Shared_Clean Shared_Dirty Private_Clean Private_Dirty Referenced Anonymous
LazyFree AnonHugePages ShmemPmdMapped Shared_Hugetlb Private_Hugetlb Swap SwapPss
Locked THPeligible ProtectionKey            VmFlags Mapping
[...]
```

These extra fields are kernel version dependent. They include details of huge page use, swap use, and the proportional set size (**Pss**) for mappings (highlighted). PSS shows how much private memory a mapping has, plus shared memory divided by the number of users. This provides a more realistic value for the main memory usage.

7.5.10   perf

perf(1) is the official Linux profiler, a multi-tool with many capabilities. Chapter 13 provides as a summary of perf(1). This section covers its usage for memory analysis. Also see Chapter 6 for perf(1) analysis of memory PMCs.

One-Liners

The following one-liners are both useful and demonstrate different perf(1) capabilities for memory analysis.

Sample page faults (RSS growth) with stack traces system wide, until Ctrl-C:

```
perf record -e page-faults -a -g
```

Record all page faults with stack traces for PID 1843, for 60 seconds:

```
perf record -e page-faults -c 1 -p 1843 -g -- sleep 60
```

Record heap growth via brk(2), until Ctrl-C:

```
perf record -e syscalls:sys_enter_brk -a -g
```

Record page migrations on NUMA systems:

```
perf record -e migrate:mm_migrate_pages -a
```

Count all kmem events, printing a report every second:

```
perf stat -e 'kmem:*' -a -I 1000
```

Count all vmscan events, printing a report every second:

```
perf stat -e 'vmscan:*' -a -I 1000
```

Count all memory compaction events, printing a report every second:

```
perf stat -e 'compaction:*' -a -I 1000
```

Trace kswapd wakeup events with stack traces, until Ctrl-C:

```
perf record -e vmscan:mm_vmscan_wakeup_kswapd -ag
```

Profile memory accesses for the given command:

```
perf mem record command
```

Summarize a memory profile:

```
perf mem report
```

For commands that record or sample events, use perf report to summarize the profile or perf script --header to print them all.

See Chapter 13, perf, Section 13.2, One-Liners, for more perf(1) one-liners, and Section 7.5.13, bpftrace, which builds observability programs on many of the same events.

Page Fault Sampling

perf(1) can record the stack trace on page faults, showing the code path that triggered this event. Since page faults occur as a process increases its resident set size (RSS), analyzing them can explain why the main memory of a process is growing. See Figure 7.2 for the role of page faults during memory usage.

In the following example, the page-fault software event is traced across all CPUs (-a[9]) with stack traces (-g) for 60 seconds, and then the stacks are printed:

```
# perf record -e page-faults -a -g -- sleep 60
[ perf record: Woken up 4 times to write data ]
[ perf record: Captured and wrote 1.164 MB perf.data (2584 samples) ]
# perf script
[...]
sleep  4910 [001] 813638.716924:          1 page-faults:
        ffffffff9303f31e __clear_user+0x1e ([kernel.kallsyms])
        ffffffff9303f37b clear_user+0x2b ([kernel.kallsyms])
```

---

[9] The -a option became the default in Linux 4.11.

```
            ffffffff92941683 load_elf_binary+0xf33 ([kernel.kallsyms])
            ffffffff928d25cb search_binary_handler+0x8b ([kernel.kallsyms])
            ffffffff928d38ae __do_execve_file.isra.0+0x4fe ([kernel.kallsyms])
            ffffffff928d3e09 __x64_sys_execve+0x39 ([kernel.kallsyms])
            ffffffff926044ca do_syscall_64+0x5a ([kernel.kallsyms])
            ffffffff9320008c entry_SYSCALL_64_after_hwframe+0x44 ([kernel.kallsyms])
                7fb53524401b execve+0xb (/usr/lib/x86_64-linux-gnu/libc-2.30.so)
[...]
mysqld  4918 [000] 813641.075298:             1 page-faults:
                7fc6252d7001 [unknown] (/usr/lib/x86_64-linux-gnu/libc-2.30.so)
                562cacaeb282 pfs_malloc_array+0x42 (/usr/sbin/mysqld)
                562cacafd582 PFS_buffer_scalable_container<PFS_prepared_stmt, 1024, 1024,
PFS_buffer_default_array<PFS_prepared_stmt>,
PFS_buffer_default_allocator<PFS_prepared_stmt> >::allocate+0x262 (/usr/sbin/mysqld)
                562cacafd820 create_prepared_stmt+0x50 (/usr/sbin/mysqld)
                562cacadbbef [unknown] (/usr/sbin/mysqld)
                562cab3719ff mysqld_stmt_prepare+0x9f (/usr/sbin/mysqld)
                562cab3479c8 dispatch_command+0x16f8 (/usr/sbin/mysqld)
                562cab348d74 do_command+0x1a4 (/usr/sbin/mysqld)
                562cab464fe0 [unknown] (/usr/sbin/mysqld)
                562cacad873a [unknown] (/usr/sbin/mysqld)
                7fc625ceb669 start_thread+0xd9 (/usr/lib/x86_64-linux-gnu/libpthread-
2.30.so)
[...]
```

Only two stacks have been included here. The first is from the dummy sleep(1) command that
perf(1) invoked, and the second is a MySQL server. When tracing system-wide, you may see
many stacks from short-lived processes that briefly grew in memory, triggering page faults,
before exiting. You can use -p PID instead of -a to match on a process.

The full output is 222,582 lines; perf report summarizes code paths as a hierarchy, but the output is still 7,592 lines. Flame graphs can be used to visualize the entire profile more effectively.

Page Fault Flame Graphs

Figure 7.12 shows a page fault flame graph generated from the previous profile.

The Figure 7.12 flame graph shows that more than half of the memory growth in MySQL server
was from the JOIN::optimize() code path (left large tower). A mouse-over of JOIN::optimize()
shows that it and its child calls were responsible for 3,226 page faults; with 4 Kbyte pages, this
amounts to around 12 Mbytes of main memory growth.

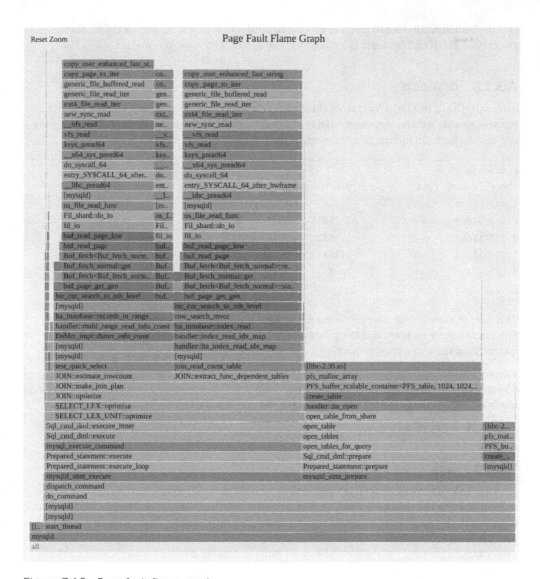

Figure 7.12 Page fault flame graph

The commands used to generate this flame graph, including the perf(1) command to record page faults, are:

```
# perf record -e page-faults -a -g -- sleep 60
# perf script --header > out.stacks
$ git clone https://github.com/brendangregg/FlameGraph; cd FlameGraph
$ ./stackcollapse-perf.pl < ../out.stacks | ./flamegraph.pl --hash \
    --bgcolor=green --count=pages --title="Page Fault Flame Graph" > out.svg
```

I set the background color to green as a visual reminder that this is not a typical CPU flame graph (yellow background) but is a memory flame graph (green background).

7.5.11   drsnoop

drsnoop(8)[10] is a BCC tool for tracing the direct reclaim approach to freeing memory, showing the process affected and the latency: the time taken for the reclaim. It can be used to quantify the application performance impact of a memory-constrained system. For example:

```
# drsnoop -T
TIME(s)        COMM          PID     LAT(ms) PAGES
0.000000000    java          11266    1.72   57
0.004007000    java          11266    3.21   57
0.011856000    java          11266    2.02   43
0.018315000    java          11266    3.09   55
0.024647000    acpid         1209     6.46   73
[...]
```

This output shows some direct reclaims for Java, taking between one and seven milliseconds. The rates of these reclaims and their duration in milliseconds (`LAT(ms)`) can be considered in quantifying the application impact.

This tool works by tracing the vmscan mm_vmscan_direct_reclaim_begin and mm_vmscan_direct_reclaim_end tracepoints. These are expected to be low-frequency events (usually happening in bursts), so the overhead should be negligible.

drsnoop(8) supports a `-T` option to include timestamps, and `-p PID` to match a single process.

7.5.12   wss

wss(8) is an experimental tool I developed to show how a process working set size (WSS) can be measured using the page table entry (PTE) "accessed" bit. This was part of a longer study to summarize different ways working set size can be determined [Gregg 18c]. I've included wss(8) here because working set size (the amount of frequently accessed memory) is an important metric for understanding memory usage, and having an experimental tool with warnings is better than no tool.

The following output shows wss(8) measuring the WSS of a MySQL database server (mysqld), printing the cumulative WSS every one second:

```
# ./wss.pl $(pgrep -n mysqld) 1
Watching PID 423 page references grow, output every 1 seconds...
Est(s)     RSS(MB)    PSS(MB)    Ref(MB)
1.014       403.66     400.59     86.00
2.034       403.66     400.59     90.75
```

---

[10] Origin: This was created by Wenbo Zhang on 10-Feb-2019.

3.054	403.66	400.59	94.29
4.074	403.66	400.59	97.53
5.094	403.66	400.59	100.33
6.114	403.66	400.59	102.44
7.134	403.66	400.59	104.58
8.154	403.66	400.59	106.31
9.174	403.66	400.59	107.76
10.194	403.66	400.59	109.14

The output shows that by the five-second mark, mysqld had touched around 100 Mbytes of memory. The RSS for mysqld was 400 Mbytes. The output also includes the estimated time for the interval, including the time taken to set and read the accessed bit (Est(s)), and the proportional set size (PSS), which accounts for sharing pages with other processes.

This tool works by resetting the PTE accessed bit for every page in a process, pausing for an interval, and then checking the bits to see which have been set. Since this is page-based, the resolution is the page size, typically 4 Kbytes. Consider the numbers it reports to have been rounded up to the page size.

WARNINGS: This tool uses /proc/PID/clear_refs and /proc/PID/smaps, which can cause slightly higher application latency (e.g., 10%) while the kernel walks page structures. For large processes (> 100 Gbytes), this duration of higher latency can last over one second, during which this tool is consuming system CPU time. Keep these overheads in mind. This tool also resets the referenced flag, which might confuse the kernel as to which pages to reclaim, especially if swapping is active. Further, it also activates some old kernel code that may not have been used in your environment before. Test first in a lab environment to make sure you understand the overheads.

7.5.13 bpftrace

bpftrace is a BPF-based tracer that provides a high-level programming language, allowing the creation of powerful one-liners and short scripts. It is well suited for custom application analysis based on clues from other tools. The bpftrace repository contains additional tools for memory analysis, including oomkill.bt [Robertson 20].

bpftrace is explained in Chapter 15, BPF. This section shows some examples for memory analysis.

One-liners

The following one-liners are useful and demonstrate different bpftrace capabilities.

Sum libc malloc() request bytes by user stack and process (high overhead):

```
bpftrace -e 'uprobe:/lib/x86_64-linux-gnu/libc.so.6:malloc {
    @[ustack, comm] = sum(arg0); }'
```

Sum libc malloc() request bytes by user stack for PID 181 (high overhead):

```
bpftrace -e 'uprobe:/lib/x86_64-linux-gnu/libc.so.6:malloc /pid == 181/ {
    @[ustack] = sum(arg0); }'
```

Show libc malloc() request bytes by user stack for PID 181 as a power-of-2 histogram (high overhead):

```
bpftrace -e 'uprobe:/lib/x86_64-linux-gnu/libc.so.6:malloc /pid == 181/ {
   @[ustack] = hist(arg0); }'
```

Sum kernel kmem cache allocation bytes by kernel stack trace:

```
bpftrace -e 't:kmem:kmem_cache_alloc { @bytes[kstack] = sum(args->bytes_alloc); }'
```

Count process heap expansion (brk(2)) by code path:

```
bpftrace -e 'tracepoint:syscalls:sys_enter_brk { @[ustack, comm] = count(); }'
```

Count page faults by process:

```
bpftrace -e 'software:page-fault:1 { @[comm, pid] = count(); }'
```

Count user page faults by user-level stack trace:

```
bpftrace -e 't:exceptions:page_fault_user { @[ustack, comm] = count(); }'
```

Count vmscan operations by tracepoint:

```
bpftrace -e 'tracepoint:vmscan:* { @[probe] = count(); }'
```

Count swapins by process:

```
bpftrace -e 'kprobe:swap_readpage { @[comm, pid] = count(); }'
```

Count page migrations:

```
bpftrace -e 'tracepoint:migrate:mm_migrate_pages { @ = count(); }'
```

Trace compaction events:

```
bpftrace -e 't:compaction:mm_compaction_begin { time(); }'
```

List USDT probes in libc:

```
bpftrace -l 'usdt:/lib/x86_64-linux-gnu/libc.so.6:*'
```

List kernel kmem tracepoints:

```
bpftrace -l 't:kmem:*'
```

List all memory subsystem (mm) tracepoints:

```
bpftrace -l 't:*:mm_*'
```

User Allocation Stacks

User-level allocations can be traced from the allocation functions used. For this example, the malloc(3) function from libc is traced for PID 4840, a MySQL database server. The allocation requested size is recorded as a histogram keyed by user-level stack trace:

```
# bpftrace -e 'uprobe:/lib/x86_64-linux-gnu/libc.so.6:malloc /pid == 4840/ {
    @[ustack] = hist(arg0); }'
Attaching 1 probe...
^C
[...]


    __libc_malloc+0
    Filesort_buffer::allocate_sized_block(unsigned long)+52
    0x562cab572344
    filesort(THD*, Filesort*, RowIterator*, Filesort_info*, Sort_result*, unsigned
long long*)+4017
    SortingIterator::DoSort(QEP_TAB*)+184
    SortingIterator::Init()+42
    SELECT_LEX_UNIT::ExecuteIteratorQuery(THD*)+489
    SELECT_LEX_UNIT::execute(THD*)+266
    Sql_cmd_dml::execute_inner(THD*)+563
    Sql_cmd_dml::execute(THD*)+1062
    mysql_execute_command(THD*, bool)+2380
    Prepared_statement::execute(String*, bool)+2345
    Prepared_statement::execute_loop(String*, bool)+172
    mysqld_stmt_execute(THD*, Prepared_statement*, bool, unsigned long, PS_PARAM*)
+385
    dispatch_command(THD*, COM_DATA const*, enum_server_command)+5793
    do_command(THD*)+420
    0x562cab464fe0
    0x562cacad873a
    start_thread+217
]:
[32K, 64K)          676 |@@@@@@@@@@@@@@@@@@@@@@@@@@@@@@@@@@@@@@@@@@@@@@@@@@@@@@@@|
[64K, 128K)         338 |@@@@@@@@@@@@@@@@@@@@@@@@@@@                            |
```

The output shows that, while tracing, this code path had 676 malloc() requests sized between 32 and 64 Kbytes, and 338 sized between 64 Kbytes and 128 Kbytes.

malloc() Bytes Flame Graph

The output from the previous one-liner was many pages long, so is more easily understood as a flame graph. One can be generated using the following steps:

```
# bpftrace -e 'u:/lib/x86_64-linux-gnu/libc.so.6:malloc /pid == 4840/ {
    @[ustack] = hist(arg0); }' > out.stacks
$ git clone https://github.com/brendangregg/FlameGraph; cd FlameGraph
$ ./stackcollapse-bpftrace.pl < ../out.stacks | ./flamegraph.pl --hash \
    --bgcolor=green --count=bytes --title="malloc() Bytes Flame Graph" > out.svg
```

WARNING: user-level allocation requests can be a frequent activity, occurring many millions of times per second. While the instrumentation cost is small, when multiplied by a high rate, it can lead to significant CPU overhead while tracing, slowing down the target by a factor of two or more—use sparingly. Because it is low-cost, I first use CPU profiling of stack traces to get a handle on allocation paths, or page fault tracing shown in the next section.

Page Fault Flame Graphs

Tracing page faults shows when a process grows in memory size. The previous malloc() one-liner traced the allocation path. Page fault tracing was performed earlier in Section 7.5.10, perf, and from it a flame graph was generated. An advantage of using bpftrace instead is that the stack traces can be aggregated in kernel space for efficiency, and only the unique stacks and counts written to user space.

The following commands use bpftrace to collect page fault stack traces and then generate a flame graph from them:

```
# bpftrace -e 't:exceptions:page_fault_user { @[ustack, comm] = count(); }
    ' > out.stacks
$ git clone https://github.com/brendangregg/FlameGraph; cd FlameGraph
$ ./stackcollapse-bpftrace.pl < ../out.stacks | ./flamegraph.pl --hash \
    --bgcolor=green --count=pages --title="Page Fault Flame Graph" > out.svg
```

See Section 7.5.10, perf, for an example page fault stack trace and flame graph.

Memory Internals

If needed, you can develop custom tools to explore memory allocation and internals in more depth. Start by trying tracepoints for the kernel memory events, and USDT probes for library allocators such as libc. Listing tracepoints:

```
# bpftrace -l 'tracepoint:kmem:*'
tracepoint:kmem:kmalloc
tracepoint:kmem:kmem_cache_alloc
tracepoint:kmem:kmalloc_node
tracepoint:kmem:kmem_cache_alloc_node
tracepoint:kmem:kfree
```

```
tracepoint:kmem:kmem_cache_free
[...]
# bpftrace -l 't:*:mm_*'
tracepoint:huge_memory:mm_khugepaged_scan_pmd
tracepoint:huge_memory:mm_collapse_huge_page
tracepoint:huge_memory:mm_collapse_huge_page_isolate
tracepoint:huge_memory:mm_collapse_huge_page_swapin
tracepoint:migrate:mm_migrate_pages
tracepoint:compaction:mm_compaction_isolate_migratepages
tracepoint:compaction:mm_compaction_isolate_freepages
[...]
```

Each of these tracepoints have arguments that can be listed using -lv. On this kernel (5.3) there are 12 kmem tracepoints, and 47 tracepoints beginning with "mm_".

Listing USDT probes for libc on Ubuntu:

```
# bpftrace -l 'usdt:/lib/x86_64-linux-gnu/libc.so.6'
usdt:/lib/x86_64-linux-gnu/libc.so.6:libc:setjmp
usdt:/lib/x86_64-linux-gnu/libc.so.6:libc:longjmp
usdt:/lib/x86_64-linux-gnu/libc.so.6:libc:longjmp_target
usdt:/lib/x86_64-linux-gnu/libc.so.6:libc:lll_lock_wait_private
usdt:/lib/x86_64-linux-gnu/libc.so.6:libc:memory_mallopt_arena_max
usdt:/lib/x86_64-linux-gnu/libc.so.6:libc:memory_mallopt_arena_test
usdt:/lib/x86_64-linux-gnu/libc.so.6:libc:memory_tunable_tcache_max_bytes
[...]
```

For this libc version (6) there are 33 USDT probes.

If the tracepoints and USDT probes are insufficient, consider using dynamic instrumentation with kprobes and uprobes.

There is also the watchpoint probe type for memory watchpoints: events when a specified memory address is read, written, or executed.

Since memory events can be very frequent, instrumenting them can consume significant overhead. malloc(3) functions from user space can be called millions of times per second, and with the current uprobes overhead (see Chapter 4, Observability Tools, Section 4.3.7, uprobes), tracing them can slow a target two-fold or more. Use caution and find ways to reduce this overhead, such as using maps to summarize statistics instead of printing per-event details, and tracing the fewest possible events.

7.5.14 Other Tools

Memory observability tools included in other chapters of this book, and in *BPF Performance Tools* [Gregg 19], are listed in Table 7.6.

Table 7.6 **Other memory observability tools**

Section	Tool	Description
6.6.11	pmcarch	CPU cycle usage including LLC misses
6.6.12	tlbstat	Summarizes TLB cycles
8.6.2	free	Cache capacity statistics
8.6.12	cachestat	Page cache statistics
[Gregg 19]	oomkill	Shows extra info on OOM kill events
[Gregg 19]	memleak	Shows possible memory leak code paths
[Gregg 19]	mmapsnoop	Traces mmap(2) calls system-wide
[Gregg 19]	brkstack	Shows brk() calls with user stack traces
[Gregg 19]	shmsnoop	Traces shared memory calls with details
[Gregg 19]	faults	Shows page faults, by user stack trace
[Gregg 19]	ffaults	Shows page faults, by filename
[Gregg 19]	vmscan	Measures VM scanner shrink and reclaim times
[Gregg 19]	swapin	Shows swap-ins by process
[Gregg 19]	hfaults	Shows huge page faults, by process

Other Linux memory observability tools and sources include the following:

- **dmesg**: Check for "Out of memory" messages from the OOM killer.

- **dmidecode**: Shows BIOS information for memory banks.

- **tiptop**: A version of top(1) that displays PMC statistics by process.

- **valgrind**: A performance analysis suite, including memcheck, a wrapper for user-level allocators for memory usage analysis including leak detection. This costs significant overhead; the manual advises that it can cause the target to run 20 to 30 times slower [Valgrind 20].

- **iostat**: If the swap device is a physical disk or slice, device I/O may be observable using iostat(1), which indicates that the system is paging.

- **/proc/zoneinfo**: Statistics for memory zones (DMA, etc.).

- **/proc/buddyinfo**: Statistics for the kernel buddy allocator for pages.

- **/proc/pagetypeinfo**: Kernel free memory page statistics; can be used to help debug issues of kernel memory fragmentation.

- **/sys/devices/system/node/node*/numastat**: Statistics for NUMA nodes.

- **SysRq m**: Magic SysRq has an "m" key to dump memory info to the console.

Here is an example output from dmidecode(8), showing a bank of memory:

```
# dmidecode
[...]
Memory Device
        Array Handle: 0x0003
        Error Information Handle: Not Provided
        Total Width: 64 bits
        Data Width: 64 bits
        Size: 8192 MB
        Form Factor: SODIMM
        Set: None
        Locator: ChannelA-DIMM0
        Bank Locator: BANK 0
        Type: DDR4
        Type Detail: Synchronous Unbuffered (Unregistered)
        Speed: 2400 MT/s
        Manufacturer: Micron
        Serial Number: 00000000
        Asset Tag: None
        Part Number: 4ATS1G64HZ-2G3A1
        Rank: 1
        Configured Clock Speed: 2400 MT/s
        Minimum Voltage: Unknown
        Maximum Voltage: Unknown
        Configured Voltage: 1.2 V
[...]
```

This output is useful information for static performance tuning (e.g., it shows the type is DDR4 and not DDR5). Unfortunately, this information is typically unavailable to cloud guests.

Here is some sample output from the SysRq "m" trigger:

```
# echo m > /proc/sysrq-trigger
# dmesg
[...]
[334849.389256] sysrq: Show Memory
[334849.391021] Mem-Info:
[334849.391025] active_anon:110405 inactive_anon:24 isolated_anon:0
                 active_file:152629 inactive_file:137395 isolated_file:0
                 unevictable:4572 dirty:311 writeback:0 unstable:0
                 slab_reclaimable:31943 slab_unreclaimable:14385
                 mapped:37490 shmem:186 pagetables:958 bounce:0
                 free:37403 free_pcp:478 free_cma:2289
```

```
[334849.391028] Node 0 active_anon:441620kB inactive_anon:96kB active_file:610516kB
inactive_file:549580kB unevictable:18288kB isolated(anon):0kB isolated(file):0kB
mapped:149960kB dirty:1244kB writeback:0kB shmem:744kB shmem_thp: 0kB
shmem_pmdmapped: 0kB anon_thp: 2048kB writeback_tmp:0kB unstable:0kB
all_unreclaimable? no
[334849.391029] Node 0 DMA free:12192kB min:360kB low:448kB high:536kB ...
[...]
```

This can be useful if the system has locked up, as it may still be possible to request this information using the SysRq key sequence on the console keyboard, if available [Linux 20g].

Applications and virtual machines (e.g., the Java VM) may also provide their own memory analysis tools. See Chapter 5, Applications.

7.6 Tuning

The most important memory tuning you can do is to ensure that applications remain in main memory, and that paging and swapping do not occur frequently. Identifying this problem was covered in Section 7.4, Methodology, and Section 7.5, Observability Tools. This section discusses other memory tuning: kernel tunable parameters, configuring large pages, allocators, and resource controls.

The specifics of tuning—the options available and what to set them to—depend on the operating system version and the intended workload. The following sections, organized by tuning type, provide examples of which tunable parameters may be available, and why they may need to be tuned.

7.6.1 Tunable Parameters

This section describes tunable parameter examples for recent Linux kernels.

Various memory tunable parameters are described in the kernel source documentation in Documentation/sysctl/vm.txt and can be set using sysctl(8). The examples in Table 7.7 are from a 5.3 kernel, with defaults from Ubuntu 19.10 (those listed in the first edition of this book have not changed since then).

Table 7.7 **Example Linux memory tunables**

Option	Default	Description
vm.dirty_background_bytes	0	Amount of dirty memory to trigger pdflush background write-back
vm.dirty_background_ratio	10	Percentage of dirty system memory to trigger pdflush background write-back
vm.dirty_bytes	0	Amount of dirty memory that causes a writing process to start write-back

Option	Default	Description
vm.dirty_ratio	20	Ratio of dirty system memory to cause a writing process to begin write-back
vm.dirty_expire_centisecs	3,000	Minimum time for dirty memory to be eligible for pdflush (promotes *write cancellation*)
vm.dirty_writeback_centisecs	500	pdflush wake-up interval (0 to disable)
vm.min_free_kbytes	dynamic	sets the desired free memory amount (some kernel atomic allocations can consume this)
vm.watermark_scale_factor	10	The distance between kswapd watermarks (min, low, high) that control waking up and sleeping (unit is fractions of 10000, such that 10 means 0.1% of system memory)
vm.watermark_boost_factor	5000	How far past the high watermark kswapd scans when memory is fragmented (recent fragmentation events occurred); unit is fractions of 10000, so 5000 means kswapd can boost up to 150% of the high watermark; 0 to disable
vm.percpu_pagelist_fraction	0	This can override the default max fraction of pages that can be allocated to per-cpu page lists (a value of 10 limits to 1/10th of pages)
vm.overcommit_memory	0	0 = Use a heuristic to allow reasonable overcommits; 1 = always overcommit; 2 = don't overcommit
vm.swappiness	60	The degree to favor swapping (paging) for freeing memory over reclaiming it from the page cache
vm.vfs_cache_pressure	100	The degree to reclaim cached directory and inode objects; lower values retain them more; 0 means never reclaim—can easily lead to out-of-memory conditions
kernel.numa_balancing	1	Enables automatic NUMA page balancing
kernel.numa_balancing_scan_size_mb	256	How many Mbytes of pages are scanned for each NUMA balancing scan

The tunables use a consistent naming scheme that includes the units. Note that dirty_background_bytes and dirty_background_ratio are mutually exclusive, as are dirty_bytes and dirty_ratio (when one is set it overrides the other).

The size of vm.min_free_kbytes is set dynamically as a fraction of main memory. The algorithm to choose this is not linear, as needs for free memory do not linearly scale with main memory size. (For reference, this is documented in the Linux source in mm/page_alloc.c.) vm.min_free_kbytes can be reduced to free up some memory for applications, but that can also cause the kernel to be overwhelmed during memory pressure and resort to using OOM sooner. Increasing it can help avoid OOM kills.

Another parameter for avoiding OOM is vm.overcommit_memory, which can be set to 2 to disable overcommit and avoid cases where this leads to OOM. If you want to control the OOM killer on a per-process basis, check your kernel version for /proc tunables such as oom_adj or oom_score_adj. These are described in Documentation/filesystems/proc.txt.

The vm.swappiness tunable can significantly affect performance if it begins swapping application memory earlier than desired. The value of this tunable can be between 0 and 100, with high values favoring swapping applications and therefore retaining the page cache. It may be desirable to set this to zero, so that application memory is retained as long as possible at the expense of the page cache. When there is still a memory shortage, the kernel can still use swapping.

At Netflix, kernel.numa_balancing was set to zero for earlier kernels (around Linux 3.13) because overly aggressive NUMA scanning consumed too much CPU [Gregg 17d]. This was fixed in later kernels, and there are other tunables including kernel.numa_balancing_scan_size_mb for adjusting the aggressiveness of NUMA scanning.

7.6.2   Multiple Page Sizes

Large page sizes can improve memory I/O performance by improving the hit ratio of the TLB cache (increasing its reach). Most modern processors support multiple page sizes, such as a 4 Kbyte default and a 2 Mbyte large page.

On Linux, large pages (called *huge pages*) can be configured in a number of ways. For reference, see Documentation/vm/hugetlbpage.txt.

These usually begin with the creation of huge pages:

```
# echo 50 > /proc/sys/vm/nr_hugepages
# grep Huge /proc/meminfo
AnonHugePages:         0 kB
HugePages_Total:      50
HugePages_Free:       50
HugePages_Rsvd:        0
HugePages_Surp:        0
Hugepagesize:       2048 kB
```

One way for an application to consume huge pages is via the shared memory segments, and the SHM_HUGETLBS flag to shmget(2). Another way involves creating a huge page-based file system for applications to map memory from:

```
# mkdir /mnt/hugetlbfs
# mount -t hugetlbfs none /mnt/hugetlbfs -o pagesize=2048K
```

Other ways include the MAP_ANONYMOUS|MAP_HUGETLB flags to mmap(2) and use of the libhugetlbfs API [Gorman 10].

Finally, *transparent huge pages* (THP) is another mechanism that uses huge pages by automatically promoting and demoting normal pages to huge, without an application needing to specify huge pages [Corbet 11]. In the Linux source see Documentation/vm/transhuge.txt and admin-guide/mm/transhuge.rst.[11]

7.6.3 Allocators

Different user-level allocators may be available, offering improved performance for multithreaded applications. These may be selected at compile time, or at execution time by setting the LD_PRELOAD environment variable.

For example, the libtcmalloc allocator could be selected using:

```
export LD_PRELOAD=/usr/lib/x86_64-linux-gnu/libtcmalloc_minimal.so.4
```

This may be placed in its startup script.

7.6.4 NUMA Binding

On NUMA systems, the numactl(8) command can be used to bind processes to NUMA nodes. This can improve performance for applications that do not need more than a single NUMA node of main memory. Example usage:

```
# numactl --membind=0 3161
```

This binds PID 3161 to NUMA node 0. Future memory allocations for this process will fail if they cannot be satisfied from this node. When using this option, you should also investigate using the --physcpubind option to also restrict CPU usage to CPUs connected to that NUMA node. I commonly use both NUMA and CPU bindings to restrict a process to a single socket, to avoid the performance penalty of CPU interconnect access.

Use numastat(8) (Section 7.5.6) to list available NUMA nodes.

7.6.5 Resource Controls

Basic resource controls, including setting a main memory limit and a virtual memory limit, may be available using ulimit(1).

For Linux, the container groups (cgroups) memory subsystem provides various additional controls. These include:

- **memory.limit_in_bytes**: The maximum allowed user memory, including file cache usage, in bytes

---

[11] Note that historically there were performance issues with transparent huge pages, deterring its usage. These issues have hopefully been fixed.

- **memory.memsw.limit_in_bytes**: The maximum allowed memory and swap space, in bytes (when swap is in use)

- **memory.kmem.limit_in_bytes**: The maximum allowed kernel memory, in bytes

- **memory.tcp.limit_in_bytes**: The maximum tcp buffer memory, in bytes.

- **memory.swappiness**: Similar to vm.swappiness described earlier but can be set for a cgroup

- **memory.oom_control**: Can be set to 0, to allow the OOM killer for this cgroup, or 1, to disable it

Linux also allows system-wide configuration in /etc/security/limits.conf.

For more on resource controls, see Chapter 11, Cloud Computing.

7.7   Exercises

1. Answer the following questions about memory terminology:

   - What is a page of memory?

   - What is resident memory?

   - What is virtual memory?

   - Using Linux terminology, what is the difference between paging and swapping?

2. Answer the following conceptual questions:

   - What is the purpose of demand paging?

   - Describe memory utilization and saturation.

   - What is the purpose of the MMU and the TLB?

   - What is the role of the page-out daemon?

   - What is the role of the OOM killer?

3. Answer the following deeper questions:

   - What is anonymous paging, and why is it more important to analyze than file system paging?

   - Describe the steps the kernel takes to free up more memory when free memory becomes exhausted on Linux-based systems.

   - Describe the performance advantages of slab-based allocation.

4. Develop the following procedures for your operating system:

   - A USE method checklist for memory resources. Include how to fetch each metric (e.g., which command to execute) and how to interpret the result. Try to use existing OS observability tools before installing or using additional software products.

   - Create a workload characterization checklist for memory resources. Include how to fetch each metric, and try to use existing OS observability tools first.

5. Perform these tasks:

- Choose an application, and summarize code paths that lead to memory allocation (malloc(3)).

- Choose an application that has some degree of memory growth (calling brk(2) or sbrk(2)), and summarize code paths that lead to this growth.

- Describe the memory activity visible in the following Linux output alone:

```
# vmstat 1
procs -----------memory-------- ---swap-- -----io---- --system-- -----cpu-----
 r  b   swpd   free  buff cache  si   so    bi    bo   in   cs us sy id wa st
 2  0 413344  62284    72  6972   0    0    17    12    1    1  0  0 100  0  0
 2  0 418036  68172    68  3808   0 4692  4520  4692 1060 1939 61 38  0  1  0
 2  0 418232  71272    68  1696   0  196 23924   196 1288 2464 51 38  0 11  0
 2  0 418308  68792    76  2456   0   76  3408    96 1028 1873 58 39  0  3  0
 1  0 418308  67296    76  3936   0    0  1060     0 1020 1843 53 47  0  0  0
 1  0 418308  64948    76  3936   0    0     0     0 1005 1808 36 64  0  0  0
 1  0 418308  62724    76  6120   0    0  2208     0 1030 1870 62 38  0  0  0
 1  0 422320  62772    76  6112   0 4012     0  4016 1052 1900 49 51  0  0  0
 1  0 422320  62772    76  6144   0    0     0     0 1007 1826 62 38  0  0  0
 1  0 422320  60796    76  6144   0    0     0     0 1008 1817 53 47  0  0  0
 1  0 422320  60788    76  6144   0    0     0     0 1006 1812 49 51  0  0  0
 3  0 430792  65584    64  5216   0 8472  4912  8472 1030 1846 54 40  0  6  0
 1  0 430792  64220    72  6496   0    0  1124    16 1024 1857 62 38  0  0  0
 2  0 434252  68188    64  3704   0 3460  5112  3460 1070 1964 60 40  0  0  0
 2  0 434252  71540    64  1436   0    0 21856     0 1300 2478 55 41  0  4  0
 1  0 434252  66072    64  3912   0    0  2020     0 1022 1817 60 40  0  0  0
[...]
```

6. (optional, advanced) Find or develop metrics to show how well the kernel NUMA memory locality policies are working in practice. Develop "known" workloads that have good or poor memory locality for testing the metrics.

7.8 References

[**Corbató 68**] Corbató, F. J., *A Paging Experiment with the Multics System*, MIT Project MAC Report MAC-M-384, 1968.

[**Denning 70**] Denning, P., "Virtual Memory," *ACM Computing Surveys (CSUR)* 2, no. 3, 1970.

[**Peterson 77**] Peterson, J., and Norman, T., "Buddy Systems," *Communications of the ACM*, 1977.

[**Thompson 78**] Thompson, K., *UNIX Implementation*, Bell Laboratories, 1978.

[**Babaoglu 79**] Babaoglu, O., Joy, W., and Porcar, J., *Design and Implementation of the Berkeley Virtual Memory Extensions to the UNIX Operating System*, Computer Science Division, Deptartment of Electrical Engineering and Computer Science, University of California, Berkeley, 1979.

[**Bach 86**] Bach, M. J., *The Design of the UNIX Operating System*, Prentice Hall, 1986.

[**Bonwick 94**] Bonwick, J., "The Slab Allocator: An Object-Caching Kernel Memory Allocator," USENIX, 1994.

[**Bonwick 01**] Bonwick, J., and Adams, J., "Magazines and Vmem: Extending the Slab Allocator to Many CPUs and Arbitrary Resources," USENIX, 2001.

[**Corbet 04**] Corbet, J., "2.6 swapping behavior," *LWN.net*, http://lwn.net/Articles/83588, 2004

[**Gorman 04**] Gorman, M., *Understanding the Linux Virtual Memory Manager*, Prentice Hall, 2004.

[**McDougall 06a**] McDougall, R., Mauro, J., and Gregg, B., *Solaris Performance and Tools: DTrace and MDB Techniques for Solaris 10 and OpenSolaris*, Prentice Hall, 2006.

[**Ghemawat 07**] Ghemawat, S., "TCMalloc : Thread-Caching Malloc," https://gperftools.github.io/gperftools/tcmalloc.html, 2007.

[**Lameter 07**] Lameter, C., "SLUB: The unqueued slab allocator V6," *Linux kernel mailing list*, http://lwn.net/Articles/229096, 2007.

[**Hall 09**] Hall, A., "Thanks for the Memory, Linux," Andrew Hall, https://www.ibm.com/developerworks/library/j-nativememory-linux, 2009.

[**Gorman 10**] Gorman, M., "Huge pages part 2: Interfaces," *LWN.net*, http://lwn.net/Articles/375096, 2010.

[**Corbet 11**] Corbet, J., "Transparent huge pages in 2.6.38," *LWN.net*, http://lwn.net/Articles/423584, 2011.

[**Facebook 11**] "Scalable memory allocation using jemalloc," *Facebook Engineering*, https://www.facebook.com/notes/facebook-engineering/scalable-memory-allocation-using-jemalloc/480222803919, 2011.

[**Evans 17**] Evans, J., "Swapping, memory limits, and cgroups," https://jvns.ca/blog/2017/02/17/mystery-swap, 2017.

[**Gregg 17d**] Gregg, B., "AWS re:Invent 2017: How Netflix Tunes EC2," http://www.brendangregg.com/blog/2017-12-31/reinvent-netflix-ec2-tuning.html, 2017.

[**Corbet 18a**] Corbet, J., "Is it time to remove ZONE_DMA?" *LWN.net*, https://lwn.net/Articles/753273, 2018.

[**Crucial 18**] "The Difference between RAM Speed and CAS Latency," https://www.crucial.com/articles/about-memory/difference-between-speed-and-latency, 2018.

[**Gregg 18c**] Gregg, B., "Working Set Size Estimation," http://www.brendangregg.com/wss.html, 2018.

[Facebook 19] "Getting Started with PSI," *Facebook Engineering*, https://facebookmicrosites.github.io/psi/docs/overview, 2019.

[Gregg 19] Gregg, B., *BPF Performance Tools: Linux System and Application Observability*, Addison-Wesley, 2019.

[Intel 19a] *Intel 64 and IA-32 Architectures Software Developer's Manual,* Combined Volumes: 1, 2A, 2B, 2C, 3A, 3B and 3C, Intel, 2019.

[Amazon 20] "Amazon EC2 High Memory Instances," https://aws.amazon.com/ec2/instance-types/high-memory, accessed 2020.

[Linux 20g] "Linux Magic System Request Key Hacks," *Linux documentation*, https://www.kernel.org/doc/html/latest/admin-guide/sysrq.html, accessed 2020.

[Robertson 20] Robertson, A., "bpftrace," https://github.com/iovisor/bpftrace, last updated 2020.

[Valgrind 20] "Valgrind Documentation," http://valgrind.org/docs/manual, May 2020.

Chapter 8

File Systems

File system performance often matters more to the application than disk or storage device performance, because it is the file system that applications interact with and wait for. File systems can use caching, buffering, and asynchronous I/O to avoid subjecting applications to disk-level (or remote storage system) latency.

System performance analysis and monitoring tools have historically focused on disk performance, leaving file system performance as a blind spot. This chapter sheds light on file systems, showing how they work and how to measure their latency and other details. This often makes it possible to rule out file systems and their underlying disk devices as the source of poor performance, allowing investigation to move on to other areas.

The learning objectives of this chapter are:

- Understand file system models and concepts.
- Understand how file system workloads affect performance.
- Become familiar with file system caches.
- Become familiar with file system internals and performance features.
- Follow various methodologies for file system analysis.
- Measure file system latency to identify modes and outliers.
- Investigate file system usage using tracing tools.
- Test file system performance using microbenchmarks.
- Become aware of file system tunable parameters.

This chapter consists of six parts, the first three providing the basis for file system analysis and the last three showing its practical application to Linux-based systems. The parts are as follows:

- **Background** introduces file system-related terminology and basic models, illustrating file system principles and key file system performance concepts.
- **Architecture** introduces generic and specific file system architecture.
- **Methodology** describes performance analysis methodologies, both observational and experimental.

- **Observability Tools** shows file system observability tools for Linux-based systems, including static and dynamic instrumentation.

- **Experimentation** summarizes file system benchmark tools.

- **Tuning** describes file system tunable parameters.

8.1   Terminology

For reference, file system–related terminology used in this chapter includes:

- **File system**: An organization of data as files and directories, with a file-based interface for accessing them, and file permissions to control access. Additional content may include special file types for devices, sockets, and pipes, and metadata including file access timestamps.

- **File system cache**: An area of main memory (usually DRAM) used to cache file system contents, which may include different caches for various data and metadata types.

- **Operations**: File system operations are requests of the file system, including read(2), write(2), open(2), close(2), stat(2), mkdir(2), and other operations.

- **I/O**: Input/output. File system I/O can be defined in several ways; here it is used to mean only operations that directly read and write (performing I/O), including read(2), write(2), stat(2) (read statistics), and mkdir(2) (write a new directory entry). I/O does not include open(2) and close(2) (although those calls update metadata and can cause indirect disk I/O).

- **Logical I/O**: I/O issued by the application to the file system.

- **Physical I/O**: I/O issued directly to disks by the file system (or via raw I/O).

- **Block size**: Also known as *record size*, is the size of file system on-disk data groups. See Block vs. Extent in Section 8.4.4, File System Features.

- **Throughput**: The current data transfer rate between applications and the file system, measured in bytes per second.

- **inode**: An index node (inode) is a data structure containing metadata for a file system object, including permissions, timestamps, and data pointers.

- **VFS**: Virtual file system, a kernel interface to abstract and support different file system types.

- **Volume**: An instance of storage providing more flexibility than using a whole storage device. A volume may be a portion of a device, or multiple devices.

- **Volume manager**: Software for managing physical storage devices in a flexible way, creating *virtual volumes* for use by the OS.

Other terms are introduced throughout this chapter. The Glossary includes basic terminology for reference, including *fsck*, *IOPS*, *operation rate*, and *POSIX*. Also see the terminology sections in Chapters 2 and 3.

8.2 Models

The following simple models illustrate some basic principles of file systems and their performance.

8.2.1 File System Interfaces

A basic model of a file system is shown in Figure 8.1, in terms of its interfaces.

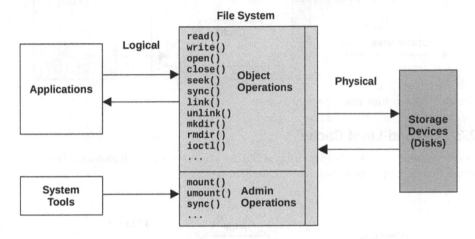

Figure 8.1 File system interfaces

The locations where *logical* and *physical* operations occur are also labeled in the figure. See Section 8.3.12, Logical vs. Physical I/O, for more about these.

Figure 8.1 shows generic object operations. Kernels may implement additional variants: for example, Linux provides readv(2), writev(2), openat(2), and more.

One approach for studying file system performance is to treat it as a black box, focusing on the latency of the object operations. This is explained in more detail in Section 8.5.2, Latency Analysis.

8.2.2 File System Cache

A generic file system cache stored in main memory is pictured in Figure 8.2, servicing a read operation.

The read returns data either from cache (*cache hit*) or from disk (*cache miss*). Cache misses are stored in the cache, populating the cache (warming it up).

The file system cache may also buffer writes to be written (flushed) later. The mechanisms for doing this differ for different file system types, and are described in Section 8.4, Architecture.

Kernels often provide a way to bypass the cache if desired. See Section 8.3.8, Raw and Direct I/O.

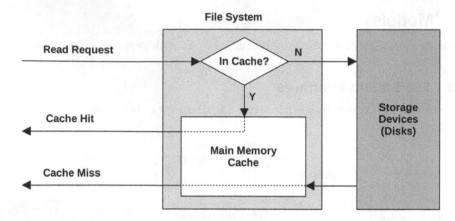

Figure 8.2   File system main memory cache

8.2.3 Second-Level Cache

Second-level cache may be any memory type; Figure 8.3 shows it as flash memory. This cache type was first developed by myself in 2007, for ZFS.

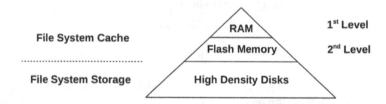

Figure 8.3   File system second-level cache

8.3 Concepts

The following are a selection of important file system performance concepts.

8.3.1 File System Latency

File system latency is the primary metric of file system performance, measured as the time from a logical file system request to its completion. It includes time spent in the file system and disk I/O subsystem, and waiting on disk devices—the physical I/O. Application threads often block during an application request in order to wait for file system requests to complete—in this way, file system latency *directly* and *proportionally* affects application performance.

Cases where applications may not be directly affected include the use of non-blocking I/O, prefetch (Section 8.3.4), and when I/O is issued from an asynchronous thread (e.g., a background flush thread). It may be possible to identify these cases from the application, if it provides detailed metrics for its file system usage. If not, a generic approach is to use a kernel tracing tool that can show the user-level stack trace that led to a logical file system I/O. This stack trace can then be studied to see which application routines issued it.

Operating systems have not historically made file system latency readily observable, instead providing disk device-level statistics. But there are many cases where such statistics are unrelated to application performance, and where they are also misleading. An example of this is where file systems perform background flushing of written data, which may appear as bursts of high-latency disk I/O. From the disk device-level statistics, this looks alarming; however, no application is waiting on these to complete. See Section 8.3.12, Logical vs. Physical I/O, for more cases.

8.3.2 Caching

The file system will typically use main memory (RAM) as a cache to improve performance. For applications, this process is transparent: application logical I/O latency becomes much lower (better), as it can be served from main memory rather than the much slower disk devices.

Over time, the cache grows, while free memory for the operating system shrinks. This can alarm new users, but is perfectly normal. The principle is: If there is spare main memory, do something useful with it. When applications need more memory, the kernel should quickly free it from the file system cache for use.

File systems use caching to improve read performance, and buffering (in the cache) to improve write performance. Multiple types of cache are typically used by the file system and the block device subsystem, which may include those in Table 8.1.

Table 8.1 **Example cache types**

Cache	Example
Page cache	Operating system page cache
File system primary cache	ZFS ARC
File system secondary cache	ZFS L2ARC
Directory cache	dentry cache
inode cache	inode cache
Device cache	ZFS vdev
Block device cache	Buffer cache

Specific cache types are described in Section 8.4, Architecture, while Chapter 3, Operating Systems, has the full list of caches (including application- and device-level).

8.3.3 Random vs. Sequential I/O

A series of logical file system I/O can be described as *random* or *sequential*, based on the file offset of each I/O. With sequential I/O, each I/O offset begins at the end of the previous I/O. Random I/O have no apparent relationship between them, and the offset changes randomly. A random file system workload may also refer to accessing many different files at random.

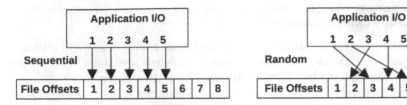

Figure 8.4 Sequential and random file I/O

Figure 8.4 illustrates these access patterns, showing an ordered series of I/O and example file offsets.

Due to the performance characteristics of certain storage devices (described in Chapter 9, Disks), file systems have historically attempted to reduce random I/O by placing file data on disk sequentially and contiguously. The term *fragmentation* describes what happens file systems do this poorly, causing files to be scattered over a drive, so that sequential logical I/O yields random physical I/O.

File systems may measure logical I/O access patterns so that they can identify sequential workloads, and then improve their performance using prefetch or read-ahead. This is helpful for rotational disks; less so for flash drives.

8.3.4 Prefetch

A common file system workload involves reading a large amount of file data sequentially, for example, for a file system backup. This data may be too large to fit in the cache, or it may be read only once and is unlikely to be retained in the cache (depending on the cache eviction policy). Such a workload would perform relatively poorly, as it would have a low cache hit ratio.

Prefetch is a common file system feature for solving this problem. It can detect a sequential read workload based on the current and previous file I/O offsets, and then predict and issue disk reads before the application has requested them. This populates the file system cache, so that if the application does perform the expected read, it results in a cache hit (the data needed was already in the cache). An example scenario is as follows:

1. An application issues a file read(2), passing execution to the kernel.

2. The data is not cached, so the file system issues the read to disk.

3. The previous file offset pointer is compared to the current location, and if they are sequential, the file system issues additional reads (prefetch).

4. The first read completes, and the kernel passes the data and execution back to the application.

5. Any prefetch reads complete, populating the cache for future application reads.

6. Future sequential application reads complete quickly via the cache in RAM.

This scenario is also illustrated in Figure 8.5, where application reads to offsets 1 and then 2 trigger prefetch of the next three offsets.

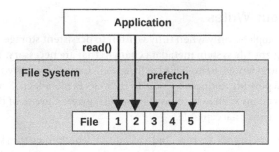

Figure 8.5 File system prefetch

When prefetch detection works well, applications show significantly improved sequential read performance; the disks keep ahead of application requests (provided they have the bandwidth to do so). When prefetch detection works poorly, unnecessary I/O is issued that the application does not need, polluting the cache and consuming disk and I/O transport resources. File systems typically allow prefetch to be tuned as needed.

8.3.5 Read-Ahead

Historically, prefetch has also been known as *read-ahead*. Linux uses the read-ahead term for a system call, readahead(2), that allows applications to explicitly warm up the file system cache.

8.3.6 Write-Back Caching

Write-back caching is commonly used by file systems to improve write performance. It works by treating writes as completed after the transfer to main memory, and writing them to disk sometime later, *asynchronously*. The file system process for writing this "dirty" data to disk is called *flushing*. An example sequence is as follows:

1. An application issues a file write(2), passing execution to the kernel.

2. Data from the application address space is copied to the kernel.

3. The kernel treats the write(2) syscall as completed, passing execution back to the application.

4. Sometime later, an asynchronous kernel task finds the written data and issues disk writes.

The trade-off is reliability. DRAM-based main memory is volatile, and dirty data can be lost in the event of a power failure. Data could also be written to disk *incompletely*, leaving a *corrupted* on-disk state.

If file system metadata becomes corrupted, the file system may no longer load. Such a state may be recoverable only from system backups, causing prolonged downtime. Worse, if the corruption affects file contents that the application reads and uses, the business may be in jeopardy.

To balance needs for both speed and reliability, file systems can offer write-back caching by default, and a *synchronous write* option to bypass this behavior and write directly to persistent storage devices.

8.3.7 Synchronous Writes

A synchronous write completes only when fully written to persistent storage (e.g., disk devices), which includes writing any file system metadata changes that are necessary. These are much slower than asynchronous writes (write-back caching), since synchronous writes incur disk device I/O latency (and possibly multiple I/O due to file system metadata). Synchronous writes are used by some applications such as database log writers, where the risk of data corruption from asynchronous writes is unacceptable.

There are two forms of synchronous writes: individual I/O, which is written synchronously, and groups of previous writes, which are synchronously committed.

Individual Synchronous Writes

Write I/O is synchronous when a file is opened using the flag O_SYNC or one of the variants, O_DSYNC and O_RSYNC (which as of Linux 2.6.31 are mapped by glibc to O_SYNC). Some file systems have mount options to force all write I/O to all files to be synchronous.

Synchronously Committing Previous Writes

Rather than synchronously writing individual I/O, an application may synchronously commit previous asynchronous writes at checkpoints in their code, using the fsync(2) system call. This can improve performance by grouping the writes, and can also avoid multiple metadata updates by use of write cancellation.

There are other situations that will commit previous writes, such as closing file handles, or when there are too many uncommitted buffers on a file. The former is often noticeable as long pauses when unpacking an archive of many files, especially over NFS.

8.3.8 Raw and Direct I/O

These are other types of I/O that an application may use, if supported by the kernel or file system:

Raw I/O is issued directly to disk offsets, bypassing the file system altogether. It has been used by some applications, especially databases, that can manage and cache their own data better than the file system cache. A drawback is more complexity in the software, and administration difficulties: the regular file system toolset can't be used for backup/restore or observability.

Direct I/O allows applications to use a file system but bypass the file system cache, for example, by using the O_DIRECT open(2) flag on Linux. This is similar to synchronous writes (but without the guarantees that O_SYNC offers), and it works for reads as well. It isn't as direct as raw device I/O, since mapping of file offsets to disk offsets must still be performed by file system code, and I/O may also be resized to match the size used by the file system for on-disk layout (its record size) or it may error (EINVAL). Depending on the file system, this may not only disable read caching and write buffering but may also disable prefetch.

8.3.9 Non-Blocking I/O

Normally, file system I/O will either complete immediately (e.g., from cache) or after waiting (e.g., for disk device I/O). If waiting is required, the application thread will *block* and leave CPU, allowing other threads to execute while it waits. While the blocked thread cannot perform other work, this typically isn't a problem since multithreaded applications can create additional threads to execute while some are blocked.

In some cases, non-blocking I/O is desirable, such as when avoiding the performance or resource overhead of thread creation. Non-blocking I/O may be performed by using the O_NONBLOCK or O_NDELAY flags to the open(2) syscall, which cause reads and writes to return an EAGAIN error instead of blocking, which tells the application to try again later. (Support for this depends on the file system, which may honor non-blocking only for advisory or mandatory file locks.)

The OS may also provide a separate asynchronous I/O interface, such as aio_read(3) and aio_write(3). Linux 5.1 added a new asynchronous I/O interface called io_uring, with improved ease of use, efficiency, and performance [Axboe 19].

Non-blocking I/O was also discussed in Chapter 5, Applications, Section 5.2.6, Non-Blocking I/O.

8.3.10 Memory-Mapped Files

For some applications and workloads, file system I/O performance can be improved by mapping files to the process address space and accessing memory offsets directly. This avoids the syscall execution and context switch overheads incurred when calling read(2) and write(2) syscalls to access file data. It can also avoid double copying of data, if the kernel supports directly mapping the file data buffer to the process address space.

Memory mappings are created using the mmap(2) syscall and removed using munmap(2). Mappings can be tuned using madvise(2), as summarized in Section 8.8, Tuning. Some applications provide an option to use the mmap syscalls (which may be called "mmap mode") in their configuration. For example, the Riak database can use mmap for its in-memory data store.

I've noticed a tendency to try using mmap(2) to solve file system performance issues without first analyzing them. If the issue is high I/O latency from disk devices, avoiding the small syscall overheads with mmap(2) may accomplish very little, when the high disk I/O latency is still present and dominant.

A disadvantage of using mappings on multiprocessor systems can be the overhead to keep each CPU MMU in sync, specifically the CPU cross calls to remove mappings (*TLB shootdowns*). Depending on the kernel and mapping, these may be minimized by delaying TLB updates (*lazy shootdowns*) [Vahalia 96].

8.3.11 Metadata

While *data* describes the contents of files and directories, *metadata* describes information about them. Metadata may refer to information that can be read from the file system interface (POSIX) or information needed to implement the file system on-disk layout. These are called logical and physical metadata, respectively.

Logical Metadata

Logical metadata is information that is read and written to the file system by consumers (applications), either:

- **Explicitly:** Reading file statistics (stat(2)), creating and deleting files (creat(2), unlink(2)) and directories (mkdir(2), rmdir(2)), setting file properties (chown(2), chmod(2))

- **Implicitly:** File system access timestamp updates, directory modification timestamp updates, used-block bitmap updates, free space statistics

A workload that is "metadata-heavy" typically refers to logical metadata, for example, web servers that stat(2) files to ensure they haven't changed since caching, at a much greater rate than reading file data contents.

Physical Metadata

Physical metadata refers to the on-disk layout metadata necessary to record all file system information. The metadata types in use depend on the file system and may include superblocks, inodes, blocks of data pointers (primary, secondary...), and free lists.

Logical and physical metadata are one reason for the difference between logical and physical I/O.

8.3.12   Logical vs. Physical I/O

Although it may seem counterintuitive, I/O requested by applications to the file system (logical I/O) may not match disk I/O (physical I/O), for several reasons.

File systems do much more than present persistent storage (the disks) as a file-based interface. They cache reads, buffer writes, map files to address spaces, and create additional I/O to maintain the on-disk physical layout metadata that they need to record where everything is. This can cause disk I/O that is unrelated, indirect, implicit, inflated, or deflated as compared to application I/O. Examples follow.

Unrelated

This is disk I/O that is not related to the application and may be due to:

- **Other applications**

- **Other tenants**: The disk I/O is from another cloud tenant (visible via system tools under some virtualization technologies).

- **Other kernel tasks**: For example, when the kernel is rebuilding a software RAID volume or performing asynchronous file system checksum verification (see Section 8.4, Architecture).

- **Administration tasks**: Such as backups.

Indirect

This is disk I/O caused by the application but without an immediate corresponding application I/O. This may be due to:

- **File system prefetch:** Adding additional I/O that may or may not be used by the application.
- **File system buffering:** The use of write-back caching to defer and coalesce writes for later flushing to disk. Some systems may buffer writes for tens of seconds before writing, which then appear as large, infrequent bursts.

Implicit

This is disk I/O triggered directly by application events other than explicit file system reads and writes, such as:

- **Memory mapped load/stores:** For memory mapped (mmap(2)) files, load and store instructions may trigger disk I/O to read or write data. Writes may be buffered and written later on. This can be confusing when analyzing file system operations (read(2), write(2)) and failing to find the source of the I/O (since it is triggered by instructions and not syscalls).

Deflated

Disk I/O that is smaller than the application I/O, or even nonexistent. This may be due to:

- **File system caching:** Satisfying reads from main memory instead of disk.
- **File system write cancellation:** The same byte offsets are modified multiple times before being flushed once to disk.
- **Compression:** Reducing the data volume from logical to physical I/O.
- **Coalescing:** Merging sequential I/O before issuing them to disk (this reduces the I/O count, but not the total size).
- **In-memory file system:** Content that may never be written to disk (e.g., tmpfs[1]).

Inflated

Disk I/O that is larger than the application I/O. This is the typical case due to:

- **File system metadata:** Adding additional I/O.
- **File system record size:** Rounding up I/O size (inflating bytes), or fragmenting I/O (inflating count).
- **File system journaling:** If employed, this can double disk writes, one write for the journal and the other for the final destination.
- **Volume manager parity:** Read-modify-write cycles, adding additional I/O.
- **RAID inflation:** Writing extra parity data, or data to mirrored volumes.

---

[1] Although tmpfs can also be written to swap devices.

Example

To show how these factors can occur in concert, the following example describes what can happen with a 1-byte application write:

1. An application performs a 1-byte write to an existing file.

2. The file system identifies the location as part of a 128 Kbyte file system record, which is not cached (but the metadata to reference it is).

3. The file system requests that the record be loaded from disk.

4. The disk device layer breaks the 128 Kbyte read into smaller reads suitable for the device.

5. The disks perform multiple smaller reads, totaling 128 Kbytes.

6. The file system now replaces the 1 byte in the record with the new byte.

7. Sometime later, the file system or kernel requests that the 128 Kbyte dirty record be written back to disk.

8. The disks write the 128 Kbyte record (broken up if needed).

9. The file system writes new metadata, for example, to update references (for copy-on-write) or access time.

10. The disks perform more writes.

So, while the application performed only a single 1-byte write, the disks performed multiple reads (128 Kbytes in total) and more writes (over 128 Kbytes).

8.3.13   Operations Are Not Equal

As is clear from the previous sections, file system operations can exhibit different performance based on their type. You can't tell much about a workload of "500 operations/s" from the rate alone. Some operations may return from the file system cache at main memory speeds; others may return from disk and be orders of magnitude slower. Other determinant factors include whether operations are random or sequential, reads or writes, synchronous writes or asynchronous writes, their I/O size, whether they include other operation types, their CPU execution cost (and how CPU-loaded the system is), and the storage device characteristics.

It is common practice to micro-benchmark different file system operations to determine these performance characteristics. As an example, the results in Table 8.2 are from a ZFS file system, on an otherwise idle Intel Xeon 2.4 GHz multi-core processor.

Table 8.2   **Example file system operation latencies**

Operation	Average (µs)
open(2) (cached[2])	2.2
close(2) (clean[3])	0.7

---

[2]With the file inode cached.

[3]Without dirty data that needs to be flushed to disk.

Operation	Average (µs)
read(2) 4 Kbytes (cached)	3.3
read(2) 128 Kbytes (cached)	13.9
write(2) 4 Kbytes (async)	9.3
write(2) 128 Kbytes (async)	55.2

These tests did not involve the storage devices but are a test of the file system software and CPU speed. Some special file systems never access persistent storage devices.

These tests were also single-threaded. Parallel I/O performance may be affected by the type and organization of file system locks in use.

8.3.14 Special File Systems

The intent of a file system is usually to store data persistently, but there are special file system types used on Linux for other purposes, including temporary files (/tmp), kernel device paths (/dev), system statistics (/proc), and system configuration (/sys).[4]

8.3.15 Access Timestamps

Many file systems support access timestamps, which record the time that each file and directory was accessed (read). This causes file metadata to be updated whenever files are read, creating a write workload that consumes disk I/O resources. Section 8.8, Tuning, shows how to turn off these updates.

Some file systems optimize access timestamp writes by deferring and grouping them to reduce interference with the active workload.

8.3.16 Capacity

When file systems fill, performance may degrade for a couple of reasons. First, when writing new data, it may take more CPU time and disk I/O to find free blocks on disk.[5] Second, areas of free space on disk are likely to be smaller and more sparsely located, degrading performance due to smaller I/O or random I/O.

How much of a problem this is depends on the file system type, its on-disk layout, its use of copy-on-write, and its storage devices. Various file system types are described in the next section.

---

[4] For a list of special file system types on Linux that do not use storage devices: grep '^nodev' /proc/filesystems

[5] ZFS, for example, switches to a different and slower free-block-finding algorithm when the pool storage exceeds a threshold (originally 80%, later 99%). See "Pool performance can degrade when a pool is very full" [Oracle 12].

8.4   Architecture

This section introduces generic and specific file system architecture, beginning with the I/O stack, VFS, file system caches and features, common file system types, volumes, and pools. Such background is useful when determining which file system components to analyze and tune. For deeper internals and other file system topics, refer to source code, if available, and external documentation. Some of these are listed at the end of this chapter.

8.4.1   File System I/O Stack

Figure 8.6 depicts a general model of the file system I/O stack, focusing on the file system interface. Specific components, layers, and APIs depend on the operating system type, version, and file systems used. A higher-level I/O stack figure is included in Chapter 3, Operating Systems, and another showing the disk components in more detail is in Chapter 9, Disks.

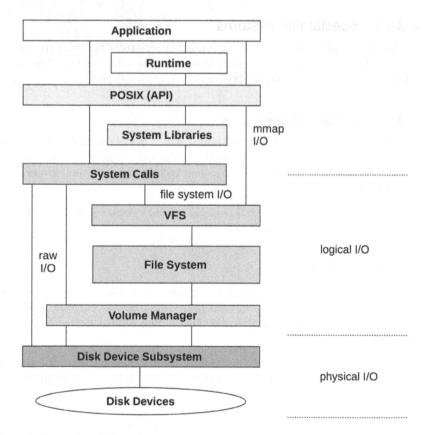

Figure 8.6   Generic file system I/O stack

This shows the path of I/O from applications and system libraries to syscalls and through the kernel. The path from system calls directly to the disk device subsystem is *raw I/O*. The path via VFS and the file system is file system I/O, including direct I/O, which skips the file system cache.

8.4.2   VFS

VFS (the virtual file system interface) provides a common interface for different file system types. Its location is shown in Figure 8.7.

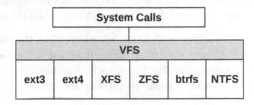

Figure 8.7   Virtual file system interface

VFS originated in SunOS and has become the standard abstraction for file systems.

The terminology used by the Linux VFS interface can be a little confusing, since it reuses the terms *inodes* and *superblocks* to refer to VFS objects—terms that originated from Unix file system on-disk data structures. The terms used for Linux on-disk data structures are usually prefixed with their file system type, for example, ext4_inode and ext4_super_block. The VFS inodes and VFS superblocks are in memory only.

The VFS interface can also serve as a common location for measuring the performance of any file system. Doing this may be possible using operating system–supplied statistics, or static or dynamic instrumentation.

8.4.3   File System Caches

Unix originally had only the buffer cache to improve the performance of block device access. Nowadays, Linux has multiple different cache types. Figure 8.8 gives an overview of file system caches on Linux, showing generic caches available for standard file system types.

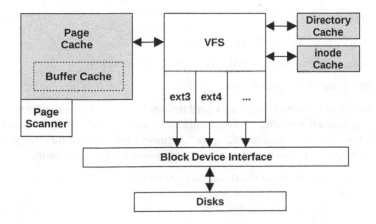

Figure 8.8   Linux file system caches

Buffer Cache

Unix used a buffer cache at the block device interface to cache disk device blocks. This was a separate, fixed-size cache and, with the later addition of the page cache, presented tuning problems when balancing different workloads between them, as well as the overheads of double caching and synchronization. These problems have largely been addressed by using the page cache to store the buffer cache, an approach introduced by SunOS and called the *unified buffer cache*.

Linux originally used a buffer cache as with Unix. Since Linux 2.4, the buffer cache has also been stored in the page cache (hence the dotted border in Figure 8.8) avoiding the double caching and synchronization overhead. The buffer cache functionality still exists, improving the performance of block device I/O, and the term still appears in Linux observability tools (e.g., free(1)).

The size of the buffer cache is dynamic and is observable from /proc.

Page Cache

The page cache was first introduced to SunOS during a virtual memory rewrite in 1985 and added to SVR4 Unix [Vahalia 96]. It cached virtual memory pages, including mapped file system pages, improving the performance of file and directory I/O. It was more efficient for file access than the buffer cache, which required translation from file offset to disk offset for each lookup. Multiple file system types could use the page cache, including the original consumers UFS and NFS. The size was dynamic: the page cache would grow to use available memory, freeing it again when applications needed it.

Linux has a page cache with the same attributes. The size of the Linux page cache is also dynamic, with a tunable to set the balance between evicting from the page cache and swapping (swappiness; see Chapter 7, Memory).

Pages of memory that are dirty (modified) and are needed for use by a file system are flushed to disk by kernel threads. Prior to Linux 2.6.32, there was a pool of page dirty flush (*pdflush*) threads, between two and eight as needed. These have since been replaced by the *flusher threads* (named *flush*), which are created per device to better balance the per-device workload and improve throughput. Pages are flushed to disk for the following reasons:

- After an interval (30 seconds)
- The sync(2), fsync(2), msync(2) system calls
- Too many dirty pages (the dirty_ratio and dirty_bytes tunables)
- No available pages in the page cache

If there is a system memory deficit, another kernel thread, the page-out daemon (*kswapd*, also known as the *page scanner*), may also find and schedule dirty pages to be written to disk so that it can free the memory pages for reuse (see Chapter 7, Memory). For observability, the kswapd and flush threads are visible as kernel tasks from operating system performance tools.

See Chapter 7, Memory, for more details about the page scanner.

Dentry Cache

The *dentry cache* (Dcache) remembers mappings from directory entry (struct dentry) to VFS inode, similar to an earlier Unix *directory name lookup cache* (DNLC). The Dcache improves the performance of path name lookups (e.g., via open(2)): when a path name is traversed, each name lookup can check the Dcache for a direct inode mapping, instead of stepping through the directory contents. The Dcache entries are stored in a hash table for fast and scalable lookup (hashed by the parent dentry and directory entry name).

Performance has been further improved over the years, including with the *read-copy-update-walk* (RCU-walk) algorithm [Corbet 10]. This attempts to walk the path name without updating dentry reference counts, which were causing scalability issues due to cache coherency with high rates of path name lookups on multi-CPU systems. If a dentry is encountered that isn't in the cache, RCU-walk reverts to the slower reference-count walk (ref-walk), since reference counts will be necessary during file system lookup and blocking. For busy workloads, it's expected that the dentry data will likely be cached, and the RCU-walk approach will succeed.

The Dcache also performs *negative caching*, which remembers lookups for nonexistent entries. This improves the performance of failed lookups, which commonly occur when searching for shared libraries.

The Dcache grows dynamically, shrinking via LRU (least recently used) when the system needs more memory. Its size can be seen via /proc.

Inode Cache

This cache contains VFS inodes (struct inodes), each describing properties of a file system object, many of which are returned via the stat(2) system call. These properties are frequently accessed for file system workloads, such as checking permissions when opening files, or updating time-stamps during modification. These VFS inodes are stored in a hash table for fast and scalable lookup (hashed by inode number and file system superblock), although most of the lookups will be done via the Dentry cache.

The inode cache grows dynamically, holding at least all inodes mapped by the Dcache. When there is system memory pressure, the inode cache will shrink, dropping inodes that do not have associated dentries. Its size can be seen via the /proc/sys/fs/inode* files.

8.4.4   File System Features

Additional key file system features that affect performance are described here.

Block vs. Extent

Block-based file systems store data in fixed-size blocks, referenced by pointers stored in meta-data blocks. For large files, this can require many block pointers and metadata blocks, and the placement of blocks may become scattered, leading to random I/O. Some block-based file systems attempt to place blocks contiguously to avoid this. Another approach is to use *variable block sizes*, so that larger sizes can be used as the file grows, which also reduces the metadata overhead.

Extent-based file systems preallocate contiguous space for files (extents), growing them as needed. These extents are variable in length, representing one or many contiguous blocks.

This improves streaming performance and can improve random I/O performance as file data is localized. It also improves metadata performance as there are fewer objects to track, without sacrificing space of unused blocks in an extent.

Journaling

A file system journal (or *log*) records changes to the file system so that, in the event of a system crash or power failure, changes can be replayed atomically—either succeeding in their entirety or failing. This allows file systems to quickly recover to a consistent state. Non-journaled file systems can become corrupted during a system crash, if data and metadata relating to a change were incompletely written. Recovering from such a crash requires walking all file system structures, which can take hours for large (terabytes) file systems.

The journal is written to disk synchronously, and for some file systems it can be configured to use a separate device. Some journals record both data and metadata, which consumes more storage I/O resources as all I/O is written twice. Others write only metadata and maintain data integrity by employing copy-on-write.

There is a file system type that consists of only a journal: a *log-structured file system*, where all data and metadata updates are written to a continuous and circular log. This optimizes write performance, as writes are always sequential and can be merged to use larger I/O sizes.

Copy-on-Write

A copy-on-write (COW) file system does not overwrite existing blocks but instead follows these steps:

1. Write blocks to a new location (a new copy).
2. Update references to new blocks.
3. Add old blocks to the free list.

This helps maintain file system integrity in the event of a system failure, and also improves performance by turning random writes into sequential ones.

When a file system approaches capacity, COW can cause a file's on-disk data layout to be fragmented, reducing performance (especially for HDDs). File system defragmentation, if available, may help restore performance.

Scrubbing

This is a file system feature that asynchronously reads all data blocks and verifies checksums to detect failed drives as early as possible, ideally while the failure is still recoverable due to RAID. However, scrubbing read I/O can hurt performance, so it should be issued at a low priority or at times of low workload.

Other Features

Other file system features that can affect performance include snapshots, compression, built-in redundancy, deduplication, trim support, and more. The following section describes various such features for specific file systems.

8.4.5   File System Types

Much of this chapter describes generic *characteristics* that can be applied to all file system types. The following sections summarize specific performance features for commonly used file systems. Their analysis and tuning are covered in later sections.

FFS

Many file systems are ultimately based on the Berkeley *fast file system* (FFS), which was designed to address issues with the original Unix file system.[6] Some background can help explain the state of file systems today.

The original Unix file system on-disk layout consisted of a table of inodes, 512-byte storage blocks, and a superblock of information used when allocating resources [Ritchie 74][Lions 77]. The inode table and storage blocks divided disk partitions into two ranges, which caused performance issues when seeking between them. Another issue was the use of the small fixed-block size, 512 bytes, which limited throughput and increased the amount of metadata (pointers) required to store large files. An experiment to double this to 1024 bytes, and the bottleneck then encountered was described by [McKusick 84]:

> Although the throughput had doubled, the old file system was still using only about four percent of the disk bandwidth. The main problem was that although the free list was initially ordered for optimal access, it quickly became scrambled as files were created and removed. Eventually the free list became entirely random, causing files to have their blocks allocated randomly over the disk. This forced a seek before every block access. Although old file systems provided transfer rates of up to 175 kilobytes per second when they were first created, this rate deteriorated to 30 kilobytes per second after a few weeks of moderate use because of this randomization of data block placement.

This excerpt describes free list *fragmentation*, which decreases performance over time as the file system is used.

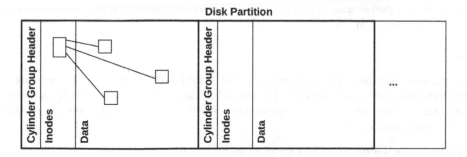

Figure 8.9   Cylinder groups

---

[6] The original Unix file system is not to be confused with later file systems called UFS, which are based on FFS.

FFS improved performance by splitting the partition into numerous *cylinder groups*, shown in Figure 8.9, each with its own inode array and data blocks. File inodes and data were kept within one cylinder group where possible, as pictured in Figure 8.9, reducing disk seek. Other related data was also placed nearby, including the inodes for a directory and its entries. The design of an inode was similar, with a hierarchy of pointers and data blocks, as pictured in Figure 8.10 (triply indirect blocks, which have three levels of pointers, are not shown here) [Bach 86].

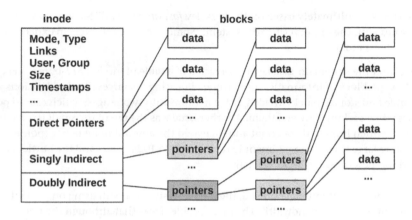

Figure 8.10   Inode data structure

The block size was increased to a 4 Kbyte minimum, improving throughput. This reduced the number of data blocks necessary to store a file, and therefore the number of indirect blocks needed to refer to the data blocks. The number of required indirect pointer blocks was further reduced because they were also larger. For space efficiency with small files, each block could be split into 1 Kbyte fragments.

Another performance feature of FFS was *block interleaving*: placing sequential file blocks on disk with a spacing between them of one or more blocks [Doeppner 10]. These extra blocks gave the kernel and the processor time to issue the next sequential file read. Without interleaving, the next block might pass the (rotational) disk head before it is ready to issue the read, causing latency as it waits for a full rotation.

ext3

The Linux extended file system (ext) was developed in 1992 as the first file system for Linux and its VFS, based on the original Unix file system. The second version, ext2 (1993), included multiple timestamps and cylinder groups from FFS. The third version, ext3 (1999), included file system growth and journaling.

Key performance features, including those added since its release, are:

- **Journaling**: Either *ordered mode,* for metadata only, or *journal mode,* for metadata and data. Journaling improves boot performance after a system crash, avoiding the need to run fsck. It may also improve the performance of some write workloads by coalescing metadata writes.

- **Journal device:** An external journal device can be used, so that the journal workload doesn't contend with the read workload.

- **Orlov block allocator:** This spreads top-level directories across cylinder groups, so that the subdirectories and contents are more likely to be co-located, reducing random I/O.

- **Directory indexes:** These add hashed B-trees to the file system for faster directory lookups.

Configurable features are documented in the mke2fs(8) man page.

ext4

The Linux ext4 file system was released in 2008, extending ext3 with new features and performance improvements: extents, large capacity, preallocation with fallocate(2), delayed allocation, journal checksumming, faster fsck, multiblock allocator, nanosecond timestamps, and snapshots.

Key performance features, including those added since its release, are:

- **Extents:** Extents improve contiguous placement, reducing random I/O and increasing the I/O size for sequential I/O. They are introduced in Section 8.4.4, File System Features.

- **Preallocation:** Via the fallocate(2) syscall, this allows applications to preallocate space that is likely contiguous, improving later write performance.

- **Delayed allocation:** Block allocation is delayed until it is flushed to disk, allowing writes to group (via the *multiblock allocator*), reducing fragmentation.

- **Faster fsck:** Unallocated blocks and inode entries are marked, reducing fsck time.

The state of some features can be seen via the /sys file system. For example:

```
# cd /sys/fs/ext4/features
# grep . *
batched_discard:supported
casefold:supported
encryption:supported
lazy_itable_init:supported
meta_bg_resize:supported
metadata_csum_seed:supported
```

Configurable features are documented in the mke2fs(8) man page. Some features, such as extents, can also be applied to ext3 file systems.

XFS

XFS was created by Silicon Graphics in 1993 for their IRIX operating system, to solve scalability limitations in the previous IRIX file system, EFS (which was based on FFS) [Sweeney 96]. XFS patches were merged into the Linux kernel in the early 2000s. Today, XFS is supported by most Linux distributions and can be used for the root file system. Netflix, for example, uses XFS for its

Cassandra database instances due to its high performance for that workload (and uses ext4 for the root file system).

Key performance features, including those added since its release, are:

- **Allocation Groups:** The partition is divided into equal-sized allocation groups (AG) that can be accessed in parallel. To limit contention, metadata such as inodes and free block lists of each AG are managed independently, while files and directories can span AGs.

- **Extents:** (See previous description in ext4.)

- **Journalling:** Journaling improves boot performance after a system crash, avoiding the need to run fsck(8). It may also improve the performance of some write workloads by coalescing metadata writes.

- **Journal device:** An external journal device can be used, so that the journal workload does not contend with the data workload.

- **Striped allocation:** If the file system is created on a striped RAID or LVM device, a stripe unit for data and the journal can be provided to ensure data allocations are optimized for the underlying hardware.

- **Delayed allocation:** Extent allocation is delayed until the data is flushed to disk, allowing writes to group and reduce fragmentation. Blocks are reserved for files in memory so that there is space available when the flush occurs.

- **Online defragmentation:** XFS provides a defrag utility that can operate on a file system while being actively used. While XFS uses extents and delayed allocation to prevent fragmentation, certain workloads and conditions can fragment the filesystem.

Configurable features are documented in the mkfs.xfs(8) man page. Internal performance data for XFS can be seen via /prov/fs/xfs/stat. The data is designed for advanced analysis: for more information see the XFS website [XFS 06][XFS 10].

ZFS

ZFS was developed by Sun Microsystems and released in 2005, combining the file system with the volume manager and including numerous enterprise features, making it an attractive choice for file servers (*filers*). ZFS was released as open source and is in use by several operating systems, although typically as an add-on because ZFS uses the CDDL license. Most development is occurring in the OpenZFS project, which in 2019 announced support for Linux as the primary OS [Ahrens 19]. While it is seeing growing support and usage in Linux, there is still resistance due to the source license, including from Linus Torvalds [Torvalds 20a].

Key ZFS performance features, including those added since its release, are:

- **Pooled storage:** All assigned storage devices are placed in a pool, from which file systems are created. This allows all devices to be used in parallel for maximum throughput and IOPS. Different RAID types can be used: 0, 1, 10, Z (based on RAID-5), Z2 (double-parity), and Z3 (triple-parity).

- **COW:** Copies modified blocks, then groups and writes them sequentially.

- **Logging**: ZFS flushes *transaction groups* (TXGs) of changes as batches, which succeed or fail as a whole so that the on-disk format is always consistent.

- **ARC**: The Adaptive Replacement Cache achieves a high cache hit rate by using multiple cache algorithms at the same time: most recently used (MRU) and most frequently used (MFU). Main memory is balanced between these based on their performance, which is known by maintaining extra metadata (*ghost lists*) to see how each would perform if it ruled all of main memory.

- **Intelligent prefetch**: ZFS applies different types of prefetch as appropriate: for metadata, for znodes (file contents), and for vdevs (virtual devices).

- **Multiple prefetch streams**: Multiple streaming readers on one file can create a random I/O workload as the file system seeks between them. ZFS tracks individual prefetch streams, allowing new streams to join them.

- **Snapshots**: Due to the COW architecture, snapshots can be created nearly instantaneously, deferring the copying of new blocks until needed.

- **ZIO pipeline**: Device I/O is processed by a pipeline of stages, each stage serviced by a pool of threads to improve performance.

- **Compression**: Multiple algorithms are supported, which usually reduce performance due to the CPU overhead. The lzjb (Lempel-Ziv Jeff Bonwick) option is lightweight and can marginally improve storage performance by reducing I/O load (as it is compressed), at the cost of some CPU.

- **SLOG**: The ZFS separate intent log allows synchronous writes to be written to separate devices, avoiding contention with the pool disks' workload. Writes to the SLOG are read only in the event of system failure, for replay.

- **L2ARC**: The Level 2 ARC is a second level of cache after main memory, for caching random read workloads on flash memory-based solid-state disks (SSDs). It does not buffer write workloads, and contains only clean data that already resides on the storage pool disks. It can also duplicate data in the ARC, so that the system can recover more quickly in the event of a main memory flushing perturbation.

- **Data deduplication**: A file-system-level feature that avoids recording multiple copies of the same data. This feature has significant performance implications, both good (reduced device I/O) and bad (when the hash table no longer fits in main memory, device I/O becomes inflated, perhaps significantly). The initial version is intended only for workloads where the hash table is expected to always fit in main memory.

There is a behavior of ZFS that can reduce performance in comparison with other file systems: by default, ZFS issues cache flush commands to the storage devices, to ensure that writes have completed in the case of a power outage. This is one of the ZFS integrity features; however, it comes at a cost: it can induce latency for ZFS operations that must wait for the cache flush.

btrfs

The B-tree file system (btrfs) is based on copy-on-write B-trees. This is a modern file system and volume manager combined architecture, similar to ZFS, and is expected to eventually offer a similar feature set. Current features include pooled storage, large capacity, extents, COW, volume growth and shrinking, subvolumes, block device addition and removal, snapshots, clones, compression, and various checksums (including crc32c, xxhash64, sha256, and blake2b). Development was begun by Oracle in 2007.

Key performance features include the following:

- **Pooled storage:** Storage devices are placed in a combined volume, from which file systems are created. This allows all devices to be used in parallel for maximum throughput and IOPS. RAID 0, 1, and 10 can be used.

- **COW:** Groups and writes data sequentially.

- **Online balancing:** Objects may be moved between storage devices to balance their workload.

- **Extents:** Improve sequential layout and performance.

- **Snapshots:** Due to the COW architecture, snapshots can be created nearly instantaneously, deferring the copying of new blocks until needed.

- **Compression:** Supports zlib and LZO.

- **Journaling:** A per-subvolume log tree can be created to journal synchronous COW workloads.

Planned performance-related features include RAID-5 and 6, object-level RAID, incremental dumps, and data deduplication.

8.4.6 Volumes and Pools

Historically, file systems were built upon a single disk or disk partition. Volumes and pools allow file systems to be built upon multiple disks and can be configured using different RAID strategies (see Chapter 9, Disks).

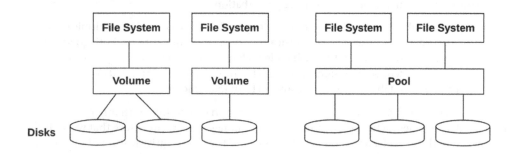

Figure 8.11   Volumes and pools

Volumes present multiple disks as one virtual disk, upon which the file system is built. When built upon whole disks (and not slices or partitions), volumes isolate workloads, reducing performance issues of contention.

Volume management software includes the Logical Volume Manager (LVM) for Linux-based systems. Volumes, or virtual disks, may also be provided by hardware RAID controllers.

Pooled storage includes multiple disks in a storage pool, from which multiple file systems can be created. This is shown in Figure 8.11 with volumes for comparison. Pooled storage is more flexible than volume storage, as file systems can grow and shrink regardless of the backing devices. This approach is used by modern file systems, including ZFS and btrfs, and is also possible using LVM.

Pooled storage can use all disk devices for all file systems, improving performance. Workloads are not isolated; in some cases, multiple pools may be used to separate workloads, given the trade-off of some flexibility, as disk devices must be initially placed in one pool or another. Note that pooled disks may be of different types and sizes, whereas volumes may be restricted to uniform disks within a volume.

Additional performance considerations when using either software volume managers or pooled storage include the following:

- **Stripe width**: Matching this to the workload.

- **Observability**: The virtual device utilization can be confusing; check the separate physical devices.

- **CPU overhead**: Especially when performing RAID parity computation. This has become less of an issue with modern, faster CPUs. (Parity computation can also be offloaded to hardware RAID controllers.)

- **Rebuilding**: Also called *resilvering*, this is when an empty disk is added to a RAID group (e.g., replacing a failed disk) and it is populated with the necessary data to join the group. This can significantly affect performance as it consumes I/O resources and may last for hours or even days.

Rebuilding is a worsening problem, as the capacity of storage devices increases faster than their throughput, increasing rebuild time, and making the risk of a failure or medium errors during rebuild greater. When possible, offline rebuilds of unmounted drives can improve rebuild times.

8.5 Methodology

This section describes various methodologies and exercises for file system analysis and tuning. The topics are summarized in Table 8.3.

Table 8.3 **File system performance methodologies**

Section	Methodology	Types
8.5.1	Disk analysis	Observational analysis
8.5.2	Latency analysis	Observational analysis
8.5.3	Workload characterization	Observational analysis, capacity planning
8.5.4	Performance monitoring	Observational analysis, capacity planning

Section	Methodology	Types
8.5.5	Static performance tuning	Observational analysis, capacity planning
8.5.6	Cache tuning	Observational analysis, tuning
8.5.7	Workload separation	Tuning
8.5.8	Micro-benchmarking	Experimental analysis

See Chapter 2, Methodologies, for more strategies and the introduction to many of these.

These may be followed individually or used in combination. My suggestion is to use the following strategies to start with, in this order: latency analysis, performance monitoring, workload characterization, micro-benchmarking, and static performance tuning. You may come up with a different combination and ordering that works best in your environment.

Section 8.6, Observability Tools, shows operating system tools for applying these methods.

8.5.1   Disk Analysis

A common troubleshooting strategy has been to ignore the file system and focus on *disk* performance instead. This assumes that the worst I/O is disk I/O, so by analyzing only the disks you have conveniently focused on the expected source of problems.

With simpler file systems and smaller caches, this generally worked. Nowadays, this approach becomes confusing and misses entire classes of issues (see Section 8.3.12, Logical vs. Physical I/O).

8.5.2   Latency Analysis

For latency analysis, begin by measuring the latency of file system operations. This should include all object operations, not just I/O (e.g., include sync(2)).

operation latency = time (operation completion) - time (operation request)

These times can be measured from one of four layers, as shown in Table 8.4.

Table 8.4   **Targets (layers) for analyzing file system latency**

Layer	Pros	Cons
Application	Closest measure of the effect of file system latency on the application; can also inspect application context to determine if latency is occurring during the application's primary function, or if it is asynchronous.	Technique varies between applications and application software versions.

Layer	Pros	Cons
Syscall interface	Well-documented interface. Commonly observable via operating system tools and static tracing.	Syscalls catch all file system types, including non-storage file systems (statistics, sockets), which may be confusing unless filtered. Adding to the confusion, there may also be multiple syscalls for the same file system function. For example, for read, there may be read(2), pread64(2), preadv(2), preadv2(2), etc., all of which need to be measured.
VFS	Standard interface for all file systems; one call for file system operations (e.g., vfs_write())	VFS traces all file system types, including non-storage file systems, which may be confusing unless filtered.
Top of file system	Target file system type traced only; some file system internal context for extended details.	File system-specific; tracing technique may vary between file system software versions (although the file system may have a VFS-like interface that maps to VFS, and as such doesn't change often).

Choosing the layer may depend on tool availability. Check the following:

- **Application documentation:** Some applications already provide file system latency metrics, or the ability to enable their collection.

- **Operating system tools:** Operating systems may also provide metrics, ideally as separate statistics for each file system or application.

- **Dynamic instrumentation:** If your system has dynamic instrumentation (Linux kprobes and uprobes, used by various tracers), all layers can be inspected via custom tracing programs, without restarting anything.

Latency may be presented as per-interval averages, distributions (e.g., histograms or heat maps: see Section 8.6.18), or as a list of every operation and its latency. For file systems that have a high cache hit rate (over 99%), per-interval averages can become dominated by cache hit latency. This may be unfortunate when there are isolated instances of high latency (outliers) that are important to identify but difficult to see from an average. Examining full distributions or per-operation latency allows such outliers to be investigated, along with the effect of different tiers of latency, including file system cache hits and misses.

Once high latency has been found, continue with drill-down analysis into the file system to determine the origin.

Transaction Cost

Another way to present file system latency is as the total time spent waiting on the file system during an application transaction (e.g., a database query):

percent time in file system = 100 * total blocking file system latency/application transaction time

This allows the cost of file system operations to be quantified in terms of application performance, and performance improvements to be predicted. The metric may be presented as the average either for all transactions during an interval, or for individual transactions.

Figure 8.12 shows the time spent on an application thread that is servicing a transaction. This transaction issues a single file system read; the application blocks and waits for its completion, transitioning to off-CPU. The total blocking time in this case is the time for the single file system read. If multiple blocking I/O were called during a transaction, the total time is their sum.

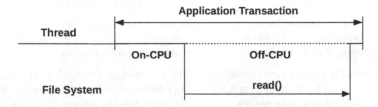

Figure 8.12   Application and file system latency

As a specific example, an application transaction takes 200 ms, during which it waits for a total of 180 ms on multiple file system I/O. The time that the application was blocked by the file system is 90% (100 * 180 ms/200 ms). Eliminating file system latency may improve performance by up to 10x.

As another example, if an application transaction takes 200 ms, during which only 2 ms was spent in the file system, the file system—and the entire disk I/O stack—is contributing only 1% to the transaction runtime. This result is incredibly useful, as it can steer the performance investigation to the real source of latency.

If the application were issuing I/O as *non-blocking*, the application can continue to execute on-CPU while the file system responds. In this case, the blocking file system latency measures only the time the application was blocked off-CPU.

8.5.3   Workload Characterization

Characterizing the load applied is an important exercise when capacity planning, benchmarking, and simulating workloads. It can also lead to some of the largest performance gains by identifying unnecessary work that can be eliminated.

Here are the basic attributes that characterize the file system workload:

- Operation rate and operation types
- File I/O throughput
- File I/O size
- Read/write ratio
- Synchronous write ratio
- Random versus sequential file offset access

Operation rate and throughput are defined in Section 8.1, Terminology. Synchronous writes and random versus sequential were described in Section 8.3, Concepts.

These characteristics can vary from second to second, especially for timed application tasks that execute at intervals. To better characterize the workload, capture maximum values as well as averages. Better still, examine the full distribution of values over time.

Here is an example workload description, to show how these attributes can be expressed together:

> On a financial trading database, the file system has a random read workload, averaging 18,000 reads/s with an average read size of 4 Kbytes. The total operation rate is 21,000 ops/s, which includes reads, stats, opens, closes, and around 200 synchronous writes/s. The write rate is steady while the read rate varies, up to a peak of 39,000 reads/s.

These characteristics may be described in terms of a single file system instance, or all instances on a system of the same type.

Advanced Workload Characterization/Checklist

Additional details may be included to characterize the workload. These have been listed here as questions for consideration, which may also serve as a checklist when studying file system issues thoroughly:

- What is the file system cache hit ratio? Miss rate?
- What are the file system cache capacity and current usage?
- What other caches are present (directory, inode, buffer), and what are their statistics?
- Have any attempts been made to tune the file system in the past? Are any file system parameters set to values other than their defaults?
- Which applications or users are using the file system?
- What files and directories are being accessed? Created and deleted?
- Have any errors been encountered? Was this due to invalid requests, or issues from the file system?
- Why is file system I/O issued (user-level call path)?
- To what degree do applications directly (synchronously) request file system I/O?
- What is the distribution of I/O arrival times?

Many of these questions can be posed per application or per file. Any of them may also be checked over time, to look for maximums, minimums, and time-based variations. Also see Section 2.5.10, Workload Characterization, in Chapter 2, Methodologies, which provides a higher-level summary of the characteristics to measure (who, why, what, how).

Performance Characterization

The previous workload characterization lists examine the workload applied. The following examines the resulting performance:

- What is the average file system operation latency?
- Are there any high-latency outliers?
- What is the full distribution of operation latency?
- Are system resource controls for file system or disk I/O present and active?

The first three questions may be asked for each operation type separately.

Event Tracing

Tracing tools can be used to record all file system operations and details to a log for later analysis. This can include the operating type, operation arguments, file pathname, start and end timestamps, completion status, and process ID and name, for every I/O. While this may be the ultimate tool for workload characterization, in practice it can cost significant overhead due to the rate of file system operations, often making it impractical unless heavily filtered (e.g., only including slow I/O in the log: see the ext4slower(8) tool in Section 8.6.14).

8.5.4   Performance Monitoring

Performance monitoring can identify active issues and patterns of behavior over time. Key metrics for file system performance are:

- Operation rate
- Operation latency

The operation rate is the most basic characteristic of the applied workload, and the latency is the resulting performance. The value for normal or bad latency depends on your workload, environment, and latency requirements. If you aren't sure, micro-benchmarks of known-to-be-good versus bad workloads may be performed to investigate latency (e.g., workloads that usually hit the file system cache versus those that usually miss). See Section 8.7, Experimentation.

The operation latency metric may be monitored as a per-second average, and can include other values such as the maximum and standard deviation. Ideally, it would be possible to inspect the full distribution of latency, for example by using a histogram or heat map, to look for outliers and other patterns.

Both rate and latency may also be recorded for each operation type (read, write, stat, open, close, etc.). Doing this will greatly help investigations of workload and performance changes, by identifying differences in particular operation types.

For systems that impose file system-based resource controls, statistics can be included to show if and when throttling was in use.

Unfortunately, in Linux there are usually no readily available statistics for file system operations (exceptions include, for NFS, via nfsstat(8)).

8.5.5   Static Performance Tuning

Static performance tuning focuses on issues of the configured environment. For file system performance, examine the following aspects of the static configuration:

- How many file systems are mounted and actively used?
- What is the file system record size?
- Are access timestamps enabled?
- What other file system options are enabled (compression, encryption...)?
- How has the file system cache been configured? Maximum size?
- How have other caches (directory, inode, buffer) been configured?
- Is a second-level cache present and in use?
- How many storage devices are present and in use?
- What is the storage device configuration? RAID?
- Which file system types are used?
- What is the version of the file system (or kernel)?
- Are there file system bugs/patches that should be considered?
- Are there resource controls in use for file system I/O?

Answering these questions can reveal configuration choices that have been overlooked. Sometimes a system has been configured for one workload, and then repurposed for another. This method will remind you to revisit those choices.

8.5.6   Cache Tuning

The kernel and file system may use many different caches, including a buffer cache, directory cache, inode cache, and file system (page) cache. Various caches were described in Section 8.4, Architecture. These can be examined and often tuned, depending on the tunable options available.

8.5.7   Workload Separation

Some types of workloads perform better when configured to use their own exclusive file systems and disk devices. This approach has been known as using "separate spindles," since creating random I/O by seeking between two different workload locations is particularly bad for rotational disks (see Chapter 9, Disks).

For example, a database may benefit from having separate file systems and disks for its log files and its database files. The installation guide for the database frequently contains advice on the placement of its data stores.

8.5.8 Micro-Benchmarking

Benchmark tools for file system and disk benchmarking (of which there are many) can be used to test the performance of different file system types or settings within a file system, for given workloads. Typical factors that may be tested include

- **Operation types:** The rate of reads, writes, and other file system operations
- **I/O size:** 1 byte up to 1 Mbyte and larger
- **File offset pattern:** Random or sequential
- **Random-access pattern:** Uniform, random, or Pareto distribution
- **Write type:** Asynchronous or synchronous (O_SYNC)
- **Working set size:** How well it fits in the file system cache
- **Concurrency:** Number parallel I/O or number of threads performing I/O
- **Memory mapping:** File access via mmap(2), instead of read(2)/write(2)
- **Cache state:** Whether the file system cache is "cold" (unpopulated) or "warm"
- **File system tunables:** May include compression, data deduplication, and so on

Common combinations include random read, sequential read, random write, and sequential write. I have not included direct I/O in this list, as its intent with micro-benchmarking is to bypass the file system and test disk device performance (see Chapter 9, Disks).

A critical factor when micro-benchmarking file systems is the *working set size* (WSS): the volume of data that is accessed. Depending on the benchmark, this may be the total size of the files in use. A small working set size may return entirely from the file system cache in main memory (DRAM), unless a direct I/O flag is used. A large working set size may return mostly from storage devices (disks). The performance difference can be multiple orders of magnitude. Running a benchmark against a newly mounted file system and then a second time after caches have been populated and comparing the results of the two is often a good illustration of WSS. (Also see Section 8.7.3, Cache Flushing.)

Consider the general expectations for different benchmarks, which include the total size of the files (WSS), in Table 8.5.

Table 8.5 **File system benchmark expectations**

System Memory	Total File Size (WSS)	Benchmark	Expectation
128 Gbytes	10 Gbytes	Random read	100% cache hits
128 Gbytes	10 Gbytes	Random read, direct I/O	100% disk reads (due to direct I/O)
128 Gbytes	1,000 Gbytes	Random read	Mostly disk reads, with ~12% cache hits
128 Gbytes	10 Gbytes	Sequential read	100% cache hits
128 Gbytes	1,000 Gbytes	Sequential read	Mixture of cache hits (most due to prefetch) and disk reads

System Memory	Total File Size (WSS)	Benchmark	Expectation
128 Gbytes	10 Gbytes	Buffered writes	Mostly cache hits (buffering), with some blocking on writes depending on file system behavior
128 Gbytes	10 Gbytes	Synchronous writes	100% disk writes

Some file system benchmark tools do not make clear what they are testing, and may imply a *disk* benchmark but use a small total file size, which returns entirely from cache and so does not test the disks. See Section 8.3.12, Logical vs. Physical I/O, to understand the difference between testing the file system (logical I/O) and testing the disks (physical I/O).

Some *disk* benchmark tools operate via the file system by using direct I/O to avoid caching and buffering. The file system still plays a minor role, adding code path overheads and mapping differences between file and on-disk placement.

See Chapter 12, Benchmarking, for more on this general topic.

8.6 Observability Tools

This section introduces file system observability tools for Linux-based operating systems. See the previous section for strategies to follow when using these.

The tools in this section are listed in Table 8.6.

Table 8.6 **File system observability tools**

Section	Tool	Description
8.6.1	mount	List file systems and their mount flags
8.6.2	free	Cache capacity statistics
8.6.3	top	Includes memory usage summary
8.6.4	vmstat	Virtual memory statistics
8.6.5	sar	Various statistics, including historic
8.6.6	slabtop	Kernel slab allocator statistics
8.6.7	strace	System call tracing
8.6.8	fatrace	Trace file system operations using fanotify
8.6.9	latencytop	Show system-wide latency sources
8.6.10	opensnoop	Trace files opened
8.6.11	filetop	Top files in use by IOPS and bytes
8.6.12	cachestat	Page cache statistics

Section	Tool	Description
8.6.13	ext4dist (xfs, zfs, btrfs, nfs)	Show ext4 operation latency distribution
8.6.14	ext4slower (xfs, zfs, btrfs, nfs)	Show slow ext4 operations
8.6.15	bpftrace	Custom file system tracing

This is a selection of tools and capabilities to support Section 8.5, Methodology. It begins with traditional and then covers tracing-based tools. Some of the traditional tools are likely available on other Unix-like operating systems where they originated, including: mount(8), free(1), top(1), vmstat(8), and sar(1). Many of the tracing tools are BPF-based, and use BCC and bpftrace frontends (Chapter 15); they are: opensnoop(8), filetop(8), cachestat(8), ext4dist(8), and ext4slower(8).

See the documentation for each tool, including its man pages, for full references of its features.

8.6.1   mount

The Linux mount(1) command lists mounted file systems and their mount flags:

```
$ mount
/dev/nvme0n1p1 on / type ext4 (rw,relatime,discard)
devtmpfs on /dev type devtmpfs (rw,relatime,size=986036k,nr_inodes=246509,mode=755)
sysfs on /sys type sysfs (rw,nosuid,nodev,noexec,relatime)
proc on /proc type proc (rw,nosuid,nodev,noexec,relatime)
securityfs on /sys/kernel/security type securityfs (rw,nosuid,nodev,noexec,relatime)
tmpfs on /dev/shm type tmpfs (rw,nosuid,nodev)
[...]
```

The first line shows that an ext4 file system stored on /dev/nvme0n1p1 is mounted on /, with the mount flags rw, relatime, and discard. relatime is a performance improving option that reduces inode access time updates, and the subsequent disk I/O cost, by only updating the access time when the modify or change times are also being updated, or if the last update was more than a day ago.

8.6.2   free

The Linux free(1) command shows memory and swap statistics. The following two commands show the normal and wide (-w) output, both as megabytes (-m):

```
$ free -m
              total        used        free      shared  buff/cache   available
Mem:           1950         568         163           0        1218        1187
Swap:             0           0           0
$ free -mw
              total        used        free      shared     buffers       cache   available
Mem:           1950         568         163           0          84        1133        1187
Swap:             0           0           0
```

The wide output shows a buffers column for the buffer cache size, and a cached column for the page cache size. The default output combines these as buff/cache.

An important column is available (a new addition to free(1)), which shows how much memory is available for applications without needing to swap. It takes into account memory that cannot be reclaimed immediately.

These fields can also be read from /proc/meminfo, which provides them in kilobytes.

8.6.3 top

Some versions of the top(1) command include file system cache details. These lines from the Linux version of top(1) include the buff/cache and available (avail Mem) statistics printed by free(1):

```
MiB Mem :   1950.0 total,    161.2 free,    570.3 used,   1218.6 buff/cache
MiB Swap:      0.0 total,      0.0 free,      0.0 used.   1185.9 avail Mem
```

See Chapter 6, CPUs, for more about top(1).

8.6.4 vmstat

The vmstat(1) command, like top(1), also may include details on the file system cache. For more details on vmstat(1), see Chapter 7, Memory.

The following runs vmstat(1) with an interval of 1 to provide updates every second:

```
$ vmstat 1
procs -----------memory---------- ---swap-- -----io---- -system-- ------cpu-----
 r  b   swpd   free   buff  cache   si   so    bi    bo   in   cs us sy id wa st
 0  0      0 167644  87032 1161112    0    0     7    14   14    1  4  2 90  0  5
 0  0      0 167636  87032 1161152    0    0     0     0  162  376  0  0 100  0  0
[...]
```

The buff column shows the buffer cache size, and cache shows the page cache size, both in kilobytes.

8.6.5 sar

The system activity reporter, sar(1), provides various file system statistics and may be configured to record these periodically. sar(1) is mentioned in various chapters in this book for the different statistics it provides, and introduced in Section 4.4, sar.

Executing sar(1) with a one-second interval for reporting current activity:

```
# sar -v 1
Linux 5.3.0-1009-aws (ip-10-1-239-218)    02/08/20    _x86_64_  (2 CPU)

21:20:24    dentunusd   file-nr  inode-nr    pty-nr
21:20:25        27027      1344     52945         2
```

```
21:20:26        27012      1312      52922        2
21:20:27        26997      1248      52899        2
[...]
```

The **-v** option provides the following columns:

- **dentunusd**: Directory entry cache unused count (available entries)
- **file-nr**: Number of file handles in use
- **inode-nr**: Number of inodes in use
- **pty-nr**: Number of pseudo-terminals in use

There is also a **-r** option, which prints kbbuffers and kbcached columns for buffer cache and page cache sizes, in kilobytes.

8.6.6 slabtop

The Linux slabtop(1) command prints information about the kernel slab caches, some of which are used for file system caches:

```
# slabtop -o
 Active / Total Objects (% used)    : 604675 / 684235 (88.4%)
 Active / Total Slabs (% used)      : 24040 / 24040 (100.0%)
 Active / Total Caches (% used)     : 99 / 159 (62.3%)
 Active / Total Size (% used)       : 140593.95K / 160692.10K (87.5%)
 Minimum / Average / Maximum Object : 0.01K / 0.23K / 12.00K

  OBJS ACTIVE   USE OBJ SIZE   SLABS OBJ/SLAB CACHE SIZE NAME
165945 149714   90%    0.10K    4255       39     17020K buffer_head
107898  66011   61%    0.19K    5138       21     20552K dentry
 67350  67350  100%    0.13K    2245       30      8980K kernfs_node_cache
 41472  40551   97%    0.03K     324      128      1296K kmalloc-32
 35940  31460   87%    1.05K    2396       15     38336K ext4_inode_cache
 33514  33126   98%    0.58K    2578       13     20624K inode_cache
 24576  24576  100%    0.01K      48      512       192K kmalloc-8
[...]
```

Some file system-related slab caches can be seen in the output: dentry, ext4_inode_cache, and inode_cache. Without the **-o** (once) output mode, slabtop(1) will refresh and update the screen.

Slabs may include:

- **buffer_head**: Used by the buffer cache
- **dentry**: dentry cache
- **inode_cache**: inode cache
- **ext3_inode_cache**: inode cache for ext3

- **ext4_inode_cache**: inode cache for ext4

- **xfs_inode**: inode cache for XFS

- **btrfs_inode**: inode cache for btrfs

slabtop(1) uses /proc/slabinfo, which exists if CONFIG_SLAB is enabled.

8.6.7 strace

File system latency can be measured at the syscall interface using tracing tools including strace(1) for Linux. However, the current ptrace(2)-based implementation of strace(1) can severely hurt performance and may be suitable for use only when the performance overhead is acceptable and other methods to analyze latency are not possible. See Chapter 5, Section 5.5.4, strace, for more on strace(1).

This example shows strace(1) timing reads on an ext4 file system:

```
$ strace -ttT -p 845
[...]
18:41:01.513110 read(9, "\334\260/\224\356k..."..., 65536) = 65536 <0.018225>
18:41:01.531646 read(9, "\371X\265|\244\317..."..., 65536) = 65536 <0.000056>
18:41:01.531984 read(9, "\357\311\347\1\241..."..., 65536) = 65536 <0.005760>
18:41:01.538151 read(9, "*\263\264\204|\370..."..., 65536) = 65536 <0.000033>
18:41:01.538549 read(9, "\205q\327\304f\370..."..., 65536) = 65536 <0.002033>
18:41:01.540923 read(9, "6\2738>zw\321\353..."..., 65536) = 65536 <0.000032>
```

The **-tt** option prints the relative timestamps on the left, and **-T** prints the syscall times on the right. Each read(2) was for 64 Kbytes, the first taking 18 ms, followed by 56 µs (likely cached), then 5 ms. The reads were to file descriptor 9. To check that this is to a file system (and isn't a socket), either the open(2) syscall will be visible in earlier strace(1) output, or another tool such as lsof(8) can be used. You can also find information on FD 9 in the /proc file system: /proc/845/fd{,info}/9}.

Given the current overheads of strace(1), the measured latency can be skewed by observer effect. See newer tracing tools, including ext4slower(8), which use per-CPU buffered tracing and BPF to greatly reduce overhead, providing more accurate latency measurements.

8.6.8 fatrace

fatrace(1) is a specialized tracer that uses the Linux fanotify API (file access notify). Example output:

```
# fatrace
sar(25294): O /etc/ld.so.cache
sar(25294): RO /lib/x86_64-linux-gnu/libc-2.27.so
sar(25294): C /etc/ld.so.cache
sar(25294): O /usr/lib/locale/locale-archive
sar(25294): O /usr/share/zoneinfo/America/Los_Angeles
```

```
sar(25294): RC /usr/share/zoneinfo/America/Los_Angeles
sar(25294): RO /var/log/sysstat/sa09
sar(25294): R /var/log/sysstat/sa09
[...]
```

Each line shows the process name, PID, type of event, full path, and optional status. The type of event can be opens (O), reads (R), writes (W), and closes (C). fatrace(1) can be used for workload characterization: understanding the files accessed, and looking for unnecessary work that could be eliminated.

However, for a busy file system workload, fatrace(1) can produce tens of thousands of lines of output every second, and can cost significant CPU resources. This may be alleviated somewhat by filtering to one type of event. BPF-based tracing tools, including opensnoop(8) (Section 8.6.10), also greatly reduce overhead.

8.6.9   LatencyTOP

LatencyTOP is a tool for reporting sources of latency, aggregated system-wide and per process. File system latency is reported by LatencyTOP. For example:

```
Cause                                    Maximum      Percentage
Reading from file                     209.6 msec         61.9 %
synchronous write                      82.6 msec         24.0 %
Marking inode dirty                     7.9 msec          2.2 %
Waiting for a process to die            4.6 msec          1.5 %
Waiting for event (select)              3.6 msec         10.1 %
Page fault                              0.2 msec          0.2 %

Process gzip (10969)           Total: 442.4 msec
Reading from file                     209.6 msec         70.2 %
synchronous write                      82.6 msec         27.2 %
Marking inode dirty                     7.9 msec          2.5 %
```

The upper section is the system-wide summary, and the bottom is for a single gzip(1) process, which is compressing a file. Most of the latency for gzip(1) is due to Reading from file at 70.2%, with 27.2% in synchronous write as the new compressed file is written.

LatencyTOP was developed by Intel, but it has not been updated in a while, and its website is no longer online. It also requires kernel options that are not commonly enabled.[7] You may find it easier to measure file system latency using BPF tracing tools instead: see Sections 8.6.13 to 8.6.15.

---

[7] CONFIG_LATENCYTOP and CONFIG_HAVE_LATENCYTOP_SUPPORT

8.6.10 opensnoop

opensnoop(8)[8] is a BCC and bpftrace tool that traces file opens. It is useful for discovering the
location of data files, log files, and configuration files. It can also discover performance problems caused by frequent opens, or help troubleshoot issues caused by missing files. Here is some
example output, with –T to include timestamps:

```
# opensnoop -T
TIME(s)         PID     COMM            FD ERR PATH
0.000000000     26447   sshd             5   0 /var/log/btmp
[...]
1.961686000     25983   mysqld           4   0 /etc/mysql/my.cnf
1.961715000     25983   mysqld           5   0 /etc/mysql/conf.d/
1.961770000     25983   mysqld           5   0 /etc/mysql/conf.d/mysql.cnf
1.961799000     25983   mysqld           5   0 /etc/mysql/conf.d/mysqldump.cnf
1.961818000     25983   mysqld           5   0 /etc/mysql/mysql.conf.d/
1.961843000     25983   mysqld           5   0 /etc/mysql/mysql.conf.d/mysql.cnf
1.961862000     25983   mysqld           5   0 /etc/mysql/mysql.conf.d/mysqld.cnf
[...]
2.438417000     25983   mysqld           4   0 /var/log/mysql/error.log
[...]
2.816953000     25983   mysqld          30   0 ./binlog.000024
2.818827000     25983   mysqld          31   0 ./binlog.index_crash_safe
2.820621000     25983   mysqld           4   0 ./binlog.index
[...]
```

This output includes the startup of a MySQL database, and opensnoop(2) has revealed the configuration files, log file, data files (binary logs), and more.

opensnoop(8) works by only tracing the open(2) variant syscalls: open(2) and openat(2). The
overhead is expected to be negligible as opens are typically infrequent.

Options for the BCC version include:

- **–T**: Include a timestamp column
- **–x**: Only show failed opens
- **–p PID**: Trace this process only
- **–n NAME**: Only show opens when the process name contains NAME

The –x option can be used for troubleshooting: focusing on cases where applications are unable
to open files.

[8] Origin: I created the first opensnoop in 2004, the BCC version on 17-Sep-2015, and the bpftrace version on
8-Sep-2018.

8.6.11   filetop

filetop(8)[9] is a BCC tool that is like top(1) for files, showing the most frequently read or written filenames. Example output:

```
# filetop
Tracing... Output every 1 secs. Hit Ctrl-C to end

19:16:22 loadavg: 0.11 0.04 0.01 3/189 23035

TID     COMM            READS  WRITES R_Kb    W_Kb    T FILE
23033   mysqld          481    0      7681    0       R sb1.ibd
23033   mysqld          3      0      48      0       R mysql.ibd
23032   oltp_read_only. 3      0      20      0       R oltp_common.lua
23031   oltp_read_only. 3      0      20      0       R oltp_common.lua
23032   oltp_read_only. 1      0      19      0       R Index.xml
23032   oltp_read_only. 4      0      16      0       R openssl.cnf
23035   systemd-udevd   4      0      16      0       R sys_vendor
[...]
```

By default, the top twenty files are shown, sorted by the read bytes column. The top line shows mysqld did 481 reads from an sb1.ibd file, totaling 7,681 Kbytes.

This tool is used for workload characterization and general file system observability. Just as you can discover an unexpected CPU-consuming process using top(1), this may help you discover an unexpected I/O-busy file.

filetop by default also only shows regular files. The –a option shows all files, including TCP sockets and device nodes:

```
# filetop -a
[...]
TID     COMM            READS  WRITES R_Kb    W_Kb    T FILE
21701   sshd            1      0      16      0       O ptmx
23033   mysqld          1      0      16      0       R sbtest1.ibd
23335   sshd            1      0      8       0       S TCP
1       systemd         4      0      4       0       R comm
[...]
```

The output now contains file type other (O) and socket (S). In this case, the type other file, ptmx, is a character-special file in /dev.

Options include:

- **–C**: Don't clear the screen: rolling output
- **–a**: Show all file types

---

[9] Origin: I created this for BCC on 6-Feb-2016, inspired by top(1) by William LeFebvre.

- **-r ROWS**: Print this many rows (default 20)

- **-p PID**: Trace this process only

The screen is refreshed every second (like top(1)) unless **-c** is used. I prefer using **-c** so that the output is in the terminal scrollback buffer, in case I need to refer to it later.

8.6.12 cachestat

cachestat(8)[10] is a BCC tool that shows page cache hit and miss statistics. This can be used to check the hit ratio and efficiency of the page cache, and run while investigating system and application tuning for feedback on cache performance. Example output:

```
$ cachestat -T 1
TIME        HITS   MISSES  DIRTIES HITRATIO   BUFFERS_MB  CACHED_MB
21:00:48     586        0     1870 100.00%          208        775
21:00:49     125        0     1775 100.00%          208        776
21:00:50     113        0     1644 100.00%          208        776
21:00:51      23        0     1389 100.00%          208        776
21:00:52     134        0     1906 100.00%          208        777
[...]
```

This output shows a read workload that is entirely cached (HITS with a 100% HITRATIO) and a higher write workload (DIRTIES). Ideally, the hit ratio is close to 100% so that application reads are not blocking on disk I/O.

If you encounter a low hit ratio that may be hurting performance, you may be able to tune the application's memory size to be a little smaller, leaving more room for the page cache. If swap devices are configured, there is also the swappiness tunable to prefer evicting from the page cache versus swapping.

Options include **-T** to print a timestamp.

While this tool provides crucial insight for the page cache hit ratio, it is also an experimental tool that uses kprobes to trace certain kernel functions, so it will need maintenance to work on different kernel versions. Even better, if tracepoints or /proc statistics are added, this tool can be rewritten to use them and become stable. Its best use today may be simply to show that such a tool is possible.

8.6.13 ext4dist (xfs, zfs, btrfs, nfs)

ext4dist(8)[11] is a BCC and bpftrace tool to instrument the ext4 file system and show the distribution of latencies as histograms for common operations: reads, writes, opens, and fsync. There are versions for other file systems: xfsdist(8), zfsdist(8), btrfsdist(8), and nfsdist(8). Example output:

---

[10] Origin: I created this as an experimental Ftrace-tool on 28-Dec-2014. Allan McAleavy ported it to BCC on 6-Nov-2015.

[11] Origin: I created the BCC tool on 12-Feb-2016, and the bpftrace version on 02-Feb-2019 for [Gregg 19]. These are based on an earlier ZFS tool I developed in 2012.

```
# ext4dist 10 1
Tracing ext4 operation latency... Hit Ctrl-C to end.

21:09:46:


operation = read
     usecs               : count    distribution
        0 -> 1           : 783      |**********************                  |
        2 -> 3           : 88       |**                                      |
        4 -> 7           : 449      |*************                           |
        8 -> 15          : 1306     |****************************************|
       16 -> 31          : 48       |*                                       |
       32 -> 63          : 12       |                                        |
       64 -> 127         : 39       |*                                       |
      128 -> 255         : 11       |                                        |
      256 -> 511         : 158      |****                                    |
      512 -> 1023        : 110      |***                                     |
     1024 -> 2047        : 33       |*                                       |


operation = write
     usecs               : count    distribution
        0 -> 1           : 1073     |***************************             |
        2 -> 3           : 324      |********                                |
        4 -> 7           : 1378     |***********************************     |
        8 -> 15          : 1505     |****************************************|
       16 -> 31          : 183      |****                                    |
       32 -> 63          : 37       |                                        |
       64 -> 127         : 11       |                                        |
      128 -> 255         : 9        |                                        |


operation = open
     usecs               : count    distribution
        0 -> 1           : 672      |****************************************|
        2 -> 3           : 10       |                                        |


operation = fsync
     usecs               : count    distribution
      256 -> 511         : 485      |*********                               |
      512 -> 1023        : 308      |******                                  |
     1024 -> 2047        : 1779     |****************************************|
     2048 -> 4095        : 79       |*                                       |
     4096 -> 8191        : 26       |                                        |
     8192 -> 16383       : 4        |                                        |
```

This used an interval of 10 seconds and a count of 1 to show a single 10-second trace. It shows a bi-modal read latency distribution, with one mode between 0 and 15 microseconds, likely memory cache hits, and another between 256 and 2048 microseconds, likely disk reads. Distributions of other operations can be studied as well. The writes are fast, likely due to buffering that is later flushed to disk using the slower fsync operation.

This tool and its companion ext4slower(8) (next section) show latencies that applications can experience. Measuring latency down at the disk level is possible, and is shown in Chapter 9, but the applications may not be blocking on disk I/O directly, making those measurements harder to interpret. Where possible, I use the ext4dist(8)/ext4slower(8) tools first before disk I/O latency tools. See Section 8.3.12 for differences between logical I/O to the file systems, as measured by this tool, and physical I/O to the disks.

Options include:

- **-m**: Print output in milliseconds
- **-p PID**: Trace this process only

The output from this tool can be visualized as a latency heat map. For more information on slow file system I/O, run ext4slower(8) and its variants.

8.6.14 ext4slower (xfs, zfs, btrfs, nfs)

ext4slower(8)[12] traces common ext4 operations and prints per-event details for those that were slower than a given threshold. The operations traced are reads, writes, opens, and fsync. Example output:

```
# ext4slower
Tracing ext4 operations slower than 10 ms
TIME      COMM         PID    T BYTES   OFF_KB   LAT(ms)  FILENAME
21:36:03 mysqld       22935  S 0        0         12.81   sbtest1.ibd
21:36:15 mysqld       22935  S 0        0         12.13   ib_logfile1
21:36:15 mysqld       22935  S 0        0         10.46   binlog.000026
21:36:15 mysqld       22935  S 0        0         13.66   ib_logfile1
21:36:15 mysqld       22935  S 0        0         11.79   ib_logfile1
[...]
```

The columns show the time (TIME), process name (COMM), and pid (PID), type of operation (T: R is reads, W is writes, O is opens, and S is syncs), offset in Kbytes (OFF_KB), latency of the operation in milliseconds (LAT(ms)), and the filename (FILENAME).

The output shows a number of sync operations (S) that exceeded 10 milliseconds, the default threshold for ext4slower(8). The threshold can be provided as an argument; selecting 0 milliseconds shows all operations:

---

[12] Origin: I developed this on 11-Feb-2016, based on an earlier ZFS tool I had developed in 2011.

```
# ext4slower 0
Tracing ext4 operations
21:36:50 mysqld          22935  W 917504  2048          0.42 ibdata1
21:36:50 mysqld          22935  W 1024    14165         0.00 ib_logfile1
21:36:50 mysqld          22935  W 512     14166         0.00 ib_logfile1
21:36:50 mysqld          22935  S 0       0             3.21 ib_logfile1
21:36:50 mysqld          22935  W 1746    21714         0.02 binlog.000026
21:36:50 mysqld          22935  S 0       0             5.56 ibdata1
21:36:50 mysqld          22935  W 16384   4640          0.01 undo_001
21:36:50 mysqld          22935  W 16384   11504         0.01 sbtest1.ibd
21:36:50 mysqld          22935  W 16384   13248         0.01 sbtest1.ibd
21:36:50 mysqld          22935  W 16384   11808         0.01 sbtest1.ibd
21:36:50 mysqld          22935  W 16384   1328          0.01 undo_001
21:36:50 mysqld          22935  W 16384   6768          0.01 undo_002
[...]
```

A pattern can be seen in the output: mysqld performs writes to files followed by a later sync operation.

Tracing all operations can produce a large amount of output with associated overheads. I only do this for short durations (e.g., ten seconds) to understand patterns of file system operations that are not visible in other summaries (ext4dist(8)).

Options include –p PID to trace a single process only, and –j to produce parsable (CSV) output.

8.6.15   bpftrace

bpftrace is a BPF-based tracer that provides a high-level programming language, allowing the creation of powerful one-liners and short scripts. It is well suited for custom file system analysis based on clues from other tools.

bpftrace is explained in Chapter 15, BPF. This section shows some examples for file system analysis: one-liners, syscall tracing, VFS tracing, and file system internals.

One-Liners

The following one-liners are useful and demonstrate different bpftrace capabilities.

Trace files opened via openat(2) with process name:

```
bpftrace -e 't:syscalls:sys_enter_openat { printf("%s %s\n", comm,
    str(args->filename)); }'
```

Count read syscalls by syscall type:

```
bpftrace -e 'tracepoint:syscalls:sys_enter_*read* { @[probe] = count(); }'
```

Count write syscalls by syscall type:

```
bpftrace -e 'tracepoint:syscalls:sys_enter_*write* { @[probe] = count(); }'
```

Show the distribution of read() syscall request sizes:

```
bpftrace -e 'tracepoint:syscalls:sys_enter_read { @ = hist(args->count); }'
```

Show the distribution of read() syscall read bytes (and errors):

```
bpftrace -e 'tracepoint:syscalls:sys_exit_read { @ = hist(args->ret); }'
```

Count read() syscall errors by error code:

```
bpftrace -e 't:syscalls:sys_exit_read /args->ret < 0/ { @[- args->ret] = count(); }'
```

Count VFS calls:

```
bpftrace -e 'kprobe:vfs_* { @[probe] = count(); }'
```

Count VFS calls for PID 181:

```
bpftrace -e 'kprobe:vfs_* /pid == 181/ { @[probe] = count(); }'
```

Count ext4 tracepoints:

```
bpftrace -e 'tracepoint:ext4:* { @[probe] = count(); }'
```

Count xfs tracepoints:

```
bpftrace -e 'tracepoint:xfs:* { @[probe] = count(); }'
```

Count ext4 file reads by process name and user-level stack:

```
bpftrace -e 'kprobe:ext4_file_read_iter { @[ustack, comm] = count(); }'
```

Trace ZFS spa_sync() times:

```
bpftrace -e 'kprobe:spa_sync { time("%H:%M:%S ZFS spa_sync()\n"); }'
```

Count dcache references by process name and PID:

```
bpftrace -e 'kprobe:lookup_fast { @[comm, pid] = count(); }'
```

Syscall Tracing

Syscalls are a great target for tracing and are the instrumentation source for many tracing tools. However, some syscalls lack file system context, making them confusing to use. I'll provide an example of things working (openat(2) tracing) and not working (read(2) tracing), with suggested remedies.

openat(2)

Tracing the open(2) family of syscalls shows files that are opened. Nowadays the openat(2) variant is more commonly used. Tracing it:

```
# bpftrace -e 't:syscalls:sys_enter_openat { printf("%s %s\n", comm,
    str(args->filename)); }'
Attaching 1 probe...
sa1 /etc/sysstat/sysstat
sadc /etc/ld.so.cache
sadc /lib/x86_64-linux-gnu/libsensors.so.5
sadc /lib/x86_64-linux-gnu/libc.so.6
sadc /lib/x86_64-linux-gnu/libm.so.6
sadc /sys/class/i2c-adapter
sadc /sys/bus/i2c/devices
sadc /sys/class/hwmon
sadc /etc/sensors3.conf
[...]
```

This output caught the execution of sar(1) for archiving statistics, and the files it was opening. bpftrace used the filename argument from the tracepoint; all arguments can be listed using -lv:

```
# bpftrace -lv t:syscalls:sys_enter_openat
tracepoint:syscalls:sys_enter_openat
    int __syscall_nr;
    int dfd;
    const char * filename;
    int flags;
    umode_t mode;
```

The arguments are the syscall number, file descriptor, filename, open flags, and open mode: enough information for use by one-liners and tools, such as opensnoop(8).

read(2)

read(2) should be a useful tracing target for understanding file system read latency. However, consider the tracepoint arguments (see if you can spot the problem):

```
# bpftrace -lv t:syscalls:sys_enter_read
tracepoint:syscalls:sys_enter_read
    int __syscall_nr;
    unsigned int fd;
    char * buf;
    size_t count;
```

read(2) can be called for file systems, sockets, /proc, and other targets, and the arguments do not differentiate between them. To show how confusing this is, the following counts read(2) syscalls by process name:

```
# bpftrace -e 't:syscalls:sys_enter_read { @[comm] = count(); }'
Attaching 1 probe...
^C

@[systemd-journal]: 13
@[sshd]: 141
@[java]: 3472
```

While tracing, Java performed 3,472 read(2) syscalls, but are they from a file system, a socket, or something else? (The sshd reads are probably socket I/O.)

What read(2) does provide is the file descriptor (FD) as an integer, but it is just a number and does not show the FD type (and bpftrace is running in a restricted kernel mode: it can't look up FD information in /proc). There are at least four solutions to this:

- Print the PID and FD from bpftrace, and later look up the FDs using lsof(8) or /proc to see what they are.
- An upcoming BPF helper, get_fd_path(), can return the pathname for an FD. This will help differentiate file system reads (that have a pathname) from other types.
- Trace from VFS instead, where more data structures are available.
- Trace file system functions directly, which exclude other I/O types. This approach is used by ext4dist(8) and ext4slower(8).

The following section on VFS Latency Tracing shows the VFS-based solution.

VFS Tracing

As the virtual file system (VFS) abstracts all file systems (and other devices), tracing its calls provides a single point from which to observe all file systems.

VFS Counts

Counting VFS calls provides a high-level overview of the operation types in use. The following counts kernel functions beginning with "vfs_" using kprobes:

```
# bpftrace -e 'kprobe:vfs_* { @[func] = count(); }'
Attaching 65 probes...
^C
[...]
@[vfs_statfs]: 36
@[vfs_readlink]: 164
```

```
@[vfs_write]: 364
@[vfs_lock_file]: 516
@[vfs_iter_read]: 2551
@[vfs_statx]: 3141
@[vfs_statx_fd]: 4214
@[vfs_open]: 5271
@[vfs_read]: 5602
@[vfs_getattr_nosec]: 7794
@[vfs_getattr]: 7795
```

This shows the different operation types occurring system-wide. While tracing, there were 7,795 vfs_read()s.

VFS Latency

As with syscalls, VFS reads can be for file systems, sockets, and other targets. The following bpftrace program fetches the type from a kernel structure (inode superblock name), providing a breakdown of vfs_read() latency in microseconds by type:

```
# vfsreadlat.bt
Tracing vfs_read() by type... Hit Ctrl-C to end.
^C
[...]
@us[sockfs]:
[0]                  141 |@@@@@@@@@@@@@@@@@@@@@@@@@@@@@@@@@@@@@@@@@@@@@@@@@@@@|
[1]                   91 |@@@@@@@@@@@@@@@@@@@@@@@@@@@@@@@@@@@               |
[2, 4)                57 |@@@@@@@@@@@@@@@@@@@@@                            |
[4, 8)                53 |@@@@@@@@@@@@@@@@@@@                              |
[8, 16)               86 |@@@@@@@@@@@@@@@@@@@@@@@@@@@@@@@@@                 |
[16, 32)               2 |                                                |
[...]

@us[proc]:
[0]                  242 |@@@@@@@@@@@@@@@@@@@@@@@@@@@@@@@@@@@@@@@@@@@@@@@@@@@@|
[1]                   41 |@@@@@@@@                                         |
[2, 4)                40 |@@@@@@@@                                         |
[4, 8)                61 |@@@@@@@@@@@@                                     |
[8, 16)               44 |@@@@@@@@@                                        |
[16, 32)              40 |@@@@@@@@                                         |
[32, 64)               6 |@                                                |
[64, 128)              3 |                                                 |
```

```
@us[ext4]:
[0]                653 |@@@@@@@@@@@@@@@@@@@@@@@@@@@@@@@@@@@@@@@@@@@@@     |
[1]                447 |@@@@@@@@@@@@@@@@@@@@@@@@@@@@@@@@@               |
[2, 4)              70 |@@@@                                          |
[4, 8)             774 |@@@@@@@@@@@@@@@@@@@@@@@@@@@@@@@@@@@@@@@@@@@@@@@@@@@|
[8, 16)            417 |@@@@@@@@@@@@@@@@@@@@@@@@@@@@                   |
[16, 32)            25 |@                                             |
[32, 64)             7 |                                              |
[64, 128)          170 |@@@@@@@@@@                                    |
[128, 256)          55 |@@@                                           |
[256, 512)          59 |@@@                                           |
[512, 1K)          118 |@@@@@@@                                       |
[1K, 2K)             3 |@@                                            |
```

The output (truncated) also included latency histograms for: sysfs, devpts, pipefs, devtmpfs, tmpfs, and anon_inodefs.

The source code is:

```
#!/usr/local/bin/bpftrace
#include <linux/fs.h>

BEGIN
{
        printf("Tracing vfs_read() by type... Hit Ctrl-C to end.\n");
}

kprobe:vfs_read
{
        @file[tid] = ((struct file *)arg0)->f_inode->i_sb->s_type->name;
        @ts[tid] = nsecs;
}

kretprobe:vfs_read
/@ts[tid]/
{
        @us[str(@file[tid])] = hist((nsecs - @ts[tid]) / 1000);
        delete(@file[tid]); delete(@ts[tid]);
}

END
```

```
{
        clear(@file); clear(@ts);
}
```

You can extend this tool to include other operations, such as vfs_readv(), vfs_write(), vfs_writev(), etc. To understand this code, begin with Section 15.2.4, Programming, which explains the basics of timing vfs_read().

Note that this latency may or may not directly affect application performance, as mentioned in Section 8.3.1, File System Latency. It depends on whether the latency is encountered during an application request, or if it occurs during an asynchronous background task. To answer this, you can include the user stack trace (ustack) as an additional histogram key, which may reveal whether or not the vfs_read() call took place during an application request.

File System Internals

If needed, you can develop custom tools that show the behavior of file system internals. Start by trying the tracepoints, if available. Listing them for ext4:

```
# bpftrace -l 'tracepoint:ext4:*'
tracepoint:ext4:ext4_other_inode_update_time
tracepoint:ext4:ext4_free_inode
tracepoint:ext4:ext4_request_inode
tracepoint:ext4:ext4_allocate_inode
tracepoint:ext4:ext4_evict_inode
tracepoint:ext4:ext4_drop_inode
[...]
```

Each of these has arguments that can be listed using –lv. If the tracepoints are insufficient (or not available for your file system type), consider using dynamic instrumentation with kprobes. Listing kprobe targets for ext4:

```
# bpftrace -lv 'kprobe:ext4_*'
kprobe:ext4_has_free_clusters
kprobe:ext4_validate_block_bitmap
kprobe:ext4_get_group_number
kprobe:ext4_get_group_no_and_offset
kprobe:ext4_get_group_desc
kprobe:ext4_wait_block_bitmap
[...]
```

In this kernel version (5.3) there are 105 ext4 tracepoints and 538 possible ext4 kprobes.

8.6.17   Other Tools

File system observability tools included in other chapters of this book, and in *BPF Performance Tools* [Gregg 19], are listed in Table 8.7.

Table 8.7   **Other file system observability tools**

Section	Tool	Description
5.5.6	syscount	Counts syscalls including file system-related
[Gregg 19]	statsnoop	Trace calls to stat(2) varieties
[Gregg 19]	syncsnoop	Trace sync(2) and variety calls with timestamps
[Gregg 19]	mmapfiles	Count mmap(2) files
[Gregg 19]	scread	Count read(2) files
[Gregg 19]	fmapfault	Count file map faults
[Gregg 19]	filelife	Trace short-lived files with their lifespan in seconds
[Gregg 19]	vfsstat	Common VFS operation statistics
[Gregg 19]	vfscount	Count all VFS operations
[Gregg 19]	vfssize	Show VFS read/write sizes
[Gregg 19]	fsrwstat	Show VFS reads/writes by file system type
[Gregg 19]	fileslower	Show slow file reads/writes
[Gregg 19]	filetype	Show VFS reads/writes by file type and process
[Gregg 19]	ioprofile	Count stacks on I/O to show code paths
[Gregg 19]	writesync	Show regular file writes by sync flag
[Gregg 19]	writeback	Show write-back events and latencies
[Gregg 19]	dcstat	Directory cache hit statistics
[Gregg 19]	dcsnoop	Trace directory cache lookups
[Gregg 19]	mountsnoop	Trace mount and umounts system-wide
[Gregg 19]	icstat	Inode cache hit statistics
[Gregg 19]	bufgrow	Buffer cache growth by process and bytes
[Gregg 19]	readahead	Show read ahead hits and efficiency

Other Linux file system–related tools include:

- **df(1)**: report file system usage and capacity statistics
- **inotify**: a Linux framework for monitoring file system events

Some file system types have their own specific performance tools, in addition to those provided by the operating system, for example, ZFS.

ZFS

ZFS comes with zpool(1M), which has an iostat suboption for observing ZFS pool statistics. It reports pool operation rates (reads and writes) and throughput.

A popular add-on has been the arcstat.pl tool, which reports ARC and L2ARC size and hit and miss rates. For example:

```
$ arcstat 1
    time   read  miss  miss%  dmis  dm%  pmis  pm%  mmis  mm%  arcsz    c
04:45:47       0     0      0     0    0     0    0     0    0    14G  14G
04:45:49     15K    10      0    10    0     0    0     1    0    14G  14G
04:45:50     23K    81      0    81    0     0    0     1    0    14G  14G
04:45:51     65K    25      0    25    0     0    0     4    0    14G  14G
[...]
```

The statistics are per interval and are:

- **read**, **miss**: Total ARC accesses, misses
- **miss%**, **dm%**, **pm%**, **mm%**: ARC miss percent total, demand, prefetch, metadata
- **dmis**, **pmis**, **mmis**: Misses for demand, prefetch, metadata
- **arcsz**, **c**: ARC size, ARC target size

arcstat.pl is a Perl program that reads statistics from kstat.

8.6.18   Visualizations

The load applied to file systems can be plotted over time as a line graph, to help identify time-based usage patterns. It can be useful to plot separate graphs for reads, writes, and other file system operations.

The distribution of file system latency is expected to be bimodal: one mode at low latency for file system cache hits, and another at high latency for cache misses (storage device I/O). For this reason, representing the distribution as a single value—such as a mean, mode, or median—is misleading.

One way to solve this problem is to use a visualization that shows the full distribution, such as a heat map. Heat maps were introduced in Chapter 2, Methodologies, Section 2.10.3, Heat Maps. An example file system latency heat map is shown in Figure 8.13: it shows the passage of time on the x-axis and I/O latency on the y-axis [Gregg 09a].

This heat map shows the difference enabling an L2ARC device makes to NFSv3 latency. An L2ARC device is a secondary ZFS cache, after main memory, and typically uses flash memory (it was mentioned in Section 8.3.2, Caching). The system in Figure 8.13 had 128 Gbytes of main memory (DRAM) and 600 Gbytes of L2ARC (read-optimized SSDs). The left half of the heat map shows no L2ARC device (the L2ARC was disabled), and the right half shows the latency with an L2ARC device.

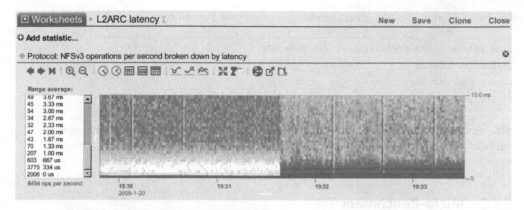

Figure 8.13   File system latency heat map

For the left half, file system latency is either low or high, separated by a gap. The low latencies are the blue line at the bottom, around 0 milliseconds, which is likely main memory cache hits. The high latencies begin at around 3 milliseconds and extended to the top, appearing as a "cloud," which is likely rotational disk latency. This bi-modal latency distribution is typical for file system latency when backed by rotational disks.

For the right half, the L2ARC was enabled and latency is now often lower than 3 milliseconds, and there are fewer higher disk latencies. You can see how the L2ARC's latency filled in range where there was a gap on the left of the heat map, reducing file system latency overall.

8.7   Experimentation

This section describes tools for actively testing file system performance. See Section 8.5.8, Micro-Benchmarking, for a suggested strategy to follow.

When using these tools, it is a good idea to leave iostat(1) continually running to confirm that the workload reaches the disks as expected, which may mean not at all. For example, when testing a working set size that should easily fit in the file system cache, the expectation with a read workload is 100% cache hits, so iostat(1) should *not* show substantial disk I/O. iostat(1) is covered in Chapter 9, Disks.

8.7.1   Ad Hoc

The dd(1) command (device-to-device copy) can be used to perform ad hoc tests of sequential file system performance. The following commands write, and then read a 1 Gbyte file named file1 with a 1 Mbyte I/O size:

```
write: dd if=/dev/zero of=file1 bs=1024k count=1k
read: dd if=file1 of=/dev/null bs=1024k
```

The Linux version of dd(1) prints statistics on completion. For example:

```
$ dd if=/dev/zero of=file1 bs=1024k count=1k
1024+0 records in
1024+0 records out
1073741824 bytes (1.1 GB, 1.0 GiB) copied, 0.76729 s, 1.4 GB/s
```

 This shows a file system write throughput of 1.4 Gbytes/s (write-back caching is in use, so this only dirtied memory and will be flushed later to disk, depending on the vm.dirty_* tunable settings: see Chapter 7, Memory, Section 7.6.1, Tunable Parameters).

8.7.2   Micro-Benchmark Tools

There are many file system benchmark tools available, including Bonnie, Bonnie++, iozone, tiobench, SysBench, fio, and FileBench. A few are discussed here, in order of increasing complexity. Also see Chapter 12, Benchmarking. My personal recommendation is to use fio.

Bonnie, Bonnie++

The Bonnie tool is a simple C program to test several workloads on a single file, from a single thread. It was originally written by Tim Bray in 1989 [Bray 90]. Usage is straightforward, not requiring arguments (defaults will be used):

```
$ ./Bonnie
File './Bonnie.9598', size: 104857600
[...]
              -------Sequential Output-------- ---Sequential Input-- --Random--
              -Per Char- --Block--- -Rewrite-- -Per Char- --Block--- --Seeks---
Machine    MB K/sec %CPU K/sec %CPU K/sec %CPU K/sec %CPU K/sec %CPU  /sec %CPU
           100 123396 100.0 1258402 100.0 996583 100.0 126781 100.0 2187052 100.0
164190.1 299.0
```

The output includes the CPU time during each test, which at 100% is an indicator that Bonnie never blocked on disk I/O, instead always hitting from cache and staying on-CPU. The reason is that the target file size is 100 Mbytes, which is entirely cached on this system. You can change the file size using -s size.

There is a 64-bit version called Bonnie-64, which allows larger files to be tested. There is also a rewrite in C++ called Bonnie++ by Russell Coker [Coker 01].

Unfortunately, file system benchmark tools like Bonnie can be misleading, unless you clearly understand what is being tested. The first result, a putc(3) test, can vary based on the system library implementation, which then becomes the target of the test rather than the file system. See the example in Chapter 12, Benchmarking, Section 12.3.2, Active Benchmarking.

fio

The Flexible IO Tester (fio) by Jens Axboe is a customizable file system benchmark tool with many advanced features [Axboe 20]. Two that have led me to use it instead of other benchmark tools are:

- **Non-uniform random distributions**, which can more accurately simulate a real-world access pattern (e.g., -random_distribution=pareto:0.9)

- **Reporting of latency percentiles**, including 99.00, 99.50, 99.90, 99.95, 99.99

Here is an example output, showing a random read workload with an 8 Kbyte I/O size, a 5 Gbyte working set size, and a non-uniform access pattern (pareto:0.9):

```
# fio --runtime=60 --time_based --clocksource=clock_gettime --name=randread --
numjobs=1 --rw=randread --random_distribution=pareto:0.9 --bs=8k --size=5g --
filename=fio.tmp
randread: (g=0): rw=randread, bs=8K-8K/8K-8K/8K-8K, ioengine=sync, iodepth=1
fio-2.0.13-97-gdd8d
Starting 1 process
Jobs: 1 (f=1): [r] [100.0% done] [3208K/0K/0K /s] [401 /0 /0  iops] [eta 00m:00s]
randread: (groupid=0, jobs=1): err= 0: pid=2864: Tue Feb  5 00:13:17 2013
  read : io=247408KB, bw=4122.2KB/s, iops=515 , runt= 60007msec
    clat (usec): min=3 , max=67928 , avg=1933.15, stdev=4383.30
     lat (usec): min=4 , max=67929 , avg=1934.40, stdev=4383.31
    clat percentiles (usec):
     |  1.00th=[    5],  5.00th=[    5], 10.00th=[    5], 20.00th=[    6],
     | 30.00th=[    6], 40.00th=[    6], 50.00th=[    7], 60.00th=[  620],
     | 70.00th=[  692], 80.00th=[ 1688], 90.00th=[ 7648], 95.00th=[10304],
     | 99.00th=[19584], 99.50th=[24960], 99.90th=[39680], 99.95th=[51456],
     | 99.99th=[63744]
    bw (KB/s)  : min= 1663, max=71232, per=99.87%, avg=4116.58, stdev=6504.45
    lat (usec) : 4=0.01%, 10=55.62%, 20=1.27%, 50=0.28%, 100=0.13%
    lat (usec) : 500=0.01%, 750=15.21%, 1000=4.15%
    lat (msec) : 2=3.72%, 4=2.57%, 10=11.50%, 20=4.57%, 50=0.92%
    lat (msec) : 100=0.05%
  cpu          : usr=0.18%, sys=1.39%, ctx=13260, majf=0, minf=42
  IO depths    : 1=100.0%, 2=0.0%, 4=0.0%, 8=0.0%, 16=0.0%, 32=0.0%, >=64=0.0%
     submit    : 0=0.0%, 4=100.0%, 8=0.0%, 16=0.0%, 32=0.0%, 64=0.0%, >=64=0.0%
     complete  : 0=0.0%, 4=100.0%, 8=0.0%, 16=0.0%, 32=0.0%, 64=0.0%, >=64=0.0%
     issued    : total=r=30926/w=0/d=0, short=r=0/w=0/d=0
```

The latency percentiles (clat) show very low latencies up to the 50th percentile, which I would assume, based on the latency (5 to 7 microseconds), to be cache hits. The remaining percentiles show the effect of cache misses, including the tail of the queue; in this case, the 99.99th percentile is showing a 63 ms latency.

While these percentiles lack information to really understand what is probably a multimode distribution, they do focus on the most interesting part: the tail of the slower mode (disk I/O).

For a similar but simpler tool, you can try SysBench (an example of using SysBench for CPU analysis in Chapter 6, Section 6.8.2, SysBench). On the other hand, if you want even more control, try FileBench.

FileBench

FileBench is a programmable file system benchmark tool, where application workloads can be simulated by describing them in its Workload Model Language. This allows threads with different behaviors to be simulated, and for synchronous thread behavior to be specified. It ships with a variety of these configurations, called *personalities*, including one to simulate the Oracle database I/O model. Unfortunately, FileBench is not an easy tool to learn and use, and may be of interest only to those working on file systems full-time.

8.7.3   Cache Flushing

Linux provides a way to flush (drop entries from) file system caches, which may be useful for benchmarking performance from a consistent and "cold" cache state, as you would have after system boot. This mechanism is described very simply in the kernel source documentation (Documentation/sysctl/vm.txt) as:

```
To free pagecache:
        echo 1 > /proc/sys/vm/drop_caches
To free reclaimable slab objects (includes dentries and inodes):
        echo 2 > /proc/sys/vm/drop_caches
To free slab objects and pagecache:
        echo 3 > /proc/sys/vm/drop_caches
```

It can be especially useful to free everything (3) before other benchmark runs, so that the system begins in a consistent state (a cold cache), helping to provide consistent benchmark results.

8.8   Tuning

Many tuning approaches have already been covered in Section 8.5, Methodology, including cache tuning and workload characterization. The latter can lead to the highest tuning wins by identifying and eliminating unnecessary work. This section includes specific tuning parameters (tunables).

The specifics of tuning—the options available and what to set them to—depend on the operating system version, the file system type, and the intended workload. The following sections provide examples of what may be available and why they may need to be tuned. I cover application calls and two example file system types: ext4 and ZFS. For tuning of the page cache, see Chapter 7, Memory.

8.8.1 Application Calls

Section 8.3.7, Synchronous Writes, mentioned how performance of synchronous write workloads can be improved by using fsync(2) to flush a logical group of writes, instead of individually when using the O_DSYNC/O_RSYNC open(2) flags.

Other calls that can improve performance include posix_fadvise() and madvise(2), which provide hints for cache eligibility.

posix_fadvise()

This library call (a wrapper to the fadvise64(2) syscall) operates on a region of a file and has the function prototype:

```
int posix_fadvise(int fd, off_t offset, off_t len, int advice);
```

The advice may be as shown in Table 8.8.

Table 8.8 **Linux posix_fadvise() advice flags**

Advice	Description
POSIX_FADV_SEQUENTIAL	The specified data range will be accessed sequentially.
POSIX_FADV_RANDOM	The specified data range will be accessed randomly.
POSIX_FADV_NOREUSE	The data will not be reused.
POSIX_FADV_WILLNEED	The data will be used again in the near future.
POSIX_FADV_DONTNEED	The data will not be used again in the near future.

The kernel can use this information to improve performance, helping it decide when best to prefetch data, and when best to cache data. This can improve the cache hit ratio for higher-priority data, as advised by the application. See the man page on your system for the full list of advice arguments.

madvise()

This system call operates on a memory mapping and has the synopsis:

```
int madvise(void *addr, size_t length, int advice);
```

The advice may be as shown in Table 8.9.

Table 8.9 **Linux madvise(2) advice flags**

Advice	Description
MADV_RANDOM	Offsets will be accessed in random order.
MADV_SEQUENTIAL	Offsets will be accessed in sequential order.
MADV_WILLNEED	Data will be needed again (please cache).
MADV_DONTNEED	Data will not be needed again (no need to cache).

As with posix_fadvise(), the kernel can use this information to improve performance, including making better caching decisions.

8.8.2   ext4

On Linux, the ext2, ext3, and ext4 file systems can be tuned in one of four ways:

- mount options
- the tune2fs(8) command
- /sys/fs/ext4 property files
- the e2fsck(8) command

mount and tune2fs

The mount options can be set at mount time, either manually with the mount(8) command, or at boot time in /boot/grub/menu.lst and /etc/fstab. The options available are in the man pages for mount(8). Some example options:

```
# man mount
[...]
FILESYSTEM-INDEPENDENT MOUNT OPTIONS
[...]
       atime  Do not use the noatime feature, so the inode access time is con-
              trolled  by  kernel  defaults.  See also the descriptions of the
              relatime and strictatime mount options.

       noatime
              Do not update inode access times on this  filesystem  (e.g.  for
              faster access on the news spool to speed up news servers).  This
[...]
       relatime
              Update  inode  access  times  relative to modify or change time.
              Access time is only updated if the previous access time was ear-
              lier  than  the  current  modify  or  change  time.  (Similar to
              noatime, but it doesn't break mutt or  other  applications  that
              need  to know if a file has been read since the last time it was
              modified.)
```

> Since Linux 2.6.30, the kernel defaults to the behavior provided
> by this option (unless noatime was specified), and the
> strictatime option is required to obtain traditional semantics.
> In addition, since Linux 2.6.30, the file's last access time is
> always updated if it is more than 1 day old.

[...]

The noatime option has historically been used to improve performance by avoiding access timestamp updates and their associated disk I/O. As described in this output, relatime is now the default, which also reduces these updates.

The mount(8) man page covers both generic mount options and file system–specific mount options; however, in the case of ext4 the file system–specific mount options have their own man page, ext4(5):

---

man ext4
[...]
Mount options for ext4
[...]

    The options journal_dev, journal_path, norecovery, noload, data, com-
    mit, orlov, oldalloc, [no]user_xattr, [no]acl, bsddf, minixdf, debug,
    errors, data_err, grpid, bsdgroups, nogrpid, sysvgroups, resgid, re-
    suid, sb, quota, noquota, nouid32, grpquota, usrquota, usrjquota, gr-
    pjquota, and jqfmt are backwardly compatible with ext3 or ext2.

    journal_checksum | nojournal_checksum
        The journal_checksum option enables checksumming of the journal
        transactions. This will allow the recovery code in e2fsck and

[...]

The current mount settings can be seen using tune2fs -1 *device* and mount (no options). tune2fs(8) can set or clear various mount options, as described by its own man page.

A commonly used mount option to improve performance is noatime: it avoids file access timestamp updates, which—if not needed for the file system users—will reduce back-end I/O.

/sys/fs Property Files

Some additional tunables can be set live via the /sys file system. For ext4:

```
# cd /sys/fs/ext4/nvme0n1p1
# ls
delayed_allocation_blocks  last_error_time         msg_ratelimit_burst
err_ratelimit_burst        lifetime_write_kbytes   msg_ratelimit_interval_ms
err_ratelimit_interval_ms  max_writeback_mb_bump   reserved_clusters
errors_count               mb_group_prealloc       session_write_kbytes
```

```
extent_max_zeroout_kb        mb_max_to_scan           trigger_fs_error
first_error_time             mb_min_to_scan           warning_ratelimit_burst
inode_goal                   mb_order2_req            warning_ratelimit_interval_ms
inode_readahead_blks         mb_stats
journal_task                 mb_stream_req
# cat inode_readahead_blks
32
```

This output shows that ext4 will read ahead at most 32 inode table blocks. Not all of these files are tunables: some are for information only. They are documented in the Linux source under Documentation/admin-guide/ext4.rst [Linux 20h], which also documents the mount options.

e2fsck

Lastly, the e2fsck(8) command can be used to reindex directories in an ext4 file system, which may help improve performance. For example:

```
e2fsck -D -f /dev/hdX
```

The other options for e2fsck(8) are related to checking and repairing a file system.

8.8.3 ZFS

ZFS supports a large number of tunable parameters (called *properties*) per file system, with a smaller number that can be set system-wide. These can be listed using the zfs(1) command. For example:

```
# zfs get all zones/var
NAME        PROPERTY        VALUE           SOURCE
[...]
zones/var   recordsize      128K            default
zones/var   mountpoint      legacy          local
zones/var   sharenfs        off             default
zones/var   checksum        on              default
zones/var   compression     off             inherited from zones
zones/var   atime           off             inherited from zones
[...]
```

The (truncated) output includes columns for the property name, current value, and source. The source shows how it was set: whether it was inherited from a higher-level ZFS dataset, the default, or set locally for that file system.

The parameters can also be set using the zfs(1M) command and are described in its man page. Key parameters related to performance are listed in Table 8.10.

Table 8.10   **Key ZFS dataset tunable parameters**

Parameter	Options	Description
recordsize	512 to 128 K	Suggested block size for files
compression	on | off | lzjb | gzip | gzip-[1–9] | zle | lz4	Lightweight algorithms (e.g., lzjb) can improve performance in some situations, by relieving back-end I/O congestion
atime	on | off	Access timestamp updates (causes some writes after reads)
primarycache	all | none | metadata	ARC policy; cache pollution due to low-priority file systems (e.g., archives) can be reduced by using "none" or "metadata" (only)
secondarycache	all | none | metadata	L2ARC policy
logbias	latency | throughput	Advice for synchronous writes: "latency" uses log devices, whereas "throughput" uses pool devices
sync	standard | always | disabled	Synchronous write behavior

The most important parameter to tune is usually record size, to match the application I/O. It usually defaults to 128 Kbytes, which can be inefficient for small, random I/O. Note that this does not apply to files that are smaller than the record size, which are saved using a dynamic record size equal to their file length. Disabling atime can also improve performance if those timestamps are not needed.

ZFS also provides system-wide tunables, including for tuning the transaction group (TXG) sync time (zfs_txg_synctime_ms, zfs_txg_timeout), and a threshold for metaslabs to switch to space-instead of time-optimizing allocation (metaslab_df_free_pct). Tuning TXGs to be smaller can improve performance by reducing contention and queueing with other I/O.

As with other kernel tunables, check their documentation for the full list, descriptions, and warnings.

8.9   Exercises

1. Answer the following questions about file system terminology:

   - What is the difference between logical I/O and physical I/O?

   - What is the difference between random and sequential I/O?

   - What is direct I/O?

   - What is non-blocking I/O?

   - What is the working set size?

2. Answer the following conceptual questions:

- What is the role of VFS?

- Describe file system latency, specifically where it can be measured from.

- What is the purpose of prefetch (read-ahead)?

- What is the purpose of direct I/O?

3. Answer the following deeper questions:

- Describe the advantages of using fsync(2) over O_SYNC.

- Describe the pros and cons of mmap(2) over read(2)/write(2).

- Describe reasons why logical I/O becomes *inflated* by the time it becomes physical I/O.

- Describe reasons why logical I/O becomes *deflated* by the time it becomes physical I/O.

- Explain how file system copy-on-write can improve performance.

4. Develop the following procedures for your operating system:

- A file system cache tuning checklist. This should list the file system caches that exist, how to check their current size and usage, and hit rate.

- A workload characterization checklist for file system operations. Include how to fetch each detail, and try to use existing OS observability tools first.

5. Perform these tasks:

- Choose an application, and measure file system operations and latency. Include:

   □ the full distribution of file system operation latency, not just the average.

   □ the portion of each second that each application thread spends in file system operations.

- Using a micro-benchmark tool, determine the size of the file system cache experimentally. Explain your choices when using the tool. Also show the performance degradation (using any metric) when the working set no longer caches.

6. (optional, advanced) Develop an observability tool that provides metrics for synchronous versus asynchronous file system writes. This should include their rate and latency and be able to identify the process ID that issued them, making it suitable for workload characterization.

7. (optional, advanced) Develop a tool to provide statistics for indirect and inflated file system I/O: additional bytes and I/O not issued directly by applications. The tool should break down this additional I/O into different types to explain their reason.

8.10 References

[**Ritchie 74**] Ritchie, D. M., and Thompson, K., "The UNIX Time-Sharing System," *Communications of the ACM* 17, no. 7, pp. 365–75, July 1974

[**Lions 77**] Lions, J., *A Commentary on the Sixth Edition UNIX Operating System*, University of New South Wales, 1977.

[McKusick 84] McKusick, M. K., Joy, W. N., Leffler, S. J., and Fabry, R. S., "A Fast File System for UNIX." *ACM Transactions on Computer Systems (TOCS)* 2, no. 3, August 1984.

[Bach 86] Bach, M. J., *The Design of the UNIX Operating System*, Prentice Hall, 1986.

[Bray 90] Bray, T., "Bonnie," http://www.textuality.com/bonnie, 1990.

[Sweeney 96] Sweeney, A., "Scalability in the XFS File System," *USENIX Annual Technical Conference*, https://www.cs.princeton.edu/courses/archive/fall09/cos518/papers/xfs.pdf, 1996.

[Vahalia 96] Vahalia, U., *UNIX Internals: The New Frontiers*, Prentice Hall, 1996.

[Coker 01] Coker, R., "bonnie++," https://www.coker.com.au/bonnie++, 2001.

[XFS 06] "XFS User Guide," https://xfs.org/docs/xfsdocs-xml-dev/XFS_User_Guide/tmp/en-US/html/index.html, 2006.

[Gregg 09a] Gregg, B., "L2ARC Screenshots," http://www.brendangregg.com/blog/2009-01-30/l2arc-screenshots.html, 2009.

[Corbet 10] Corbet, J., "Dcache scalability and RCU-walk," *LWN.net*, http://lwn.net/Articles/419811, 2010.

[Doeppner 10] Doeppner, T., *Operating Systems in Depth: Design and Programming*, Wiley, 2010.

[XFS 10] "Runtime Stats," https://xfs.org/index.php/Runtime_Stats, 2010.

[Oracle 12] "ZFS Storage Pool Maintenance and Monitoring Practices," *Oracle Solaris Administration: ZFS File Systems*, https://docs.oracle.com/cd/E36784_01/html/E36835/storage-9.html, 2012.

[Ahrens 19] Ahrens, M., "State of OpenZFS," *OpenZFS Developer Summit 2019*, https://drive.google.com/file/d/197jS8_MWtfdW2LyvIFnH58uUasHuNszz/view, 2019.

[Axboe 19] Axboe, J., "Efficient IO with io_uring," https://kernel.dk/io_uring.pdf, 2019.

[Gregg 19] Gregg, B., *BPF Performance Tools: Linux System and Application Observability*, Addison-Wesley, 2019.

[Axboe 20] Axboe, J., "Flexible I/O Tester," https://github.com/axboe/fio, last updated 2020.

[Linux 20h] "ext4 General Information," *Linux documentation*, https://www.kernel.org/doc/html/latest/admin-guide/ext4.html, accessed 2020.

[Torvalds 20a] Torvalds, L., "Re: Do not blame anyone. Please give polite, constructive criticism," https://www.realworldtech.com/forum/?threadid=189711&curpostid=189841, 2020.

Chapter 9

Disks

Disk I/O can cause significant application latency, and is therefore an important target of systems performance analysis. Under high load, disks become a bottleneck, leaving CPUs idle as the system waits for disk I/O to complete. Identifying and eliminating these bottlenecks can improve performance and application throughput by orders of magnitude.

The term *disks* refers to the primary storage devices of the system. They include flash-memory-based solid-state disks (SSDs) and magnetic rotating disks. SSDs were introduced primarily to improve disk I/O performance, which they do. However, demands for capacity, I/O rates, and throughput are also increasing, and flash memory devices are not immune to performance issues.

The learning objectives of this chapter are:

- Understand disk models and concepts.
- Understand how disk access patterns affect performance.
- Understand the perils of interpreting disk utilization.
- Become familiar with disk device characteristics and internals.
- Become familiar with the kernel path from file systems to devices.
- Understand RAID levels and their performance.
- Follow different methodologies for disk performance analysis.
- Characterize system-wide and per-process disk I/O.
- Measure disk I/O latency distributions and identify outliers.
- Identify applications and code paths requesting disk I/O.
- Investigate disk I/O in detail using tracers.
- Become aware of disk tunable parameters.

This chapter consists of six parts, the first three providing the basis for disk I/O analysis and the last three showing its practical application to Linux-based systems. The parts are as follows:

- **Background** introduces storage-related terminology, basic models of disk devices, and key disk performance concepts.

- **Architecture** provides generic descriptions of storage hardware and software architecture.

- **Methodology** describes performance analysis methodology, both observational and experimental.

- **Observability Tools** shows disk performance observability tools for Linux-based systems, including tracing and visualizations.

- **Experimentation** summarizes disk benchmark tools.

- **Tuning** describes example disk tunable parameters.

The previous chapter covered the performance of file systems built upon disks, and is a better target of study for understanding application performance.

9.1 Terminology

Disk-related terminology used in this chapter includes:

- **Virtual disk:** An emulation of a storage device. It appears to the system as a single physical disk, but it may be constructed from multiple disks or a fraction of a disk.

- **Transport:** The physical bus used for communication, including data transfers (I/O) and other disk commands.

- **Sector:** A block of storage on disk, traditionally 512 bytes in size, but today often 4 Kbytes.

- **I/O:** Strictly speaking, I/O includes only disk reads and writes, and would not include other disk commands. I/O can be described by, at least, the direction (read or write), a disk address (location), and a size (bytes).

- **Disk commands:** Disks may be commanded to perform other non-data-transfer commands (e.g., a cache flush).

- **Throughput:** With disks, throughput commonly refers to the current data transfer rate, measured in bytes per second.

- **Bandwidth:** This is the maximum possible data transfer rate for storage transports or controllers; it is limited by hardware.

- **I/O latency:** Time for an I/O operation from start to end. Section 9.3.1, Measuring Time, defines more precise time terminology. Be aware that networking uses the term *latency* to refer to the time needed to initiate an I/O, followed by data transfer time.

- **Latency outliers:** Disk I/O with unusually high latency.

Other terms are introduced throughout this chapter. The Glossary includes basic terminology for reference if needed, including *disk, disk controller, storage array, local disks, remote disks,* and *IOPS*. Also see the terminology sections in Chapters 2 and 3.

9.2 Models

The following simple models illustrate some basic principles of disk I/O performance.

9.2.1 Simple Disk

Modern disks include an on-disk queue for I/O requests, as depicted in Figure 9.1.

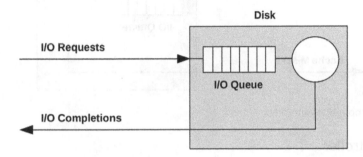

Figure 9.1   Simple disk with queue

I/O accepted by the disk may be either waiting on the queue or being serviced. This simple model is similar to a grocery store checkout, where customers queue to be serviced. It is also well suited for analysis using queueing theory.

While this may imply a first-come, first-served queue, the on-disk controller can apply other algorithms to optimize performance. These algorithms could include elevator seeking for rotational disks (see the discussion in Section 9.4.1, Disk Types), or separate queues for read and write I/O (especially for flash memory-based disks).

9.2.2 Caching Disk

The addition of an on-disk cache allows some read requests to be satisfied from a faster memory type, as shown in Figure 9.2. This may be implemented as a small amount of memory (DRAM) that is contained within the physical disk device.

While cache hits return with very low (good) latency, cache misses are still frequent, returning with high disk-device latency.

The on-disk cache may also be used to improve *write* performance, by using it as a *write-back* cache. This signals writes as having completed after the data transfer to cache and before the slower transfer to persistent disk storage. The counter-term is the *write-through* cache, which completes writes only after the full transfer to the next level.

In practice, storage write-back caches are often coupled with batteries, so that buffered data can still be saved in the event of a power failure. Such batteries may be on the disk or disk controller.

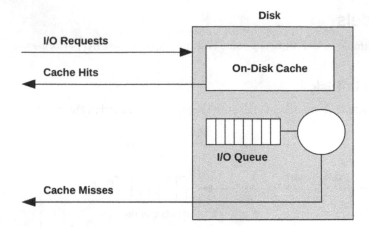

Figure 9.2   Simple disk with on-disk cache

9.2.3   Controller

A simple type of disk controller is shown in Figure 9.3, bridging the CPU I/O transport with the storage transport and attached disk devices. These are also called *host bus adapters* (HBAs).

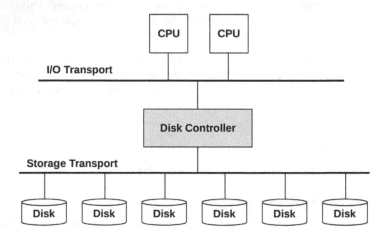

Figure 9.3   Simple disk controller and connected transports

Performance may be limited by either of these buses, the disk controller, or the disks. See Section 9.4, Architecture, for more about disk controllers.

9.3 Concepts

The following are important concepts in disk performance.

9.3.1 Measuring Time

I/O time can be measured as:

- **I/O request time (also called *I/O response time*)**: The entire time from issuing an I/O to its completion

- **I/O wait time**: The time spent waiting on a queue

- **I/O service time**: The time during which the I/O was processed (not waiting)

These are pictured in Figure 9.4.

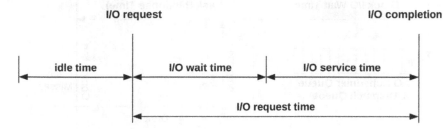

Figure 9.4   I/O time terminology (generic)

The term *service time* originates from when disks were simpler devices managed directly by the operating system, which therefore knew when the disk was actively servicing I/O. Disks now do their own internal queueing, and the operating system service time includes time spent waiting on kernel queues.

Where possible, I use clarifying terms to state what is being measured, from which start event to which end event. The start and end events can be kernel-based or disk-based, with kernel-based times measured from the block I/O interface for disk devices (pictured in Figure 9.7).

From the kernel:

- **Block I/O wait time** (also called **OS wait time**) is the time spent from when a new I/O was created and inserted into a kernel I/O queue to when it left the final kernel queue and was issued to the disk device. This may span multiple kernel-level queues, including a block I/O layer queue and a disk device queue.

- **Block I/O service time** is the time from issuing the request to the device to its completion interrupt from the device.

- **Block I/O request time** is both block I/O wait time and block I/O service time: the full time from creating an I/O to its completion.

From the disk:

- *Disk wait time* is the time spent on an on-disk queue.

- *Disk service time* is the time after the on-disk queue needed for an I/O to be actively processed.

- *Disk request time* (also called *disk response time* and *disk I/O latency*) is both the disk wait time and disk service time, and is equal to the block I/O service time.

These are pictured in Figure 9.5, where DWT is disk wait time, and DST is disk service time. This diagram also shows an on-disk cache, and how disk cache hits can result in a much shorter disk service time (DST).

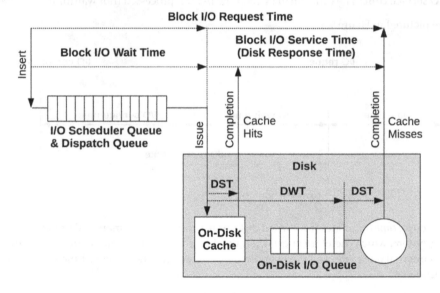

Figure 9.5   Kernel and disk time terminology

I/O latency is another commonly used term, introduced in Chapter 1. As with other terms, what this means depends on where it is measured. I/O latency alone may refer to the block I/O request time: the entire I/O time. Applications and performance tools commonly use the term *disk I/O latency* to refer to the disk request time: the entire time on the device. If you were talking to a hardware engineer from the perspective of the device, they may use the term *disk I/O latency* to refer to the disk wait time.

Block I/O service time is generally treated as a measure of current disk performance (this is what older versions of iostat(1) show); however, you should be aware that this is a simplification. In Figure 9.7, a generic I/O stack is pictured, which shows three possible driver layers beneath the block device interface. Any of these may implement its own queue, or may block on mutexes, adding latency to the I/O. This latency is included in the block I/O service time.

Calculating Time

Disk service time is typically not observable by kernel statistics directly, but an average disk service time can be inferred using IOPS and utilization:

disk service time = utilization/IOPS

For example, a utilization of 60% and an IOPS of 300 gives an average service time of 2 ms (600 ms/300 IOPS). This assumes that the utilization reflects a single device (or *service center*), which can process only one I/O at a time. Disks can typically process multiple I/O in parallel, making this calculation inaccurate.

Instead of using kernel statistics, event tracing can be used to provide an accurate disk service time by measuring high-resolution timestamps for the issue and completion for disk I/O. This can be done using tools described later in this chapter (e.g., biolatency(8) in Section 9.6.6, biolatency).

9.3.2   Time Scales

The time scale for disk I/O can vary by orders of magnitude, from tens of microseconds to thousands of milliseconds. At the slowest end of the scale, poor application response time can be caused by a single slow disk I/O; at the fastest end, disk I/O may become an issue only in great numbers (the sum of many fast I/O equaling a slow I/O).

For context, Table 9.1 provides a general idea of the possible range of disk I/O latencies. For precise and current values, consult the disk vendor documentation, and perform your own micro-benchmarking. Also see Chapter 2, Methodologies, for time scales other than disk I/O.

To better illustrate the orders of magnitude involved, the Scaled column shows a comparison based on an imaginary on-disk cache hit latency of one second.

Table 9.1   **Example time scale of disk I/O latencies**

Event	Latency	Scaled
On-disk cache hit	< 100 μs[1]	1 s
Flash memory read	~100 to 1,000 μs (small to large I/O)	1 to 10 s
Rotational disk sequential read	~1 ms	10 s
Rotational disk random read (7,200 rpm)	~8 ms	1.3 minutes
Rotational disk random read (slow, queueing)	> 10 ms	1.7 minutes
Rotational disk random read (dozens in queue)	> 100 ms	17 minutes
Worst-case virtual disk I/O (hardware controller, RAID-5, queueing, random I/O)	> 1,000 ms	2.8 hours

---

[1] 10 to 20 μs for Non-Volatile Memory express (NVMe) storage devices: these are typically flash memory attached via a PCIe bus card.

These latencies may be interpreted differently based on the environment requirements. While working in the enterprise storage industry, I considered any disk I/O taking over 10 ms to be unusually slow and a potential source of performance issues. In the cloud computing industry, there is greater tolerance for high latencies, especially in web-facing applications that already expect high latency between the network and client browser. In those environments, disk I/O may become an issue only beyond 50 ms (individually, or in total during an application request).

This table also illustrates that a disk can return two types of latency: one for on-disk cache hits (less than 100 µs) and one for misses (1–8 ms and higher, depending on the access pattern and device type). Since a disk will return a mixture of these, expressing them together as an *average* latency (as iostat(1) does) can be misleading, as this is really a distribution with two modes. See Figure 2.23 in Chapter 2, Methodologies, for an example of disk I/O latency distribution as a histogram.

9.3.3   Caching

The best disk I/O performance is none at all. Many layers of the software stack attempt to avoid disk I/O by caching reads and buffering writes, right down to the disk itself. The full list of these caches is in Table 3.2 of Chapter 3, Operating Systems, which includes application-level and file system caches. At the disk device driver level and below, they may include the caches listed in Table 9.2.

Table 9.2   **Disk I/O caches**

Cache	Example
Device cache	ZFS vdev
Block cache	Buffer cache
Disk controller cache	RAID card cache
Storage array cache	Array cache
On-disk cache	Disk data controller (DDC) attached DRAM

The block-based buffer cache was described in Chapter 8, File Systems. These disk I/O caches have been particularly important to improve the performance of random I/O workloads.

9.3.4   Random vs. Sequential I/O

The disk I/O workload can be described using the terms *random* and *sequential*, based on the relative location of the I/O on disk (*disk offset*). These terms were discussed in Chapter 8, File Systems, with regard to file access patterns.

Sequential workloads are also known as *streaming workloads*. The term *streaming* is usually used at the application level, to describe streaming reads and writes "to disk" (file system).

Random versus sequential disk I/O patterns were important to study during the era of magnetic rotational disks. For these, random I/O incurs additional latency as the disk heads seek and the platter rotates between I/O. This is shown in Figure 9.6, where both seek and rotation are necessary for the disk heads to move between sectors 1 and 2 (the actual path taken will be as direct as possible). Performance tuning involved identifying random I/O and trying to eliminate it in a number of ways, including caching, isolating random I/O to separate disks, and disk placement to reduce seek distance.

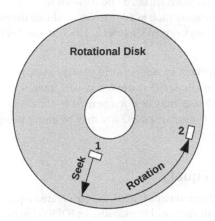

Figure 9.6   Rotational disk

Other disk types, including flash-based SSDs, usually perform no differently on random and sequential read patterns. Depending on the drive, there may be a small difference due to other factors, for example, an address lookup cache that can span sequential access but not random. Writes smaller than the block size may encounter a performance penalty due to a read-modify-write cycle, especially for random writes.

Note that the disk offsets as seen from the operating system may not match the offsets on the physical disk. For example, a hardware-provided virtual disk may map a contiguous range of offsets across multiple disks. Disks may remap offsets in their own way (via the disk data controller). Sometimes random I/O isn't identified by inspecting the offsets but may be inferred by measuring increased disk service time.

9.3.5 Read/Write Ratio

Apart from identifying random versus sequential workloads, another characteristic measure is the ratio of reads to writes, referring to either IOPS or throughput. This can be expressed as the ratio over time, as a percentage, for example, "The system has run at 80% reads since boot."

Understanding this ratio helps when designing and configuring systems. A system with a high read rate may benefit most from adding cache. A system with a high write rate may benefit most from adding more disks to increase maximum available throughput and IOPS.

The reads and writes may themselves show different workload patterns: reads may be random I/O, while writes may be sequential (especially for copy-on-write file systems). They may also exhibit different I/O sizes.

9.3.6   I/O Size

The average I/O size (bytes), or distribution of I/O sizes, is another workload characteristic. Larger I/O sizes typically provide higher throughput, although for longer per-I/O latency.

The I/O size may be altered by the disk device subsystem (for example, quantized to 512-byte sectors). The size may also have been inflated and deflated since the I/O was issued at the application level, by kernel components such as file systems, volume managers, and device drivers. See the Inflated and Deflated sections in Chapter 8, File Systems, Section 8.3.12, Logical vs. Physical I/O.

Some disk devices, especially flash-based, perform very differently with different read and write sizes. For example, a flash-based disk drive may perform optimally with 4 Kbyte reads and 1 Mbyte writes. Ideal I/O sizes may be documented by the disk vendor or identified using micro-benchmarking. The currently used I/O size may be found using observation tools (see Section 9.6, Observability Tools).

9.3.7   IOPS Are Not Equal

Because of those last three characteristics, IOPS are not created equal and cannot be directly compared between different devices and workloads. An IOPS value on its own doesn't mean a lot.

For example, with rotational disks, a workload of 5,000 sequential IOPS may be much faster than one of 1,000 random IOPS. Flash-memory-based IOPS are also difficult to compare, since their I/O performance is often relative to I/O size and direction (read or write).

IOPS may not even matter that much to the application workload. A workload that consists of random requests is typically latency-sensitive, in which case a high IOPS rate is desirable. A streaming (sequential) workload is throughput-sensitive, which may make a lower IOPS rate of larger I/O more desirable.

To make sense of IOPS, include the other details: random or sequential, I/O size, read/write, buffered/direct, and number of I/O in parallel. Also consider using time-based metrics, such as utilization and service time, which reflect resulting performance and can be more easily compared.

9.3.8   Non-Data-Transfer Disk Commands

Disks can be sent other commands besides I/O reads and writes. For example, disks with an on-disk cache (RAM) may be commanded to flush the cache to disk. Such a command is not a data transfer; the data was previously sent to the disk via writes.

Another example command is used to discard data: the ATA TRIM command, or SCSI UNMAP command. This tells the drive that a sector range is no longer needed, and can help SSD drives maintain write performance.

These disk commands can affect performance and can cause a disk to be utilized while other I/O wait.

9.3.9 Utilization

Utilization can be calculated as the time a disk was busy actively performing work during an interval.

A disk at 0% utilization is "idle," and a disk at 100% utilization is continually busy performing I/O (and other disk commands). Disks at 100% utilization are a likely source of performance issues, especially if they remain at 100% for some time. However, any rate of disk utilization can contribute to poor performance, as disk I/O is typically a slow activity.

There may also be a point between 0% and 100% (say, 60%) at which the disk's performance is no longer satisfactory due to the increased likelihood of queueing, either on-disk queues or in the operating system. The exact utilization value that becomes a problem depends on the disk, workload, and latency requirements. See the M/D/1 and 60% Utilization section in Chapter 2, Methodologies, Section 2.6.5, Queueing Theory.

To confirm whether high utilization is causing application issues, study the disk response time and whether the application is blocking on this I/O. The application or operating system may be performing I/O asynchronously, such that slow I/O is not directly causing the application to wait.

Note that utilization is an interval summary. Disk I/O can occur in bursts, especially due to write flushing, which can be disguised when summarizing over longer intervals. See Chapter 2, Methodologies, Section 2.3.11, Utilization, for a further discussion about the utilization metric type.

Virtual Disk Utilization

For virtual disks supplied by hardware (e.g., a disk controller, or network-attached storage), the operating system may be aware of when the virtual disk was busy, but know nothing about the performance of the underlying disks upon which it is built. This leads to scenarios where virtual disk utilization, as reported by the operating system, is significantly different from what is happening on the actual disks (and is counterintuitive):

- A virtual disk that is 100% busy, and is built upon multiple physical disks, may be able to accept more work. In this case, 100% may mean that some disks were busy all the time, but not all the disks all the time, and therefore some disks were idle.

- Virtual disks that include a write-back cache may not appear very busy during write workloads, since the disk controller returns write completions immediately, even though the underlying disks are busy for some time afterward.

- Disks may be busy due to hardware RAID rebuild, with no corresponding I/O seen by the operating system.

For the same reasons, it can be difficult to interpret the utilization of virtual disks created by operating system software (software RAID). However, the operating system should be exposing utilization for the physical disks as well, which can be inspected.

Once a physical disk reaches 100% utilization and more I/O is requested, it becomes saturated.

9.3.10 Saturation

Saturation is a measure of work queued beyond what the resource can deliver. For disk devices, it can be calculated as the average length of the device wait queue in the operating system (assuming it does queueing).

This provides a measure of performance beyond the 100% utilization point. A disk at 100% utilization may have no saturation (queueing), or it may have a lot, significantly affecting performance due to the queueing of I/O.

You might assume that disks at less than 100% utilization have no saturation, but this actually depends on the utilization interval: 50% disk utilization during an interval may mean 100% utilized for half that time and idle for the rest. Any interval summary can suffer from similar issues. When it is important to know exactly what occurred, tracing tools can be used to examine I/O events.

9.3.11 I/O Wait

I/O wait is a per-CPU performance metric showing time spent idle, when there are threads on the CPU dispatcher queue (in sleep state) that are blocked on disk I/O. This divides CPU idle time into time spent with nothing to do, and time spent blocked on disk I/O. A high rate of I/O wait per CPU shows that the disks may be a bottleneck, leaving the CPU idle while it waits on them.

I/O wait can be a very confusing metric. If another CPU-hungry process comes along, the I/O wait value can drop: the CPUs now have something to do, instead of being idle. However, the same disk I/O is still present and blocking threads, despite the drop in the I/O wait metric. The reverse has sometimes happened when system administrators have upgraded application software and the newer version is more efficient and uses fewer CPU cycles, *revealing* I/O wait. This can make the system administrator think that the upgrade has caused a disk issue and made performance worse, when in fact disk performance is the same, but CPU performance is improved.

A more reliable metric is the time that application threads are blocked on disk I/O. This captures the pain endured by application threads caused by the disks, regardless of what other work the CPUs may be doing. This metric can be measured using static or dynamic instrumentation.

I/O wait is still a popular metric on Linux systems and, despite its confusing nature, it is used successfully to identify a type of disk bottleneck: disks busy, CPUs idle. One way to interpret it is to treat any wait I/O as a sign of a system bottleneck, and then tune the system to minimize it—even if the I/O is still occurring concurrently with CPU utilization. Concurrent I/O is more likely to be non-blocking I/O, and less likely to cause a direct issue. Non-concurrent I/O, as identified by I/O wait, is more likely to be application blocking I/O, and a bottleneck.

9.3.12 Synchronous vs. Asynchronous

It can be important to understand that disk I/O latency may not directly affect application performance, if the application I/O and disk I/O operate asynchronously. This commonly occurs with write-back caching, where the application I/O completes early, and the disk I/O is issued later.

Applications may use read-ahead to perform asynchronous reads, which may not block the application while the disk completes the I/O. The file system may initiate this itself to warm the cache (prefetch).

Even if an application is synchronously waiting for I/O, that application code path may be non-critical and asynchronous to client application requests. It could be an application I/O worker thread, created to manage I/O while other threads continue to process work.

Kernels also typically support *asynchronous* or *non-blocking I/O*, where an API is provided for the application to request I/O and to be notified of its completion sometime later. For more on these topics, see Chapter 8, File Systems, Sections 8.3.9, Non-Blocking I/O; 8.3.5, Read-Ahead; 8.3.4, Prefetch; and 8.3.7, Synchronous Writes.

9.3.13 Disk vs. Application I/O

Disk I/O is the end result of various kernel components, including file systems and device drivers. There are many reasons why the rate and volume of this disk I/O may not match the I/O issued by the application. These include:

- File system inflation, deflation, and unrelated I/O. See Chapter 8, File Systems, Section 8.3.12, Logical vs. Physical I/O.

- Paging due to a system memory shortage. See Chapter 7, Memory, Section 7.2.2, Paging.

- Device driver I/O size: rounding up I/O size, or fragmenting I/O.

- RAID writing mirror or checksum blocks, or verifying read data.

This mismatch can be confusing when unexpected. It can be understood by learning the architecture and performing analysis.

9.4 Architecture

This section describes disk architecture, which is typically studied during capacity planning to determine the limits for different components and configuration choices. It should also be checked during the investigation of later performance issues, in case the problem originates from architectural choices rather than the current load and tuning.

9.4.1 Disk Types

The two most commonly used disk types at present are magnetic rotational and flash-memory-based SSDs. Both of these provide permanent storage; unlike volatile memory, their stored content is still available after a power cycle.

9.4.1.1 Magnetic Rotational

Also termed a *hard disk drive* (HDD), this type of disk consists of one or more discs, called *platters*, impregnated with iron oxide particles. A small region of these particles can be magne-tized in one of two directions; this orientation is used to store a bit. The platters rotate, while a mechanical arm with circuitry to read and write data reaches across the surface. This circuitry includes the *disk heads*, and an arm may have more than one head, allowing it to read and write multiple bits simultaneously. Data is stored on the platter in circular tracks, and each track is divided into sectors.

Being mechanical devices, these perform relatively slowly, especially for random I/O. With advances in flash memory-based technology, SSDs are displacing rotational disks, and it is conceivable that one day rotational disks will be obsolete (along with other older storage technologies: drum disks and core memory). In the meantime, rotational disks are still competitive in some scenarios, such as economical high-density storage (low cost per megabyte), especially for data warehousing.[2]

The following topics summarize factors in rotational disk performance.

Seek and Rotation

Slow I/O for magnetic rotational disks is usually caused by the seek time for the disk heads and the rotation time of the disk platter, both of which may take milliseconds. Best case is when the next requested I/O is located at the end of the currently servicing I/O, so that the disk heads don't need to seek or wait for additional rotation. As described earlier, this is known as *sequential I/O*, while I/O that requires head seeking or waiting for rotation is called *random I/O*.

There are many strategies to reduce seek and rotation wait time, including:

- Caching: eliminating I/O entirely.
- File system placement and behavior, including copy-on-write (which makes writes sequential, but may make later reads random).
- Separating different workloads to different disks, to avoid seeking between workload I/O.
- Moving different workloads to different systems (some cloud computing environments can do this to reduce multitenancy effects).
- Elevator seeking, performed by the disk itself.
- Higher-density disks, to tighten the workload location.
- Partition (or "slice") configuration, for example, short-stroking.

An additional strategy to reduce rotation wait time is to use faster disks. Disks are available in different rotational speeds, including 5400, 7200, 10 K, and 15 K revolutions per minute (rpm). Note that higher speeds can result in lower disk life-spans, due to increased heat and wear.

Theoretical Maximum Throughput

If the maximum sectors per track of a disk is known, disk throughput can be calculated using the following formula:

max throughput = max sectors per track × sector size × rpm/60 s

---

[2] The Netflix Open Connect Appliances (OCAs) that host videos for streaming might sound like another use case for HDDs, but supporting large numbers of simultaneous customers per server can result in random I/O. Some OCAs have switched to flash drives [Netflix 20].

This formula was more useful for older disks that exposed this information accurately. Modern disks provide a virtual image of the disk to the operating system, and expose only synthetic values for these attributes.

Short-Stroking

Short-stroking is where only the outer tracks of the disk are used for the workload; the remainder are either unused, or used for low-throughput workloads (e.g., archives). This reduces seek time as head movement is bounded by a smaller range, and the disk may put the heads at rest at the outside edge, reducing the first seek after idle. The outer tracks also usually have better throughput due to sector zoning (see the next section). Keep an eye out for short-stroking when examining published disk benchmarks, especially benchmarks that don't include price, where many short-stroked disks may have been used.

Sector Zoning

The length of disk tracks varies, with the shortest at the center of the disk and the longest at the outside edge. Instead of the number of sectors (and bits) per track being fixed, sector zoning (also called *multiple-zone recording*) increases the sector count for the longer tracks, since more sectors can be physically written. Because the rotation speed is constant, the longer outside-edge tracks deliver higher throughput (megabytes per second) than the inner tracks.

Sector Size

The storage industry has developed a new standard for disk devices, called Advanced Format, to support larger sector sizes, particularly 4 Kbytes. This reduces I/O computational overhead, improving throughput as well as reducing overheads for the disk's per-sector stored metadata. Sectors of 512 bytes can still be provided by disk firmware via an emulation standard called Advanced Format 512e. Depending on the disk, this may increase write overheads, invoking a read-modify-write cycle to map 512 bytes to a 4 Kbyte sector. Other performance issues to be aware of include misaligned 4 Kbyte I/O, which span two sectors, inflating sector I/O to service them.

On-Disk Cache

A common component of these disks is a small amount of memory (RAM) used to cache the result of reads and to-buffer writes. This memory also allows I/O (commands) to be queued on the device and reordered more efficiently. With SCSI, this is Tagged Command Queueing (TCQ); with SATA, it is called Native Command Queueing (NCQ).

Elevator Seeking

The *elevator algorithm* (also known as *elevator seeking*) is one way that a command queue can improve efficiency. It reorders I/O based on their on-disk location, to minimize travel of the disk heads. The result is similar to a building elevator, which does not service floors based on the order in which the floor buttons were pushed, but makes sweeps up and down the building, stopping at the currently requested floors.

This behavior becomes apparent when inspecting disk I/O traces and finding that sorting I/O by completion time doesn't match sorting by start time: I/O are completing out of order.

While this seems like an obvious performance win, contemplate the following scenario: A disk has been sent a batch of I/O near offset 1,000, and a single I/O at offset 2,000. The disk heads are currently at 1,000. When will the I/O at offset 2,000 be serviced? Now consider that, while servicing the I/O near 1,000, more arrive near 1,000, and more, and more—enough continual I/O to keep the disk busy near offset 1,000 for 10 seconds. When will the 2,000 offset I/O be serviced, and what is its final I/O latency?

Data Integrity

Disks store an error-correcting code (ECC) at the end of each sector for data integrity, so that the drive can verify data was read correctly, or correct any errors that may have occurred. If the sector was not read correctly, the disk heads may retry the read on the next rotation (and may retry several times, varying the location of the head slightly each time). This may be the explanation for unusually slow I/O. The drive may provide soft errors to the OS to explain what happened. It can be beneficial to monitor the rate of soft errors, as an increase can indicate that a drive may soon fail.

One benefit of the industry switch from 512 byte to 4 Kbyte sectors is that fewer ECC bits are required for the same volume of data, as ECC is more efficient for the larger sector size [Smith 09].

Note that other checksums may also be in use to verify data. For example, a cyclic redundancy check (CRC) may be used to verify data transfers to the host, and other checksums may be in use by file systems.

Vibration

While disk device vendors were well aware of vibration issues, those issues weren't commonly known or taken seriously by the industry. In 2008, while investigating a mysterious performance issue, I conducted a vibration-inducing experiment by *shouting* at a disk array while it performed a write benchmark, which caused a burst of very slow I/O. My experiment was immediately videoed and put on YouTube, where it went viral, and it has been described as the first demonstration of the impact of vibration on disk performance [Turner 10]. The video has had over 1,700,000 views, promoting awareness of disk vibration issues [Gregg 08]. Based on emails I've received, I also seem to have accidentally spawned an industry in soundproofing data centers: you can now hire professionals who will analyze data center sound levels and improve disk performance by damping vibrations.

Sloth Disks

A current performance issue with some rotational disks is the discovery of what has been called *sloth disks*. These disks sometimes return very slow I/O, over one second, without any reported errors. This is much longer than ECC-based retries should take. It might actually be better if such disks returned a failure instead of taking so long, so that the operating system or disk controllers could take corrective action, such as offlining the disk in redundant environments and reporting the failure. Sloth disks are a nuisance, especially when they are part of a virtual disk presented by a storage array where the operating system has no direct visibility, making them harder to identify.[3]

---

[3] If the Linux Distributed Replicated Block Device (DRBD) system is in use, it does provide a "disk-timeout" parameter.

SMR

Shingled Magnetic Recording (SMR) drives provide higher density by using narrower tracks. These tracks are too narrow for the write head to record, but not for the (smaller) read head to read, so it writes them by partially overlapping other tracks, in a style similar to roof shingles (hence its name). Drives using SMR increase in density by around 25%, at the cost of degraded write performance, as the overlapped data is destroyed and must also be re-written. These drives are suitable for archival workloads that are written once then mostly read, but are not suited for write-heavy workloads in RAID configurations [Mellor 20].

Disk Data Controller

Mechanical disks present a simple interface to the system, implying a fixed sectors-per-track ratio and a contiguous range of addressable offsets. What actually happens on the disk is up to the disk data controller—a disk internal microprocessor, programmed by firmware. Disks may implement algorithms including sector zoning, affecting how the offsets are laid out. This is something to be aware of, but it's difficult to analyze—the operating system cannot see into the disk data controller.

9.4.1.2 Solid-State Drives

These are also called solid-state disks (SSDs). The term solid-state refers to their use of solid-state electronics, which provides programmable nonvolatile memory with typically much better performance than rotational disks. Without moving parts, these disks are also physically durable and not susceptible to performance issues caused by vibration.

The performance of this disk type is usually consistent across different offsets (no rotational or seek latency) and predictable for given I/O sizes. The random or sequential characteristic of workloads matters much less than with rotational disks. All of this makes them easier to study and do capacity planning for. However, if they do encounter performance pathologies, understanding them can be just as complex as with rotational disks, due to how they operate internally.

Some SSDs use nonvolatile DRAM (NV-DRAM). Most use flash memory.

Flash Memory

Flash-memory-based SSDs offer high read performance, particularly random read performance that can beat rotational disks by orders of magnitude. Most are built using NAND flash memory, which uses electron-based trapped-charge storage media that can store electrons persistently[4] in a no-power state [Cornwell 12]. The name "flash" relates to how data is written, which requires erasing an entire block of memory at a time (including multiple pages, usually 8 or 64 KBytes per page) and rewriting the contents. Because of these write overheads, flash memory has asymmetrical read/write performance: fast reads and slower writes. Drives typically mitigate this using write-back caches to improve write performance, and a small capacitor as a battery backup in case of a power failure.

---

[4] But not indefinitely. Data retention errors for modern MLC may occur in a matter of mere months when powered off [Cassidy 12][Cai 15].

Flash memory comes in different types:

- **Single-level cell (SLC)**: Stores data bits in individual cells.
- **Multi-level cell (MLC)**: Stores multiple bits per cell (usually two, which requires four voltage levels).
- **Enterprise multi-level cell (eMLC)**: MLC with advanced firmware intended for enterprise use.
- **Tri-level cell (TLC)**: Stores three bits (eight voltage levels).
- **Quad-level cell (QLC)**: Stores four bits.
- **3D NAND / Vertical NAND (V-NAND)**: This stacks layers of flash memory (e.g., TLC) to increase the density and storage capacity.

This list is in rough chronological order, with the newest technologies listed last: 3D NAND has been commercially available since 2013.

SLC tends to have higher performance and reliability compared to other types and was preferred for enterprise use, although with higher costs. MLC is now often used in the enterprise for its higher density, in spite of its lower reliability. Flash reliability is often measured as the number of block writes (program/erase cycles) a drive is expected to support. For SLC, this expectation is around 50,000 to 100,000 cycles; for MLC around 5,000 to 10,000 cycles; for TLC around 3,000 cycles; and for QLC around 1,000 cycles [Liu 20].

Controller

The controller for an SSD has the following task [Leventhal 13]:

- **Input**: Reads and writes occur per page (usually 8 Kbytes); writes can occur only to erased pages; pages are erased in blocks of 32 to 64 (256–512 Kbytes).
- **Output**: Emulates a hard drive block interface: reads or writes of arbitrary sectors (512 bytes or 4 Kbytes).

Translating between input and output is performed by the controller's flash translation layer (FTL), which must also track free blocks. It essentially uses its own file system to do this, such as a log-structured file system.

The write characteristics can be a problem for write workloads, especially when writing I/O sizes that are smaller than the flash memory block size (which may be as large as 512 Kbytes). This can cause *write amplification*, where the remainder of the block is copied elsewhere before erasure, and also latency for at least the erase-write cycle. Some flash memory drives mitigate the latency issue by providing an on-disk buffer (RAM-based) backed by a battery, so that writes can be buffered and written later, even in the event of a power failure.

The most common enterprise-grade flash memory drive I've used performs optimally with 4 Kbyte reads and 1 Mbyte writes, due to the flash memory layout. These values vary for different drives and may be found via micro-benchmarking of I/O sizes.

Given the disparity between the native operations of flash and the exposed block interface, there has been room for improvement by the operating system and its file systems. The TRIM command is an example: it informs the SSD that a region is no longer in use, allowing the SSD to more easily assemble its pool of free blocks, reducing write amplification. (For SCSI, this can be implemented using the UNMAP or WRITE SAME commands; for ATA, the DATA SET MANAGEMENT command. Linux support includes the discard mount option, and the fstrim(8) command.)

Lifespan

There are various problems with NAND flash as a storage medium, including burnout, data fade, and read disturbance [Cornwell 12]. These can be solved by the SSD controller, which can move data to avoid problems. It will typically employ *wear leveling*, which spreads writes across different blocks to reduce the write cycles on individual blocks, and *memory overprovisioning*, which reserves extra memory that can be mapped into service when needed.

While these techniques improve lifespan, the SSD still has a limited number of write cycles per block, depending on the type of flash memory and the mitigation features employed by the drive. Enterprise-grade drives use memory overprovisioning and the most reliable type of flash memory, SLC, to achieve write cycle rates of 1 million and higher. Consumer-grade drives based on MLC may offer as few as 1,000 cycles.

Pathologies

Here are some flash memory SSD pathologies to be aware of:

- Latency outliers due to aging, and the SSD trying harder to extract correct data (which is checked using ECC).
- Higher latency due to fragmentation (reformatting may fix this by cleaning up the FTL block maps).
- Lower throughput performance if the SSD implements internal compression.

Check for other developments with SSD performance features and issues encountered.

9.4.1.3 Persistent Memory

Persistent memory, in the form of battery-backed[5] DRAM, is used for storage controller write-back caches. The performance of this type is orders of magnitude faster than flash, but its cost and limited battery life span have limited it to only specialized uses.

A new type of persistent memory called 3D XPoint, developed by Intel and Micron, will allow persistent memory to be used for many more applications at a compelling price/performance, in between DRAM and flash memory. 3D XPoint works by storing bits in a stackable cross-gridded data access array, and is byte-addressable. An Intel performance comparison reported 14 microsecond access latency for 3D XPoint compared to 200 microseconds for 3D NAND SSD [Hady 18]. 3D XPoint also showed consistent latency for their test, whereas 3D NAND had a wider latency distribution reaching up to 3 milliseconds.

3D XPoint has been commercially available since 2017. Intel uses the brand name Optane, and releases it as Intel Optane persistent memory in a DIMM package, and as Intel Optane SSDs.

---

[5] A battery or a super capacitor.

9.4.2　Interfaces

The interface is the protocol supported by the drive for communication with the system, usually via a disk controller. A brief summary of the SCSI, SAS, SATA, FC, and NVMe interfaces follows. You will need to check what the current interfaces and supported bandwidths are, as they change over time when new specifications are developed and adopted.

SCSI

The Small Computer System Interface was originally a parallel transport bus, using multiple electrical connectors to transport bits in parallel. The first version, SCSI-1 in 1986, had a data bus width of 8 bits, allowing one byte to be transferred per clock, and delivered a bandwidth of 5 Mbytes/s. This was connected using a 50-pin Centronics C50. Later parallel SCSI versions used wider data buses and more pins for the connectors, up to 80 pins, and bandwidths in the hundreds of megabytes.

Because parallel SCSI is a shared bus, it can suffer performance issues due to bus contention, for example when a scheduled system backup saturates the bus with low-priority I/O. Workarounds included putting low-priority devices on their own SCSI bus or controller.

Clocking of parallel buses also becomes a problem at higher speeds which, along with the other issues (including limited devices and the need for SCSI terminator packs), has led to a switch to the serial version: SAS.

SAS

The Serial Attached SCSI interface is designed as a high-speed point-to-point transport, avoiding the bus contention issues of parallel SCSI. The initial SAS-1 specification was 3 Gbits/s (released in 2003), followed by SAS-2 supporting 6 Gbits/s (2009), SAS-3 supporting 12 Gbits/s (2012), and SAS-4 supporting 22.5 Gbit/s (2017). Link aggregations are supported, so that multiple ports can combine to deliver higher bandwidths. The actual data transfer rate is 80% of bandwidth, due to 8b/10b encoding.

Other SAS features include dual porting of drives for use with redundant connectors and architectures, I/O multipathing, SAS domains, hot swapping, and compatibility support for SATA devices. These features have made SAS popular for enterprise use, especially with redundant architectures.

SATA

For similar reasons as for SCSI and SAS, the parallel ATA (aka IDE) interface standard has evolved to become the Serial ATA interface. Created in 2003, SATA 1.0 supported 1.5 Gbits/s; later major versions are SATA 2.0 supporting 3.0 Gbits/s (2004), and SATA 3.0 supporting 6.0 Gbits/s (2008). Additional features have been added in major and minor releases, including native command queueing support. SATA uses 8b/10b encoding, so the data transfer rate is 80% of bandwidth. SATA has been in common use for consumer desktops and laptops.

FC

Fibre Channel (FC) is a high-speed interface standard for data transfer, originally intended only for fibre optic cable (hence its name) and later supporting copper as well. FC is commonly used in enterprise environments to create storage area networks (SANs) where multiple storage devices can be connected to multiple servers via a Fibre Channel Fabric. This offers greater scalability and accessibility than other interfaces, and is similar to connecting multiple hosts via a network. And, like networking, FC can involve using *switches* to connect together multiple local endpoints (server and storage). Development of a Fibre Channel standard began in 1988 with the first version approved by ANSI in 1994 [FICA 20]. There have since been many variants and speed improvements, with the recent Gen 7 256GFC standard reaching up to 51,200 MB/s full duplex [FICA 18].

NVMe

Non-Volatile Memory express (NVMe) is a PCIe bus specification for storage devices. Rather than connecting storage devices to a storage controller card, an NVMe device is itself a card that connects directly to the PCIe bus. Created in 2011, the first NVMe specification was 1.0e (released in 2013), and the latest is 1.4 (2019) [NVMe 20]. Newer specifications add various features, for example, thermal management features and commands for self-testing, verifying data, and sanitizing data (making recovery impossible). The bandwidth of NVMe cards is bounded by the PCIe bus; PCIe version 4.0, commonly used today, has a single-direction bandwidth of 31.5 Gbytes/s for a x16 card (link width).

An advantage with NVMe over traditional SAS and SATA is its support for multiple hardware queues. These queues can be used from the same CPU to promote cache warmth (and with Linux multi-queue support, shared kernel locks are also avoided). These queues also allow much greater buffering, supporting up to 64 thousand commands in each queue, whereas typical SAS and SATA are limited to 256 and 32 commands respectively.

NVMe also supports SR-IOV for improving virtual machine storage performance (see Chapter 11, Cloud Computing, Section 11.2, Hardware Virtualization).

NVMe is used for low-latency flash devices, with an expected I/O latency of less than 20 microseconds.

9.4.3 Storage Types

Storage can be provided to a server in a number of ways; the following sections describe four general architectures: disk devices, RAID, storage arrays, and network-attached storage (NAS).

Disk Devices

The simplest architecture is a server with internal disks, individually controlled by the operating system. The disks connect to a disk controller, which is circuitry on the main board or an expander card, and which allows the disk devices to be seen and accessed. In this architecture the disk controller merely acts as a conduit so that the system can communicate with the disks. A typical personal computer or laptop has a disk attached in this way for primary storage.

This architecture is the easiest to analyze using performance tools, as each disk is known to the operating system and can be observed separately.

Some disk controllers support this architecture, where it is called *just a bunch of disks* (JBOD).

RAID

Advanced disk controllers can provide the redundant array of independent disks (RAID) architecture for disk devices (originally the redundant array of *inexpensive* disks [Patterson 88]). RAID can present multiple disks as a single big, fast, and reliable virtual disk. These controllers often include an on-board cache (RAM) to improve read and write performance.

Providing RAID by a disk controller card is called *hardware* RAID. RAID can also be implemented by operating system software, but hardware RAID has been preferred as CPU-expensive checksum and parity calculations can be performed more quickly on dedicated hardware, plus such hardware can include a battery backup unit (BBU) for improved resiliency. However, advances in processors have produced CPUs with a surplus of cycles and cores, reducing the need to offload parity calculations. A number of storage solutions have moved back to software RAID (for example, using ZFS), which reduces complexity and hardware cost and improves observability from the operating system. In the case of a major failure, software RAID may also be easier to repair than hardware RAID (imagine a dead RAID card).

The following sections describe the performance characteristics of RAID. The term *stripe* is often used: this refers to when data is grouped as blocks that are written across multiple drives (like drawing a stripe through them all).

Types

Various RAID types are available to meet varying needs for capacity, performance, and reliability. This summary focuses on the performance characteristics shown in Table 9.3.

Table 9.3 **RAID types**

Level	Description	Performance
0 (concat.)	Drives are filled one at a time.	Eventually improves random read performance when multiple drives can take part.
0 (stripe)	Drives are used in parallel, splitting (striping) I/O across multiple drives.	Expected best random and sequential I/O performance (depends on stripe size and workload pattern).
1 (mirror)	Multiple drives (usually two) are grouped, storing identical content for redundancy.	Good random and sequential read performance (can read from all drives simultaneously, depending on implementation). Writes limited by slowest disk in mirror, and throughput overheads doubled (two drives).
10	A combination of RAID-0 stripes across groups of RAID-1 drives, providing capacity and redundancy.	Similar performance characteristics to RAID-1 but allows more groups of drives to take part, like RAID-0, increasing bandwidth.
5	Data is stored as stripes across multiple disks, along with extra parity information for redundancy.	Poor write performance due to read-modify-write cycle and parity calculations.
6	RAID-5 with two parity disks per stripe.	Similar to RAID-5 but worse.

While RAID-0 striping performs the best, it has no redundancy, making it impractical for most production use. Possible exceptions include fault-tolerant cloud computing environments that does not store critical data and where a failed instance will automatically be replaced, and storage servers used for caching only.

Observability

As described in the earlier section on virtual disk utilization, the use of hardware-supplied virtual disk devices can make observability more difficult in the operating system, which does not know what the physical disks are doing. If RAID is supplied via software, individual disk devices can usually be observed, as the operating system manages them directly.

Read-Modify-Write

When data is stored as a stripe including a parity, as with RAID-5, write I/O can incur additional read I/O and compute time. This is because writes that are smaller than the stripe size may require the entire stripe to be read, the bytes modified, the parity recalculated, and then the stripe rewritten. An optimization for RAID-5 may be in use to avoid this: instead of reading the entire stripe, only the portions of the stripe (strips) are read that include the modified data, along with the parity. By a sequence of XOR operations, an updated parity can be calculated and written along with the modified strips.

Writes that span the entire stripe can write over the previous contents, without needing to read them first. Performance in this environment may be improved by balancing the size of the stripe with the average I/O size of the writes, to reduce the additional read overhead.

Caches

Disk controllers that implement RAID-5 can mitigate read-write-modify performance by use of a write-back cache. These caches must be battery-backed, so that in the event of a power failure they can still complete buffered writes.

Additional Features

Be aware that advanced disk controller cards can provide advanced features that can affect performance. It is a good idea to browse the vendor documentation so that you're at least aware of what may be in play. For example, here are a couple of features from Dell PERC 5 cards [Dell 20]:

- **Patrol read**: Every several days, all disk blocks are read and their checksums verified. If the disks are busy servicing requests, the resources given to the patrol read function are reduced, to avoid competing with the system workload.

- **Cache flush interval**: The time in seconds between flushing dirty data in the cache to disk. Longer times may reduce disk I/O due to write cancellation and better aggregate writes; however, they may also cause higher read latency during the larger flushes.

Both of these can have a significant effect on performance.

Storage Arrays

Storage arrays allow many disks to be connected to the system. They use advanced disk controllers so that RAID can be configured, and they usually provide a large cache (gigabytes) to improve read and write performance. These caches are also typically battery-backed, allowing them to operate in write-back mode. A common policy is to switch to write-through mode if the battery fails, which may be noticed as a sudden drop in write performance due to waiting for the read-modify-write cycle.

An additional performance consideration is how the storage array is attached to the system—usually via an external storage controller card. The card, and the transport between it and the storage array, will both have limits for IOPS and throughput. For improvements in both performance and reliability, storage arrays are often dual-attachable, meaning they can be connected using two physical cables, to one or two different storage controller cards.

Network-Attached Storage

NAS is provided to the system over the existing network via a network protocol, such as NFS, SMB/CIFS, or iSCSI, usually from dedicated systems known as NAS appliances. These are separate systems and should be analyzed as such. Some performance analysis may be done on the client, to inspect the workload applied and I/O latencies. The performance of the network also becomes a factor, and issues can arise from network congestion and from multiple-hop latency.

9.4.4   Operating System Disk I/O Stack

The components and layers in a disk I/O stack will depend on the operating system, version, and software and hardware technologies used. Figure 9.7 depicts a general model. See Chapter 3, Operating Systems, for a similar model including the application.

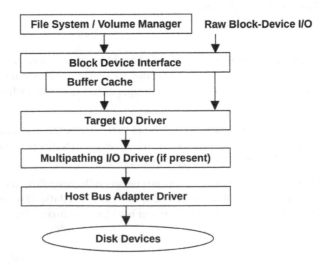

Figure 9.7   Generic disk I/O stack

Block Device Interface

The block device interface was created in early Unix for accessing storage devices in units of blocks of 512 bytes, and to provide a buffer cache to improve performance. The interface exists in Linux, although the role of the buffer cache has diminished as other file system caches have been introduced, as described in Chapter 8, File Systems.

Unix provided a path to bypass the buffer cache, called *raw block device I/O* (or just *raw I/O*), which could be used via character special device files (see Chapter 3, Operating Systems). These files are no longer commonly available by default in Linux. Raw block device I/O is different from, but in some ways similar to, the "direct I/O" file system feature described in Chapter 8, File Systems.

The block I/O interface can usually be observed from operating system performance tools (iostat(1)). It is also a common location for static instrumentation and more recently can be explored with dynamic instrumentation as well. Linux has enhanced this area of the kernel with additional features.

Linux

The main components of the Linux block I/O stack are shown in Figure 9.8.

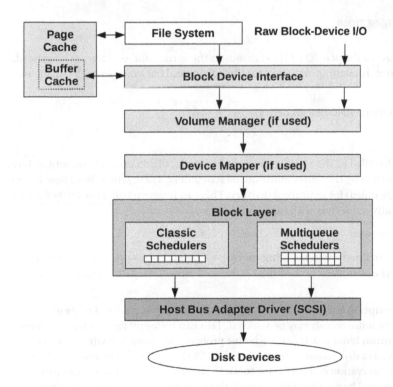

Figure 9.8 Linux I/O stack

Linux has enhanced block I/O with the addition of I/O merging and I/O schedulers for improving performance, volume managers for grouping multiple devices, and a device mapper for creating virtual devices.

I/O merging

When I/O requests are created, Linux can merge and coalesce them as shown in Figure 9.9.

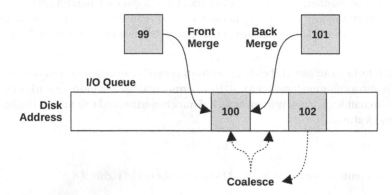

Figure 9.9   I/O merging types

This groups I/O, reducing the per-I/O CPU overheads in the kernel storage stack and overheads on the disk, improving throughput. Statistics for these front and back merges are available in iostat(1).

After merging, I/O is then scheduled for delivery to the disks.

I/O Schedulers

I/O is queued and scheduled in the block layer either by classic schedulers (only present in Linux versions older than 5.0) or by the newer multi-queue schedulers. These schedulers allow I/O to be reordered (or rescheduled) for optimized delivery. This can improve and more fairly balance performance, especially for devices with high I/O latencies (rotational disks).

Classic schedulers include:

- **Noop:** This doesn't perform scheduling (noop is CPU-talk for no-operation) and can be used when the overhead of scheduling is deemed unnecessary (for example, in a RAM disk).

- **Deadline:** Attempts to enforce a latency deadline; for example, read and write expiry times in units of milliseconds may be selected. This can be useful for real-time systems, where determinism is desired. It can also solve problems of *starvation*: where an I/O request is starved of disk resources as newly issued I/O jump the queue, resulting in a latency outlier. Starvation can occur due to *writes starving reads*, and as a consequence of elevator seeking and heavy I/O to one area of disk starving I/O to another. The deadline scheduler solves this, in part, by using three separate queues for I/O: read FIFO, write FIFO, and sorted [Love 10].

- **CFQ:** The completely fair queueing scheduler allocates I/O time slices to processes, similar to CPU scheduling, for fair usage of disk resources. It also allows priorities and classes to be set for user processes, via the ionice(1) command.

A problem with the classic schedulers was their use of a single request queue, protected by a single lock, which became a performance bottleneck at high I/O rates. The multi-queue driver (blk-mq, added in Linux 3.13) solves this by using separate submission queues for each CPU, and multiple dispatch queues for the devices. This delivers better performance and lower latency for I/O versus classic schedulers, as requests can be processed in parallel and on the same CPU where the I/O was initiated. This was necessary to support flash memory-based and other device types capable of handling millions of IOPS [Corbet 13b].

Multi-queue schedulers include:

- **None:** No queueing.

- **BFQ:** The budget fair queueing scheduler, similar to CFQ, but allocates bandwidth as well as I/O time. It creates a queue for each process performing disk I/O, and maintains a budget for each queue measured in sectors. There is also a system-wide budget timeout to prevent one process from holding a device for too long. BFQ supports cgroups.

- **mq-deadline:** A blk-mq version of deadline (described earlier).

- **Kyber:** A scheduler that adjusts read and write dispatch queue lengths based on performance so that target read or write latencies can be met. It is a simple scheduler that only has two tunables: the target read latency (read_lat_nsec) and target synchronous write latency (write_lat_nsec). Kyber has shown improved storage I/O latencies in the Netflix cloud, where it is used by default.

Since Linux 5.0, the multi-queue schedulers are the default (the classic schedulers are no longer included).

I/O schedulers are documented in detail in the Linux source under Documentation/block.

After I/O scheduling, the request is placed on the block device queue for issuing to the device.

9.5   Methodology

This section describes various methodologies and exercises for disk I/O analysis and tuning. The topics are summarized in Table 9.4.

Table 9.4   Disk performance methodologies

Section	Methodology	Types
9.5.1	Tools method	Observational analysis
9.5.2	USE method	Observational analysis
9.5.3	Performance monitoring	Observational analysis, capacity planning
9.5.4	Workload characterization	Observational analysis, capacity planning
9.5.5	Latency analysis	Observational analysis

Section	Methodology	Types
9.5.6	Static performance tuning	Observational analysis, capacity planning
9.5.7	Cache tuning	Observational analysis, tuning
9.5.8	Resource controls	Tuning
9.5.9	Micro-benchmarking	Experimentation analysis
9.5.10	Scaling	Capacity planning, tuning

See Chapter 2, Methodologies, for more methodologies and the introduction to many of these.

These methods may be followed individually or used in combination. When investigating disk issues, my suggestion is to use the following strategies, in this order: the USE method, performance monitoring, workload characterization, latency analysis, micro-benchmarking, static analysis, and event tracing.

Section 9.6, Observability Tools, shows operating system tools for applying these methods.

9.5.1   Tools Method

The tools method is a process of iterating over available tools, examining key metrics they provide. While a simple methodology, it can overlook issues for which the tools provide poor or no visibility, and it can be time-consuming to perform.

For disks, the tools method can involve checking the following (for Linux):

- **iostat:** Using extended mode to look for busy disks (over 60% utilization), high average service times (over, say, 10 ms), and high IOPS (depends)

- **iotop/biotop:** To identify which process is causing disk I/O

- **biolatency:** To examine the distribution of I/O latency as a histogram, looking for multi-modal distributions and latency outliers (over, say, 100 ms)

- **biosnoop:** To examine individual I/O

- **perf(1)/BCC/bpftrace:** For custom analysis including viewing user and kernel stacks that issued I/O

- **Disk-controller-specific tools** (from the vendor)

If an issue is found, examine all fields from the available tools to learn more context. See Section 9.6, Observability Tools, for more about each tool. Other methodologies can also be used, which can identify more types of issues.

9.5.2   USE Method

The USE method is for identifying bottlenecks and errors across all components, early in a performance investigation. The sections that follow describe how the USE method can be applied to disk devices and controllers, while Section 9.6, Observability Tools, shows tools for measuring specific metrics.

Disk Devices

For each disk device, check for:

- **Utilization:** The time the device was busy
- **Saturation:** The degree to which I/O is waiting in a queue
- **Errors:** Device errors

Errors may be checked first. They sometimes get overlooked because the system functions correctly—albeit more slowly—in spite of disk failures: disks are commonly configured in a redundant pool of disks designed to tolerate some failure. Apart from standard disk error counters from the operating system, disk devices may support a wider variety of error counters that can be retrieved by special tools (for example, SMART data[6]).

If the disk devices are physical disks, utilization should be straightforward to find. If they are virtual disks, utilization may not reflect what the underlying physical disks are doing. See Section 9.3.9, Utilization, for more discussion on this.

Disk Controllers

For each disk controller, check for:

- **Utilization:** Current versus maximum throughput, and the same for operation rate
- **Saturation:** The degree to which I/O is waiting due to controller saturation
- **Errors:** Controller errors

Here the utilization metric is not defined in terms of time, but rather in terms of the limitations of the disk controller card: throughput (bytes per second) and operation rate (operations per second). Operations are inclusive of read/write and other disk commands. Either throughput or operation rate may also be limited by the transport connecting the disk controller to the system, just as it may also be limited by the transport from the controller to the individual disks. Each transport should be checked the same way: errors, utilization, saturation.

You may find that the observability tools (e.g., Linux iostat(1)) do not present per-controller metrics but provide them only per disk. There are workarounds for this: if the system has only one controller, you can determine the controller IOPS and throughput by summing those metrics for all disks. If the system has multiple controllers, you will need to determine which disks belong to which, and sum the metrics accordingly.

Performance of disk controllers and transports is often overlooked. Fortunately, they are not common sources of system bottlenecks, as their capacity typically exceeds that of the attached disks. If total disk throughput or IOPS always levels off at a certain rate, even under different workloads, this may be a clue that the disk controllers or transports are in fact causing the problems.

---

[6] On Linux, see tools such as MegaCLI and smartctl (covered later), cciss-vol-status, cpqarrayd, varmon, and dpt-i2o-raidutils.

9.5.3   Performance Monitoring

Performance monitoring can identify active issues and patterns of behavior over time. Key metrics for disk I/O are:

- Disk utilization
- Response time

Disk utilization at 100% for multiple seconds is very likely an issue. Depending on your environment, over 60% may also cause poor performance due to increased queueing. The value for "normal" or "bad" depends on your workload, environment, and latency requirements. If you aren't sure, micro-benchmarks of known-to-be-good versus bad workloads may be performed to show how these can be found via disk metrics. See Section 9.8, Experimentation.

These metrics should be examined on a per-disk basis, to look for unbalanced workloads and individual poorly performing disks. The response time metric may be monitored as a per-second average and can include other values such as the maximum and standard deviation. Ideally, it would be possible to inspect the full distribution of response times, such as by using a histogram or heat map, to look for latency outliers and other patterns.

If the system imposes disk I/O resource controls, statistics to show if and when these were in use can also be collected. Disk I/O may be a bottleneck as a consequence of the imposed limit, not the activity of the disk itself.

Utilization and response time show the result of disk performance. More metrics may be added to characterize the workload, including IOPS and throughput, providing important data for use in capacity planning (see the next section and Section 9.5.10, Scaling).

9.5.4   Workload Characterization

Characterizing the load applied is an important exercise in capacity planning, benchmarking, and simulating workloads. It can also lead to some of the largest performance gains, by identifying unnecessary work that can be eliminated.

The following are basic attributes for characterizing disk I/O workload:

- I/O rate
- I/O throughput
- I/O size
- Read/write ratio
- Random versus sequential

Random versus sequential, the read/write ratio, and I/O size are described in Section 9.3, Concepts. I/O rate (IOPS) and I/O throughput are defined in Section 9.1, Terminology.

These characteristics can vary from second to second, especially for applications and file systems that buffer and flush writes at intervals. To better characterize the workload, capture maximum values as well as averages. Better still, examine the full distribution of values over time.

Here is an example workload description, to show how these attributes can be expressed together:

> The system disks have a light random read workload, averaging 350 IOPS with a throughput of 3 Mbytes/s, running at 96% reads. There are occasional short bursts of sequential writes, lasting between 2 and 5 seconds, which drive the disks to a maximum of 4,800 IOPS and 560 Mbytes/s. The reads are around 8 Kbytes in size, and the writes around 128 Kbytes.

Apart from describing these characteristics system-wide, they can also be used to describe per-disk and per-controller I/O workloads.

Advanced Workload Characterization/Checklist

Additional details may be included to characterize the workload. These have been listed here as questions for consideration, which may also serve as a checklist when studying disk issues thoroughly:

- What is the IOPS rate system-wide? Per disk? Per controller?
- What is the throughput system-wide? Per disk? Per controller?
- Which applications or users are using the disks?
- What file systems or files are being accessed?
- Have any errors been encountered? Were they due to invalid requests, or issues on the disk?
- How balanced is the I/O over available disks?
- What is the IOPS for each transport bus involved?
- What is the throughput for each transport bus involved?
- What non-data-transfer disk commands are being issued?
- Why is disk I/O issued (kernel call path)?
- To what degree is disk I/O application-synchronous?
- What is the distribution of I/O arrival times?

IOPS and throughput questions can be posed for reads and writes separately. Any of these may also be checked over time, to look for maximums, minimums, and time-based variations. Also see Chapter 2, Methodologies, Section 2.5.11, Workload Characterization, which provides a higher-level summary of the characteristics to measure (who, why, what, how).

Performance Characterization

The previous workload characterization lists examine the workload applied. The following examines the resulting performance:

- How busy is each disk (utilization)?
- How saturated is each disk with I/O (wait queueing)?
- What is the average I/O service time?

- What is the average I/O wait time?
- Are there I/O outliers with high latency?
- What is the full distribution of I/O latency?
- Are system resource controls, such as I/O throttling, present and active?
- What is the latency of non data-transfer disk commands?

Event Tracing

Tracing tools can be used to record all file system operations and details to a log for later analysis (e.g., Section 9.6.7, biosnoop). This can include the disk device ID, I/O or command type, offset, size, issue and completion timestamps, completion status, and originating process ID and name (when possible). With the issue and completion timestamps, the I/O latency can be calculated (or it can be directly included in the log). By studying the sequence of request and completion timestamps, I/O reordering by the device can also be identified. While this may be the ultimate tool for workload characterization, in practice it may cost noticeable overhead to capture and save, depending on the rate of disk operations. If the disk writes for the event trace are included in the trace, it may not only pollute the trace, but also create a feedback loop and a performance problem.

9.5.5   Latency Analysis

Latency analysis involves drilling deeper into the system to find the source of latency. With disks, this will often end at the disk interface: the time between an I/O request and the completion interrupt. If this matches the I/O latency at the application level, it's usually safe to assume that the I/O latency originates from the disks, allowing you to focus your investigation on them. If the latency differs, measuring it at different levels of the operating system stack will identify the origin.

Figure 9.10 pictures a generic I/O stack, with the latency shown at different levels of two I/O outliers, A and B.

The latency of I/O A is similar at each level from the application down to the disk drivers. This correlation points to the disks (or the disk driver) as the cause of the latency. This could be inferred if the layers were measured independently, based on the similar latency values between them.

The latency of B appears to originate at the file system level (locking or queueing?), with the I/O latency at lower levels contributing much less time. Be aware that different layers of the stack may inflate or deflate I/O, which means the size, count, and latency will differ from one layer to the next. The B example may be a case of only observing one I/O at the lower levels (of 10 ms), but failing to account for other related I/O that occurred to service the same file system I/O (e.g., metadata).

The latency at each level may be presented as:

- **Per-interval I/O averages:** As typically reported by operating system tools.
- **Full I/O distributions:** As histograms or heat maps; see Section 9.7.3, Latency Heat Maps.
- **Per-I/O latency values:** See the earlier Event Tracing section.

The last two are useful for tracking the origin of outliers and can help identify cases where I/O has been split or coalesced.

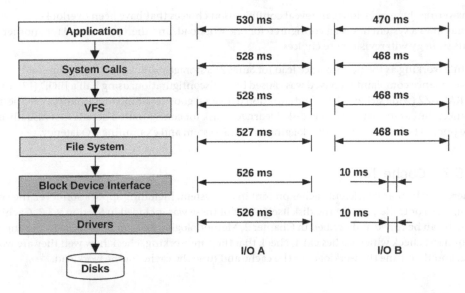

Figure 9.10   Stack latency analysis

9.5.6   Static Performance Tuning

Static performance tuning focuses on issues of the configured environment. For disk performance, examine the following aspects of the static configuration:

- How many disks are present? Of which types (e.g., SMR, MLC)? Sizes?
- What version is the disk firmware?
- How many disk controllers are present? Of which interface types?
- Are disk controller cards connected to high-speed slots?
- How many disks are connected to each HBA?
- If disk/controller battery backups are present, what is their power level?
- What version is the disk controller firmware?
- Is RAID configured? How exactly, including stripe width?
- Is multipathing available and configured?
- What version is the disk device driver?
- What is the server main memory size? In use by the page and buffer caches?
- Are there operating system bugs/patches for any of the storage device drivers?
- Are there resource controls in use for disk I/O?

Be aware that performance bugs may exist in device drivers and firmware, which are ideally fixed by updates from the vendor.

Answering these questions can reveal configuration choices that have been overlooked. Sometimes a system has been configured for one workload, and then repurposed for another. This strategy will revisit those choices.

While working as the performance lead for Sun's ZFS storage product, the most common performance complaint I received was caused by a misconfiguration: using half a JBOD (12 disks) of RAID-Z2 (wide stripes). This configuration delivered good reliability but unimpressive performance, similar to that of a single disk. I learned to ask for configuration details first (usually over the phone) before spending time logging in to the system and examining I/O latency.

9.5.7   Cache Tuning

There may be many different caches present in the system, including application-level, file system, disk controller, and on the disk itself. A list of these was included in Section 9.3.3, Caching, which can be tuned as described in Chapter 2, Methodologies, Section 2.5.18, Cache Tuning. In summary, check which caches exist, check that they are working, check how well they are working, and then tune the workload for the cache and tune the cache for the workload.

9.5.8   Resource Controls

The operating system may provide controls for allocating disk I/O resources to processes or groups of processes. These may include fixed limits for IOPS and throughput, or shares for a more flexible approach. How these work are implementation-specific, as discussed in Section 9.9, Tuning.

9.5.9   Micro-Benchmarking

Micro-benchmarking disk I/O was introduced in Chapter 8, File Systems, which explains the difference between testing file system I/O and testing disk I/O. Here we would like to test disk I/O, which usually means testing via the operating system's device paths, particularly the raw device path if available, to avoid all file system behavior (including caching, buffering, I/O splitting, I/O coalescing, code path overheads, and offset mapping differences).

Factors for micro-benchmarking include:

- **Direction**: Reads or writes
- **Disk offset pattern**: Random or sequential
- **Range of offsets**: Full disk or tight ranges (e.g., offset 0 only)
- **I/O size**: 512 bytes (typical minimum) up to 1 Mbyte
- **Concurrency**: Number of I/O in flight, or number of threads performing I/O
- **Number of devices**: Single disk tests, or multiple disks (to explore controller and bus limits)

The next two sections show how these factors can be combined to test disk and disk controller performance. See Section 9.8, Experimentation, for details of the specific tools that can be used to perform these tests.

Disks

Micro-benchmarking can be performed on a per-disk basis to determine the following, along with suggested workloads:

- **Maximum disk throughput** (Mbytes per second): 128 Kbyte or 1 Mbyte reads, sequential
- **Maximum disk operation rate** (IOPS): 512-byte reads,[7] offset 0 only
- **Maximum disk random reads** (IOPS): 512-byte reads, random offsets
- **Read latency profile** (average microseconds): Sequential reads, repeat for 512 bytes, 1K, 2K, 4K, and so on
- **Random I/O latency profile** (average microseconds): 512-byte reads, repeat for full offset span, beginning offsets only, end offsets only

These tests can be repeated for writes. The use of "offset 0 only" is intended to cache the data in the on-disk cache, so that cache access time can be measured.[8]

Disk Controllers

Disk controllers may be micro-benchmarked by applying a workload to multiple disks, designed to hit limits in the controller. These tests may be performed using the following, along with suggested workloads for the disks:

- **Maximum controller throughput** (Mbytes per second): 128 Kbytes, offset 0 only
- **Maximum controller operation rate** (IOPS): 512-byte reads, offset 0 only

Apply the workload to the disks one by one, watching for limits. It may take over a dozen disks to find the limit in a disk controller.

9.5.10 Scaling

Disks and disk controllers have throughput and IOPS limits, which can be demonstrated via micro-benchmarking as described previously. Tuning can improve performance only up to these limits. If more disk performance is needed, and other strategies such as caching won't work, the disks will need to scale.

Here is a simple method, based on capacity planning of resources:

1. Determine the target disk workload, in terms of throughput and IOPS. If this is a new system, see Chapter 2, Methodologies, Section 2.7, Capacity Planning. If the system already has a workload, express the user population in terms of current disk throughput and IOPS, and scale these numbers to the target user population. (If cache is not scaled at the same time, the disk workload may increase, because the cache-per-user ratio becomes smaller.)

2. Calculate the number of disks required to support this workload. Factor in RAID configuration. Do not use the maximum throughput and IOPS values per disk, as this would

---

[7] This size is intended to match the smallest disk block size. Many disks today use 4 Kbytes.

[8] I've heard a rumor that some drive manufacturers have firmware routines to accelerate sector 0 I/O, inflating performance for such a test. You can verify by testing sector 0 versus sector *your_favorite_number*.

result in driving disks at 100% utilization, leading to immediate performance issues due to saturation and queueing. Pick a target utilization (say, 50%) and scale values accordingly.

3. Calculate the number of disk controllers required to support this workload.

4. Check that transport limits have not been exceeded, and scale transports if necessary.

5. Calculate CPU cycles per disk I/O, and the number of CPUs required (this may necessitate multiple CPUs and parallel I/O).

The maximum per-disk throughput and IOPS numbers used will depend on their type and the disk type. See Section 9.3.7, IOPS Are Not Equal. Micro-benchmarking can be used to find specific limits for a given I/O size and I/O type, and workload characterization can be used on existing workloads to see which sizes and types matter.

To deliver the disk workload requirement, it's not uncommon to find servers requiring dozens of disks, connected via storage arrays. We used to say, "Add more spindles." We may now say, "Add more flash."

9.6 Observability Tools

This section introduces disk I/O observability tools for Linux-based operating systems. See the previous section for strategies to follow when using them.

The tools in this section are listed in Table 9.5.

Table 9.5 **Disk observability tools**

Section	Tool	Description
9.6.1	iostat	Various per-disk statistics
9.6.2	sar	Historical disk statistics
9.6.3	PSI	Disk pressure stall information
9.6.4	pidstat	Disk I/O usage by process
9.6.5	perf	Record block I/O tracepoints
9.6.6	biolatency	Summarize disk I/O latency as a histogram
9.6.7	biosnoop	Trace disk I/O with PID and latency
9.6.8	iotop, biotop	Top for disks: summarize disk I/O by process
9.6.9	biostacks	Show disk I/O with initialization stacks
9.6.10	blktrace	Disk I/O event tracing
9.6.11	bpftrace	Custom disk tracing
9.6.12	MegaCli	LSI controller statistics
9.6.13	smartctl	Disk controller statistics

This is a selection of tools to support Section 9.5, Methodology, beginning with traditional tools and statistics, then tracing tools, and finally disk controller statistics. Some of the traditional tools are likely available on other Unix-like operating systems where they originated, including: iostat(8) and sar(1). Many of the tracing tools are BPF-based, and use BCC and bpftrace frontends (Chapter 15); they are: biolatency(8), biosnoop(8), biotop(8), and biostacks(8).

See the documentation for each tool, including its man pages, for full references of its features.

9.6.1   iostat

iostat(1) summarizes per-disk I/O statistics, providing metrics for workload characterization, utilization, and saturation. It can be executed by any user and is typically the first command used to investigate disk I/O issues at the command line. The statistics it provides are also typically shown by monitoring software, so it can be worthwhile to learn iostat(1) in detail to deepen your understanding of monitoring statistics. These statistics are enabled by default by the kernel,[9] so the overhead of this tool is considered negligible.

The name "iostat" is short for "I/O statistics," although it might have been better to call it "diskiostat" to reflect the type of I/O it reports. This has led to occasional confusion when a user knows that an application is performing I/O (to the file system) but wonders why it can't be seen via iostat(1) (the disks).

iostat(1) was written in the early 1980s for Unix, and different versions are available on the different operating systems. It can be added to Linux-based systems via the sysstat package. The following describes the Linux version.

iostat Default Output

Without any arguments or options, a summary-since-boot for CPU and disk statistics is printed. It's covered here as an introduction to this tool; however, you are not expected to use this mode, as the extended mode covered later is more useful.

```
$ iostat
Linux 5.3.0-1010-aws (ip-10-1-239-218)    02/12/20      _x86_64_   (2 CPU)

avg-cpu:   %user   %nice %system %iowait  %steal   %idle
           0.29    0.01    0.18    0.03    0.21   99.28

Device            tps    kB_read/s    kB_wrtn/s    kB_read    kB_wrtn
loop0            0.00         0.05         0.00       1232          0
[...]
nvme0n1          3.40        17.11        36.03     409902     863344
```

The first output line is a summary of the system, including the kernel version, host name, date, architecture, and CPU count. Subsequent lines show summary-since-boot statistics for the CPUs (avg-cpu; these statistics were covered in Chapter 6, CPUs) and disk devices (under Device:).

---

[9] Statistics can be disabled via the /sys/block/<dev>/queue/iostats file. I don't know of anyone ever doing so.

Each disk device is shown as a row, with basic details in the columns. I've highlighted the column headers in bold; they are:

- **tps**: Transactions per second (IOPS)
- **kB_read/s**, **kB_wrtn/s**: Kilobytes read per second, and written per second
- **kB_read**, **kB_wrtn**: Total kilobytes read and written

Some SCSI devices, including CD-ROMs, may not be shown by iostat(1). SCSI tape drives can be examined using tapestat(1) instead, also in the sysstat package. Also note that, while iostat(1) reports block device reads and writes, it may exclude some other types of disk device commands depending on the kernel (see the logic in the kernel function blk_do_io_stat()). The iostat(1) extended mode includes extra fields for these device commands.

iostat Options

iostat(1) can be executed with various options, followed by an optional interval and count. For example:

```
# iostat 1 10
```

will print one-second summaries ten times. And:

```
# iostat 1
```

will print one-second summaries without end (until Ctrl-C is typed).

Commonly used options are:

- **-c**: Display CPU report
- **-d**: Display disk report
- **-k**: Use kilobytes instead of (512-byte) blocks
- **-m**: Use megabytes instead of (512-byte) blocks
- **-p**: Include per-partition statistics
- **-t**: Timestamp output
- **-x**: Extended statistics
- **-s**: Short (narrow) output
- **-z**: Skip displaying zero-activity summaries

There is also an environment variable, POSIXLY_CORRECT=1, to output blocks (512 bytes each) instead of Kbytes. Some older versions included an option for NFS statistics, -n. Since sysstat version 9.1.3, this was moved to the separate nfsiostat command.

iostat Extended Short Output

Extended output (-x) provides extra columns that are useful for the methodologies covered earlier. These extra columns include IOPS and throughput metrics for workload characterization, utilization and queue lengths for the USE method, and disk response times for performance characterization and latency analysis.

Over the years, the extended output has gained more and more fields, and the latest release (12.3.1, Dec. 2019) produces output that is 197 characters wide. This not only does not fit in this book, it does not fit in many wide terminals either, making the output difficult to read due to line wraps. A solution was added in 2017, the -s option, to provide a "short" or narrow output that is intended to fit within an 80-character width.

Here is an example of short (-s) extended (-x) statistics, and skipping zero-activity devices (-z):

```
$ iostat -sxz 1
[...]
avg-cpu:  %user   %nice %system %iowait  %steal   %idle
          15.82    0.00   10.71   31.63    1.53   40.31


Device             tps     kB/s    rqm/s   await aqu-sz  areq-sz  %util
nvme0n1        1642.00  9064.00   664.00    0.44   0.00     5.52 100.00
[...]
```

The disk columns are:

- **tps**: Transactions issued per second (IOPS)

- **kB/s**: Kbytes per second

- **rqm/s**: Requests queued and merged per second

- **await**: Average I/O response time, including time queued in the OS and the I/O response time of the device (ms)

- **aqu-sz**: Average number of requests both waiting in the driver request queue and active on the device

- **areq-sz**: Average request size in Kbytes

- **%util**: Percent of time the device was busy processing I/O requests (utilization)

The most important metric for delivered performance is await, showing the average total wait time for I/O. What constitutes "good" or "bad" depends on your needs. In the example output, await was 0.44 ms, which is satisfactory for this database server. It can increase for a number of reasons: queueing (load), larger I/O sizes, random I/O on rotational devices, and device errors.

For resource usage and capacity planning, %util is important, but bear in mind that it is only a measure of busyness (non-idle time) and may mean little for virtual devices backed by multiple disks. Those devices may be better understood by the load applied: tps (IOPS) and kB/s (throughput).

Nonzero counts in the rqm/s column show that contiguous requests were merged before delivery to the device, to improve performance. This metric is also a sign of a sequential workload.

Since areq-sz is after merging, small sizes (8 Kbytes or less) are an indicator of a random I/O workload that could not be merged. Large sizes may be either large I/O or a merged sequential workload (indicated by earlier columns).

iostat Extended Output

Without the -s option, -x prints many more columns. Here is the summary since boot (no interval or count) for sysstat version 12.3.2 (from Apr 2020):

```
$ iostat -x
[...]
Device              r/s      rkB/s    rrqm/s  %rrqm r_await rareq-sz     w/s      wkB/s
wrqm/s  %wrqm w_await wareq-sz    d/s      dkB/s    drqm/s  %drqm d_await dareq-sz
f/s f_await  aqu-sz  %util
nvme0n1            0.23       9.91      0.16  40.70    0.56   43.01     3.10      33.09
0.92   22.91    0.89   10.66    0.00       0.00      0.00   0.00    0.00     0.00
0.00     0.00    0.00    0.12
```

These break down many of the -sx metrics into read and write components, and also includes discards and flushes.

The extra columns are:

- **r/s, w/s, d/s, f/s**: Read, write, discard, and flush requests completed from the disk device per second (after merges)

- **rkB/s, wkB/s, dkB/s**: Read, write, and discard Kbytes from the disk device per second

- **%rrqm/s, %wrqm/s, %drqm/s**: Read, write, and discard requests queued and merged as a percentage of the total requests for that type

- **r_await, w_await, d_await, f_await**: Read, write, discard, and flush average response time, including time queued in the OS and the response time from the device (ms)

- **rareq-sz, wareq-sz, dareq-sz**: Read, write, and discard average size (Kbytes)

Examining reads and writes separately is important. Applications and file systems commonly use techniques to mitigate write latency (e.g., write-back caching), so the application is less likely to be blocked on disk writes. This means that any metrics that group reads and writes are skewed by a component that may not directly matter (the writes). By splitting them, you can start examining r_wait, which shows average read latency, and is likely to be the most important metric for application performance.

The reads and writes as IOPS (r/s, w/s) and throughput (rkB/s, wkB/s) are important for workload characterization.

The discard and flush statistics are new additions to iostat(1). Discard operations free up blocks on the drive (the ATA TRIM command), and their statistics were added in the Linux 4.19 kernel. Flush statistics were added in Linux 5.5. These can help to narrow down the reason for disk latency.

Here is another useful iostat(1) combination:

```
$ iostat -dmstxz -p ALL 1
Linux 5.3.0-1010-aws (ip-10-1-239-218)      02/12/20       _x86_64_   (2 CPU)
```

```
02/12/20 17:39:29
Device             tps     MB/s    rqm/s   await   areq-sz  aqu-sz  %util
nvme0n1           3.33     0.04     1.09    0.87     12.84    0.00    0.12
nvme0n1p1         3.31     0.04     1.09    0.87     12.91    0.00    0.12

02/12/20 17:39:30
Device             tps     MB/s    rqm/s   await   areq-sz  aqu-sz  %util
nvme0n1        1730.00    14.97   709.00    0.54      8.86    0.02   99.60
nvme0n1p1      1538.00    14.97   709.00    0.61      9.97    0.02   99.60
[...]
```

The first output is the summary since boot, followed by one-second intervals. The -d focuses on disk statistics only (no CPU), -m for Mbytes, and -t for the timestamp, which can be useful when comparing the output to other timestamped sources, and -p ALL includes per-partition statistics.

Unfortunately, the current version of iostat(1) does not include disk errors; otherwise all USE method metrics could be checked from one tool!

9.6.2   sar

The system activity reporter, sar(1), can be used to observe current activity and can be configured to archive and report historical statistics. It is introduced in Section 4.4, sar, and mentioned in various other chapters in this book for the different statistics it provides.

The sar(1) disk summary is printed using the -d option, demonstrated in the following examples with an interval of one second. The output is wide, so it is included here in two parts (sysstat 12.3.2):

```
$ sar -d 1
Linux 5.3.0-1010-aws (ip-10-0-239-218)     02/13/20        _x86_64_   (2 CPU)

09:10:22          DEV      tps     rkB/s     wkB/s    dkB/s   areq-sz \ ...
09:10:23      dev259-0  1509.00  11100.00  12776.00    0.00     15.82 / ...
[...]
```

Here are the remaining columns:

```
$ sar -d 1
09:10:22      \ ... \   aqu-sz    await    %util
09:10:23      / ... /     0.02     0.60    94.00
[...]
```

These columns also appear in iostat(1) -x output, and were described in the previous section. This output shows a mixed read/write workload with an await of 0.6 ms, driving the disk to 94% utilization.

Previous versions of sar(1) included a svctm (service time) column: the average (inferred) disk response time, in milliseconds. See Section 9.3.1, Measuring Time, for background on service time. Since its simplistic calculation was no longer accurate for modern disks that perform I/O in parallel, svctm has been removed in later versions.

9.6.3   PSI

Linux pressure stall information (PSI), added in Linux 4.20, includes statistics for I/O saturation. These not only show if there is I/O pressure, but how it is changing over the last five minutes. Example output:

```
# cat /proc/pressure/io
some avg10=63.11 avg60=32.18 avg300=8.62 total=667212021
full avg10=60.76 avg60=31.13 avg300=8.35 total=622722632
```

This output shows that I/O pressure is increasing, with a higher 10-second average (63.11) than the 300-second average (8.62). These averages are percentages of time that a task was I/O stalled. The some line shows when some tasks (threads) were affected, and the full line shows when all runnable tasks were affected.

As with load averages, this can be a high-level metric used for alerting. Once you become aware that there is a disk performance issue, you can use other tools to find the root causes, including pidstat(8) for disk statistics by process.

9.6.4   pidstat

The Linux pidstat(1) tool prints CPU usage by default and includes a -d option for disk I/O statistics. This is available on kernels 2.6.20 and later. For example:

```
$ pidstat -d 1
Linux 5.3.0-1010-aws (ip-10-0-239-218)     02/13/20        _x86_64_   (2 CPU)

09:47:41      UID      PID    kB_rd/s    kB_wr/s kB_ccwr/s iodelay  Command
09:47:42        0     2705   32468.00       0.00      0.00       5  tar
09:47:42        0     2706       0.00    8192.00      0.00       0  gzip

[...]
09:47:56      UID      PID    kB_rd/s    kB_wr/s kB_ccwr/s iodelay  Command
09:47:57        0      229       0.00      72.00      0.00       0  systemd-journal
09:47:57        0      380       0.00       4.00      0.00       0  auditd
09:47:57        0     2699       4.00       0.00      0.00      10  kworker/
u4:1-flush-259:0
09:47:57        0     2705   15104.00       0.00      0.00       0  tar
09:47:57        0     2706       0.00    6912.00      0.00       0  gzip
```

Columns include:

- **kB_rd/s**: Kilobytes read per second
- **kB_wd/s**: Kilobytes issued for write per second
- **kB_ccwr/s**: Kilobytes canceled for write per second (e.g., overwritten or deleted before flush)
- **iodelay**: The time the process was blocked on disk I/O (clock ticks), including swapping

The workload seen in the output was a `tar` command reading the file system to a pipe, and `gzip` reading the pipe and writing a compressed archive file. The `tar` reads caused iodelay (5 clock ticks), whereas the `gzip` writes did not, due to write-back caching in the page cache. Some time later the page cache was flushed, as can be seen in the second interval output by the `kworker/u4:1-flush-259:0` process, which experienced iodelay.

iodelay is a recent addition and shows the magnitude of performance issues: how much the application waited. The other columns show the workload applied.

Note that only superusers (root) can access disk statistics for processes that they do not own. These are read via /proc/PID/io.

9.6.5 perf

The Linux perf(1) tool (Chapter 13) can record block tracepoints. Listing them:

```
# perf list 'block:*'

List of pre-defined events (to be used in -e):

  block:block_bio_backmerge                          [Tracepoint event]
  block:block_bio_bounce                             [Tracepoint event]
  block:block_bio_complete                           [Tracepoint event]
  block:block_bio_frontmerge                         [Tracepoint event]
  block:block_bio_queue                              [Tracepoint event]
  block:block_bio_remap                              [Tracepoint event]
  block:block_dirty_buffer                           [Tracepoint event]
  block:block_getrq                                  [Tracepoint event]
  block:block_plug                                   [Tracepoint event]
  block:block_rq_complete                            [Tracepoint event]
  block:block_rq_insert                              [Tracepoint event]
  block:block_rq_issue                               [Tracepoint event]
  block:block_rq_remap                               [Tracepoint event]
  block:block_rq_requeue                             [Tracepoint event]
  block:block_sleeprq                                [Tracepoint event]
  block:block_split                                  [Tracepoint event]
  block:block_touch_buffer                           [Tracepoint event]
  block:block_unplug                                 [Tracepoint event]
```

For example, the following records block device issues with stack traces. A `sleep 10` command is provided as the duration of tracing.

```
# perf record -e block:block_rq_issue -a -g sleep 10
[ perf record: Woken up 22 times to write data ]
[ perf record: Captured and wrote 5.701 MB perf.data (19267 samples) ]
# perf script --header
[...]
mysqld  1965 [001] 160501.158573: block:block_rq_issue: 259,0 WS 12288 () 10329704 +
24 [mysqld]
        ffffffffb12d5040 blk_mq_start_request+0xa0 ([kernel.kallsyms])
        ffffffffb12d5040 blk_mq_start_request+0xa0 ([kernel.kallsyms])
        ffffffffb1532b4c nvme_queue_rq+0x16c ([kernel.kallsyms])
        ffffffffb12d7b46 __blk_mq_try_issue_directly+0x116 ([kernel.kallsyms])
        ffffffffb12d87bb blk_mq_request_issue_directly+0x4b ([kernel.kallsyms])
        ffffffffb12d8896 blk_mq_try_issue_list_directly+0x46 ([kernel.kallsyms])
        ffffffffb12dce7e blk_mq_sched_insert_requests+0xae ([kernel.kallsyms])
        ffffffffb12d86c8 blk_mq_flush_plug_list+0x1e8 ([kernel.kallsyms])
        ffffffffb12cd623 blk_flush_plug_list+0xe3 ([kernel.kallsyms])
        ffffffffb12cd676 blk_finish_plug+0x26 ([kernel.kallsyms])
        ffffffffb119771c ext4_writepages+0x77c ([kernel.kallsyms])
        ffffffffb10209c3 do_writepages+0x43 ([kernel.kallsyms])
        ffffffffb1017ed5 __filemap_fdatawrite_range+0xd5 ([kernel.kallsyms])
        ffffffffb10186ca file_write_and_wait_range+0x5a ([kernel.kallsyms])
        ffffffffb118637f ext4_sync_file+0x8f ([kernel.kallsyms])
        ffffffffb1105869 vfs_fsync_range+0x49 ([kernel.kallsyms])
        ffffffffb11058fd do_fsync+0x3d ([kernel.kallsyms])
        ffffffffb1105944 __x64_sys_fsync+0x14 ([kernel.kallsyms])
        ffffffffb0e044ca do_syscall_64+0x5a ([kernel.kallsyms])
        ffffffffb1a0008c entry_SYSCALL_64_after_hwframe+0x44 ([kernel.kallsyms])
            7f2285d1988b fsync+0x3b (/usr/lib/x86_64-linux-gnu/libpthread-2.30.so)
            55ac10a05ebe Fil_shard::redo_space_flush+0x44e (/usr/sbin/mysqld)
            55ac10a06179 Fil_shard::flush_file_redo+0x99 (/usr/sbin/mysqld)
            55ac1076ff1c [unknown] (/usr/sbin/mysqld)
            55ac10777030 log_flusher+0x520 (/usr/sbin/mysqld)
            55ac10748d61
std::thread::_State_impl<std::thread::_Invoker<std::tuple<Runnable, void (*)(log_t*),
log_t*> > >::_M_run+0xc1 (/usr/sbin/mysql
            7f228559df74 [unknown] (/usr/lib/x86_64-linux-gnu/libstdc++.so.6.0.28)
            7f226c3652c0 [unknown] ([unknown])
            55ac107499f0
std::thread::_State_impl<std::thread::_Invoker<std::tuple<Runnable, void (*)(log_t*),
log_t*> > >::~_State_impl+0x0 (/usr/sbin/
          5441554156415741 [unknown] ([unknown])
[...]
```

The output is a one-line summary for each event, followed by the stack trace that led to it. The one-line summary begins with default fields from perf(1): the process name, thread ID, CPU ID, timestamp, and event name (see Chapter 13, perf, Section 13.11, perf script). The remaining fields are specific to the tracepoint: for this block:block_rq_issue tracepoint, they are, along with the field contents:

- **Disk major and minor numbers:** 259,0
- **I/O type:** WS (synchronous writes)
- **I/O size:** 12288 (bytes)
- **I/O command string:** ()
- **Sector address:** 10329704
- **Number of sectors:** 24
- **Process:** mysqld

These fields are from the format string of the tracepoint (see Chapter 4, Observability Tools, Section 4.3.5, Tracepoints, under Tracepoints Arguments and Format String).

The stack trace can help explain the nature of the disk I/O. In this case, it is from the mysqld log_flusher() routine that called fsync(2). The kernel code path shows it was handled by the ext4 file system, and became a disk I/O issue via blk_mq_try_issue_list_directly().

Often I/O will be queued and then issued later by a kernel thread, and tracing the block:block_rq_issue tracepoint will not show the originating process or user-level stack trace. In those cases you can try tracing block:block_rq_insert instead, which is for queue insertion. Note that it misses I/O that did not queue.

One-Liners

The following one-liners demonstrate using filters with the block tracepoints.

Trace all block completions, of size at least 100 Kbytes, until Ctrl-C[10]:

```
perf record -e block:block_rq_complete --filter 'nr_sector > 200'
```

Trace all block completions, synchronous writes only, until Ctrl-C:

```
perf record -e block:block_rq_complete --filter 'rwbs == "WS"'
```

Trace all block completions, all types of writes, until Ctrl-C:

```
perf record -e block:block_rq_complete --filter 'rwbs ~ "*W*"'
```

Disk I/O Latency

Disk I/O latency (described earlier as *disk request time*) can also be determined by recording both the disk issue and completion events for later analysis. The following records them for 60 seconds then writes the events to a out.disk01.txt file:

---

[10]With a sector size of 512 bytes, 100 Kbytes means 200 sectors.

```
perf record -e block:block_rq_issue,block:block_rq_complete -a sleep 60
perf script --header > out.disk01.txt
```

You can post-process the output file using whatever is convenient: awk(1), Perl, Python, R, Google Spreadsheets, etc. Associate issues with completions and use the recorded timestamps to calculate the latency.

The following tools, biolatency(8) and biosnoop(8), calculate disk I/O latency efficiently in kernel space using a BPF program, and include the latency directly in the output.

9.6.6   biolatency

biolatency(8)[11] is a BCC and bpftrace tool to show disk I/O latency as a histogram. The term *I/O latency* used here refers to the time from issuing a request to the device, to when it completes (aka disk request time).

The following shows biolatency(8) from BCC tracing block I/O for 10 seconds:

```
# biolatency 10 1
Tracing block device I/O... Hit Ctrl-C to end.

     usecs               : count    distribution
         0 -> 1          : 0        |                                        |
         2 -> 3          : 0        |                                        |
         4 -> 7          : 0        |                                        |
         8 -> 15         : 0        |                                        |
        16 -> 31         : 2        |                                        |
        32 -> 63         : 0        |                                        |
        64 -> 127        : 0        |                                        |
       128 -> 255        : 1065     |****************                        |
       256 -> 511        : 2462     |****************************************|
       512 -> 1023       : 1949     |*******************************         |
      1024 -> 2047       : 373      |******                                  |
      2048 -> 4095       : 1815     |*****************************           |
      4096 -> 8191       : 591      |*********                               |
      8192 -> 16383      : 397      |******                                  |
     16384 -> 32767      : 50       |                                        |
```

This output shows a bi-modal distribution, with one mode between 128 and 1023 microseconds, and another between 2048 and 4095 microseconds (2.0 to 4.1 milliseconds.) Now that I know that the device latency is bi-modal, understanding why may lead to tuning that moves more I/O to the faster mode. For example, the slower I/O could be random I/O or larger-sized I/O (which

---

[11] Origin: I created biolatency for BCC on 20-Sep-2015 and bpftrace on 13-Sep-2018, based on an earlier iolatency tool I developed. I added the "b" to these tools to make it clear it refers to block I/O.

can be determined using other BPF tools), or different I/O flags (shown using the **-F** option). The slowest I/O in this output reached the 16- to 32-millisecond range: this sounds like queueing on the device.

The BCC version of biolatency(8) supports options including:

- **-m**: Output in milliseconds
- **-Q**: Include OS queued I/O time (*OS request time*)
- **-F**: Show a histogram for each I/O flag set
- **-D**: Show a histogram for each disk device

Using **-Q** makes biolatency(8) report the full I/O time from creation and insertion on a kernel queue to device completion, described earlier as the *block I/O request time*.

The BCC biolatency(8) also accepts optional interval and count arguments, in seconds.

Per-Flag

The **-F** option is especially useful, breaking down the distribution for each I/O flag. For example, with **-m** for millisecond histograms:

```
# biolatency -Fm 10 1
Tracing block device I/O... Hit Ctrl-C to end.

flags = Sync-Write
    msecs              : count    distribution
        0 -> 1         : 2        |****************************************|

flags = Flush
    msecs              : count    distribution
        0 -> 1         : 1        |****************************************|

flags = Write
    msecs              : count    distribution
        0 -> 1         : 14       |****************************************|
        2 -> 3         : 1        |**                                      |
        4 -> 7         : 10       |****************************            |
        8 -> 15        : 11       |*******************************         |
       16 -> 31        : 11       |*******************************         |

flags = NoMerge-Write
    msecs              : count    distribution
        0 -> 1         : 95       |**********                              |
        2 -> 3         : 152      |****************                        |
        4 -> 7         : 266      |****************************            |
        8 -> 15        : 350      |*************************************** |
       16 -> 31        : 298      |********************************        |
```

```
flags = Read
    msecs                  : count    distribution
       0 -> 1              : 11       |****************************************|

flags = ReadAhead-Read
    msecs                  : count    distribution
       0 -> 1              : 5261     |****************************************|
       2 -> 3              : 1238     |*********                               |
       4 -> 7              : 481      |***                                     |
       8 -> 15             : 5        |                                        |
      16 -> 31             : 2        |                                        |
```

These flags may be handled differently by the storage device; separating them allows us to study them in isolation. The previous output shows that writes were slower than reads, and can explain the earlier bi-modal distribution.

biolatency(8) summarizes disk I/O latency. To examine it for each I/O, use biosnoop(8).

9.6.7 biosnoop

biosnoop(8)[12] is a BCC and bpftrace tool that prints a one-line summary for each disk I/O. For example:

```
# biosnoop
TIME(s)        COMM             PID    DISK      T   SECTOR     BYTES    LAT(ms)
0.009165000    jbd2/nvme0n1p1   174    nvme0n1   W   2116272    8192     0.43
0.009612000    jbd2/nvme0n1p1   174    nvme0n1   W   2116288    4096     0.39
0.011836000    mysqld           1948   nvme0n1   W   10434672   4096     0.45
0.012363000    jbd2/nvme0n1p1   174    nvme0n1   W   2116296    8192     0.49
0.012844000    jbd2/nvme0n1p1   174    nvme0n1   W   2116312    4096     0.43
0.016809000    mysqld           1948   nvme0n1   W   10227712   262144   1.82
0.017184000    mysqld           1948   nvme0n1   W   10228224   262144   2.19
0.017679000    mysqld           1948   nvme0n1   W   10228736   262144   2.68
0.018056000    mysqld           1948   nvme0n1   W   10229248   262144   3.05
0.018264000    mysqld           1948   nvme0n1   W   10229760   262144   3.25
0.018657000    mysqld           1948   nvme0n1   W   10230272   262144   3.64
0.018954000    mysqld           1948   nvme0n1   W   10230784   262144   3.93
0.019053000    mysqld           1948   nvme0n1   W   10231296   131072   4.03
0.019731000    jbd2/nvme0n1p1   174    nvme0n1   W   2116320    8192     0.49
0.020243000    jbd2/nvme0n1p1   174    nvme0n1   W   2116336    4096     0.46
0.020593000    mysqld           1948   nvme0n1   R   4495352    4096     0.26
[...]
```

---

[12] Origin: I created the BCC version on 16-Sep-2015, and the bpftrace version on 15-Nov-2017, based on an earlier tool of mine from 2003. The full origin is described in [Gregg 19].

This output shows a write workload to disk nvme0n1, mostly from mysqld, PID 174, with varying I/O sizes. The columns are:

- **TIME(s)**: I/O completion time in seconds
- **COMM**: Process name (if known by this tool)
- **PID**: Process ID (if known by this tool)
- **DISK**: Storage device name
- **T**: Type: R == reads, W == writes
- **SECTOR**: Address on disk in units of 512-byte sectors
- **BYTES**: Size of the I/O request
- **LAT(ms)**: Duration of the I/O from device issue to device completion (disk request time)

Around the middle of the example output is a series of 262,144 byte writes, beginning with a latency of 1.82 ms and increasing in latency for each subsequent I/O, ending with 4.03 ms. This is a pattern I commonly see, and the likely reason can be calculated from another column in the output: TIME(s). If you subtract the LAT(ms) column from the TIME(s) column, you have the starting time of the I/O, and these started around the same time. This appears to be a group of writes that were sent at the same time, queued on the device, and then completed in turn, with increasing latency for each.

By careful examination of the start and end times, reordering on the device can also be identified. Since the output can many thousands of lines, I have often used the R statistical software to plot the output as a scatter plot, to help in identifying these patterns (see Section 9.7, Visualizations).

Outlier Analysis

Here is a method for finding and analyzing latency outliers using biosnoop(8).

1. Write the output to a file:

```
# biosnoop > out.biosnoop01.txt
```

2. Sort the output by the latency column, and print the last five entries (those with the highest latency):

```
# sort -n -k 8,8 out.biosnoop01.txt | tail -5
31.344175    logger        10994    nvme0n1 W 15218056    262144    30.92
31.344401    logger        10994    nvme0n1 W 15217544    262144    31.15
31.344757    logger        10994    nvme0n1 W 15219080    262144    31.49
31.345260    logger        10994    nvme0n1 W 15218568    262144    32.00
46.059274    logger        10994    nvme0n1 W 15198896    4096      64.86
```

3. Open the output in a text editor (e.g., vi(1) or vim(1)):

```
# vi out.biosnoop01.txt
```

4. Work through the outliers from slowest to fastest, searching for the time in the first column. The slowest was 64.86 milliseconds, with the completion time of 46.059274 (seconds). Searching for 46.059274:

```
[...]
45.992419    jbd2/nvme0n1p1  174    nvme0n1  W  2107232    8192    0.45
45.992988    jbd2/nvme0n1p1  174    nvme0n1  W  2107248    4096    0.50
46.059274    logger          10994  nvme0n1  W  15198896   4096    64.86
[...]
```

5. Look at events that occurred prior to the outlier, to see whether they had similar latency and therefore this was the result of queueing (similar to the 1.82 to 4.03 ms ramp seen in the first biosnoop(8) example output), or for any other clues. That's not the case here: the previous event was around 6 ms earlier, with a latency of 0.5 ms. The device may have reordered events and completed the others first. If the previous completion event was around 64 ms ago, then the gap in completions from the device may be explained by other factors: e.g., this system is a VM instance, and can be de-scheduled by the hypervisor during I/O, adding that time to the I/O time.

Queued Time

A -Q option to BCC biosnoop(8) can be used to show the time spent between the creation of the I/O and the issue to the device (previously called the *block I/O wait time* or *OS wait time*). This time is mostly spent on OS queues, but could also include memory allocation and lock acquisition. For example:

```
# biosnoop -Q
TIME(s)      COMM          PID    DISK     T SECTOR     BYTES  QUE(ms) LAT(ms)
0.000000     kworker/u4:0  9491   nvme0n1  W 5726504    4096    0.06    0.60
0.000039     kworker/u4:0  9491   nvme0n1  W 8128536    4096    0.05    0.64
0.000084     kworker/u4:0  9491   nvme0n1  W 8128584    4096    0.05    0.68
0.000138     kworker/u4:0  9491   nvme0n1  W 8128632    4096    0.05    0.74
0.000231     kworker/u4:0  9491   nvme0n1  W 8128664    4096    0.05    0.83
[...]
```

The queued time is shown in the QUE(ms) column.

9.6.8   iotop, biotop

I wrote the first iotop in 2005 for Solaris-based systems [McDougall 06a]. There are now many versions, including a Linux iotop(1) tool based on kernel accounting statistics[13] [Chazarain 13], and my own biotop(8) based on BPF.

---

[13] iotop(1) requires CONFIG_TASK_DELAY_ACCT, CONFIG_TASK_IO_ACCOUNTING, CONFIG_TASKSTATS, and CONFIG_VM_EVENT_COUNTERS.

iotop

iotop can typically be installed via an iotop package. When run without arguments, it refreshes the screen every second, showing the top disk I/O processes. Batch mode (-b) can be used to provide a rolling output (no screen clear); it is demonstrated here with I/O processes only (-o) and an interval of 5 s (-d5):

```
# iotop -bod5
Total DISK READ:       4.78 K/s | Total DISK WRITE:      15.04 M/s
  TID  PRIO  USER     DISK READ  DISK WRITE  SWAPIN     IO    COMMAND
22400 be/4 root       4.78 K/s    0.00 B/s  0.00 % 13.76 % [flush-252:0]
  279 be/3 root       0.00 B/s 1657.27 K/s  0.00 %  9.25 % [jbd2/vda2-8]
22446 be/4 root       0.00 B/s   10.16 M/s  0.00 %  0.00 % beam.smp -K true ...
Total DISK READ:       0.00 B/s | Total DISK WRITE:      10.75 M/s
  TID  PRIO  USER     DISK READ  DISK WRITE  SWAPIN     IO    COMMAND
  279 be/3 root       0.00 B/s    9.55 M/s  0.00 %  0.01 % [jbd2/vda2-8]
22446 be/4 root       0.00 B/s   10.37 M/s  0.00 %  0.00 % beam.smp -K true ...
  646 be/4 root       0.00 B/s  272.71 B/s  0.00 %  0.00 % rsyslogd -n -c 5
[...]
```

The output shows the `beam.smp` process (Riak) performing a disk write workload of around 10 Mbytes/s. The columns include:

- **DISK READ**: Read Kbytes/s
- **DISK WRITE**: Write Kbytes/s
- **SWAPIN**: Percent of time the thread spent waiting for swap-in I/O
- **IO**: Percent of time the thread spent waiting for I/O

iotop(8) supports various other options, including -a for accumulated statistics (instead of per-interval), -p PID to match a process, and -d SEC to set the interval.

I recommend that you test iotop(8) with a known workload and check that the numbers match. I just tried (iotop version 0.6) and found that it greatly undercounts write workloads. You can also use biotop(8), which uses a different instrumentation source and *does* match my test workload.

biotop

biotop(8) is a BCC tool, and is another top(1) for disks. Example output:

```
# biotop
Tracing... Output every 1 secs. Hit Ctrl-C to end

08:04:11 loadavg: 1.48 0.87 0.45 1/287 14547

PID    COMM          D MAJ MIN DISK    I/O  Kbytes  AVGms
14501  cksum         R 202 1   xvda1   361  28832   3.39
```

```
6961    dd                R 202 1    xvda1    1628    13024    0.59
13855   dd                R 202 1    xvda1    1627    13016    0.59
326     jbd2/xvda1-8      W 202 1    xvda1       3      168    3.00
1880    supervise         W 202 1    xvda1       2        8    6.71
1873    supervise         W 202 1    xvda1       2        8    2.51
1871    supervise         W 202 1    xvda1       2        8    1.57
1876    supervise         W 202 1    xvda1       2        8    1.22
[...]
```

This shows cksum(1) and dd(1) commands performing reads, and supervise processes performing some writes. This is a quick way to identify who is performing disk I/O, and by how much. The columns are:

- **PID**: Cached process ID (best effort)

- **COMM**: Cached process name (best effort)

- **D**: Direction (R == read, W == write)

- **MAJ MIN**: Disk major and minor numbers (a kernel identifier)

- **DISK**: Disk name

- **I/O**: Number of disk I/O during interval

- **Kbytes**: Total disk throughput during interval (Kbytes)

- **AVGms**: Average time for the I/O (latency) from the issue to the device, to its completion (milliseconds)

By the time disk I/O is issued to the device, the requesting process may no longer be on CPU, and identifying it can be difficult. biotop(8) uses a best-effort approach: the PID and COMM columns will usually match the correct process, but this is not guaranteed.

biotop(8) supports optional interval and count columns (the default interval is one second), -C to not clear the screen, and -r MAXROWS to specify the top number of processes to display.

9.6.9   biostacks

biostacks(8)[14] is a bpftrace tool that traces the block I/O request time (from OS enqueue to device completion) with the I/O initialization stack trace. For example:

```
# biostacks.bt
Attaching 5 probes...
Tracing block I/O with init stacks. Hit Ctrl-C to end.
^C
[...]
```

---

14 Origin: I created it on 19-Mar-2019 for [Gregg 19].

```
@usecs[
    blk_account_io_start+1
    blk_mq_make_request+1069
    generic_make_request+292
    submit_bio+115
    submit_bh_wbc+384
    ll_rw_block+173
    ext4_bread+102
    __ext4_read_dirblock+52
    ext4_dx_find_entry+145
    ext4_find_entry+365
    ext4_lookup+129
    lookup_slow+171
    walk_component+451
    path_lookupat+132
    filename_lookup+182
    user_path_at_empty+54
    sys_access+175
    do_syscall_64+115
    entry_SYSCALL_64_after_hwframe+61
]:
[2K, 4K)             2 |@@                                                      |
[4K, 8K)            37 |@@@@@@@@@@@@@@@@@@@@@@@@@@@@@@@@@@@@@@@@@@@@@@@@@@@@@@@@@@@|
[8K, 16K)           15 |@@@@@@@@@@@@@@@@@@@@@@                                   |
[16K, 32K)           9 |@@@@@@@@@@@@@                                           |
[32K, 64K)           1 |@                                                       |
```

The output shows a latency histogram (in microseconds) for disk I/O, along with the requesting I/O stack: via the access(2) syscall, filename_lookup(), and ext4_lookup(). This I/O was caused by looking up pathnames during file permission checks. The output included many such stacks, and these show that I/O are caused by activity other than reads and writes.

I have seen cases where there was mysterious disk I/O without any application causing it. The reason turned out to be background file system tasks. (In one case it was ZFS's background scrubber, which periodically verifies checksums.) biostacks(8) can identify the real reason for disk I/O by showing the kernel stack trace.

9.6.10 blktrace

blktrace(8) is a custom tracing facility for block device I/O events on Linux that uses the kernel blktrace tracer. This is a specialized tracer controlled via BLKTRACE ioctl(2) syscalls to disk device files. The frontend tools include blktrace(8), blkparse(1), and btrace(8).

blktrace(8) enables kernel block driver tracing and retrieves the raw trace data, which can be processed using blkparse(1). For convenience, the btrace(8) tool runs both blktrace(8) and blkparse(1), such that the following are equivalent:

```
# blktrace -d /dev/sda -o - | blkparse -i -
# btrace /dev/sda
```

blktrace(8) is a low-level tool that shows multiple events per I/O.

Default Output

The following shows the default output of btrace(8) and captures a single disk read event by the cksum(1) command:

```
# btrace /dev/sdb
  8,16   3        1     0.429604145 20442  A   R 184773879 + 8 <- (8,17) 184773816
  8,16   3        2     0.429604569 20442  Q   R 184773879 + 8 [cksum]
  8,16   3        3     0.429606014 20442  G   R 184773879 + 8 [cksum]
  8,16   3        4     0.429607624 20442  P   N [cksum]
  8,16   3        5     0.429608804 20442  I   R 184773879 + 8 [cksum]
  8,16   3        6     0.429610501 20442  U   N [cksum] 1
  8,16   3        7     0.429611912 20442  D   R 184773879 + 8 [cksum]
  8,16   1        1     0.440227144     0  C   R 184773879 + 8 [0]
[...]
```

Eight lines of output were reported for this single disk I/O, showing each action (event) involving the block device queue and the device.

By default, there are seven columns:

1. Device major, minor number

2. CPU ID

3. Sequence number

4. Action time, in seconds

5. Process ID

6. Action identifier: the type of event (see the Action Identifiers heading)

7. RWBS description: I/O flags (see the RWBS Description heading)

These output columns may be customized using the -f option. They are followed by custom data based on the action.

The final data depends on the action. For example, 184773879 + 8 [cksum] means an I/O at block address 184773879 with size 8 (sectors), from the process named cksum.

Action Identifiers

These are described in the blkparse(1) man page:

A	IO was remapped to a different device
B	IO bounced
C	IO completion
D	IO issued to driver
F	IO front merged with request on queue
G	Get request
I	IO inserted onto request queue
M	IO back merged with request on queue
P	Plug request
Q	IO handled by request queue code
S	Sleep request
T	Unplug due to timeout
U	Unplug request
X	Split

This list has been included because it also shows the events that the blktrace framework can observe.

RWBS Description

For tracing observability, the kernel provides a way to describe the type of each I/O using a character string named *rwbs*. rwbs is used by blktrace(8) and other disk tracing tools. It is defined in the kernel blk_fill_rwbs() function and uses the characters:

- R: Read
- W: Write
- M: Metadata
- S: Synchronous
- A: Read-ahead
- F: Flush or force unit access
- D: Discard
- E: Erase
- N: None

The characters can be combined. For example, "WM" is for writes of metadata.

Action Filtering

The blktrace(8) and btrace(8) commands can filter actions to show only the event type of interest. For example, to trace only the D actions (I/O issued), use the filter option -a issue:

```
# btrace -a issue /dev/sdb
  8,16   1        1     0.000000000    448  D   W 38978223 + 8 [kjournald]
  8,16   1        2     0.000306181    448  D   W 104685503 + 24 [kjournald]
  8,16   1        3     0.000496706    448  D   W 104685527 + 8 [kjournald]
  8,16   1        1     0.010441458  20824  D   R 184944151 + 8 [tar]
[...]
```

Other filters are described in the blktrace(8) man page, including options to trace only reads (-a read), writes (-a write), or synchronous operations (-a sync).

Analyze

The blktrace package includes btt(1) to analyze I/O traces. Here is an example invocation, now using blktrace(8) on /dev/nvme0n1p1 to write trace files (a new directory is used since these commands create several files):

```
# mkdir tracefiles; cd tracefiles
# blktrace -d /dev/nvme0n1p1 -o out -w 10
=== nvme0n1p1 ===
  CPU  0:                   20135 events,       944 KiB data
  CPU  1:                   38272 events,      1795 KiB data
  Total:                   58407 events (dropped 0),     2738 KiB data
# blkparse -i out.blktrace.* -d out.bin
259,0   1        1     0.000000000   7113  A   RM 161888 + 8 <- (259,1) 159840
259,0   1        1     0.000000000   7113  A   RM 161888 + 8 <- (259,1) 159840
[...]
# btt -i out.bin
==================== All Devices ====================

                 ALL           MIN           AVG           MAX           N
--------------- ------------- ------------- ------------- -----------

Q2Q             0.000000001   0.000365336   2.186239507        24625
Q2A             0.000037519   0.000476609   0.001628905         1442
Q2G             0.000000247   0.000007117   0.006140020        15914
G2I             0.000001949   0.000027449   0.000081146          602
Q2M             0.000000139   0.000000198   0.000021066         8720
I2D             0.000002292   0.000008148   0.000030147          602
M2D             0.000001333   0.000188409   0.008407029         8720
```

D2C	0.000195685	0.000885833	0.006083538	12308
Q2C	0.000198056	0.000964784	0.009578213	12308
[...]				

These statistics are in units of seconds, and show times for each stage of I/O processing. Interesting times include:

- **Q2C**: The total time from the I/O request to completion (time in block layer)
- **D2C**: The device issue to completion (disk I/O latency)
- **I2D**: The time from device queue insertion to device issue (request queue time)
- **M2D**: The time from I/O merge to issue

The output shows an average D2C time of 0.86 ms, and a max M2D of 8.4 ms. Maximums such as these can cause I/O latency outliers.

For more information, see the btt User Guide [Brunelle 08].

Visualizations

The blktrace(8) tool can record events to trace files that can be visualized using iowatcher(1), also provided in the blktrace package, and also visualized using Chris Mason's seekwatcher [Mason 08].

9.6.11   bpftrace

bpftrace is a BPF-based tracer that provides a high-level programming language, allowing the creation of powerful one-liners and short scripts. It is well suited for custom disk analysis based on clues from other tools.

bpftrace is explained in Chapter 15. This section shows some examples for disk analysis: one-liners, disk I/O size, and disk I/O latency.

One-Liners

The following one-liners are useful and demonstrate different bpftrace capabilities.

Count block I/O tracepoints events:

```
bpftrace -e 'tracepoint:block:* { @[probe] = count(); }'
```

Summarize block I/O size as a histogram:

```
bpftrace -e 't:block:block_rq_issue { @bytes = hist(args->bytes); }'
```

Count block I/O request user stack traces:

```
bpftrace -e 't:block:block_rq_issue { @[ustack] = count(); }'
bpftrace -e 't:block:block_rq_insert { @[ustack] = count(); }'
```

Count block I/O type flags:

```
bpftrace -e 't:block:block_rq_issue { @[args->rwbs] = count(); }'
```

Trace block I/O errors with device and I/O type:

```
bpftrace -e 't:block:block_rq_complete /args->error/ {
    printf("dev %d type %s error %d\n", args->dev, args->rwbs, args->error); }'
```

Count SCSI opcodes:

```
bpftrace -e 't:scsi:scsi_dispatch_cmd_start { @opcode[args->opcode] =
    count(); }'
```

Count SCSI result codes:

```
bpftrace -e 't:scsi:scsi_dispatch_cmd_done { @result[args->result] = count(); }'
```

Count SCSI driver functions:

```
bpftrace -e 'kprobe:scsi* { @[func] = count(); }'
```

Disk I/O Size

Sometimes disk I/O is slow simply because it is large, especially for SSD drives. Another size-based issue is when an application requests many small I/O, which instead could be aggregated into larger sizes to reduce I/O stack overheads. Both of these issues can be investigated by examining the I/O size distribution.

Using bpftrace, the following shows a disk I/O size distribution broken down by the requesting process name:

```
# bpftrace -e 't:block:block_rq_issue /args->bytes/ { @[comm] = hist(args->bytes); }'
Attaching 1 probe...
^C
[...]

@[kworker/3:1H]:
[4K, 8K)               1 |@@@@@@@@@                                           |
[8K, 16K)              0 |                                                    |
[16K, 32K)             0 |                                                    |
[32K, 64K)             0 |                                                    |
[64K, 128K)            0 |                                                    |
[128K, 256K)           0 |                                                    |
[256K, 512K)           0 |                                                    |
[512K, 1M)             5 |@@@@@@@@@@@@@@@@@@@@@@@@@@@@@@@@@@@@@@@@@@@@@@@@@@@@@@|
[1M, 2M)               3 |@@@@@@@@@@@@@@@@@@@@@@@@@@@@@@@@                     |
```

```
@[dmcrypt_write]:
[4K, 8K)           103 |@@@@@@@@@@@@@@@@@@@@@@@@@@@@@@@@@@@@@@@@@@@@@@@@@@@@|
[8K, 16K)           46 |@@@@@@@@@@@@@@@@@@@@@@@@                           |
[16K, 32K)          11 |@@@@@                                             |
[32K, 64K)           0 |                                                 |
[64K, 128K)          1 |                                                 |
[128K, 256K)         1 |                                                 |
```

The output shows processes named dmcrypt_write performing small I/O, mostly in the 4 to 32 Kbyte range.

The tracepoint block:block_rq_issue shows when I/O were sent to the device driver for delivery to the disk device. There is no guarantee that the originating process is still on CPU, especially if the I/O is queued by a scheduler, so the process name shown may be for a later kernel worker thread that reads I/O from a queue for device delivery. You can switch the tracepoint to block:block_rq_insert to measure from the insertion of the queue, which may improve the accuracy of the process name, but it may also miss instrumenting I/O that bypasses queueing (this was also mentioned in Section 9.6.5, perf).

If you add args->rwbs as a histogram key, the output will be further broken down by I/O type:

```
# bpftrace -e 't:block:block_rq_insert /args->bytes/ { @[comm, args->rwbs] =
    hist(args->bytes); }'
Attaching 1 probe...
^C
[...]

@[dmcrypt_write, WS]:
[4K, 8K)             4 |@@@@@@@@@@@@@@@@@@@@@@@@@@@@@@@@@@@@@@@@@@@@@@@@@@@@|
[8K, 16K)            1 |@@@@@@@@@@@@                                      |
[16K, 32K)           0 |                                                 |
[32K, 64K)           1 |@@@@@@@@@@@@                                      |
[64K, 128K)          1 |@@@@@@@@@@@@                                      |
[128K, 256K)         1 |@@@@@@@@@@@@                                      |

@[dmcrypt_write, W]:
[512K, 1M)           8 |@@@@@@@@@@                                        |
[1M, 2M)            38 |@@@@@@@@@@@@@@@@@@@@@@@@@@@@@@@@@@@@@@@@@@@@@@@@@@@@|
```

The output now includes W for writes, WS for synchronous writes, etc. See the earlier RWBS Description section for an explanation of these letters.

Disk I/O Latency

The disk response time, often referred to as disk I/O latency, can be measured by instrumenting device issue to completion events. The biolatency.bt tool does this, showing disk I/O latency as a histogram. For example:

```
# biolatency.bt
Attaching 4 probes...
Tracing block device I/O... Hit Ctrl-C to end.
^C

@usecs:
[32, 64)               2 |@                                                    |
[64, 128)              1 |                                                     |
[128, 256)             1 |                                                     |
[256, 512)            27 |@@@@@@@@@@@@@@@@@@@@@@@@@@                            |
[512, 1K)             43 |@@@@@@@@@@@@@@@@@@@@@@@@@@@@@@@@@@@@@@@@@              |
[1K, 2K)              54 |@@@@@@@@@@@@@@@@@@@@@@@@@@@@@@@@@@@@@@@@@@@@@@@@@@@@@@@@|
[2K, 4K)              41 |@@@@@@@@@@@@@@@@@@@@@@@@@@@@@@@@@@@@@@@@               |
[4K, 8K)              47 |@@@@@@@@@@@@@@@@@@@@@@@@@@@@@@@@@@@@@@@@@@@@@@         |
[8K, 16K)             16 |@@@@@@@@@@@@@@@                                      |
[16K, 32K)             4 |@@@                                                  |
```

This output shows that I/O were typically completing between 256 microseconds and 16 milliseconds (16K microseconds).

The source code is:

```
#!/usr/local/bin/bpftrace
BEGIN
{
        printf("Tracing block device I/O... Hit Ctrl-C to end.\n");
}


tracepoint:block:block_rq_issue
{
        @start[args->dev, args->sector] = nsecs;
}


tracepoint:block:block_rq_complete
/@start[args->dev, args->sector]/
{
        @usecs = hist((nsecs - @start[args->dev, args->sector]) / 1000);
        delete(@start[args->dev, args->sector]);
}
```

```
END
{
        clear(@start);
}
```

Measuring I/O latency requires storing a custom timestamp for the start of each I/O, and then referring to it when the I/O has completed in order to calculate the elapsed time. When VFS latency was measured in Chapter 8, File Systems, Section 8.6.15, bpftrace, the start timestamp was stored in a BPF map keyed by the thread ID: that worked because the same thread ID will be on CPU for the start and completion events. That is not the case with disk I/O, as the completion event will interrupt whatever else is on CPU. The unique ID in biolatency.bt has been constructed from the device and sector number: it assumes that only one I/O will be in flight to a given sector at a time.

As with the I/O size one-liner, you can add `args->rwbs` to the map key to break down by I/O type.

Disk I/O Errors

I/O error status is an argument to the block:block_rq_complete tracepoint, and the following bioerr(8) tool[15] uses it to print details for I/O operations that error (a one-liner version of this was included earlier):

```
#!/usr/local/bin/bpftrace

BEGIN
{
        printf("Tracing block I/O errors. Hit Ctrl-C to end.\n");
}

tracepoint:block:block_rq_complete
/args->error != 0/
{
        time("%H:%M:%S ");
        printf("device: %d,%d, sector: %d, bytes: %d, flags: %s, error: %d\n",
            args->dev >> 20, args->dev & ((1 << 20) - 1), args->sector,
            args->nr_sector * 512, args->rwbs, args->error);
}
```

Finding more information on a disk error may require lower-level disk tools, such as the next three (MegaCli, smartctl, SCSI logging).

---

[15] Origin: I created it for the BPF book on 19-Mar-2019 [Gregg 19].

9.6.12 MegaCli

Disk controllers (host bus adapters) consist of hardware and firmware that are external to the system. Operating system analysis tools, even dynamic tracers, cannot directly observe their internals. Sometimes their workings can be inferred by observing the input and output carefully (including via kernel static or dynamic instrumentation), to see how the disk controller responds to a series of I/O.

There are some analysis tools for specific disk controllers, such as LSI's MegaCli. The following shows recent controller events:

```
# MegaCli -AdpEventLog -GetLatest 50 -f lsi.log -aALL
# more lsi.log
seqNum: 0x0000282f
Time: Sat Jun 16 05:55:05 2012
Code: 0x00000023
Class: 0
Locale: 0x20
Event Description: Patrol Read complete
Event Data:
===========
None

seqNum: 0x000027ec
Time: Sat Jun 16 03:00:00 2012
Code: 0x00000027
Class: 0
Locale: 0x20
Event Description: Patrol Read started
[...]
```

The last two events show that a patrol read (which can affect performance) occurred between 3:00 and 5:55 a.m. Patrol reads were mentioned in Section 9.4.3, Storage Types; they read disk blocks and verify their checksums.

MegaCli has many other options, which can show the adapter information, disk device information, virtual device information, enclosure information, battery status, and physical errors. These help identify issues of configuration and errors. Even with this information, some types of issues can't be analyzed easily, such as exactly why a particular I/O took hundreds of milliseconds.

Check the vendor documentation to see what interface, if any, exists for disk controller analysis.

9.6.13 smartctl

The disk has logic to control disk operation, including queueing, caching, and error handling. Similarly to disk controllers, the internal behavior of the disk is not directly observable by the operating system and instead is usually inferred by observing I/O requests and their latency.

Many modern drives provide SMART (Self-Monitoring, Analysis and Reporting Technology) data, which provides various health statistics. The following output of smartctl(8) on Linux shows the sort of data available (this is accessing the first disk in a virtual RAID device, using -d megaraid,0):

```
# smartctl --all -d megaraid,0 /dev/sdb
smartctl 5.40 2010-03-16 r3077 [x86_64-unknown-linux-gnu] (local build)
Copyright (C) 2002-10 by Bruce Allen, http://smartmontools.sourceforge.net

Device: SEAGATE  ST3600002SS      Version: ER62
Serial number: 3SS0LM01
Device type: disk
Transport protocol: SAS
Local Time is: Sun Jun 17 10:11:31 2012 UTC
Device supports SMART and is Enabled
Temperature Warning Disabled or Not Supported
SMART Health Status: OK

Current Drive Temperature:     23 C
Drive Trip Temperature:        68 C
Elements in grown defect list: 0
Vendor (Seagate) cache information
  Blocks sent to initiator = 3172800756
  Blocks received from initiator = 2618189622
  Blocks read from cache and sent to initiator = 854615302
  Number of read and write commands whose size <= segment size = 30848143
  Number of read and write commands whose size > segment size = 0
Vendor (Seagate/Hitachi) factory information
  number of hours powered up = 12377.45
  number of minutes until next internal SMART test = 56

Error counter log:
          Errors Corrected by      Total  Correction  Gigabytes  Total
              ECC         rereads/  errors  algorithm   processed uncorrected
          fast | delayed rewrites  corrected invocations [10^9 bytes] errors
read:   7416197        0        0  7416197   7416197    1886.494          0
write:        0        0        0        0         0    1349.999          0
verify: 142475069      0        0 142475069 142475069  22222.134          0

Non-medium error count:    2661

SMART Self-test log
Num  Test                Status     segment  LifeTime  LBA_first_err [SK ASC ASQ]
     Description                     number   (hours)
```

```
# 1   Background long    Completed    16      3                  - [-   -    -]
# 2   Background short   Completed    16      0                  - [-   -    -]

Long (extended) Self Test duration: 6400 seconds [106.7 minutes]
```

While this is very useful, it does not have the resolution to answer questions about individual slow disk I/O, as kernel tracing frameworks do. The corrected errors information should be useful for monitoring, to help predict disk failure before it happens, as well as to confirm that a disk has failed or is failing.

9.6.14   SCSI Logging

Linux has a built-in facility for SCSI event logging. It can be enabled via sysctl(8) or /proc. For example, both of these commands set the logging to the maximum for all event types (warning: depending on your disk workload, this may flood your system log):

```
# sysctl -w dev.scsi.logging_level=03333333333
# echo 03333333333 > /proc/sys/dev/scsi/logging_level
```

The format of the number is a bitfield that sets the logging level from 1 to 7 for 10 different event types (written here in octal; as hexadecimal it is 0x1b6db6db). This bitfield is defined in drivers/scsi/scsi_logging.h. The sg3-utils package provides a scsi_logging_level(8) tool for setting these. For example:

```
# scsi_logging_level -s --all 3
```

Example events:

```
# dmesg
[...]
[542136.259412] sd 0:0:0:0: tag#0 Send: scmd 0x0000000001fb89dc
[542136.259422] sd 0:0:0:0: tag#0 CDB: Test Unit Ready 00 00 00 00 00 00
[542136.261103] sd 0:0:0:0: tag#0 Done: SUCCESS Result: hostbyte=DID_OK
driverbyte=DRIVER_OK
[542136.261110] sd 0:0:0:0: tag#0 CDB: Test Unit Ready 00 00 00 00 00 00
[542136.261115] sd 0:0:0:0: tag#0 Sense Key : Not Ready [current]
[542136.261121] sd 0:0:0:0: tag#0 Add. Sense: Medium not present
[542136.261127] sd 0:0:0:0: tag#0 0 sectors total, 0 bytes done.
[...]
```

This can be used to help debug errors and timeouts. While timestamps are provided (the first column), using them to calculate I/O latency is difficult without unique identifying details.

9.6.15 Other Tools

Disk tools included in other chapters of this book and in *BPF Performance Tools* [Gregg 19] are listed in Table 9.6.

Table 9.6 **Other disk observability tools**

Section	Tool	Description
7.5.1	vmstat	Virtual memory statistics including swapping
7.5.3	swapon	Swap device usage
[Gregg 19]	seeksize	Show requested I/O seek distances
[Gregg 19]	biopattern	Identify random/sequential disk access patterns
[Gregg 19]	bioerr	Trace disk errors
[Gregg 19]	mdflush	Trace md flush requests
[Gregg 19]	iosched	Summarize I/O scheduler latency
[Gregg 19]	scsilatency	Show SCSI command latency distributions
[Gregg 19]	scsiresult	Show SCSI command result codes
[Gregg 19]	nvmelatency	Summarize NVME driver command latency

Other Linux disk observability tools and sources include the following:

- **/proc/diskstats**: High-level per-disk statistics
- **seekwatcher**: Visualizes disk access patterns [Mason 08]

The disks vendors may have additional tools that access firmware statistics, or by installing a debug version of the firmware.

9.7 Visualizations

There are many types of visualizations that can help in analyzing disk I/O performance. This section demonstrates these with screenshots from various tools. See Chapter 2, Methodologies, Section 2.10, Visualization, for a discussion about visualizations in general.

9.7.1 Line Graphs

Performance monitoring solutions commonly graph disk IOPS, throughput, and utilization measurements over time as line graphs. This helps illustrate time-based patterns, such as changes in load during the day, or recurring events such as file system flush intervals.

Note the metric that is graphed. Average latency can hide multi-modal distributions, and outliers. Averages across all disk devices can hide unbalanced behavior, including single-device outliers. Averages across long time periods can also hide shorter-term fluctuations.

9.7.2   Latency Scatter Plots

Scatter plots are useful for visualizing I/O latency per-event, which may include thousands of events. The x-axis can show completion time, and the y-axis I/O response time (latency). The example in Figure 9.11 plots 1,400 I/O events from a production MySQL database server, captured using iosnoop(8) and plotted using R.

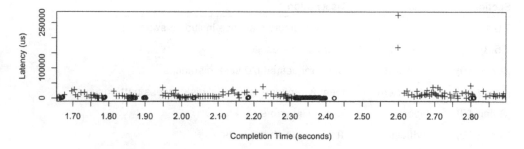

Figure 9.11   Scatter plot of disk read and write latency

The scatter plot shows reads (+) and writes (o) differently. Other dimensions could be plotted, for example, disk block address on the y-axis instead of latency.

A couple of read outliers can be seen here, with latencies over 150 ms. The reason for these outliers was previously not known. This scatter plot, and others that included similar outliers, showed that they occur after a burst of writes. The writes have low latency since they returned from a RAID controller write-back cache, which will write them to the device after returning the completions. I suspect that the reads are queueing behind the device writes.

This scatter plot showed a single server for a few seconds. Multiple servers or longer intervals can capture many more events, which when plotted merge together and become difficult to read. At that point, consider using a latency heat map.

9.7.3   Latency Heat Maps

A *heat map* can be used to visualize latency, placing the passage of time on the x-axis, the I/O latency on the y-axis, and the number of I/O in a particular time and latency range on the z-axis, shown by color (darker means more). Heat maps were introduced in Chapter 2, Methodologies, Section 2.10.3, Heat Maps. An interesting disk example is shown in Figure 9.12.

The workload visualized was experimental: I was applying sequential reads to multiple disks one by one to explore bus and controller limits. The resulting heat map was unexpected (it has been described as a pterodactyl) and shows the information that would be missed when only considering averages. There are technical reasons for each of the details seen: e.g., the "beak" ends at eight disks, equal to the number of SAS ports connected (two x4 ports) and the "head" begins at nine disks once those ports begin suffering contention.

I invented latency heat maps to visualize latency over time, inspired by taztool, described in the next section. Figure 9.12 is from Analytics in the Sun Microsystems ZFS Storage appliance [Gregg 10a]: I collected this and other interesting latency heat maps to share publicly and promote their use.

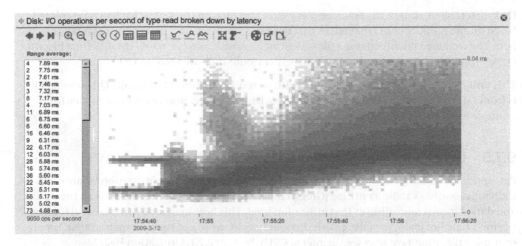

Figure 9.12   Disk latency pterodactyl

The x- and y-axis are the same as a latency scatter plot. The main advantage of heat maps is that they can scale to millions of events, whereas the scatter plot becomes "paint." This problem was discussed in Sections 2.10.2, Scatter Plots, and 2.10.3, Heat Maps.

9.7.4   Offset Heat Maps

I/O location, or offset, can also be visualized as a heat map (and predates latency heat maps in computing). Figure 9.13 shows an example.

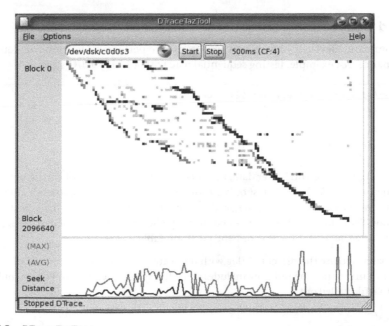

Figure 9.13   DTraceTazTool

Disk offset (block address) is shown on the y-axis, and time on the x-axis. Each pixel is colored based on the number of I/O that fell in that time and latency range, darker colors for larger numbers. The workload visualized was a file system archive, which creeps across the disk from block 0. Darker lines indicate a sequential I/O, and lighter clouds indicate random I/O.

This visualization was introduced in 1995 with taztool by Richard McDougall. This screenshot is from DTraceTazTool, a version I wrote in 2006. Disk I/O offset heat maps are available from multiple tools, including seekwatcher (Linux).

9.7.5 Utilization Heat Maps

Per-device utilization may also be shown as a heat map, so that device utilization balance and individual outliers can be identified [Gregg 11b]. In this case percent utilization is on the y-axis, and darker means more disks at that utilization level. This heat map type can be useful for identifying single hot disks, including sloth disks, as lines at the top of the heat map (100%). For an example utilization heat map see Chapter 6, CPUs, Section 6.7.1, Utilization Heat Map.

9.8 Experimentation

This section describes tools for actively testing disk I/O performance. See Section 9.5.9, Micro-Benchmarking, for a suggested methodology to follow.

When using these tools, it's a good idea to leave iostat(1) continually running so that any result can be immediately double-checked. Some micro-benchmarking tools may require a "direct" mode of operation to bypass the file system cache, and focus on disk device performance.

9.8.1 Ad Hoc

The dd(1) command (device-to-device copy) can be used to perform ad hoc tests of sequential disk performance. For example, testing sequential read with a 1 Mbyte I/O size:

```
# dd if=/dev/sda1 of=/dev/null bs=1024k count=1k
1024+0 records in
1024+0 records out
1073741824 bytes (1.1 GB) copied, 7.44024 s, 144 MB/s
```

Since the kernel can cache and buffer data, the dd(1) measured throughput can be of the cache and disk and not the disk alone. To test only the disk's performance, you can use a character special device for the disk: On Linux, the raw(8) command (where available) can create these under /dev/raw. Sequential write can be tested similarly; however, beware of destroying all data on disk, including the master boot record and partition table!

A safer approach is to use the direct I/O flag with dd(1) and file system files instead of disk devices. Bear in mind that the test now includes some file system overheads. For example, doing a write test to a file called out1:

```
# dd if=/dev/zero of=out1 bs=1024k count=1000 oflag=direct
1000+0 records in
1000+0 records out
1048576000 bytes (1.0 GB, 1000 MiB) copied, 1.79189 s, 585 MB/s
```

iostat(1) in another terminal session confirmed that the disk I/O write throughput was around 585 Mbytes/sec.

Use `iflag=direct` for direct I/O with input files.

9.8.2 Custom Load Generators

To test custom workloads, you can write your own load generator and measure resulting performance using iostat(1). A custom load generator can be a short C program that opens the device path and applies the intended workload. On Linux, the block special devices files can be opened with O_DIRECT, to avoid buffering. If you use higher-level languages, try to use system-level interfaces that avoid library buffering (e.g., sysread() in Perl) at least, and preferably avoid kernel buffering as well (e.g., O_DIRECT).

9.8.3 Micro-Benchmark Tools

Available disk benchmark tools include, for example, hdparm(8) on Linux:

```
# hdparm -Tt /dev/sdb

/dev/sdb:
 Timing cached reads:    16718 MB in  2.00 seconds = 8367.66 MB/sec
 Timing buffered disk reads:  846 MB in  3.00 seconds = 281.65 MB/sec
```

The -T option tests cached reads, and -t tests disk device reads. The results show the dramatic difference between on-disk cache hits and misses.

Study the tool documentation to understand any caveats, and see Chapter 12, Benchmarking, for more background on micro-benchmarking. Also see Chapter 8, File Systems, for tools that test disk performance via the file system (for which many more are available).

9.8.4 Random Read Example

As an example experiment, I wrote a custom tool to perform a random 8 Kbyte read workload of a disk device path. From one to five instances of the tool were run concurrently, with iostat(1) running. The write columns, which contained zeros, have been removed:

```
Device:    rrqm/s     r/s    rkB/s avgrq-sz  aqu-sz r_await  svctm  %util
sda        878.00  234.00  2224.00    19.01    1.00    4.27   4.27 100.00
[...]
```

Device:	rrqm/s	r/s	rkB/s	avgrq-sz	aqu-sz	r_await	svctm	%util
sda	1233.00	311.00	3088.00	19.86	2.00	6.43	3.22	100.00
[...]								
Device:	rrqm/s	r/s	rkB/s	avgrq-sz	aqu-sz	r_await	svctm	%util
sda	1366.00	358.00	3448.00	19.26	3.00	8.44	2.79	100.00
[...]								
Device:	rrqm/s	r/s	rkB/s	avgrq-sz	aqu-sz	r_await	svctm	%util
sda	1775.00	413.00	4376.00	21.19	4.01	9.66	2.42	100.00
[...]								
Device:	rrqm/s	r/s	rkB/s	avgrq-sz	aqu-sz	r_await	svctm	%util
sda	1977.00	423.00	4800.00	22.70	5.04	12.08	2.36	100.00

Note the stepped increases in aqu-sz, and the increased latency of r_await.

9.8.5   ioping

ioping(1) is an interesting disk micro-benchmark tool that resembles the ICMP ping(8) utility. Running ioping(1) on the nvme0n1 disk device:

```
# ioping /dev/nvme0n1
4 KiB <<< /dev/nvme0n1 (block device 8 GiB): request=1 time=438.7 us (warmup)
4 KiB <<< /dev/nvme0n1 (block device 8 GiB): request=2 time=421.0 us
4 KiB <<< /dev/nvme0n1 (block device 8 GiB): request=3 time=449.4 us
4 KiB <<< /dev/nvme0n1 (block device 8 GiB): request=4 time=412.6 us
4 KiB <<< /dev/nvme0n1 (block device 8 GiB): request=5 time=468.8 us
^C
--- /dev/nvme0n1 (block device 8 GiB) ioping statistics ---
4 requests completed in 1.75 ms, 16 KiB read, 2.28 k iops, 8.92 MiB/s
generated 5 requests in 4.37 s, 20 KiB, 1 iops, 4.58 KiB/s
min/avg/max/mdev = 412.6 us / 437.9 us / 468.8 us / 22.4 us
```

By default ioping(1) issues a 4 Kbyte read per second and prints its I/O latency in microseconds. When terminated, various statistics are printed.

What makes ioping(1) different to other benchmark tools is that its workload is lightweight. Here is some iostat(1) output while ioping(1) was running:

```
$ iostat -xsz 1
[...]
Device           tps    kB/s   rqm/s   await aqu-sz  areq-sz   %util
nvme0n1         1.00    4.00    0.00    0.00   0.00     4.00    0.40
```

The disk was driven to only 0.4% utilization. ioping(1) could possibly be used to debug issues in production environments where other micro-benchmarks would be unsuitable, as they typically drive the target disks to 100% utilization.

9.8.6 fio

The flexible IO tester (fio) is a file system benchmark tool that can also shed light on disk device performance, especially when used with the `--direct=true` option to use non-buffered I/O (when non-buffered I/O is supported by the file system). It was introduced in Chapter 8, File Systems, Section 8.7.2, Micro-Benchmark Tools.

9.8.7 blkreplay

The block I/O replay tool (blkreplay) can replay block I/O loads captured with blktrace (Section 9.6.10, blktrace) or Windows DiskMon [Schöbel-Theuer 12]. This can be useful when debugging disk issues that are difficult to reproduce with micro-benchmark tools.

See Chapter 12, Benchmarking, Section 12.2.3, replay, for an example of how disk I/O replays can be misleading if the target system has changed.

9.9 Tuning

Many tuning approaches were covered in Section 9.5, Methodology, including cache tuning, scaling, and workload characterization, which can help you identify and eliminate unnecessary work. Another important area of tuning is the storage configuration, which can be studied as part of a static performance tuning methodology.

The following sections show areas that can be tuned: the operating system, disk devices, and disk controller. Available tunable parameters vary between versions of an operating system, models of disks, disk controllers, and their firmware; see their respective documentation. While changing tunables can be easy to do, the default settings are usually reasonable and rarely need much adjusting.

9.9.1 Operating System Tunables

These include ionice(1), resource controls, and kernel tunable parameters.

ionice

On Linux, the ionice(1) command can be used to set an I/O scheduling class and priority for a process. The scheduling classes are identified numerically:

- **0, none:** No class specified, so the kernel will pick a default—best effort, with a priority based on the process nice value.

- **1, real-time:** Highest-priority access to the disk. If misused, this can starve other processes (just like the RT CPU scheduling class).

- **2, best effort:** Default scheduling class, supporting priorities 0–7, with 0 being the highest.

- **3, idle:** Disk I/O allowed only after a grace period of disk idleness.

Example usage:

```
# ionice -c 3 -p 1623
```

This puts process ID 1623 in the idle I/O scheduling class. This may be desirable for long-running backup jobs so that they are less likely to interfere with the production workload.

Resource Controls

Modern operating systems provide resource controls for managing disk or file system I/O usage in custom ways.

For Linux, the container groups (cgroups) block I/O (blkio) subsystem provides storage device resource controls for processes or process groups. This can be a proportional weight (like a share) or a fixed limit. Limits can be set for read and write independently, and for either IOPS or throughput (bytes per second). For more detail, see Chapter 11, Cloud Computing.

Tunable Parameters

Example Linux tunables include:

- **/sys/block/*/queue/scheduler**: To select the I/O scheduler policy: these may include noop, deadline, cfq, etc. See the earlier descriptions of these in Section 9.4, Architecture.

- **/sys/block/*/queue/nr_requests**: The number of read or write requests that can be allocated by the block layer.

- **/sys/block/*/queue/read_ahead_kb**: Maximum read ahead Kbytes for file systems to request.

As with other kernel tunables, check the documentation for the full list, descriptions, and warnings. In the Linux source, see Documentation/block/queue-sysfs.txt.

9.9.2   Disk Device Tunables

On Linux, the hdparm(8) tool can set various disk device tunables, including power management and spindown timeouts [Archlinux 20]. Be very careful when using this tool and study the hdparm(8) man page—various options are marked "DANGEROUS" because they can result in data loss.

9.9.3   Disk Controller Tunables

The available disk controller tunable parameters depend on the disk controller model and vendor. To give you an idea of what these may include, the following shows some of the settings from a Dell PERC 6 card, viewed using the MegaCli command:

```
# MegaCli -AdpAllInfo -aALL
[...]
Predictive Fail Poll Interval    : 300sec
Interrupt Throttle Active Count  : 16
```

```
Interrupt Throttle Completion     : 50us
Rebuild Rate                      : 30%
PR Rate                           : 0%
BGI Rate                          : 1%
Check Consistency Rate            : 1%
Reconstruction Rate               : 30%
Cache Flush Interval              : 30s
Max Drives to Spinup at One Time  : 2
Delay Among Spinup Groups         : 12s
Physical Drive Coercion Mode      : 128MB
Cluster Mode                      : Disabled
Alarm                             : Disabled
Auto Rebuild                      : Enabled
Battery Warning                   : Enabled
Ecc Bucket Size                   : 15
Ecc Bucket Leak Rate              : 1440 Minutes
Load Balance Mode                 : Auto
[...]
```

Each setting has a reasonably descriptive name and is described in more detail in the vendor documentation.

9.10 Exercises

1. Answer the following questions about disk terminology:

   - What are IOPS?

   - What is the difference between service time and wait time?

   - What is disk I/O wait time?

   - What is a latency outlier?

   - What is a non-data-transfer disk command?

2. Answer the following conceptual questions:

   - Describe disk utilization and saturation.

   - Describe the performance differences between random and sequential disk I/O.

   - Describe the role of an on-disk cache for read and write I/O.

3. Answer the following deeper questions:

   - Explain why utilization (percent busy) of virtual disks can be misleading.

   - Explain why the "I/O wait" metric can be misleading.

   - Describe performance characteristics of RAID-0 (striping) and RAID-1 (mirroring).

- Describe what happens when disks are overloaded with work, including the effect on application performance.

- Describe what happens when the storage controller is overloaded with work (either throughput or IOPS), including the effect on application performance.

4. Develop the following procedures for your operating system:

- A USE method checklist for disk resources (disks and controllers). Include how to fetch each metric (e.g., which command to execute) and how to interpret the result. Try to use existing OS observability tools before installing or using additional software products.

- A workload characterization checklist for disk resources. Include how to fetch each metric, and try to use existing OS observability tools first.

5. Describe disk behavior visible in this Linux iostat(1) output alone:

```
$ iostat -x 1
[...]
avg-cpu:   %user   %nice %system %iowait  %steal   %idle
            3.23    0.00   45.16   31.18    0.00   20.43


Device:            rrqm/s   wrqm/s     r/s     w/s    rkB/s     wkB/s avgrq-sz
avgqu-sz   await r_await w_await  svctm  %util
vda                 39.78 13156.99  800.00  151.61  3466.67 41200.00    93.88
11.99      7.49    0.57   44.01   0.49  46.56
vdb                  0.00     0.00    0.00    0.00     0.00     0.00     0.00
0.00       0.00    0.00    0.00   0.00   0.00
```

6. (optional, advanced) Develop a tool to trace all disk commands *except* for reads and writes. This may require tracing at the SCSI level.

9.11 References

[**Patterson 88**] Patterson, D., Gibson, G., and Kats, R., "A Case for Redundant Arrays of Inexpensive Disks," *ACM SIGMOD*, 1988.

[**McDougall 06a**] McDougall, R., Mauro, J., and Gregg, B., *Solaris Performance and Tools: DTrace and MDB Techniques for Solaris 10 and OpenSolaris*, Prentice Hall, 2006.

[**Brunelle 08**] Brunelle, A., "btt User Guide," *blktrace package*, /usr/share/doc/blktrace/btt.pdf, 2008.

[**Gregg 08**] Gregg, B., "Shouting in the Datacenter," https://www.youtube.com/watch?v=tDacjrSCeq4, 2008.

[**Mason 08**] Mason, C., "Seekwatcher," https://oss.oracle.com/~mason/seekwatcher, 2008.

[**Smith 09**] Smith, R., "Western Digital's Advanced Format: The 4K Sector Transition Begins," https://www.anandtech.com/show/2888, 2009.

[**Gregg 10a**] Gregg, B., "Visualizing System Latency," *Communications of the ACM*, July 2010.

[**Love 10**] Love, R., *Linux Kernel Development*, 3rd Edition, Addison-Wesley, 2010.

[**Turner 10**] Turner, J., "Effects of Data Center Vibration on Compute System Performance," *USENIX SustainIT*, 2010.

[**Gregg 11b**] Gregg, B., "Utilization Heat Maps," http://www.brendangregg.com/HeatMaps/ utilization.html, published 2011.

[**Cassidy 12**] Cassidy, C., "SLC vs MLC: Which Works Best for High-Reliability Applications?" https://www.eetimes.com/slc-vs-mlc-which-works-best-for-high-reliability-applications/#, 2012.

[**Cornwell 12**] Cornwell, M., "Anatomy of a Solid-State Drive," *Communications of the ACM*, December 2012.

[**Schöbel-Theuer 12**] Schöbel-Theuer, T., "blkreplay - a Testing and Benchmarking Toolkit," http://www.blkreplay.org, 2012.

[**Chazarain 13**] Chazarain, G., "Iotop," http://guichaz.free.fr/iotop, 2013.

[**Corbet 13b**] Corbet, J., "The multiqueue block layer," *LWN.net*, https://lwn.net/ Articles/552904, 2013.

[**Leventhal 13**] Leventhal, A., "A File System All Its Own," *ACM Queue*, March 2013.

[**Cai 15**] Cai, Y., Luo, Y., Haratsch, E. F., Mai, K., and Mutlu, O., "Data Retention in MLC NAND Flash Memory: Characterization, Optimization, and Recovery," *IEEE 21st International Symposium on High Performance Computer Architecture (HPCA)*, 2015. https://users.ece.cmu.edu/~omutlu/pub/flash-memory-data-retention_hpca15.pdf

[**FICA 18**] "Industry's Fastest Storage Networking Speed Announced by Fibre Channel Industry Association—64GFC and Gen 7 Fibre Channel," *Fibre Channel Industry Association*, https://fibrechannel.org/industrys-fastest-storage-networking-speed-announced-by-fibre-channel-industry-association-%E2%94%80-64gfc-and-gen-7-fibre-channel, 2018.

[**Hady 18**] Hady, F., "Achieve Consistent Low Latency for Your Storage-Intensive Workloads," https://www.intel.com/content/www/us/en/architecture-and-technology/optane-technology/ low-latency-for-storage-intensive-workloads-article-brief.html, 2018.

[**Gregg 19**] Gregg, B., *BPF Performance Tools: Linux System and Application Observability*, Addison-Wesley, 2019.

[**Archlinux 20**] "hdparm," https://wiki.archlinux.org/index.php/Hdparm, last updated 2020.

[**Dell 20**] "PowerEdge RAID Controller," https://www.dell.com/support/article/en-us/ sln312338/poweredge-raid-controller?lang=en, accessed 2020.

[**FCIA 20**] "Features," *Fibre Channel Industry Association*, https://fibrechannel.org/ fibre-channel-features, accessed 2020.

[**Liu 20**] Liu, L., "Samsung QVO vs EVO vs PRO: What's the Difference? [Clone Disk]," https://www.partitionwizard.com/clone-disk/samsung-qvo-vs-evo.html, 2020.

[Mellor 20] Mellor, C., "Western Digital Shingled Out in Lawsuit for Sneaking RAID-unfriendly Tech into Drives for RAID arrays," *TheRegister*, https://www.theregister.com/2020/05/29/wd_class_action_lawsuit, 2020.

[Netflix 20] "Open Connect Appliances," https://openconnect.netflix.com/en/appliances, accessed 2020.

[NVMe 20] "NVM Express," https://nvmexpress.org, accessed 2020.

Chapter 10

Network

As systems become more distributed, especially with cloud computing environments, the network plays a bigger role in performance. Common tasks in network performance include improving network latency and throughput, and eliminating latency outliers, which can be caused by dropped or delayed packets.

Network analysis spans hardware and software. The hardware is the physical network, which includes the network interface cards, switches, routers, and gateways (these typically have software, too). The software is the kernel network stack including network device drivers, packet queues, and packet schedulers, and the implementation of network protocols. Lower-level protocols are typically kernel software (IP, TCP, UDP, etc.) and higher-level protocols are typically library or application software (e.g., HTTP).

The network is often blamed for poor performance given the potential for congestion and its inherent complexity (blame the unknown). This chapter will show how to figure out what is really happening, which may exonerate the network so that analysis can move on.

The learning objectives of this chapter are:

- Understand networking models and concepts.
- Understand different measures of network latency.
- Have a working knowledge of common network protocols.
- Become familiar with network hardware internals.
- Become familiar with the kernel path from sockets and devices.
- Follow different methodologies for network analysis.
- Characterize system-wide and per-process network I/O.
- Identify issues caused by TCP retransmits.
- Investigate network internals using tracing tools.
- Become aware of network tunable parameters.

This chapter consists of six parts, the first three providing the basis for network analysis, and the last three showing its practical application to Linux-based systems. The parts are as follows:

- **Background** introduces network-related terminology, models, and key network performance concepts.

- **Architecture** provides generic descriptions of physical network components and the network stack.

- **Methodology** describes performance analysis methodologies, both observational and experimental.

- **Observability Tools** shows network performance observability tools for Linux-based systems.

- **Experimentation** summarizes network benchmark and experiment tools.

- **Tuning** describes example tunable parameters.

Network basics, such as the role of TCP and IP, are assumed knowledge for this chapter.

10.1 Terminology

For reference, network-related terminology used in this chapter includes:

- **Interface**: The term *interface port* refers to the physical network connector. The term *interface* or *link* refers to the logical instance of a network interface port, as seen and configured by the OS. (Not all OS interfaces are backed by hardware: some are virtual.)

- **Packet**: The term *packet* refers to a message in a packet-switched network, such as IP packets.

- **Frame**: A physical network-level message, for example an Ethernet frame.

- **Socket**: An API originating from BSD for network endpoints.

- **Bandwidth**: The maximum rate of data transfer for the network type, usually measured in bits per second. "100 GbE" is Ethernet with a bandwidth of 100 Gbits/s. There may be bandwidth limits for each direction, so a 100 GbE may be capable of 100 Gbits/s transmit and 100 Gbit/s receive in parallel (200 Gbit/sec total throughput).

- **Throughput**: The current data transfer rate between the network endpoints, measured in bits per second or bytes per second.

- **Latency**: Network *latency* can refer to the time it takes for a message to make a round-trip between endpoints, or the time required to establish a connection (e.g., TCP handshake), excluding the data transfer time that follows.

Other terms are introduced throughout this chapter. The Glossary includes basic terminology for reference, including *client, Ethernet, host, IP, RFC, server, SYN, ACK*. Also see the terminology sections in Chapters 2 and 3.

10.2 Models

The following simple models illustrate some basic principles of networking and network performance. Section 10.4, Architecture, digs much deeper, including implementation-specific details.

10.2.1 Network Interface

A network interface is an operating system endpoint for network connections; it is an abstraction configured and managed by the system administrators.

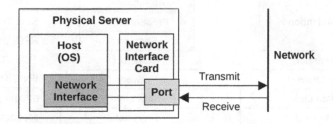

Figure 10.1   Network interface

A network interface is pictured in Figure 10.1. Network interfaces are mapped to physical network ports as part of their configuration. Ports connect to the network and typically have separate transmit and receive channels.

10.2.2 Controller

A *network interface card* (NIC) provides one or more network ports for the system and houses a *network controller*: a microprocessor for transferring packets between the ports and the system I/O transport. An example controller with four ports is pictured in Figure 10.2, showing the physical components involved.

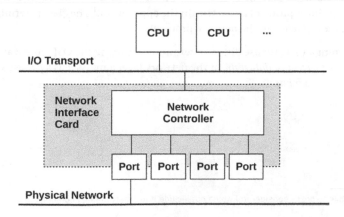

Figure 10.2   Network controller

The controller is typically provided as a separate expansion card or is built into the system board. (Other options include via USB.)

10.2.3   Protocol Stack

Networking is accomplished by a stack of protocols, each layer of which serves a particular purpose. Two stack models are shown in Figure 10.3, with example protocols.

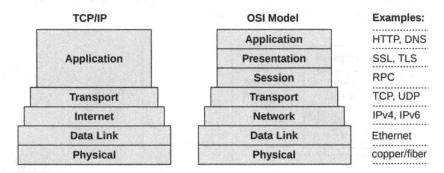

Figure 10.3   Network protocol stacks

Lower layers are drawn wider to indicate protocol encapsulation. Sent messages move down the stack from the application to the physical network. Received messages move up.

Note that the Ethernet standard also describes the physical layer, and how copper or fiber is used.

There may be additional layers, for example, if Internet Protocol Security (IPsec) or Linux WireGuard are in use, they are above the Internet layer to provide security between IP endpoints. Also, if tunneling is in use (e.g., Virtual Extensible LAN (VXLAN)), then one protocol stack may be encapsulated in another.

While the TCP/IP stack has become standard, I think it can be useful to briefly consider the OSI model as well, as it shows protocol layers within the application.[1] The "layer" terminology is from OSI, where *Layer 3* refers to the network protocols.

Messages at different layers also use different terminology. Using the OSI model: at the transport layer a message is a *segment* or *datagram*; at the network layer a message is a *packet*; and at the data link layer a message is a *frame*.

---

[1] I think it's worthwhile to *briefly* consider it; I would not include it in a networking knowledge test.

10.3 Concepts

The following are a selection of important concepts in networking and network performance.

10.3.1 Networks and Routing

A network is a group of connected hosts, related by network protocol addresses. Having multiple networks—instead of one giant worldwide network—is desirable for a number of reasons, particularly scalability. Some network messages will be *broadcast* to all neighboring hosts. By creating smaller subnetworks, such broadcast messages can be isolated locally so they do not create a flooding problem at scale. This is also the basis for isolating the transmission of regular messages to only the networks between source and destination, making more efficient usage of network infrastructure.

Routing manages the delivery of messages, called *packets*, across these networks. The role of routing is pictured in Figure 10.4.

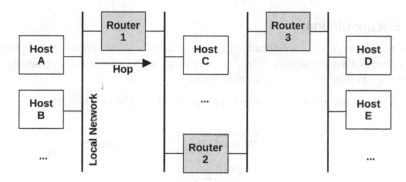

Figure 10.4   Networks connected via routers

From the perspective of host A, the *localhost* is host A itself. All other hosts pictured are *remote hosts*.

Host A can connect to host B via the local network, usually driven by a network switch (see Section 10.4, Architecture). Host A can connect to host C via router 1, and to host D via routers 1, 2, and 3. Since network components such as routers are shared, contention from other traffic (e.g., host C to host E) can hurt performance.

Connections between pairs of hosts involve *unicast* transmission. *Multicast* transmission allows a sender to transmit to multiple destinations simultaneously, which may span multiple networks. This must be supported by the router configuration to allow delivery. In public cloud environments it may be blocked.

Apart from routers, a typical network will also use *firewalls* to improve security, blocking unwanted connections between hosts.

The address information needed to route packets is contained in an IP header.

10.3.2 Protocols

Network protocol standards, such as those for IP, TCP, and UDP, are a necessary requirement for communication between systems and devices. Communication is performed by transferring routable messages called *packets*, typically by encapsulation of payload data.

Network protocols have different performance characteristics, arising from the original protocol design, extensions, or special handling by software or hardware. For example, the different versions of the IP protocol, IPv4 and IPv6, may be processed by different kernel code paths and can exhibit different performance characteristics. Other protocols perform differently by design, and may be selected when they suit the workload: examples include Stream Control Transmission Protocol (SCTP), Multipath TCP (MPTCP), and QUIC.

Often, there are also system tunable parameters that can affect protocol performance, by changing settings such as buffer sizes, algorithms, and various timers. These differences for specific protocols are described in later sections.

Protocols typically transmit data by use of encapsulation.

10.3.3 Encapsulation

Encapsulation adds metadata to a payload at the start (a *header*), at the end (a *footer*), or both. This doesn't change the payload data, though it does increase the total size of the message slightly, which costs some overhead for transmission.

Figure 10.5 shows an example of encapsulation for a TCP/IP stack with Ethernet.

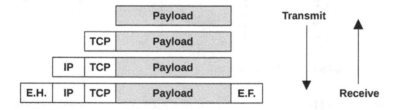

Figure 10.5 Network protocol encapsulation

E.H. is the Ethernet header, and E.F. is the optional Ethernet footer.

10.3.4 Packet Size

The size of the packets and their payload affect performance, with larger sizes improving throughput and reducing packet overheads. For TCP/IP and Ethernet, packets can be between 54 and 9,054 bytes, including the 54 bytes (or more, depending on options or version) of protocol headers.

Packet size is usually limited by the network interface *maximum transmission unit* (MTU) size, which for many Ethernet networks is configured to be 1,500 bytes. The origin of the 1500 MTU size was from the early versions of Ethernet, and the need to balance factors such as NIC buffer memory cost and transmission latency [Nosachev 20]. Hosts competed to use a shared medium (coax or an Ethernet hub), and larger sizes increased the latency for hosts to wait their turn.

Ethernet now supports larger packets (frames) of up to approximately 9,000 bytes, termed *jumbo frames*. These can improve network throughput performance, as well as the latency of data transfers, by requiring fewer packets.

The confluence of two components has interfered with the adoption of jumbo frames: older network hardware and misconfigured firewalls. Older hardware that does not support jumbo frames can either fragment the packet using the IP protocol (causing a performance cost for the packet reassembly) or respond with an ICMP "can't fragment" error, letting the sender know to reduce the packet size. Now the misconfigured firewalls come into play: there have been ICMP-based attacks in the past (including the "ping of death") to which some firewall administrators have responded by blocking all ICMP. This prevents the helpful "can't fragment" messages from reaching the sender and causes network packets to be silently dropped once their packet size increases beyond 1,500. If the ICMP message is received and fragmentation occurs, there is also the risk of fragmented packets getting dropped by devices that do not support them. To avoid these problems, many systems stick to the 1,500 MTU default.

The performance of 1,500 MTU frames has been improved by network interface card features, including *TCP offload* and *large segment offload*. These send larger buffers to the network card, which can then split them into smaller frames using dedicated and optimized hardware. This has, to some degree, narrowed the gap between 1,500 and 9,000 MTU network performance.

10.3.5 Latency

Latency is an important metric for network performance and can be measured in different ways, including name resolution latency, ping latency, connection latency, first-byte latency, round-trip time, and connection life span. These are described as measured by a client connecting to a server.

Name Resolution Latency

When establishing connections to remote hosts, a host name is usually resolved to an IP address, for example, by DNS resolution. The time this takes can be measured separately as name resolution latency. Worst case for this latency involves name resolution time-outs, which can take tens of seconds.

Operating systems often provide a name resolution service that provides caching, so that subsequent DNS lookups can resolve quickly from a cache. Sometimes applications only use IP addresses and not names, and so DNS latency is avoided entirely.

Ping Latency

This is the time for an ICMP echo request to echo response, as measured by the ping(1) command. This time is used to measure network latency between hosts, including hops in between, and is measured as the time needed for a network request to make a round-trip. It is in common use because it is simple and often readily available: many operating systems will respond to ping by default. It may not exactly reflect the round-trip time of application requests, as ICMP may be handled with a different priority by routers.

Example ping latencies are shown in Table 10.1.

Table 10.1 **Example ping latencies**

From	To	Via	Latency	Scaled
Localhost	Localhost	Kernel	0.05 ms	1 s
Host	Host (same subnet)	10 GbE	0.2 ms	4 s
Host	Host (same subnet)	1 GbE	0.6 ms	12 s
Host	Host (same subnet)	Wi-Fi	3 ms	1 minute
San Francisco	New York	Internet	40 ms	13 minutes
San Francisco	United Kingdom	Internet	81 ms	27 minutes
San Francisco	Australia	Internet	183 ms	1 hour

To better illustrate the orders of magnitude involved, the Scaled column shows a comparison based on an imaginary localhost ping latency of one second.

Connection Latency

Connection latency is the time to establish a network connection, before any data is transferred. For *TCP connection latency*, this is the TCP handshake time. Measured from the client, it is the time from sending the SYN to receiving the corresponding SYN-ACK. Connection latency might be better termed *connection establishment latency* to clearly differentiate it from connection life span.

Connection latency is similar to ping latency, although it exercises more kernel code to establish a connection and includes time to retransmit any dropped packets. The TCP SYN packet, in particular, can be dropped by the server if its backlog is full, causing the client to send a timer-based retransmit of the SYN. This occurs during the TCP handshake, so connection latency can include retransmission latency, adding one or more seconds.

Connection latency is followed by first-byte latency.

First-Byte Latency

Also known as *time to first byte* (TTFB), first-byte latency is the time from when the connection has been established to when the first byte of data is received. This includes the time for the remote host to accept a connection, schedule the thread that services it, and for that thread to execute and send the first byte.

While ping and connection latency measures the latency incurred by the network, first-byte latency includes the think time of the target server. This may include latency if the server is overloaded and needs time to process the request (e.g., TCP backlog) and to schedule the server (CPU scheduler latency).

Round-Trip Time

Round-trip time (RTT) describes the time needed for a network request to make a round trip between the endpoints. This includes the signal propagation time and the processing time at each network hop. The intended use is to determine the latency of the network, so ideally RTT is dominated by the time that the request and reply packets spend on the network (and not the time the remote host spends servicing the request). RTT for ICMP echo requests is often studied, as the remote host processing time is minimal.

Connection Life Span

Connection life span is the time from when a network connection is established to when it is closed. Some protocols use a *keep-alive* strategy, extending the duration of connections so that future operations can use existing connections and avoid the overheads and latency of connection establishment (and TLS establishment).

For more network latency measurements, see Section 10.5.4, Latency Analysis, which describes using them to diagnose network performance.

10.3.6 Buffering

Despite various network latencies that may be encountered, network throughput can be sustained at high rates by use of buffering on the sender and receiver. Larger buffers can mitigate the effects of higher round-trip times by continuing to send data before blocking and waiting for an acknowledgment.

TCP employs buffering, along with a sliding send window, to improve throughput. Network sockets also have buffers, and applications may also employ their own, to aggregate data before sending.

Buffering can also be performed by external network components, such as switches and routers, in an effort to improve their own throughput. Unfortunately, the use of large buffers on these components can lead to *bufferbloat*, where packets are queued for long intervals. This causes TCP congestion avoidance on the hosts, which throttles performance. Features have been added to the Linux 3.x kernels to address this problem (including byte queue limits, the CoDel queueing discipline [Nichols 12], and TCP small queues). There is also a website for discussing the issue [Bufferbloat 20].

The function of buffering (or large buffering) may be best served by the endpoints—the hosts—and not the intermediate network nodes, following a principle called *end-to-end arguments* [Saltzer 84].

10.3.7 Connection Backlog

Another type of buffering is for the initial connection requests. TCP implements a backlog, where SYN requests can queue in the kernel before being accepted by the user-land process. When there are too many TCP connection requests for the process to accept in time, the backlog reaches a limit and SYN packets are dropped, to be later retransmitted by the client. The retransmission of these packets causes latency for the client connect time. The limit is tunable: it is a parameter of the listen(2) syscall, and the kernel may also provide system-wide limits.

Backlog drops and SYN retransmits are indicators of host overload.

10.3.8   Interface Negotiation

Network interfaces may operate with different modes, autonegotiated between the connected transceivers. Some examples are:

- **Bandwidth:** For example, 10, 100, 1,000, 10,000, 40,000, 100,000 Mbits/s
- **Duplex:** Half or full duplex

These examples are from Ethernet, which tends to use round base-10 numbers for bandwidth limits. Other physical-layer protocols, such as SONET, have a different set of possible bandwidths.

Network interfaces are usually described in terms of their highest bandwidth and protocol, for example, 1 Gbit/s Ethernet (1 GbE). This interface may, however, autonegotiate to lower speeds if needed. This can occur if the other endpoint cannot operate faster, or to accommodate physical problems with the connection medium (bad wiring).

Full-duplex mode allows bidirectional simultaneous transmission, with separate paths for transmit and receive that can each operate at full bandwidth. Half-duplex mode allows only one direction at a time.

10.3.9   Congestion Avoidance

Networks are shared resources that can become congested when traffic loads are high. This can cause performance problems: for example, routers or switches may drop packets, causing latency-inducing TCP retransmits. Hosts can also become overwhelmed when receiving high packet rates, and may drop packets themselves.

There are many mechanisms to avoid these problems; these mechanisms should be studied, and tuned if necessary, to improve scalability under load. Examples for different protocols include:

- **Ethernet:** An overwhelmed host may send *pause frames* to a transmitter, requesting that they pause transmission (IEEE 802.3x). There are also priority classes and *priority pause frames* for each class.
- **IP:** Includes an Explicit Congestion Notification (ECN) field.
- **TCP:** Includes a congestion window, and various *congestion control algorithms* may be used.

Later sections describe IP ECN and TCP congestion control algorithms in more detail.

10.3.10   Utilization

Network interface utilization can be calculated as the current throughput over the maximum bandwidth. Given variable bandwidth and duplex due to autonegotiation, calculating this isn't as straightforward as it sounds.

For full duplex, utilization applies to each direction and is measured as the current throughput for that direction over the current negotiated bandwidth. Usually it is just one direction that matters most, as hosts are commonly asymmetric: servers are transmit-heavy, and clients are receive-heavy.

Once a network interface direction reaches 100% utilization, it becomes a bottleneck, limiting performance.

Some performance tools report activity only in terms of packets, not bytes. Since packet size can vary greatly (as mentioned earlier), it is not possible to relate packet counts to byte counts for calculating either throughput or (throughput-based) utilization.

10.3.11 Local Connections

Network connections can occur between two applications on the same system. These are *localhost* connections and use a virtual network interface: *loopback*.

Distributed application environments are often split into logical parts that communicate over the network. These can include web servers, database servers, caching servers, proxy servers, and application servers. If they are running on the same host, their connections are to localhost.

Connecting via IP to localhost is the *IP sockets* technique of inter-process communication (IPC). Another technique is Unix domain sockets (UDS), which create a file on the file system for communication. Performance may be better with UDS, as the kernel TCP/IP stack can be bypassed, skipping kernel code and the overheads of protocol packet encapsulation.

For TCP/IP sockets, the kernel may detect the localhost connection after the handshake, and then shortcut the TCP/IP stack for data transfers, improving performance. This was developed as a Linux kernel feature, called *TCP friends*, but was not merged [Corbet 12]. BPF can now be used on Linux for this purpose, as is done by the Cilium software for container networking performance and security [Cilium 20a].

10.4 Architecture

This section introduces network architecture: protocols, hardware, and software. These have been summarized as background for performance analysis and tuning, with a focus on performance characteristics. For more details, including general networking topics, see networking texts [Stevens 93][Hassan 03], RFCs, and vendor manuals for networking hardware. Some of these are listed at the end of the chapter.

10.4.1 Protocols

In this section, performance features and characteristics of IP, TCP, UDP, and QUIC are summarized. How these protocols are implemented in hardware and software (including features such as segmentation offload, connection queues, and buffering) is described in the later hardware and software sections.

IP

The Internet Protocol (IP) versions 4 and 6 include a field to set the desired performance of a connection: the Type of Service field in IPv4, and the Traffic Class field in IPv6. These fields have since been redefined to contain a Differentiated Services Code Point (DSCP) (RFC 2474) [Nichols 98] and an Explicit Congestion Notification (ECN) field (RFC 3168) [Ramakrishnan 01].

The DSCP is intended to support different *service classes*, each of which have different characteristics including packet drop probability. Example service classes include: telephony, broadcast video, low-latency data, high-throughput data, and low-priority data.

ECN is a mechanism that allows servers, routers, or switches on the path to explicitly signal the presence of congestion by setting a bit in the IP header, instead of dropping a packet. The receiver will echo this signal back to the sender, which can then throttle transmission. This provides the benefits of congestion avoidance without incurring the penalty of packet drops (provided that the ECN bit is used correctly across the network).

TCP

The Transmission Control Protocol (TCP) is a commonly used Internet standard for creating reliable network connections. TCP is specified by RFC 793 [Postel 81] and later additions.

In terms of performance, TCP can provide a high rate of throughput even on high-latency networks, by use of buffering and a *sliding window*. TCP also employs congestion control and a *congestion window* set by the sender, so that it can maintain a high but also reliable rate of transmission across different and varying networks. Congestion control avoids sending too many packets, which would cause congestion and a performance breakdown.

The following is a summary of TCP performance features, including additions since the original specification:

- **Sliding window:** This allows multiple packets up to the size of the window to be sent on the network before acknowledgments are received, providing high throughput even on high-latency networks. The size of the window is advertised by the receiver to indicate how many packets it is willing to receive at that time.

- **Congestion avoidance:** To prevent sending too much data and causing saturation, which can cause packet drops and worse performance.

- **Slow-start:** Part of TCP congestion control, this begins with a small congestion window and then increases it as acknowledgments (ACKs) are received within a certain time. When they are not, the congestion window is reduced.

- **Selective acknowledgments** (SACKs): Allow TCP to acknowledge discontinuous packets, reducing the number of retransmits required.

- **Fast retransmit:** Instead of waiting on a timer, TCP can retransmit dropped packets based on the arrival of duplicate ACKs. These are a function of round-trip time and not the typically much slower timer.

- **Fast recovery:** This recovers TCP performance after detecting duplicate ACKs, by resetting the connection to perform slow-start.

- **TCP fast open:** Allows a client to include data in a SYN packet, so that server request processing can begin earlier and not wait for the SYN handshake (RFC7413). This can use a cryptographic cookie to authenticate the client.

- **TCP timestamps:** Includes a timestamp for sent packets that is returned in the ACK, so that round-trip time can be measured (RFC 1323) [Jacobson 92].

- **TCP SYN cookies:** Provides cryptographic cookies to clients during possible SYN flood attacks (full backlogs) so that legitimate clients can continue to connect, and without the server needing to store extra data for these connection attempts.

In some cases these features are implemented by use of extended TCP options added to the protocol header.

Important topics for TCP performance include the three-way handshake, duplicate ACK detection, congestion control algorithms, Nagle, delayed ACKs, SACK, and FACK.

Three-Way Handshake

Connections are established using a three-way handshake between the hosts. One host passively listens for connections; the other actively initiates the connection. To clarify terminology: *passive* and *active* are from RFC 793 [Postel 81]; however, they are commonly called *listen* and *connect*, respectively, after the socket API. For the client/server model, the server performs listen and the client performs connect.

The three-way handshake is pictured in Figure 10.6.

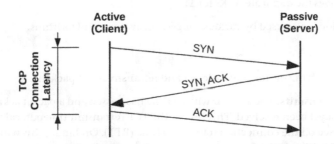

Figure 10.6 TCP three-way handshake

Connection latency from the client is indicated, which completes when the final ACK is sent. After that, data transfer may begin.

This figure shows best-case latency for a handshake. A packet may be dropped, adding latency as it is timed out and retransmitted.

Once the three-way handshake is complete, the TCP session is placed in the ESTABLISHED state.

States and Timers

TCP sessions switch between TCP states based on packets and socket events. The states are LISTEN, SYN-SENT, SYN-RECEIVED, ESTABLISHED, FIN-WAIT-1, FIN-WAIT-2, CLOSE-WAIT, CLOSING, LAST-ACK, TIME-WAIT, and CLOSED [Postal 80]. Performance analysis typically focuses on those in the ESTABLISHED state, which are the active connections. Such connections may be transferring data, or idle awaiting the next event: a data transfer or close event.

A session that has fully closed enters the TIME_WAIT[2] state so that late packets are not mis-associated with a new connection on the same ports. This can lead to a performance issue of port exhaustion, explained in Section 10.5.7, TCP Analysis.

Some states have timers associated with them. TIME_WAIT is typically two minutes (some kernels, such as the Windows kernel, allow it to be tuned). There may also be a "keep alive" timer on ESTABLISHED, set to a long duration (e.g., two hours), to trigger probe packets to check that the remote host is still alive.

Duplicate ACK Detection

Duplicate ACK detection is used by the fast retransmit and fast recovery algorithms to quickly detect when a sent packet (or its ACK) has been lost. It works as follows:

1. The sender sends a packet with sequence number 10.

2. The receiver replies with an ACK for sequence number 11.

3. The sender sends 11, 12, and 13.

4. Packet 11 is dropped.

5. The receiver replies to both 12 and 13 by sending an ACK for 11, which it is still expecting.

6. The sender receives the duplicate ACKs for 11.

Duplicate ACK detection is also used by various congestion avoidance algorithms.

Retransmits

Two commonly used mechanisms for TCP to detect and retransmits lost packets are:

- **Timer-based retransmits:** These occur when a time has passed and a packet acknowledgment has not yet been received. This time is the TCP retransmit timeout, calculated dynamically based on the connection round-trip time (RTT). On Linux, this will be at least 200 ms (TCP_RTO_MIN) for the first retransmit,[3] and subsequent retransmits will be much slower, following an exponential backoff algorithm that doubles the timeout.

- **Fast retransmits:** When duplicate ACKs arrive, TCP can assume that a packet was dropped and retransmit it immediately.

To further improve performance, additional mechanisms have been developed to avoid the timer-based retransmit. One problem occurs is when the last transmitted packet is lost, and there are no subsequent packets to trigger duplicate ACK detection. (Consider the prior example with a loss on packet 13.) This is solved by Tail Loss Probe (TLP), which sends an additional packet (probe) after a short timeout on the last transmission to help detect packet loss [Dukkipati 13].

Congestion control algorithms may also throttle throughput in the presence of retransmits.

---

[2]While it is often written (and programmed) as TIME_WAIT, RFC 793 uses TIME-WAIT.

[3]This seems to violate RFC6298, which stipulates a one second RTO minimum [Paxson 11].

Congestion Controls

Congestion control algorithms have been developed to maintain performance on congested networks. Some operating systems (including Linux-based) allow the algorithm to be selected as part of system tuning. These algorithms include:

- **Reno**: Triple duplicate ACKs trigger: halving of the congestion window, halving of the slow-start threshold, fast retransmit, and fast recovery.

- **Tahoe**: Triple duplicate ACKs trigger: fast retransmit, halving the slow-start threshold, congestion window set to one maximum segment size (MSS), and slow-start state. (Along with Reno, Tahoe was first developed for 4.3BSD.)

- **CUBIC**: Uses a cubic function (hence the name) to scale the window, and a "hybrid start" function to exit slow start. CUBIC tends to be more aggressive than Reno, and is the default in Linux.

- **BBR**: Instead of window-based, BBR builds an explicit model of the network path characteristics (RTT and bandwidth) using probing phases. BBR can provide dramatically better performance on some network paths, while hurting performance on others. BBRv2 is currently in development and promises to fix some of the deficiencies of v1.

- **DCTCP**: DataCenter TCP relies on switches configured to emit Explicit Congestion Notification (ECN) marks at a very shallow queue occupancy to rapidly ramp up to the available bandwidth (RFC 8257) [Bensley 17]. This makes DCTCP unsuitable for deployment across the Internet, but in a suitably configured controlled environment it can improve performance significantly.

Other algorithms not listed previously include Vegas, New Reno, and Hybla.

The congestion control algorithm can make a large difference to network performance. The Netflix cloud services, for example, use BBR and found it can improve throughput threefold during heavy packet loss [Ather 17]. Understanding how these algorithms react under different network conditions is an important activity when analyzing TCP performance.

Linux 5.6, released in 2020, added support for developing new congestion control algorithms in BPF [Corbet 20]. This allows them to be defined by the end user and loaded on demand.

Nagle

This algorithm (RFC 896) [Nagle 84] reduces the number of small packets on the network by delaying their transmission to allow more data to arrive and be coalesced. This delays packets only if there is data in the pipeline and delays are already being encountered.

The system may provide a tunable parameter or socket option to disable Nagle, which may be necessary if its operation conflicts with delayed ACKs (see Section 10.8.2, Socket Options).

Delayed ACKs

This algorithm (RFC 1122) [Braden 89] delays the sending of ACKs up to 500 ms, so that multiple ACKs may be combined. Other TCP control messages can also be combined, reducing the number of packets on the network.

As with Nagle, the system may provide a tunable parameter to disable this behavior.

SACK, FACK, and RACK

The TCP selective acknowledgment (SACK) algorithm allows the receiver to inform the sender that it received a noncontiguous block of data. Without this, a packet drop would eventually cause the entire send window to be retransmitted, to preserve a sequential acknowledgment scheme. This harms TCP performance and is avoided by most modern operating systems that support SACK.

SACK has been extended by forward acknowledgments (FACK), which are supported in Linux by default. FACKs track additional state and better regulate the amount of outstanding data in the network, improving overall performance [Mathis 96].

Both SACK and FACK are used to improve packet loss recovery. A newer algorithm, Recent ACKnowledgment (RACK; now called RACK-TLP with the incorporation of TLP) uses time information from ACKs for even better loss detection and recovery, rather than ACK sequences alone [Cheng 20]. For FreeBSD, Netflix has developed a new refactored TCP stack called RACK based on RACK, TLP, and other features [Stewart 18].

Initial Window

The initial window (IW) is the number of packets a TCP sender will transmit at the beginning of a connection before waiting for acknowledgment from the sender. For short flows, such as typical HTTP connections, an IW large enough to span the transmitted data can greatly reduce completion time, improving performance. Larger IWs, however, can risk congestion and packet drops. This is especially compounded when multiple flows start up at the same time.

The Linux default (10 packets, aka IW10) can be too high on slow links or when many connections start up; other operating systems default to 2 or 4 packets (IW2 or IW4).

UDP

The User Datagram Protocol (UDP) is a commonly used Internet standard for sending messages, called *datagrams*, across a network (RFC 768) [Postel 80]. In terms of performance, UDP provides:

- **Simplicity:** Simple and small protocol headers reduce overheads of computation and size.
- **Statelessness:** Lower overheads for connections and transmission.
- **No retransmits:** These add significant latencies for TCP connections.

While simple and often high-performing, UDP is not intended to be reliable, and data can be missing or received out of order. This makes it unsuitable for many types of connections. UDP also has no congestion avoidance and can therefore contribute to congestion on the network.

Some services, including versions of NFS, can be configured to operate over TCP or UDP as desired. Others that perform broadcast or multicast data may be able to use only UDP.

A major use for UDP has been DNS. Due to the simplicity of UDP, a lack of congestion control, and Internet support (it is not typically firewalled) there are now new protocols built upon UDP that implement their own congestion control and other features. An example is QUIC.

QUIC and HTTP/3

QUIC is a network protocol designed by Jim Roskind at Google as a higher-performing, lower-latency alternative to TCP, optimized for HTTP and TLS [Roskind 12]. QUIC is built upon UDP, and provides several features on top of it, including:

- The ability to multiplex several application-defined streams on top of the same "connection."

- A TCP-like reliable in-order stream transport that can be optionally turned off for individual substreams.

- Connection resumption when a client changes its network address, based on cryptographic authentication of connection IDs.

- Full encryption of the payload data, including QUIC headers.

- 0-RTT connection handshakes including cryptography (for peers that have previously communicated).

QUIC is in heavy use by the Chrome web browser.

While QUIC was initially developed by Google, the Internet Engineering Task Force (IETF) is in the process of standardizing both the QUIC transport itself, and the specific configuration of using HTTP over QUIC (the latter combination is named HTTP/3).

10.4.2 Hardware

Networking hardware includes interfaces, controllers, switches, routers, and firewalls. An understanding of their operation is useful, even if they are managed by other staff (network administrators).

Interfaces

Physical network interfaces send and receive messages, called *frames*, on the attached network. They manage the electrical, optical, or wireless signaling involved, including the handling of transmission errors.

Interface types are based on layer 2 standards, each providing a maximum bandwidth. Higher-bandwidth interfaces provide lower data-transfer latency, at a higher cost. When designing new servers, a key decision is often how to balance the price of the server with the desired network performance.

For Ethernet, choices include copper or optical, with maximum speeds of 1 Gbit/s (1 GbE), 10 GbE, 40 GbE, 100 GbE, 200 GbE, and 400 GbE. Numerous vendors manufacture Ethernet interface controllers, although your operating system may not have driver support for some of them.

Interface utilization can be examined as the current throughput divided by the current negotiated bandwidth. Most interfaces have separate channels for transmit and receive, and when operating in full-duplex mode, each channel's utilization must be studied separately.

Wireless interfaces can suffer performance issues due to poor signal strength and interference.[4]

Controllers

Physical network interfaces are provided to the system via controllers, either built into the system board or provided via expander cards.

Controllers are driven by microprocessors and are attached to the system via an I/O transport (e.g., PCI). Either of these can become the limiter for network throughput or IOPS.

For example, a dual 10 GbE network interface card is connected to a four-channel PCI express (PCIe) Gen 2 slot. The card has a maximum send or receive bandwidth of 2 × 10 GbE = 20 Gbits/s, and bidirectional, 40 Gbit/s. The slot has a maximum bandwidth of 4 × 4 Gbits/s = 16 Gbits/s. Therefore, network throughput on both ports will be limited by PCIe Gen 2 bandwidth, and it will not be possible to drive them both at line rate at the same time (I know this from practice!).

Switches and Routers

Switches provide a dedicated communication path between any two connected hosts, allowing multiple transmissions between pairs of hosts without interference. This technology replaced hubs (and before that, shared physical buses: the commonly used thick-Ethernet coaxial cable), which shared all packets with all hosts. This sharing led to contention when hosts transmitted simultaneously, identified by the interface as a *collision* using a "carrier sense multiple access with collision detection" (CSMA/CD) algorithm. This algorithm would exponentially back off and retransmit until successful, creating performance issues under load. With the use of switches this is behind us, but some observability tools still have collision counters—even though these usually occur only due to errors (negotiation or bad wiring).

Routers deliver packets between networks and use network protocols and routing tables to determine efficient delivery paths. Delivering a packet between two cities may involve a dozen or more routers, plus other network hardware. The routers and routes are usually configured to update dynamically, so that the network can automatically respond to network and router outages, and to balance load. This means that at a given point in time, no one can be sure what path a packet is actually taking. With multiple paths possible, there is also the potential for packets to be delivered out of order, which can cause TCP performance problems.

This element of mystery on the network is often blamed for poor performance: perhaps heavy network traffic—from other unrelated hosts—is saturating a router between the source and destination? Network administration teams are therefore frequently required to exonerate their infrastructure. They can do so using advanced real-time monitoring tools to check all routers and other network components involved.

---

[4]I developed BPF software that turns Linux Wi-Fi signal strength into an audible pitch, and demonstrated it in an AWS re:Invent 2019 talk [Gregg 19b]. I would include it in this chapter, but I have not yet used it for enterprise or cloud environments, which so far are all wired.

Both routers and switches include buffers and microprocessors, which themselves can become performance bottlenecks under load. As an extreme example, I once found that an early 10 GbE switch could drive no more than 11 Gbits/s in total across all ports, due to its limited CPU capacity.

Note that switches and routers are also often where *rate transitions* occur (switching from one bandwidth to another, e.g., a 10 Gbps link transitions to a 1 Gbps link). When this happens, some buffering is necessary to avoid excessive drops, but many switches and routers over-buffer (see the bufferbloat issue in Section 10.3.6, Buffering), leading to high latencies. Better queue management algorithms can help eliminate this problem, but not all network device vendors support them. Pacing at the source can also be a way to alleviate issues with rate transitions by making the traffic less bursty.

Firewalls

Firewalls are often in use to permit only authorized communications based on a configured rule set, improving the security of the network. They may be present as both physical network devices and kernel software.

Firewalls can become a performance bottleneck, especially when configured to be stateful. Stateful rules store metadata for each seen connection, and the firewall may experience excessive memory load when processing many connections. This can happen due to a denial of service (DoS) attack that attempts to inundate a target with connections. It can also happen with a heavy rate of outbound connections, as they may require similar connection tracking.

As firewalls are custom hardware or software, the tools available to analyze them depends on each firewall product. See their respective documentation.

The use of extended BPF to implement firewalls on commodity hardware is growing, due to its performance, programmability, ease of use, and final cost. Companies adopting BPF firewalls and DDoS solutions include Facebook [Deepak 18], Cloudflare [Majkowski 18], and Cilium [Cilium 20a].

Firewalls can also be a nuisance during performance testing: performing a bandwidth experiment when debugging an issue may involve modifying firewall rules to allow the connection (and coordinating that with the security team).

Others

Your environment may include other physical network devices, such as hubs, bridges, repeaters, and modems. Any of these can be a source of performance bottlenecks and dropped packets.

10.4.3 Software

Networking software includes the network stack, TCP, and device drivers. Topics related to performance are discussed in this section.

Network Stack

The components and layers involved depend on the operating system type, version, protocols, and interfaces in use. Figure 10.7 depicts a general model, showing the software components.

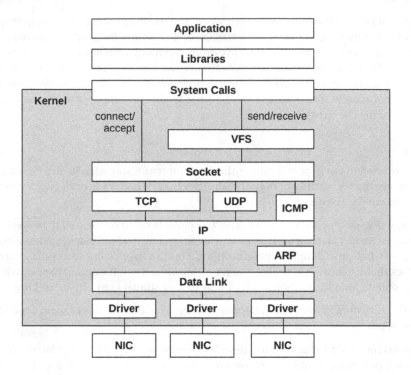

Figure 10.7   Generic network stack

On modern kernels the stack is multithreaded, and inbound packets can be processed by multiple CPUs.

Linux

The Linux network stack is pictured in Figure 10.8, including the location of socket send/receive buffers and packet queues.

On Linux systems, the network stack is a core kernel component, and device drivers are additional modules. Packets are passed through these kernel components as the struct sk_buff (socket buffer) data type. Note that there may also be queueing in the IP layer (not pictured) for packet reassembly.

The following sections discuss Linux implementation details related to performance: TCP connection queues, TCP buffering, queueing disciplines, network device drivers, CPU scaling, and kernel bypass. The TCP protocol was described in the previous section.

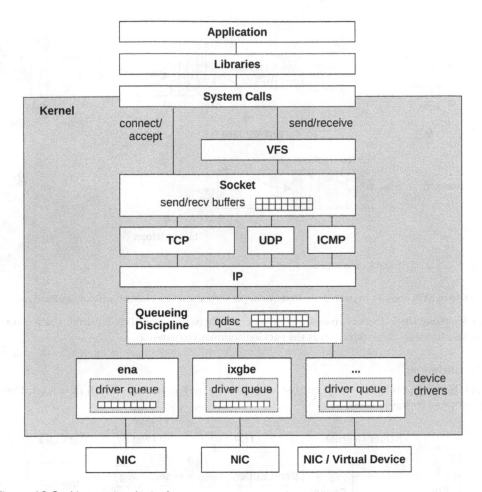

Figure 10.8   Linux network stack

TCP Connection Queues

Bursts of inbound connections are handled by using backlog queues. There are two such queues, one for incomplete connections while the TCP handshake completes (also known as the *SYN backlog*), and one for established sessions waiting to be accepted by the application (also known as the *listen backlog*). These are pictured in Figure 10.9.

Only one queue was used in earlier kernels, and it was vulnerable to SYN floods. A SYN flood is a type of DoS attack that involves sending numerous SYNs to the listening TCP port from bogus IP addresses. This fills the backlog queue while TCP waits to complete the handshake, preventing real clients from connecting.

With two queues, the first can act as a staging area for potentially bogus connections, which are promoted to the second queue only once the connection is established. The first queue can be made long to absorb SYN floods and optimized to store only the minimum amount of metadata necessary.

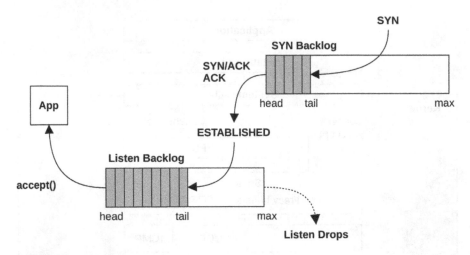

Figure 10.9   TCP backlog queues

The use of SYN cookies bypasses the first queue, as they show the client is already authorized.

The length of these queues can be tuned independently (see Section 10.8, Tuning). The second can also be set by the application as the backlog argument to listen(2).

TCP Buffering

Data throughput is improved by using send and receive buffers associated with the socket. These are pictured in Figure 10.10.

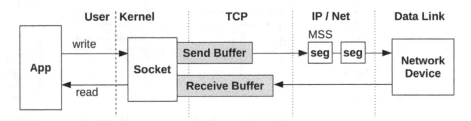

Figure 10.10   TCP send and receive buffers

The size of both the send and receive buffers is tunable. Larger sizes improve throughput performance, at the cost of more main memory spent per connection. One buffer may be set to be larger than the other if the server is expected to perform more sending or receiving. The Linux kernel will also dynamically increase the size of these buffers based on connection activity, and allows tuning of their minimum, default, and maximum sizes.

Segmentation Offload: GSO and TSO

Network devices and networks accept packet sizes up to a maximum segment size (MSS) that may be as small as 1500 bytes. To avoid the network stack overheads of sending many small packets, Linux uses generic segmentation offload (GSO) to send packets up to 64 Kbytes in size ("super packets"), which are split into MSS-sized segments just before delivery to the network device. If the NIC and driver support TCP segmentation offload (TSO), GSO leaves splitting to the device, improving network stack throughput.[5] There is also a generic receive offload (GRO) complement to GSO [Linux 20i].[6] GRO and GSO are implemented in kernel software, and TSO is implemented by NIC hardware.

Queueing Discipline

This is an optional layer for managing traffic classification (tc), scheduling, manipulation, filtering, and shaping of network packets. Linux provides numerous queueing discipline algorithms (qdiscs), which can be configured using the tc(8) command. As each has a man page, the man(1) command can be used to list them:

```
# man -k tc-
tc-actions (8)        - independently defined actions in tc
tc-basic (8)          - basic traffic control filter
tc-bfifo (8)          - Packet limited First In, First Out queue
tc-bpf (8)            - BPF programmable classifier and actions for ingress/egress
queueing disciplines
tc-cbq (8)            - Class Based Queueing
tc-cbq-details (8)    - Class Based Queueing
tc-cbs (8)            - Credit Based Shaper (CBS) Qdisc
tc-cgroup (8)         - control group based traffic control filter
tc-choke (8)          - choose and keep scheduler
tc-codel (8)          - Controlled-Delay Active Queue Management algorithm
tc-connmark (8)       - netfilter connmark retriever action
tc-csum (8)           - checksum update action
tc-drr (8)            - deficit round robin scheduler
tc-ematch (8)         - extended matches for use with "basic" or "flow" filters
tc-flow (8)           - flow based traffic control filter
tc-flower (8)         - flow based traffic control filter
tc-fq (8)             - Fair Queue traffic policing
tc-fq_codel (8)       - Fair Queuing (FQ) with Controlled Delay (CoDel)
[...]
```

The Linux kernel sets pfifo_fast as the default qdisc, whereas systemd is less conservative and sets it to fq_codel to reduce potential bufferbloat, at the cost of slightly higher complexity in the qdisc layer.

BPF can enhance the capabilities of this layer with the programs of type BPF_PROG_TYPE_SCHED_CLS and BPF_PROG_TYPE_SCHED_ACT. These BPF programs can be attached to kernel ingress and egress points for packet filtering, mangling, and forwarding, as used by load balancers and firewalls.

---

[5] Some network cards provide a TCP offload engine (TOE) to offload part or all of TCP/IP protocol processing. Linux does not support TOE for various reasons, including security, complexity, and even performance [Linux 16].

[6] UDP support for GSO and GRO was added to Linux in 2018, with QUIC a key use case [Bruijn 18].

Network Device Drivers

The network device driver usually has an additional buffer—a ring buffer—for sending and receiving packets between kernel memory and the NIC. This was pictured in Figure 10.8 as the driver queue.

A performance feature that has become more common with high-speed networking is the use of *interrupt coalescing mode*. Instead of interrupting the kernel for every arrived packet, an interrupt is sent only when either a timer (polling) or a certain number of packets is reached. This reduces the rate at which the kernel communicates with the NIC, allowing larger transfers to be buffered, resulting in greater throughput, though at some cost in latency.

The Linux kernel uses a new API (NAPI) framework that uses an interrupt mitigation technique: for low packet rates, interrupts are used (processing is scheduled via a softirq); for high packet rates, interrupts are disabled, and polling is used to allow coalescing [Corbet 03][Corbet 06b]. This provides low latency or high throughput, depending on the workload. Other features of NAPI include:

- Packet throttling, which allows early packet drop in the network adapter to prevent the system from being overwhelmed by packet storms.

- Interface scheduling, where a quota is used to limit the buffers processed in a polling cycle, to ensure fairness between busy network interfaces.

- Support for the SO_BUSY_POLL socket option, where user-level applications can reduce network receive latency by requesting to *busy wait* (spin on CPU until an event occurs) on a socket [Dumazet 17a].

Coalescing can be especially important for improving virtual machine networking, and is used by the ena network driver used by AWS EC2.

NIC Send and Receive

For sent packets, the NIC is notified and typically reads the packet (frame) from kernel memory using direct memory access (DMA) for efficiency. NICs provide transmit descriptors for managing DMA packets; if the NIC does not have free descriptors, the network stack will pause transmission to allow the NIC to catch up.[7]

For received packets, NICs can use DMA to place the packet into kernel ring-buffer memory and then notify the kernel using an interrupt (which may be ignored to allow coalescing). The interrupt triggers a softirq to deliver the packet to the network stack for further processing.

CPU Scaling

High packet rates can be achieved by engaging multiple CPUs to process packets and the TCP/IP stack. Linux supports various methods for multi-CPU packet processing (see Documentation/networking/scaling.txt):

- **RSS: Receive Side Scaling**: For modern NICs that support multiple queues and can hash packets to different queues, which are in turn processed by different CPUs, interrupting

---

[7] Byte Queue Limits (BQL), summarized under the heading Other Optimizations, usually prevent TX descriptor exhaustion.

them directly. This hash may be based on the IP address and TCP port numbers, so that packets from the same connection end up being processed by the same CPU.[8]

- **RPS: Receive Packet Steering**: A software implementation of RSS, for NICs that do not support multiple queues. This involves a short interrupt service routine to map the inbound packet to a CPU for processing. A similar hash can be used to map packets to CPUs, based on fields from the packet headers.

- **RFS: Receive Flow Steering**: This is similar to RPS, but with affinity for where the socket was last processed on-CPU, to improve CPU cache hit rates and memory locality.

- **Accelerated Receive Flow Steering**: This achieves RFS in hardware, for NICs that support this functionality. It involves updating the NIC with flow information so that it can determine which CPU to interrupt.

- **XPS: Transmit Packet Steering**: For NICs with multiple transmit queues, this supports transmission by multiple CPUs to the queues.

Without a CPU load-balancing strategy for network packets, a NIC may interrupt only one CPU, which can reach 100% utilization and become a bottleneck. This may show up as high softirq CPU time on a single CPU (e.g., using Linux mpstat(1): see Chapter 6, CPUs, Section 6.6.3, mpstat). This may especially happen for load balancers or proxy servers (e.g., nginx), as their intended workload is a high rate of inbound packets.

Mapping interrupts to CPUs based on factors such as cache coherency, as is done by RFS, can noticeably improve network performance. This can also be accomplished by the irqbalance process, which assigns interrupt request (IRQ) lines to CPUs.

Kernel Bypass

Figure 10.8 shows the path most commonly taken through the TCP/IP stack. Applications can bypass the kernel network stack using technologies such as the Data Plane Development Kit (DPDK) in order to achieve higher packet rates and performance. This involves an application implementing its own network protocols in user-space, and making writes to the network driver via a DPDK library and a kernel user space I/O (UIO) or virtual function I/O (VFIO) driver. The expense of copying packet data can be avoided by directly accessing memory on the NIC.

The eXpress Data Path (XDP) technology provides another path for network packets: a programmable fast path that uses extended BPF and that integrates into the existing kernel stack rather than bypassing it [Høiland-Jørgensen 18]. (DPDK now supports XDP for receiving packets, moving some functionality back to the kernel [DPDK 20].)

With kernel network stack bypass, instrumentation using traditional tools and metrics is not available because the counters and tracing events they use are also bypassed. This makes performance analysis more difficult.

Apart from full stack bypass, there are capabilities for avoiding the expense of copying data: the MSG_ZEROCOPY send(2) flag, and zero-copy receive via mmap(2) [Linux 20c][Corbet 18b].

---

[8]The Netflix FreeBSD CDN uses RSS to assist TCP large receive offload (LRO), allowing packets for the same connection to be aggregated, even when separated by other packets [Gallatin 17].

Other Optimizations

There are other algorithms in use throughout the Linux network stack to improve performance. Figure 10.11 shows these for the TCP send path (many of these are called from the tcp_write_xmit() kernel function).

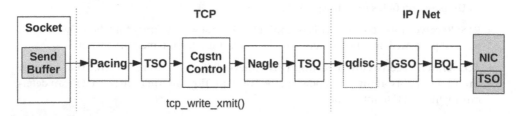

Figure 10.11 TCP send path

Some of these components and algorithms were described earlier (socket send buffers, TSO,[9] congestion controls, Nagle, and qdiscs); others include:

- **Pacing:** This controls when to send packets, spreading out transmissions (pacing) to avoid bursts that may hurt performance (this may help avoid TCP micro-bursts that can lead to queueing delay, or even cause network switches to drop packets. It may also help with the *incast* problem, when many end points transmit to one at the same time [Fritchie 12]).

- **TCP Small Queues (TSQ):** This controls (reduces) how much is queued by the network stack to avoid problems including bufferbloat [Bufferbloat 20].

- **Byte Queue Limits (BQL):** These automatically size the driver queues large enough to avoid starvation, but also small enough to reduce the maximum latency of queued packets, and to avoid exhausting NIC TX descriptors [Hrubý 12]. It works by pausing the addition of packets to the driver queue when necessary, and was added in Linux 3.3 [Siemon 13].

- **Earliest Departure Time (EDT):** This uses a timing wheel instead of a queue to order packets sent to the NIC. Timestamps are set on every packet based on policy and rate configuration. This was added in Linux 4.20, and has BQL- and TSQ-like capabilities [Jacobson 18].

These algorithms often work in combination to improve performance. A TCP sent packet can be processed by any of the congestion controls, TSO, TSQ, pacing, and queueing disciplines, before it ever arrives at the NIC [Cheng 16].

10.5 Methodology

This section describes methodologies and exercises for network analysis and tuning. Table 10.2 summarizes the topics.

---

[9]Note that TSO appears twice in the diagram: first, after Pacing to build a super packet, and then in the NIC for final segmentation.

Table 10.2 **Network performance methodologies**

Section	Methodology	Types
10.5.1	Tools method	Observational analysis
10.5.2	USE method	Observational analysis
10.5.3	Workload characterization	Observational analysis, capacity planning
10.5.4	Latency analysis	Observational analysis
10.5.5	Performance monitoring	Observational analysis, capacity planning
10.5.6	Packet sniffing	Observational analysis
10.5.7	TCP analysis	Observational analysis
10.5.8	Static performance tuning	Observational analysis, capacity planning
10.5.9	Resource controls	Tuning
10.5.10	Micro-benchmarking	Experimental analysis

See Chapter 2, Methodologies, for more strategies and the introduction to many of these.

These may be followed individually or used in combination. My suggestion is to use the following strategies to start with, in this order: performance monitoring, the USE method, static performance tuning, and workload characterization.

Section 10.6, Observability Tools, shows operating system tools for applying these methods.

10.5.1 Tools Method

The tools method is a process of iterating over available tools, examining key metrics they provide. It may overlook issues for which the tools provide poor or no visibility, and it can be time-consuming to perform.

For networking, the tools method can involve checking:

- **nstat/netstat -s**: Look for a high rate of retransmits and out-of-order packets. What constitutes a "high" retransmit rate depends on the clients: an Internet-facing system with unreliable remote clients should have a higher retransmit rate than an internal system with clients in the same data center.

- **ip -s link/netstat -i**: Check interface error counters, including "errors," "dropped," "overruns."

- **ss -tiepm**: Check for the limiter flag for important sockets to see what their bottleneck is, as well as other statistics showing socket health.

- **nicstat/ip -s link**: Check the rate of bytes transmitted and received. High throughput may be limited by a negotiated data link speed, or an external network throttle. It could also cause contention and delays between network users on the system.

- **tcplife**: Log TCP sessions with process details, duration (lifespan), and throughput statistics.

- **tcptop**: Watch top TCP sessions live.

- **tcpdump**: While this can be expensive to use in terms of the CPU and storage costs, using tcpdump(8) for short periods may help you identify unusual network traffic or protocol headers.

- **perf(1)/BCC/bpftrace**: Inspect selected packets between the application and the wire, including examining kernel state.

If an issue is found, examine all fields from the available tools to learn more context. See Section 10.6, Observability Tools, for more about each tool. Other methodologies can identify more types of issues.

10.5.2   USE Method

The USE method is for quickly identifying bottlenecks and errors across all components. For each network interface, and in each direction—transmit (TX) and receive (RX)—check for:

- **Utilization:** The time the interface was busy sending or receiving frames

- **Saturation:** The degree of extra queueing, buffering, or blocking due to a fully utilized interface

- **Errors:** For receive: bad checksum, frame too short (less than the data link header) or too long, collisions (unlikely with switched networks); for transmit: late collisions (bad wiring)

Errors may be checked first, since they are typically quick to check and the easiest to interpret.

Utilization is not commonly provided by operating system or monitoring tools directly (nicstat(1) is an exception). It can be calculated as the current throughput divided by the current negotiated speed, for each direction (RX, TX). The current throughput should be measured as bytes per second on the network, including all protocol headers.

For environments that implement network bandwidth limits (resource controls), as occurs in some cloud computing environments, network utilization may need to be measured in terms of the imposed limit, in addition to the physical limit.

Saturation of the network interface is difficult to measure. Some network buffering is normal, as applications can send data much more quickly than an interface can transmit it. It may be possible to measure as the time application threads spend blocked on network sends, which should increase as saturation increases. Also check if there are other kernel statistics more closely related to interface saturation, for example, Linux "overruns." Note that Linux uses BQL to regulate the NIC queue size, which helps avoid NIC saturation.

Retransmits at the TCP level are usually readily available as statistics and can be an indicator of network saturation. However, they are measured across the network between the server and its clients and could be caused by problems at any hop.

The USE method can also be applied to network controllers, and the transports between them and the processors. Since observability tools for these components are sparse, it may be easier to infer metrics based on network interface statistics and topology. For example, if network controller A houses ports A0 and A1, the network controller throughput can be calculated as the sum of the interface throughputs A0 + A1. With a known maximum throughput, utilization of the network controller can then be calculated.

10.5.3 Workload Characterization

Characterizing the load applied is an important exercise when capacity planning, benchmarking, and simulating workloads. It can also lead to some of the largest performance gains by identifying unnecessary work that can be eliminated.

The following are the most basic characteristics to measure:

- **Network interface throughput**: RX and TX, bytes per second
- **Network interface IOPS**: RX and TX, frames per second
- **TCP connection rate**: Active and passive, connections per second

The terms *active* and *passive* were described in the Three-Way Handshake section of Section 10.4.1, Protocols.

These characteristics can vary over time, as usage patterns change throughout the day. Monitoring over time is described in Section 10.5.5, Performance Monitoring.

Here is an example workload description, to show how these attributes can be expressed together:

> The network throughput varies based on users and performs more writes (TX) than reads (RX). The peak write rate is 200 Mbytes/s and 210,000 packets/s, and the peak read rate is 10 Mbytes/s with 70,000 packets/s. The inbound (passive) TCP connection rate reaches 3,000 connections/s.

Apart from describing these characteristics system-wide, they can also be expressed per interface. This allows interface bottlenecks to be determined, if the throughput can be observed to have reached line rate. If network bandwidth limits (resource controls) are present, they may throttle network throughput before line rate is reached.

Advanced Workload Characterization/Checklist

Additional details may be included to characterize the workload. These have been listed here as questions for consideration, which may also serve as a checklist when studying CPU issues thoroughly:

- What is the average packet size? RX, TX?
- What is the protocol breakdown for each layer? For transport protocols: TCP, UDP (which can include QUIC).
- What TCP/UDP ports are active? Bytes per second, connections per second?
- What are the broadcast and multicast packet rates?
- Which processes are actively using the network?

The sections that follow answer some of these questions. See Chapter 2, Methodologies, for a higher-level summary of this methodology and the characteristics to measure (who, why, what, how).

10.5.4   Latency Analysis

Various times (latencies) can be studied to help understand and express network performance. Some were introduced in Section 10.3.5, Latency, and a longer list is provided as Table 10.3. Measure as many of these as you can to narrow down the real source of latency.

Table 10.3   **Network latencies**

Latency	Description
Name resolution latency	The time for a host to be resolved to an IP address, usually by DNS resolution—a common source of performance issues.
Ping latency	The time from an ICMP echo request to a response. This measures the network and kernel stack handling of the packet on each host.
TCP connection initialization latency	The time from when a SYN is sent to when the SYN,ACK is received. Since no applications are involved, this measures the network and kernel stack latency on each host, similar to ping latency, with some additional kernel processing for the TCP session. TCP Fast Open (TFO) may be used to reduce this latency.
TCP first-byte latency	Also known as the time-to-first-byte latency (TTFB), this measures the time from when a connection is established to when the first data byte is received by the client. This includes CPU scheduling and application think time for the host, making it a more a measure of application performance and current load than TCP connection latency.
TCP retransmits	If present, can add thousands of milliseconds of latency to network I/O.
TCP TIME_WAIT latency	The duration that locally closed TCP sessions are left waiting for late packets.
Connection/session lifespan	The duration of a network connection from initialization to close. Some protocols like HTTP can use a keep-alive strategy, leaving connections open and idle for future requests, to avoid the overheads and latency of repeated connection establishment.
System call send/ receive latency	Time for the socket read/write calls (any syscalls that read/write to sockets, including read(2), write(2), recv(2), send(2), and variants).
System call connect latency	For connection establishment; note that some applications perform this as a non-blocking syscall.
Network round-trip time	The time for a network request to make a round-trip between endpoints. The kernel may use such measurements with congestion control algorithms.

Latency	Description
Interrupt latency	Time from a network controller interrupt for a received packet to when it is serviced by the kernel.
Inter-stack latency	Time for a packet to move through the kernel TCP/IP stack.

Latency may be presented as:

- **Per-interval averages:** Best performed per client/server pair, to isolate differences in the intermediate network
- **Full distributions:** As histograms or heat maps
- **Per-operation latency:** Listing details for each event, including source and destination IP addresses

A common source of issues is the presence of latency outliers caused by TCP retransmits. These can be identified using full distributions or per-operation latency tracing, including by filtering for a minimum latency threshold.

Latencies may be measured using tracing tools and, for some latencies, socket options. On Linux, the socket options include SO_TIMESTAMP for incoming packet time (and SO_TIMESTAMPNS for nanosecond resolution) and SO_TIMESTAMPING for per-event timestamps [Linux 20j]. SO_TIMESTAMPING can identify transmission delays, network round-trip time, and inter-stack latencies; this can be especially helpful when analyzing complex packet latency involving tunneling [Hassas Yeganeh 19].

Note that some sources of extra latency are transient and only occur during system load. For more realistic measurements of network latency, it is important to measure not only an idle system, but also a system under load.

10.5.5 Performance Monitoring

Performance monitoring can identify active issues and patterns of behavior over time, including daily patterns of end users, and scheduled activities including network backups.

Key metrics for network monitoring are

- **Throughput:** Network interface bytes per second for both receive and transmit, ideally for each interface
- **Connections:** TCP connections per second, as another indication of network load
- **Errors:** Including dropped packet counters
- **TCP retransmits:** Also useful to record for correlation with network issues
- **TCP out-of-order packets:** *Can also* cause performance problems

For environments that implement network bandwidth limits (resource controls), as in some cloud computing environments, statistics related to the imposed limits may also be collected.

10.5.6   Packet Sniffing

Packet sniffing (aka *packet capture*) involves capturing the packets from the network so that their protocol headers and data can be inspected on a packet-by-packet basis. For observational analysis this may be the last resort, as it can be expensive to perform in terms of CPU and storage overhead. Network kernel code paths are typically cycle-optimized, since they need to handle up to millions of packets per second and are sensitive to any extra overhead. To reduce this overhead, ring buffers may be used by the kernel to pass packet data to the user-level trace tool via a shared memory map—for example,[10] using BPF with perf(1)'s output ring buffer, and also using AF_XDP [Linux 20k]. A different way to solve overhead is to use an out-of-band packet sniffer: a separate server connected to a "tap" or "mirror" port of a switch. Public cloud providers such as Amazon and Google provide this as a service [Amazon 19][Google 20b].

Packet sniffing typically involves capturing packets to a file, and then analyzing that file in different ways. One way is to produce a log, which can contain the following for each packet:

- Timestamp
- Entire packet, including
  - All protocol headers (e.g., Ethernet, IP, TCP)
  - Partial or full payload data
- Metadata: number of packets, number of drops
- Interface name

As an example of packet capture, the following shows the default output of the Linux tcpdump(8) tool:

```
# tcpdump -ni eth4
tcpdump: verbose output suppressed, use -v or -vv for full protocol decode
listening on eth4, link-type EN10MB (Ethernet), capture size 65535 bytes
01:20:46.769073 IP 10.2.203.2.22 > 10.2.0.2.33771: Flags [P.], seq
4235343542:4235343734, ack 4053030377, win 132, options [nop,nop,TS val 328647671 ecr
2313764364], length 192
01:20:46.769470 IP 10.2.0.2.33771 > 10.2.203.2.22: Flags [.], ack 192, win 501,
options [nop,nop,TS val 2313764392 ecr 328647671], length 0
01:20:46.787673 IP 10.2.203.2.22 > 10.2.0.2.33771: Flags [P.], seq 192:560, ack 1,
win 132, options [nop,nop,TS val 328647672 ecr 2313764392], length 368
01:20:46.788050 IP 10.2.0.2.33771 > 10.2.203.2.22: Flags [.], ack 560, win 501,
options [nop,nop,TS val 2313764394 ecr 328647672], length 0
01:20:46.808491 IP 10.2.203.2.22 > 10.2.0.2.33771: Flags [P.], seq 560:896, ack 1,
win 132, options [nop,nop,TS val 328647674 ecr 2313764394], length 336
[...]
```

---

[10] Another option is to use PF_RING instead of the per-packet PF_PACKET, although PF_RING has not been included in the Linux kernel [Deri 04].

This output has a line summarizing each packet, including details of the IP addresses, TCP ports, and other TCP header details. This can be used to debug a variety of issues including message latency and missing packets.

Because packet capture can be a CPU-expensive activity, most implementations include the ability to drop events instead of capturing them when overloaded. The count of dropped packets may be included in the log.

Apart from the use of ring buffers to reduce overhead, packet capture implementations commonly allow a filtering expression to be supplied by the user and perform this filtering in the kernel. This reduces overhead by not transferring unwanted packets to user level. The filter expression is typically optimized using Berkeley Packet Filter (BPF), which compiles the expression to BPF bytecode that can be JIT-compiled to machine code by the kernel. In recent years, BPF has been extended in Linux to become a general-purpose execution environment, which powers many observability tools: see Chapter 3, Operating Systems, Section 3.4.4, Extended BPF, and Chapter 15, BPF.

10.5.7 TCP Analysis

Apart from what was covered in Section 10.5.4, Latency Analysis, other specific TCP behavior can be investigated, including:

- Usage of TCP (socket) send/receive buffers
- Usage of TCP backlog queues
- Kernel drops due to the backlog queue being full
- Congestion window size, including zero-size advertisements
- SYNs received during a TCP TIME_WAIT interval

The last behavior can become a scalability problem when a server is connecting frequently to another on the same destination port, using the same source and destination IP addresses. The only distinguishing factor for each connection is the client source port—the *ephemeral port*—which for TCP is a 16-bit value and may be further constrained by operating system parameters (minimum and maximum). Combined with the TCP TIME_WAIT interval, which may be 60 seconds, a high rate of connections (more than 65,536 during 60 seconds) can encounter a clash for new connections. In this scenario, a SYN is sent while that ephemeral port is still associated with a previous TCP session that is in TIME_WAIT, and the new SYN may be rejected if it is misidentified as part of the old connection (a collision). To avoid this issue, the Linux kernel attempts to reuse or recycle connections quickly (which usually works well). The use of multiple IP addresses by the server is another possible solution, as is the SO_LINGER socket option with a low linger time.

10.5.8 Static Performance Tuning

Static performance tuning focuses on issues of the configured environment. For network performance, examine the following aspects of the static configuration:

- How many network interfaces are available for use? Are currently in use?
- What is the maximum speed of the network interfaces?

- What is the currently negotiated speed of the network interfaces?

- Are network interfaces negotiated as half or full duplex?

- What MTU is configured for the network interfaces?

- Are network interfaces trunked?

- What tunable parameters exist for the device driver? IP layer? TCP layer?

- Have any tunable parameters been changed from the defaults?

- How is routing configured? What is the default gateway?

- What is the maximum throughput of network components in the data path (all components, including switch and router backplanes)?

- What is the maximum MTU for the datapath and does fragmentation occur?

- Are any wireless connections in the data path? Are they suffering interference?

- Is forwarding enabled? Is the system acting as a router?

- How is DNS configured? How far away is the server?

- Are there known performance issues (bugs) with the version of the network interface firmware, or any other network hardware?

- Are there known performance issues (bugs) with the network device driver? Kernel TCP/IP stack?

- What firewalls are present?

- Are there software-imposed network throughput limits present (resource controls)? What are they?

The answers to these questions may reveal configuration choices that have been overlooked.

The last question is especially relevant for cloud computing environments, where there may be imposed limits on network throughput.

10.5.9   Resource Controls

The operating system may provide controls to limit network resources for types of connections, processes, or groups of processes. These can include the following types of controls:

- **Network bandwidth limits:** A permitted bandwidth (maximum throughput) for different protocols or applications, applied by the kernel.

- **IP quality of service (QoS):** The prioritization of network traffic, performed by network components (e.g., routers). This can be implemented in different ways: the IP header includes type-of-service (ToS) bits, including a priority; those bits have since been redefined for newer QoS schemes, including Differentiated Services (see Section 10.4.1, Protocols, under the heading IP). There may be other priorities implemented by other protocol layers, for the same purpose.

- **Packet latency:** Additional packet latency (e.g., using Linux tc-netem(8)), which can be used to simulate other networks when testing performance.

Your network may have a mix of traffic that can be classified as low or high priority. Low priority may include the transfer of backups and performance-monitoring traffic. High priority may be the traffic between the production server and clients. Either resource control scheme can be used to throttle the low-priority traffic, producing more favorable performance for the high-priority traffic.

How these work is implementation-specific: see Section 10.8, Tuning.

10.5.10   Micro-Benchmarking

There are many benchmark tools for networking. They are especially useful when investigating throughput issues for a distributed application environment, to confirm that the network can at least achieve the expected network throughput. If it cannot, network performance can be investigated via a network micro-benchmark tool, which is typically much less complex and faster to debug than the application. After the network has been tuned to the desired speed, attention can return to the application.

Typical factors that can be tested include:

- **Direction**: Send or receive
- **Protocol**: TCP or UDP, and port
- **Number of threads**
- **Buffer size**
- **Interface MTU size**

Faster network interfaces, such as 100 Gbits/s, may require multiple client threads to be driven to maximum bandwidth.

An example network micro-benchmark tool, iperf(1), is introduced in Section 10.7.4, iperf, and others are listed in Section 10.7, Experimentation.

10.6   Observability Tools

This section introduces network performance observability tools for Linux-based operating systems. See the previous section for strategies to follow when using them.

The tools in this section are listed in Table 10.4.

Table 10.4   **Network observability tools**

Section	Tool	Description
10.6.1	ss	Socket statistics
10.6.2	ip	Network interface and route statistics
10.6.3	ifconfig	Network interface statistics
10.6.4	nstat	Network stack statistics

Section	Tool	Description
10.6.5	netstat	Various network stack and interface statistics
10.6.6	sar	Historical statistics
10.6.7	nicstat	Network interface throughput and utilization
10.6.8	ethtool	Network interface driver statistics
10.6.9	tcplife	Trace TCP session lifespans with connection details
10.6.10	tcptop	Show TCP throughput by host and process
10.6.11	tcpretrans	Trace TCP retransmits with address and TCP state
10.6.12	bpftrace	TCP/IP stack tracing: connections, packets, drops, latency
10.6.13	tcpdump	Network packet sniffer
10.6.14	Wireshark	Graphical network packet inspection

This is a selection of tools and capabilities to support Section 10.5, Methodology, beginning with traditional tools and statistics, then tracing tools, and finally packet capture tools. Some of the traditional tools are likely available on other Unix-like operating systems where they originated, including: ifconfig(8), netstat(8), and sar(1). The tracing tools are BPF-based, and use BCC and bpftrace frontends (Chapter 15); they are: socketio(8), tcplife(8), tcptop(8), and tcpretrans(8).

The first statistical tools covered are ss(8), ip(8), and nstat(8), as these are from the iproute2 package that is maintained by the network kernel engineers. Tools from this package are most likely to support the latest Linux kernel features. Similar tools from the net-tools package, namely ifconfig(8) and netstat(8), are also covered as they are in widespread use, although Linux kernel network engineers consider these deprecated.

10.6.1   ss

ss(8) is a socket statistics tool that summarizes open sockets. The default output provides high-level information about sockets, for example:

```
# ss
Netid State    Recv-Q  Send-Q    Local Address:Port      Peer Address:Port
[...]
tcp   ESTAB    0       0         100.85.142.69:65264     100.82.166.11:6001
tcp   ESTAB    0       0         100.85.142.69:6028      100.82.16.200:6101
[...]
```

This output is a snapshot of the current state. The first column shows the protocol used by the sockets: these are TCP. Since this output lists all established connections with IP address information, it can be used to characterize the current workload, and answer questions including how many client connections are open, how many concurrent connections there are to a dependency service, etc.

Similar per-socket information is available using the older netstat(8) tool. ss(8), however, can show much more information when using options. For example, showing TCP sockets only (-t), with TCP internal info (-i), extended socket info (-e), process info (-p), and memory usage (-m):

```
# ss -tiepm
State     Recv-Q  Send-Q    Local Address:Port     Peer Address:Port


ESTAB     0       0         100.85.142.69:65264    100.82.166.11:6001
 users:(("java",pid=4195,fd=10865)) uid:33 ino:2009918 sk:78 <->
        skmem:(r0,rb12582912,t0,tb12582912,f266240,w0,o0,bl0,d0) ts sack bbr ws
cale:9,9 rto:204 rtt:0.159/0.009 ato:40 mss:1448 pmtu:1500 rcvmss:1448 advmss:14
48 cwnd:152 bytes_acked:347681 bytes_received:1798733 segs_out:582 segs_in:1397
data_segs_out:294 data_segs_in:1318 bbr:(bw:328.6Mbps,mrtt:0.149,pacing_gain:2.8
8672,cwnd_gain:2.88672) send 11074.0Mbps lastsnd:1696 lastrcv:1660 lastack:1660
pacing_rate 2422.4Mbps delivery_rate 328.6Mbps app_limited busy:16ms rcv_rtt:39.
822 rcv_space:84867 rcv_ssthresh:3609062 minrtt:0.139
[...]
```

Highlighted in bold are the endpoint addresses and the following details:

- **"java",pid=4195**: Process name "java", PID 4195.
- **fd=10865**: File descriptor 10865 (for PID 4195).
- **rto:204**: TCP retransmission timeout: 204 milliseconds.
- **rtt:0.159/0.009**: Average round-trip time is 0.159 milliseconds, with 0.009 milliseconds mean deviation.
- **mss:1448**: Maximum segment size: 1448 bytes.
- **cwnd:152**: Congestion window size: 152 × MSS.
- **bytes_acked:347681**: 340 Kbytes successfully transmitted.
- **bytes_received:1798733**: 1.72 Mbytes received.
- **bbr:...**: BBR congestion control statistics.
- **pacing_rate 2422.4Mbps**: Pacing rate of 2422.4 Mbps.
- **app_limited**: Shows that the congestion window is not fully utilized, suggesting that the connection is application-bound.
- **minrtt:0.139**: Minimum round-trip time in millisecond. Compare to the average and mean deviation (listed earlier) to get an idea of network variation and congestion.

This particular connection is flagged as application-limited (app_limited), with a low RTT to the remote endpoint, and low total bytes transferred. The possible "limited" flags ss(1) can print are:

- **app_limited**: Application limited.
- **rwnd_limited:Xms**: Limited by the receive window. Includes the time limited in milliseconds.

- **sndbuf_limited:Xms**: Limited by the send buffer. Includes the time limited in milliseconds.

One detail missing from the output is the age of the connection, which is needed to calculate the average throughput. A workaround I've found is to use the change timestamp on the file descriptor file in /proc: for this connection, I would run stat(1) on /proc/4195/fd/10865.

netlink

ss(8) reads these extended details from the netlink(7) interface, which operates via sockets of family AF_NETLINK to fetch information from the kernel. You can see this in action using strace(1) (see Chapter 5, Applications, Section 5.5.4, strace, for warnings on strace(1) overhead):

```
# strace -e sendmsg,recvmsg ss -t
sendmsg(3, {msg_name={sa_family=AF_NETLINK, nl_pid=0, nl_groups=00000000},
msg_namelen=12, msg_iov=[{iov_base={{len=72, type=SOCK_DIAG_BY_FAMILY,
flags=NLM_F_REQUEST|NLM_F_DUMP, seq=123456, pid=0}, {sdiag_family=AF_INET,
sdiag_protocol=IPPROTO_TCP, idiag_ext=1<<(INET_DIAG_MEMINFO-1)|...
recvmsg(3, {msg_name={sa_family=AF_NETLINK, nl_pid=0, nl_groups=00000000},...
[...]
```

netstat(8) sources information using /proc/net files instead:

```
# strace -e openat netstat -an
[...]
openat(AT_FDCWD, "/proc/net/tcp", O_RDONLY) = 3
openat(AT_FDCWD, "/proc/net/tcp6", O_RDONLY) = 3
[...]
```

Because the /proc/net files are text, I've found them handy as a source for ad hoc reporting, requiring nothing more than awk(1) for processing. Serious monitoring tools should use the netlink(7) interface instead, which passes information in binary format and avoids the overhead of text parsing.

10.6.2 ip

ip(8) is a tool for managing routing, network devices, interfaces, and tunnels. For observability, it can be used to print statistics on: link, address, route, etc. For example, printing extra statistics (-s) on interfaces (link):

```
# ip -s link
1: lo: <LOOPBACK,UP,LOWER_UP> mtu 65536 qdisc noqueue state UNKNOWN mode DEFAULT
group default qlen 1000
    link/loopback 00:00:00:00:00:00 brd 00:00:00:00:00:00
    RX: bytes  packets  errors  dropped overrun mcast
    26550075   273178   0       0       0       0
    TX: bytes  packets  errors  dropped carrier collsns
    26550075   273178   0       0       0       0
```

```
2: eth0: <BROADCAST,MULTICAST,UP,LOWER_UP> mtu 1500 qdisc mq state UP mode DEFAULT
group default qlen 1000
    link/ether 12:c0:0a:b0:21:b8 brd ff:ff:ff:ff:ff:ff
    RX: bytes  packets  errors  dropped overrun mcast
    512473039143 568704184 0        0       0      0
    TX: bytes  packets  errors  dropped carrier collsns
    573510263433 668110321 0        0       0      0
```

Examining the configuration of all interfaces can be useful during static performance tuning, to check for misconfigurations. Error metrics are also included in the output: for receive (RX): receive errors, drops, and overruns; for transmit (TX): transmit errors, drops, carrier errors, and collisions. Such errors can be a source of performance issues and, depending on the error, may be caused by faulty network hardware. These are global counters showing all errors since the interface was activated (in network speak, it was brought "UP").

Specifying the -s option twice (-s -s) provides even more statistics for error types.

Although ip(8) provides RX and TX byte counters, it does not include an option to print the current throughput over an interval. For that, use sar(1) (Section 10.6.6, sar).

Route Table

ip(1) does have observability for other networking components. For example, the route object shows the routing table:

```
# ip route
default via 100.85.128.1 dev eth0
default via 100.85.128.1 dev eth0 proto dhcp src 100.85.142.69 metric 100
100.85.128.0/18 dev eth0 proto kernel scope link src 100.85.142.69
100.85.128.1 dev eth0 proto dhcp scope link src 100.85.142.69 metric 100
```

Misconfigured routes can also be a source of performance problems (for example, when specific route entries were added by an administrator but are no longer needed, and now perform worse than the default route).

Monitoring

Use the monitoring subcommand ip monitor to watch for netlink messages.

10.6.3 ifconfig

The ifconfig(8) command is the traditional tool for interface administration, and can also list the configuration of all interfaces. The Linux version includes statistics with the output[11]:

---

[11]It also shows a tunable parameter, txqueuelen, but not all drivers use this value (it calls a netdevice notifier with NETDEV_CHANGE_TX_QUEUE_LEN, which is not implemented by some drivers), and byte queue limits auto-tune the device queues.

```
$ ifconfig
eth0      Link encap:Ethernet  HWaddr 00:21:9b:97:a9:bf
          inet addr:10.2.0.2  Bcast:10.2.0.255  Mask:255.255.255.0
          inet6 addr: fe80::221:9bff:fe97:a9bf/64 Scope:Link
          UP BROADCAST RUNNING MULTICAST  MTU:1500  Metric:1
          RX packets:933874764 errors:0 dropped:0 overruns:0 frame:0
          TX packets:1090431029 errors:0 dropped:0 overruns:0 carrier:0
          collisions:0 txqueuelen:1000
          RX bytes:584622361619 (584.6 GB)  TX bytes:537745836640 (537.7 GB)
          Interrupt:36 Memory:d6000000-d6012800

eth3      Link encap:Ethernet  HWaddr 00:21:9b:97:a9:c5
[...]
```

The counters are the same as those described for the ip(8) command.

On Linux, ifconfig(8) is considered obsolete, replaced by ip(8).

10.6.4   nstat

nstat(8) prints the various network metrics maintained by the kernel, with their SNMP names. For example, using -s to avoid resetting the counters:

```
# nstat -s
#kernel
IpInReceives            462657733           0.0
IpInDelivers            462657733           0.0
IpOutRequests           497050986           0.0
IpOutDiscards           42                  0.0
IpFragOKs               2298                0.0
IpFragCreates           13788               0.0
IcmpInMsgs              91                  0.0
[...]
TcpActiveOpens          362997              0.0
TcpPassiveOpens         9663983             0.0
TcpAttemptFails         12718               0.0
TcpEstabResets          14591               0.0
TcpInSegs               462181482           0.0
TcpOutSegs              938958577           0.0
TcpRetransSegs          129212              0.0
TcpOutRsts              52362               0.0
UdpInDatagrams          476072              0.0
UdpNoPorts              88                  0.0
```

```
UdpOutDatagrams            476197           0.0
UdpIgnoredMulti            2                0.0
Ip6OutRequests             29               0.0
[...]
```

Key metrics include:

- **IpInReceives**: Inbound IP packets.

- **IpOutRequests**: Outbound IP packets.

- **TcpActiveOpens**: TCP active connections (the connect(2) socket syscall).

- **TcpPassiveOpens**: TCP passive connections (the accept(2) socket syscall).

- **TcpInSegs**: TCP inbound segments.

- **TcpOutSegs**: TCP outbound segments.

- **TcpRetransSegs**: TCP retransmitted segments. Compare with TcpOutSegs for the ratio of retransmits.

If the -s option is not used, the default behavior of nstat(8) is to reset the kernel counters. This can be useful, as you can then run nstat(8) a second time and see counts that spanned that interval, rather than totals since boot. If you had a network problem that could be reproduced with a command, then nstat(8) can be run before and after the command to show which counters changed.

If you forgot to use -s and have reset the counters by mistake, you can use -rs to set them back to their summary since boot values.

nstat(8) also has a daemon mode (-d) to collect interval statistics, which when used are shown in the last column.

10.6.5 netstat

The netstat(8) command reports various types of network statistics, based on the options used. It is like a multi-tool with several different functions. These include the following:

- **(default)**: Lists connected sockets

- **-a**: Lists information for all sockets

- **-s**: Network stack statistics

- **-i**: Network interface statistics

- **-r**: Lists the route table

Other options can modify the output, including -n to not resolve IP addresses to host names, and -v for verbose details where available.

Here is an example of netstat(8) interface statistics:

```
$ netstat -i
Kernel Interface table
Iface    MTU      RX-OK RX-ERR RX-DRP RX-OVR     TX-OK TX-ERR TX-DRP TX-OVR Flg
eth0    1500 933760207      0    0 0        1090211545      0      0      0 BMRU
eth3    1500 718900017      0    0 0         587534567      0      0      0 BMRU
lo     16436 21126497       0    0 0          21126497      0      0      0 LRU
ppp5    1496      4225      0    0 0              3736      0      0      0 MOPRU
ppp6    1496      1183      0    0 0              1143      0      0      0 MOPRU
tun0    1500    695581      0    0 0            692378      0      0      0 MOPRU
tun1    1462         0      0    0 0                 4      0      0      0 PRU
```

The columns include the network interface (`Iface`), `MTU`, and a series of metrics for receive (`RX-`) and transmit (`TX-`):

- **`-OK`:** Packets transferred successfully
- **`-ERR`:** Packet errors
- **`-DRP`:** Packet drops
- **`-OVR`:** Packet overruns

The packet drops and overruns are indications of network interface *saturation* and can be examined along with errors as part of the USE method.

The `-c` continuous mode can be used with `-i`, which prints these cumulative counters every second. This provides the data for calculating the rate of packets.

Here is an example of netstat(8) network stack statistics (truncated):

```
$ netstat -s
Ip:
    Forwarding: 2
    454143446 total packets received
    0 forwarded
    0 incoming packets discarded
    454143446 incoming packets delivered
    487760885 requests sent out
    42 outgoing packets dropped
    2260 fragments received ok
    13560 fragments created
Icmp:
    91 ICMP messages received
[...]
Tcp:
    359286 active connection openings
    9463980 passive connection openings
```

```
        12527 failed connection attempts
        14323 connection resets received
        13545 connections established
        453673963 segments received
        922299281 segments sent out
        127247 segments retransmitted
        0 bad segments received
        51660 resets sent
Udp:
        469302 packets received
        88 packets to unknown port received
        0 packet receive errors
        469427 packets sent
        0 receive buffer errors
        0 send buffer errors
        IgnoredMulti: 2
TcpExt:
        21 resets received for embryonic SYN_RECV sockets
        12252 packets pruned from receive queue because of socket buffer overrun
        201219 TCP sockets finished time wait in fast timer
        11727438 delayed acks sent
        1445 delayed acks further delayed because of locked socket
        Quick ack mode was activated 17624 times
        169257582 packet headers predicted
        76058392 acknowledgments not containing data payload received
        111925821 predicted acknowledgments
        TCPSackRecovery: 1703
        Detected reordering 876 times using SACK
        Detected reordering 19 times using time stamp
        2 congestion windows fully recovered without slow start
        19 congestion windows partially recovered using Hoe heuristic
        TCPDSACKUndo: 164
        88 congestion windows recovered without slow start after partial ack
        TCPLostRetransmit: 901
        TCPSackFailures: 31
        28248 fast retransmits
        709 retransmits in slow start
        TCPTimeouts: 12684
        TCPLossProbes: 73383
        TCPLossProbeRecovery: 132
        TCPSackRecoveryFail: 24
        805315 packets collapsed in receive queue due to low socket buffer
[...]
```

```
TCPAutoCorking: 13520259
TCPFromZeroWindowAdv: 257
TCPToZeroWindowAdv: 257
TCPWantZeroWindowAdv: 18941
TCPSynRetrans: 24816
[...]
```

The output lists various network statistics, mostly from TCP, grouped by their protocol. Fortunately, many of these have long descriptive names, so their meaning may be obvious. A number of these statistics have been highlighted in bold, to show the kind of performance-related information available. Many of these require an advanced understanding of TCP behavior, including the newer features and algorithms that have been introduced in recent years. Some example statistics to look for:

- A high rate of forwarded versus total packets received: check that the server is supposed to be forwarding (routing) packets.

- Passive connection openings: this can be monitored to show load in terms of client connections.

- A high rate of segments retransmitted versus segments sent out: can show an unreliable network. This may be expected (Internet clients).

- TCPSynRetrans: shows retransmitted SYNs, which can be caused by the remote endpoint dropping SYNs from the listen backlog due to load.

- Packets pruned from the receive queue because of socket buffer overrun: This is a sign of network saturation and may be fixable by increasing socket buffers, provided there are sufficient system resources for the application to keep up.

Some of the statistic names include typos (e.g., `packetes rejected`). These can be problematic to simply fix, if other monitoring tools have been built upon the same output. Such tools should be better served by processing nstat(8) output, which uses standard SNMP names, or even better, to read the /proc sources for these statistics directly, which are /proc/net/snmp and /proc/net/netstat. For example:

```
$ grep ^Tcp /proc/net/snmp
Tcp: RtoAlgorithm RtoMin RtoMax MaxConn ActiveOpens PassiveOpens AttemptFails
EstabResets CurrEstab InSegs OutSegs RetransSegs InErrs OutRsts InCsumErrors
Tcp: 1 200 120000 -1 102378 126946 11940 19495 24 627115849 325815063 346455 5 24183
0
```

These /proc/net/snmp statistics also include the SNMP management information bases (MIBs). MIB documentation describes what each statistic is supposed to be (if the kernel has correctly implemented it). Extended statistics are in /proc/net/netstat.

An interval, in seconds, can be used with netstat(8) so that it continually prints the cumulative counters every interval. This output could then be post-processed to calculate the rate of each counter.

10.6.6 sar

The system activity reporter, sar(1), can be used to observe current activity and can be configured to archive and report historical statistics. It is introduced in Chapter 4, Observability Tools, and mentioned in other chapters as appropriate.

The Linux version provides network statistics via the following options:

- **-n DEV**: Network interface statistics
- **-n EDEV**: Network interface errors
- **-n IP**: IP datagram statistics
- **-n EIP**: IP error statistics
- **-n TCP**: TCP statistics
- **-n ETCP**: TCP error statistics
- **-n SOCK**: Socket usage

Statistics provided include those shown in Table 10.5.

Table 10.5 **Linux sar network statistics**

Option	Statistic	Description	Units
-n DEV	rxpkt/s	Received packets	Packets/s
-n DEV	txpkt/s	Transmitted packets	Packets/s
-n DEV	rxkB/s	Received kilobytes	Kilobytes/s
-n DEV	txkB/s	Transmitted kilobytes	Kilobytes/s
-n DEV	rxcmp/s	Received compressed packets	Packets/s
-n DEV	txcmp/s	Transmitted compressed packets	Packets/s
-n DEV	rxmcst/s	Received multicast packets	Packets/s
-n DEV	%ifutil	Interface utilization: for full duplex, the greater of rx or tx	Percent
-n EDEV	rxerr/s	Received packet errors	Packets/s
-n EDEV	txerr/s	Transmitted packet errors	Packets/s
-n EDEV	coll/s	Collisions	Packets/s
-n EDEV	rxdrop/s	Received packets dropped (buffer full)	Packets/s
-n EDEV	txdrop/s	Transmitted packets dropped (buffer full)	Packets/s
-n EDEV	txcarr/s	Transmission carrier errors	Errors/s
-n EDEV	rxfram/s	Received alignment errors	Errors/s
-n EDEV	rxfifo/s	Received packets FIFO overrun errors	Packets/s
-n EDEV	txfifo/s	Transmitted packets FIFO overrun errors	Packets/s

Option	Statistic	Description	Units
-n IP	irec/s	Input datagrams (received)	Datagrams/s
-n IP	fwddgm/s	Forwarded datagrams	Datagrams/s
-n IP	idel/s	Input IP datagrams (including ICMP)	Datagrams/s
-n IP	orq/s	Output datagram requests (transmit)	Datagrams/s
-n IP	asmrq/s	IP fragments received	Fragments/s
-n IP	asmok/s	IP datagrams reassembled	Datagrams/s
-n IP	fragok/s	IP datagrams fragmented	Datagrams/s
-n IP	fragcrt/s	IP datagram fragments created	Fragments/s
-n EIP	ihdrerr/s	IP header errors	Datagrams/s
-n EIP	iadrerr/s	Invalid IP destination address errors	Datagrams/s
-n EIP	iukwnpr/s	Unknown protocol errors	Datagrams/s
-n EIP	idisc/s	Input discards (e.g., buffer full)	Datagrams/s
-n EIP	odisc/s	Output discards (e.g., buffer full)	Datagram/s
-n EIP	onort/s	Output datagram no route error	Datagrams/s
-n EIP	asmf/s	IP reassembly failures	Failures/s
-n EIP	fragf/s	IP don't fragment discards	Datagrams/s
-n TCP	active/s	New active TCP connections (connect(2))	Connections/s
-n TCP	passive/s	New passive TCP connections (accept(2))	Connections/s
-n TCP	iseg/s	Input segments (received)	Segments/s
-n TCP	oseg/s	Output segments (received)	Segments/s
-n ETCP	atmptf/s	Active TCP connection fails	Connections/s
-n ETCP	estres/s	Established resets	Resets/s
-n ETCP	retrans/s	TCP segments retransmitted	Segments/s
-n ETCP	isegerr/s	Segment errors	Segments/s
-n ETCP	orsts/s	Sent resets	Segments/s
-n SOCK	totsck	Total sockets in use	Sockets
-n SOCK	tcpsck/s	Total TCP sockets in use	Sockets
-n SOCK	udpsck/s	Total UDP sockets in use	Sockets
-n SOCK	rawsck/s	Total RAW sockets in use	Sockets
-n SOCK	ip-frag	IP fragments currently queued	Fragments
-n SOCK	tcp-tw	TCP sockets in TIME_WAIT	Sockets

Not listed are the ICMP, NFS, and SOFT (software network processing) groups, and IPv6 variants: IP6, EIP6, SOCK6, and UDP6. See the man page for the full list of statistics, which also notes some equivalent SNMP names (e.g., ipInReceives for irec/s). Many of the sar(1) statistic names are easy to remember in practice, as they include the direction and units measured: rx for "received," i for "input," seg for "segments," and so on.

This example prints TCP statistics every second:

```
$ sar -n TCP 1
Linux 5.3.0-1010-aws (ip-10-1-239-218)    02/27/20      _x86_64_   (2 CPU)

07:32:45    active/s passive/s    iseg/s    oseg/s
07:32:46        0.00    12.00     186.00  28837.00
07:32:47        0.00    13.00     203.00  33584.00
07:32:48        0.00    11.00    1999.00  24441.00
07:32:49        0.00     7.00      92.00   8908.00
07:32:50        0.00    10.00     114.00  13795.00
[...]
```

The output shows a passive connection rate (inbound) of around 10 per second.

When examining network devices (DEV) the network interface statistics column (IFACE) lists all interfaces; however, often only one is of interest. The following example uses a little awk(1) to filter the output:

```
$ sar -n DEV 1 | awk 'NR == 3 || $2 == "ens5"'
07:35:41 IFACE  rxpck/s   txpck/s  rxkB/s   txkB/s rxcmp/s txcmp/s rxmcst/s %ifutil
07:35:42 ens5    134.00  11483.00   10.22  6328.72    0.00    0.00     0.00    0.00
07:35:43 ens5    170.00  20354.00   13.62  6925.27    0.00    0.00     0.00    0.00
07:35:44 ens5    185.00  28228.00   14.33  8586.79    0.00    0.00     0.00    0.00
07:35:45 ens5    180.00  23093.00   14.59  7452.49    0.00    0.00     0.00    0.00
07:35:46 ens5   1525.00  19594.00  137.48  7044.81    0.00    0.00     0.00    0.00
07:35:47 ens5    146.00  10282.00   12.05  6876.80    0.00    0.00     0.00    0.00
[...]
```

This shows network throughput for transmit and receive, and other statistics.

The atop(1) tool is also able to archive statistics.

10.6.7 nicstat

nicstat(1)[12] prints network interface statistics, including throughput and utilization. It follows the style of the traditional resource statistic tools, iostat(1) and mpstat(1).

---

[12] I developed the original version for Solaris; Tim Cook developed the Linux version [Cook 09].

Here is output for version 1.92 on Linux:

```
# nicstat -z 1
      Time      Int   rKB/s   wKB/s    rPk/s    wPk/s    rAvs   wAvs %Util    Sat
01:20:58     eth0    0.07    0.00    0.95    0.02    79.43   64.81 0.00    0.00
01:20:58     eth4    0.28    0.01    0.20    0.10    1451.3  80.11 0.00    0.00
01:20:58  vlan123    0.00    0.00    0.00    0.02    42.00   64.81 0.00    0.00
01:20:58      br0    0.00    0.00    0.00    0.00    42.00   42.07 0.00    0.00
      Time      Int   rKB/s   wKB/s    rPk/s    wPk/s    rAvs   wAvs %Util    Sat
01:20:59     eth4 42376.0   974.5 28589.4 14002.1   1517.8  71.27 35.5    0.00
      Time      Int   rKB/s   wKB/s    rPk/s    wPk/s    rAvs   wAvs %Util    Sat
01:21:00     eth0    0.05    0.00    1.00    0.00    56.00    0.00 0.00    0.00
01:21:00     eth4 41834.7   977.9 28221.5 14058.3   1517.9  71.23 35.1    0.00
      Time      Int   rKB/s   wKB/s    rPk/s    wPk/s    rAvs   wAvs %Util    Sat
01:21:01     eth4 42017.9   979.0 28345.0 14073.0   1517.9  71.24 35.2    0.00
```

The first output is the summary-since-boot, followed by interval summaries. The interval summaries show that the eth4 interface is running at 35% utilization (this is reporting the highest current utilization from either the RX or TX direction) and is reading at 42 Mbytes/s.

The fields include the interface name (Int), the maximum utilization (%Util), a value reflecting interface saturation statistics (Sat), and a series of statistics prefixed with r for "read" (receive) and w for "write" (transmit):

- **KB/s**: Kbytes per second
- **Pk/s**: packets per second
- **Avs/s**: Average packet size, bytes

Options supported in this version include -z to skip lines of zeros (idle interfaces) and -t for TCP statistics.

nicstat(1) is particularly useful for the USE method, as it provides utilization and saturation values.

10.6.8   ethtool

ethtool(8) can be used to check the static configuration of the network interfaces with -i and -k options, and also print driver statistics with -S. For example:

```
# ethtool -S eth0
NIC statistics:
     tx_timeout: 0
     suspend: 0
     resume: 0
     wd_expired: 0
     interface_up: 1
     interface_down: 0
```

```
        admin_q_pause: 0
        queue_0_tx_cnt: 100219217
        queue_0_tx_bytes: 84830086234
        queue_0_tx_queue_stop: 0
        queue_0_tx_queue_wakeup: 0
        queue_0_tx_dma_mapping_err: 0
        queue_0_tx_linearize: 0
        queue_0_tx_linearize_failed: 0
        queue_0_tx_napi_comp: 112514572
        queue_0_tx_tx_poll: 112514649
        queue_0_tx_doorbells: 52759561
[...]
```

This fetches statistics from the kernel ethtool framework, which many network device drivers support. Device drivers can define their own ethtool statistics.

The -i option shows driver details, and -k shows interface tunables. For example:

```
# ethtool -i eth0
driver: ena
version: 2.0.3K
[...]
# ethtool -k eth0
Features for eth0:
rx-checksumming: on
[...]
tcp-segmentation-offload: off
        tx-tcp-segmentation: off [fixed]
        tx-tcp-ecn-segmentation: off [fixed]
        tx-tcp-mangleid-segmentation: off [fixed]
        tx-tcp6-segmentation: off [fixed]
udp-fragmentation-offload: off
generic-segmentation-offload: on
generic-receive-offload: on
large-receive-offload: off [fixed]
rx-vlan-offload: off [fixed]
tx-vlan-offload: off [fixed]
ntuple-filters: off [fixed]
receive-hashing: on
highdma: on
[...]
```

This example is a cloud instance with the ena driver, with tcp-segmentation-offload off. The -K option can be used to change these tunables.

10.6.9   tcplife

tcplife(8)[13] is a BCC and bpftrace tool to trace the lifespan of TCP sessions, showing their duration, address details, throughput, and, when possible, the responsible process ID and name.

The following shows tcplife(8) from BCC, on a 48-CPU production instance:

```
# tcplife
PID     COMM    LADDR         LPORT  RADDR         RPORT  TX_KB  RX_KB  MS
4169    java    100.1.111.231  32648  100.2.0.48     6001      0      0  3.99
4169    java    100.1.111.231  32650  100.2.0.48     6001      0      0  4.10
4169    java    100.1.111.231  32644  100.2.0.48     6001      0      0  8.41
4169    java    100.1.111.231  40158  100.2.116.192  6001      7     33  3590.91
4169    java    100.1.111.231  56940  100.5.177.31   6101      0      0  2.48
4169    java    100.1.111.231  6001   100.2.176.45   49482     0      0  17.94
4169    java    100.1.111.231  18926  100.5.102.250  6101      0      0  0.90
4169    java    100.1.111.231  44530  100.2.31.140   6001      0      0  2.64
4169    java    100.1.111.231  44406  100.2.8.109    6001     11     28  3982.11
34781   sshd    100.1.111.231  22     100.2.17.121   41566     5      7  2317.30
4169    java    100.1.111.231  49726  100.2.9.217    6001     11     28  3938.47
4169    java    100.1.111.231  58858  100.2.173.248  6001      9     30  2820.51
[...]
```

This output shows a series of connections that were either short-lived (less than 20 milliseconds)
or long-lived (over three seconds), as shown in the duration column (MS for milliseconds). This is
an application server pool that listens on port 6001. Most of the sessions in this screenshot show
connections to port 6001 on remote application servers, with only one connection to the local
port 6001. An ssh session was also seen, owned by sshd and local port 22—an inbound session.

The BCC version of tcplife(8) supports options including:

- **-t**: Include time column (HH:MM:SS)
- **-w**: Wider columns (to better fit IPv6 addresses)
- **-p PID**: Trace this process only
- **-L PORT[,PORT[,...]]**: Trace only sessions with these local ports
- **-D PORT[,PORT[,...]]**: Trace only sessions with these remote ports

This tool works by tracing TCP socket state-change events, and prints the summary details when
the state changes to TCP_CLOSE. These state-change events are much less frequent than packets,
making this approach much less costly in overhead than per-packet sniffers. This has made
tcplife(8) acceptable to run continuously as a TCP flow logger on Netflix production servers.[14]

Creating udplife(8) for tracing UDP sessions is a Chapter 10 exercise in the *BPF Performance Tools*
book [Gregg 19]; I have posted an initial solution [Gregg 19d].

---

[13] Origin: I created tcplife(8) on 18-Oct-2016 based on an idea by Julia Evans, and the bpftrace version on 17-Apr-2019.
[14] It is coupled with snapshots of all open sessions.

10.6.10   tcptop

tcptop(8)[15] is a BCC tool that shows top processes using TCP. For example, from a 36-CPU production Hadoop instance:

```
# tcptop
09:01:13 loadavg: 33.32 36.11 38.63 26/4021 123015

PID     COMM     LADDR                RADDR                 RX_KB   TX_KB
118119  java     100.1.58.46:36246    100.2.52.79:50010     16840      0
122833  java     100.1.58.46:52426    100.2.6.98:50010          0   3112
122833  java     100.1.58.46:50010    100.2.50.176:55396     3112      0
120711  java     100.1.58.46:50010    100.2.7.75:23358       2922      0
121635  java     100.1.58.46:50010    100.2.5.101:56426      2922      0
121219  java     100.1.58.46:50010    100.2.62.83:40570      2858      0
121219  java     100.1.58.46:42324    100.2.4.58:50010          0   2858
122927  java     100.1.58.46:50010    100.2.2.191:29338      2351      0
[...]
```

This output shows one connection at the top receiving over 16 Mbytes during this interval. By default, the screen is updated every second.

This works by tracing the TCP send and receive code path, and summarizing data in a BPF map efficiency. Even so, these events can be frequent, and on high network throughput systems the overhead may become measurable.

Options include:

- **-C**: Don't clear the screen.
- **-p PID**: Measure this process only.

tcptop(8) also accepts an optional interval and count.

10.6.11   tcpretrans

tcpretrans(8)[16] is a BCC and bpftrace tool to trace TCP retransmits, showing IP address and port details and the TCP state. The following shows tcpretrans(8) from BCC, on a production instance:

```
# tcpretrans
Tracing retransmits ... Hit Ctrl-C to end
TIME      PID     IP LADDR:LPORT         T> RADDR:RPORT         STATE
00:20:11  72475   4  100.1.58.46:35908   R> 100.2.0.167:50010   ESTABLISHED
00:20:11  72475   4  100.1.58.46:35908   R> 100.2.0.167:50010   ESTABLISHED
```

---

[15] Origin: I created the BCC version on 02-Sep-2016, based on an earlier tcptop tool I had created in 2005, which itself was inspired by the original top(1) by William LeFebvre.

[16] Origin: I created similar tools in 2011, an Ftrace tcpretrans(8) in 2014, and this BCC version on 14-Feb-2016. Dale Hamel created the bpftrace version on 23-Nov-2018.

```
00:20:11 72475   4   100.1.58.46:35908      R> 100.2.0.167:50010      ESTABLISHED
00:20:12 60695   4   100.1.58.46:52346      R> 100.2.6.189:50010      ESTABLISHED
00:20:12 60695   4   100.1.58.46:52346      R> 100.2.6.189:50010      ESTABLISHED
00:20:12 60695   4   100.1.58.46:52346      R> 100.2.6.189:50010      ESTABLISHED
00:20:12 60695   4   100.1.58.46:52346      R> 100.2.6.189:50010      ESTABLISHED
00:20:13 60695   6   ::ffff:100.1.58.46:13562 R> ::ffff:100.2.51.209:47356 FIN_WAIT1
00:20:13 60695   6   ::ffff:100.1.58.46:13562 R> ::ffff:100.2.51.209:47356 FIN_WAIT1
[...]
```

This output shows a low rate of retransmits, a few per second (TIME column), which were mostly for sessions in the ESTABLISHED state. A high rate in the ESTABLISHED state can point to an external network problem. A high rate in the SYN_SENT state can point to an overloaded server application that is not consuming its SYN backlog fast enough.

This works by tracing TCP retransmit events in the kernel. Since these should occur infrequently, the overhead should be negligible. Compare this to how retransmits are historically analyzed using a packet sniffer to capture all packets, and then post-processing to find retransmits—both steps can cost significant CPU overhead. Packet-capture can only see details that are on the wire, whereas tcpretrans(8) prints the TCP state directly from the kernel, and can be enhanced to print more kernel state if needed.

Options for the BCC version include:

- **-l**: Include tail loss probe attempts (adds a kprobe for tcp_send_loss_probe())
- **-c**: Count retransmits per flow

The **-c** option changes the behavior of tcpretrans(8), causing it to print a summary of counts rather than per-event details.

10.6.12   bpftrace

bpftrace is a BPF-based tracer that provides a high-level programming language, allowing the creation of powerful one-liners and short scripts. It is well suited for custom networking analysis based on clues from other tools. It can examine network events from within the kernel and applications, including socket connections, socket I/O, TCP events, packet transmission, backlog drops, TCP retransmits, and other details. These abilities support workload characterization and latency analysis.

bpftrace is explained in Chapter 15. This section shows some examples for network analysis: one-liners, socket tracing, and TCP tracing.

One-Liners

The following one-liners are useful and demonstrate different bpftrace capabilities.

Count socket accept(2)s by PID and process name:

```
bpftrace -e 't:syscalls:sys_enter_accept* { @[pid, comm] = count(); }'
```

Count socket connect(2)s by PID and process name:

```
bpftrace -e 't:syscalls:sys_enter_connect { @[pid, comm] = count(); }'
```

Count socket connect(2)s by user stack trace:

```
bpftrace -e 't:syscalls:sys_enter_connect { @[ustack, comm] = count(); }'
```

Count socket send/receives by direction, on-CPU PID, and process name[17]:

```
bpftrace -e 'k:sock_sendmsg,k:sock_recvmsg { @[func, pid, comm] = count(); }'
```

Count socket send/receive bytes by on-CPU PID and process name:

```
bpftrace -e 'kr:sock_sendmsg,kr:sock_recvmsg /(int32)retval > 0/ { @[pid, comm] =
    sum((int32)retval); }'
```

Count TCP connects by on-CPU PID and process name:

```
bpftrace -e 'k:tcp_v*_connect { @[pid, comm] = count(); }'
```

Count TCP accepts by on-CPU PID and process name:

```
bpftrace -e 'k:inet_csk_accept { @[pid, comm] = count(); }'
```

Count TCP send/receives by on-CPU PID and process name:

```
bpftrace -e 'k:tcp_sendmsg,k:tcp_recvmsg { @[func, pid, comm] = count(); }'
```

TCP send bytes as a histogram:

```
bpftrace -e 'k:tcp_sendmsg { @send_bytes = hist(arg2); }'
```

TCP receive bytes as a histogram:

```
bpftrace -e 'kr:tcp_recvmsg /retval >= 0/ { @recv_bytes = hist(retval); }'
```

Count TCP retransmits by type and remote host (assumes IPv4):

```
bpftrace -e 't:tcp:tcp_retransmit_* { @[probe, ntop(2, args->saddr)] = count(); }'
```

Count all TCP functions (adds high overhead to TCP):

```
bpftrace -e 'k:tcp_* { @[func] = count(); }'
```

Count UDP send/receives by on-CPU PID and process name:

```
bpftrace -e 'k:udp*_sendmsg,k:udp*_recvmsg { @[func, pid, comm] = count(); }'
```

---

[17] The earlier socket syscalls are in process context, where PID and comm are reliable. These kprobes are deeper in the kernel, and the process endpoint for these connections my not be currently on-CPU, meaning the pid and comm shown by bpftrace could be unrelated. They usually work, but that may not always be the case.

UDP send bytes as a histogram:

```
bpftrace -e 'k:udp_sendmsg { @send_bytes = hist(arg2); }'
```

UDP receive bytes as a histogram:

```
bpftrace -e 'kr:udp_recvmsg /retval >= 0/ { @recv_bytes = hist(retval); }'
```

Count transmit kernel stack traces:

```
bpftrace -e 't:net:net_dev_xmit { @[kstack] = count(); }'
```

Show receive CPU histogram for each device:

```
bpftrace -e 't:net:netif_receive_skb { @[str(args->name)] = lhist(cpu, 0, 128, 1); }'
```

Count ieee80211 layer functions (adds high overhead to packets):

```
bpftrace -e 'k:ieee80211_* { @[func] = count(); }'
```

Count all ixgbevf device driver functions (adds high overhead to ixgbevf):

```
bpftrace -e 'k:ixgbevf_* { @[func] = count(); }'
```

Count all iwl device driver tracepoints (adds high overhead to iwl):

```
bpftrace -e 't:iwlwifi:*,t:iwlwifi_io:* { @[probe] = count(); }'
```

Socket Tracing

Tracing network events at the socket layer has the advantage that the responsible process is still on-CPU, making it straightforward to identify the application and code-path responsible. For example, counting the applications calling the accept(2) syscall:

```
# bpftrace -e 't:syscalls:sys_enter_accept { @[pid, comm] = count(); }'
Attaching 1 probe...
^C

@[573, sshd]: 2
@[1948, mysqld]: 41
```

The output shows that during tracing mysqld called accept(2) 41 times, and sshd called accept(2) 2 times.

The stack trace can be included to show the code path that led to accept(2). For example, counting by the user-level stack trace and process name:

```
# bpftrace -e 't:syscalls:sys_enter_accept { @[ustack, comm] = count(); }'
Attaching 1 probe...
^C
```

```
@[

    accept+79

    Mysqld_socket_listener::listen_for_connection_event()+283

    mysqld_main(int, char**)+15577

    __libc_start_main+243

    0x49564100fe8c4b3d

, mysqld]: 22
```

This output shows that mysqld was accepting connections via a code path that included
Mysqld_socket_listener::listen_for_connection_event(). By changing "accept" to "connect",
this one-liner will identify the code paths leading to connect(2). I have used such one-liners to
explain mysterious network connections, showing the code paths calling them.

sock Tracepoints

Apart from socket syscalls, there are socket tracepoints. From a 5.3 kernel:

```
# bpftrace -l 't:sock:*'
tracepoint:sock:sock_rcvqueue_full
tracepoint:sock:sock_exceed_buf_limit
tracepoint:sock:inet_sock_set_state
```

The sock:inet_sock_set_state tracepoint is used by the earlier tcplife(8) tool. Here is an example
one-liner that uses it to count source and destination IPv4 addresses for new connections:

```
# bpftrace -e 't:sock:inet_sock_set_state
    /args->newstate == 1 && args->family == 2/ {
    @[ntop(args->saddr), ntop(args->daddr)] = count() }'
Attaching 1 probe...
^C
@[127.0.0.1, 127.0.0.1]: 2
@[10.1.239.218, 10.29.225.81]: 18
```

This one-liner is getting long, and it would be easier to save to a bpftrace program file (.bt) for
editing and execution. As a file, it can also include the appropriate kernel headers so that the
filter line can be rewritten to use constant names rather than hard-coded numbers (which are
unreliable), like this:

```
/args->newstate == TCP_ESTABLISHED && args->family == AF_INET/ {
```

The next example is of a program file: socketio.bt.

socketio.bt

As a more complex example, the socketio(8) tool shows socket I/O with the process details, direction, protocol, and port. Example output:

```
# ./socketio.bt
Attaching 2 probes...
^C
[...]
@io[sshd, 21925, read, UNIX, 0]: 40
@io[sshd, 21925, read, TCP, 37408]: 41
@io[systemd, 1, write, UNIX, 0]: 51
@io[systemd, 1, read, UNIX, 0]: 57
@io[systemd-udevd, 241, write, NETLINK, 0]: 65
@io[systemd-udevd, 241, read, NETLINK, 0]: 75
@io[dbus-daemon, 525, write, UNIX, 0]: 98
@io[systemd-logind, 526, read, UNIX, 0]: 105
@io[systemd-udevd, 241, read, UNIX, 0]: 127
@io[snapd, 31927, read, NETLINK, 0]: 150
@io[dbus-daemon, 525, read, UNIX, 0]: 160
@io[mysqld, 1948, write, TCP, 55010]: 8147
@io[mysqld, 1948, read, TCP, 55010]: 24466
```

This shows that the most socket I/O was by mysqld, with reads and writes to TCP port 55010, the ephemeral port a client is using.

The source to socketio(8) is:

```
#!/usr/local/bin/bpftrace

#include <net/sock.h>

kprobe:sock_recvmsg
{
        $sock = (struct socket *)arg0;
        $dport = $sock->sk->__sk_common.skc_dport;
        $dport = ($dport >> 8) | (($dport << 8) & 0xff00);
        @io[comm, pid, "read", $sock->sk->__sk_common.skc_prot->name, $dport] =
            count();
}

kprobe:sock_sendmsg
{
        $sock = (struct socket *)arg0;
        $dport = $sock->sk->__sk_common.skc_dport;
        $dport = ($dport >> 8) | (($dport << 8) & 0xff00);
        @io[comm, pid, "write", $sock->sk->__sk_common.skc_prot->name, $dport] =
            count();
}
```

This is an example of fetching details from a kernel struct, in this case struct socket, which provides the protocol name and destination port. The destination port is big endian, and is converted to little endian (for this x86 processor) by the tool before inclusion in the @io map.[18] This script could be modified to show the bytes transferred instead of the I/O counts.

TCP Tracing

Tracing at the TCP level provides insight for TCP protocol events and internals, as well as events not associated with a socket (e.g., a TCP port scan).

TCP Tracepoints

Instrumenting TCP internals often requires using kprobes, but there are some TCP tracepoints available. From a 5.3 kernel:

```
# bpftrace -l 't:tcp:*'
tracepoint:tcp:tcp_retransmit_skb
tracepoint:tcp:tcp_send_reset
tracepoint:tcp:tcp_receive_reset
tracepoint:tcp:tcp_destroy_sock
tracepoint:tcp:tcp_rcv_space_adjust
tracepoint:tcp:tcp_retransmit_synack
tracepoint:tcp:tcp_probe
```

The tcp:tcp_retransmit_skb tracepoint is used by the earlier tcpretrans(8) tool. Tracepoints are preferable for their stability, but when they cannot solve your problem you can use kprobes on the kernel TCP functions. Counting them:

```
# bpftrace -e 'k:tcp_* { @[func] = count(); }'
Attaching 336 probes...
^C
@[tcp_try_keep_open]: 1
@[tcp_ooo_try_coalesce]: 1
@[tcp_reset]: 1
[...]
@[tcp_push]: 3191
@[tcp_established_options]: 3584
@[tcp_wfree]: 4408
@[tcp_small_queue_check.isra.0]: 4617
@[tcp_rate_check_app_limited]: 7022
@[tcp_poll]: 8898
@[tcp_release_cb]: 18330
```

---

[18] For this to work on big-endian processors, the tool should test for processor endianness and use a conversion only if necessary; for example, by use of #ifdef LITTLE_ENDIAN.

```
@[tcp_send_mss]: 28168
@[tcp_sendmsg]: 31450
@[tcp_sendmsg_locked]: 31949
@[tcp_write_xmit]: 33276
@[tcp_tx_timestamp]: 33485
```

This showed that the most frequently called function was tcp_tx_timestamp(), called 33,485 times while tracing. Counting functions can identify targets for tracing in more detail. Note that counting all TCP calls may add noticeable overhead due to the number and frequency of functions traced. For this particular task I would use Ftrace function profiling instead via my funccount(8) perf-tools tool, as its overhead and initialization time are much lower. See Chapter 14, Ftrace.

tcpsynbl.bt

The tcpsynbl(8)[19] tool is an example of instrumenting TCP using kprobes. It shows the length of the listen(2) backlog queues broken down by queue length so that you can tell how close the queues are to overflowing (which causes drops of TCP SYN packets). Example output:

```
# tcpsynbl.bt
Attaching 4 probes...
Tracing SYN backlog size. Ctrl-C to end.
04:44:31 dropping a SYN.
04:44:31 dropping a SYN.
04:44:31 dropping a SYN.
04:44:31 dropping a SYN.
04:44:31 dropping a SYN.
[...]
^C
@backlog[backlog limit]: histogram of backlog size

@backlog[128]:
[0]                    473 |@                                                  |
[1]                    502 |@                                                  |
[2, 4)                1001 |@@@                                                |
[4, 8)                1996 |@@@@@@                                             |
[8, 16)               3943 |@@@@@@@@@@@                                        |
[16, 32)              7718 |@@@@@@@@@@@@@@@@@@@@@@                              |
[32, 64)             14460 |@@@@@@@@@@@@@@@@@@@@@@@@@@@@@@@@@@@@@@@@@@@          |
[64, 128)            17246 |@@@@@@@@@@@@@@@@@@@@@@@@@@@@@@@@@@@@@@@@@@@@@@@@@@@@@|
[128, 256)            1844 |@@@@@                                              |
```

---

[19] Origin: I created tcpsynbl.bt on 19-Apr-2019 for [Gregg 19].

While running, tcpsynbl.bt prints timestamps and SYN drops if they occur when tracing. When terminated (by typing Ctrl-C), a histogram of backlog size is printed for each backlog limit in use. This output shows several SYN drops occurring at 4:44:31, and the histogram summary shows a limit of 128 and a distribution where that limit was reached 1844 times (the 128 to 256 bucket). This distribution shows the backlog length when SYNs arrive.

By monitoring the backlog length, you can check whether it is growing over time, giving you an early warning that SYN drops are imminent. This is something you can do as part of capacity planning.

The source to tcpsynbl(8) is:

```
#!/usr/local/bin/bpftrace

#include <net/sock.h>

BEGIN
{
        printf("Tracing SYN backlog size. Ctrl-C to end.\n");
}

kprobe:tcp_v4_syn_recv_sock,
kprobe:tcp_v6_syn_recv_sock
{
        $sock = (struct sock *)arg0;
        @backlog[$sock->sk_max_ack_backlog & 0xffffffff] =
            hist($sock->sk_ack_backlog);
        if ($sock->sk_ack_backlog > $sock->sk_max_ack_backlog) {
                time("%H:%M:%S dropping a SYN.\n");
        }
}

END
{
        printf("\n@backlog[backlog limit]: histogram of backlog size\n");
}
```

The shape of the earlier printed distribution has much to do with the log2 scale used by hist(), where later buckets span larger ranges. You can change hist() to lhist() using:

```
        lhist($sock->sk_ack_backlog, 0, 1000, 10);
```

This will print a linear histogram with even ranges for each bucket: in this case, for the range 0 to 1000 with a bucket size of 10. For more bpftrace programming, see Chapter 15, BPF.

Event Sources

bpftrace can instrument much more; Table 10.6 shows event sources for instrumenting different network events.

Table 10.6 **Network events and sources**

Network Event	Event Source
Application protocols	uprobes
Sockets	syscalls tracepoints
TCP	tcp tracepoints, kprobes
UDP	kprobes
IP and ICMP	kprobes
Packets	skb tracepoints, kprobes
QDiscs and driver queues	qdisc and net tracepoints, kprobes
XDP	xdp tracepoints
Network device drivers	kprobes, some have tracepoints

Use tracepoints wherever possible, as they are a stable interface.

10.6.13   tcpdump

Network packets can be captured and inspected on Linux using the tcpdump(8) utility. This can either print packet summaries on STDOUT or write packet data to a file for later analysis. The latter is usually more practical: packet rates can be too high to follow their summaries in real time.

Dumping packets from the eth4 interface to a file in /tmp:

```
# tcpdump -i eth4 -w /tmp/out.tcpdump
tcpdump: listening on eth4, link-type EN10MB (Ethernet), capture size 65535 bytes
^C273893 packets captured
275752 packets received by filter
1859 packets dropped by kernel
```

The output notes how many packets were dropped by the kernel instead of being passed to tcpdump(8), as occurs when the rate of packets is too high. Note that you can use -i any to c apture packets from all interfaces.

Inspecting packets from a dump file:

```
# tcpdump -nr /tmp/out.tcpdump
reading from file /tmp/out.tcpdump, link-type EN10MB (Ethernet)
02:24:46.160754 IP 10.2.124.2.32863 > 10.2.203.2.5001: Flags [.], seq
3612664461:3612667357, ack 180214943, win 64436, options [nop,nop,TS val 692339741
ecr 346311608], length 2896
```

```
02:24:46.160765 IP 10.2.203.2.5001 > 10.2.124.2.32863: Flags [.], ack 2896, win
18184, options [nop,nop,TS val 346311610 ecr 692339740], length 0
02:24:46.160778 IP 10.2.124.2.32863 > 10.2.203.2.5001: Flags [.], seq 2896:4344, ack
1, win 64436, options [nop,nop,TS val 692339741 ecr 346311608], length 1448
02:24:46.160807 IP 10.2.124.2.32863 > 10.2.203.2.5001: Flags [.], seq 4344:5792, ack
1, win 64436, options [nop,nop,TS val 692339741 ecr 346311608], length 1448
02:24:46.160817 IP 10.2.203.2.5001 > 10.2.124.2.32863: Flags [.], ack 5792, win
18184, options [nop,nop,TS val 346311610 ecr 692339741], length 0
[...]
```

Each line of output shows the time of the packet (with microsecond resolution), its source and destination IP addresses, and TCP header values. By studying these, the operation of TCP can be understood in detail, including how well advanced features are working for your workload.

The -n option was used to not resolve IP addresses as host names. Other options include printing verbose details where available (-v), link-layer headers (-e), and hex-address dumps (-x or -X). For example:

```
# tcpdump -enr /tmp/out.tcpdump -vvv -X
reading from file /tmp/out.tcpdump, link-type EN10MB (Ethernet)
02:24:46.160754 80:71:1f:ad:50:48 > 84:2b:2b:61:b6:ed, ethertype IPv4 (0x0800),
length 2962: (tos 0x0, ttl 63, id 46508, offset 0, flags [DF], proto TCP (6), length
2948)
    10.2.124.2.32863 > 10.2.203.2.5001: Flags [.], cksum 0x667f (incorrect ->
0xc4da), seq 3612664461:3612667357, ack 180214943, win 64436, options [nop,nop,TS val
692339741 ecr 346311608], length 289
6
        0x0000:  4500 0b84 b5ac 4000 3f06 1fbf 0a02 7c02  E.....@.?.....|.
        0x0010:  0a02 cb02 805f 1389 d754 e28d 0abd dc9f  ....._...T......
        0x0020:  8010 fbb4 667f 0000 0101 080a 2944 441d  ....f.......)DD.
        0x0030:  14a4 4bb8 3233 3435 3637 3839 3031 3233  ..K.234567890123
        0x0040:  3435 3637 3839 3031 3233 3435 3637 3839  4567890123456789
[...]
```

During performance analysis, it can be useful to change the timestamp column to show delta times between packets (-ttt), or elapsed time since the first packet (-tttt).

An expression can also be provided to describe how to filter packets (see pcap-filter(7)) to focus on the packets of interest. This is performed in-kernel for efficiency (except on Linux 2.0 and older) using BPF.

Packet capture is expensive to perform in terms of both CPU cost and storage. If possible, use tcpdump(8) only for short periods to limit the performance cost, and look for ways to use efficient BPF-based tools such as bpftrace instead.

tshark(1) is a similar command-line packet capture tool that provides better filtering and output options. It is the CLI version of Wireshark.

10.6.14   Wireshark

While tcpdump(8) works fine for casual investigations, for deeper analysis it can be time-consuming to use at the command line. The Wireshark tool (formerly Ethereal) provides a graphical interface for packet capture and inspection and can also import packet dump files from tcpdump(8) [Wireshark 20]. Useful features include identifying network connections and their related packets, so that they can be studied separately, and also translation of hundreds of protocol headers.

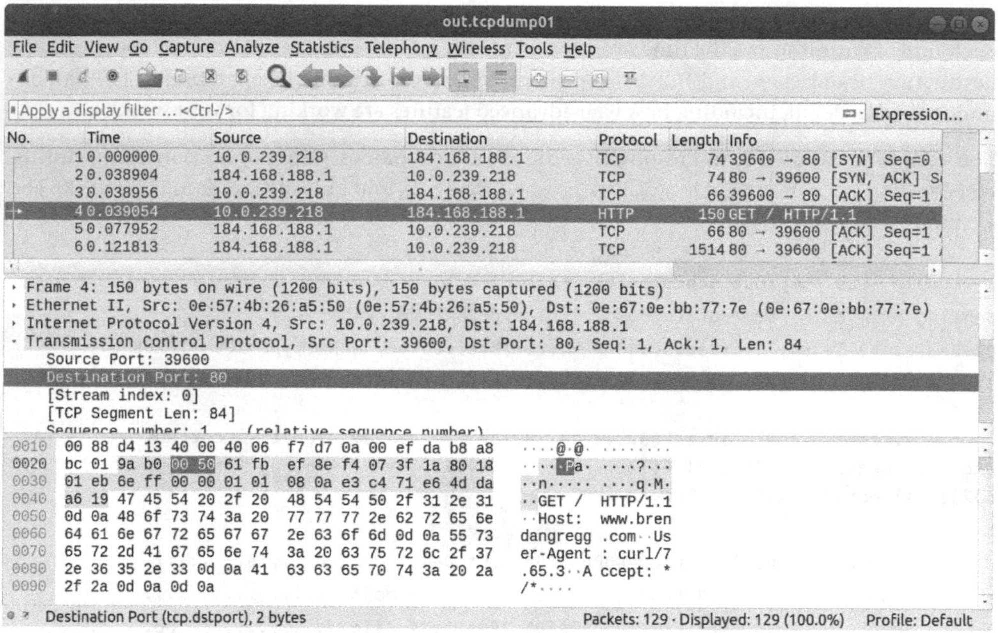

Figure 10.12   Wireshark screenshot

Figure 10.12 shows an example screenshot of Wireshark. The window is split horizontally into three parts. At the top is a table showing packets as rows and details as columns. The middle section shows protocol details: in this example the TCP protocol was expanded and the destination port selected. The bottom section shows the raw packet as hexadecimal on the left and text on the right: the location of the TCP destination port is highlighted.

10.6.15   Other Tools

Network analysis tools included in other chapters of this book, and in *BPF Performance Tools* [Gregg 19], are listed in Table 10.7.

Table 10.7 **Other network analysis tools**

Section	Tool	Description
5.5.3	offcputime	Off-CPU profiling can show network I/O
[Gregg 19]	sockstat	High-level socket statistics
[Gregg 19]	sofamily	Count address families for new sockets, by process
[Gregg 19]	soprotocol	Count transport protocols for new sockets, by process
[Gregg 19]	soconnect	Trace socket IP-protocol connections with details
[Gregg 19]	soaccept	Trace socket IP-protocol accepts with details
[Gregg 19]	socketio	Summarize socket details with I/O counts
[Gregg 19]	socksize	Show socket I/O sizes as per-process histograms
[Gregg 19]	sormem	Show socket receive buffer usage and overflows
[Gregg 19]	soconnlat	Summarize IP socket connection latency with stacks
[Gregg 19]	so1stbyte	Summarize IP socket first byte latency
[Gregg 19]	tcpconnect	Trace TCP active connections (connect())
[Gregg 19]	tcpaccept	Trace TCP passive connections (accept())
[Gregg 19]	tcpwin	Trace TCP send congestion window parameters
[Gregg 19]	tcpnagle	Trace TCP Nagle usage and transmit delays
[Gregg 19]	udpconnect	Trace new UDP connections from localhost
[Gregg 19]	gethostlatency	Trace DNS lookup latency via library calls
[Gregg 19]	ipecn	Trace IP inbound explicit congestion notification
[Gregg 19]	superping	Measure ICMP echo times from the network stack
[Gregg 19]	qdisc-fq (...)	Show FQ qdisc queue latency
[Gregg 19]	netsize	Show net device I/O sizes
[Gregg 19]	nettxlat	Show net device transmission latency
[Gregg 19]	skbdrop	Trace sk_buff drops with kernel stack traces
[Gregg 19]	skblife	Lifespan of sk_buff as inter-stack latency
[Gregg 19]	ieee80211scan	Trace IEEE 802.11 WiFi scanning

Other Linux network observability tools and sources include:

- **strace(1)**: Trace socket-related syscalls and examine the options used (note that strace(1) has high overhead)

- **lsof(8)**: List open files by process ID, including socket details

- **nfsstat(8)**: NFS server and client statistics

- **ifpps(8)**: Top-like network and system statistics

- **iftop(8)**: Summarize network interface throughput by host (sniffer)
- **perf(1)**: Count and record network tracepoints and kernel functions.
- **/proc/net**: Contains many network statistics files
- **BPF iterator**: Allows BPF programs to export custom statistics in /sys/fs/bpf

There are also many network monitoring solutions, either based on SNMP or running their own custom agents.

10.7   Experimentation

Network performance is commonly tested using tools that perform an experiment rather than just observing the state of the system. Such experimental tools include ping(8), traceroute(8), and network micro-benchmarks such as iperf(8). These can be used to determine network health between hosts, which can be used to help determine whether end-to-end network throughput is a problem when debugging application performance issues.

10.7.1   ping

The ping(8) command tests network connectivity by sending ICMP echo request packets. For example:

```
# ping www.netflix.com
PING www.netflix.com(2620:108:700f::3423:46a1 (2620:108:700f::3423:46a1)) 56 data
bytes
64 bytes from 2620:108:700f::3423:46a1 (2620:108:700f::3423:46a1): icmp_seq=1 ttl=43
time=32.3 ms
64 bytes from 2620:108:700f::3423:46a1 (2620:108:700f::3423:46a1): icmp_seq=2 ttl=43
time=34.3 ms
64 bytes from 2620:108:700f::3423:46a1 (2620:108:700f::3423:46a1): icmp_seq=3 ttl=43
time=34.0 ms
^C
--- www.netflix.com ping statistics ---
3 packets transmitted, 3 received, 0% packet loss, time 2003ms
rtt min/avg/max/mdev = 32.341/33.579/34.389/0.889 ms
```

The output includes the round-trip time (`time`) for each packet and has a summary showing various statistics.

Older versions of ping(8) measured the round-trip time from user space, slightly inflating times due to kernel execution and scheduler latency. Newer kernels and ping(8) versions use kernel timestamp support (SIOCGSTAMP or SO_TIMESTAMP) to improve the accuracy of the reported ping times.

The ICMP packets used may be treated by routers at a lower priority than application protocols, and latency may show higher variance than usual.[20]

10.7.2   traceroute

The traceroute(8) command sends a series of test packets to experimentally determine the current route to a host. This is performed by increasing the IP protocol time to live (TTL) by one for each packet, causing the sequence of gateways to the host to reveal themselves by sending ICMP time exceeded response messages (provided a firewall doesn't block them).

For example, testing the current route from a California host to my website:

```
# traceroute www.brendangregg.com
traceroute to www.brendangregg.com (184.168.188.1), 30 hops max, 60 byte packets
 1  _gateway (10.0.0.1)  3.453 ms  3.379 ms  4.769 ms
 2  196.120.89.153 (196.120.89.153)  19.239 ms  19.217 ms  13.507 ms
 3  be-10006-rur01.sanjose.ca.sfba.comcast.net (162.151.1.145)  19.141 ms  19.102 ms
19.050 ms
 4  be-231-rar01.santaclara.ca.sfba.comcast.net (162.151.78.249)  19.018 ms  18.987
ms  18.941 ms
 5  be-299-ar01.santaclara.ca.sfba.comcast.net (68.86.143.93)  21.184 ms  18.849 ms
21.053 ms
 6  lag-14.ear3.SanJose1.Level3.net (4.68.72.105)  18.717 ms  11.950 ms  16.471 ms
 7  4.69.216.162 (4.69.216.162)  24.905 ms 4.69.216.158 (4.69.216.158)  21.705 ms
28.043 ms
 8  4.53.228.238 (4.53.228.238)  35.802 ms  37.202 ms  37.137 ms
 9  ae0.ibrsa0107-01.lax1.bb.godaddy.com (148.72.34.5)  24.640 ms  24.610 ms  24.579
ms
10  148.72.32.16 (148.72.32.16)  33.747 ms  35.537 ms  33.598 ms
11  be38.trmc0215-01.ars.mgmt.phx3.gdg (184.168.0.69)  33.646 ms  33.590 ms  35.220
ms
12  * * *
13  * * *
[...]
```

Each hop shows a series of three RTTs, which can be used as a coarse source of network latency statistics. As with ping(8), the packets used are low-priority and may show higher latency than for other application protocols. Some tests show "*": an ICMP time exceeded message was not returned. All three tests showing "*" can be due to a hop not returning ICMP at all, or ICMP being blocked by a firewall. A workaround can be to switch to TCP instead of ICMP, using the -T option (also provided as the command tcptraceroute(1); a more advanced version is astraceroute(8), which can customize flags).

---

[20] Although some networks may instead treat ICMP with a higher priority, to perform better on ping-based benchmarks.

The path taken can also be studied as part of static performance tuning. Networks are designed to be dynamic and responsive to outages, and performance may have degraded as the path has changed. Note that the path can also change during a traceroute(8) run: hop 7 in the previous output first returned from 4.69.216.162, and then 4.69.216.158. If the address changes, it is printed; otherwise only the RTT time is printed for the subsequent tests.

For advanced details on interpreting traceroute(8), see [Steenbergen 09].

traceroute(8) was first written by Van Jacobson. He later created an amazing tool called pathchar.

10.7.3   pathchar

pathchar is similar to traceroute(8) but includes the bandwidth between hops. This is determined by sending a series of network packets in various sizes many times and performing statistical analysis. Here is example output:

```
# pathchar 192.168.1.10
pathchar to 192.168.1.1 (192.168.1.1)
 doing 32 probes at each of 64 to 1500 by 32
 0 localhost
 |     30 Mb/s,    79 us (562 us)
 1 neptune.test.com (192.168.2.1)
 |     44 Mb/s,   195 us (1.23 ms)
 2 mars.test.com (192.168.1.1)
 2 hops, rtt 547 us (1.23 ms), bottleneck  30 Mb/s, pipe 7555 bytes
```

Unfortunately, pathchar somehow missed becoming popular (perhaps because the source code was not released, as far as I know), and it is difficult to run the original version (the most recent Linux binary on the pathchar site is for Linux 2.0.30 published in 1997 [Jacobson 97]). A new version by Bruce A. Mah, called pchar(8), is more readily available. pathchar was also very time-consuming to run, taking tens of minutes depending on the number of hops, although methods have been proposed to reduce this time [Downey 99].

10.7.4   iperf

iperf(1) is an open-source tool for testing maximum TCP and UDP throughput. It supports a variety of options, including parallel mode where multiple client threads are used, which can be necessary to drive a network to its limit. iperf(1) must be executed on both the server and the client.

For example, executing iperf(1) on the server:

```
$ iperf -s -l 128k
------------------------------------------------------------
Server listening on TCP port 5001
TCP window size: 85.3 KByte (default)
------------------------------------------------------------
```

This increased the socket buffer size to 128 Kbytes (-l 128k), from the default of 8 Kbytes.

The following was executed on the client:

```
# iperf -c 10.2.203.2 -l 128k -P 2 -i 1 -t 60
------------------------------------------------------------
Client connecting to 10.2.203.2, TCP port 5001
TCP window size: 48.0 KByte (default)
------------------------------------------------------------
[  4] local 10.2.124.2 port 41407 connected with 10.2.203.2 port 5001
[  3] local 10.2.124.2 port 35830 connected with 10.2.203.2 port 5001
[ ID] Interval       Transfer     Bandwidth
[  4]  0.0- 1.0 sec  6.00 MBytes  50.3 Mbits/sec
[  3]  0.0- 1.0 sec  22.5 MBytes   189 Mbits/sec
[SUM]  0.0- 1.0 sec  28.5 MBytes   239 Mbits/sec
[  3]  1.0- 2.0 sec  16.1 MBytes   135 Mbits/sec
[  4]  1.0- 2.0 sec  12.6 MBytes   106 Mbits/sec
[SUM]  1.0- 2.0 sec  28.8 MBytes   241 Mbits/sec
[...]
[  4]  0.0-60.0 sec   748 MBytes   105 Mbits/sec
[  3]  0.0-60.0 sec   996 MBytes   139 Mbits/sec
[SUM]  0.0-60.0 sec  1.70 GBytes   244 Mbits/sec
```

This used the following options:

- **-c host**: Connect to the host name or IP address
- **-l 128k**: Use a 128 Kbyte socket buffer
- **-P 2**: Run in parallel mode with two client threads
- **-i 1**: Print interval summaries every second
- **-t 60**: Total duration of the test: 60 seconds

The final line shows the average throughput during the test, summed across all parallel threads: 244 Mbits/s.

The per-interval summaries can be inspected to see the variance over time. The --reportstyle c option can be used to output CSV, so that it can then be imported by other tools, such as graphing software.

10.7.5 netperf

netperf(1) is an advanced micro-benchmark tool that can test request/response performance [HP 18]. I use netperf(1) to measure TCP round-trip latency; here is some example output:

```
server$ netserver -D -p 7001
Starting netserver with host 'IN(6)ADDR_ANY' port '7001' and family AF_UNSPEC
[...]
```

```
client$ netperf -v 100 -H 100.66.63.99 -t TCP_RR -p 7001
MIGRATED TCP REQUEST/RESPONSE TEST from 0.0.0.0 (0.0.0.0) port 0 AF_INET to
100.66.63.99 () port 0 AF_INET : demo : first burst 0
Alignment      Offset        RoundTrip Trans   Throughput
Local Remote   Local Remote  Latency   Rate    10^6bits/s
Send  Recv     Send  Recv    usec/Tran per sec Outbound  Inbound
   8     0        0     0     98699.102  10.132 0.000     0.000
```

This shows a TCP round-trip latency of 98.7 ms.

10.7.6   tc

The traffic control utility, tc(8), allows various queueing disciplines (qdiscs) to be selected to improve or manage performance. For experimentation, there are also qdiscs that can throttle or perturb performance, which can be useful for testing and simulation. This section demonstrates the network emulator (netem) qdisc.

To start with, the following command lists the current qdisc configuration for the interface eth0:

```
# tc qdisc show dev eth0
qdisc noqueue 0: root refcnt 2
```

Now the netem qdisc will be added. Each qdisc supports different tunable parameters. For this example, I will use the packet loss parameters for netem, and set packet loss to 1%:

```
# tc qdisc add dev eth0 root netem loss 1%
# tc qdisc show dev eth0
qdisc netem 8001: root refcnt 2 limit 1000 loss 1%
```

Subsequent network I/O on eth0 will now suffer a 1% packet loss.

The -s option to tc(8) shows statistics:

```
# tc -s qdisc show dev eth0
qdisc netem 8001: root refcnt 2 limit 1000 loss 1%
 Sent 75926119 bytes 89538 pkt (dropped 917, overlimits 0 requeues 0)
 backlog 0b 0p requeues 0
```

This output shows counts for the number of dropped packets.

To remove the qdisc:

```
# tc qdisc del dev eth0 root
# tc qdisc show dev eth0
qdisc noqueue 0: root refcnt 2
```

See the man page for each qdisc for the full list of options (for netem, the man page is tc-netem(8)).

10.7.7 Other Tools

Other experimental tools worth mentioning:

- **pktgen**: A packet generator included in the Linux kernel [Linux 20l].

- **Flent**: The FLExible Network Tester launches multiple micro-benchmarks and graphs the results [Høiland-Jørgensen 20].

- **mtr(8)**: A traceroute-like tool that includes ping statistics.

- **tcpreplay(1)**: A tool that replays previously captured network traffic (from tcpdump(8)), including simulating packet timing. While more useful for general debugging than performance testing, there might be performance issues that only occur with a certain sequence of packets or bit patterns, and this tool may be able to reproduce them.

10.8 Tuning

Network tunable parameters are usually already tuned to provide high performance. The network stack is also usually designed to respond dynamically to different workloads, providing optimum performance.

Before trying tunable parameters, it can be worthwhile to first understand network usage. This may also identify unnecessary work that can be eliminated, leading to much greater performance wins. Try the workload characterization and static performance tuning methodologies using the tools in the previous section.

Available tunables vary between versions of an operating system. See their documentation. The sections that follow provide an idea of what may be available and how they are tuned; they should be treated as a starting point to revise based on your workload and environment.

10.8.1 System-Wide

On Linux, system-wide tunable parameters can be viewed and set using the sysctl(8) command and written to /etc/sysctl.conf. They can also be read and written from the /proc file system, under /proc/sys/net.

For example, to see what is currently available for TCP, the parameters can be searched for the text "tcp" from sysctl(8):

```
# sysctl -a | grep tcp
net.ipv4.tcp_abort_on_overflow = 0
net.ipv4.tcp_adv_win_scale = 1
net.ipv4.tcp_allowed_congestion_control = reno cubic
net.ipv4.tcp_app_win = 31
net.ipv4.tcp_autocorking = 1
net.ipv4.tcp_available_congestion_control = reno cubic
net.ipv4.tcp_available_ulp =
```

```
net.ipv4.tcp_base_mss = 1024
net.ipv4.tcp_challenge_ack_limit = 1000
net.ipv4.tcp_comp_sack_delay_ns = 1000000
net.ipv4.tcp_comp_sack_nr = 44
net.ipv4.tcp_congestion_control = cubic
net.ipv4.tcp_dsack = 1
[...]
```

On this kernel (5.3) there are 70 containing "tcp" and many more under "net." including parameters for IP, Ethernet, routing, and network interfaces.

Some of these settings can be tuned on a per-socket basis. For example, net.ipv4.tcp_congestion_control is the system-wide default congestion control algorithm, which can be set per socket using the TCP_CONGESTION socket option (see Section 10.8.2, Socket Options).

Production Example

The following shows how Netflix tunes their cloud instances [Gregg 19c]; it is applied in a start script during boot:

```
net.core.default_qdisc = fq
net.core.netdev_max_backlog = 5000
net.core.rmem_max = 16777216
net.core.somaxconn = 1024
net.core.wmem_max = 16777216
net.ipv4.ip_local_port_range = 10240 65535
net.ipv4.tcp_abort_on_overflow = 1
net.ipv4.tcp_congestion_control = bbr
net.ipv4.tcp_max_syn_backlog = 8192
net.ipv4.tcp_rmem = 4096 12582912 16777216
net.ipv4.tcp_slow_start_after_idle = 0
net.ipv4.tcp_syn_retries = 2
net.ipv4.tcp_tw_reuse = 1
net.ipv4.tcp_wmem = 4096 12582912 16777216
```

This sets only 14 tunables out of those possible, and is provided as a point-in-time example, not a recipe. Netflix is considering updating two of these during 2020 (setting net.core.netdev_max_backlog to 1000, and net.core.somaxconn to 4096)[21] pending non-regression testing.

The following sections discuss individual tunables.

---

[21] Thanks to Daniel Borkmann for the suggestions, made during the review of this book. These new values are already in use by Google [Dumazet 17b][Dumazet 19].

Socket and TCP Buffers

The maximum socket buffer size for all protocol types, for both reads (`rmem_max`) and writes (`wmem_max`), can be set using:

```
net.core.rmem_max = 16777216
net.core.wmem_max = 16777216
```

The value is in bytes. This may need to be set to 16 Mbytes or higher to support full-speed 10 GbE connections.

Enabling auto-tuning of the TCP receive buffer:

```
net.ipv4.tcp_moderate_rcvbuf = 1
```

Setting the auto-tuning parameters for the TCP read and write buffers:

```
net.ipv4.tcp_rmem = 4096 87380 16777216
net.ipv4.tcp_wmem = 4096 65536 16777216
```

Each has three values: the minimum, default, and maximum number of bytes to use. The size used is auto-tuned from the default. To improve TCP throughput, try increasing the maximum value. Increasing minimum and default will consume more memory per connection, which may not be necessary.

TCP Backlog

First backlog queue, for half-open connections:

```
net.ipv4.tcp_max_syn_backlog = 4096
```

Second backlog queue, the listen backlog, for passing connections to accept(2):

```
net.core.somaxconn = 1024
```

Both of these may need to be increased from their defaults, for example, to 4,096 and 1,024, or higher, to better handle bursts of load.

Device Backlog

Increasing the length of the network device backlog queue, per CPU:

```
net.core.netdev_max_backlog = 10000
```

This may need to be increased, such as to 10,000, for 10 GbE NICs.

TCP Congestion Control

Linux supports pluggable congestion-control algorithms. Listing those currently available:

```
# sysctl net.ipv4.tcp_available_congestion_control
net.ipv4.tcp_available_congestion_control = reno cubic
```

Some may be available but not currently loaded. For example, adding htcp:

```
# modprobe tcp_htcp
# sysctl net.ipv4.tcp_available_congestion_control
net.ipv4.tcp_available_congestion_control = reno cubic htcp
```

The current algorithm may be selected using:

```
net.ipv4.tcp_congestion_control = cubic
```

TCP Options

Other TCP parameters that may be set include:

```
net.ipv4.tcp_sack = 1
net.ipv4.tcp_fack = 1
net.ipv4.tcp_tw_reuse = 1
net.ipv4.tcp_tw_recycle = 0
```

SACK and the FACK extensions may improve throughput performance over high-latency networks, at the cost of some CPU load.

The `tcp_tw_reuse` tunable allows a TIME_WAIT session to be reused when it appears safe to do so. This can allow higher rates of connections between two hosts, such as between a web server and a database, without hitting the 16-bit ephemeral port limit with sessions in TIME_WAIT.

`tcp_tw_recycle` is another way to reuse TIME_WAIT sessions, although not as safe as `tcp_tw_reuse`.

ECN

Explicit Congestion Notification can be controlled using:

```
net.ipv4.tcp_ecn = 1
```

Values are 0 to disable ECN, 1 to allow for incoming connections and request ECN on outgoing connections, and 2 to allow for incoming and not request ECN on outgoing. The default is 2.

There is also net.ipv4.tcp_ecn_fallback, set to 1 (true) by default, which will disable ECN for a connection if the kernel detects that it has misbehaved.

Byte Queue Limits

This can be tuned via /sys. Showing the contents of the control files for these limits (the path, truncated in this output, will be different for your system and interface):

```
# grep . /sys/devices/pci.../net/ens5/queues/tx-0/byte_queue_limits/limit*
/sys/devices/pci.../net/ens5/queues/tx-0/byte_queue_limits/limit:16654
/sys/devices/pci.../net/ens5/queues/tx-0/byte_queue_limits/limit_max:1879048192
/sys/devices/pci.../net/ens5/queues/tx-0/byte_queue_limits/limit_min:0
```

The limit for this interface is 16654 bytes, set by auto-tuning. To control this value, set limit_min and limit_max to clamp the accepted range.

Resource Controls

The container groups (cgroups) network priority (net_prio) subsystem can be used to apply a priority to outgoing network traffic, for processes or groups of processes. This can be used to favor high-priority network traffic, such as production load, over low-priority traffic, such as backups or monitoring. There is also the network classifier (net_cls) cgroup for tagging packets belonging to a cgroup with a class ID: these IDs can then be used by a queueing discipline for applying packet or bandwidth limits, and also by BPF programs. BPF programs can also use other information such as the cgroup v2 ID for container awareness, and can improve scalability by moving classification, measurement, and remarking to the tc egress hook, relieving pressure on the root qdisc lock [Fomichev 20].

For more information on resource controls see the Network I/O heading in Chapter 11, Cloud Computing, Section 11.3.3, Resource Controls.

Queueing Disciplines

Described in Section 10.4.3, Software, and pictured in Figure 10.8, queueing disciplines (qdiscs) are algorithms for scheduling, manipulating, filtering, and shaping network packets. Section 10.7.6, tc, showed using the netem qdisc for creating packet loss. There are also various qdiscs that may improve performance for different workloads. You can list the qdiscs on your system using:

```
# man -k tc-
```

Each qdisc has its own man page. Qdiscs can be used to set packet rate or bandwidth policies, set the IP ECN flags, and more.

The default qdisc can be viewed and set using:

```
# sysctl net.core.default_qdisc
net.core.default_qdisc = fq_codel
```

Many Linux distributions have already switched to fq_codel as the default because it provides good performance in most cases.

The Tuned Project

With so many tunables available, it can be laborious to work through them. The Tuned Project provides automatic tuning for some of these tunables based on selectable profiles, and supports Linux distributions including RHEL, Fedora, Ubuntu, and CentOS [Tuned Project 20]. After installing tuned, the available profiles can be listed using:

```
# tuned-adm list
Available profiles:
[...]
- balanced                 - General non-specialized tuned profile
[...]
- network-latency          - Optimize for deterministic performance at the cost of
increased power consumption, focused on low latency network performance
- network-throughput       - Optimize for streaming network throughput, generally
only necessary on older CPUs or 40G+ networks
[...]
```

This output is truncated: the full list shows 28 profiles. To activate the network-latency profile:

```
# tuned-adm profile network-latency
```

To see which tunables this profile sets, its configuration file can be read from the tuned source [Škarvada 20]:

```
$ more tuned/profiles/network-latency/tuned.conf
[...]
[main]
summary=Optimize for deterministic performance at the cost of increased power
consumption, focused on low latency network performance
include=latency-performance

[vm]
transparent_hugepages=never

[sysctl]
net.core.busy_read=50
net.core.busy_poll=50
net.ipv4.tcp_fastopen=3
kernel.numa_balancing=0

[bootloader]
cmdline_network_latency=skew_tick=1
```

Note that this has an `include` directive that includes the tunables in the latency-performance profile as well.

10.8.2 Socket Options

Sockets can be tuned individually by applications via the setsockopt(2) syscall. This may only be possible if you are developing or recompiling software, and can make modifications to the source.[22]

setsockopt(2) allows different layers to be tuned (e.g., socket, TCP). Table 10.8 shows some tuning possibilities on Linux.

Table 10.8 **Sample socket options**

Option Name	Description
SO_SNDBUF, SO_RCVBUF	Send and receive buffer sizes (these can be tuned up to the system limits described earlier; there is also SO_SNDBUFFORCE to override the send limit).
SO_REUSEPORT	Allows multiple processes or threads to bind to the same port, allowing the kernel to distribute load across them for scalability (since Linux 3.9).
SO_MAX_PACING_RATE	Sets the maximum pacing rate, in bytes per second (see tc-fq(8)).
SO_LINGER	Can be used to reduce TIME_WAIT latency.
SO_TXTIME	Request time-based packet transmission, where deadlines can be supplied (since Linux 4.19) [Corbet 18c] (used for UDP pacing [Bruijn 18]).
TCP_NODELAY	Disables Nagle, sending segments as soon as possible. This may improve latency at the cost of higher network utilization (more packets).
TCP_CORK	Pause transmission until full packets can be sent, improving throughput. (There is also a system-wide setting for the kernel to automatically attempt corking: net.ipv4.tcp_autocorking.)
TCP_QUICKACK	Send ACKs immediately (can increase send bandwidth).
TCP_CONGESTION	Congestion control algorithm for the socket.

For available socket options, see the man pages for socket(7), tcp(7), udp(7), etc.

There are also some socket I/O syscall flags that can affect performance. For example, Linux 4.14 added the MSG_ZEROCOPY flag for send(2) syscalls: it allows the user space buffer to be used during transmission, to avoid the expense of copying it to kernel space[23] [Linux 20c].

---

[22] There are some dangerous ways to hack it into a running binary, but it would be irresponsible to show them here.

[23] Using MSG_ZEROCOPY is not as simple as just setting the flag: the send(2) syscall may return before the data has been sent, so the sending application must wait for a kernel notification to know when freeing or reusing the buffer memory is allowed.

10.8.3 Configuration

The following configuration options may also be available for tuning network performance:

- **Ethernet jumbo frames:** Increasing the default MTU from 1,500 to ~9,000 can improve network throughput performance, if the network infrastructure supports jumbo frames.

- **Link aggregation:** Multiple network interfaces can be grouped together so that they act as one with the combined bandwidth. This requires switch support and configuration to work properly.

- **Firewall configuration:** For example, iptables or BPF programs on the egress hook can be used to set the IP ToS (DSCP) level in the IP headers based on a firewall rule. This could be used to prioritize traffic based on port, as well as other use cases.

10.9 Exercises

1. Answer the following questions about network terminology:

   - What is the difference between bandwidth and throughput?

   - What is TCP connection latency?

   - What is first-byte latency?

   - What is round-trip time?

2. Answer the following conceptual questions:

   - Describe network interface utilization and saturation.

   - What is the TCP listen backlog, and how is it used?

   - Describe the pros and cons of interrupt coalescing.

3. Answer the following deeper questions:

   - For a TCP connection, explain how a network frame (or packet) error could hurt performance.

   - Describe what happens when a network interface is overloaded with work, including the effect on application performance.

4. Develop the following procedures for your operating system:

   - A USE method checklist for network resources (network interfaces and controllers). Include how to fetch each metric (e.g., which command to execute) and how to interpret the result. Try to use existing OS observability tools before installing or using additional software products.

5. A workload characterization checklist for network resources. Include how to Perform these tasks (may require use of dynamic tracing):

   - Measure first-byte latency for outbound (active) TCP connections.

   - Measure TCP connect latency. The script should handle non-blocking connect(2) calls.

6. (optional, advanced) Measure TCP/IP inter-stack latency for RX and TX. For RX, this measures time from interrupt to socket read; for TX, the time from socket write to device transmit. Test under load. Can additional information be included to explain the cause of any latency outliers?

10.10 References

[**Postel 80**] Postel, J., "RFC 768: User Datagram Protocol," *Information Sciences Institute*, https://tools.ietf.org/html/rfc768, 1980.

[**Postel 81**] Postel, J., "RFC 793: Transmission Control Protocol," *Information Sciences Institute*, https://tools.ietf.org/html/rfc768, 1981.

[**Nagle 84**] Nagle, J., "RFC 896: Congestion Control in IP/TCP Internetworks," https://tools.ietf.org/html/rfc896,1984.

[**Saltzer 84**] Saltzer, J., Reed, D., and Clark, D., "End-to-End Arguments in System Design," *ACM TOCS*, November 1984.

[**Braden 89**] Braden, R., "RFC 1122: Requirements for Internet Hosts—Communication Layers," https://tools.ietf.org/html/rfc1122, 1989.

[**Jacobson 92**] Jacobson, V., et al., "TCP Extensions for High Performance," *Network Working Group*, https://tools.ietf.org/html/rfc1323, 1992.

[**Stevens 93**] Stevens, W. R., *TCP/IP Illustrated, Volume 1*, Addison-Wesley, 1993.

[**Mathis 96**] Mathis, M., and Mahdavi, J., "Forward Acknowledgement: Refining TCP Congestion Control," *ACM SIGCOMM*, 1996.

[**Jacobson 97**] Jacobson, V., "pathchar-a1-linux-2.0.30.tar.gz," ftp://ftp.ee.lbl.gov/pathchar, 1997.

[**Nichols 98**] Nichols, K., Blake, S., Baker, F., and Black, D., "Definition of the Differentiated Services Field (DS Field) in the IPv4 and IPv6 Headers," *Network Working Group*, https://tools.ietf.org/html/rfc2474, 1998.

[**Downey 99**] Downey, A., "Using pathchar to Estimate Internet Link Characteristics," *ACM SIGCOMM*, October 1999.

[**Ramakrishnan 01**] Ramakrishnan, K., Floyd, S., and Black, D., "The Addition of Explicit Congestion Notification (ECN) to IP," *Network Working Group*, https://tools.ietf.org/html/rfc3168, 2001.

[**Corbet 03**] Corbet, J., "Driver porting: Network drivers," *LWN.net*, https://lwn.net/Articles/30107, 2003.

[**Hassan 03**] Hassan, M., and R. Jain., *High Performance TCP/IP Networking*, Prentice Hall, 2003.

[**Deri 04**] Deri, L., "Improving Passive Packet Capture: Beyond Device Polling," *Proceedings of SANE*, 2004.

[**Corbet 06b**] Corbet, J., "Reworking NAPI," *LWN.net*, https://lwn.net/Articles/214457, 2006.

[Cook 09] Cook, T., "nicstat - the Solaris and Linux Network Monitoring Tool You Did Not Know You Needed," https://blogs.oracle.com/timc/entry/nicstat_the_solaris_and_linux, 2009.

[Steenbergen 09] Steenbergen, R., "A Practical Guide to (Correctly) Troubleshooting with Traceroute," https://archive.nanog.org/meetings/nanog47/presentations/Sunday/RAS_Traceroute_N47_Sun.pdf, 2009.

[Paxson 11] Paxson, V., Allman, M., Chu, J., and Sargent, M., "RFC 6298: Computing TCP's Retransmission Timer," *Internet Engineering Task Force (IETF)*, https://tools.ietf.org/html/rfc6298, 2011.

[Corbet 12] "TCP friends," *LWN.net*, https://lwn.net/Articles/511254, 2012.

[Fritchie 12] Fritchie, S. L., "quoted," https://web.archive.org/web/20120119110658/http://www.snookles.com/slf-blog/2012/01/05/tcp-incast-what-is-it, 2012.

[Hrubý 12] Hrubý, T., "Byte Queue Limits," Linux Plumber's Conference, https://blog.linuxplumbersconf.org/2012/wp-content/uploads/2012/08/bql_slide.pdf, 2012.

[Nichols 12] Nichols, K., and Jacobson, V., "Controlling Queue Delay," *Communications of the ACM*, July 2012.

[Roskind 12] Roskind, J., "QUIC: Quick UDP Internet Connections," https://docs.google.com/document/d/1RNHkx_VvKWyWg6Lr8SZ-saqsQx7rFV-ev2jRFUoVD34/edit#, 2012.

[Dukkipati 13] Dukkipati, N., Cardwell, N., Cheng, Y., and Mathis, M., "Tail Loss Probe (TLP): An Algorithm for Fast Recovery of Tail Losses," *TCP Maintenance Working Group*, https://tools.ietf.org/html/draft-dukkipati-tcpm-tcp-loss-probe-01, 2013.

[Siemon 13] Siemon, D., "Queueing in the Linux Network Stack," https://www.coverfire.com/articles/queueing-in-the-linux-network-stack, 2013.

[Cheng 16] Cheng, Y., and Cardwell, N., "Making Linux TCP Fast," *netdev 1.2*, https://netdevconf.org/1.2/papers/bbr-netdev-1.2.new.new.pdf, 2016.

[Linux 16] "TCP Offload Engine (TOE)," https://wiki.linuxfoundation.org/networking/toe, 2016.

[Ather 17] Ather, A., "BBR TCP congestion control offers higher network utilization and throughput during network congestion (packet loss, latencies)," https://twitter.com/amernetflix/status/892787364598132736, 2017.

[Bensley 17] Bensley, S., et al., "Data Center TCP (DCTCP): TCP Congestion Control for Data Centers," *Internet Engineering Task Force (IETF)*, https://tools.ietf.org/html/rfc8257, 2017.

[Dumazet 17a] Dumazet, E., "Busy Polling: Past, Present, Future," *netdev 2.1*, https://netdevconf.info/2.1/slides/apr6/dumazet-BUSY-POLLING-Netdev-2.1.pdf, 2017.

[Dumazet 17b] Dumazet, E., "Re: Something hitting my total number of connections to the server," *netdev mailing list*, https://lore.kernel.org/netdev/1503423863.2499.39.camel@edumazet-glaptop3.roam.corp.google.com, 2017.

[Gallatin 17] Gallatin, D., "Serving 100 Gbps from an Open Connect Appliance," *Netflix Technology Blog,* https://netflixtechblog.com/serving-100-gbps-from-an-open-connect-appliance-cdb51dda3b99, 2017.

[Bruijn 18] Bruijn, W., and Dumazet, E., "Optimizing UDP for Content Delivery: GSO, Pacing and Zerocopy," *Linux Plumber's Conference,* http://vger.kernel.org/lpc_net2018_talks/willemdebruijn-lpc2018-udpgso-paper-DRAFT-1.pdf, 2018.

[Corbet 18b] Corbet, J., "Zero-copy TCP receive," *LWN.net,* https://lwn.net/Articles/752188, 2018.

[Corbet 18c] Corbet, J., "Time-based packet transmission," *LWN.net,* https://lwn.net/Articles/748879, 2018.

[Deepak 18] Deepak, A., "eBPF / XDP firewall and packet filtering," *Linux Plumber's Conference,* http://vger.kernel.org/lpc_net2018_talks/ebpf-firewall-LPC.pdf, 2018.

[Jacobson 18] Jacobson, V., "Evolving from AFAP: Teaching NICs about Time," netdev 0x12, July 2018, https://www.files.netdevconf.org/d/4ee0a09788fe49709855/files/?p=/Evolving%20from%20AFAP%20%E2%80%93%20Teaching%20NICs%20about%20time.pdf, 2018.

[Høiland-Jørgensen 18] Høiland-Jørgensen, T., et al., "The eXpress Data Path: Fast Programmable Packet Processing in the Operating System Kernel," Proceedings of the 14th International Conference on emerging Networking EXperiments and Technologies, 2018.

[HP 18] "Netperf," https://github.com/HewlettPackard/netperf, 2018.

[Majkowski 18] Majkowski, M., "How to Drop 10 Million Packets per Second," https://blog.cloudflare.com/how-to-drop-10-million-packets, 2018.

[Stewart 18] Stewart, R., "This commit brings in a new refactored TCP stack called Rack," https://reviews.freebsd.org/rS334804, 2018.

[Amazon 19] "Announcing Amazon VPC Traffic Mirroring for Amazon EC2 Instances," https://aws.amazon.com/about-aws/whats-new/2019/06/announcing-amazon-vpc-traffic-mirroring-for-amazon-ec2-instances, 2019.

[Dumazet 19] Dumazet, E., "Re: [LKP] [net] 19f92a030c: apachebench.requests_per_second -37.9% regression," *netdev mailing list,* https://lore.kernel.org/lkml/20191113172102.GA23306@1wt.eu, 2019.

[Gregg 19] Gregg, B., *BPF Performance Tools: Linux System and Application Observability,* Addison-Wesley, 2019.

[Gregg 19b] Gregg, B., "BPF Theremin, Tetris, and Typewriters," http://www.brendangregg.com/blog/2019-12-22/bpf-theremin.html, 2019.

[Gregg 19c] Gregg, B., "LISA2019 Linux Systems Performance," *USENIX LISA,* http://www.brendangregg.com/blog/2020-03-08/lisa2019-linux-systems-performance.html, 2019.

[Gregg 19d] Gregg, B., "udplife.bt," https://github.com/brendangregg/bpf-perf-tools-book/blob/master/exercises/Ch10_Networking/udplife.bt, 2019.

[Hassas Yeganeh 19] Hassas Yeganeh, S., and Cheng, Y., "TCP SO_TIMESTAMPING with OPT_STATS for Performance Analytics," *netdev 0x13*, https://netdevconf.info/0x13/session. html?talk-tcp-timestamping, 2019.

[Bufferbloat 20] "Bufferbloat," https://www.bufferbloat.net, 2020.

[Cheng 20] Cheng, Y., Cardwell, N., Dukkipati, N., and Jha, P., "RACK-TLP: A Time-Based Efficient Loss Detection for TCP," *TCP Maintenance Working Group*, https://tools.ietf.org/html/ draft-ietf-tcpm-rack-09, 2020.

[Cilium 20a] "API-aware Networking and Security," https://cilium.io, accessed 2020.

[Corbet 20] Corbet, J., "Kernel operations structures in BPF," *LWN.net*, https://lwn.net/ Articles/811631, 2020.

[DPDK 20] "AF_XDP Poll Mode Driver," *DPDK documentation*, http://doc.dpdk.org/guides/ index.html, accessed 2020.

[Fomichev 20] Fomichev, S., et al., "Replacing HTB with EDT and BPF," *netdev 0x14*, https://netdevconf.info/0x14/session.html?talk-replacing-HTB-with-EDT-and-BPF, 2020.

[Google 20b] "Packet Mirroring Overview," https://cloud.google.com/vpc/docs/packet-mirroring, accessed 2020.

[Høiland-Jørgensen 20] Høiland-Jørgensen, T., "The FLExible Network Tester," https://flent.org, accessed 2020.

[Linux 20i] "Segmentation Offloads," *Linux documentation*, https://www.kernel.org/doc/ Documentation/networking/segmentation-offloads.rst, accessed 2020.

[Linux 20c] "MSG_ZEROCOPY," *Linux documentation*, https://www.kernel.org/doc/html/ latest/networking/msg_zerocopy.html, accessed 2020.

[Linux 20j] "timestamping.txt," *Linux documentation*, https://www.kernel.org/doc/ Documentation/networking/timestamping.txt, accessed 2020.

[Linux 20k] "AF_XDP," *Linux documentation*, https://www.kernel.org/doc/html/latest/ networking/af_xdp.html, accessed 2020.

[Linux 20l] "HOWTO for the Linux Packet Generator," *Linux documentation*, https://www.kernel.org/doc/html/latest/networking/pktgen.html, accessed 2020.

[Nosachev 20] Nosachev, D., "How 1500 Bytes Became the MTU of the Internet," https://blog.benjojo.co.uk/post/why-is-ethernet-mtu-1500, 2020.

[Škarvada 20] Škarvada, J., "network-latency/tuned.conf," https://github.com/redhat-performance/tuned/blob/master/profiles/network-latency/tuned.conf, last updated 2020.

[Tuned Project 20] "The Tuned Project," https://tuned-project.org, accessed 2020.

[Wireshark 20] "Wireshark," https://www.wireshark.org, accessed 2020.

Chapter 11

Cloud Computing

The rise of cloud computing solves some old problems in the field of performance while creating new ones. A cloud environment can be created instantly and scaled on demand, without the typical overheads of building and managing an on-premises data center. Clouds also allow better granularity for deployments—fractions of a server can be used by different customers as needed. However, this brings its own challenges: the performance overhead of virtualization technologies, and resource contention with neighboring tenants.

The learning objectives of this chapter are:

- Understand cloud computing architecture and its performance implications.

- Understand the types of virtualization: hardware, OS, and lightweight hardware.

- Become familiar with virtualization internals, including the use of I/O proxies, and tuning techniques.

- Have a working knowledge of the expected overheads for different workloads under each virtualization type.

- Diagnose performance issues from hosts and guests, understanding how tool usage may vary depending on which virtualization is in use.

While this entire book is applicable to cloud performance analysis, this chapter focuses on performance topics unique to the cloud: how hypervisors and virtualization work, how resource controls can be applied to guests, and how observability works from the host and guests. Cloud vendors typically provide their own custom services and APIs, which are not covered here: see the documentation that each cloud vendor provides for their own set of services.

This chapter consists of four main parts:

- **Background** presents general cloud computing architecture and the performance implications thereof.

- **Hardware virtualization**, where a hypervisor manages multiple guest operating system instances as virtual machines, each running its own kernel with virtualized devices. This section uses the Xen, KVM, and Amazon Nitro hypervisors as examples.

- **OS virtualization**, where a single kernel manages the system, creating virtual OS instances that are isolated from each other. This section uses Linux containers as the example.

- **Lightweight hardware virtualization** provides a best-of-both-worlds solution, where lightweight hardware virtualized instances run with dedicated kernels, with boot times and density benefits similar to containers. This section uses AWS Firecracker as the example hypervisor.

The virtualization sections are ordered by when they were made widely available in the cloud. For example, the Amazon Elastic Compute Cloud (EC2) offered hardware virtualized instances in 2006, OS virtualized containers in 2017 (Amazon Fargate), and lightweight virtualized machines in 2019 (Amazon Firecracker).

11.1   Background

Cloud computing allows computing resources to be delivered as a service, scaling from small fractions of a server to multi-server systems. The building blocks of your cloud depend on how much of the software stack is installed and configured. This chapter focuses on the following cloud offerings, both of which provide *server instances* that may be:

- **Hardware instances**: Also known as *infrastructure as a service* (IaaS), provided using hardware virtualization. Each server instance is a virtual machine.

- **OS instances**: For providing light-weight instances, typically via OS virtualization.

Together, these may be referred to as *server instances*, *cloud instances*, or just *instances*. Examples of cloud providers that support these are Amazon Web Services (AWS), Microsoft Azure, and Google Cloud Platform (GCP). There are also other types of cloud primitives including functions as a service (FaaS) (see Section 11.5, Other Types).

To summarize key cloud terminology: *cloud computing* describes a dynamic provisioning framework for instances. One or more instances run as *guests* of a physical *host* system. The guests are also called *tenants*, and the term *multitenancy* is used to describe them running on the same host. The host may be managed by cloud providers who operate a *public cloud*, or may be managed by your company for internal use only as part of a *private cloud*. Some companies construct a *hybrid cloud* that spans both public and private clouds.[1] The cloud guests (tenants) are managed by their end users.

For hardware virtualization, a technology called a *hypervisor* (or *virtual machine monitor*, VMM) creates and manages *virtual machine* instances, which appear as dedicated computers and allow entire operating systems and kernels to be installed.

Instances can typically be created (and destroyed) in minutes or seconds and immediately put into production use. A *cloud API* is commonly provided so that this provisioning can be automated by another program.

---

[1]Google Anthos, for example, is an application management platform that supports on-premises Google Kubernetes Engine (GKE) with GCP instances, as well as other clouds.

Cloud computing can be understood further by discussing various performance-related topics: instance types, architecture, capacity planning, storage, and multitenancy. These are summarized in the following sections.

11.1.1   Instance Types

Cloud providers typically offer different instance types and sizes.

Some instance types are generic and balanced across the resources. Others may be optimized for a certain resource: memory, CPUs, disks, etc. As an example, AWS groups types as "families" (abbreviated by a letter) and generations (a number), currently offering:

- **m5**: General purpose (balanced)
- **c5**: Compute optimized
- **i3, d2**: Storage optimized
- **r4, x1**: Memory optimized
- **p1, g3, f1**: Accelerated computing (GPUs, FPGAs, etc.)

Within each family there are a variety of sizes. The AWS m5 family, for example, ranges from an m5.large (2 vCPUs and 8 Gbytes of main memory) to an m5.24xlarge (twenty-four extra-large: 96 vCPUs and 384 Gbytes of main memory).

There is typically a fairly consistent price/performance ratio across the sizes, allowing customers to pick the size that best suits their workload.

Some providers, such as Google Cloud Platform, also offer custom machine types where the amount of resources can be selected.

With so many options and the ease of redeploying instances, the instance type has become like a tunable parameter that can be modified as needed. This is a great improvement over the traditional enterprise model of selecting and ordering physical hardware that the company might be unable to change for years.

11.1.2   Scalable Architecture

Enterprise environments have historically used a *vertical scalability* approach for handling load: building larger single systems (mainframes). This approach has its limitations. There is a practical limit to the physical size to which a computer can be built (which may be bounded by the size of elevator doors or shipping containers), and there are increasing difficulties with CPU cache coherency as the CPU count scales, as well as power and cooling. The solution to these limitations has been to scale load across many (perhaps small) systems; this is called *horizontal scalability*. In enterprise, it has been used for computer farms and clusters, especially with high-performance computing (HPC, where its use predates the cloud).

Cloud computing is also based on horizontal scalability. An example environment is shown in Figure 11.1, which includes load balancers, web servers, application servers, and databases.

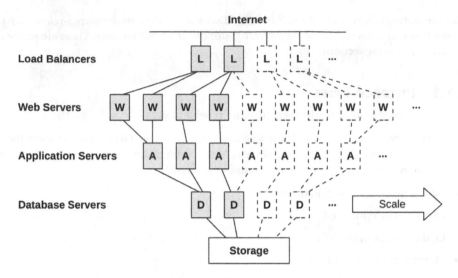

Figure 11.1   Cloud architecture: horizontal scaling

Each environment layer is composed of one or more server instances running in parallel, with more added to handle load. Instances may be added individually, or the architecture may be divided into vertical partitions, where a group composed of database servers, application servers, and web servers is added as a single unit.[2]

A challenge of this model is the deployment of traditional databases, where one database instance must be primary. Data for these databases, such as MySQL, can be split logically into groups called *shards*, each of which is managed by its own database (or primary/secondary pair). Distributed database architectures, such as Riak, handle parallel execution dynamically, spreading load over available instances. There are now *cloud-native databases*, designed for use on the cloud, including Cassandra, CockroachDB, Amazon Aurora, and Amazon DynamoDB.

With the per-server instance size typically being small, say, 8 Gbytes (on physical hosts with 512 Gbytes and more of DRAM), fine-grained scaling can be used to attain optimum price/performance, rather than investing up front in huge systems that may remain mostly idle.

11.1.3   Capacity Planning

On-premises servers can be a significant infrastructure cost, both for the hardware and for service contract fees that may go on for years. It can also take months for new servers to be put into production: time spent in approvals, waiting for part availability, shipping, racking, installing, and testing. Capacity planning is critically important, so that appropriately sized systems can be purchased: too small means failure, too large is costly (and, with service contracts, may be costly for years to come). Capacity planning is also needed to predict increases in demand well in advance, so that lengthy purchasing procedures can be completed in time.

---

[2] Shopify, for example, calls these units "pods" [Denis 18].

On-premises servers, and data centers, were the norm for enterprise environments. Cloud computing is very different. Server instances are inexpensive, and can be created and destroyed almost instantly. Instead of spending time planning what may be needed, companies can increase the number of server instances they use *as needed*, in reaction to real load. This can be done automatically via the cloud API, based on metrics from performance monitoring software. A small business or startup can grow from a single small instance to thousands, without a detailed capacity planning study as would be expected in enterprise environments.[3]

For growing startups, another factor to consider is the pace of code changes. Sites commonly update their production code weekly, daily, or even multiple times a day. A capacity planning study can take weeks and, because it is based on a snapshot of performance metrics, may be out of date by the time it is completed. This differs from enterprise environments running commercial software, which may change no more than a few times per year.

Activities performed in the cloud for capacity planning include:

- **Dynamic sizing**: Automatically adding and removing server instances
- **Scalability testing**: Purchasing a large cloud environment for a short duration, in order to test scalability versus synthetic load (this is a *benchmarking* activity)

Bearing in mind the time constraints, there is also the potential for modeling scalability (similar to enterprise studies) to estimate how actual scalability falls short of where it theoretically should be.

Dynamic Sizing (Auto Scaling)

Cloud vendors typically support deploying groups of server instances that can automatically scale up as load increases (e.g., an AWS *auto scaling group* (ASG)). This also supports a *microservice* architecture, where the application is split into smaller networked parts that can individually scale as needed.

Auto scaling can solve the need to quickly respond to changes in load, but it also risks *over-provisioning*, as pictured in Figure 11.2. For example, a DoS attack may appear as an increase in load, triggering an expensive increase in server instances. There is a similar risk with application changes that regress performance, requiring more instances to handle the same load. Monitoring is important to verify that these increases make sense.

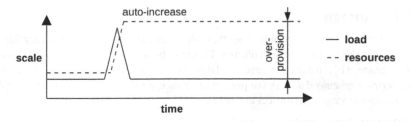

Figure 11.2   Dynamic sizing

---

[3] Things may get complex as a company scales to hundreds of thousands of instances, as cloud providers may temporarily run out of available instances of a given type due to demand. If you get to this scale, talk to your account representative about ways to mitigate this (e.g., purchasing reserve capacity).

Cloud providers bill by the hour, minute, or even second, allowing users to scale up *and down* quickly. Cost savings can be realized immediately when they downsize. This can be automated so that the instance count matches a daily pattern, only provisioning enough capacity for each minute of the day as needed.[4] Netflix does this for its cloud, adding and removing tens of thousands of instances daily to match its daily streams per second pattern, an example of which is shown in Figure 11.3 [Gregg 14b].

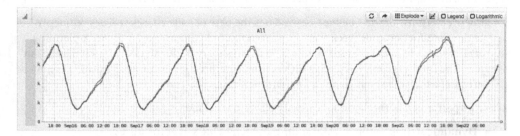

Figure 11.3   Netflix streams per second

As other examples, in December 2012, Pinterest reported cutting costs from $54/hour to $20/hour by automatically shutting down its cloud systems after hours in response to traffic load [Hoff 12], and in 2018 Shopify moved to the cloud and saw large infrastructure savings: moving from servers with 61% average idle time to cloud instances with 19% average idle time [Kwiatkowski 19]. Immediate savings can also be a result of performance tuning, where the number of instances required to handle load is reduced.

Some cloud architectures (see Section 11.3, OS Virtualization) can dynamically allocate more CPU resources instantly, if available, using a strategy called *bursting*. This can be provided at no extra cost and is intended to help prevent overprovisioning by providing a buffer during which the increased load can be checked to determine if it is real and likely to continue. If so, more instances can be provisioned so that resources are guaranteed going forward.

Any of these techniques should be considerably more efficient than enterprise environments—especially those with a fixed size chosen to handle expected peak load for the lifetime of the server: such servers may run mostly idle.

11.1.4   Storage

A cloud instance requires storage for the OS, application software, and temporary files. On Linux systems, this is the root and other volumes. This may be served by local physical storage or by network storage. This instance storage is volatile and is destroyed when the instance is destroyed (and are termed *ephemeral drives*). For persistent storage, an independent service is typically used, which provides storage to instances as either a:

- **File store:** For example, files over NFS
- **Block store:** Such as blocks over iSCSI
- **Object store:** Over an API, commonly HTTP-based

---

[4]Note that automating this can be complicated, for both scale up and scale down. Down scaling may involve waiting not just for requests to finish, but also for long-running batch jobs to finish, and databases to transfer local data.

These operate over a network, and both the network infrastructure and storage devices are shared with other tenants. For these reasons, performance can be much less predictable than with local disks, although performance consistency can be improved by the use of resource controls by the cloud provider.

Cloud providers typically provide their own services for these. For example, Amazon provides the Amazon Elastic File System (EFS) as a file store, the Amazon Elastic Block Store (EBS) as a block store, and the Amazon Simple Storage Service (S3) as an object store.

Both local and network storage are pictured in Figure 11.4.

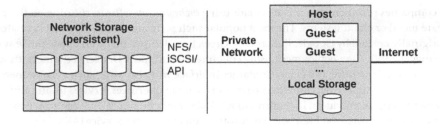

Figure 11.4   Cloud storage

The increased latency for network storage access is typically mitigated by using in-memory caches for frequently accessed data.

Some storage services allow an IOPS rate to be purchased when reliable performance is desired (e.g., Amazon EBS Provisioned IOPS volume).

11.1.5   Multitenancy

Unix is a multitasking operating system, designed to deal with multiple users and processes accessing the same resources. Later additions by Linux have provided resource limits and controls to share these resources more fairly, and observability to identify and quantify when there are performance issues involving resource contention.

Cloud computing differs in that entire operating system instances can coexist on the same physical system. Each guest is its own isolated operating system: guests (typically[5]) cannot observe users and processes from other guests on the same host—that would be considered an information leak—even though they share the same physical resources.

Since resources are shared among tenants, performance issues may be caused by *noisy neighbors*. For example, another guest on the same host might perform a full database dump during your peak load, interfering with your disk and network I/O. Worse, a neighbor could be evaluating the cloud provider by executing micro-benchmarks that deliberately saturate resources in order to find their limit.

---

[5] Linux containers can be assembled in different ways from namespaces and cgroups. It should be possible to create containers that share the process namespace with each other, which may be used for an introspection ("sidecar") container that can debug other container processes. In Kubernetes, the main abstraction is a Pod, which shares a network namespace.

There are some solutions to this problem. Multitenancy effects can be controlled by *resource management*: setting operating system *resource controls* that provide *performance isolation* (also called *resource isolation*). This is where per-tenant limits or priorities are imposed for the usage of system resources: CPU, memory, disk or file system I/O, and network throughput.

Apart from limiting resource usage, being able to observe multitenancy contention can help cloud operators tune the limits and better balance tenants on available hosts. The degree of observability depends on the virtualization type.

11.1.6   Orchestration (Kubernetes)

Many companies run their own private clouds using *orchestration software* running on their own bare metal or cloud systems. The most popular such software is Kubernetes (abbreviated as k8s), originally created by Google. Kubernetes, Greek for "Helmsman," is an open-source system that manages application deployment using containers (commonly Docker containers, though any runtime implementing the Open Container Interface will also work, such as containerd) [Kubernetes 20b]. Public cloud providers have also created Kubernetes services to simplify deployment to those providers, including Google Kubernetes Engine (GKE), Amazon Elastic Kubernetes Service (Amazon EKS), and Microsoft Azure Kubernetes Service (AKS).

Kubernetes deploys containers as co-located groups called *Pods*, where containers can share resources and communicate with each other locally (localhost). Each Pod has its own IP address that can be used to communicate (via networking) with other Pods. A Kubernetes *service* is an abstraction for endpoints provided by a group of Pods with metadata including an IP address, and is a persistent and stable interface to these endpoints, while the Pods themselves may be added and removed, allowing them to be treated as disposable. Kubernetes services support the micro-services architecture. Kubernetes includes auto-scaling strategies, such as the "Horizontal Pod Autoscaler" that can scale replicas of a Pod based on a target resource utilization or other metric. In Kubernetes, physical machines are called *Nodes*, and a group of Nodes belong to a Kubernetes *cluster* if they connect to the same Kubernetes API server.

Performance challenges in Kubernetes include scheduling (where to run containers on a cluster to maximize performance), and network performance, as extra components are used to implement container networking and load balancing.

For scheduling, Kubernetes takes into account CPU and memory requests and limits, and metadata such as *node taints* (where Nodes are marked to be excluded from scheduling) and *label selectors* (custom metadata). Kubernetes does not currently limit block I/O (support for this, using the blkio cgroup, may be added in the future [Xu 20]) making disk contention a possible source of performance issues.

For networking, Kubernetes allows different networking components to be used, and determining which to use is an important activity for ensuring maximum performance. Container networking can be implemented by plugin container network interface (CNI) software; example CNI software includes Calico, based on netfilter or iptables, and Cilium, based on BPF. Both are open source [Calico 20][Cilium 20b]. For load balancing, Cilium also provides a BPF replacement for kube-proxy [Borkmann 19].

11.2 Hardware Virtualization

Hardware virtualization creates a virtual machine (VM) that can run an entire operating system, including its own kernel. VMs are created by hypervisors, also called virtual machine managers (VMMs). A common classification of hypervisors identifies them as Type 1 or 2 [Goldberg 73], which are:

- **Type 1** executes directly on the processors. Hypervisor administration may be performed by a privileged guest that can create and launch new guests. Type 1 is also called *native hypervisor* or *bare-metal hypervisor*. This hypervisor includes its own CPU scheduler for guest VMs. A popular example is the Xen hypervisor.

- **Type 2** is executed within a host OS, which has privileges to administer the hypervisor and launch new guests. For this type, the system boots a conventional OS that then runs the hypervisor. This hypervisor is scheduled by the host kernel CPU scheduler, and guests appear as processes on the host.

Although you may still encounter the terms Type 1 and Type 2, with advances in hypervisor technologies this classification is no longer strictly applicable [Liguori, 07]—Type 2 has been made Type 1-ish by using kernel modules so that parts of the hypervisor have direct access to hardware. A more practical classification is shown in Figure 11.5, illustrating two common configurations that I have named Config A and B [Gregg 19].

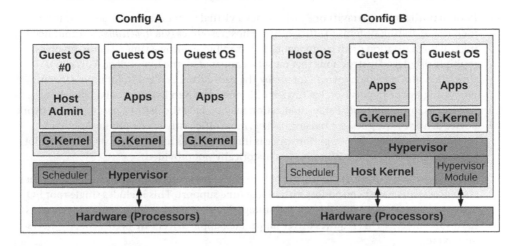

Figure 11.5 Common hypervisor configurations

These configurations are:

- **Config A:** Also called a native hypervisor or a bare-metal hypervisor. The hypervisor software runs directly on the processors, creates domains for running guest virtual machines, and schedules virtual guest CPUs onto the real CPUs. A privileged domain (number 0 in Figure 11.5) can administer the others. A popular example is the Xen hypervisor.

- **Config B:** The hypervisor software is executed by a host OS kernel, and may be composed of kernel-level modules and user-level processes. The host OS has privileges to administer the hypervisor, and its kernel schedules the VM CPUs along with other processes on the host. By use of kernel modules, this configuration also provides direct access to hardware. A popular example is the KVM hypervisor.

Both configurations may involve running an I/O proxy (e.g., using the QEMU software) in domain 0 (Xen) or the host OS (KVM), for serving guest I/O. This adds overhead to I/O, and over the years has been optimized by adding shared memory transports and other techniques.

The original hardware hypervisor, pioneered by VMware in 1998, used *binary translations* to perform full hardware virtualization [VMware 07]. This involved rewriting privileged instructions such as syscalls and page table operations before execution. Non-privileged instructions could be run directly on the processor. This provided a complete virtual system composed of virtualized hardware components onto which an unmodified operating system could be installed. The high-performance overhead for this was often acceptable for the savings provided by server consolidation.

This has since been improved by:

- **Processor virtualization support:** The AMD-V and Intel VT-x extensions were introduced in 2005–2006 to provide faster hardware support for VM operations by the processor. These extensions improved the speed of virtualizing privileged instructions and the MMU.

- **Paravirtualization** (paravirt or PV): Provides a virtual system that includes an interface for guest operating systems to efficiently use host resources (via *hypercalls*), without needing full virtualization of all components. For example, arming a timer usually involves multiple privileged instructions that must be emulated by the hypervisor. This can be simplified into a single hypercall for use by the paravirtualized guest, for more efficient processing by the hypervisor. For further efficiency, the Xen hypervisor batches these hypercalls into a *multicall*. Paravirtualization may include the use of a paravirtual network device driver by the guest for passing packets more efficiently to the physical network interfaces in the host. While performance is improved, this relies on guest OS support for paravirtualization (which Windows has historically not provided).

- **Device hardware support:** To further optimize VM performance, hardware devices other than processors have been adding virtual machine support. This includes single root I/O virtualization (SR-IOV) for network and storage devices, which allows guest VMs to access hardware directly. This requires driver support (example drivers are ixgbe, ena, hv_netvsc, and nvme).

Over the years, Xen has evolved and improved its performance. Modern Xen VMs often boot in hardware VM mode (HVM) and then use PV drivers with HVM support for improved performance: a configuration called PVHVM. This can further be improved by depending entirely on hardware virtualization for some drivers, such as SR-IOV for network and storage devices.

11.2.1   Implementation

There are many different implementations of hardware virtualization, and some have already been mentioned (Xen and KVM). Examples are:

- **VMware ESX**: First released in 2001, VMware ESX is an enterprise product for server consolidation and is a key component of the VMware vSphere cloud computing product. Its hypervisor is a microkernel that runs on bare metal, and the first virtual machine is called the *service console*, which can administer the hypervisor and new virtual machines.

- **Xen**: First released in 2003, Xen began as a research project at the University of Cambridge and was later acquired by Citrix. Xen is a Type 1 hypervisor that runs paravirtualized guests for high performance; support was later added for hardware-assisted guests for unmodified OS support (Windows). Virtual machines are called *domains*, with the most privileged being *dom0*, from which the hypervisor is administered and new domains launched. Xen is open source and can be launched from Linux. The Amazon Elastic Compute Cloud (EC2) was previously based on Xen.

- **Hyper-V**: Released with Windows Server 2008, Hyper-V is a Type 1 hypervisor that creates *partitions* for executing guest operating systems. The Microsoft Azure public cloud may be running a customized version of Hyper-V (exact details are not publicly available).

- **KVM**: This was developed by Qumranet, a startup that was bought by Red Hat in 2008. KVM is a Type 2 hypervisor, executing as a kernel module. It supports hardware-assisted extensions and, for high performance, uses paravirtualization for certain devices where supported by the guest OS. To create a complete hardware-assisted virtual machine instance, it is paired with a user process called QEMU (Quick Emulator), a VMM (hypervisor) that can create and manage virtual machines. QEMU was originally a high-quality open-source Type 2 hypervisor that used binary translation, written by Fabrice Bellard. KVM is open source, and is used by Google for the Google Compute Engine [Google 20c].

- **Nitro**: Launched by AWS in 2017, this hypervisor uses parts based on KVM with hardware support for all main resources: processors, network, storage, interrupts, and timers [Gregg 17e]. No QEMU proxy is used. Nitro provides near bare-metal performance to guest VMs.

The following sections describe performance topics related to hardware virtualization: overhead, resource controls, and observability. These differ based on the implementation and its configuration.

11.2.2 Overhead

Understanding when and when not to expect performance overhead from virtualization is important in investigating cloud performance issues.

Hardware virtualization is accomplished in various ways. Resource access may require proxying and translation by the hypervisor, adding overhead, or it may use hardware-based technologies to avoid these overheads. The following sections summarize the performance overheads for CPU execution, memory mapping, memory size, performing I/O, and contention from other tenants.

CPU

In general, the guest applications execute directly on the processors, and CPU-bound applications may experience virtually the same performance as a bare-metal system. CPU overheads may be encountered when making privileged processor calls, accessing hardware, and mapping main memory, depending on how they are handled by the hypervisor. The following describe how CPU instructions are handled by the different hardware virtualization types:

- **Binary translation:** Guest kernel instructions that operate on physical resources are identified and translated. Binary translation was used before hardware-assisted virtualization was available. Without hardware support for virtualization, the scheme used by VMware involved running a virtual machine monitor (VMM) in processor ring 0 and moving the guest kernel to ring 1, which had previously been unused (applications run in ring 3, and most processors provide four rings; protection rings were introduced in Chapter 3, Operating Systems, Section 3.2.2, Kernel and User Modes). Because some guest kernel instructions assume they are running in ring 0, in order to execute from ring 1 they need to be translated, calling into the VMM so that virtualization can be applied. This translation is performed during runtime, costing significant CPU overhead.

- **Paravirtualization:** Instructions in the guest OS that must be virtualized are replaced with hypercalls to the hypervisor. Performance can be improved if the guest OS is modified to optimize the hypercalls, making it aware that it is running on virtualized hardware.

- **Hardware-assisted:** Unmodified guest kernel instructions that operate on hardware are handled by the hypervisor, which runs a VMM at a ring level below 0. Instead of translating binary instructions, the guest kernel privileged instructions are forced to trap to the higher-privileged VMM, which can then emulate the privilege to support virtualization [Adams 06].

Hardware-assisted virtualization is generally preferred, depending on the implementation and workload, while paravirtualization is used to improve the performance of some workloads (especially I/O) if the guest OS supports it.

As an example of implementation differences, VMware's binary translation model has been heavily optimized over the years, and as they wrote in 2007 [VMware 07]:

> Due to high hypervisor to guest transition overhead and a rigid programming model, VMware's binary translation approach currently outperforms first generation hardware assist implementations in most circumstances. The rigid programming model in the first generation implementation leaves little room for software flexibility in managing either the frequency or the cost of hypervisor to guest transitions.

The rate of transitions between the guest and hypervisor, as well as the time spent in the hypervisor, can be studied as a metric of CPU overhead. These events are commonly referred to as *guest exits*, as the virtual CPU must stop executing inside the guest when this happens. Figure 11.6 shows CPU overhead related to guest exits inside KVM.

The figure shows the flow of guest exits between the user process, the host kernel, and the guest. The time spent outside of the guest-handling exits is the CPU overhead of hardware virtualization; the more time spent handling exits, the greater the overhead. When the guest exits, a subset of the events can be handled directly in the kernel. Those that cannot must leave the kernel and return to the user process; this induces even greater overhead compared to exits that can be handled by the kernel.

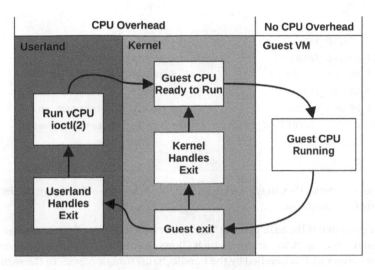

Figure 11.6 Hardware virtualization CPU overhead

For example, with the Linux KVM implementation, these overheads can be studied via their guest exit functions, which are mapped in the source code as follows (from arch/x86/kvm/vmx/vmx.c in Linux 5.2, truncated):

```
/*
 * The exit handlers return 1 if the exit was handled fully and guest execution
 * may resume.  Otherwise they set the kvm_run parameter to indicate what needs
 * to be done to userspace and return 0.
 */
static int (*kvm_vmx_exit_handlers[])(struct kvm_vcpu *vcpu) = {
        [EXIT_REASON_EXCEPTION_NMI]             = handle_exception,
        [EXIT_REASON_EXTERNAL_INTERRUPT]        = handle_external_interrupt,
        [EXIT_REASON_TRIPLE_FAULT]              = handle_triple_fault,
        [EXIT_REASON_NMI_WINDOW]                = handle_nmi_window,
        [EXIT_REASON_IO_INSTRUCTION]            = handle_io,
        [EXIT_REASON_CR_ACCESS]                 = handle_cr,
        [EXIT_REASON_DR_ACCESS]                 = handle_dr,
        [EXIT_REASON_CPUID]                     = handle_cpuid,
        [EXIT_REASON_MSR_READ]                  = handle_rdmsr,
        [EXIT_REASON_MSR_WRITE]                 = handle_wrmsr,
        [EXIT_REASON_PENDING_INTERRUPT]         = handle_interrupt_window,
        [EXIT_REASON_HLT]                       = handle_halt,
        [EXIT_REASON_INVD]                      = handle_invd,
        [EXIT_REASON_INVLPG]                    = handle_invlpg,
        [EXIT_REASON_RDPMC]                     = handle_rdpmc,
        [EXIT_REASON_VMCALL]                    = handle_vmcall,
```

```
[...]
        [EXIT_REASON_XSAVES]                       = handle_xsaves,
        [EXIT_REASON_XRSTORS]                      = handle_xrstors,
        [EXIT_REASON_PML_FULL]                     = handle_pml_full,
        [EXIT_REASON_INVPCID]                      = handle_invpcid,
        [EXIT_REASON_VMFUNC]                        = handle_vmx_instruction,
        [EXIT_REASON_PREEMPTION_TIMER]             = handle_preemption_timer,
        [EXIT_REASON_ENCLS]                        = handle_encls,
};
```

While the names are terse, they may provide an idea of the reasons a guest may call into a hypervisor, incurring CPU overhead.

One common guest exit is the halt instruction, usually called by the idle thread when the kernel can find no more work to perform (which allows the processor to operate in low-power modes until interrupted). It is handled by the handle_halt() function (seen in the earlier listing for EXIT_REASON_HLT), which ultimately calls kvm_vcpu_halt() (arch/x86/kvm/x86.c):

```
int kvm_vcpu_halt(struct kvm_vcpu *vcpu)
{
        ++vcpu->stat.halt_exits;
        if (lapic_in_kernel(vcpu)) {
                vcpu->arch.mp_state = KVM_MP_STATE_HALTED;
                return 1;
        } else {
                vcpu->run->exit_reason = KVM_EXIT_HLT;
                return 0;
        }
}
```

As with many guest exit types, the code is kept small to minimize CPU overhead. This example begins with a vcpu statistic increment, which tracks how many halts occurred. The remaining code performs the hardware emulation required for this privileged instruction. These functions can be instrumented on Linux using kprobes on the hypervisor host, to track their type and the duration of their exits. Exits can also be tracked globally using the kvm:kvm_exit tracepoint, which is used in Section 11.2.4, Observability.

Virtualizing hardware devices such as the interrupt controller and high-resolution timers also incur some CPU (and a small amount of memory) overhead.

Memory Mapping

As described in Chapter 7, Memory, the operating system works with the MMU to create page mappings from virtual to physical memory, caching them in the TLB to improve performance.

For virtualization, mapping a new page of memory (page fault) from the guest to the hardware involves two steps:

1. Virtual-to-guest physical translation, as performed by the guest kernel

2. Guest-physical-to-host-physical (actual) translation, as performed by the hypervisor VMM

The mapping, from guest virtual to host physical, can then be cached in the TLB, so that subsequent accesses can operate at normal speed—not requiring additional translation. Modern processors support MMU virtualization, so that mappings that have left the TLB can be recalled more quickly in hardware alone (page walk), without calling in to the hypervisor. The feature that supports this is called *extended page tables* (EPT) on Intel and *nested page tables* (NPT) on AMD [Milewski 11].

Without EPT/NPT, another approach to improve performance is to maintain *shadow page tables* of guest-virtual-to-host-physical mappings, which are managed by the hypervisor and then accessed during guest execution by overwriting the guest's CR3 register. With this strategy, the guest kernel maintains its own page tables, which map from guest virtual to guest physical, as normal. The hypervisor intercepts changes to these page tables and creates equivalent mappings to the host physical pages in the shadow pages. Then, during guest execution, the hypervisor overwrites the CR3 register to point to the shadow pages.

Memory Size

Unlike OS virtualization, there are some additional consumers of memory when using hardware virtualization. Each guest runs its own kernel, which consumes a small amount of memory. The storage architecture may also lead to double caching, where both the guest and host cache the same data. KVM-style hypervisors also run a VMM process for each VM, such as QEMU, which itself consumes some main memory.

I/O

Historically, I/O was the largest source of overhead for hardware virtualization. This was because every device I/O had to be translated by the hypervisor. For high-frequency I/O, such as 10 Gbit/s networking, a small degree of overhead per I/O (packet) could cause a significant overall reduction in performance. Technologies have been created to mitigate these I/O overheads, culminating with hardware support for eliminating these overheads entirely. Such hardware support includes I/O MMU virtualization (AMD-Vi and Intel VT-d).

One method for improving I/O performance is the use of paravirtualized drivers, which can coalesce I/O and perform fewer device interrupts to reduce the hypervisor overhead.

Another technique is *PCI pass-through*, which assigns a PCI device directly to the guest, so it can be used as it would on a bare-metal system. PCI pass-through can provide the best performance of the available options, but it reduces flexibility when configuring the system with multiple tenants, as some devices are now owned by guests and cannot be shared. This may also complicate live migration [Xen 19].

There are some technologies to improve the flexibility of using PCI devices with virtualization, including single root I/O virtualization (SR-IOV, mentioned earlier) and multiroot I/O virtualization (MR-IOV). These terms refer to the number of root complex PCI topologies that are exposed, providing hardware virtualization in different ways. The Amazon EC2 cloud has been adopting these technologies to accelerate first networking and then storage I/O, which are in use by default with the Nitro hypervisor [Gregg 17e].

Common configurations of the Xen, KVM, and Nitro hypervisors are pictured in Figure 11.7.

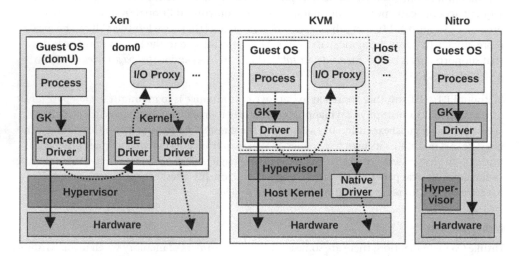

Figure 11.7   Xen, KVM, and Nitro I/O path

GK is "guest kernel," and BE is "back end." The dotted arrows indicate the *control path*, where components inform each other, either synchronously or asynchronously, that more data is ready to transfer. The *data path* (solid arrows) may be implemented in some cases by shared memory and ring buffers. A control path is not shown for Nitro, as it uses the same data path for direct access to hardware.

There are different ways to configure Xen and KVM, not pictured here. This figure shows them using I/O proxy processes (typically the QEMU software), which are created per guest VM. But they can also be configured to use SR-IOV, allowing guest VMs to access hardware directly (not pictured for Xen or KVM in Figure 11.7). Nitro requires such hardware support, eliminating the need for I/O proxies.

Xen improves its I/O performance using a *device channel*—an asynchronous shared memory transport between dom0 and the guest domains (domU). This avoids the CPU and bus overhead of creating an extra copy of I/O data as it is passed between the domains. It may also use separate domains for performing I/O, as described in Section 11.2.3, Resource Controls.

The number of steps in the I/O path, both control and data, is critical for performance: the fewer, the better. In 2006, the KVM developers compared a privileged-guest system like Xen with KVM and found that KVM could perform I/O using half as many steps (five versus ten, although the test was performed without paravirtualization so does not reflect most modern configurations) [Qumranet 06].

As the Nitro hypervisor eliminates extra I/O steps, I would expect all large cloud providers seeking maximum performance to follow suit, using hardware support to eliminate I/O proxies.

Multi-Tenant Contention

Depending on the hypervisor configuration and how much CPUs and CPU caches are shared between tenants, there may be CPU stolen time and CPU cache pollution caused by other tenants, reducing performance. This is typically a larger problem with containers than VMs, as containers promote such sharing to support CPU bursting.

Other tenants performing I/O may cause interrupts that interrupt execution, depending on the hypervisor configuration.

Contention for resources can be managed by resource controls.

11.2.3   Resource Controls

As part of the guest configuration, CPU and main memory are typically configured with resource limits. The hypervisor software may also provide resource controls for network and disk I/O.

For KVM-like hypervisors, the host OS ultimately controls the physical resources, and resource controls available from the OS may also be applied to the guests, in addition to the controls the hypervisor provides. For Linux, this means cgroups, tasksets, and other resource controls. See Section 11.3, OS Virtualization, for more about the resource controls that may be available from the host OS. The following sections describe resource controls from the Xen and KVM hypervisors, as examples.

CPUs

CPU resources are usually allocated to guests as virtual CPUs (vCPUs). These are then scheduled by the hypervisor. The number of vCPUs assigned coarsely limits CPU resource usage.

For Xen, a fine-grained CPU quota for guests can be applied by a hypervisor CPU scheduler. Schedulers include [Cherkasova 07][Matthews 08]:

- **Borrowed virtual time (BVT)**: A fair-share scheduler based on the allocation of virtual time, which can be borrowed in advance to provide low-latency execution for real-time and interactive applications
- **Simple earliest deadline first (SEDF)**: A real-time scheduler that allows runtime guarantees to be configured, with the scheduler giving priority to the earliest deadline
- **Credit-based**: Supports priorities (*weights*) and caps for CPU usage, and load balancing across multiple CPUs

For KVM, fine-grained CPU quotas can be applied by the host OS, for example when using the host kernel *fair-share scheduler* described earlier. On Linux, this can be applied using the cgroup CPU bandwidth controls.

There are limitations on how either technology can respect guest *priorities*. A guest's CPU usage is typically opaque to the hypervisor, and guest kernel thread priorities cannot typically be seen or respected. For example, a low-priority log rotation daemon in one guest may have the same hypervisor priority as a critical application server in another guest.

For Xen, CPU resource usage can be further complicated by high-I/O workloads that consume extra CPU resources in dom0. The back-end driver and I/O proxy in the guest domain alone may consume more than their CPU allocation but are not accounted for [Cherkasova 05]. A solution has been to create isolated driver domains (IDDs), which separate out I/O servicing for security, performance isolation, and accounting. This is pictured in Figure 11.8.

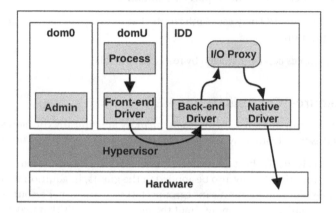

Figure 11.8   Xen with isolated driver domains

The CPU usage by IDDs can be monitored, and the guests can be charged for this usage. From [Gupta 06]:

> Our modified scheduler, SEDF-DC for SEDF-Debt Collector, periodically receives feedback from XenMon about the CPU consumed by IDDs for I/O processing on behalf of guest domains. Using this information, SEDF-DC constrains the CPU allocation to guest domains to meet the specified combined CPU usage limit.

A more recent technique used in Xen is *stub domains*, which run a mini-OS.

CPU Caches

Apart from the allocation of vCPUs, CPU cache usage can be controlled using Intel cache allocation technology (CAT). It allows the LLC to be partitioned between guests, and partitions to be shared. While this can prevent a guest polluting another guest's cache, it can also hurt performance by limiting cache usage.

Memory Capacity

Memory limits are imposed as part of the guest configuration, with the guest seeing only the set amount of memory. The guest kernel then performs its own operations (paging, swapping) to remain within its limit.

In an effort to increase flexibility from the static configuration, VMware developed a *balloon driver* [Waldspurger 02], which is able to reduce the memory consumed by the running guest by "inflating" a balloon module inside it, which consumes guest memory. This memory is then reclaimed by the hypervisor for use by other guests. The balloon can also be deflated, returning memory to the guest kernel for use. During this process, the guest kernel executes its normal memory management routines to free memory (e.g., paging). VMware, Xen, and KVM all have support for balloon drivers.

When balloon drivers are in use (to check from the guest, search for "balloon" in the output of dmesg(1)), I would be on the lookout for performance issues that they may cause.

File System Capacity

Guests are provided with virtual disk volumes from the host. For KVM-like hypervisors, these may be software volumes created by the OS and sized accordingly. For example, the ZFS file system can create virtual volumes of a desired size.

Device I/O

Resource controls by hardware virtualization software have historically focused on controlling CPU usage, which can indirectly control I/O usage.

Network throughput may be throttled by external dedicated devices or, in the case of KVM-like hypervisors, by host kernel features. For example, Linux has network bandwidth controls from cgroups as well as different qdiscs, which can be applied to guest network interfaces.

Network performance isolation for Xen has been studied, with the following conclusion [Adamczyk 12]:

> ...when the network virtualization is considered, the weak point of Xen is its lack of proper performance isolation.

The authors of [Adamczyk 12] also propose a solution for Xen network I/O scheduling, which adds tunable parameters for network I/O priority and rate. If you are using Xen, check whether this or a similar technology has been made available.

For hypervisors with full hardware support (e.g., Nitro), I/O limits may be supported by the hardware, or by external devices. In the Amazon EC2 cloud, network I/O and disk I/O to network-attached devices are throttled to quotas using external systems.

11.2.4 Observability

What is observable on virtualized systems depends on the hypervisor and the location from which the observability tools are launched. In general:

- **From the privileged guest (Xen) or host (KVM):** All physical resources should be observable using standard OS tools covered in previous chapters. Guest I/O can be observed by analyzing I/O proxies, if in use. Per-guest resource usage statistics should be made available from the hypervisor. Guest internals, including their processes, cannot be observed directly. Some I/O may not be observable if the device uses pass-through or SR-IOV.

- **From the hardware-supported host (Nitro):** The use of SR-IOV may make device I/O more difficult to observe from the hypervisor as the guest is accessing hardware directly, and not via a proxy or host kernel. (How Amazon actually does hypervisor observability on Nitro is not public knowledge.)

- **From the guests:** Virtualized resources and their usage by the guest can be seen, and physical problems inferred. Since the VM has its own dedicated kernel, kernel internals can be analyzed, and kernel tracing tools, including BPF-based tools, all work.

From the privileged guest or host (Xen or KVM hypervisors), physical resource usage can typically be observed at a high level: utilization, saturation, errors, IOPS, throughput, I/O type. These factors can usually be expressed per guest, so that heavy users can be quickly identified. Details of which guest processes are performing I/O and their application call stacks cannot be observed directly. They can be observed by logging in to the guest (provided that a means to do so is authorized and configured, e.g., SSH) and using the observability tools that the guest OS provides.

When pass-through or SR-IOV is used, the guest may be making I/O calls directly to hardware. This may bypass I/O paths in the hypervisor, and the statistics they typically collect. The result is that I/O can become invisible to the hypervisor, and not appear in iostat(1) or other tools. A possible workaround is to use PMCs to examine I/O-related counters, and infer I/O that way.

To identify the root cause of a guest performance issue, the cloud operator may need to log in to both the hypervisor and the guest and execute observability tools from both. Tracing the path of I/O becomes complex due to the steps involved and may also include analysis of hypervisor internals and an I/O proxy, if used.

From the guest, physical resource usage may not be observable at all. This may tempt the guest customers to blame mysterious performance issues on resource contention caused by noisy neighbors. To give cloud customers peace of mind (and reduce support tickets) information about physical resource usage (redacted) may be provided via other means, including SNMP or a cloud API.

To make container performance easier to observe and understand, there are various monitoring solutions that present graphs, dashboards, and directed graphs to show your container environment. Such software includes Google cAdvisor [Google 20d] and Cilium Hubble [Cilium 19] (both are open source).

The following sections demonstrate the raw observability tools that can be used from different locations, and describe a strategy for analyzing performance. Xen and KVM are used to demonstrate the kind of information that virtualization software may provide (Nitro is not included as it is Amazon proprietary).

11.2.4.1 Privileged Guest/Host

All system resources (CPUs, memory, file system, disk, network) should be observable using the tools covered in previous chapters (with the exception of I/O via pass-through/SR-IOV).

Xen

For Xen-like hypervisors, the guest vCPUs exist in the hypervisor and are not visible from the privileged guest (dom0) using standard OS tools. For Xen, the xentop(1) tool can be used instead:

```
# xentop
xentop - 02:01:05   Xen 3.3.2-rc1-xvm
2 domains: 1 running, 1 blocked, 0 paused, 0 crashed, 0 dying, 0 shutdown
Mem: 50321636k total, 12498976k used, 37822660k free    CPUs: 16 @ 2394MHz
       NAME  STATE  CPU(sec) CPU(%)    MEM(k) MEM(%)  MAXMEM(k) MAXMEM(%) VCPUS NETS
NETTX(k) NETRX(k) VBDS   VBD_OO   VBD_RD   VBD_WR SSID
   Domain-0 -----r   6087972    2.6   9692160   19.3   no limit       n/a    16    0
0        0    0        0        0        0    0
Doogle_Win --b---     172137    2.0   2105212    4.2   2105344       4.2     1    2
0        0    2        0        0        0    0
[...]
```

The fields include

- **CPU(%)**: CPU usage percentage (sum for multiple CPUs)
- **MEM(k)**: Main memory usage (Kbytes)
- **MEM(%)**: Main memory percentage of system memory
- **MAXMEM(k)**: Main memory limit size (Kbytes)
- **MAXMEM(%)**: Main memory limit as a percentage of system memory
- **VCPUS**: Count of assigned VCPUs
- **NETS**: Count of virtualized network interfaces
- **NETTX(k)**: Network transmit (Kbytes)
- **NETRX(k)**: Network receive (Kbytes)
- **VBDS**: Count of virtual block devices
- **VBD_OO**: Virtual block device requests blocked and queued (saturation)
- **VBD_RD**: Virtual block device read requests
- **VBD_WR**: Virtual block device write requests

The xentop(1) output is updated every 3 seconds by default and is selectable using -d *delay_secs*.

> For advanced Xen analysis there is the xentrace(8) tool, which can retrieve a log of fixed event types from the hypervisor. This can then be viewed using xenanalyze for investigating scheduling issues with the hypervisor and CPU scheduler used. There is also xenoprof, the system-wide profiler for Xen (MMU and guests) in the Xen source.

KVM

For KVM-like hypervisors, the guest instances are visible within the host OS. For example:

```
host$ top
top - 15:27:55 up 26 days, 22:04,  1 user,  load average: 0.26, 0.24, 0.28
Tasks: 499 total,   1 running, 408 sleeping,   2 stopped,   0 zombie
%Cpu(s): 19.9 us,  4.8 sy,  0.0 ni, 74.2 id,  1.1 wa,  0.0 hi,  0.1 si,  0.0 st
KiB Mem : 24422712 total,  6018936 free, 12767036 used,  5636740 buff/cache
KiB Swap: 32460792 total, 31868716 free,   592076 used.  8715220 avail Mem

  PID USER      PR  NI    VIRT    RES    SHR S  %CPU %MEM     TIME+ COMMAND
24881 libvirt+  20   0 6161864 1.051g  19448 S 171.9  4.5   0:25.88 qemu-system-x86

21897 root       0 -20       0      0      0 I   2.3  0.0   0:00.47 kworker/u17:8
23445 root       0 -20       0      0      0 I   2.3  0.0   0:00.24 kworker/u17:7
15476 root       0 -20       0      0      0 I   2.0  0.0   0:01.23 kworker/u17:2
23038 root       0 -20       0      0      0 I   2.0  0.0   0:00.28 kworker/u17:0

22784 root       0 -20       0      0      0 I   1.7  0.0   0:00.36 kworker/u17:1
[...]
```

The `qemu-system-x86` process is a KVM guest, which includes threads for each vCPU and threads for I/O proxies. The total CPU usage for the guest can be seen in the previous top(1) output, and per-vCPU usage can be examined using other tools. For example, using pidstat(1):

```
host$ pidstat -tp 24881 1
03:40:44 PM   UID  TGID    TID  %usr %system %guest %wait   %CPU CPU Command
03:40:45 PM 64055 24881      - 17.00   17.00 147.00  0.00 181.00   0 qemu-system-x86
03:40:45 PM 64055     - 24881  9.00    5.00   0.00  0.00  14.00   0 |__qemu-system-x86
03:40:45 PM 64055     - 24889  0.00    0.00   0.00  0.00   0.00   6 |__qemu-system-x86
03:40:45 PM 64055     - 24897  1.00    3.00  69.00  1.00  73.00   4 |__CPU 0/KVM
03:40:45 PM 64055     - 24899  1.00    4.00  79.00  0.00  84.00   5 |__CPU 1/KVM
03:40:45 PM 64055     - 24901  0.00    0.00   0.00  0.00   0.00   2 |__vnc_worker
03:40:45 PM 64055     - 25811  0.00    0.00   0.00  0.00   0.00   7 |__worker
03:40:45 PM 64055     - 25812  0.00    0.00   0.00  0.00   0.00   6 |__worker
[...]
```

This output shows the CPU threads, named `CPU 0/KVM` and `CPU 1/KVM` consuming 73% and 84% CPU.

Mapping QEMU processes to their guest instance names is usually a matter of examining their process arguments (ps -wwfp PID) to read the -name option.

Another important area for analysis is guest vCPU exits. The types of exits that occur can show what a guest is doing: whether a given vCPU is idle, performing I/O, or performing compute. On Linux, the perf(1) kvm subcommand provides high-level statistics for KVM exits. For example:

```
host# perf kvm stat live
11:12:07.687968


Analyze events for all VMs, all VCPUs:


            VM-EXIT Samples Samples%   Time%  Min Time   Max Time      Avg time


         MSR_WRITE   1668   68.90%    0.28%   0.67us     31.74us     3.25us ( +-  2.20% )
               HLT    466   19.25%   99.63%   2.61us 100512.98us  4160.68us ( +- 14.77% )
   PREEMPTION_TIMER    112    4.63%    0.03%   2.53us     10.42us     4.71us ( +-  2.68% )
  PENDING_INTERRUPT     82    3.39%    0.01%   0.92us     18.95us     3.44us ( +-  6.23% )
 EXTERNAL_INTERRUPT     53    2.19%    0.01%   0.82us      7.46us     3.22us ( +-  6.57% )
    IO_INSTRUCTION     37    1.53%    0.04%   5.36us     84.88us    19.97us ( +- 11.87% )
          MSR_READ      2    0.08%    0.00%   3.33us      4.80us     4.07us ( +- 18.05% )
      EPT_MISCONFIG      1    0.04%    0.00%  19.94us     19.94us    19.94us ( +-  0.00% )


Total Samples:2421, Total events handled time:1946040.48us.
[...]
```

This shows the reasons for virtual machine exit, and statistics for each reason. The longest-duration exits in this example output were for HLT (halt), as virtual CPUs enter the idle state. The columns are:

- **VM-EXIT**: Exit type
- **Samples**: Number of exits while tracing
- **Samples%**: Number of exits as an overall percent
- **Time%**: Time spent in exits as an overall percent
- **Min Time**: Minimum exit time
- **Max Time**: Maximum exit time
- **Avg time**: Average exit time

While it may not be easy for an operator to directly see inside a guest virtual machine, examining the exits lets you characterize how the overhead of hardware virtualization may or may not be affecting a tenant. If you see a low number of exits and a high percentage of those are HLT, you know that the guest CPU is fairly idle. On the other hand, if you have a high number of I/O operations, with interrupts both generated and injected into the guest, then it is very likely that the guest is doing I/O over its virtual NICs and disks.

For advanced KVM analysis, there are many tracepoints:

```
host# perf list | grep kvm
  kvm:kvm_ack_irq                             [Tracepoint event]
  kvm:kvm_age_page                            [Tracepoint event]
  kvm:kvm_apic                                [Tracepoint event]
```

```
kvm:kvm_apic_accept_irq                        [Tracepoint event]
kvm:kvm_apic_ipi                               [Tracepoint event]
kvm:kvm_async_pf_completed                     [Tracepoint event]
kvm:kvm_async_pf_doublefault                   [Tracepoint event]
kvm:kvm_async_pf_not_present                   [Tracepoint event]
kvm:kvm_async_pf_ready                         [Tracepoint event]
kvm:kvm_avic_incomplete_ipi                    [Tracepoint event]
kvm:kvm_avic_unaccelerated_access              [Tracepoint event]
kvm:kvm_cpuid                                  [Tracepoint event]
kvm:kvm_cr                                     [Tracepoint event]
kvm:kvm_emulate_insn                           [Tracepoint event]
kvm:kvm_enter_smm                              [Tracepoint event]
kvm:kvm_entry                                  [Tracepoint event]
kvm:kvm_eoi                                    [Tracepoint event]
kvm:kvm_exit                                   [Tracepoint event]
[...]
```

Of particular interest are kvm:kvm_exit (mentioned earlier) and kvm:kvm_entry. Listing kvm:kvm_exit arguments using bpftrace:

```
host# bpftrace -lv t:kvm:kvm_exit
tracepoint:kvm:kvm_exit
    unsigned int exit_reason;
    unsigned long guest_rip;
    u32 isa;
    u64 info1;
    u64 info2;
```

This provides the exit reason (exit_reason), guest return instruction pointer (guest_rip), and other details. Along with kvm:kvm_entry, which shows when the KVM guest was entered (or put differently, when the exit completed), the duration of the exit can be measured along with its exit reason. In *BPF Performance Tools* [Gregg 19] I published kvmexits.bt, a bpftrace tool for showing exit reasons as a histogram (it is also open source and online [Gregg 19e]). Sample output:

```
host# kvmexits.bt
Attaching 4 probes...
Tracing KVM exits. Ctrl-C to end
^C
[...]

@exit_ns[30, IO_INSTRUCTION]:
[1K, 2K)               1 |                                                    |
[2K, 4K)              12 |@@@                                                 |
[4K, 8K)              71 |@@@@@@@@@@@@@@@@@@@@                                 |
```

```
[8K, 16K)          198 |@@@@@@@@@@@@@@@@@@@@@@@@@@@@@@@@@@@@@@@@@@@@@@@@@@@@@|
[16K, 32K)         129 |@@@@@@@@@@@@@@@@@@@@@@@@@@@@@@@@@@@@                |
[32K, 64K)          94 |@@@@@@@@@@@@@@@@@@@@@@@@@                          |
[64K, 128K)         37 |@@@@@@@@@                                         |
[128K, 256K)        12 |@@@                                               |
[256K, 512K)        23 |@@@@@@                                            |
[512K, 1M)           2 |                                                  |
[1M, 2M)             0 |                                                  |
[2M, 4M)             1 |                                                  |
[4M, 8M)             2 |                                                  |

@exit_ns[48, EPT_VIOLATION]:
[512, 1K)         6160 |@@@@@@@@@@@@@@@@@@@@@@@@@@@@@@@@@@@@@@@@@@@@        |
[1K, 2K)          6885 |@@@@@@@@@@@@@@@@@@@@@@@@@@@@@@@@@@@@@@@@@@@@@@@     |
[2K, 4K)          7686 |@@@@@@@@@@@@@@@@@@@@@@@@@@@@@@@@@@@@@@@@@@@@@@@@@@@@@|
[4K, 8K)          2220 |@@@@@@@@@@@@@@@                                   |
[8K, 16K)          582 |@@@                                               |
[16K, 32K)         244 |@                                                 |
[32K, 64K)          47 |                                                  |
[64K, 128K)          3 |                                                  |
```

The output includes histograms for each exit: only two are included here. This shows IO_ INSTRUCTION exits are typically taking less than 512 microseconds, with a few outliers reaching the 2 to 8 millisecond range.

Another example of advanced analysis is profiling the contents of the CR3 register. Every process in the guest has its own address space and set of page tables describing the virtual-to-physical memory translations. The root of this page table is stored in the register CR3. By sampling the CR3 register from the host (e.g., using bpftrace) you may identify whether a single process is active in the guest (same CR3 value) or if it is switching between processes (different CR3 values).

For more information, you must log in to the guest.

11.2.4.2 Guest

From a hardware virtualized guest, only the virtual devices can be seen (unless pass-through/ SR-IOV is used). This includes CPUs, which shows the vCPUs allocated to the guest. For example, examining CPUs from a KVM guest using mpstat(1):

```
kvm-guest$ mpstat -P ALL 1
Linux 4.15.0-91-generic (ubuntu0)    03/22/2020       _x86_64_  (2 CPU)

10:51:34 PM CPU   %usr  %nice   %sys %iowait  %irq  %soft %steal %guest %gnice  %idle
10:51:35 PM all  14.95   0.00  35.57    0.00  0.00   0.00   0.00   0.00   0.00  49.48
10:51:35 PM   0  11.34   0.00  28.87    0.00  0.00   0.00   0.00   0.00   0.00  59.79
10:51:35 PM   1  17.71   0.00  42.71    0.00  0.00   0.00   0.00   0.00   0.00  39.58
```

```
10:51:35 PM CPU   %usr %nice   %sys %iowait  %irq %soft %steal %guest %gnice  %idle
10:51:36 PM all  11.56  0.00  37.19    0.00  0.00  0.00   0.50   0.00   0.00  50.75
10:51:36 PM   0   8.05  0.00  22.99    0.00  0.00  0.00   0.00   0.00   0.00  68.97
10:51:36 PM   1  15.04  0.00  48.67    0.00  0.00  0.00   0.00   0.00   0.00  36.28
[...]
```

The output shows the status of the two guest CPUs only.

The Linux vmstat(8) command includes a column for CPU percent stolen (st), which is a rare example of a virtualization-aware statistic. Stolen shows CPU time not available to the guest: it may be consumed by other tenants or other hypervisor functions (such as processing your own I/O, or throttling due to the instance type):

```
xen-guest$ vmstat 1
procs -----------memory---------- ---swap-- -----io---- --system-- -----cpu-----
 r  b   swpd   free   buff  cache   si   so    bi    bo   in   cs us sy id wa st
 1  0      0 107500 141348 301680    0    0     0     0 1006    9 99  0  0  0  1
 1  0      0 107500 141348 301680    0    0     0     0 1006   11 97  0  0  0  3
 1  0      0 107500 141348 301680    0    0     0     0  978    9 95  0  0  0  5
 3  0      0 107500 141348 301680    0    0     0     4  912   15 99  0  0  0  1
 2  0      0 107500 141348 301680    0    0     0     0   33    7  3  0  0  0 97
 3  0      0 107500 141348 301680    0    0     0     0   34    6 100 0  0  0  0
 5  0      0 107500 141348 301680    0    0     0     0   35    7  1  0  0  0 99
 2  0      0 107500 141348 301680    0    0     0    48   38   16  2  0  0  0 98
[...]
```

In this example, a Xen guest with an aggressive CPU limiting policy was tested. For the first 4 seconds, over 90% of CPU time was in user mode of the guest, with a few percent stolen. This behavior then begins to change aggressively, with most of the CPU time stolen.

Understanding CPU usage at the cycle level often requires the use of hardware counters (see Chapter 4, Observability Tools, Section 4.3.9, Hardware Counters (PMCs)). These may or may not be available to the guest, depending on the hypervisor configuration. Xen, for example, has a virtual performance monitoring unit (vpmu) to support PMC usage by the guests, and tuning to specify which PMCs to allow [Gregg 17f].

Since disk and network devices are virtualized, an important metric to analyze is *latency*, showing how the device is responding given virtualization, limits, and other tenants. Metrics such as percent busy are difficult to interpret without knowing what the underlying device is.

Device latency in detail can be studied using kernel tracing tools, including perf(1), Ftrace, and BPF (Chapters 13, 14, and 15). Fortunately, these all should work in the guests since they run dedicated kernels, and the root user has full kernel access. For example, running the BPF-based biosnoop(8) in a KVM guest:

```
kvm-guest# biosnoop
TIME(s)          COMM            PID   DISK   T   SECTOR     BYTES    LAT(ms)
0.000000000      systemd-journa  389   vda    W   13103112   4096        3.41
0.001647000      jbd2/vda2-8     319   vda    W   8700872    360448      0.77
0.011814000      jbd2/vda2-8     319   vda    W   8701576    4096        0.20
1.711989000      jbd2/vda2-8     319   vda    W   8701584    20480       0.72
1.718005000      jbd2/vda2-8     319   vda    W   8701624    4096        0.67
[...]
```

The output shows the virtual disk device latency. Note that with containers (Section 11.3, OS Virtualization) these kernel tracing tools may not work, so the end user may not be able to examine device I/O and various other targets in detail.

11.2.4.3   Strategy

Previous chapters have covered analysis techniques for the physical system resources, which can be followed by the administrators of the physical systems to look for bottlenecks and errors. Resource controls imposed on the guests can also be checked, to see if guests are consistently at their limit and should be informed and encouraged to upgrade. Not much more can be identified by the administrators without logging in to the guests, which may be necessary for any serious performance investigation.[6]

For the guests, the tools and strategies for analyzing resources covered in previous chapters can be applied, bearing in mind that the resources in this case are typically virtual. Some resources may not be driven to their limits, due to unseen resource controls by the hypervisor or contention from other tenants. Ideally, the cloud software or vendor provides a means for customers to check redacted physical resource usage, so that they can investigate performance issues further on their own. If not, contention and limits may be deduced from increases in I/O and CPU scheduling latency. Such latency can be measured either at the syscall layer or in the guest kernel.

A strategy I use to identify disk and network resource contention from the guest is careful analysis of I/O patterns. This can involve logging the output of biosnoop(8) (see the prior example) and then examining the sequence of I/O to see if any latency outliers are present, and if they are caused by either their size (large I/O is slower), their access pattern (e.g., reads queueing behind a write flush), or neither, in which case it is likely a physical contention or device issue.

11.3   OS Virtualization

OS virtualization partitions the operating system into instances that Linux calls *containers*, which act like separate guest servers and can be administrated and rebooted independently of the host. These provide small, efficient, fast-booting instances for cloud customers, and high-density servers for cloud operators. OS-virtualized guests are pictured in Figure 11.9.

---

[6]A reviewer pointed out another possible technique (note that this is not a recommendation): a snapshot of the guest's storage (provided it isn't encrypted) could be analyzed. For example, given a log of prior disk I/O addresses, a snapshot of file system state can be used to determine which files may have been accessed.

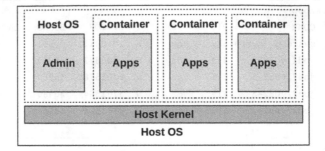

Figure 11.9   Operating system virtualization

This approach has origins in the Unix chroot(8) command, which isolates a process to a subtree of the Unix global file system (it changes the top-level directory, "/" as seen by the process, to point to somewhere else). In 1998, FreeBSD developed this further as *FreeBSD jails*, providing secure compartments that act as their own servers. In 2005, Solaris 10 included a version called *Solaris Zones*, with various resource controls. Meanwhile Linux had been adding process isolation capabilities in parts, with *namespaces* first added in 2002 for Linux 2.4.19, and *control groups* (cgroups) first added in 2008 for Linux 2.6.24 [Corbet 07a][Corbet 07b][Linux 20m]. Namespaces and cgroups are combined to create containers, which typically use seccomp-bpf as well to control syscall access.

A key difference from hardware virtualization technologies is that only one kernel is running. The following are the performance advantages of containers over hardware VMs (Section 11.2, Hardware Virtualization):

- Fast initialization time: typically measured in milliseconds.
- Guests can use memory entirely for applications (no extra kernel).
- There is a unified file system cache—this can avoid double-caching scenarios between the host and guest.
- More fine-grained control of resource sharing (cgroups).
- For the host operators: improved performance observability, as guest processes are directly visible along with their interactions.
- Containers may be able to share memory pages for common files, freeing space in the page cache and improving the CPU cache hit ratio.
- CPUs are real CPUs; assumptions by adaptive mutex locks remain valid.

And there are disadvantages:

- Increased contention for kernel resources (locks, caches, buffers, queues).
- For the guests: reduced performance observability, as the kernel typically cannot be analyzed.
- Any kernel panic affects all guests.
- Guests cannot run custom kernel modules.

- Guests cannot run longer-run PGO kernels (see Section 3.5.1, PGO Kernels).

- Guests cannot run different kernel versions or kernels.[7]

Consider the first two disadvantages together: A guest moving from a VM to a container will more likely encounter kernel contention issues, while also losing the ability to analyze them. They will become more dependent on the host operator for this kind of analysis.

A non-performance disadvantage for containers is that they are considered less secure because they share a kernel.

All of these disadvantages are solved by lightweight virtualization, covered in Section 11.4, Lightweight Virtualization, although at the cost of some advantages.

The following sections describe Linux OS virtualization specifics: implementation, overhead, resource controls, and observability.

11.3.1 Implementation

In the Linux kernel there is no notion of a container. There are, however, namespaces and cgroups, which user-space software (for example, Docker) uses to create what it calls *containers*.[8] A typical container configuration is pictured in Figure 11.10.

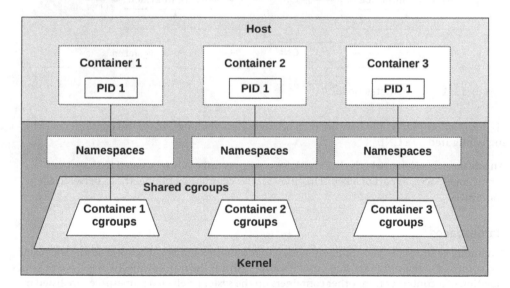

Figure 11.10 Linux containers

---

[7] There are technologies that emulate a different syscall interface so that a different OS can run under a kernel, but this has performance implications in practice. For example, such emulations typically only offer a basic set of syscall features, where advanced performance features return ENOTSUP (error not supported).

[8] The kernel does use a struct nsproxy to link to the namespaces for a process. Since this struct defines how a process is contained, it can be considered the best notion the kernel has of a container.

Despite each container having a process with ID 1 within the container, these are different processes as they belong to different namespaces.

Because many container deployments use Kubernetes, its architecture is pictured in Figure 11.11. Kubernetes was introduced in Section 11.1.6, Orchestration (Kubernetes).

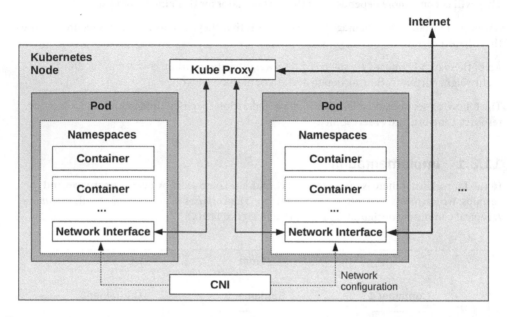

Figure 11.11   Kubernetes node

Figure 11.11 also shows the network path between Pods via Kube Proxy, and container networking configured by a CNI.

An advantage of Kubernetes is that multiple containers can easily be created to share the same namespaces, as part of a Pod. This allows faster communication methods between the containers.

Namespaces

A namespace filters the view of the system so that containers can only see and administer their own processes, mount points, and other resources. This is the primary mechanism that provides isolation of a container from other containers on the system. Selected namespaces are listed in Table 11.1

Table 11.1   **Selected Linux namespaces**

Namespace	Description
cgroup	For cgroup visibility
ipc	For interprocess communication visibility

Namespace	Description
mnt	For file system mounts
net	For network stack isolation; filters the interfaces, sockets, routes, etc., that are seen
pid	For process visibility; filters /proc
time	For separate system clocks per container
user	For user IDs
uts	For host information; the uname(2) syscall

The current namespaces on a system can be listed with lsns(8):

```
# lsns
        NS TYPE    NPROCS   PID USER          COMMAND
4026531835 cgroup     105     1 root          /sbin/init
4026531836 pid        105     1 root          /sbin/init
4026531837 user       105     1 root          /sbin/init
4026531838 uts        102     1 root          /sbin/init
4026531839 ipc        105     1 root          /sbin/init
4026531840 mnt         98     1 root          /sbin/init
4026531860 mnt          1    19 root          kdevtmpfs
4026531992 net        105     1 root          /sbin/init
4026532166 mnt          1   241 root          /lib/systemd/systemd-udevd
4026532167 uts          1   241 root          /lib/systemd/systemd-udevd
[...]
```

This lsns(8) output shows the init process has six different namespaces, in use by over 100 processes.

There is some documentation for namespaces in the Linux source, as well as in man pages, starting with namespaces(7).

Control Groups

Control groups (cgroups) limit the usage of resources. There are two versions of cgroups in the Linux kernel, v1 and v2[9]; many projects such as Kubernetes are still using v1 (v2 is in the works). The v1 cgroups include those listed in Table 11.2.

---

[9] There are also mixed-mode configurations that use parts of both v1 and v2 in parallel.

Table 11.2   **Selected Linux cgroups**

cgroup	Description
blkio	Limits block I/O (disk I/O): bytes and IOPS
cpu	Limits CPU usage based on shares
cpuacct	Accounting for CPU usage for process groups
cpuset	Assigns CPU and memory nodes to containers
devices	Controls device administration
hugetlb	Limits huge pages usage
memory	Limits process memory, kernel memory, and swap usage
net_cls	Sets classids on packets for use by qdiscs and firewalls
net_prio	Sets network interface priorities
perf_event	Allows perf to monitor processes in a cgroup
pids	Limits the number of processes that can be created
rdma	Limits RDMA and InfiniBand resource usage

These cgroups can be configured to limit resource contention between containers, for example by putting a hard limit on CPU and memory usage, or softer limits (share-based) for CPU and disk usage. There can also be a hierarchy of cgroups, including system cgroups that are shared between the containers, as pictured in Figure 11.10.

cgroups v2 is hierarchy-based and solves various shortcomings of v1. It is expected that container technologies will migrate to v2 in the coming years, with v1 eventually being deprecated. The Fedora 31 OS, released in 2019, has already switched to cgroups v2.

There is some documentation for namespaces in the Linux source under Documentation/cgroup-v1 and Documentation/admin-guide/cgroup-v2.rst, as well as in the cgroups(7) man page.

The following sections describe container virtualization topics: overhead, resource controls, and observability. These differ based on the specific container implementation and its configuration.

11.3.2   Overhead

The overhead of container execution should be lightweight: application CPU and memory usage should experience bare-metal performance, though there may be some extra calls within the kernel for I/O due to layers in the file system and network path. The biggest performance problems are caused by multitenancy contention, as containers promote heavier sharing of kernel and physical resources. The following sections summarize the performance overheads for CPU execution, memory usage, performing I/O, and contention from other tenants.

CPU

When a container thread is running in user mode, there are no direct CPU overheads: threads run on-CPU directly until they either yield or are preempted. On Linux, there are also no extra CPU overheads for running processes in namespaces and cgroups: all processes already run in a default namespace and cgroups set, whether containers are in use or not.

CPU performance is most likely degraded due to contention with other tenants (see the later section, Multi-Tenant Contention).

With orchestrators such as Kubernetes, additional network components can add some CPU overheads for handling network packets (e.g., with many services (thousands); kube-proxy encounters first-packet overheads when having to process large iptables rule sets due to a high number of Kubernetes services used. This overhead can be overcome by replacing kube-proxy with BPF instead [Borkmann 20]).

Memory Mapping

Memory mapping, loads, and stores should execute without overhead.

Memory Size

Applications can make use of the entire amount of allocated memory for the container. Compare this to hardware VMs, which run a kernel per tenant, each kernel costing a small amount of main memory.

A common container configuration (the use of OverlayFS) allows sharing the page cache between containers that are accessing the same file. This can free up some memory compared to VMs, which duplicate common files (e.g., system libraries) in memory.

I/O

The I/O overhead depends on the container configuration, as it may include extra layers for isolation for:

- **file system I/O**: E.g., overlayfs
- **network I/O**: E.g., bridge networking

The following is a kernel stack trace showing a container file system write that was handled by overlayfs (and backed by the XFS file system):

```
blk_mq_make_request+1
generic_make_request+420
submit_bio+108
_xfs_buf_ioapply+798
__xfs_buf_submit+226
xlog_bdstrat+48
xlog_sync+703
```

```
__xfs_log_force_lsn+469
xfs_log_force_lsn+143
xfs_file_fsync+244
xfs_file_buffered_aio_write+629
do_iter_readv_writev+316
do_iter_write+128
ovl_write_iter+376
__vfs_write+274
vfs_write+173
ksys_write+90
do_syscall_64+85
entry_SYSCALL_64_after_hwframe+68
```

Overlayfs can be seen in the stack as the ovl_write_iter() function.

How much this matters is dependent on the workload and its rate of IOPS. For low-IOPS servers (say, <1000 IOPS) it should cost negligible overhead.

Multi-Tenant Contention

The presence of other running tenants is likely to cause resource contention and interrupts that hurt performance, including:

- CPU caches may have a lower hit ratio, as other tenants are consuming and evicting entries. For some processors and kernel configurations, context switching to other container threads may even flush the L1 cache.[10]

- TLB caches may also have a lower hit ratio due to other tenant usage, and also flushing on context switches (which may be avoided if PCID is in use).

- CPU execution may be interrupted for short periods for other tenant devices (e.g., network I/O) performing interrupt service routines.

- Kernel execution can encounter additional contention for buffers, caches, queues, and locks, because a multi-tenant container system can increase their load by an order of magnitude or more. Such contention can slightly degrade application performance, depending on the kernel resource and its scalability characteristics.

- Network I/O can encounter CPU overhead due to the use of iptables to implement container networking.

- There may be contention for system resources (CPUs, disks, network interfaces) from other tenants who are using them.

---

[10] For example, in June 2020, Linus Torvalds rejected a kernel patch that allowed processes to opt in to L1 data cache flushing [Torvalds 20b]. The patch was a security precaution for cloud environments, but was rejected due to concerns over the performance cost in cases where it was unnecessary. While not included in Linux mainline, I would not be surprised if this patch was running in some Linux distributions in the cloud.

A post by Gianluca Borello describes how a container's performance was found to slowly and steadily deteriorate over time when certain other containers were on the system [Borello 17]. He tracked it down to find that lstat(2) latency was higher, caused by the other container's workload and its effect on the dcache.

Another issue, reported by Maxim Leonovich, showed how moving from single-tenant VMs to multi-tenant containers increased the rate of posix_fadvise() calls for the kernel, creating a bottleneck [Leonovich 18].

The last item on the list is managed by resource controls. While some of these factors exist in a traditional multi-user environment, they are much more prevalent in a multi-tenant container system.

11.3.3 Resource Controls

Resource controls throttle access to resources so they can be shared more fairly. On Linux, these are mostly provided via cgroups.

Individual resource controls can be classified as *priorities* or *limits*. Priorities steer resource consumption to balance usage between neighbors based on an importance value. Limits are a ceiling value of resource consumption. Either is used as appropriate—for some resources, that means both. Examples are listed in Table 11.3.

Table 11.3 Linux container resource controls

Resource	Priority	Limit
CPU	CFS shares	cpusets (whole CPUs), CFS bandwidth (fractional CPUs)
Memory capacity	Memory soft limits	Memory limits
Swap capacity	-	Swap limits
File system capacity	-	File system quotas/limits
File system cache	-	Kernel memory limits
Disk I/O	blkio weights	blkio IOPS limits blkio throughput limits
Network I/O	net_prio priorities qdiscs (fq, etc.) Custom BPF	qdiscs (fq, etc.) Custom BPF

These are described in the following sections in general terms, based on cgroup v1. The steps to configure these depend on the container platform you are using (Docker, Kubernetes, etc.); see their associated documentation.

CPUs

CPUs can be allocated across containers using the cpusets cgroup, and shares and bandwidth from the CFS scheduler.

cpusets

The cpusets cgroup allows whole CPUs to be allocated to specific containers. The benefit is that those containers can run on CPU without interruption by others, and that the CPU capacity available to them is consistent. The downside is that idle CPU capacity is unavailable to other containers to use.

Shares and Bandwidth

CPU *shares*, provided by the CFS scheduler, is a different approach for CPU allocation that allows containers to share their idle CPU capacity. Shares support the concept of *bursting*, where a container can effectively run faster by using idle CPU from other containers. When there isn't idle capacity, including when a host has been overprovisioned, shares provide a best-effort division of CPU resources among the containers that need them.

CPU shares work by assigning allocation units called shares to containers, which are used to calculate the amount of CPU a busy container will get at a given time. This calculation uses the formula:

container CPU = (all CPUs × container shares) / total busy shares on system

Consider a system that has allocated 100 shares between several containers. At one moment, only containers A and B want CPU resources. Container A has 10 shares, and container B has 30 shares. Container A can therefore use 25% of the total CPU resources on the system: all CPUs × 10/(10 + 30).

Now consider a system where all containers are busy at the same time. A given container's CPU allocation will be:

container CPU = all CPUs × container shares / total shares on system

For the scenario described, container A would get 10% of the CPU capacity (CPUs × 10/100). The share allocation provides a minimum guarantee of CPU usage. Bursting may allow the container to use more. Container A can use anything from 10% to 100% of the CPU capacity, depending on how many other containers are busy.

A problem with shares is that bursting can confuse capacity planning, especially since many monitoring systems do not show bursting statistics (they should). An end user testing a container may be satisfied with its performance, unaware that this performance is only made possible by bursting. Later on, when other tenants move in, their container can no longer burst and will suffer lower performance. Imagine container A initially testing on an idle system and getting 100% CPU, but later on only getting 10% as other containers have since been added. I've seen this scenario happen in real life on numerous occasions, where the end user thinks that there must be a system performance issue and asks me to help debug it. They are then disappointed to learn that the system is working as intended, and that ten-times slower is the new norm because other containers have moved in. To the customer, this can feel like bait and switch.

It's possible to reduce the problem of excessive bursting by limiting it so that the performance drop is not as severe (even though this also limits performance). On Linux this is accomplished using CFS *bandwidth* controls, which can set an upper limit for CPU usage. For example, container A could have bandwidth set at 20% of system-wide CPU capacity, such that with shares it now operates in the range of 10 to 20%, depending on idle availability. This range from a share-based minimum CPU to the bandwidth maximum is pictured in Figure 11.12. It assumes that there are sufficient busy threads in each container to use the available CPUs (otherwise containers become CPU-limited due to their own workloads, before hitting system-imposed limits).

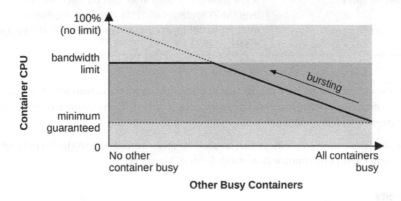

Figure 11.12   CPU shares and bandwidth

Bandwidth controls are typically exposed as a percentage of whole CPUs: 2.5 would mean two and a half CPUs. This maps to the kernel settings, which are actually *periods* and *quotas* in microseconds: a container gets a quota of CPU microseconds every period.

A different way to manage bursting is for container operators to notify their end users when they are bursting for some period of time (e.g., days) so that they do not develop wrong expectations about performance. End users can then be encouraged to upgrade their container size so that they get more shares, and a higher minimum guarantee of CPU allocation.

CPU Caches

CPU cache usage can be controlled using Intel cache allocation technology (CAT) to avoid a container polluting the CPU caches. This was described in Section 11.2.3, Resource Controls, and has the same caveat: limiting cache access also hurts performance.

Memory Capacity

The memory cgroup provides four mechanisms to manage memory usage. Table 11.4 describes them via their memory cgroup setting name.

Table 11.4   **Linux memory cgroup settings**

Name	Description
memory.limit_in_bytes	A size limit, in bytes. If a container tries to use more than the allocated size, it encounters swapping (if configured) or the OOM killer.
memory.soft_limit_in_bytes	A size limit, in bytes. A best-effort approach that involves reclaiming memory to steer containers towards their soft limit.
memory.kmem.limit_in_bytes	A size limit for kernel memory, in bytes.
memory.kmem.tcp.limit_in_bytes	A size limit for TCP buffer memory, in bytes.
memory.pressure_level	A low memory notifier that can be used via the eventfd(2) system call. This requires application support to configure the pressure level and use the system call.

There are also notification mechanisms so that applications can take action when memory is running low: memory.pressure_level and memory.oom_control. These require configuring notifications via the eventfd(2) system call.

Note that a container's unused memory can be used by other containers in the kernel page cache, improving their performance (a memory form of bursting).

Swap Capacity

The memory cgroup also allows a swap limit to be configured. The actual setting is memory. memsw.limit_in_bytes, which is memory plus swap.

File System Capacity

File system capacity can usually be limited by the file system. For example, the XFS file system supports both soft and hard quotas for users, groups, and projects, where soft limits allow some temporary excess usage under the hard limit. ZFS and btrfs also have quotas.

File System Cache

In Linux, memory used by the file system page cache for a container is accounted to the container in the memory cgroup: no additional setting is required. If the container configures swap, the degree between favoring swapping over page cache eviction can be controlled by the memory.swappiness setting, similar to the system-wide vm.swappinness (Chapter 7, Memory, Section 7.6.1, Tunable Parameters).

Disk I/O

The blkio cgroup provides mechanisms to manage disk I/O. Table 11.5 describes them via their blkio cgroup setting name.

Table 11.5 **Linux blkio cgroup settings**

Name	Description
blkio.weight	A cgroup weight that controls the share of disk resources during load, similar to CPU shares. It is used with the BFQ I/O scheduler.
blkio.weight_device	A weight setting for a specific device.
blkio.throttle.read_bps_device	A limit for read bytes/s.
blkio.throttle.write_bps_device	A limit for write bytes/s.
blkio.throttle.read_iops_device	A limit for read IOPS.
blkio.throttle.write_iops_device	A limit for write IOPS.

As with CPU shares and bandwidths, the blkio weights and throttle settings allow disk I/O resources to be shared based on a policy of priorities and limits.

Network I/O

The net_prio cgroup allows priorities to be set for outbound network traffic. These are the same as the SO_PRIORITY socket option (see socket(7)), and control the priority of packet processing in the network stack. The net_cls cgroup can tag packets with a class ID for later management by qdiscs. (This also works for Kubernetes Pods, which can use a net_cls per Pod.)

Queueing disciplines (qdiscs, see Chapter 10, Network, Section 10.4.3, Software) can operate on class IDs or be assigned to container virtual network interfaces to prioritize and throttle network traffic. There are over 50 different qdisc types, each with their own policies, features, and tunables. For example, the Kubernetes kubernetes.io/ingress-bandwidth and kubernetes.io/egress-bandwidth settings are implemented by creating a token bucket filter (tbf) qdisc [CNI 18]. Section 10.7.6, tc, provides an example of adding and removing a qdisc to a network interface.

BPF programs can be attached to cgroups for custom programmatic resource controls and firewalls. An example is the Cilium software, which uses a combination of BPF programs at various layers such as XDP, cgroup, and tc (qdiscs), to support security, load balancing, and firewall capabilities between containers [Cilium 20a].

11.3.4 Observability

What is observable depends on the location from which the observability tools are launched and the security settings of the host. Because containers can be configured in many different ways, I will describe the typical case. In general:

- **From the host** (most privileged namespace): Everything can be observed, including hardware resources, file systems, guest processes, guest TCP sessions, and so on. Guest processes can be seen and analyzed without logging into the guests. Guest file systems can also be easily browsed from the host (the cloud provider).

- **From the guests:** The container can typically only see its own processes, file systems, network interfaces, and TCP sessions. A major exception is system-wide statistics, such as for CPUs and disks: these often show the host rather than just the container. The status of these statistics is typically undocumented (I have written my own documentation in the following section, Traditional Tools). Kernel internals typically cannot be inspected, so performance tools that use kernel tracing frameworks (Chapters 13 to 15) usually do not work.

The last point was described earlier: containers are more likely to encounter kernel contention issues, at the same time that they remove the end user's ability to diagnose those issues.

A common concern for container performance analysis is the possible presence of "noisy neighbors," other container tenants that are aggressively consuming resources and causing access contention for others. Since these container processes are all under one kernel and can be analyzed simultaneously from the host, this is not dissimilar to traditional performance analysis of multiple processes running on one time-sharing system. The main difference is that cgroups may impose additional software limits (resource controls) that are encountered before the hardware limits.

Many monitoring tools written for stand-alone systems have yet to develop support for OS virtualization (containers), and are blind to cgroup and other software limits. Customers attempting to use these in the containers may find that they appear to work, but are in fact only showing physical system resources. Without support for observing cloud resource controls, these tools may falsely report that systems have headroom when in fact they have hit software limits. They may also show high resource usage that is actually due to other tenants.

On Linux, container observability from both the host and guests is made still more complex and time-consuming by the fact that there is currently no container ID in the kernel,[11] nor much container support from traditional performance tools.

These challenges are described in the following sections that summarize the state of traditional performance tools, explore observability from the host and containers, and describe a strategy for analyzing performance.

11.3.4.1 Traditional Tools

As a summary of traditional performance tools, Table 11.6 describes what various tools show when run from the host and from a typical container (one that uses process and mount namespaces) on a Linux 5.2 kernel. Situations that may be unexpected, such as when the container can observe host statistics, are highlighted in bold.

---

[11] Container management software may name cgroups after the container ID, in which case the in-kernel cgroup names do show the user-level container name. The default cgroup v2 ID is another candidate for an in-kernel ID, and is used for this purpose by BPF and bpftrace. Section 11.3.4, Observability, under the BPF Tracing section, shows another possible solution: the nodename from the uts namespace, which is typically set to the container name.

Table 11.6   **Linux traditional tools**

Tool	From the Host	From the Container
`top`	The summary heading shows the host; the process table shows all host and container processes	**The summary heading shows mixed statistics; some are from the host and some from the container.** The process table shows container processes
`ps`	Shows all processes	Shows container processes
`uptime`	Shows host (system-wide) load averages	**Shows host load averages**
`mpstat`	Shows host CPUs and host usage	**Shows host CPUs, and host CPU usage**
`vmstat`	Shows host CPUs, memory, and other statistics	**Shows host CPUs, memory, and other statistics**
`pidstat`	Shows all processes	Shows container processes
`free`	Shows host memory	**Shows host memory**
`iostat`	Shows host disks	**Shows host disks**
`pidstat -d`	Shows all process disk I/O	Shows container process disk I/O
`sar -n DEV, TCP 1`	Shows host network interfaces and TCP statistics	Shows container network interfaces and TCP statistics
`perf`	Can profile everything	**Either fails to run, or can be enabled and then can profile other tenants**
`tcpdump`	Can sniff all interfaces	Only sniffs container interfaces
`dmesg`	Shows the kernel log	**Fails to run**

Over time, container support for tools may improve so that they only show container-specific statistics when run from the container or, even better, show a breakdown of container versus host statistics. The host tools can show everything, and they, too, could be improved by adding support for breakdowns and filters by container or cgroup. These topics are explained more in the following sections on host and guest observability.

11.3.4.2   Host

When logged in to the host, all system resources (CPUs, memory, file system, disk, network) can be inspected using the tools covered in previous chapters. There are two additional factors to examine when using containers:

- Statistics per container
- Effect of resource controls

As described in Section 11.3.1, Implementation, there is no notion of a container in the kernel: a container is just a collection of namespaces and cgroups. The container ID you see is created and managed by user-space software. Here are example container IDs from Kubernetes (in this case, a Pod with a single container) and Docker:

```
# kubectl get pod
NAME                          READY    STATUS              RESTARTS    AGE
kubernetes-b94cb9bff-kqvml    0/1      ContainerCreating   0           3m
[...]
# docker ps
CONTAINER ID   IMAGE    COMMAND    CREATED        STATUS        PORTS   NAMES
6280172ea7b9   ubuntu   "bash"     4 weeks ago    Up 4 weeks            eager_bhaskara
[...]
```

This presents a problem for traditional performance tools such as ps(1), top(1), and so on. To show a container ID, they would need support for Kubernetes, Docker, and every other container platform. If, instead, there was kernel support for a container ID, it would become the standard to be supported by all performance tools. This is the case with the Solaris kernel, where containers are called *zones* and have a kernel-based *zone ID* that can be observed using ps(1) and others. (The following BPF Tracing heading shows a Linux solution using the nodename from the UTS namespace for the container ID.)

In practice, performance statistics by container ID on Linux can be examined using:

- **Container tools** provided by the container platform; e.g., Docker has a tool for showing resource usage by container.

- **Performance monitoring** software, which typically has plugins for various container platforms.

- **Cgroup statistics** and the tools that use them. This requires an extra step to figure out which cgroups map to which container.

- **Namespace mapping** from the host, such as by using nsenter(1), to allow host performance tools to be run in the container. This can reduce visible processes to just those from the container, when used with the **-p** (PID namespace) option. Although performance tool statistics may not be for the container alone: see Table 11.6. The **-n** (network namespace) option is also useful for running network tools within the same network namespace (ping(8), tcpdump(8)).

- **BPF tracing**, which can read cgroup and namespace information from the kernel.

The following sections provide examples for container tools, cgroup statistics, namespace entering, and BPF tracing, as well resource control observability.

Container Tools

The Kubernetes container orchestration system provides a way to check basic resource usage using kubectl top.

Checking hosts ("nodes"):

```
# kubectl top nodes
NAME                      CPU(cores)   CPU%   MEMORY(bytes)   MEMORY%
bgregg-i-03cb3a7e46298b38e 1781m       10%    2880Mi          9%
```

The CPU(cores) time shows cumulative milliseconds of CPU time, and CPU% shows the current usage of the node.

Checking containers ("Pods"):

```
# kubectl top pods
NAME                      CPU(cores)   MEMORY(bytes)
kubernetes-b94cb9bff-p7jsp 73m         9Mi
```

This shows the cumulative CPU time and current memory size.

These commands require a metrics server to be running, which may be added by default depending on how you initialized Kubernetes. Other monitoring tools can also display these metrics in a GUI, including cAdvisor, Sysdig, and Google Cloud Monitoring [Kubernetes 20c].

The Docker container technology provides some docker(1) analysis subcommands, including stats. For example, from a production host:

```
# docker stats
CONTAINER    CPU %    MEM USAGE / LIMIT    MEM %    NET I/O      BLOCK I/O        PIDS
353426a09db1 526.81%  4.061 GiB / 8.5 GiB  47.78%   0 B / 0 B    2.818 MB / 0 B   247
6bf166a66e08 303.82%  3.448 GiB / 8.5 GiB  40.57%   0 B / 0 B    2.032 MB / 0 B   267
58dcf8aed0a7 41.01%   1.322 GiB / 2.5 GiB  52.89%   0 B / 0 B    0 B / 0 B        229
61061566ffe5 85.92%   220.9 MiB / 3.023 GiB 7.14%   0 B / 0 B    43.4 MB / 0 B    61
bdc721460293 2.69%    1.204 GiB / 3.906 GiB 30.82%  0 B / 0 B    4.35 MB / 0 B    66
[...]
```

This shows that a container with UUID 353426a09db1 was consuming a total of 527% CPU for this update interval and was using 4 Gbytes of main memory versus an 8.5 Gbyte limit. For this interval there was no network I/O, and only a small volume (Mbytes) of disk I/O.

Cgroup Statistics

Various statistics by cgroup are available from /sys/fs/cgroups. These are read and graphed by various container monitoring products and tools, and can be examined directly at the command line:

```
# cd /sys/fs/cgroup/cpu,cpuacct/docker/02a7cf65f82e3f3e75283944caa4462e82f...
# cat cpuacct.usage
1615816262506
```

```
# cat cpu.stat
nr_periods 507
nr_throttled 74
throttled_time 3816445175
```

The cpuacct.usage file shows the CPU usage of this cgroup in total nanoseconds. The cpu.stat file shows the number of times this cgroup was CPU throttled (nr_throttled), as well as the total throttled time in nanoseconds. This example shows that this cgroup was CPU throttled 74 times out of 507 time periods, for a total of 3.8 throttled seconds.

There is also a cpuacct.usage_percpu, this time showing a Kubernetes cgroup:

```
# cd /sys/fs/cgroup/cpu,cpuacct/kubepods/burstable/pod82e745...
# cat cpuacct.usage_percpu
37944772821 35729154566 35996200949 36443793055 36517861942 36156377488 36176348313
35874604278 37378190414 35464528409 35291309575 35829280628 36105557113 36538524246
36077297144 35976388595
```

The output includes 16 fields for this 16-CPU system, with total CPU time in nanoseconds. These cgroupv1 metrics are documented in the kernel source under Documentation/cgroup-v1/cpuacct.txt.

Command-line tools that read these statistics include htop(1) and systemd-cgtop(1). For example, running systemd-cgtop(1) on a production container host:

```
# systemd-cgtop
```

Control Group	Tasks	%CPU	Memory	Input/s	Output/s
/	-	798.2	45.9G	-	-
/docker	1082	790.1	42.1G	-	-
/docker/dcf3a...9d28fc4a1c72bbaff4a24834	200	610.5	24.0G	-	-
/docker/370a3...e64ca01198f1e843ade7ce21	170	174.0	3.0G	-	-
/system.slice	748	5.3	4.1G	-	-
/system.slice/daemontools.service	422	4.0	2.8G	-	-
/docker/dc277...42ab0603bbda2ac8af67996b	160	2.5	2.3G	-	-
/user.slice	5	2.0	34.5M	-	-
/user.slice/user-0.slice	5	2.0	15.7M	-	-
/user.slice/u....slice/session-c26.scope	3	2.0	13.3M	-	-
/docker/ab452...c946f8447f2a4184f3ccff2a	174	1.0	6.3G	-	-
/docker/e18bd...26ffdd7368b870aa3d1deb7a	156	0.8	2.9G	-	-
[...]					

This output shows that a cgroup named /docker/dcf3a... is consuming 610.5% total CPU for this update interval (across many CPUs) and 24 Gbytes of main memory, with 200 running tasks. The output also shows a number of cgroups created by systemd for system services (/system.slice) and user sessions (/user.slice).

Namespace Mapping

Containers typically use different namespaces for process IDs and mounts.

For process namespaces, it means that the PID in the guest is unlikely to match the PID in the host.

When diagnosing performance issues, I first log in to the container so that I can see the problem from the viewpoint of the end user. Later on, I may log in to the host to continue the investigation using system-wide tools, but the PID may not be the same. The mapping is shown in the /proc/PID/status file. For example, from the host:

```
host# grep NSpid /proc/4915/status
NSpid:   4915    753
```

This shows that PID 4915 on the host is PID 753 in the guest. Unfortunately, I typically need to do the reverse mapping: given the container PID, I need to find the host PID. One (somewhat inefficient) way to do this is to scan all status files:

```
host# awk '$1 == "NSpid:" && $3 == 753 { print $2 }' /proc/*/status
4915
```

In this case it showed that guest PID 753 was host PID 4915. Note that the output may show more than one host PID, since "753" could appear in multiple process namespaces. In that case, you will need to figure out which 753 is from the matching namespace. The /proc/PID/ns files are symlinks that contain namespace IDs, and can be used for this purpose. Examining them from the guest and then the host:

```
guest# ls -lh /proc/753/ns/pid
lrwxrwxrwx 1 root root 0 Mar 15 20:47 /proc/753/ns/pid -> 'pid:[4026532216]'
```

```
host# ls -lh /proc/4915/ns/pid
lrwxrwxrwx 1 root root 0 Mar 15 20:46 /proc/4915/ns/pid -> 'pid:[4026532216]'
```

Note the matching namespace IDs (4026532216): this confirms that host PID 4915 is the same as guest PID 753.

Mount namespaces can present similar challenges. Running the perf(1) command from the host, for example, searches in /tmp/perf-PID.map for supplemental symbol files, but container applications emit them to /tmp in the container, which is not the same as /tmp in the host. In addition, the PID is likely different due to process namespaces. Alice Goldfuss first posted a workaround for this that involved moving and renaming these symbol files so that they were available in the host [Goldfuss 17]. perf(1) has since gained namespace support to avoid this problem, and the kernel provides a /proc/PID/root mount namespace mapping for direct access to the container's root ("/"). For example:

```
host# ls -lh /proc/4915/root/tmp
total 0
-rw-r--r-- 1 root root 0 Mar 15 20:54 I_am_in_the_container.txt
```

This is listing a file in the container's /tmp.

Apart from /proc files, the nsenter(1) command can execute other commands in selected namespaces. The following runs the top(1) command from the host, in the mount (-m) and process (-p) namespaces from PID 4915 (-t 4915):

```
# nsenter -t 4915 -m -p top
top - 21:14:24 up 32 days, 23:23,  0 users,  load average: 0.32, 0.09, 0.02
Tasks:   3 total,   2 running,   1 sleeping,   0 stopped,   0 zombie
%Cpu(s):  0.2 us,  0.1 sy,  0.0 ni, 99.4 id,  0.0 wa,  0.0 hi,  0.0 si,  0.2 st
KiB Mem :  1996844 total,     98400 free,    858060 used,   1040384 buff/cache
KiB Swap:        0 total,         0 free,         0 used.    961564 avail Mem

   PID USER      PR  NI    VIRT    RES    SHR S  %CPU %MEM     TIME+ COMMAND
   753 root      20   0  818504  93428  11996 R 100.0  0.2   0:27.88 java
     1 root      20   0   18504   3212   2796 S   0.0  0.2   0:17.57 bash
   766 root      20   0   38364   3420   2968 R   0.0  0.2   0:00.00 top
```

This shows the top process is java with PID 753.

BPF Tracing

Some BPF tracing tools already have container support, but many do not. Fortunately, adding support to bpftrace tools when needed is typically not difficult; the following is an example. See Chapter 15 for an explanation of bpftrace programming.

The forks.bt tool counts the number of new processes created while tracing by instrumenting the clone(2), fork(2), and vfork(2) syscalls. The source is:

```
#!/usr/local/bin/bpftrace

tracepoint:syscalls:sys_enter_clone,
tracepoint:syscalls:sys_enter_fork,
tracepoint:syscalls:sys_enter_vfork
{
        @new_processes = count();
}
```

Example output:

```
# ./forks.bt
Attaching 3 probes...
^C

@new_processes: 590
```

This shows 590 new processes created system-wide while tracing.

To break this down by container, one approach is to print the nodename (hostname) from the uts namespace. This relies on the container software configuring this namespace, which is typically the case. The code becomes, with additions highlighted:

```
#!/usr/local/bin/bpftrace

#include <linux/sched.h>
#include <linux/nsproxy.h>
#include <linux/utsname.h>

tracepoint:syscalls:sys_enter_clone,
tracepoint:syscalls:sys_enter_fork,
tracepoint:syscalls:sys_enter_vfork
{
        $task = (struct task_struct *)curtask;
        $nodename = $task->nsproxy->uts_ns->name.nodename;
        @new_processes[$nodename] = count();
}
```

This extra code walks from the current kernel task_struct to the uts namespace nodename, and includes it in the @new_processes output map as a key.

Example output:

```
# ./forks.bt
Attaching 3 probes...
^C

@new_processes[ip-10-1-239-218]: 171
@new_processes[efe9f9be6185]: 743
```

The output is now broken down by container, showing that nodename 6280172ea7b9 (a container) created 252 processes while tracing. The other nodename, ip-10-1-239-218, is the host system.

This only works because system calls operate in task (process) context, so curtask returns the responsible task_struct from which we fetch the nodename. If process-asynchronous events are traced, for example, the completion interrupts from disk I/O, then the originating process may not be on-CPU and curtask will not identify the correct nodename.

As fetching of the uts nodename may become commonly used in bpftrace, I imagine we will add a built-in variable, nodename, so that the only addition is:

```
@new_processes[nodename] = count();
```

Check for bpftrace updates to see if this has already been added.

Resource Controls

The resource controls listed in Section 11.3.3, Resource Controls, must be observed to identify whether a container is limited by them. Traditional performance tools and documentation focus on physical resources, and are blind to these software-imposed limits.

Checking resource controls was described in the USE method (Chapter 2, Methodologies, Section 2.5.9, The USE Method), which iterates over resources and checks utilization, saturation, and errors. With resource controls present they, too, must be checked for each resource.

The earlier section called Cgroup Statistics showed the /sys/fs/cgroup/.../cpu.stat file, which provides statistics on CPU throttling (nr_throttled) and the time throttled in nanoseconds (throttled_time). This throttling refers to the CPU bandwidth limits, and it's straightforward to identify whether a container is bandwidth throttled: throttled_time will be increasing. If cpusets are used instead, their CPU utilization can be checked from per-CPU tools and metrics, including mpstat(1).

CPUs can also be managed by shares, as described in their earlier Shares and Bandwidth section. A shares-limited container is more difficult to identify, as there is no statistic. I developed the flow chart in Figure 11.13 for the process of determining if and how container CPUs are throttled [Gregg 17g]:

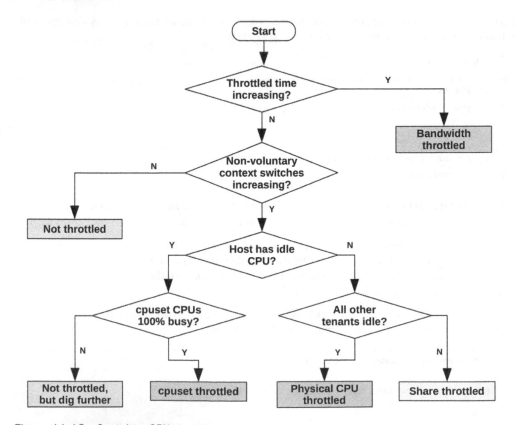

Figure 11.13   Container CPU throttling analysis

The process in Figure 11.13 determines if and how a container CPUs are throttled using five statistics:

- **Throttled time**: cpu cgroup throttled_time
- **Non-voluntary context switches**: Can be read from /proc/PID/status as an increase in nonvoluntary_ctxt_switches
- **Host has idle CPU**: Can be read from mpstat(1) `%idle`, /proc/stat, and other tools
- **cpuset CPUs 100% busy**: If cpusets are in use, their utilization can be read from mpstat(1), /proc/stat, etc.
- **All other tenants idle**: Can be determined from a container-specific tool (`docker stat`), or system tools that show the lack of competition for CPU resources (e.g., if top(1) only shows the one container consuming `%CPU`)

A similar process can be developed for other resources, and supporting statistics including the cgroup statistics should be made available in monitoring software and tools. An ideal monitoring product or tool makes the determination for you, and reports if and how each container is throttled.

11.3.4.3 Guest (Container)

You might expect that performance tools run from a container would show only container statistics, but that is often not the case. For example, running iostat(1) on an idle container:

```
container# iostat -sxz 1
[...]
avg-cpu:  %user   %nice %system %iowait  %steal   %idle
          57.29    0.00    8.54   33.17    0.00    1.01


Device             tps     kB/s    rqm/s   await aqu-sz  areq-sz  %util
nvme0n1        2578.00 12436.00   331.00    0.33   0.00     4.82 100.00


avg-cpu:  %user   %nice %system %iowait  %steal   %idle
          51.78    0.00    7.61   40.61    0.00    0.00


Device             tps     kB/s    rqm/s   await aqu-sz  areq-sz  %util
nvme0n1        2664.00 11020.00    88.00    0.32   0.00     4.14  98.80
[...]
```

This output shows both a CPU and disk workload, and yet this container is completely idle. This can be confusing for people new to OS virtualization—why is my container busy? It's because the tools are showing host statistics that include activity from other tenants.

The status of these performance tools was summarized in Section 11.3.4, Observability, subsection Traditional Tools. These tools are becoming more "container aware" over time, supporting cgroup statistics and providing container-only statistics in a container.

There are cgroup statistics for block I/O. From the same container:

```
container# cat /sys/fs/cgroup/blkio/blkio.throttle.io_serviced
259:0 Read 452
259:0 Write 352
259:0 Sync 692
259:0 Async 112
259:0 Discard 0
259:0 Total 804
Total 804
container# sleep 10
container# cat /sys/fs/cgroup/blkio/blkio.throttle.io_serviced
259:0 Read 452
259:0 Write 352
259:0 Sync 692
259:0 Async 112
259:0 Discard 0
259:0 Total 804
Total 804
```

These count types of operations. I printed them twice with a sleep 10 to set an interval: you can see that the counts did not increase during that interval; therefore, the container was not issuing disk I/O. There is another file for bytes: blkio.throttle.io_service_bytes.

Unfortunately, these counters do not provide all the statistics iostat(1) needs. More counters need to be exposed by cgroup so that iostat(1) can become container-aware.

Container Awareness

Making a tool container-aware doesn't necessarily mean restricting its view to its own container: There are benefits to a container seeing the status of physical resources. It depends on the goal for using containers, which may be:

A) **The container is an isolated server**: If this is the goal, as is typically the case for cloud vendors, then making tools container-aware means they only show the current container's activity. iostat(1), for example, should only show disk I/O called by the container and not others. This could be implemented by isolating all statistic sources to only show the current container (/proc, /sys, netlink, etc.). Such isolation would both help and hinder analysis by the guest: diagnosing issues of resource contention from other tenants will be more time-consuming and will rely on inference from unexplained increases in device latency.

B) **The container is a packaging solution**: For companies operating their own container clouds, isolating a container's statistics may not necessarily be required. Allowing containers to see host statistics (as is often currently the case anyway, as seen earlier with iostat(1)) means that end users can better understand the state of hardware devices and problems caused by noisy neighbors. To make iostat(1) more container-aware in this scenario may mean providing a breakdown showing the current container versus host or other container usage, rather than hiding those statistics.

For both scenarios, tools should also support showing resource controls where appropriate as part of container awareness. To continue with the iostat(1) example, apart from the device %util (not visible in scenario A), it could also provide a %cap based on the blkio throughput and IOPS limits, so a container knows whether disk I/O is limited by resource controls.[12]

If physical resource observability is allowed, guests will be able to rule out some types of issues, including noisy neighbors. This can lighten the support burden on container operators: people tend to blame what they cannot observe. It is also an important difference from hardware virtualization, which hides physical resources from the guests and has no way to share those statistics (unless external means are used). Ideally, there will be a future setting in Linux to control the sharing of host statistics, so that each container environment can choose between A or B as desired.

Tracing Tools

Advanced kernel-based tracing tools, such as perf(1), Ftrace, and BPF, have similar issues and work ahead of them to become container-aware. They do not currently work from within a container due to the permissions required for various system calls (perf_event_open(2), bpf(2), etc.) and access for various /proc and /sys files. Describing their future for the earlier scenarios A and B:

A) **Isolation required**: Allowing containers to use tracing tools may be possible via:

   □ **Kernel filtering**: Events and their arguments can be filtered by the kernel, so that, for example, tracing the block:block_rq_issue tracepoint only shows the current container's disk I/O.

   □ **Host API**: The host exposes access to certain tracing tools via a secure API or GUI. A container could, for example, request common BCC tools such as execsnoop(8) and biolatency(8) to execute, and the host would validate the request, execute a filtered version of the tool, and return with the output.

B) **Isolation not required**: Resources (syscalls, /proc, and /sys) are made available in the container so that tracing tools work. The tracing tools themselves can become container-aware to facilitate filtering of events to the current container only.

Making tools and statistics container-aware has been a slow process in Linux and other kernels, and will likely take many years before they are all done. This most hurts advanced users who are logging into systems to use performance tools at the command line; many users use monitoring products with agents that are already container-aware (to some degree).

11.3.4.4 Strategy

Previous chapters have covered analysis techniques for the physical system resources and included various methodologies. These can be followed for host operators, and to some extent by the guests, bearing in mind the limitations mentioned previously. For guests, high-level resource usage is typically observable, but drilling down into the kernel is usually not possible.

---

[12] iostat(1) -x currently has so many fields it doesn't fit on my widest terminal, and I hesitate to encourage adding more. I'd rather another switch be added, such as -1, to show software limit columns.

Apart from the physical resources, cloud limits imposed by resource controls should also be checked, by both the host operators and guest tenants. Since these limits, where present, are encountered long before the physical limits, they are more likely to be in effect and should be checked first.

Because many traditional observability tools were created before containers and resource controls existed (e.g., top(1), iostat(1)), they do not include resource control information by default, and users may forget to check them.

Here are some comments and strategies for checking each resource control:

- **CPU:** See the Figure 11.13 flowchart. The use of cpusets, bandwidth, and shares all need to be checked.

- **Memory:** For main memory, check current usage against any memory cgroup limits.

- **File system capacity:** This should be observable as for any other file system (including using df(1)).

- **Disk I/O:** Check the configuration of blkio cgroup throttles (/sys/fs/cgroup/blkio) and statistics from blkio.throttle.io_serviced and blkio.throttle.io_service_bytes files: if they are incrementing at the same rate as the throttles, it is evidence that disk I/O is throttle-limited. If BPF tracing is available, the blkthrot(8) tool can also be used to confirm blkio throttling [Gregg 19].

- **Network I/O:** Check current network throughput against any known bandwidth limit, which may be observable only from the host. Encountering the limit causes network I/O latency to increase, as tenants are throttled.

A final comment: much of this section describes cgroup v1 and the current state of Linux containers. Kernel capabilities are rapidly changing, leaving other areas such as vendor documentation and tool container-awareness playing catch up. To keep up to date with Linux containers you will need to check for additions in new kernel releases, and read through the Documentation directory in the Linux source. I'd also recommend reading any documentation written by Tejun Heo, the lead developer of cgroups v2, including Documentation/admin-guide/cgroup-v2.rst in the Linux source [Heo 15].

11.4   Lightweight Virtualization

Lightweight hardware virtualization has been designed to be the best of both worlds: The security of hardware virtualization with the efficiency and fast boot time of containers. They are pictured in Figure 11.14 based on Firecracker, alongside containers for comparison.

Lightweight hardware virtualization uses a lightweight hypervisor based on processor virtualization, and a minimum number of emulated devices. This is different from full-machine hardware hypervisors (Section 11.2, Hardware Virtualization), which originated with desktop virtual machines and include support for video, audio, the BIOS, the PCI bus, and other devices, as well as different levels of processor support. A hypervisor intended only for server computing does not need to support those devices, and one written today can assume that modern processor virtualization features are available.

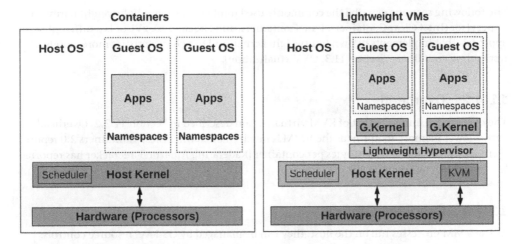

Figure 11.14   Lightweight virtualization

To describe the difference this makes: quick emulator (QEMU) is a full-machine hardware hypervisor used for KVM, and has over 1.4 million lines of code (QEMU version 4.2). Amazon Firecracker is a lightweight hypervisor and has only 50 thousand lines of code [Agache 20].

Lightweight VMs behave similarly to the config B hardware VMs described in Section 11.2. Compared to hardware VMs, lightweight VMs have much faster boot time, lower memory overheads, and improved security. Lightweight hypervisors can improve security further by configuring namespaces as another layer of security, as pictured in Figure 11.14.

Some implementations describe lightweight virtual machines as *containers*, and others use the term *MicroVM*. I prefer the term MicroVM, as the term containers is typically associated with OS virtualization.

11.4.1   Implementation

There are several lightweight hardware virtualization projects, including:

- **Intel Clear Containers**: Launched in 2015, this used Intel VT features to provide light-weight virtual machines. This project proved the potential of lightweight containers, achieving boot times of under 45 ms [Kadera 16]. In 2017, Intel Clear Containers joined the Kata Containers project, where it continues development.

- **Kata Containers**: Launched in 2017, this project is based on Intel Clear Containers and Hyper.sh RunV, and is under the governance of the OpenStack foundation. Its website slogan is: "The speed of containers, the security of VMs" [Kata Containers 20].

- **Google gVisor**: Launched in 2018 as open source, gVisor uses a specialized user-space kernel for guests, written in Go, that improves container security.

- **Amazon Firecracker**: Launched in 2019 as open source [Firecracker 20], this uses KVM with a new lightweight VMM instead of QEMU, and achieves boot times of around 100 ms (system boot) [Agache 20].

The following sections describe the commonly used implementation: a lightweight hardware hypervisor (Intel Clear Containers, Kata Containers, and Firecracker). gVisor is a different approach that implements its own lightweight kernel, and has characteristics more closely resembling containers (Section 11.3, OS Virtualization).

11.4.2   Overhead

The overhead is similar to that of KVM virtualization described in Section 11.2.2, Overhead, with a lower memory footprint as the VMM is much smaller. Intel Clear Containers 2.0 report a memory overhead of 48–50 Mbytes per container [Kadera 16]; Amazon Firecracker has reported less than 5 Mbytes [Agache 20].

11.4.3   Resource Controls

As the VMM processes run on the host, they can be managed by OS-level resource controls: cgroups, qdiscs, etc., similar to KVM virtualization described in Section 11.2.3, Resource Controls. These OS-level resource controls were also discussed in more detail for containers in Section 11.3.3, Resource Controls.

11.4.4   Observability

Observability is similar to that of KVM virtualization described in Section 11.2.4, Observability. In summary:

- **From the host**: All physical resources can be observed using standard OS tools, as covered in prior chapters. Guest VMs are visible as processes. Guest internals, including processes inside the VM and their file systems, cannot be observed directly. For a hypervisor operator to analyze guest internals, they must be granted access (e.g., SSH).

- **From the guest**: Virtualized resources and their usage by the guest can be seen, and physical problems inferred. Kernel tracing tools, including BPF-based tools, all work because the VM has its own dedicated kernel.

As an example of observability, the following shows a Firecracker VM as observed using top(1) from the host[13]:

```
host# top
top - 15:26:22 up 25 days, 22:03,  2 users,  load average: 4.48, 2.10, 1.18
Tasks: 495 total,   1 running, 398 sleeping,   2 stopped,   0 zombie
%Cpu(s): 25.4 us,  0.1 sy,  0.0 ni, 74.4 id,  0.0 wa,  0.0 hi,  0.0 si,  0.0 st
KiB Mem : 24422712 total,  8268972 free, 10321548 used,  5832192 buff/cache
KiB Swap: 32460792 total, 31906152 free,   554640 used. 11185060 avail Mem

  PID USER      PR  NI    VIRT    RES    SHR S  %CPU %MEM     TIME+ COMMAND
30785 root      20   0 1057360 297292 296772 S 200.0  1.2   0:22.03 firecracker
31568 bgregg    20   0  110076   3336   2316 R  45.7  0.0   0:01.93 sshd
```

[13] This VM was created using Weave Ignite, a microVM container manager [Weaveworks 20].

```
31437 bgregg    20   0   57028    8052   5436 R  22.8  0.0   0:01.09 ssh
30719 root      20   0  120320   16348  10756 S   0.3  0.1   0:00.83 ignite-spawn
    1 root      20   0  227044    7140   3540 S   0.0  0.0  15:32.13 systemd
[..]
```

The entire VM appears as a single process named firecracker. This output shows it is consuming 200% CPU (2 CPUs). From the host, you cannot tell which guest processes are consuming this CPU.

The following shows top(1) run **from the guest**:

```
guest# top
top - 22:26:30 up 16 min,  1 user,  load average: 1.89, 0.89, 0.38
Tasks:  67 total,   3 running,  35 sleeping,   0 stopped,   0 zombie
%Cpu(s): 81.0 us, 19.0 sy,  0.0 ni,  0.0 id,  0.0 wa,  0.0 hi,  0.0 si,  0.0 st
KiB Mem :  1014468 total,   793660 free,    51424 used,   169384 buff/cache
KiB Swap:        0 total,        0 free,        0 used.   831400 avail Mem

  PID USER      PR  NI    VIRT    RES    SHR S  %CPU %MEM     TIME+ COMMAND
 1104 root      20   0   18592   1232    700 R 100.0  0.1   0:05.77 bash
 1105 root      20   0   18592   1232    700 R 100.0  0.1   0:05.59 bash
 1106 root      20   0   38916   3468   2944 R   4.8  0.3   0:00.01 top
    1 root      20   0   77224   8352   6648 S   0.0  0.8   0:00.38 systemd
    3 root       0 -20       0      0      0 I   0.0  0.0   0:00.00 rcu_gp
[...]
```

The output now shows that the CPU was consumed by two bash programs.

Also compare the difference between the header summaries: the host has a one-minute load average of 4.48, whereas the guest has 1.89. Other details are also different, as the guest has its own kernel that is maintaining guest-only statistics. As described in Section 11.3.4, Observability, this is different for containers, where statistics seen from the guest may unexpectedly show system-wide statistics from the host.

As another example, the following shows mpstat(1) executed from the guest:

```
guest# mpstat -P ALL 1
Linux 4.19.47 (cd41e0d846509816)      03/21/20      _x86_64_   (2 CPU)

22:11:07  CPU  %usr %nice  %sys %iowait  %irq %soft %steal %guest %gnice  %idle
22:11:08  all 81.50  0.00 18.50    0.00  0.00  0.00   0.00   0.00   0.00   0.00
22:11:08    0 82.83  0.00 17.17    0.00  0.00  0.00   0.00   0.00   0.00   0.00
22:11:08    1 80.20  0.00 19.80    0.00  0.00  0.00   0.00   0.00   0.00   0.00
[...]
```

This output shows only two CPUs, as the guest has two CPUs assigned.

11.5 Other Types

Other cloud computing primitives and technologies include:

- **Functions as a service (FaaS):** The developer submits an application function to the cloud, which is run on demand. Although this simplifies the software development experience, because there is no server to manage ("serverless"), there are performance consequences. The startup time for the function may be significant, and without a server, the end user cannot run traditional command-line observability tools. Performance analysis is typically limited to application-provided timestamps.

- **Software as a service (SaaS):** This provides high-level software without the end user needing to configure the servers or applications themselves. Performance analysis is limited to the operators: without access to servers, end users can do little other than client-based timing.

- **Unikernels:** This technology compiles an application together with minimal kernel parts into a single software binary that can be executed by hardware hypervisors directly, no operating system required. While there can be performance gains, such as minimizing instruction text and therefore CPU cache pollution, as well as security gains due to stripping out unused code, Unikernels also create observability challenges as there is no OS from which to run observability tools. Kernel statistics, such as those found in /proc, may also be non-existent. Fortunately, implementations typically allow the Unikernel to be run as a normal process, providing one path for analysis (albeit in a different environment from the hypervisor). Hypervisors can also develop ways to inspect them, such as stack profiling: I developed a prototype that generated flame graphs of a running MirageOS Unikernel [Gregg 16a].

For all of these, there is no operating system for end users to log in to (or container to enter) and do traditional performance analysis. FaaS and SaaS must be analyzed by the operators. Unikernels require custom tooling and statistics, and ideally hypervisor profiling support.

11.6 Comparisons

Comparing technologies can help you better understand them, even if you are not in a position to change the technology used by your company. Performance attributes of the three technologies discussed in this chapter are compared in Table 11.7.[14]

Table 11.7   **Comparing virtualization technology performance attributes**

Attribute	Hardware Virtualization	OS Virtualization (Containers)	Lightweight Virtualization
Example	*KVM*	*Containers*	*FireCracker*
CPU performance	High (CPU support)	High	High (CPU support)

---

[14] Note that this table focuses on performance only. There are also other differences, for example, containers have been described as having weaker security [Agache 20].

Attribute	Hardware Virtualization	OS Virtualization (Containers)	Lightweight Virtualization
CPU allocation	Fixed to vCPUs	Flexible (shares + bandwidth)	Fixed to vCPUs
I/O throughput	High (with SR-IOV)	High (no intrinsic overhead)	High (with SR-IOV)
I/O latency	Low (with SR-IOV and no QEMU)	Low (no intrinsic overhead)	Low (with SR-IOV)
Memory access overhead	Some (EPT/NPT or shadow page tables)	None	Some (EPT/NPT or shadow page tables)
Memory loss	Some (extra kernels, page tables)	None	Some (extra kernels, page tables)
Memory allocation	Fixed (and possibly double caching)	Flexible (unused guest memory used for file system cache)	Fixed (and possibly double caching)
Resource controls	Most (kernel plus hypervisor controls)	Many (depends on kernel)	Most (kernel plus hypervisor controls)
Observability: from the host	Medium (resource usage, hypervisor statistics, OS inspection for KVM-like hypervisors, but cannot see guest internals)	High (see everything)	Medium (resource usage, hypervisor statistics, OS inspection for KVM-like hypervisors, but cannot see guest internals)
Observability: from the guest	High (full kernel and virtual device inspection)	Medium (user mode only, kernel counters, full kernel visibility restricted) with extra host-wide metrics (e.g., iostat(1))	High (full kernel and virtual device inspection)
Observability favors	End users	Host operators	End users
Hypervisor complexity	Highest (addition of a complex hypervisor)	Medium (OS)	High (addition of a lightweight hypervisor)
Different OS guests	Yes	Usually no (sometimes possible with syscall translation, which can add overheads)	Yes

While this table will go out of date as more features are developed for these virtualization technologies, it still serves to show the kinds of things to look for, even as entirely new virtualization technologies are developed that fit none of these categories.

Virtualization technologies are often compared using micro-benchmarking to see which performs the best. Unfortunately, this overlooks the importance of being able to observe the system, which can lead to the largest performance gains of all. Observability often makes it possible to identify and eliminate unnecessary work, making possible performance wins far greater than minor hypervisor differences.

For cloud operators, the highest observability option is containers, because from the host they can see all processes and their interaction. For end users, it is virtual machines, since those give users kernel access to run all kernel-based performance tools, including those in Chapters 13, 14, and 15. Another option is containers that have kernel access, giving operators and users full visibility of everything; however, this is only an option when the customer also runs the container host, since it lacks security isolation between containers.

Virtualization is still an evolving space, with lightweight hardware hypervisors only appearing in recent years. Given their benefits, especially for end-user observability, I expect their usage to grow.

11.7   Exercises

1. Answer the following questions about virtualization terminology:
   - What is the difference between the host and the guest?
   - What is a tenant?
   - What is a hypervisor?
   - What is hardware virtualization?
   - What is OS virtualization?

2. Answer the following conceptual questions:
   - Describe the role of performance isolation.
   - Describe the performance overheads with modern hardware virtualization (e.g., Nitro).
   - Describe the performance overheads with OS virtualization (e.g., Linux containers).
   - Describe physical system observability from a hardware-virtualized guest (either Xen or KVM).
   - Describe physical system observability from an OS-virtualized guest.
   - Explain the difference between hardware virtualization (e.g., Xen or KVM) and lightweight hardware virtualization (e.g., Firecracker).

3. Choose a virtualization technology and answer the following for the guests:
   - Describe how a memory limit is applied, and how it is visible from the guest. (What does the system administrator see when guest memory is exhausted?)
   - If there is an imposed CPU limit, describe how it is applied and how it is visible from the guest.

- If there is an imposed disk I/O limit, describe how it is applied and how it is visible from the guest.

- If there is an imposed network I/O limit, describe how it is applied and how it is visible from the guest.

4. Develop a USE method checklist for resource controls. Include how to fetch each metric (e.g., which command to execute) and how to interpret the result. Try to use existing OS observability tools before installing or using additional software products.

11.8 References

[Goldberg 73] Goldberg, R. P., *Architectural Principles for Virtual Computer Systems,* Harvard University (Thesis), 1972.

[Waldspurger 02] Waldspurger, C., "Memory Resource Management in VMware ESX Server," *Proceedings of the 5th Symposium on Operating Systems Design and Implementation*, 2002.

[Cherkasova 05] Cherkasova, L., and Gardner, R., "Measuring CPU Overhead for I/O Processing in the Xen Virtual Machine Monitor," *USENIX ATEC*, 2005.

[Adams 06] Adams, K., and Agesen, O., "A Comparison of Software and Hardware Techniques for x86 Virtualization," *ASPLOS*, 2006.

[Gupta 06] Gupta, D., Cherkasova, L., Gardner, R., and Vahdat, A., "Enforcing Performance Isolation across Virtual Machines in Xen," *ACM/IFIP/USENIX Middleware*, 2006.

[Qumranet 06] "KVM: Kernel-based Virtualization Driver," Qumranet Whitepaper, 2006.

[Cherkasova 07] Cherkasova, L., Gupta, D., and Vahdat, A., "Comparison of the Three CPU Schedulers in Xen," *ACM SIGMETRICS*, 2007.

[Corbet 07a] Corbet, J., "Process containers," *LWN.net*, https://lwn.net/Articles/236038, 2007.

[Corbet 07b] Corbet, J., "Notes from a container," *LWN.net*, https://lwn.net/Articles/256389, 2007.

[Liguori, 07] Liguori, A., "The Myth of Type I and Type II Hypervisors," http://blog.codemonkey.ws/2007/10/myth-of-type-i-and-type-ii-hypervisors.html, 2007.

[VMware 07] "Understanding Full Virtualization, Paravirtualization, and Hardware Assist," https://www.vmware.com/techpapers/2007/understanding-full-virtualization-paravirtualizat-1008.html, 2007.

[Matthews 08] Matthews, J., et al. *Running Xen: A Hands-On Guide to the Art of Virtualization*, Prentice Hall, 2008.

[Milewski 11] Milewski, B., "Virtual Machines: Virtualizing Virtual Memory," http://corensic.wordpress.com/2011/12/05/virtual-machines-virtualizing-virtual-memory, 2011.

[Adamczyk 12] Adamczyk, B., and Chydzinski, A., "Performance Isolation Issues in Network Virtualization in Xen," *International Journal on Advances in Networks and Services*, 2012.

[Hoff 12] Hoff, T., "Pinterest Cut Costs from $54 to $20 Per Hour by Automatically Shutting Down Systems," http://highscalability.com/blog/2012/12/12/pinterest-cut-costs-from-54-to-20-per-hour-by-automatically.html, 2012.

[Gregg 14b] Gregg, B., "From Clouds to Roots: Performance Analysis at Netflix," http://www.brendangregg.com/blog/2014-09-27/from-clouds-to-roots.html, 2014.

[Heo 15] Heo, T., "Control Group v2," *Linux documentation*, https://www.kernel.org/doc/Documentation/cgroup-v2.txt, 2015.

[Gregg 16a] Gregg, B., "Unikernel Profiling: Flame Graphs from dom0," http://www.brendangregg.com/blog/2016-01-27/unikernel-profiling-from-dom0.html, 2016.

[Kadera 16] Kadera, M., "Accelerating the Next 10,000 Clouds," https://www.slideshare.net/Docker/accelerating-the-next-10000-clouds-by-michael-kadera-intel, 2016.

[Borello 17] Borello, G., "Container Isolation Gone Wrong," *Sysdig blog*, https://sysdig.com/blog/container-isolation-gone-wrong, 2017.

[Goldfuss 17] Goldfuss, A., "Making FlameGraphs with Containerized Java," https://blog.alicegoldfuss.com/making-flamegraphs-with-containerized-java, 2017.

[Gregg 17e] Gregg, B., "AWS EC2 Virtualization 2017: Introducing Nitro," http://www.brendangregg.com/blog/2017-11-29/aws-ec2-virtualization-2017.html, 2017.

[Gregg 17f] Gregg, B., "The PMCs of EC2: Measuring IPC," http://www.brendangregg.com/blog/2017-05-04/the-pmcs-of-ec2.html, 2017.

[Gregg 17g] Gregg, B., "Container Performance Analysis at DockerCon 2017," http://www.brendangregg.com/blog/2017-05-15/container-performance-analysis-dockercon-2017.html, 2017.

[CNI 18] "bandwidth plugin," https://github.com/containernetworking/plugins/blob/master/plugins/meta/bandwidth/README.md, 2018.

[Denis 18] Denis, X., "A Pods Architecture to Allow Shopify to Scale," https://engineering.shopify.com/blogs/engineering/a-pods-architecture-to-allow-shopify-to-scale, 2018.

[Leonovich 18] Leonovich, M., "Another reason why your Docker containers may be slow," https://hackernoon.com/another-reason-why-your-docker-containers-may-be-slow-d37207dec27f, 2018.

[Borkmann 19] Borkmann, D., and Pumputis, M., "Kube-proxy Removal," https://cilium.io/blog/2019/08/20/cilium-16/#kubeproxy-removal, 2019.

[Cilium 19] "Announcing Hubble - Network, Service & Security Observability for Kubernetes," https://cilium.io/blog/2019/11/19/announcing-hubble/, 2019.

[Gregg 19] Gregg, B., *BPF Performance Tools: Linux System and Application Observability*, Addison-Wesley, 2019.

[Gregg 19e] Gregg, B., "kvmexits.bt," https://github.com/brendangregg/bpf-perf-tools-book/blob/master/originals/Ch16_Hypervisors/kvmexits.bt, 2019.

[Kwiatkowski 19] Kwiatkowski, A., "Autoscaling in Reality: Lessons Learned from Adaptively Scaling Kubernetes," https://conferences.oreilly.com/velocity/vl-eu/public/schedule/detail/78924, 2019.

[Xen 19] "Xen PCI Passthrough," http://wiki.xen.org/wiki/Xen_PCI_Passthrough, 2019.

[Agache 20] Agache, A., et al., "Firecracker: Lightweight Virtualization for Serverless Applications," https://www.amazon.science/publications/firecracker-lightweight-virtualization-for-serverless-applications, 2020.

[Calico 20] "Cloud Native Networking and Network Security," https://github.com/projectcalico/calico, last updated 2020.

[Cilium 20a] "API-aware Networking and Security," https://cilium.io, accessed 2020.

[Cilium 20b] "eBPF-based Networking, Security, and Observability," https://github.com/cilium/cilium, last updated 2020.

[Firecracker 20] "Secure and Fast microVMs for Serverless Computing," https://github.com/firecracker-microvm/firecracker, last updated 2020.

[Google 20c] "Google Compute Engine FAQ," https://developers.google.com/compute/docs/faq#whatis, accessed 2020.

[Google 20d] "Analyzes Resource Usage and Performance Characteristics of Running containers," https://github.com/google/cadvisor, last updated 2020.

[Kata Containers 20] "Kata Containers," https://katacontainers.io, accessed 2020.

[Linux 20m] "mount_namespaces(7)," http://man7.org/linux/man-pages/man7/mount_namespaces.7.html, accessed 2020.

[Weaveworks 20] "Ignite a Firecracker microVM," https://github.com/weaveworks/ignite, last updated 2020.

[Kubernetes 20b] "Production-Grade Container Orchestration," https://kubernetes.io, accessed 2020.

[Kubernetes 20c] "Tools for Monitoring Resources," https://kubernetes.io/docs/tasks/debug-application-cluster/resource-usage-monitoring, last updated 2020.

[Torvalds 20b] Torvalds, L., "Re: [GIT PULL] x86/mm changes for v5.8," https://lkml.org/lkml/2020/6/1/1567, 2020.

[Xu 20] Xu, P., "iops limit for pod/pvc/pv #92287," https://github.com/kubernetes/kubernetes/issues/92287, 2020.

Chapter 12

Benchmarking

There are lies, damn lies and then there are performance measures.
—Anon et al., "A Measure of Transaction Processing Power" [Anon 85]

Benchmarking tests performance in a controlled manner, allowing choices to be compared, regressions to be identified, and performance limits to be understood—before they are encountered in production. These limits may be system resources, software limits in a virtualized environment (cloud computing), or limits in the target application. Previous chapters have explored these components, describing the types of limits present and the tools used to analyze them.

Previous chapters have also introduced tools for *micro-benchmarking*, which use simple artificial workloads such as file system I/O to test components. There is also *macro-benchmarking*, which simulates client workloads to test the entire system. Macro-benchmarking may involve a client workload simulation, or a trace replay. Whichever type you use, it's important to analyze the benchmark so that you can confirm what is being measured. Benchmarks tell you only how fast the system can run the benchmark; it's up to you to understand the result and determine how it applies to your environment.

The learning objectives of this chapter are:

- Understand micro-benchmarking and macro-benchmarking.
- Become aware of numerous benchmarking failures to avoid.
- Follow an active benchmarking methodology.
- Use a benchmarking checklist to check results.
- Develop accuracy at performing and interpreting benchmarks.

This chapter discusses benchmarking in general, providing advice and methodologies to help you avoid common mistakes and accurately test your systems. This is also useful background when you need to interpret the results from others, including vendor and industry benchmarks.

12.1 Background

This section describes benchmarking activities and effective benchmarking, and summarizes common mistakes.

12.1.1 Reasons

Benchmarking may be performed for the following reasons:

- **System design**: Comparing different systems, system components, or applications. For commercial products, benchmarking may provide data to aid a purchase decision, specifically the *price/performance* ratio of the available options.[1] In some cases, results from published *industry benchmarks* can be used, which avoids the need for customers to execute the benchmarks themselves.

- **Proofs of concept**: To test the performance of software or hardware under load, before purchasing or committing to production deployment.

- **Tuning**: Testing tunable parameters and configuration options, to identify those that are worth further investigation with the production workload.

- **Development**: For both *non-regression testing* and *limit investigations* during product development. Non-regression testing may be an automated battery of performance tests that run regularly, so that any performance regression can be discovered early and quickly matched to the product change. For limit investigations, benchmarking can be used to drive products to their limit during development, in order to identify where engineering effort is best spent to improve product performance.

- **Capacity planning**: Determining system and application limits for capacity planning, either to provide data for modeling performance, or to find capacity limits directly.

- **Troubleshooting**: To verify that components can still operate at maximum performance. For example: testing maximum network throughput between hosts to check whether there may be a network issue.

- **Marketing**: Determining maximum product performance for use by marketing (also called *benchmarketing*).

In enterprise on-premises environments, benchmarking hardware during proofs of concept can be an important exercise before committing to a large hardware purchase, and may be a process that lasts weeks or months. This includes the time to ship, rack, and cable systems, and then to install operating systems before testing. Such a process may occur every year or two, when new hardware is released.

In cloud computing environments, however, resources are available on demand without an expensive initial investment in hardware, and can also be modified quickly as needed (redeploying on different instance types). These environments still involve longer-term investments

---

[1]While the price/performance ratio is commonly cited, I think in practice the performance/price ratio may be easier to comprehend, because as a mathematical ratio (and not just a saying) it has the attribute "bigger is better," which matches an assumption people tend to make about performance numbers.

when choosing which application programming language to use, and which operating system, database, web server, and load balancer to run. Some of these choices can be difficult to change down the road. Benchmarking can be performed to investigate how well the various options can scale when required. The cloud computing model makes benchmarking easy: a large-scale environment can be created in minutes, used for a benchmark run, and then destroyed, all at very little cost.

Note that a fault-tolerant and distributed cloud environment also makes experimentation easy: when new instance types are made available, the environment may allow testing them immediately with production workloads, skipping a traditional benchmarking evaluation. In that scenario, benchmarking can still be used to help explain performance differences in more detail, by comparing component performance. For example, the Netflix performance engineering team has automated software for analyzing new instance types with a variety of micro-benchmarks. This includes the automatic collection of system statistics and CPU profiles so that any differences found can be analyzed and explained.

12.1.2 Effective Benchmarking

Benchmarking is surprisingly difficult to do well, with many opportunities for mistakes and oversights. As summarized by the paper "A Nine Year Study of File System and Storage Benchmarking" [Traeger 08]:

> In this article we survey 415 file system and storage benchmarks from 106 recent papers. We found that most popular benchmarks are flawed and many research papers do not provide a clear indication of true performance.

The paper also makes recommendations for what should be done; in particular, benchmark evaluations should explain *what* was tested and *why*, and they should perform some analysis of the system's expected behavior.

The essence of a good benchmark has also been summarized as [Smaalders 06]:

- **Repeatable:** To facilitate comparisons
- **Observable:** So that performance can be analyzed and understood
- **Portable:** To allow benchmarking on competitors and across different product releases
- **Easily presented:** So that everyone can understand the results
- **Realistic:** So that measurements reflect customer-experienced realities
- **Runnable:** So that developers can quickly test changes

Another characteristic must be added when comparing different systems with the intent to purchase: the *price/performance* ratio. The price can be quantified as the five-year capital cost of the equipment [Anon 85].

Effective benchmarking is also about how you apply the benchmark: the analysis and the conclusions drawn.

Benchmark Analysis

When using benchmarks, you need to understand:

- What is being tested

- What the limiting factor or factors are

- Any perturbations that might affect the results

- What conclusions may be drawn from the results

These needs require a deep understanding of what the benchmark software is doing, how the system is responding, and how the results relate to the destination environment.

Given a benchmark tool and access to the system that runs it, these needs are best served by performance analysis of the system while the benchmark is running. A common mistake is to have junior staff execute the benchmarks, then to bring in performance experts to explain the results after the benchmark has completed. It is best to engage the performance experts during the benchmark so they can analyze the system while it is still running. This may include drill-down analysis to explain and quantify the limiting factor(s).

The following is an interesting example of analysis:

> As an experiment to investigate the performance of the resulting TCP/IP implementation, we transmitted 4 Megabytes of data between two user processes on different machines. The transfer was partitioned into 1024 byte records and encapsulated in 1068 byte Ethernet packets. Sending the data from our 11/750 to our 11/780 through TCP/IP takes 28 seconds. This includes all the time needed to set up and tear down the connections, for a user-user throughput of 1.2 Megabaud. During this time the 11/750 is CPU saturated, but the 11/780 has about 30% idle time. The time spent in the system processing the data is spread out among handling for the Ethernet (20%), IP packet processing (10%), TCP processing (30%), checksumming (25%), and user system call handling (15%), with no single part of the handling dominating the time in the system.

This quote describes checking the limiting factors ("the 11/750 is CPU saturated"[2]), then explains details of the kernel components causing them. As an aside, being able to perform this analysis and summarize where kernel CPU time is spent at a high level has only recently become easy with the use of flame graphs. This quote long predates flame graphs: it's from Bill Joy describing the original BSD TCP/IP stack in 1981 [Joy 81]!

Instead of using a given benchmark tool, you may find it more effective to develop your own custom benchmark software, or at least custom load generators. These can be kept short, focusing on only what is needed for your test, making them quick to analyze and debug.

In some cases you don't have access to the benchmark tool or the system, as when reading benchmark results from others. Consider the previous bullet list based on the materials available, and, in addition, ask, What is the system environment? How is it configured? See Section 12.4, Benchmark Questions, for more questions.

---

[2] 11/750 is short for VAX-11/750, a minicomputer manufactured by DEC in 1980.

12.1.3 Benchmarking Failures

The following sections provide a checklist of various benchmarking failures—mistakes, fallacies, and misdeeds—and how to avoid them. Section 12.3, Methodology, describes how to perform benchmarking.

1. Casual Benchmarking

To do benchmarking well is not a fire-and-forget activity. Benchmark tools provide numbers, but those numbers may not reflect what you think they do, and your conclusions about them may therefore be bogus. I summarize it as:

> Casual benchmarking: you benchmark A, but actually measure B, and conclude you've measured C.

Benchmarking well requires rigor to check what is actually measured and an understanding of what was tested in order to form valid conclusions.

For example, many tools claim or imply that they measure disk performance, but actually test file system performance. The difference can be orders of magnitude, as file systems employ caching and buffering to substitute disk I/O with memory I/O. Even though the benchmark tool may be functioning correctly and testing the file system, your conclusions about the disks will be wildly incorrect.

Understanding benchmarks is particularly difficult for the beginner, who has no instinct for whether numbers are suspicious or not. If you bought a thermometer that showed the temperature of the room you're in as 1,000 degrees Fahrenheit (or Celsius), you'd immediately know that something was amiss. The same isn't true of benchmarks, which produce numbers that are probably unfamiliar to you.

2. Blind Faith

It may be tempting to believe that a popular benchmarking tool is trustworthy, especially if it is open source and has been around for a long time. The misconception that popularity equals validity is known as *argumentum ad populum* (Latin for "appeal to the people").

Analyzing the benchmarks you're using is time-consuming and requires expertise to perform properly. And, for a popular benchmark, it may seem wasteful to analyze what *surely* must be valid.

If a popular benchmark was promoted by one of the top companies in technology, would you trust it? This has happened in the past where it was known among veteran performance engineers that the promoted micro-benchmark was flawed and should never have been used. There's no easy way to stop it from happening (I've tried).

The problem isn't even necessarily with the benchmark software—although bugs do happen—but with the interpretation of the benchmark's results.

3. Numbers Without Analysis

Bare benchmark results, provided with no analytical details, can be a sign that the author is inexperienced and has assumed that the benchmark results are trustworthy and final. Often, this is just the beginning of an investigation—an investigation that ultimately finds that the results were wrong or confusing.

Every benchmark number should be accompanied by a description of the limit encountered and the analysis performed. I've summarized the risk this way:

If you've spent less than a week studying a benchmark result, it's probably wrong.

Much of this book focuses on analyzing performance, which should be carried out during benchmarking. In cases where you don't have time for careful analysis, it is a good idea to list the assumptions that you haven't had time to check and to include them with the results, for example:

- Assuming the benchmark tool isn't buggy
- Assuming the disk I/O test actually measures disk I/O
- Assuming the benchmark tool drove disk I/O to its limit, as intended
- Assuming this type of disk I/O is relevant for this application

This can become a to-do list for further verification, if the benchmark result is later deemed important enough to spend more effort on.

4. Complex Benchmark Tools

It is important that the benchmark tool not hinder benchmark analysis by its own complexity. Ideally, the program is open source so that it can be studied, and short enough that it can be read and understood quickly.

For micro-benchmarks, it is recommended to pick those written in the C programming language. For client simulation benchmarks, it is recommended to use the same programming language as the client, to minimize differences.

A common problem is one of *benchmarking the benchmark*—where the result reported is limited by the benchmark software itself. A common cause of this is single-threaded benchmark software. Complex benchmark suites can make analysis difficult due to the volume of code to comprehend and analyze.

5. Testing the Wrong Thing

While there are numerous benchmark tools available to test a variety of workloads, many of them may not be relevant for the target application.

For example, a common mistake is to test disk performance—based on the availability of disk benchmark tools—even though the target environment workload is expected to run entirely out of file system cache and not be affected by disk I/O.

Similarly, an engineering team developing a product may standardize on a particular benchmark and spend all its performance efforts improving performance as measured by that benchmark. If it doesn't actually resemble customer workloads, however, the engineering effort will optimize for the wrong behavior [Smaalders 06].

For an existing production environment, the workload characterization methodology (covered in previous chapters) can measure the makeup of the real workload from device I/O to application requests. These measurements can guide you to choose benchmarks that are most relevant. Without a production environment to analyze, you can set up simulations to analyze, or model the intended workload. Also check with the intended audience of the benchmark data to see if they agree with the tests.

A benchmark may have tested an appropriate workload once upon a time but now hasn't been updated for years and is testing the wrong thing.

6. Ignoring the Environment

Does the production environment match the test environment? Imagine you are tasked with evaluating a new database. You configure a test server and run a database benchmark, only to later learn that you missed an important step: your test server is a default setup with default tunables parameters, default file system, etc. The production database servers are tuned for high disk IOPS, so testing on an untuned system is unrealistic: you missed first understanding the production environment.

7. Ignoring Errors

Just because a benchmark tool produces a result doesn't mean that the result reflects a *successful* test. Some—or even all—of the requests may have resulted in an error. While this issue is covered by the previous mistakes, this one in particular is so common that it's worth singling out.

I was reminded of this during a benchmark of web server performance. Those running the test reported that the average latency of the web server was too high for their needs: over one second, *on average*. One second? Some quick analysis determined what went wrong: the web server did nothing at all during the test, as all requests were blocked by a firewall. *All* requests. The latency shown was the time it took for the benchmark client to time out and error!

8. Ignoring Variance

Benchmark tools, especially micro-benchmarks, often apply a steady and consistent workload, based on the *average* of a series of measurements of real-world characteristics, such as at different times of day or during an interval. For example, a disk workload may be found to have average rates of 500 reads/s and 50 writes/s. A benchmark tool may then either simulate this rate or simulate the ratio of 10:1 reads/writes, so that higher rates can be tested.

This approach ignores *variance*: the rate of operations may be variable. The types of operations may also vary, and some types may occur orthogonally. For example, writes may be applied in bursts every 10 seconds (asynchronous write-back data flushing), whereas synchronous reads are steady. Bursts of writes may cause real issues in production, such as by queueing the reads, but are not simulated if the benchmark applies steady average rates.

One possible solution to simulating variance is the use of a Markov model by the benchmark: this can reflect the probability that a write will be followed by another write.

9. Ignoring Perturbations

Consider what external perturbations may be affecting results. Will a timed system activity, such as a system backup, execute during the benchmark run? Do monitoring agents collect statistics once per minute? For the cloud, a perturbation may be caused by unseen tenants on the same host system.

A common strategy for ironing out perturbations is to make the benchmark runs longer—minutes instead of seconds. As a rule, the duration of a benchmark should not be shorter than one second. Short tests might be unusually perturbed by device interrupts (pinning the thread while performing interrupt service routines), kernel CPU scheduling decisions (waiting before migrating queued threads to preserve CPU affinity), and CPU cache warmth effects. Try running the benchmark test several times and examining the standard deviation—this should be as small as possible.

Also collect data so that perturbations, if present, can be studied. This might include collecting the distribution of operation latency—not just the total runtime for the benchmark—so that outliers can be seen and their details recorded.

10. Changing Multiple Factors

When comparing benchmark results from two tests, be careful to understand all the factors that are different between the two.

For example, if two hosts are benchmarked over the network, is the network between them identical? What if one host was more hops away, over a slower network, or over a more congested network? Any such extra factors could make the benchmark result bogus.

In the cloud, benchmarks are sometimes performed by creating instances, testing them, and then destroying them. This creates the potential for many unseen factors: instances may be created on faster or slower systems, or on systems with higher load and contention from other tenants. I recommend testing multiple instances and take the median (or better, record the distribution) to avoid outliers caused by testing one unusually fast or slow system.

11. Benchmark Paradox

Benchmarks are often used by potential customers to evaluate your product, and they are often so inaccurate that you might as well flip a coin. A salesman once told me he'd be happy with those odds: winning half of his product evaluations would meet his sales targets. But ignoring benchmarks is a benchmarking pitfall, and the odds in practice are much worse. I've summarized it as:

> "If your product's chances of winning a benchmark are 50/50, you'll usually lose."
> [Gregg 14c]

This seeming paradox can be explained by some simple probability.

When buying a product based on performance, customers often want to be really sure it delivers. That can mean not running one benchmark, but several, and wanting the product to win them *all*. If a benchmark has a 50% probability of winning, then:

The probability of winning three benchmarks = 0.5 × 0.5 × 0.5 = 0.125 = 12.5%

The more benchmarks—with the requirement of winning them all—the worse the chances.

12. Benchmarking the Competition

Your marketing department would like benchmark results showing how your product beats the competition. This is far more difficult than it may sound.

When customers pick a product, they don't use it for five minutes; they use it for months. During that time, they analyze and tune the product for performance, perhaps shaking out the worst issues in the first few weeks.

You don't have a few weeks to spend analyzing and tuning your *competitor*. In the time available, you can only gather untuned—and therefore unrealistic—results. The customers of your competitor—the target of this marketing activity—may well see that you've posted untuned results, so your company loses credibility with the very people it was trying to impress.

If you must benchmark the competition, you'll want to spend serious time tuning their product. Analyze performance using the techniques described in earlier chapters. Also search for best practices, customer forums, and bug databases. You may even want to bring in outside expertise to tune the system. Then make the same effort for your own company before you finally perform head-to-head benchmarks.

13. Friendly Fire

When benchmarking your own products, make every effort to ensure that the top-performing system and configuration have been tested, and that the system has been driven to its true limit. Share the results with the engineering team before publication; they may spot configuration items that you have missed. And if you are on the engineering team, be on the lookout for benchmark efforts—either from your company or from contracted third parties—and help them out.

In one case, I saw an engineering team had worked hard to develop a high-performing product. Key to its performance was a new technology that had yet to be documented. For the product launch, a benchmark team had been asked to provide the numbers. They didn't understand the new technology (it wasn't documented), they misconfigured it, and then they published numbers that undersold the product.

Sometimes the system may be configured correctly but simply hasn't been pushed to its limit. Ask the question, What is the bottleneck for this benchmark? This may be a physical resource (such as CPUs, disks, or an interconnect) that has been driven to 100% utilization and can be identified using analysis. See Section 12.3.2, Active Benchmarking.

Another friendly fire issue is when benchmarking older versions of a software that has performance issues that were fixed in later versions, or on limited equipment that happens to be available, producing a result that is not the best possible. Your potential customers may assume any published company benchmark shows the best possible performance—not providing that undersells the product.

14. Misleading Benchmarks

Misleading benchmark results are common in the industry. They may be a result of unintentionally limited information about what the benchmark actually measures, or of deliberately omitted information. Often the benchmark result is technically correct but is then misrepresented to the customer.

Consider this hypothetical situation: A vendor achieves a fantastic result by building a custom product that is prohibitively expensive and would never be sold to an actual customer. The price is not disclosed with the benchmark result, which focuses on non-price/performance metrics. The marketing department liberally shares an ambiguous summary of the result ("We are 2x faster!"), associating it in customers' minds with either the company in general or a product line. This is a case of omitting details in order to favorably misrepresent products. While it may not be cheating—the numbers are not fake—it is *lying by omission*.

Such vendor benchmarks may still be useful for you as upper bounds for performance. They are values that you should not expect to exceed (with an exception for cases of friendly fire).

Consider this different hypothetical situation: A marketing department has a budget to spend on a campaign and wants a good benchmark result to use. They engage several third parties to benchmark their product and pick the best result from the group. These third parties are not picked for their expertise; they are picked to deliver a fast and inexpensive result. In fact, non-expertise might be considered advantageous: the greater the results deviate from reality, the better—ideally, one of them deviates greatly in a positive direction!

When using vendor results, be careful to check the fine print for what system was tested, what disk types were used and how many, what network interfaces were used and in which configuration, and other factors. For specifics to be wary of, see Section 12.4, Benchmark Questions.

15. Benchmark Specials

Benchmark specials is when the vendor studies a popular or industry benchmark, and then engineers the product so that it scores well on that benchmark, while disregarding actual customer performance. This is also called *optimizing for the benchmark*.

The term benchmark specials came into use in 1993 with the TPC-A benchmark, as described on the Transaction Processing Performance Council (TPC) history page [Shanley 98]:

> The Standish Group, a Massachusetts-based consulting firm, charged that Oracle had added a special option (discrete transactions) to its database software, with the sole purpose of inflating Oracle's TPC-A results. The Standish Group claimed that Oracle had "violated the spirit of the TPC" because the discrete transaction option was something a typical customer wouldn't use and was, therefore, a benchmark special. Oracle vehemently rejected the accusation, stating, with some justification, that they had followed the letter of the law in the benchmark specifications. Oracle argued that since benchmark specials, much less the spirit of the TPC, were not addressed in the TPC benchmark specifications, it was unfair to accuse them of violating anything.

TPC added an anti-benchmark special clause:

> All "benchmark special" implementations that improve benchmark results but not
> real-world performance or pricing, are prohibited.

As TPC is focused on price/performance, another strategy to inflate numbers can be to base
them on *special pricing*—deep discounts that no customer would actually get. Like special software changes, the result doesn't match reality when a real customer purchases the system. TPC
has addressed this in its price requirements [TPC 19a]:

> TPC specifications require that the total price must be within 2% of the price a
> customer would pay for the configuration.

While these examples may help explain the notion of benchmark specials, TPC addressed them
in its specifications many years ago, and you shouldn't necessarily expect them today.

16. Cheating

The last failure of benchmarking is cheating: sharing fake results. Fortunately, this is either rare
or nonexistent; I've not seen a case of purely made-up numbers being shared, even in the most
bloodthirsty of benchmarking battles.

12.2   Benchmarking Types

A spectrum of benchmark types is pictured in Figure 12.1, based on the workload they test. The
production workload is also included in the spectrum.

Figure 12.1   Benchmark types

The following sections describe the three benchmarking types: micro-benchmarks, simulations,
and trace/replay. Industry-standard benchmarks are also discussed.

12.2.1   Micro-Benchmarking

Micro-benchmarking uses artificial workloads that test a particular type of operation, for
example, performing a single type of file system I/O, database query, CPU instruction, or system
call. The advantage is the simplicity: narrowing the number of components and code paths
involved results in an easier target to study and allows performance differences to be root-caused
quickly. Tests are also usually repeatable, because variation from other components is factored

out as much as possible. Micro-benchmarks are also usually quick to test on different systems. And because they are deliberately artificial, micro-benchmarks are not easily confused with real workload simulations.

For micro-benchmark results to be consumed, they need to be mapped to the target workload. A micro-benchmark may test several dimensions, but only one or two may be relevant. Performance analysis or modeling of the target system can help determine which micro-benchmark results are appropriate, and to what degree.

Example micro-benchmark tools mentioned in previous chapters include, by resource type:

- **CPU**: SysBench
- **Memory I/O**: lmbench (in Chapter 6, CPUs)
- **File system**: fio
- **Disk**: hdparm, dd or fio with direct I/O
- **Network**: iperf

There are many, many more benchmark tools available. However, remember the warning from [Traeger 08]: "Most popular benchmarks are flawed."

You can also develop your own. Aim to keep them as simple as possible, identifying attributes of the workload that can be tested individually. (See Section 12.3.6, Custom Benchmarks, for more about this.) Use externals tools to verify that they perform the operations they claim to do.

Design Example

Consider designing a file system micro-benchmark to test the following attributes: sequential or random I/O, I/O size, and direction (read or write). Table 12.1 shows five sample tests to investigate these dimensions, along with the reason for each test.

Table 12.1   **Sample file system micro-benchmark tests**

#	Test	Intent
1	sequential 512-byte reads[3]	To test maximum (realistic) IOPS
2	sequential 1-Mbyte reads[4]	To test maximum read throughput
3	sequential 1-Mbyte writes	To test maximum write throughput
4	random 512-byte reads	To test the effect of random I/O
5	random 512-byte writes	To test the effect of rewrites

---

[3] The intent here is to maximize IOPS by using more, smaller I/O. A size of 1 byte sounds better for this purpose, but disks will at least round this up to the sector size (512 bytes or 4 Kbytes).

[4] The intent here is to maximize throughput by using fewer, larger, I/O (less time on I/O initialization). While larger is better, there may be a "sweet spot" due to the file system, kernel allocator, memory pages, and other details. For example, the Solaris kernel performed best with 128 Kbyte I/O, as that was the largest slab cache size (larger I/O moved to the oversize arena, with lower performance).

More tests can be added as desired. All of these tests are multiplied by two additional factors:

- **Working set size**: The size of the data being accessed (e.g., total file size):
  - ☐ Much smaller than main memory: So that the data caches entirely in the file system cache, and the performance of the file system software can be investigated.
  - ☐ Much larger than main memory: To minimize the effect of the file system cache and drive the benchmark toward testing disk I/O.
- **Thread count**: Assuming a small working set size:
  - ☐ Single-threaded: To test file system performance based on the current CPU clock speed.
  - ☐ Multithreaded sufficient to saturate all CPUs: To test the maximum performance of the system, file system, and CPUs.

These can quickly multiply to form a large matrix of tests. Statistical analysis techniques can be used to reduce the required set to test.

Creating benchmarks that focus on top speeds has been called *sunny day* performance testing. So that issues are not overlooked, you also want to consider *cloudy day* or *rainy day* performance testing, which involves testing non-ideal situations, including contention, perturbations, and workload variance.

12.2.2   Simulation

Many benchmarks simulate customer application workloads; these are sometimes called *macro-benchmarks*. They may be based on workload characterization of the production environment (see Chapter 2, Methodologies) to determine the characteristics to simulate. For example, you may find that a production NFS workload is composed of the following operation types and probabilities: reads, 40%; writes, 7%; getattr, 19%; readdir, 1%; and so on. Other characteristics can also be measured and simulated.

Simulations can produce results that resemble how clients will perform with the real-world workload, if not closely, at least closely enough to be useful. They can encompass many factors that would be time-consuming to investigate using micro-benchmarking. Simulations can also include the effects of complex system interactions that may be missed altogether when using micro-benchmarks.

The CPU benchmarks Whetstone and Dhrystone, introduced in Chapter 6, CPUs, are examples of simulations. Whetstone was developed in 1972 to simulate scientific workloads of the time. Dhrystone, from 1984, simulates integer-based workloads of the time.

Many companies simulate client HTTP load using in-house or external load-generating software (example software includes wrk [Glozer 19], siege [Fulmer 12], and hey [Dogan 20]). These can be used to evaluate software or hardware changes, and also to simulate peak load (e.g., "flash sales" on an online shopping platform) to expose bottlenecks that can be analyzed and solved.

A workload simulation may be *stateless*, where each server request is unrelated to the previous request. For example, the NFS server workload described previously may be simulated by requesting a series of operations, with each operation type chosen randomly based on the measured probability.

A simulation may also be *stateful*, where each request is dependent on client state, at minimum the previous request. You may find that NFS reads and writes tend to arrive in groups, such that the probability of a write following a write is much higher than a write following a read. Such a workload can be better simulated using a *Markov model*, by representing requests as states and measuring the probability of state transitions [Jain 91].

A problem with simulations is that they can ignore variance, as described in Section 12.1.3, Benchmarking Failures. Customer usage patterns can also change over time, requiring these simulations to be updated and adjusted to stay relevant. There may be resistance to this, however, if there are already published results based on the older benchmark version, which would no longer be usable for comparisons with the new version.

12.2.3   Replay

A third type of benchmarking involves attempting to replay a trace log to the target, testing its performance with the actual captured client operations. This sounds ideal—as good as testing in production, right? It is, however, problematic: when characteristics and delivered latency change on the server, the captured client workload is unlikely to respond naturally to these differences, which may prove no better than a simulated customer workload. When too much faith is placed in it, things can get worse.

Consider this hypothetical situation: A customer is considering upgrading storage infrastructure. The current production workload is traced and replayed on the new hardware. Unfortunately, performance is worse, and the sale is lost. The problem: the trace/replay operated at the disk I/O level. The old system housed 10 K rpm disks, and the new system houses slower 7,200 rpm disks. However, the new system provides 16 times the amount of file system cache and faster processors. The actual production workload would have shown improved performance, as it would have returned largely from cache—which was not simulated by replaying disk events.

While this is a case of testing the wrong thing, other subtle timing effects can mess things up, even with the correct level of trace/replay. As with all benchmarks, it is crucial to analyze and understand what's going on.

12.2.4   Industry Standards

Industry-standard benchmarks are available from independent organizations, which aim to create fair and relevant benchmarks. These are usually a collection of different micro-benchmarks and workload simulations that are well defined and documented and must be executed under certain guidelines so that the results are as intended. Vendors may participate (usually for a fee) which provides the vendor with the software to execute the benchmark. Their result usually requires full disclosure of the configured environment, which may be audited.

For the customer, these benchmarks can save a lot of time, as benchmark results may already be available for a variety of vendors and products. The task for you, then, is to find the benchmark that most closely resembles your future or current production workload. For current workloads, this may be determined by workload characterization.

The need for industry-standard benchmarks was made clear in a 1985 paper titled "A Measure of Transaction Processing Power" by Jim Gray and others [Anon 85]. It described the need to measure price/performance ratio, and detailed three benchmarks that vendors could execute, called Sort, Scan, and DebitCredit. It also suggested an industry-standard measure of transactions per second (TPS) based on DebitCredit, which could be used much like miles per gallon for cars. Jim Gray and his work later encouraged the creation of the TPC [DeWitt 08].

Apart from the TPS measure, others that have been used for the same role include:

- **MIPS:** Millions of instructions per second. While this is *a* measure of performance, the work that is performed depends on the type of instruction, which may be difficult to compare between different processor architectures.

- **FLOPS:** Floating-point operations per second—a similar role to MIPS, but for workloads that make heavy use of floating-point calculations.

Industry benchmarks typically measure a custom metric based on the benchmark, which serves only for comparisons with itself.

TPC

The Transaction Processing Performance Council (TPC) creates and administers industry benchmarks with a focus on database performance. These include:

- **TPC-C:** A simulation of a complete computing environment where a population of users executes transactions against a database.

- **TPC-DS:** A simulation of a decision support system, including queries and data maintenance.

- **TPC-E:** An online transaction processing (OLTP) workload, modeling a brokerage firm database with customers who generate transactions related to trades, account inquiries, and market research.

- **TPC-H:** A decision support benchmark, simulating ad hoc queries and concurrent data modifications.

- **TPC-VMS:** The TPC Virtual Measurement Single System allows other benchmarks to be gathered for virtualized databases.

- **TPCx-HS:** A big data benchmark using Hadoop.

- **TPCx-V:** Tests database workloads in virtual machines.

TPC results are shared online [TPC 19b] and include price/performance.

SPEC

The Standard Performance Evaluation Corporation (SPEC) develops and publishes a standardized set of industry benchmarks, including:

- **SPEC Cloud IaaS 2018:** This tests provisioning, compute, storage, and network resources, using multiple multi-instance workloads.

- **SPEC CPU 2017**: A measure of compute-intensive workloads, including integer and floating point performance, and an optional metric for energy consumption.

- **SPECjEnterprise 2018 Web Profile**: A measure of full-system performance for Java Enterprise Edition (Java EE) Web Profile version 7 or later application servers, databases, and supporting infrastructure.

- **SPECsfs2014**: A simulation of a client file access workload for NFS servers, common internet file system (CIFS) servers, and similar file systems.

- **SPECvirt_sc2013**: For virtualized environments, this measures the end-to-end performance of the virtualized hardware, the platform, and the guest operating system and application software.

SPEC's results are shared online [SPEC 20] and include details of how systems were tuned and a list of components, but not usually their price.

12.3   Methodology

This section describes methodologies and exercises for performing benchmarking, whether it be micro-benchmarking, simulations, or replays. The topics are summarized in Table 12.2.

Table 12.2   **Benchmark analysis methodologies**

Section	Methodology	Types
12.3.1	Passive benchmarking	Experimental analysis
12.3.2	Active benchmarking	Observational analysis
12.3.3	CPU profiling	Observational analysis
12.3.4	USE method	Observational analysis
12.3.5	Workload characterization	Observational analysis
12.3.6	Custom benchmarks	Software development
12.3.7	Ramping load	Experimental analysis
12.3.8	Sanity check	Observational analysis
12.3.9	Statistical analysis	Statistical analysis

12.3.1   Passive Benchmarking

This is the fire-and-forget strategy of benchmarking—where the benchmark is executed and then ignored until it has completed. The main objective is the collection of benchmark data. This is how benchmarks are commonly executed, and is described as its own anti-methodology for comparison with active benchmarking.

These are some example passive benchmarking steps:

1. Pick a benchmark tool.

2. Run it with a variety of options.

3. Make a slide deck of the results.

4. Hand the slides to management.

Problems with this approach have been discussed previously. In summary, the results may be:

- Invalid due to benchmark software bugs

- Limited by the benchmark software (e.g., single-threaded)

- Limited by a component that is unrelated to the benchmark target (e.g., a congested network)

- Limited by configuration (performance features not enabled, not a maximum configuration)

- Subject to perturbations (and not repeatable)

- Benchmarking the wrong thing entirely

Passive benchmarking is easy to perform but prone to errors. When performed by the vendor, it can create false alarms that waste engineering resources or cause lost sales. When performed by the customer, it can result in poor product choices that haunt the company later on.

12.3.2 Active Benchmarking

With active benchmarking, you analyze performance while the benchmark is running—not just after it's done—using observability tools [Gregg 14d]. You can confirm that the benchmark tests what it says it tests, and that you understand what that is. Active benchmarking can also identify the true limiters of the system under test, or of the benchmark itself. It can be very helpful to include specific details of the limit encountered when sharing the benchmark results.

As a bonus, this can be a good time to develop your skills with performance observability tools. In theory, you are examining a *known load* and can see how it appears from these tools.

Ideally, the benchmark can be configured and left running in steady state, so that analysis can be performed over a period of hours or days.

Analysis Case Study

As an example, let's look at the first test of the bonnie++ micro-benchmark tool. It is described by its man page as (emphasis mine):

```
NAME
        bonnie++ - program to test hard drive performance.
```

And on its home page [Coker 01]:

Bonnie++ is a benchmark suite that is aimed at performing a number of simple tests of hard drive and file system performance.

Running bonnie++ on Ubuntu Linux:

```
# bonnie++
[...]
Version  1.97       ------Sequential Output------ --Sequential Input- --Random-
Concurrency   1       -Per Chr- --Block-- -Rewrite- -Per Chr- --Block-- --Seeks--
Machine        Size K/sec %CP K/sec %CP K/sec %CP K/sec %CP K/sec %CP  /sec %CP
ip-10-1-239-21  4G    739  99 549247  46 308024  37 1845  99 1156838  38 +++++ +++
Latency            18699us       983ms      280ms      11065us     4505us      7762us
[...]
```

The first test is "Sequential Output" and "Per Chr", and scored 739 Kbytes/sec according to bonnie++.

Sanity check: if this really was I/O per character, it would mean the system was achieving 739,000 I/O per second. The benchmark is described as testing hard drive performance, but I doubt this system can achieve that many disk IOPS.

While running the first test, I used iostat(1) to check disk IOPS:

```
$ iostat -sxz 1
[...]
avg-cpu:  %user  %nice %system %iowait  %steal  %idle
          11.44   0.00   38.81    0.00    0.00   49.75

Device             tps     kB/s    rqm/s   await aqu-sz  areq-sz  %util

[...]
```

No disk I/O was reported.

Now using bpftrace to count block I/O events (see Chapter 9, Disks, Section 9.6.11, bpftrace):

```
# bpftrace -e 'tracepoint:block:* { @[probe] = count(); }'
Attaching 18 probes...
^C

@[tracepoint:block:block_dirty_buffer]: 808225
@[tracepoint:block:block_touch_buffer]: 1025678
```

This also shows that no block I/O was issued (no block:block_rq_issue) or completed (block:-block_rq_complete); however, buffers were dirtied. Using cachestat(8) (Chapter 8, File Systems, Section 8.6.12, cachestat) to see the state of the file system cache:

```
# cachestat 1
   HITS   MISSES  DIRTIES HITRATIO  BUFFERS_MB  CACHED_MB
      0        0        0   0.00%          49        361
```

```
     293        0    54299  100.00%           49        361
     658        0   298748  100.00%           49        361
     250        0   602499  100.00%           49        362
[...]
```

bonnie++ began execution on the second line of output, and this confirms a workload of "dirt-ies": writes to the file system cache.

Checking I/O higher up in the I/O stack, at the VFS level (see Chapter 8, File Systems, Section 8.6.15, bpftrace):

```
# bpftrace -e 'kprobe:vfs_* /comm == "bonnie++"/ { @[probe] = count(); }'
Attaching 65 probes...
^C

@[kprobe:vfs_fsync_range]: 2
@[kprobe:vfs_statx_fd]: 6
@[kprobe:vfs_open]: 7
@[kprobe:vfs_read]: 13
@[kprobe:vfs_write]: 1176936
```

This shows that there was indeed a heavy vfs_write() workload. Further drilling down with bpftrace verifies the size:

```
# bpftrace -e 'k:vfs_write /comm == "bonnie++"/ { @bytes = hist(arg2); }'
Attaching 1 probe...
^C

@bytes:
[1]                668839 |@@@@@@@@@@@@@@@@@@@@@@@@@@@@@@@@@@@@@@@@@@@@@@@@@@@@|
[2, 4)                  0 |                                                  |
[4, 8)                  0 |                                                  |
[8, 16)                 0 |                                                  |
[16, 32)                1 |                                                  |
```

The third argument to vfs_write() is the byte count, and it is usually 1 byte (the single write in the 16 to 31 byte range is likely a bonnie++ message about beginning the benchmark).

By analyzing the benchmark while it is running (active benchmarking), we've learned that the first bonnie++ test is a 1-byte file system write, which buffers in the file system cache. It does not test disk I/O, as is implied by the descriptions of bonnie++.

According to the man page, bonnie++ has a –b option for "no write buffering," calling fsync(2) after every write. I'll use strace(1) to analyze this behavior, as strace(1) prints all syscalls in human-readable ways. strace(1) also costs high overhead, so the benchmark results while using strace(1) should be discarded.

```
$ strace bonnie++ -b
[...]
write(3, "6", 1)                    = 1
write(3, "7", 1)                    = 1
write(3, "8", 1)                    = 1
write(3, "9", 1)                    = 1
write(3, ":", 1)                    = 1
[...]
```

The output shows that bonnie++ is not calling fsync(2) after every write. It also has a -D option for direct IO, however, that fails on my system. There's no way to actually do a per-character disk write test.

Some people may argue that bonnie++ isn't broken, and it does really do a "Sequential Output" and "Per Chr" test: neither of those terms promised disk I/O. For a benchmark that claims to test "hard drive" performance, this is, at least, misleading.

Bonnie++ is not an unusually bad benchmark tool; it has served people well on many occasions. I picked it for this example (and also chose the most suspicious of its tests to study) because it's well known, I've studied it before, and findings like this are not uncommon. But it is just one example.

Older versions of bonnie++ had an additional problem with this test: it allowed libc to buffer writes before they were sent to the file system, so the VFS write size was 4 Kbytes or higher, depending on the libc and OS version.[5] This made it misleading to compare bonnie++ results between different operating systems that used different libc buffering sizes. This problem was fixed in recent versions of bonnie++, but that creates another problem: new results from bonnie++ cannot be compared with old results.

For more about Bonnie++ performance analysis, see the article by Roch Bourbonnais on "Decoding Bonnie++" [Bourbonnais 08].

12.3.3 CPU Profiling

CPU profiling of both the benchmark target and the benchmark software is worth singling out as a methodology, because it can lead to some quick discoveries. It is often performed as part of an active benchmarking investigation.

The intent is to quickly check what all the software is doing, to see if anything interesting shows up. This can also narrow your study to the software components that matter the most: those in play for the benchmark.

Both user- and kernel-level stacks can be profiled. User-level CPU profiling was introduced in Chapter 5, Applications. Both were covered in Chapter 6, CPUs, with examples in Section 6.6, Observability Tools, including flame graphs.

---

[5] In case you were wondering, the libc buffer size can be tuned using setbuffer(3), and was in use due to bonnie++ using libc putc(3).

Example

A disk micro-benchmark was performed on a proposed new system with some disappointing results: disk throughput was worse than on the old system. I was asked to find out what was wrong, with the expectation that either the disks or the disk controller was inferior and should be upgraded.

I began with the USE method (Chapter 2, Methodologies) and found that the disks were not very busy. There was some CPU usage, in system-time (the kernel).

For a disk benchmark, you might not expect the CPUs to be an interesting target for analysis. Given some CPU usage in the kernel, I thought it was worth a quick check to see if anything interesting showed up, even though I didn't expect it to. I profiled and generated the flame graph shown in Figure 12.2.

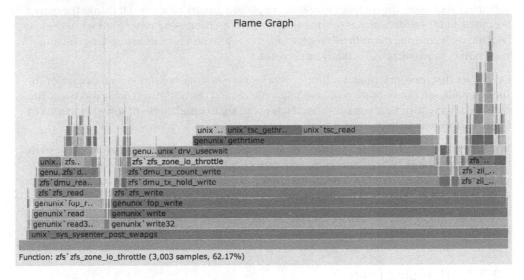

Figure 12.2   Flame graph profiling of kernel-time

Browsing the stack frames showed that 62.17% of CPU samples included a function called zfs_zone_io_throttle(). I didn't need to read the code for this function, as its name was enough of a clue: a resource control, ZFS I/O throttling, was active and *artificially* throttling the benchmark! This was a default setting on the new system (but not the older system) that had been overlooked when the benchmark was performed.

12.3.4 USE Method

The USE method was introduced in Chapter 2, Methodologies, and is described in chapters for the resources it studies. Applying the USE method during benchmarking can ensure that a limit is found. Either some component (hardware or software) has reached 100% utilization, or you are not driving the system to its limit.

12.3.5   Workload Characterization

Workload characterization was also introduced in Chapter 2, Methodologies, and discussed in later chapters. This methodology can be used to determine how well a given benchmark relates to a current production environment by characterizing the production workload for comparison.

12.3.6   Custom Benchmarks

For simple benchmarks, it may be desirable to code the software yourself. Try to keep the program as short as possible, to avoid complexity that hinders analysis.

The C programming language is usually a good choice for micro-benchmarks, as it maps closely to what is executed—although you should think carefully about how compiler optimizations will affect your code: the compiler may elide simple benchmark routines if it thinks the output is unused and therefore unnecessary to calculate. Always check using other tools while the benchmark is running to confirm its operation. It may also be worth disassembling the compiled binary to see what will actually be executed.

Languages that involve virtual machines, asynchronous garbage collection, and dynamic runtime compilation can be much more difficult to debug and control with reliable precision. You may need to use such languages anyway, if it is necessary to simulate client software written in them: macro-benchmarks.

Writing custom benchmarks can also reveal subtle details about the target that can prove useful later on. For example, when developing a database benchmark, you may discover that the API supports various options for improving performance that are not currently in use in the production environment, which was developed before the options existed.

Your software may simply generate load (a *load generator*) and leave the measurements for other tools. One way to perform this is to *ramp load*.

12.3.7   Ramping Load

This is a simple method for determining the maximum throughput a system can handle. It involves adding load in small increments and measuring the delivered throughput until a limit is reached. The results can be graphed, showing a scalability profile. This profile can be studied visually or by using scalability models (see Chapter 2, Methodologies).

As an example, Figure 12.3 shows how a file system and server scale with threads. Each thread performs 8 Kbyte random reads on a cached file, and these were added one by one.

This system peaked at almost half a million reads per second. The results were checked using VFS-level statistics, which confirmed that the I/O size was 8 Kbytes and that at peak over 3.5 Gbytes/s were transferred.

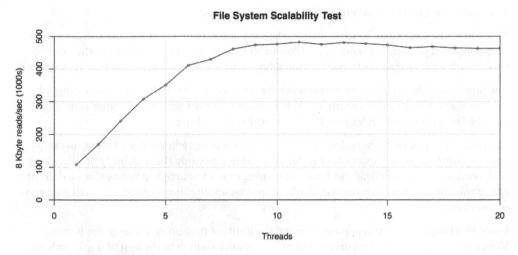

Figure 12.3 Ramping file system load

The load generator for this test was written in Perl and is short enough to include entirely as an example:

```
#!/usr/bin/perl -w
#
# randread.pl - randomly read over specified file.

use strict;

my $IOSIZE = 8192;                    # size of I/O, bytes
my $QUANTA = $IOSIZE;                 # seek granularity, bytes

die "USAGE: randread.pl filename\n" if @ARGV != 1 or not -e $ARGV[0];

my $file = $ARGV[0];
my $span = -s $file;                  # span to randomly read, bytes
my $junk;

open FILE, "$file" or die "ERROR: reading $file: $!\n";

while (1) {
        seek(FILE, int(rand($span / $QUANTA)) * $QUANTA, 0);
        sysread(FILE, $junk, $IOSIZE);
}

close FILE;
```

To avoid buffering, this uses sysread() to call the read(2) syscall directly.

This was written to micro-benchmark an NFS server and was executed in parallel from a farm of clients, each performing random reads on an NFS-mounted file. The results of the micro-benchmark (reads per second) were measured on the NFS server, using nfsstat(8) and other tools.

The number of files used and their combined size were controlled (this forms the *working set size*), so that some tests could return entirely from cache on the server, and others from disk. (See the Design Example in Section 12.2.1, Micro-Benchmarking.)

The number of instances executing on the client farm was incremented one by one, to ramp up the load until a limit was reached. This was also graphed to study the scalability profile, along with resource utilization (USE method), confirming that a resource had been exhausted. In this case it was CPU resources on the server, which spurred another investigation to further improve performance.

I used this program and this approach to find the limits of the Sun ZFS Storage Appliance [Gregg 09b]. These limits were used as the official results—which to the best of our knowledge set world records. I also had a similar set of software written in C, which I normally use, but it wasn't needed in this case: I had an abundance of client CPUs, and while the switch to C reduced their utilization, it didn't make a difference for the result as the same bottleneck was reached on the target. Other, more sophisticated benchmarks were also tried, as well as other languages, but they could not improve upon these Perl-based results.

When following this approach, measure latency as well as the throughput, especially the latency distribution. Once the system approaches its limit, queueing delays may become significant, causing latency to increase. If you push load too high, latency may become so high that it is no longer reasonable to consider the result as valid. Ask yourself if the delivered latency would be acceptable to a customer.

For example: You use a large array of clients to drive a target system to 990,000 IOPS, which responds with an average I/O latency of 5 ms. You'd really like it to break 1 million IOPS, but the system is already reaching saturation. By adding more and more clients, you manage to scrape past 1 million IOPS; however, all operations are now heavily queued, with average latency of over 50 ms, which is not acceptable! Which result do you give marketing? (Answer: 990,000 IOPS.)

12.3.8 Sanity Check

This is an exercise for checking a benchmark result by investigating whether any characteristic doesn't make sense. It includes checking whether the result would have required some component to exceed its known limits, such as network bandwidth, controller bandwidth, interconnect bandwidth, or disk IOPS. If any limit has been exceeded, it is worth investigating in more detail. In most cases, this exercise ultimately discovers that the benchmark result is bogus.

Here's an example: An NFS server is benchmarked with 8 Kbyte reads and is reported to deliver 50,000 IOPS. It is connected to the network using a single 1 Gbit/s Ethernet port. The network throughput required to drive 50,000 IOPS × 8 Kbytes = 400,000 Kbytes/s, plus protocol headers. This is over 3.2 Gbits/s—well in excess of the 1 Gbit/s known limit. Something is wrong!

Results like this usually mean the benchmark has tested *client caching* and not driven the entire workload to the NFS server.

I've used this calculation to identify numerous bogus benchmarks, which have included the following throughputs over a single 1 Gbit/s interface [Gregg 09c]:

- 120 Mbytes/s (0.96 Gbit/s)
- 200 Mbytes/s (1.6 Gbit/s)
- 350 Mbytes/s (2.8 Gbit/s)
- 800 Mbytes/s (6.4 Gbit/s)
- 1.15 Gbytes/s (9.2 Gbit/s)

These are all throughputs in a single direction. The 120 Mbyte/s result may be fine—a 1 Gbit/s interface should reach around 119 Mbyte/s, in practice. The 200 Mbyte/s result is possible only if there was heavy traffic in both directions and this was summed; however, these are single-direction results. The 350 Mbyte/s and beyond results are clearly bogus.

When you're given a benchmark result to check, look for any simple sums you can perform on the provided numbers to discover such limits.

If you have access to the system, it may be possible to further test results by constructing new observations or experiments. This can follow the scientific method: the question you're testing now is whether the benchmark result is valid. From this, hypotheses and predictions may be drawn and then tested for verification.

12.3.9   Statistical Analysis

Statistical analysis can be used to study benchmark data. It follows three phases:

1. **Selection** of the benchmark tool, its configuration, and system performance metrics to capture
2. **Execution** of the benchmark, collecting a large dataset of results and metrics
3. **Interpretation** of the data with statistical analysis, producing a report

Unlike active benchmarking, which focuses on analysis of the system while the benchmark is running, statistical analysis focuses on analyzing the results. It is also different from passive benchmarking, in which no analysis is performed at all.

This approach is used in environments where access to a large-scale system may be both time-limited and expensive. For example, there may be only one "max config" system available, but many teams want access to run tests at the same time, including:

- **Sales:** During proofs of concept, to run a simulated customer load to show what the max config system can deliver
- **Marketing:** To get the best numbers for a marketing campaign
- **Support:** To investigate pathologies that arise only on the max config system, under serious load
- **Engineering:** To test the performance of new features and code changes
- **Quality:** To perform non-regression testing and certifications

Each team may have only a limited time to run its benchmarks on the system, but much more time to analyze the results afterward.

As the collection of metrics is expensive, make an extra effort to ensure that they are reliable and trustworthy, to avoid having to redo them later if a problem is found. Apart from checking how they are generated technically, you can also collect more statistical properties so that problems can be found sooner. These may include statistics for variation, full distributions, error margins, and others (see Chapter 2, Methodologies, Section 2.8, Statistics). When benchmarking for code changes or non-regression testing, it is crucial to understand the variation and error margins, in order to make sense of a pair of results.

Also collect as much performance data as possible from the running system (without harming the result due to the collection overhead) so that forensic analysis can be performed afterward on this data. Data collection may include the use of tools such as sar(1), monitoring products, and custom tools that dump all statistics available.

For example, on Linux, a custom shell script may copy the contents of the /proc counter files before and after the run.[6] Everything possible can be included, in case it is needed. Such a script may also be executed at intervals during the benchmark, provided the performance overhead is acceptable. Other statistical tools may also be used to create logs.

Statistical analysis of results and metrics can include *scalability analysis* and *queueing theory* to model the system as a network of queues. These topics were introduced in Chapter 2, Methodologies, and are the subject of separate texts [Jain 91][Gunther 97][Gunther 07].

12.3.10   Benchmarking Checklist

Inspired by the Performance Mantras checklist (Chapter 2, Methodologies, Section 2.5.20, Performance Mantras) I have created a benchmarking checklist of questions whose answers you can seek from a benchmark to verify its accuracy [Gregg 18d]:

- Why not double?
- Did it break limits?
- Did it error?
- Does it reproduce?
- Does it matter?
- Did it even happen?

In more detail:

- **Why not double?** Why was the operation rate not double the benchmark result? This is really asking what the limiter is. Answering this can solve many benchmarking problems, when you discover that the limiter is not the intended target of the test.

- **Did it break limits?** This is a sanity check (Section 12.3.8, Sanity Check).

---

[6]Do not use tar(1) for this purpose, as it becomes confused by the zero-sized /proc files (according to stat(2)) and does not read their contents.

- **Did it error?** Errors perform differently than normal operations, and a high error rate will skew the benchmark results.

- **Does it reproduce?** How consistent are the results?

- **Does it matter?** The workload that a particular benchmark tests may not be relevant to your production needs. Some micro-benchmarks test individual syscalls and library calls, but your application may not even be using them.

- **Did it even happen?** The earlier Ignoring Errors heading in Section 12.1.3, Benchmarking Failures, described a case where a firewall blocked a benchmark from reaching the target, and reported timeout-based latency as its result.

The next section includes a much longer list of questions, which also works for scenarios where you may not have access to the target system to analyze the benchmark yourself.

12.4   Benchmark Questions

If a vendor gives you a benchmark result, there are a number of questions you can ask to better understand and apply it to your environment, even if you do not have access to the running benchmark to analyze it. The goal is to determine what is really being measured and how realistic or repeatable the result is.

- In **general**:
  - Does the benchmark relate to my production workload?
  - What was the configuration of the system under test?
  - Was a single system tested, or is this the result of a cluster of systems?
  - What is the cost of the system under test?
  - What was the configuration of the benchmark clients?
  - What was the duration of the test? How many results were collected?
  - Is the result an average or a peak? What is the average?
  - What are other distribution details (standard deviation, percentiles, or full distribution details)?
  - What was the limiting factor of the benchmark?
  - What was the operation success/fail ratio?
  - What were the operation attributes?
  - Were the operation attributes chosen to simulate a workload? How were they selected?
  - Does the benchmark simulate variance, or an average workload?
  - Was the benchmark result confirmed using other analysis tools? (Provide screenshots.)
  - Can an error margin be expressed with the benchmark result?
  - Is the benchmark result reproducible?

- For **CPU/memory**-related benchmarks:
  - What processors were used?
  - Were processors overclocked? Was custom cooling used (e.g., water cooling)?

▫ How many memory modules (e.g., DIMMs) were used? How are they attached to sockets?

▫ Were any CPUs disabled?

▫ What was the system-wide CPU utilization? (Lightly loaded systems can perform faster due to higher levels of turbo boosting.)

▫ Were the tested CPUs cores or hyperthreads?

▫ How much main memory was installed? Of what type?

▫ Were any custom BIOS settings used?

- For **storage**-related benchmarks:

  ▫ What is the storage device configuration (how many were used, their type, storage protocol, RAID configuration, cache size, write-back or write-through, etc.)?

  ▫ What is the file system configuration (what types, how many were used, their configuration such as the use of journaling, and their tuning)?

  ▫ What is the working set size?

  ▫ To what degree did the working set cache? Where did it cache?

  ▫ How many files were accessed?

- For **network**-related benchmarks:

  ▫ What was the network configuration (how many interfaces were used, their type and configuration)?

  ▫ What was the network topology?

  ▫ What protocols were used? Socket options?

  ▫ What network stack settings were tuned? TCP/UDP tunables?

When studying industry benchmarks, many of these questions may be answered from the disclosure details.

12.5   Exercises

1. Answer the following conceptual questions:

   - What is a micro-benchmark?

   - What is working set size, and how might it affect the results of storage benchmarks?

   - What is the reason for studying the price/performance ratio?

2. Choose a micro-benchmark and perform the following tasks:

   - Scale a dimension (threads, I/O size...) and measure performance.

   - Graph the results (scalability).

   - Use the micro-benchmark to drive the target to peak performance, and analyze the limiting factor.

12.6 References

[Joy 81] Joy, W., "tcp-ip digest contribution," http://www.rfc-editor.org/rfc/museum/tcp-ip-digest/tcp-ip-digest.v1n6.1, 1981.

[Anon 85] Anon et al., "A Measure of Transaction Processing Power," *Datamation*, April 1, 1985.

[Jain 91] Jain, R., *The Art of Computer Systems Performance Analysis: Techniques for Experimental Design, Measurement, Simulation, and Modeling*, Wiley, 1991.

[Gunther 97] Gunther, N., *The Practical Performance Analyst*, McGraw-Hill, 1997.

[Shanley 98] Shanley, K., "History and Overview of the TPC," http://www.tpc.org/information/about/history.asp, 1998.

[Coker 01] Coker, R., "bonnie++," https://www.coker.com.au/bonnie++, 2001.

[Smaalders 06] Smaalders, B., "Performance Anti-Patterns," *ACM Queue* 4, no. 1, February 2006.

[Gunther 07] Gunther, N., *Guerrilla Capacity Planning*, Springer, 2007.

[Bourbonnais 08] Bourbonnais, R., "Decoding Bonnie++," https://blogs.oracle.com/roch/entry/decoding_bonnie, 2008.

[DeWitt 08] DeWitt, D., and Levine, C., "Not Just Correct, but Correct and Fast," *SIGMOD Record*, 2008.

[Traeger 08] Traeger, A., Zadok, E., Joukov, N., and Wright, C., "A Nine Year Study of File System and Storage Benchmarking," *ACM Transactions on Storage*, 2008.

[Gregg 09b] Gregg, B., "Performance Testing the 7000 series, Part 3 of 3," http://www.brendangregg.com/blog/2009-05-26/performance-testing-the-7000-series3.html, 2009.

[Gregg 09c] Gregg, B., and Straughan, D., "Brendan Gregg at FROSUG, Oct 2009," http://www.beginningwithi.com/2009/11/11/brendan-gregg-at-frosug-oct-2009, 2009.

[Fulmer 12] Fulmer, J., "Siege Home," https://www.joedog.org/siege-home, 2012.

[Gregg 14c] Gregg, B., "The Benchmark Paradox," http://www.brendangregg.com/blog/2014-05-03/the-benchmark-paradox.html, 2014.

[Gregg 14d] Gregg, B., "Active Benchmarking," http://www.brendangregg.com/activebenchmarking.html, 2014.

[Gregg 18d] Gregg, B., "Evaluating the Evaluation: A Benchmarking Checklist," http://www.brendangregg.com/blog/2018-06-30/benchmarking-checklist.html, 2018.

[Glozer 19] Glozer, W., "Modern HTTP Benchmarking Tool," https://github.com/wg/wrk, 2019.

[TPC 19a] "Third Party Pricing Guideline," http://www.tpc.org/information/other/pricing_guidelines.asp, 2019.

[TPC 19b] "TPC," http://www.tpc.org, 2019.

[**Dogan 20**] Dogan, J., "HTTP load generator, ApacheBench (ab) replacement, formerly known as rakyll/boom," https://github.com/rakyll/hey, last updated 2020.

[**SPEC 20**] "Standard Performance Evaluation Corporation," https://www.spec.org, accessed 2020.

Chapter 13

perf

perf(1) is the official Linux profiler and is in the Linux kernel source under tools/perf.[1] It is a multi-tool that has profiling, tracing, and scripting capabilities, and is the front-end to the kernel perf_events observability subsystem. perf_events is also known as Performance Counters for Linux (PCL) or Linux Performance Events (LPE). perf_events and the perf(1) front-end began with performance monitoring counter (PMC) capabilities, but have since grown to support event-based tracing sources as well: tracepoints, kprobes, uprobes, and USDT.

This chapter, along with Chapter 14, Ftrace, and Chapter 15, BPF, are optional reading for those who wish to learn one or more system tracers in more detail.

Compared with other tracers, perf(1) is especially suited for CPU analysis: profiling (sampling) CPU stack traces, tracing CPU scheduler behavior, and examining PMCs to understand micro-architectural level CPU performance including cycle behavior. Its tracing capabilities allow it to analyze other targets as well, including disk I/O and software functions.

perf(1) can be used to answer questions such as:

- Which code paths are consuming CPU resources?
- Are the CPUs stalled on memory loads/stores?
- For what reasons are threads leaving the CPU?
- What is the pattern of disk I/O?

The following sections are structured to introduce perf(1), show event sources, and then show the subcommands that use them. The sections are:

- 13.1: Subcommands Overview
- 13.2: Example One-Liners
- Events:
  - 13.3: Events Overview
  - 13.4: Hardware Events

---

[1] perf(1) is unusual in that it is a large, complex user-level program that is in the Linux kernel source tree. Maintainer Arnaldo Carvalho de Melo described this situation to me as an "experiment." While this has been beneficial to perf(1) and Linux as they have been developed in lockstep, some are uncomfortable with its inclusion, and it may remain the only complex user software ever to be included in the Linux source.

Prior chapters show how to use perf(1) for the analysis of specific targets. This chapter focuses on perf(1) itself.

13.1   Subcommands Overview

perf(1)'s capabilities are invoked via subcommands. As a common usage example, the following uses two subcommands: record to instrument events and save them to a file, and then report to summarize the contents of the file. These subcommands are explained in Section 13.9, perf record, and Section 13.10, perf report.

```
# perf record -F 99 -a -- sleep 30
[ perf record: Woken up 193 times to write data ]
[ perf record: Captured and wrote 48.916 MB perf.data (11880 samples) ]
# perf report --stdio
[...]
# Overhead   Command         Shared Object           Symbol
# ........   .............   .....................   ...........................
#
    21.10%   swapper         [kernel.vmlinux]        [k] native_safe_halt
     6.39%   mysqld          [kernel.vmlinux]        [k] _raw_spin_unlock_irqrest
     4.66%   mysqld          mysqld                  [.] _Z8ut_delaym
     2.64%   mysqld          [kernel.vmlinux]        [k] finish_task_switch
[...]
```

This particular example sampled any program running on any CPU at 99 Hertz for 30 seconds, and then showed the most frequently sampled functions.

Selected subcommands from a recent perf(1) version (from Linux 5.6) are listed in Table 13.1.

Table 13.1 **Selected perf subcommands**

Section	Command	Description
-	`annotate`	Read perf.data (created by perf record) and display annotated code.
-	`archive`	Create a portable perf.data file containing debug and symbol info.
-	`bench`	System microbenchmarks.
-	`buildid-cache`	Manage build-id cache (used by USDT probes).
-	`c2c`	Cache line analysis tools.
-	`diff`	Read two perf.data files and display the differential profile.
-	`evlist`	List the event names in a perf.data file.
14.12	`ftrace`	A perf(1) interface to the Ftrace tracer.
-	`inject`	Filter to augment the events stream with additional information.
-	`kmem`	Trace/measure kernel memory (slab) properties.
11.3.3	`kvm`	Trace/measure kvm guest instances.
13.3	`list`	List event types.
-	`lock`	Analyze lock events.
-	`mem`	Profile memory access.
13.7	`probe`	Define new dynamic tracepoints.
13.9	`record`	Run a command and record its profile into perf.data.
13.10	`report`	Read perf.data (created by `perf record`) and display the profile.
6.6.13	`sched`	Trace/measure scheduler properties (latencies).
5.5.1	`script`	Read perf.data (created by `perf record`) and display trace output.
13.8	`stat`	Run a command and gather performance counter statistics.
-	`timechart`	Visualize total system behavior during a workload.
-	`top`	System profiling tool with real-time screen updates.
13.12	`trace`	A live tracer (system calls by default).

Figure 13.1 shows commonly used perf subcommands with their data sources and types of output.

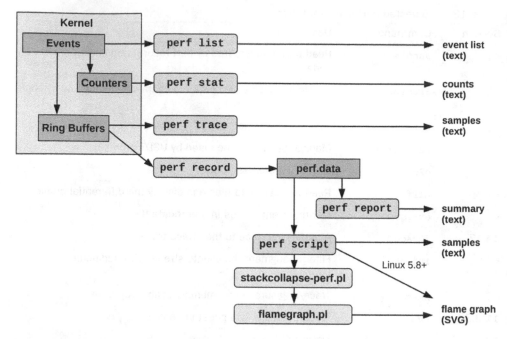

Figure 13.1   Commonly used perf subcommands

Many of these and other subcommands are explained in the following sections. Some subcommands were covered in prior chapters, as shown in Table 13.1.

Future versions of perf(1) may add more capabilities: run `perf` with no arguments for the full list of subcommands for your system.

13.2   One-Liners

The following one-liners show various perf(1) capabilities by example. These are from a larger list that I have published online [Gregg 20h], which has proven to be an effective way to explain perf(1) capabilities. The syntax of these is covered in later sections and in the man pages for perf(1).

Note that many of these one-liners use `-a` to specify all CPUs, but this became the default in Linux 4.11 and can be elided in that and later kernels.

Listing Events

List all currently known events:

```
perf list
```

List sched tracepoints:

```
perf list 'sched:*'
```

List events with names containing the string "block":

```
perf list block
```

List currently available dynamic probes:

```
perf probe -l
```

Counting Events

Show PMC statistics for the specified command:

```
perf stat command
```

Show PMC statistics for the specified PID, until Ctrl-C:

```
perf stat -p PID
```

Show PMC statistics for the entire system, for 5 seconds:

```
perf stat -a sleep 5
```

Show CPU last level cache (LLC) statistics for the command:

```
perf stat -e LLC-loads,LLC-load-misses,LLC-stores,LLC-prefetches command
```

Count unhalted core cycles using a raw PMC specification (Intel):

```
perf stat -e r003c -a sleep 5
```

Count front-end stalls using a verbose PMC raw specification (Intel):

```
perf stat -e cpu/event=0x0e,umask=0x01,inv,cmask=0x01/ -a sleep 5
```

Count syscalls per second system-wide:

```
perf stat -e raw_syscalls:sys_enter -I 1000 -a
```

Count system calls by type for the specified PID:

```
perf stat -e 'syscalls:sys_enter_*' -p PID
```

Count block device I/O events for the entire system, for 10 seconds:

```
perf stat -e 'block:*' -a sleep 10
```

Profiling

Sample on-CPU functions for the specified command, at 99 Hertz:

```
perf record -F 99 command
```

Sample CPU stack traces (via frame pointers) system-wide for 10 seconds:

```
perf record -F 99 -a -g sleep 10
```

Sample CPU stack traces for the PID, using dwarf (debuginfo) to unwind stacks:

```
perf record -F 99 -p PID --call-graph dwarf sleep 10
```

Sample CPU stack traces for a container by its /sys/fs/cgroup/perf_event cgroup:

```
perf record -F 99 -e cpu-clock --cgroup=docker/1d567f439319...etc... -a sleep 10
```

Sample CPU stack traces for the entire system, using last branch record (LBR; Intel):

```
perf record -F 99 -a --call-graph lbr sleep 10
```

Sample CPU stack traces, once every 100 last-level cache misses, for 5 seconds:

```
perf record -e LLC-load-misses -c 100 -ag sleep 5
```

Sample on-CPU user instructions precisely (e.g., using Intel PEBS), for 5 seconds:

```
perf record -e cycles:up -a sleep 5
```

Sample CPUs at 49 Hertz, and show top process names and segments, live:

```
perf top -F 49 -ns comm,dso
```

Static Tracing

Trace new processes, until Ctrl-C:

```
perf record -e sched:sched_process_exec -a
```

Sample a subset of context switches with stack traces for 1 second:

```
perf record -e context-switches -a -g sleep 1
```

Trace all context switches with stack traces for 1 second:

```
perf record -e sched:sched_switch -a -g sleep 1
```

Trace all context switches with 5-level-deep stack traces for 1 second:

```
perf record -e sched:sched_switch/max-stack=5/ -a sleep 1
```

Trace connect(2) calls (outbound connections) with stack traces, until Ctrl-C:

```
perf record -e syscalls:sys_enter_connect -a -g
```

Sample at most 100 block device requests per second, until Ctrl-C:

```
perf record -F 100 -e block:block_rq_issue -a
```

Trace all block device issues and completions (has timestamps), until Ctrl-C:

```
perf record -e block:block_rq_issue,block:block_rq_complete -a
```

Trace all block requests, of size at least 64 Kbytes, until Ctrl-C:

```
perf record -e block:block_rq_issue --filter 'bytes >= 65536'
```

Trace all ext4 calls, and write to a non-ext4 location, until Ctrl-C:

```
perf record -e 'ext4:*' -o /tmp/perf.data -a
```

Trace the http__server__request USDT event (from Node.js; Linux 4.10+):

```
perf record -e sdt_node:http__server__request -a
```

Trace block device requests with live output (no perf.data) until Ctrl-C:

```
perf trace -e block:block_rq_issue
```

Trace block device requests and completions with live output:

```
perf trace -e block:block_rq_issue,block:block_rq_complete
```

Trace system calls system-wide with live output (verbose):

```
perf trace
```

Dynamic Tracing

Add a probe for the kernel tcp_sendmsg() function entry (--add optional):

```
perf probe --add tcp_sendmsg
```

Remove the tcp_sendmsg() tracepoint (or -d):

```
perf probe --del tcp_sendmsg
```

List available variables for tcp_sendmsg(), plus externals (needs kernel debuginfo):

```
perf probe -V tcp_sendmsg --externs
```

List available line probes for tcp_sendmsg() (needs debuginfo):

```
perf probe -L tcp_sendmsg
```

List available variables for tcp_sendmsg() at line number 81 (needs debuginfo):

```
perf probe -V tcp_sendmsg:81
```

Add a probe for tcp_sendmsg() with entry argument registers (processor-specific):

```
perf probe 'tcp_sendmsg %ax %dx %cx'
```

Add a probe for tcp_sendmsg(), with an alias ("bytes") for the %cx register:

```
perf probe 'tcp_sendmsg bytes=%cx'
```

Trace previously created probe when bytes (alias) is greater than 100:

```
perf record -e probe:tcp_sendmsg --filter 'bytes > 100'
```

Add a tracepoint for tcp_sendmsg() return, and capture the return value:

```
perf probe 'tcp_sendmsg%return $retval'
```

Add a tracepoint for tcp_sendmsg(), with size and socket state (needs debuginfo):

```
perf probe 'tcp_sendmsg size sk->__sk_common.skc_state'
```

Add a tracepoint for do_sys_open() with the filename as a string (needs debuginfo):

```
perf probe 'do_sys_open filename:string'
```

Add a tracepoint for the user-level fopen(3) function from libc:

```
perf probe -x /lib/x86_64-linux-gnu/libc.so.6 --add fopen
```

Reporting

Show perf.data in an ncurses browser (TUI) if possible:

```
perf report
```

Show perf.data as a text report, with data coalesced and counts and percentages:

```
perf report -n --stdio
```

List all perf.data events, with data header (recommended):

```
perf script --header
```

List all perf.data events, with my recommended fields (needs record -a; Linux < 4.1 used -f instead of -F):

```
perf script --header -F comm,pid,tid,cpu,time,event,ip,sym,dso
```

Generate a flame graph visualization (Linux 5.8+):

```
perf script report flamegraph
```

Disassemble and annotate instructions with percentages (needs some debuginfo):

```
perf annotate --stdio
```

This is my selection of one-liners; there are more capabilities not covered here. See the subcommands in the previous section, and also later sections in this and other chapters for more perf(1) commands.

13.3 perf Events

Events can be listed using `perf list`. I've included a selection here from Linux 5.8 to show the different types of events, highlighted:

```
# perf list

List of pre-defined events (to be used in -e):

  branch-instructions OR branches              [Hardware event]
  branch-misses                                [Hardware event]
  bus-cycles                                   [Hardware event]
  cache-misses                                 [Hardware event]
[...]
  context-switches OR cs                       [Software event]
  cpu-clock                                    [Software event]
[...]
  L1-dcache-load-misses                        [Hardware cache event]
  L1-dcache-loads                              [Hardware cache event]
[...]
  branch-instructions OR cpu/branch-instructions/    [Kernel PMU event]
  branch-misses OR cpu/branch-misses/          [Kernel PMU event]
[...]
cache:
  l1d.replacement
       [L1D data line replacements] [...]
floating point:
  fp_arith_inst_retired.128b_packed_double
       [Number of SSE/AVX computational 128-bit packed double precision [...]
frontend:
  dsb2mite_switches.penalty_cycles
       [Decode Stream Buffer (DSB)-to-MITE switch true penalty cycles] [...]
memory:
  cycle_activity.cycles_l3_miss
       [Cycles while L3 cache miss demand load is outstanding] [...]
  offcore_response.demand_code_rd.l3_miss.any_snoop
       [DEMAND_CODE_RD & L3_MISS & ANY_SNOOP] [...]
```

```
other:
  hw_interrupts.received
       [Number of hardware interrupts received by the processor]
pipeline:
  arith.divider_active
       [Cycles when divide unit is busy executing divide or square root [...]
uncore:
  unc_arb_coh_trk_requests.all
       [Unit: uncore_arb Number of entries allocated. Account for Any type:
        e.g. Snoop, Core aperture, etc]
[...]
  rNNN                                          [Raw hardware event descriptor]
  cpu/t1=v1[,t2=v2,t3 ...]/modifier             [Raw hardware event descriptor]
   (see 'man perf-list' on how to encode it)
  mem:<addr>[/len][:access]                     [Hardware breakpoint]
  alarmtimer:alarmtimer_cancel                  [Tracepoint event]
  alarmtimer:alarmtimer_fired                   [Tracepoint event]
[...]
  probe:do_nanosleep                            [Tracepoint event]
[...]
  sdt_hotspot:class__initialization__clinit     [SDT event]
  sdt_hotspot:class__initialization__concurrent [SDT event]
[...]
List of pre-defined events (to be used in --pfm-events):

ix86arch:
  UNHALTED_CORE_CYCLES
     [count core clock cycles whenever the clock signal on the specific core is
running (not halted)]
  INSTRUCTION_RETIRED
[...]
```

The output has been heavily truncated in many places, as the full output is 4,402 lines on this test system. The event types are:

- **Hardware event**: Mostly processor events (implemented using PMCs)

- **Software event**: A kernel counter event

- **Hardware cache event**: Processor cache events (PMCs)

- **Kernel PMU event**: Performance Monitoring Unit (PMU) events (PMCs)

- **cache, floating point...**: Processor vendor events (PMCs) and brief descriptions

- **Raw hardware event descriptor**: PMCs specified using raw codes

- **Hardware breakpoint**: Processor breakpoint event

- **Tracepoint event**: Kernel static instrumentation events

- **SDT event**: User-level static instrumentation events (USDT)

- **pfm-events**: libpfm events (added in Linux 5.8)

The tracepoint and SDT events mostly list static instrumentation points, but if you have created some dynamic instrumentation probes, those will be listed as well. I included an example in the output: probe:do_nanosleep is described as a "Tracepoint event" that is based on a kprobe.

The perf list command accepts a search substring as an argument. For example, listing events containing "mem_load_l3" with events highlighted in bold:

```
# perf list mem_load_l3


List of pre-defined events (to be used in -e):


cache:
  mem_load_l3_hit_retired.xsnp_hit
      [Retired load instructions which data sources were L3 and cross-core snoop
hits in on-pkg core cache Supports address when precise (Precise event)]
  mem_load_l3_hit_retired.xsnp_hitm
      [Retired load instructions which data sources were HitM responses from shared
L3 Supports address when precise (Precise event)]
  mem_load_l3_hit_retired.xsnp_miss
      [Retired load instructions which data sources were L3 hit and cross-core snoop
missed in on-pkg core cache Supports address when precise (Precise event)]
  mem_load_l3_hit_retired.xsnp_none
      [Retired load instructions which data sources were hits in L3 without snoops
required Supports address when precise (Precise event)]
[...]
```

These are hardware events (PMC-based), and the output includes brief descriptions. The (Precise event) refers to precise event-based sampling (PEBS) capable events.

13.4 Hardware Events

Hardware events were introduced in Chapter 4, Observability Tools, Section 4.3.9, Hardware Counters (PMCs). They are typically implemented using PMCs, which are configured using codes specific for the processor; for example, branch instructions on Intel processors can typically be instrumented with perf(1) by using the raw hardware event descriptor "r00c4," short for the register codes: umask 0x0 and event select 0xc4. These codes are published in the processor manuals [Intel 16][AMD 18][ARM 19]; Intel also makes them available as JSON files [Intel 20c].

You are not expected to remember these codes, and you will only refer to them in the processor manuals if needed. For ease of use, perf(1) provides human-readable mappings that can be used instead. For example, the event "branch-instructions" will hopefully map to the branch instructions PMC on your system.[2] Some of these human-readable names are visible in the previous list (the hardware and PMU events).

There are many processor types, and new versions are released regularly. It is possible that human-readable mappings for your processor are not yet available in perf(1) or are in a newer kernel version. Some PMCs may never be exposed via a human-readable name. I regularly have to switch from human-readable names to raw event descriptors once I move to deeper PMCs that lack mappings. There may also be bugs in the mappings, and if you ever encounter a suspicious PMC result, you may wish to try the raw event descriptor to double-check.

13.4.1 Frequency Sampling

When using perf record with PMCs, a default sample frequency is used so that not every event is recorded. For example, recording the cycles event:

```
# perf record -vve cycles -a sleep 1
Using CPUID GenuineIntel-6-8E
intel_pt default config: tsc,mtc,mtc_period=3,psb_period=3,pt,branch
----------------------------------------------------------------
perf_event_attr:
  size                          112
  { sample_period, sample_freq }  4000
  sample_type                   IP|TID|TIME|CPU|PERIOD
  disabled                      1
  inherit                       1
  mmap                          1
  comm                          1
  freq                          1
[...]
[ perf record: Captured and wrote 3.360 MB perf.data (3538 samples) ]
```

The output shows that *frequency sampling* is enabled (freq 1) with a sample frequency of 4000. This tells the kernel to adjust the rate of sampling so that roughly 4,000 events per second per CPU are captured. This is desirable, since some PMCs instrument events that can occur billions of times per second (e.g., CPU cycles) and the overhead of recording every event would be prohibitive.[3] But this is also a gotcha: the default output of perf(1) (without the very verbose option: -vv) does not say that frequency sampling is in use, and you may be expecting to record all events. This event frequency only affects the record subcommand; stat counts all events.

---

[2] I've encountered issues with the mappings in the past, where the human-readable name is not mapping to the correct PMC. This is difficult to identify from the perf(1) output alone: you need prior experience with the PMC and have expectations on what is normal, in order to spot the abnormal. Be aware of this possibility. With the speed of processor updates, I would expect bugs with future mappings as well.

[3] Although the kernel will throttle the sampling rate and drop events to protect itself. Always check for lost events to see if this occurred (e.g., check the summary counters from: perf report -D | tail -20).

The event frequency can be modified using the -F option, or changed to a *period* using -c, which captures one-in-every-period events (also known as *overflow sampling*). As an example of using -F:

```
perf record -F 99 -e cycles -a sleep 1
```

This samples at a target rate of 99 Hertz (events per second). It is similar to the profiling one-liners in Section 13.2, One-Liners: they do not specify the event (no -e cycles), which causes perf(1) to default to cycles if PMCs are available, or to the cpu-clock software event. See Section 13.9.2, CPU Profiling, for more details.

Note that there is a limit to the frequency rate, as well as a CPU utilization percent limit for perf(1), which can be viewed and set using sysctl(8):

```
# sysctl kernel.perf_event_max_sample_rate
kernel.perf_event_max_sample_rate = 15500
# sysctl kernel.perf_cpu_time_max_percent
kernel.perf_cpu_time_max_percent = 25
```

This shows the maximum sample rate on this system to be 15,500 Hertz, and the maximum CPU utilization allowed by perf(1) (specifically the PMU interrupt) to be 25%.

13.5   Software Events

These are events that typically map to hardware events, but are instrumented in software. Like hardware events, they may have a default sample frequency, typically 4000, so that only a subset is captured when using the record subcommand.

Note the following difference between the context-switches software event, and the equivalent tracepoint. Starting with the software event:

```
# perf record -vve context-switches -a -- sleep 1
[...]
------------------------------------------------------------
perf_event_attr:
  type                                  1
  size                                  112
  config                                0x3
  { sample_period, sample_freq }        4000
  sample_type                           IP|TID|TIME|CPU|PERIOD
[...]
  freq                                  1
[...]
[ perf record: Captured and wrote 3.227 MB perf.data (660 samples) ]
```

This output shows that the software event has defaulted to frequency sampling at a rate of 4000 Hertz. Now the equivalent tracepoint:

```
# perf record -vve sched:sched_switch -a sleep 1
[...]
-------------------------------------------------------------
perf_event_attr:
  type                       2
  size                       112
  config                     0x131
  { sample_period, sample_freq }   1
  sample_type                IP|TID|TIME|CPU|PERIOD|RAW
[...]
[ perf record: Captured and wrote 3.360 MB perf.data (3538 samples) ]
```

This time, period sampling is used (no freq 1), with a sample period of 1 (equivalent to -c 1). This captures every event. You can do the same with software events by specifying -c 1, for example:

```
perf record -vve context-switches -a -c 1 -- sleep 1
```

Be careful with the volume of recording every event and the overheads involved, especially for context switches, which can be frequent. You can use perf stat to check their frequency: see Section 13.8, perf stat.

13.6 Tracepoint Events

Tracepoints were introduced in Chapter 4, Observability Tools, Section 4.3.5, Tracepoints, which includes examples of instrumenting them using perf(1). To recap, I used the block:block_rq_issue tracepoint and the following examples.

Tracing system-wide for 10 seconds and printing the events:

```
perf record -e block:block_rq_issue -a sleep 10; perf script
```

Printing arguments to this tracepoint and its format string (metadata summary):

```
cat /sys/kernel/debug/tracing/events/block/block_rq_issue/format
```

Filtering block I/O to only those larger than 65536 bytes:

```
perf record -e block:block_rq_issue --filter 'bytes > 65536' -a sleep 10
```

There are additional examples of perf(1) and tracepoints in Section 13.2, One-Liners, and in other chapters of this book.

Note that perf list will show initialized probe events including kprobes (dynamic kernel instrumentation) as "Tracepoint event"; see Section 13.7, Probe Events.

13.7 Probe Events

perf(1) uses the term *probe events* to refer to kprobes, uprobes, and USDT probes. These are "dynamic" and must first be initialized before they can be traced: they are not present in the output of perf list by default (some USDT probes may be present because they have been auto-initialized). Once initialized, they are listed as "Tracepoint event."

13.7.1 kprobes

kprobes were introduced in Chapter 4, Observability Tools, Section 4.3.6, kprobes. Here is a typical workflow for creating and using a kprobe, in this example for instrumenting the do_nanosleep() kernel function:

```
perf probe --add do_nanosleep
perf record -e probe:do_nanosleep -a sleep 5
perf script
perf probe --del do_nanosleep
```

The kprobe is created using the probe subcommand and --add (--add is optional), and when it is no longer needed, it is deleted using probe and --del. Here is output from this sequence, including listing the probe event:

```
# perf probe --add do_nanosleep
Added new event:
  probe:do_nanosleep    (on do_nanosleep)

You can now use it in all perf tools, such as:

        perf record -e probe:do_nanosleep -aR sleep 1

# perf list probe:do_nanosleep

List of pre-defined events (to be used in -e):

  probe:do_nanosleep                              [Tracepoint event]

# perf record -e probe:do_nanosleep -aR sleep 1
[ perf record: Woken up 1 times to write data ]
[ perf record: Captured and wrote 3.368 MB perf.data (604 samples) ]
# perf script
          sleep 11898 [002] 922215.458572: probe:do_nanosleep: (ffffffff83dbb6b0)
 SendControllerT 15713 [002] 922215.459871: probe:do_nanosleep: (ffffffff83dbb6b0)
 SendControllerT  5460 [001] 922215.459942: probe:do_nanosleep: (ffffffff83dbb6b0)
[...]
```

```
# perf probe --del probe:do_nanosleep
Removed event: probe:do_nanosleep
```

The output of perf script shows the do_nanosleep() calls that occurred while tracing, first from a sleep(1) command (likely the sleep(1) command that perf(1) ran) followed by calls by SendControllerT (truncated).

The return of functions can be instrumented by adding %return:

```
perf probe --add do_nanosleep%return
```

This uses a kretprobe.

kprobe Arguments

There are at least four different ways to instrument the arguments to kernel functions.

First, if kernel debuginfo is available, then information about function variables, including arguments, is available to perf(1). Listing variables for the do_nanosleep() kprobe using the --vars option:

```
# perf probe --vars do_nanosleep
Available variables at do_nanosleep
        @<do_nanosleep+0>
                enum hrtimer_mode       mode
                struct hrtimer_sleeper* t
```

This output shows variables named mode and t, which are the entry arguments to do_nanosleep(). These can be added when creating the probe so that they are included when recorded. For example, adding mode:

```
# perf probe 'do_nanosleep mode'
[...]
# perf record -e probe:do_nanosleep -a
[...]
# perf script
        svscan  1470 [012] 4731125.216396: probe:do_nanosleep: (ffffffffa8e4e440)
mode=0x1
```

This output shows mode=0x1.

Second, if kernel debuginfo is not available (as I often find in production), then arguments can be read via their register locations. One trick is to use an identical system (same hardware and kernel) and install kernel debuginfo on it for reference. This reference system can then be queried to find the register locations using the -n (dry run) and -v (verbose) options to perf probe:

```
# perf probe -nv 'do_nanosleep mode'
[...]
Writing event: p:probe/do_nanosleep _text+10806336 mode=%si:x32
[...]
```

Since it is a dry run, it does not create the event. But the output shows the location of the mode variable (highlighted in bold): it is in register %si and is printed as a 32-bit hexadecimal number (x32). (This syntax is explained in the next section on uprobes.) This can now be used on the debuginfo-less system by copying and pasting the mode declaration string (mode=%si:x32):

```
# perf probe 'do_nanosleep mode=%si:x32'
[...]
# perf record -e probe:do_nanosleep -a
[...]
# perf script
         svscan  1470 [000] 4732120.231245: probe:do_nanosleep: (fffffffa8e4e440)
mode=0x1
```

This only works if the systems have the same processor ABI and kernel versions, otherwise the wrong register locations may be instrumented.

Third, if you know the processor ABI, you can determine the register locations yourself. An example of this for uprobes is given in the following section.

Fourth, there is a new source of kernel debug information: BPF type format (BTF). This is more likely to be available by default, and a future version of perf(1) should support it as an alternate debuginfo source.

For the return of do_nanosleep, instrumented using a kretprobe, the return value can be read using the special $retval variable:

```
perf probe 'do_nanosleep%return $retval'
```

See the kernel source code to determine what the return value contains.

13.7.2 uprobes

uprobes were introduced in Chapter 4, Observability Tools, Section 4.3.7, uprobes. uprobes are created similarly to kprobes when using perf(1). For example, to create a uprobe for the libc file open function, fopen(3):

```
# perf probe -x /lib/x86_64-linux-gnu/libc.so.6 --add fopen
Added new event:
  probe_libc:fopen      (on fopen in /lib/x86_64-linux-gnu/libc-2.27.so)
```

You can now use it in all perf tools, such as:

```
perf record -e probe_libc:fopen -aR sleep 1
```

The binary path is specified using **-x**. The uprobe, named probe_libc:fopen, can now be used with perf record to record events.

When you are finished with the uprobe, you can remove it using **--del**:

```
# perf probe --del probe_libc:fopen
Removed event: probe_libc:fopen
```

The return of the function can be instrumented by adding %return:

```
perf probe -x /lib/x86_64-linux-gnu/libc.so.6 --add fopen%return
```

This uses a uretprobe.

uprobe Arguments

If your system has debuginfo for the target binary, then variable information, including arguments, may be available. This can be listed using **--vars**:

```
# perf probe -x /lib/x86_64-linux-gnu/libc.so.6 --vars fopen
Available variables at fopen
        @<_IO_vfscanf+15344>
                char*    filename
                char*    mode
```

The output shows that fopen(3) has filename and mode variables. These can be added when creating the probe:

```
perf probe -x /lib/x86_64-linux-gnu/libc.so.6 --add 'fopen filename mode'
```

Debuginfo may be provided via a -dbg or -dbgsym package. If that is unavailable on the target system but is on another, the other system can be used as a reference system, as was shown in the previous section on kprobes.

Even if debuginfo is not available anywhere, you still have options. One is to recompile the software with debuginfo (if the software is open source). Another option is to figure out the register locations yourself, based on the processor ABI. The following example is for x86_64:

```
# perf probe -x /lib/x86_64-linux-gnu/libc.so.6 --add 'fopen filename=+0(%di):string
mode=%si:u8'
[...]
# perf record -e probe_libc:fopen -a
[...]
```

```
# perf script
           run 28882 [013] 4503285.383830: probe_libc:fopen: (7fbe130e6e30)
filename="/etc/nsswitch.conf" mode=147
           run 28882 [013] 4503285.383997: probe_libc:fopen: (7fbe130e6e30)
filename="/etc/passwd" mode=17
      setuidgid 28882 [013] 4503285.384447: probe_libc:fopen: (7fed1ad56e30)
filename="/etc/nsswitch.conf" mode=147
      setuidgid 28882 [013] 4503285.384589: probe_libc:fopen: (7fed1ad56e30)
filename="/etc/passwd" mode=17
           run 28883 [014] 4503285.392096: probe_libc:fopen: (7f9be2f55e30)
filename="/etc/nsswitch.conf" mode=147
           run 28883 [014] 4503285.392251: probe_libc:fopen: (7f9be2f55e30)
filename="/etc/passwd" mode=17
         mkdir 28884 [015] 4503285.392913: probe_libc:fopen: (7fad6ea0be30)
filename="/proc/filesystems" mode=22
         chown 28885 [015] 4503285.393536: probe_libc:fopen: (7efcd22d5e30)
filename="/etc/nsswitch.conf" mode=147
[...]
```

The output includes a number of fopen(3) calls, showing filenames of /etc/nsswitch.conf, /etc/passwd, etc.

Decomposing the syntax I used:

- **filename=:** This is an alias ("filename") used to annotate the output.

- **%di, %si:** On x86_64, registers containing the first two function arguments, according to the AMD64 ABI [Matz 13].

- **+0(...):** Dereference the contents at offset zero. Without this, we would accidentally print the address as a string, rather than the contents of the address as a string.

- **:string:** Print this as a string.

- **:u8:** Print this as an unsigned 8-bit integer.

The syntax is documented in the perf-probe(1) man page.

For the uretprobe, the return value can be read using $retval:

```
perf probe -x /lib/x86_64-linux-gnu/libc.so.6 --add 'fopen%return $retval'
```

See the application source code to determine what the return value contains.

While uprobes can provide visibility into application internals, they are an unstable interface as they are instrumenting the binary directly, which can change between software versions. USDT probes are preferred whenever available.

13.7.3 USDT

USDT probes were introduced in Chapter 4, Observability Tools, Section 4.3.8, USDT. These provide a stable interface for tracing events.

Given a binary with USDT probes,[4] perf(1) can be made aware of them using the buildid-cache subcommand. For example, for a Node.js binary compiled with USDT probes (built using: ./configure --with-dtrace):

```
# perf buildid-cache --add $(which node)
```

The USDT probes can then be seen in the output of perf list:

```
# perf list | grep sdt_node
  sdt_node:gc__done                          [SDT event]
  sdt_node:gc__start                         [SDT event]
  sdt_node:http__client__request            [SDT event]
  sdt_node:http__client__response           [SDT event]
  sdt_node:http__server__request            [SDT event]
  sdt_node:http__server__response           [SDT event]
  sdt_node:net__server__connection          [SDT event]
  sdt_node:net__stream__end                 [SDT event]
```

At this point they are SDT events (statically defined tracing events): metadata that describes the location of the event in the program's instruction text. To actually instrument them, events must be created in the same fashion as uprobes from the previous section (USDT probes also use uprobes to instrument the USDT locations).[5] For example, for sdt_node:http__server_request:

```
# perf probe sdt_node:http__server__request
Added new event:
  sdt_node:http__server__request (on %http__server__request in
/home/bgregg/Build/node-v12.4.0/out/Release/node)


You can now use it in all perf tools, such as:

        perf record -e sdt_node:http__server__request -aR sleep 1

# perf list | grep http__server__request
  sdt_node:http__server__request            [Tracepoint event]
  sdt_node:http__server__request            [SDT event]
```

---

[4] You can run readelf -n on the binary to check for the existence of USDT probes: they are listed in the ELF notes section.

[5] In the future this step may become unnecessary: the following perf record command may automatically promote SDT events to tracepoints when needed.

Note that the event now shows as both the SDT event (USDT metadata) and a Tracepoint event (a trace event that can be instrumented using perf(1) and other tools). It might seem odd to see two entries for the same thing, but it is consistent with how other events work. There is a tuple for tracepoints as well, except perf(1) never lists the tracepoints, it only lists the corresponding tracepoint events (if they exist[6]).

Recording the USDT event:

```
# perf record -e sdt_node:http__server__request -a
^C[ perf record: Woken up 1 times to write data ]
[ perf record: Captured and wrote 3.924 MB perf.data (2 samples) ]
# perf script
        node 16282 [006] 510375.595203: sdt_node:http__server__request:
(55c3d8b03530) arg1=140725176825920 arg2=140725176825888 arg3=140725176829208
arg4=39090 arg5=140725176827096 arg6=140725176826040 arg7=20
        node 16282 [006] 510375.844040: sdt_node:http__server__request:
(55c3d8b03530) arg1=140725176825920 arg2=140725176825888 arg3=140725176829208
arg4=39092 arg5=140725176827096 arg6=140725176826040 arg7=20
```

The output shows that two sdt_node:http__server__request probes fired while recording. It has also printed the arguments to the USDT probe, but some of these are structs and strings, so perf(1) has printed them as pointer addresses. It *should* be possible to cast arguments to the correct type when creating the probe; for example, to cast the third argument as a string named "address":

```
perf probe --add 'sdt_node:http__server__request address=+0(arg3):string'
```

At the time of writing, this does not work.

A common problem, which has been fixed since Linux 4.20, is that some USDT probes require a semaphore in the process address space to be incremented to activate them properly. sdt_node:http__server__request is one such probe, and without incrementing the semaphore it will not record any events.

13.8 perf stat

The perf stat subcommand counts events. This can be used to measure the rate of events, or to check if an event is occurring at all. perf stat is efficient: it counts software events in kernel context and hardware events using PMC registers. This makes it suited to gauge the overhead of a more expensive perf record subcommand by first checking the event rate using perf stat.

---

[6] The kernel documentation does state that some tracepoints may not have corresponding trace events, although I have yet to encounter a case of this.

For example, counting the tracepoint sched:sched_switch (using –e for the event), system-wide (-a) and for one second (`sleep 1`: a dummy command):

```
# perf stat -e sched:sched_switch -a -- sleep 1
Performance counter stats for 'system wide':

         5,705        sched:sched_switch


     1.001892925 seconds time elapsed
```

This shows that the sched:sched_switch tracepoint fired 5,705 times during one second.

I often use a "`--`" shell separator between the perf(1) command options and the dummy command it runs, although it is not strictly necessary in this case.

The following sections explain options and usage examples.

13.8.1 Options

The `stat` subcommand supports many options, including:

- **-a**: Record across all CPUs (this became the default in Linux 4.11)
- **-e** *event*: Record this event(s)
- **--filter** *filter*: Set a Boolean filter expression for an event
- **-p** *PID*: Record this PID only
- **-t** *TID*: Record this thread ID only
- **-G** *cgroup*: Record this cgroup only (used for containers)
- **-A**: Show per-CPU counts
- **-I** *interval_ms*: Print output every interval (milliseconds)
- **-v**: Show verbose messages; **-vv** for more messages

The events can be tracepoints, software events, hardware events, kprobes, uprobes, and USDT probes (see Sections 13.3 to 13.7). Wildcards can be used to match multiple events of the file globbing style ("*" matches anything, and "?" matches any one character). For example, the following matches all tracepoints of type sched:

```
# perf stat -e 'sched:*' -a
```

Multiple -e options can be used to match multiple event descriptions. For example, to count both sched and block tracepoints, either of the following can be used:

```
# perf stat -e 'sched:*' -e 'block:*' -a
# perf stat -e 'sched:*,block:*' -a
```

If no events are specified, perf stat will default to the architectural PMCs: you can see an example of this in Chapter 4, Observability Tools, Section 4.3.9, Hardware Counters (PMCs).

13.8.2 Interval Statistics

Per-interval statistics can be printed using the -I option. For example, printing the sched:sched_switch count every 1000 milliseconds:

```
# perf stat -e sched:sched_switch -a -I 1000
#           time            counts unit events
       1.000791768           5,308      sched:sched_switch
       2.001650037           4,879      sched:sched_switch
       3.002348559           5,112      sched:sched_switch
       4.003017555           5,335      sched:sched_switch
       5.003760359           5,300      sched:sched_switch
^C     5.217339333           1,256      sched:sched_switch
```

The counts column shows the number of events since the previous interval. Browsing this column can show time-based variation. The last line shows the count between the previous line and the time I typed Ctrl-C to end perf(1). That time was 0.214 seconds, as seen by the delta in the time column.

13.8.3 Per-CPU Balance

The balance across CPUs may be examined using the -A option:

```
# perf stat -e sched:sched_switch -a -A -I 1000
#           time CPU            counts unit events
       1.000351429 CPU0          1,154      sched:sched_switch
       1.000351429 CPU1            555      sched:sched_switch
       1.000351429 CPU2            492      sched:sched_switch
       1.000351429 CPU3            925      sched:sched_switch
[...]
```

This prints the event delta per interval per logical CPU separately.

There are also --per-socket and --per-core options for CPU socket and core aggregation.

13.8.4 Event Filters

A filter may be provided for some event types (Tracepoint events) to test event arguments with a Boolean expression. The event will only be counted if the expression is true. For example, counting the sched:sched_switch event when the previous PID is 25467:

```
# perf stat -e sched:sched_switch --filter 'prev_pid == 25467' -a -I 1000
#           time            counts unit events
       1.000346518             131      sched:sched_switch
```

```
      2.000937838                   145       sched:sched_switch
      3.001370500                    11       sched:sched_switch
      4.001905444                   217       sched:sched_switch
[...]
```

See Tracepoint Arguments in Chapter 4, Observability Tools, Section 4.3.5, Tracepoints, for an explanation of these arguments. They are custom for each event, and may be listed from the format file in /sys/kernel/debug/tracing/events.

13.8.5   Shadow Statistics

perf(1) has a variety of shadow statistics that will be printed when certain combinations of events are instrumented. For example, when instrumenting the PMCs for cycles and instructions, the *instructions per cycle* (IPC) statistic is printed:

```
# perf stat -e cycles,instructions -a
^C
 Performance counter stats for 'system wide':

     2,895,806,892      cycles
     6,452,798,206      instructions              #    2.23  insn per cycle


       1.040093176 seconds time elapsed
```

In this output, IPC was 2.23. These shadow statistics are printed on the right, after a hash. The output of `perf stat` with no events has several of these shadow statistics (see Chapter 4, Observability Tools, Section 4.3.9, Hardware Counters (PMCs), for an example).

To examine events in more detail, `perf record` can be used to capture them.

13.9   perf record

The `perf record` subcommand records events to a file for later analysis. Events are specified after -e, and multiple events can be recorded simultaneously (either using multiple -e or separated by commas).

By default the output filename is perf.data. For example:

```
# perf record -e sched:sched_switch -a
^C[ perf record: Woken up 9 times to write data ]
[ perf record: Captured and wrote 6.060 MB perf.data (23526 samples) ]
```

Note that the output includes the size of the perf.data file (6.060 Mbytes), the number of samples it contains (23,526), and the number of times perf(1) woke up to record data (9 times). The data is passed from the kernel to user-space via per-CPU ring buffers, and to keep context-switch overheads to a minimum perf(1) is woken up an infrequent and dynamic number of times to read them.

The previous command recorded until Ctrl-C was typed. A dummy sleep(1) command (or any command) can be used to set the duration (as it was with perf stat earlier). For example:

```
perf record -e tracepoint -a -- sleep 1
```

This command records the tracepoint system-wide (-a) for 1 second only.

13.9.1 Options

The record subcommand supports many options, including:

- **-a**: Record across all CPUs (this became the default in Linux 4.11)
- **-e** *event*: Record this event(s)
- **--filter** *filter*: Set a Boolean filter expression for an event
- **-p** *PID*: Record this PID only
- **-t** *TID*: Record this thread ID only
- **-G** *cgroup*: Record this cgroup only (used for containers)
- **-g**: Record stack traces
- **--call-graph** *mode*: Record stack traces using a given method (fp, dwarf, or lbr)
- **-o** *file*: Set output file
- **-v**: Show verbose messages; -vv for more messages

The same events can be recorded as with perf stat and printed live (as the events occur) with perf trace.

13.9.2 CPU Profiling

A frequent use of perf(1) is as a CPU profiler. The following profiling example samples stack traces across all CPUs at 99 Hertz for 30 seconds:

```
perf record -F 99 -a -g -- sleep 30
```

The event was not specified (no -e), so perf(1) will default to the first of these that are available (many use *precise events*, introduced in Chapter 4, Observability Tools, Section 4.3.9, Hardware Counters (PMCs)):

1. **cycles:ppp**: CPU cycle-based frequency sampling with precise set to zero skid
2. **cycles:pp**: CPU cycle-based frequency sampling with precise set to requesting zero skid (which may not be zero in practice)
3. **cycles:p**: CPU cycle-based frequency sampling with precise set to requesting constant skid
4. **cycles**: CPU cycle-based frequency sampling (no precise)
5. **cpu-clock**: Software-based CPU frequency sampling

The ordering picks the most accurate CPU profiling mechanism available. The :ppp, :pp, and :p syntax activate precise event sampling modes, and can be applied to other events (apart from cycles) that support them. Events may also support different levels of precise. On Intel, precise events use PEBS; on AMD, they use IBS. These were defined in Section 4.3.9, under the PMC Challenges heading.

13.9.3 Stack Walking

Instead of using -g to specify recording stack traces, the max-stack configuration option can be used. It has two benefits: the maximum depth of the stack can be specified, and different settings can be used for different events. For example:

```
# perf record -e sched:sched_switch/max-stack=5/,sched:sched_wakeup/max-stack=1/ \
    -a -- sleep 1
```

This records sched_switch events with 5-frame stacks, and sched_wakeup events with 1 stack frame only.

Note that if stack traces appear broken, it may be due to the software not honoring the frame pointer register. This was discussed in Chapter 5, Applications, Section 5.6.2, Missing Stacks. Apart from recompiling the software with frame pointers (e.g., gcc(1) -fno-omit-frame-pointer), a different stack walking method may also work, selected using --call-graph. Options include:

- **--call-graph dwarf**: Selects debuginfo-based stack walking, which requires debuginfo for the executable to be available (for some software, it is provided by installing a package with a name ending in "-dbgsym" or "-dbg").

- **--call-graph lbr**: Selects Intel last branch record (LBR) stack walking, a processor-provided method (although it is typically limited to a stack depth of only 16 frames,[7] so its usefulness is also limited).

- **--call-graph fp**: Selects frame pointer-based stack walking (the default).

Frame pointer-based stack walking is described in Chapter 3, Operating Systems, Section 3.2.7, Stacks. Other types (dwarf, LBR, and ORC) are described in Chapter 2, Tech, Section 2.4, Stack Trace Walking, of *BPF Performance Tools* [Gregg 19].

After recording events, the events can be examined using perf report or perf script.

13.10 perf report

The perf report subcommand summarizes the contents of the perf.data file. Options include:

- **--tui**: Use the TUI interface (default)

- **--stdio**: Emit a text report

- **-i file**: Input file

---

[7]A stack depth of 16 since Haswell, and 32 since Skylake.

- **-n**: Include a column for sample counts

- **-g** *options*: Modify call graph (stack trace) display options

It is also possible to summarize perf.data using external tools. These tools may process the output of perf script, covered in Section 13.11, perf script. You may find perf report is sufficient in many situations, and use externals tools only when necessary. perf report summarizes using either an interactive text user interface (TUI) or a text report (STDIO).

13.10.1 TUI

For example, CPU profiling of the instruction pointer at 99 Hertz for 10 seconds (no stack traces) and launching the TUI:

```
# perf record -F 99 -a -- sleep 30
[ perf record: Woken up 193 times to write data ]
[ perf record: Captured and wrote 48.916 MB perf.data (11880 samples) ]
# perf report
Samples: 11K of event 'cpu-clock:pppH', Event count (approx.): 119999998800
Overhead  Command         Shared Object          Symbol
  21.10%  swapper         [kernel.vmlinux]       [k] native_safe_halt
   6.39%  mysqld          [kernel.vmlinux]       [k] _raw_spin_unlock_irqrestor
   4.66%  mysqld          mysqld                 [.] Z8ut_delaym
   2.64%  mysqld          [kernel.vmlinux]       [k] finish_task_switch
   2.59%  oltp_read_write [kernel.vmlinux]       [k] finish_task_switch
   2.03%  mysqld          [kernel.vmlinux]       [k] exit_to_usermode_loop
   1.68%  mysqld          mysqld                 [.] Z15row_search_mvccPh15pag
   1.40%  oltp_read_write [kernel.vmlinux]       [k] _raw_spin_unlock_irqrestor
[...]
```

perf report is an interactive interface where you can navigate the data, selecting functions and threads for more details.

13.10.2 STDIO

The same CPU profile was shown in Section 13.1, Subcommands Overview, using the text-based report (--stdio). It is not interactive, but is suited for redirecting to a file so that the full summary can be saved as text. Such stand-alone text reports can be useful for sharing with others over chat systems, email, and support ticketing systems. I typically use -n to include a column of sample counts.

As a different STDIO example, the following shows a CPU profile with stack traces (-g):

```
# perf record -F 99 -a -g -- sleep 30
[ perf record: Woken up 8 times to write data ]
[ perf record: Captured and wrote 2.282 MB perf.data (11880 samples) ]
# perf report --stdio
```

```
[...]
# Children     Self  Command             Shared Object                   Symbol
# ........  ........  ...............     ............................    ................
#
    50.45%    0.00%  mysqld              libpthread-2.27.so              [.] start_thread
            |
        ---start_thread
            |
            |--44.75%--pfs_spawn_thread
            |         |
            |          --44.70%--handle_connection
            |                   |
            |                    --44.55%--_Z10do_commandP3THD
            |                             |
            |                             |--42.93%--_Z16dispatch_commandP3THD
            |                             |         |
            |                             |          --40.92%--_Z19mysqld_stm
            |                             |                   |
[...]
```

Stack trace samples are merged as a hierarchy, beginning from the root function on the left and moving through child functions down and to the right. The right-most function is that of the event (in this case, the on-CPU function), and to its left is its ancestry. This path shows that the mysqld process (daemon) ran start_thread(), which called pfs_spawn_thread(), which called handle_connection(), and so on. The right-most functions are truncated in this output.

This left-to-right ordering is called *caller* by perf(1). You can flip this to *callee* ordering, where the event function is on the left and its ancestry is down and to the right using: -g callee (it was the default; perf(1) switched to the caller ordering in Linux 4.4).

13.11   perf script

The perf script subcommand by default prints each sample from perf.data, and is useful for spotting patterns over time that may be lost in a report summary. Its output may be used for generating flame graphs, and it also has the ability to run *trace scripts* that automate recording and reporting events in custom ways. These topics are summarized in this section.

To begin with, this shows output from the earlier CPU profile, which was collected without stack traces:

```
# perf script
        mysqld  8631 [000] 4142044.582702:    10101010 cpu-clock:pppH:
c08fd9 _Z19close_thread_tablesP3THD+0x49 (/usr/sbin/mysqld)
        mysqld  8619 [001] 4142044.582711:    10101010 cpu-clock:pppH:
79f81d _ZN5Field10make_fieldEP10Send_field+0x1d (/usr/sbin/mysqld)
```

```
      mysqld 22432 [002] 4142044.582713:    10101010 cpu-clock:pppH:
ffffffff95530302 get_futex_key_refs.isra.12+0x32 (/lib/modules/5.4.0-rc8-virtua...
[...]
```

The output fields are, along with the field contents from the first line of output:

- **Process name:** mysqld

- **Thread ID:** 8631

- **CPU ID:** [000]

- **Timestamp:** 4142044.582702 (seconds)

- **Period:** 10101010 (derived from -F 99); included in some sampling modes

- **Event name:** cpu-clock:pppH

- **Event arguments:** This field and those that follow are the event arguments, which
  are specific to the event. For the cpu-clock event, they are the instruction pointer, the
  function name and offset, and segment name. For the origin of these, see Chapter 4,
  Section 4.3.5, under Tracepoints Arguments and Format String.

These output fields happen to be the current default for this event, but may change in a later
version of perf(1). Other events do not include the period field.

Since it can be important to produce consistent output, especially for post-processing, you can
use the –F option to specify the fields. I frequently use it for including the process ID, as it is
missing from the default field set. I'd also recommend adding --header to include the perf.data
metadata. For example, this time showing a CPU profile with stack traces:

```
# perf script --header -F comm,pid,tid,cpu,time,event,ip,sym,dso,trace
# ========
# captured on    : Sun Jan  5 23:43:56 2020
# header version : 1
# data offset    : 264
# data size      : 2393000
# feat offset    : 2393264
# hostname : bgregg-mysql
# os release : 5.4.0
# perf version : 5.4.0
# arch : x86_64
# nrcpus online : 4
# nrcpus avail : 4
# cpudesc : Intel(R) Xeon(R) Platinum 8175M CPU @ 2.50GHz
# cpuid : GenuineIntel,6,85,4
# total memory : 15923672 kB
# cmdline : /usr/bin/perf record -F 99 -a -g -- sleep 30
# event : name = cpu-clock:pppH, , id = { 5997, 5998, 5999, 6000 }, type = 1, size =
112, { sample_period, sample_freq } = 99, sample_ty
```

```
[...]
# ========
#
mysqld 21616/8583  [000] 4142769.671581: cpu-clock:pppH:
                c36299 [unknown] (/usr/sbin/mysqld)
                c3bad4 _ZN13QEP_tmp_table8end_sendEv (/usr/sbin/mysqld)
                c3c1a5 _Z13sub_select_opP4JOINP7QEP_TABb (/usr/sbin/mysqld)
                c346a8 _ZN4JOIN4execEv (/usr/sbin/mysqld)
                ca735a _Z12handle_queryP3THDP3LEXP12Query_resultyy
[...]
```

The output includes the header, prefixed with "#", describing the system and the perf(1) command used to create the perf.data file. If you save this output to file for later use, you'll be glad you included the header, as it provides a wealth of information you may need later on. These files can be read by other tools for visualization, including for flame graphs.

13.11.1 Flame Graphs

Flame graphs visualize stack traces. While commonly used for CPU profiles, they can visualize any collection of stack traces collected by perf(1), including on context switch events to see why threads are leaving CPU, and on block I/O creation to see which code paths are creating disk I/O.

Two commonly used flame graph implementations (my own, and a d3 version) visualize the output of perf script. Flame graph support in perf(1) was added in Linux 5.8. The steps for creating flame graphs using perf(1) are included in Chapter 6, CPUs, Section 6.6.13, perf, under the heading CPU Flame Graphs. The visualization itself is explained in Section 6.7.3, Flame Graphs.

FlameScope is another tool for visualizing perf script output, combining a subsecond-offset heat map to study time-based variations with flame graphs. It is also included in Chapter 6, CPUs, Section 6.7.4, FlameScope.

13.11.2 Trace Scripts

The available perf(1) trace scripts can be listed using -l:

```
# perf script -l
List of available trace scripts:
[...]
  event_analyzing_sample          analyze all perf samples
  mem-phys-addr                   resolve physical address samples
  intel-pt-events                 print Intel PT Power Events and PTWRITE
  sched-migration                 sched migration overview
  net_dropmonitor                 display a table of dropped frames
  syscall-counts-by-pid [comm]    system-wide syscall counts, by pid
```

```
    failed-syscalls-by-pid [comm]          system-wide failed syscalls, by pid
   export-to-sqlite [database name] [columns] [calls] export perf data to a sqlite3
database
   stackcollapse                        produce callgraphs in short form for scripting
use
```

These can be executed as arguments to `perf script`. You can also develop additional trace scripts in either Perl or Python.

13.12 perf trace

The `perf trace` subcommand will trace system calls by default and print output live (no perf. data file). It was introduced in Chapter 5, Applications, Section 5.5.1, perf, as a lower-overhead version of strace(1) that can trace system-wide. `perf trace` can also inspect any event using similar syntax to `perf record`.

For example, tracing disk I/O issues and completions:

```
# perf trace -e block:block_rq_issue,block:block_rq_complete
    0.000 auditd/391 block:block_rq_issue:259,0 WS 8192 () 16046032 + 16 [auditd]
    0.566 systemd-journa/28651 block:block_rq_complete:259,0 WS () 16046032 + 16 [0]
    0.748 jbd2/nvme0n1p1/174 block:block_rq_issue:259,0 WS 61440 () 2100744 + 120
[jbd2/nvme0n1p1-]
    1.436 systemd-journa/28651 block:block_rq_complete:259,0 WS () 2100744 + 120 [0]
    1.515 kworker/0:1H-k/365 block:block_rq_issue:259,0 FF 0 () 0 + 0 [kworker/0:1H]
    1.543 kworker/0:1H-k/365 block:block_rq_issue:259,0 WFS 4096 () 2100864 + 8
[kworker/0:1H]
    2.074 sshd/6463 block:block_rq_complete:259,0 WFS () 2100864 + 8 [0]
    2.077 sshd/6463 block:block_rq_complete:259,0 WFS () 2100864 + 0 [0]
 1087.562 kworker/0:1H-k/365 block:block_rq_issue:259,0 W 4096 () 16046040 + 8
[kworker/0:1H]
[...]
```

As with `perf record`, filters can also be used on events. These filters can include some string constants, generated from kernel headers. For example, tracing mmap(2) syscalls where the flags are MAP_SHARED using the string "SHARED":

```
# perf trace -e syscalls:*enter_mmap --filter='flags==SHARED'
     0.000 env/14780 syscalls:sys_enter_mmap(len: 27002, prot: READ, flags: SHARED,
fd: 3)
    16.145 grep/14787 syscalls:sys_enter_mmap(len: 27002, prot: READ, flags: SHARED,
fd: 3)
    18.704 cut/14791 syscalls:sys_enter_mmap(len: 27002, prot: READ, flags: SHARED,
fd: 3)
[...]
```

Note that perf(1) is also using strings to improve readability of the format string: instead of "prot: 1" it has printed "prot: READ". perf(1) refers to this capability as "beautification."

13.12.1 Kernel Versions

Prior to Linux 4.19, perf trace would instrument all syscalls by default (the --syscalls option) in addition to the specified events (-e). To disable tracing other syscalls, specify --no-syscalls (which is now the default). For example:

```
# perf trace -e block:block_rq_issue,block:block_rq_complete --no-syscalls
```

Note that tracing across all CPUs (-a) has been the default since Linux 3.8. Filters (--filter) were added in Linux 5.5.

13.13   Other Commands

There are more perf(1) subcommands and functionality, and some are used in other chapters. To recap additional subcommands (see Table 13.1 for the full list):

- **perf c2c** (Linux 4.10+): Cache-to-cache and cache line false sharing analysis
- **perf kmem**: Kernel memory allocation analysis
- **perf kvm**: KVM guest analysis
- **perf lock**: Lock analysis
- **perf mem**: Memory access analysis
- **perf sched**: Kernel scheduler statistics
- **perf script**: Custom perf tooling

Advanced additional capabilities include launching BPF programs on events, and using hardware tracing such as Intel processor trace (PT) or ARM CoreSight for per-instruction analysis [Hunter 20].

The following is a basic example of Intel processor trace. This records user-mode cycles for the date(1) command:

```
# perf record -e intel_pt/cyc/u date
Sat Jul 11 05:52:40 PDT 2020
[ perf record: Woken up 1 times to write data ]
[ perf record: Captured and wrote 0.049 MB perf.data ]
```

This can be printed as an instruction trace (instructions highlighted in bold):

```
# perf script --insn-trace
        date 31979 [003] 653971.670163672:       7f3bfbf4d090 _start+0x0 (/lib/x86_64-
linux-gnu/ld-2.27.so) insn: 48 89 e7
```

```
        date 31979 [003] 653971.670163672:        7f3bfbf4d093 _start+0x3 (/lib/x86_64-
linux-gnu/ld-2.27.so) insn: e8 08 0e 00 00
[...]
```

This output includes the instructions as machine code. Installing and using the Intel X86 Encoder Decoder (XED) prints the instructions as assembly [Intelxed 19]:

```
# perf script --insn-trace --xed
date 31979 [003] 653971.670163672: ... (/lib/x86_64-linux-gnu/ld-2.27.so) mov %rsp,
%rdi
date 31979 [003] 653971.670163672: ... (/lib/x86_64-linux-gnu/ld-2.27.so) callq
0x7f3bfbf4dea0
date 31979 [003] 653971.670163672: ... (/lib/x86_64-linux-gnu/ld-2.27.so) pushq %rbp
[...]
date 31979 [003] 653971.670439432: ... (/bin/date) xor %ebp, %ebp
date 31979 [003] 653971.670439432: ... (/bin/date) mov %rdx, %r9
date 31979 [003] 653971.670439432: ... (/bin/date) popq %rsi
date 31979 [003] 653971.670439432: ... (/bin/date) mov %rsp, %rdx
date 31979 [003] 653971.670439432: ... (/bin/date) and $0xfffffffffffffff0, %rsp
[...]
```

While this is incredible detail, it is also verbose. The full output was 266,105 lines, and that's just for the date(1) command. See the perf(1) wiki for other examples [Hunter 20].

13.14   perf Documentation

Each subcommand should also have a man page for reference beginning with "perf-", for example, perf-record(1) for the record subcommand. These are in the Linux source tree under tools/perf/Documentation.

There is a perf(1) tutorial on wiki.kernel.org [Perf 15], an unofficial perf(1) page by Vince Weaver [Weaver 11], and another unofficial perf(1) examples page by myself [Gregg 20f].

My own page contains the full perf(1) one-liner list, as well as many more examples.

As perf(1) frequently gains new features, check for updates in later kernel versions. A good source is the perf section of the changelog for each kernel published on KernelNewbies [KernelNewbies 20].

13.15   References

[Weaver 11] Weaver, V., "The Unofficial Linux Perf Events Web-Page," http://web.eece.maine.edu/~vweaver/projects/perf_events, 2011.

[Matz 13] Matz, M., Hubička, J., Jaeger, A., and Mitchell, M., "System V Application Binary Interface, AMD64 Architecture Processor Supplement, Draft Version 0.99.6," http://x86-64.org/documentation/abi.pdf, 2013.

[**Perf 15**] "Tutorial: Linux kernel profiling with perf," *perf wiki*, https://perf.wiki.kernel.org/index.php/Tutorial, last updated 2015.

[**Intel 16**] *Intel 64 and IA-32 Architectures Software Developer's Manual Volume 3B: System Programming Guide, Part 2, September 2016,* https://www.intel.com/content/www/us/en/architecture-and-technology/64-ia-32-architectures-software-developer-vol-3b-part-2-manual.html, 2016.

[**AMD 18**] *Open-Source Register Reference for AMD Family 17h Processors Models 00h-2Fh,* https://developer.amd.com/resources/developer-guides-manuals, 2018.

[**ARM 19**] *Arm® Architecture Reference Manual Armv8, for Armv8-A architecture profile,* https://developer.arm.com/architectures/cpu-architecture/a-profile/docs?_ga=2.78191124.1893781712.1575908489-930650904.1559325573, 2019.

[**Intelxed 19**] "Intel XED," https://intelxed.github.io, 2019.

[**Gregg 20h**] Gregg, B., "One-Liners," http://www.brendangregg.com/perf.html#OneLiners, last updated 2020.

[**Gregg 20f**] Gregg, B., "perf Examples," http://www.brendangregg.com/perf.html, last updated 2020.

[**Hunter 20**] Hunter, A., "Perf tools support for Intel® Processor Trace," https://perf.wiki.kernel.org/index.php/Perf_tools_support_for_Intel%C2%AE_Processor_Trace, last updated 2020.

[**Intel 20c**] "/perfmon/," https://download.01.org/perfmon, accessed 2020.

[**KernelNewbies 20**] "KernelNewbies: LinuxVersions," https://kernelnewbies.org/LinuxVersions, accessed 2020.

Chapter 14

Ftrace

Ftrace is the official Linux tracer, a multi-tool composed of different tracing utilities. Ftrace was created by Steven Rostedt and first added to Linux 2.6.27 (2008). It can be used without any additional user-level front end, making it especially suited for embedded Linux environments where storage space is at a premium. It is also useful for server environments.

This chapter, along with Chapter 13, perf, and Chapter 15, BPF, are optional reading for those wishing to learn one or more system tracers in more detail.

Ftrace can be used to answer questions such as:

- How often are certain kernel functions called?
- What code path led to calling this function?
- What child functions does this kernel function call?
- What is the highest latency caused by preemption disabled code paths?

The following sections are structured to introduce Ftrace, show some of its profilers and tracers, and then show the front ends that use them. The sections are:

- 14.1: Capabilities Overview
- 14.2: tracefs (/sys)
- Profilers:
  - 14.3: Ftrace Function Profiler
  - 14.10: Ftrace Hist Triggers
- Tracers:
  - 14.4: Ftrace Function Tracing
  - 14.5: Tracepoints
  - 14.6: kprobes
  - 14.7: uprobes
  - 14.8: Ftrace function_graph
  - 14.9: Ftrace hwlat

- Front ends:
    - 14.11: trace-cmd
    - 14.12: perf ftrace
    - 14.13: perf-tools
- 14.14: Ftrace Documentation
- 14.15: References

Ftrace hist triggers is an advanced topic that requires covering both profilers and tracers first, hence its later location in this chapter. The kprobes and uprobes sections also include basic profiling capabilities.

Figure 14.1 is an overview of Ftrace and its front ends, with arrows showing the path from events to output types.

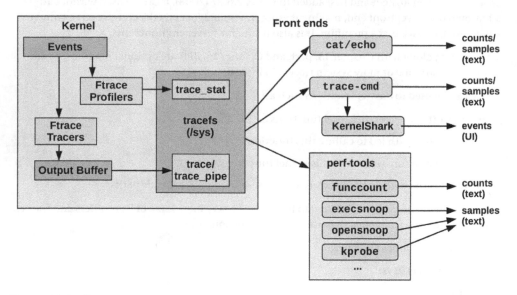

Figure 14.1   Ftrace profilers, tracers, and front ends

These are explained in the following sections.

14.1   Capabilities Overview

While perf(1) uses subcommands for different functionality, Ftrace has *profilers* and *tracers*. Profilers provide statistical summaries such as counts and histograms, and tracers provide per-event details.

As an example of Ftrace, the following funcgraph(8) tool uses an Ftrace tracer to show the child calls of the vfs_read() kernel function:

```
# funcgraph vfs_read
Tracing "vfs_read"... Ctrl-C to end.
 1)               |  vfs_read() {
 1)               |    rw_verify_area() {
 1)               |      security_file_permission() {
 1)               |        apparmor_file_permission() {
 1)               |          common_file_perm() {
 1)   0.763 us    |            aa_file_perm();
 1)   2.209 us    |          }
 1)   3.329 us    |        }
 1)   0.571 us    |        __fsnotify_parent();
 1)   0.612 us    |        fsnotify();
 1)   7.019 us    |      }
 1)   8.416 us    |    }
 1)               |    __vfs_read() {
 1)               |      new_sync_read() {
 1)               |        ext4_file_read_iter() {
[...]
```

The output shows that vfs_read() called rw_verify_area(), which called security_file_permission() and so on. The second column shows the duration in each function ("us" is microseconds) so that you can do performance analysis, identifying the child functions that caused a parent function to be slow. This particular Ftrace capability is called function graph tracing (and is covered in Section 14.8, Ftrace function_graph).

Ftrace profilers and tracers from a recent Linux version (5.2) are listed in Tables 14.1 and 14.2, along with the Linux *event tracers*: tracepoints, kprobes, and uprobes. These event tracers are Ftrace-like, sharing similar configuration and output interfaces, and are included in this chapter. The monospace tracer names shown in Table 14.2 are the Ftrace tracers, and are also the command line keywords used to configure them.

Table 14.1 **Ftrace profilers**

Profiler	Description	Section
function	Kernel function statistics	14.3
kprobe profiler	Enabled kprobe counts	14.6.5
uprobe profiler	Enabled uprobe counts	14.7.4
hist triggers	Custom histograms on events	14.10

Table 14.2 **Ftrace and event tracers**

Tracer	Description	Section
function	Kernel function call tracer	14.4
tracepoints	Kernel static instrumentation (event tracer)	14.5

Tracer	Description	Section
kprobes	Kernel dynamic instrumentation (event tracer)	14.6
uprobes	User-level dynamic instrumentation (event tracer)	14.7
function_graph	Kernel function call tracing with a hierarchical graph of child calls.	14.8
wakeup	Measures max CPU scheduler latency	-
wakeup_rt	Measures max CPU scheduler latency for real-time (RT) tasks	-
irqsoff	Traces IRQs off events with code location and latency (interrupts disabled latency)[1]	-
preemptoff	Traces preemption disabled events with code location and latency	-
preemptirqsoff	A tracer combining irqsoff and preemptoff	-
blk	Block I/O tracer (used by blktrace(8)).	-
hwlat	Hardware latency tracer: can detect external perturbations causing latency	14.9
mmiotrace	Traces calls that a module makes to hardware	-
nop	A special tracer to disable other tracers	-

You can list the Ftrace tracers available on your kernel version using:

```
# cat /sys/kernel/debug/tracing/available_tracers
hwlat blk mmiotrace function_graph wakeup_dl wakeup_rt wakeup function nop
```

This is using the tracefs interface mounted under /sys, which is introduced in the next section. Subsequent sections cover profilers, tracers, and the tools that use them.

If you wish to jump straight to Ftrace-based tools, take a look at Section 14.13, perf-tools, which includes funcgraph(8) shown earlier.

Future kernel versions may add more profilers and tracers to Ftrace: check the Ftrace documentation in the Linux source under Documentation/trace/ftrace.rst [Rostedt 08].

14.2   tracefs (/sys)

The interface for using Ftrace capabilities is the tracefs file system. It should be mounted on /sys/kernel/tracing; for example, by using:

```
mount -t tracefs tracefs /sys/kernel/tracing
```

---

[1]This (and preemptoff, preemptirqsoff) require CONFIG_PREEMPTIRQ_EVENTS to be enabled.

Ftrace was originally part of the debugfs file system until it was split into its own tracefs. When debugfs is mounted, it still preserves the original directory structure by mounting tracefs as a tracing subdirectory. You can list both debugfs and tracefs mount points using:

```
# mount -t debugfs,tracefs
debugfs on /sys/kernel/debug type debugfs (rw,relatime)
tracefs on /sys/kernel/debug/tracing type tracefs (rw,relatime)
```

This output is from Ubuntu 19.10, which shows that tracefs is mounted in /sys/kernel/debug/ tracing. The examples in the sections that follow use this location as it is still in widespread use, but in the future it should change to /sys/kernel/tracing.

Note that if tracefs fails to mount, one possible reason is that your kernel has been built without the Ftrace config options (CONFIG_FTRACE, etc.).

14.2.1   tracefs Contents

Once tracefs is mounted, you should be able to see the control and output files in the tracing directory:

```
# ls -F /sys/kernel/debug/tracing
available_events                max_graph_depth           stack_trace_filter
available_filter_functions      options/                  synthetic_events
available_tracers               per_cpu/                  timestamp_mode
buffer_percent                  printk_formats            trace
buffer_size_kb                  README                    trace_clock
buffer_total_size_kb            saved_cmdlines            trace_marker
current_tracer                  saved_cmdlines_size       trace_marker_raw
dynamic_events                  saved_tgids               trace_options
dyn_ftrace_total_info           set_event                 trace_pipe
enabled_functions               set_event_pid             trace_stat/
error_log                       set_ftrace_filter         tracing_cpumask
events/                         set_ftrace_notrace        tracing_max_latency
free_buffer                     set_ftrace_pid            tracing_on
function_profile_enabled        set_graph_function        tracing_thresh
hwlat_detector/                 set_graph_notrace         uprobe_events
instances/                      snapshot                  uprobe_profile
kprobe_events                   stack_max_size
kprobe_profile                  stack_trace
```

The names of many of these are intuitive. Key files and directories include those listed in Table 14.3.

Table 14.3 **tracefs key files**

File	Access	Description
`available_tracers`	read	Lists available tracers (see Table 14.2)
`current_tracer`	read/write	Shows the current enabled tracer
`function_profile_enabled`	read/write	Enables the function profiler
`available_filter_functions`	read	Lists available functions to trace
`set_ftrace_filter`	read/write	Select functions to trace
`tracing_on`	read/write	A switch to enable/disable the output ring buffer
`trace`	read/write	Output of tracers (ring buffer)
`trace_pipe`	read	Output of tracers; this version consumes the trace and blocks for input
`trace_options`	read/write	Options to customize the trace buffer output
`trace_stat` (directory)	read/write	Output of the function profiler
`kprobe_events`	read/write	Enabled kprobe configuration
`uprobe_events`	read/write	Enabled uprobe configuration
`events` (directory)	read/write	Event tracer control files: tracepoints, kprobes, uprobes
`instances` (directory)	read/write	Ftrace instances for concurrent users

This /sys interface is documented in the Linux source under Documentation/trace/ftrace.rst [Rostedt 08]. It can be used directly from the shell or by front ends and libraries. As an example, to see whether any of the Ftrace tracers are currently in use you can cat(1) the current_tracer file:

```
# cat /sys/kernel/debug/tracing/current_tracer
nop
```

The output shows nop (no operation), which means that no tracer is currently in use. To enable a tracer, write its name to this file. For example, to enable the blk tracer:

```
# echo blk > /sys/kernel/debug/tracing/current_tracer
```

Other Ftrace control and output files can also be used via echo(1) and cat(1). This means that Ftrace has virtually zero dependencies to be used (only a shell is needed[2]).

---

[2]echo(1) is a shell builtin, cat(1) can be approximated: function shellcat { (while read line; do echo "$line"; done) < $1; }. Or busybox could be used to include a shell, cat(1), and other basics.

Steven Rostedt built Ftrace for his own use while developing the realtime patch set, and initially it did not support concurrent users. For example, the current_tracer file can only be set to one tracer at a time. Concurrent user support was added later, in the form of instances that can be created in the "instances" directory. Each instance has its own current_tracer and output files so that it can perform tracing independently.

The following sections (14.3 to 14.10) show more /sys interface examples; then later sections (14.11 to 14.13) show the front ends built upon it: trace-cmd, the perf(1) `ftrace` subcommand, and perf-tools.

14.3   Ftrace Function Profiler

The function profiler provides statistics on kernel function calls, and is suited for exploring which kernel functions are in use and identifying which are the slowest. I frequently use the function profiler as a starting point for understanding kernel code execution for a given workload, especially because it is efficient and costs relatively low overhead. Using it, I can identify functions to analyze using more expensive per-event tracing. It requires the CONFIG_FUNCTION_PROFILER=y kernel option.

The function profiler works by using compiled-in profiling calls at the start of every kernel function. This approach is based on how compiler profilers work, such as gcc(1)'s -pg option, which inserts mcount() calls for use with gprof(1). Since gcc(1) version 4.6, this mcount() call is now __fentry__(). Adding calls to *every* kernel function sounds like it should cost significant overhead, which would be a concern for something that may rarely be used, but the overhead problem has been solved: when not in use, these calls are typically replaced with fast nop instructions, and only switched to the __fentry__() calls when needed [Gregg 19f].

The following demonstrates the function profiler using the tracefs interface in /sys. For reference, the following shows the original not-enabled state of the function profiler:

```
# cd /sys/kernel/debug/tracing
# cat set_ftrace_filter
#### all functions enabled ####
# cat function_profile_enabled
0
```

Now (from the same directory) these commands use the function profiler to count all kernel calls beginning with "tcp" for around 10 seconds:

```
# echo 'tcp*' > set_ftrace_filter
# echo 1 > function_profile_enabled
# sleep 10
# echo 0 > function_profile_enabled
# echo > set_ftrace_filter
```

The sleep(1) command was used to set a (rough) duration of the profile. The commands that came after that disabled function profiling and reset the filter. Tip: be sure to use "0 >" and not "0>"—they are not the same; the latter is a redirection of file descriptor 0. Likewise avoid "1>" as it is a redirection of file descriptor 1.

The profile statistics can now be read from the trace_stat directory, which keeps them in "function" files for each CPU. This is a 2-CPU system. Using head(1) to only show the first ten lines from each file:

```
# head trace_stat/function*
==> trace_stat/function0 <==
 Function               Hit     Time           Avg          s^2
 --------               ---     ----           ---          ---
 tcp_sendmsg            955912  2788479 us     2.917 us     3734541 us
 tcp_sendmsg_locked     955912  2248025 us     2.351 us     2600545 us
 tcp_push               955912  852421.5 us    0.891 us     1057342 us
 tcp_write_xmit         926777  674611.1 us    0.727 us     1386620 us
 tcp_send_mss           955912  504021.1 us    0.527 us     95650.41 us
 tcp_current_mss        964399  317931.5 us    0.329 us     136101.4 us
 tcp_poll               966848  216701.2 us    0.224 us     201483.9 us
 tcp_release_cb         956155  102312.4 us    0.107 us     188001.9 us

==> trace_stat/function1 <==
 Function               Hit     Time           Avg          s^2
 --------               ---     ----           ---          ---
 tcp_sendmsg            317935  936055.4 us    2.944 us     13488147 us
 tcp_sendmsg_locked     317935  770290.2 us    2.422 us     8886817 us
 tcp_write_xmit         348064  423766.6 us    1.217 us     226639782 us
 tcp_push               317935  310040.7 us    0.975 us     4150989 us
 tcp_tasklet_func       38109   189797.2 us    4.980 us     2239985 us
 tcp_tsq_handler        38109   180516.6 us    4.736 us     2239552 us
 tcp_tsq_write.part.0   29977   173955.7 us    5.802 us     1037352 us
 tcp_send_mss           317935  165881.9 us    0.521 us     352309.0 us
```

The columns show the function name (Function), the call count (Hit), the total time in the function (Time), the average function time (Avg), and standard deviation (s^2). The output shows that the tcp_sendmsg() function was most frequent on both CPUs; it was called over 955k times on CPU0 and over 317k times on CPU1. Its average duration was 2.9 microseconds.

A small amount of overhead is added to the profiled functions during profiling. If the set_ftrace_filter is left blank, all kernel functions are profiled (as we were warned by the initial state seen earlier: "all functions enabled"). Bear this in mind when using the profiler, and try to use the function filter to limit the overhead.

The Ftrace front ends, covered later, automate these steps and can combine the per-CPU output into a system-wide summary.

14.4 Ftrace Function Tracing

The function tracer prints per-event details for kernel function calls, and uses the function profiling instrumentation described in the previous section. This can show the sequence of various functions, timestamp-based patterns, and the on-CPU process name and PID that may be responsible. The overhead of function tracing is higher than function profiling, and so tracing is best suited for relatively infrequent functions (less than 1,000 calls per second). You can use function profiling from the previous section to find out the rate of functions before tracing them.

The key tracefs files involved in function tracing are shown in Figure 14.2.

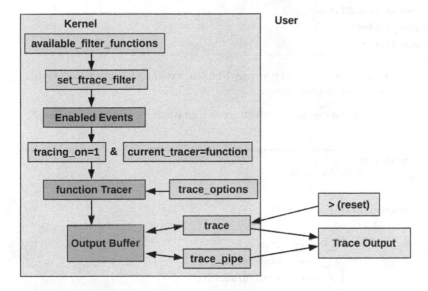

Figure 14.2   Ftrace function tracing tracefs files

The final trace output is read from either the `trace` or `trace_pipe` files, described in the following sections. Both of these interfaces also have ways to clear the output buffer (hence the arrows back to the buffer).

14.4.1 Using trace

The following demonstrates function tracing with the `trace` output file. For reference, the following shows the original not-enabled state of the function tracer:

```
# cd /sys/kernel/debug/tracing
# cat set_ftrace_filter
#### all functions enabled ####
# cat current_tracer
nop
```

No other tracer is currently in use.

For this example, all kernel functions ending with "sleep" are traced, and the events are ultimately saved to a /tmp/out.trace01.txt file. A dummy sleep(1) command is used to collect at least 10 seconds of tracing. This command sequence finishes by disabling the function tracer and returning the system back to normal:

```
# cd /sys/kernel/debug/tracing
# echo 1 > tracing_on
# echo '*sleep' > set_ftrace_filter
# echo function > current_tracer
# sleep 10
# cat trace > /tmp/out.trace01.txt
# echo nop > current_tracer
# echo > set_ftrace_filter
```

Setting tracing_on may be an unnecessary step (on my Ubuntu system, it is set to 1 by default). I've included it in case it is not set on your system.

The dummy sleep(1) command was captured in the trace output while we were tracing "sleep" function calls:

```
# more /tmp/out.trace01.txt
# tracer: function
#
# entries-in-buffer/entries-written: 57/57    #P:2
#
#                              _-----=> irqs-off
#                             / _----=> need-resched
#                            | / _---=> hardirq/softirq
#                            || / _--=> preempt-depth
#                            ||| /     delay
#           TASK-PID    CPU#  ||||    TIMESTAMP  FUNCTION
#              | |       |    ||||       |          |
      multipathd-348   [001] ....  332762.532877: __x64_sys_nanosleep <-do_syscall_64
      multipathd-348   [001] ....  332762.532879: hrtimer_nanosleep <-
__x64_sys_nanosleep
      multipathd-348   [001] ....  332762.532880: do_nanosleep <-hrtimer_nanosleep
          sleep-4203   [001] ....  332762.722497: __x64_sys_nanosleep <-do_syscall_64
          sleep-4203   [001] ....  332762.722498: hrtimer_nanosleep <-
__x64_sys_nanosleep
          sleep-4203   [001] ....  332762.722498: do_nanosleep <-hrtimer_nanosleep
      multipathd-348   [001] ....  332763.532966: __x64_sys_nanosleep <-do_syscall_64
[...]
```

The output includes field headers and trace metadata. This example shows a process named multipathd with process ID 348 calling sleep functions, as well as the sleep(1) command. The final fields show the current function and the parent function that called it. For example, for the first line, the function was __x64_sys_nanosleep() and was called by do_syscall_64().

The `trace` file is an interface to the trace events buffer. Reading it shows the buffer contents; you can clear the contents by writing a newline to it:

```
# > trace
```

The trace buffer is also cleared when the `current_tracer` is set back to nop as I did in the example steps to disable tracing. It is also cleared when trace_pipe is used.

14.4.2 Using trace_pipe

The `trace_pipe` file is a different interface for reading the trace buffer. Reads from this file return an endless stream of events. It also consumes events, so after reading them once they are no longer in the trace buffer.

For example, using `trace_pipe` to watch sleep events live:

```
# echo '*sleep' > set_ftrace_filter
# echo function > current_tracer
# cat trace_pipe
     multipathd-348    [001] ....  332624.519190: __x64_sys_nanosleep <-do_syscall_64
     multipathd-348    [001] ....  332624.519192: hrtimer_nanosleep <-
__x64_sys_nanosleep
     multipathd-348    [001] ....  332624.519192: do_nanosleep <-hrtimer_nanosleep
     multipathd-348    [001] ....  332625.519272: __x64_sys_nanosleep <-do_syscall_64
     multipathd-348    [001] ....  332625.519274: hrtimer_nanosleep <-
__x64_sys_nanosleep
     multipathd-348    [001] ....  332625.519275: do_nanosleep <-hrtimer_nanosleep
          cron-504    [001] ....  332625.560150: __x64_sys_nanosleep <-do_syscall_64
          cron-504    [001] ....  332625.560152: hrtimer_nanosleep <-
__x64_sys_nanosleep
          cron-504    [001] ....  332625.560152: do_nanosleep <-hrtimer_nanosleep
^C
# echo nop > current_tracer
# echo > set_ftrace_filter
```

The output shows a number of sleeps from `multipathd` and `cron` processes. The fields are the same as the trace file output shown previously, but this time without the column headers.

The `trace_pipe` file is handy for watching low-frequency events, but for high-frequency events you will want to capture them to a file for later analysis using the `trace` file shown earlier.

14.4.3 Options

Ftrace provides options for customizing the trace output, which can be controlled from a trace_options file or the options directory. For example (from the same directory) disabling the flags column (in the previous output this was "..."):

```
# echo 0 > options/irq-info
# cat trace
# tracer: function
#
# entries-in-buffer/entries-written: 3300/3300    #P:2
#
#           TASK-PID    CPU#   TIMESTAMP  FUNCTION
#              | |        |        |          |
     multipathd-348    [001]   332762.532877: __x64_sys_nanosleep <-do_syscall_64
     multipathd-348    [001]   332762.532879: hrtimer_nanosleep <-__x64_sys_nanosleep
     multipathd-348    [001]   332762.532880: do_nanosleep <-hrtimer_nanosleep
[...]
```

Now the flags file is not present in the output. You can set this back using:

```
# echo 1 > options/irq-info
```

There are many more options, which you can list from the options directory; they have somewhat intuitive names.

```
# ls options/
annotate            funcgraph-abstime   hex               stacktrace
bin                 funcgraph-cpu       irq-info          sym-addr
blk_cgname          funcgraph-duration  latency-format    sym-offset
blk_cgroup          funcgraph-irqs      markers           sym-userobj
blk_classic         funcgraph-overhead  overwrite         test_nop_accept
block               funcgraph-overrun   print-parent      test_nop_refuse
context-info        funcgraph-proc      printk-msg-only   trace_printk
disable_on_free     funcgraph-tail      raw               userstacktrace
display-graph       function-fork       record-cmd        verbose
event-fork          function-trace      record-tgid
func_stack_trace    graph-time          sleep-time
```

These options include `stacktrace` and `userstacktrace`, which will append kernel and user stack traces to the output: this is useful for understanding why functions were called. All of these options are documented in the Ftrace documentation in the Linux source [Rostedt 08].

14.5 Tracepoints

Tracepoints are kernel static instrumentation, and were introduced in Chapter 4, Observability Tools, Section 4.3.5, Tracepoints. Tracepoints are technically just the tracing functions placed in kernel source; they are used from a trace event interface that defines and formats their arguments. Trace events are visible in tracefs, and share output and control files with Ftrace.

As an example, the following enables the block:block_rq_issue tracepoint and watches the events live. This example finishes by disabling the tracepoint:

```
# cd /sys/kernel/debug/tracing
# echo 1 > events/block/block_rq_issue/enable
# cat trace_pipe
          sync-4844   [001] ....  343996.918805: block_rq_issue: 259,0 WS 4096 ()
2048 + 8 [sync]
          sync-4844   [001] ....  343996.918808: block_rq_issue: 259,0 WSM 4096 ()
10560 + 8 [sync]
          sync-4844   [001] ....  343996.918809: block_rq_issue: 259,0 WSM 4096 ()
38424 + 8 [sync]
          sync-4844   [001] ....  343996.918809: block_rq_issue: 259,0 WSM 4096 ()
4196384 + 8 [sync]
          sync-4844   [001] ....  343996.918810: block_rq_issue: 259,0 WSM 4096 ()
4462592 + 8 [sync]
^C
# echo 0 > events/block/block_rq_issue/enable
```

The first five columns are the same as shown in 4.6.4, and are: process name "-" PID, CPU ID, flags, timestamp (seconds), and event name. The remainder are the format string for the tracepoint, described in Section 4.3.5.

As can be seen in this example, tracepoints have control files in a directory structure under events. There is a directory for each trace system (e.g., "block") and within those subdirectories for each event (e.g., "block_rq_issue"). Listing this directory:

```
# ls events/block/block_rq_issue/
enable  filter  format  hist  id  trigger
```

These control files are documented in the Linux source under Documentation/trace/events.rst [Ts'o 20]. In this example, the enable file was used to turn on and off the tracepoint. Other files provide filtering and triggered capabilities.

14.5.1 Filter

A filter can be included to record the event only when a Boolean expression has been met. It has a restricted syntax:

```
field operator value
```

The field is from the format file described in Section 4.3.5, under the heading Tracepoints Arguments and Format String (these fields are also printed in the format string described earlier). The operator for numbers is one of: ==, !=, <, <=, >, >=, &; and for strings: ==, !=, ~. The "~" operator performs a shell glob-style match, with wildcards: *, ?, []. These Boolean expressions can be grouped with parentheses and combined using: &&, ||.

As an example, the following sets a filter on an already-enabled block:block_rq_insert tracepoint to only trace events where the bytes field was larger than 64 Kbytes:

```
# echo 'bytes > 65536' > events/block/block_rq_insert/filter
# cat trace_pipe
    kworker/u4:1-7173   [000]  ....  378115.779394: block_rq_insert: 259,0 W 262144 ()
5920256 + 512 [kworker/u4:1]
    kworker/u4:1-7173   [000]  ....  378115.784654: block_rq_insert: 259,0 W 262144 ()
5924336 + 512 [kworker/u4:1]
    kworker/u4:1-7173   [000]  ....  378115.789136: block_rq_insert: 259,0 W 262144 ()
5928432 + 512 [kworker/u4:1]
^C
```

The output now only contains larger I/O.

```
# echo 0 > events/block/block_rq_insert/filter
```

This echo 0 resets the filter.

14.5.2   Trigger

A trigger runs an extra tracing command when an event fires. That command may be to enable or disable other tracing, print a stack trace, or take a snapshot of the tracing buffer. Available trigger commands can be listed from the trigger file when no trigger is currently set. For example:

```
# cat events/block/block_rq_issue/trigger
# Available triggers:
# traceon traceoff snapshot stacktrace enable_event disable_event enable_hist
disable_hist hist
```

One use case for triggers is when you wish to see events that led to an error condition: a trigger can be placed on the error condition that either disables tracing (traceoff) so that the trace buffer only contains the prior events, or takes a snapshot (snapshot) to preserve it.

Triggers can be combined with filters, shown in the previous section, by using an if keyword. This may be necessary to match an error condition or an interesting event. For example, to stop recording events when a block I/O larger than 64 Kbytes was queued:

```
# echo 'traceoff if bytes > 65536' > events/block/block_rq_insert/trigger
```

More complex actions can be performed using hist triggers, introduced in Section 14.10 , Ftrace Hist Triggers.

14.6 kprobes

kprobes are kernel dynamic instrumentation, and were introduced in Chapter 4, Observability Tools, Section 4.3.6, kprobes. kprobes create kprobe events for tracers to use, which share tracefs output and control files with Ftrace. kprobes are similar to the Ftrace function tracer, covered in Section 14.4, in that they trace kernel functions. kprobes, however, can be customized further, can be placed on function offsets (individual instructions), and can report function argument and return values.

This section covers kprobe event tracing and the Ftrace kprobe profiler.

14.6.1 Event Tracing

As an example, the following uses kprobes to instrument the do_nanosleep() kernel function:

```
# echo 'p:brendan do_nanosleep' >> kprobe_events
# echo 1 > events/kprobes/brendan/enable
# cat trace_pipe
     multipathd-348    [001] ....  345995.823380: brendan: (do_nanosleep+0x0/0x170)
     multipathd-348    [001] ....  345996.823473: brendan: (do_nanosleep+0x0/0x170)
     multipathd-348    [001] ....  345997.823558: brendan: (do_nanosleep+0x0/0x170)
^C
# echo 0 > events/kprobes/brendan/enable
# echo '-:brendan' >> kprobe_events
```

The kprobe is created and deleted by appending a special syntax to kprobe_events. After it has been created, it appears in the events directory alongside tracepoints, and can be used in a similar fashion.

The kprobe syntax is fully explained in the kernel source under Documentation/trace/kprobetrace.rst [Hiramatsu 20]. kprobes are able to trace the entry and return of kernel functions as well as function offsets. The synopsis is:

```
 p[:[GRP/]EVENT] [MOD:]SYM[+offs]|MEMADDR [FETCHARGS]   : Set a probe
 r[MAXACTIVE][:[GRP/]EVENT] [MOD:]SYM[+0] [FETCHARGS]   : Set a return probe
 -:[GRP/]EVENT                                          : Clear a probe
```

In my example, the string "p:brendan do_nanosleep" creates a probe (p:) of name "brendan" for the kernel symbol do_nanosleep(). The string "-:brendan" deletes the probe of name "brendan".

Custom names have proven useful for differentiating different users of kprobes. The BCC tracer (covered in Chapter 15, BPF, Section 15.1, BCC) uses names that include the traced function, the string "bcc", and the BCC PID. For example:

```
# cat /sys/kernel/debug/tracing/kprobe_events
p:kprobes/p_blk_account_io_start_bcc_19454 blk_account_io_start
p:kprobes/p_blk_mq_start_request_bcc_19454 blk_mq_start_request
```

Note that, on newer kernels, BCC has switched to using a perf_event_open(2)-based interface to use kprobes instead of the kprobe_events file (and events enabled using perf_event_open(2) do not appear in kprobe_events).

14.6.2 Arguments

Unlike function tracing (Section 14.4, Ftrace Function Tracing), kprobes can inspect function arguments and return values. As an example, here is the declaration for the do_nanosleep() function traced earlier, from kernel/time/hrtimer.c, with the argument variable types highlighted:

```
static int __sched do_nanosleep(struct hrtimer_sleeper *t, enum hrtimer_mode mode)
{
[...]
```

Tracing the first two arguments on an Intel x86_64 system and printing them as hexadecimal (the default):

```
# echo 'p:brendan do_nanosleep hrtimer_sleeper=$arg1 hrtimer_mode=$arg2' >>
kprobe_events
# echo 1 > events/kprobes/brendan/enable
# cat trace_pipe
     multipathd-348    [001] .... 349138.128610: brendan: (do_nanosleep+0x0/0x170)
hrtimer_sleeper=0xffffaa6a4030be80 hrtimer_mode=0x1
     multipathd-348    [001] .... 349139.128695: brendan: (do_nanosleep+0x0/0x170)
hrtimer_sleeper=0xffffaa6a4030be80 hrtimer_mode=0x1
     multipathd-348    [001] .... 349140.128785: brendan: (do_nanosleep+0x0/0x170)
hrtimer_sleeper=0xffffaa6a4030be80 hrtimer_mode=0x1
^C
# echo 0 > events/kprobes/brendan/enable
# echo '-:brendan' >> kprobe_events
```

There is additional syntax added to the event description in the first line: the string "hrtimer_sleeper=$arg1", for example, traces the first argument to the function and uses the custom name "hrtimer_sleeper". This has been highlighted in the output.

Accessing arguments to functions as $arg1, $arg2, etc., was added in Linux 4.20. Prior Linux versions required the use of register names.[3] Here is the equivalent kprobe definition using register names:

```
# echo 'p:brendan do_nanosleep hrtimer_sleeper=%di hrtimer_mode=%si' >> kprobe_events
```

To use register names, you need to know the processor type and the function calling convention in use. x86_64 uses the AMD64 ABI [Matz 13], so the first two arguments are available in the

---

[3]This may also be necessary for processor architectures where the aliases have yet to be added.

registers rdi and rsi.[4] This syntax is also used by perf(1), and I provided a more complex example of it in Chapter 13, perf, Section 13.7.2, uprobes, which dereferenced a string pointer.

14.6.3 Return Values

The special alias $retval for the return value is available for use with kretprobes. The following example uses it to show the return value of do_nanosleep():

```
# echo 'r:brendan do_nanosleep ret=$retval' >> kprobe_events
# echo 1 > events/kprobes/brendan/enable
# cat trace_pipe
     multipathd-348   [001] d... 349782.180370: brendan:
(hrtimer_nanosleep+0xce/0x1e0 <- do_nanosleep) ret=0x0
     multipathd-348   [001] d... 349783.180443: brendan:
(hrtimer_nanosleep+0xce/0x1e0 <- do_nanosleep) ret=0x0
     multipathd-348   [001] d... 349784.180530: brendan:
(hrtimer_nanosleep+0xce/0x1e0 <- do_nanosleep) ret=0x0
^C
# echo 0 > events/kprobes/brendan/enable
# echo '-:brendan' >> kprobe_events
```

This output shows that, while tracing, the return value of do_nanosleep() was always "0" (success).

14.6.4 Filters and Triggers

Filters and triggers can be used from the events/kprobes/... directory, as they were with tracepoints (see Section 14.5, Tracepoints). Here is the format file for the earlier kprobe on do_nanosleep() with arguments (from Section 14.6.2, Arguments):

```
# cat events/kprobes/brendan/format
name: brendan
ID: 2024
format:
        field:unsigned short common_type;   offset:0;   size:2;    signed:0;
        field:unsigned char common_flags;   offset:2;   size:1;    signed:0;
        field:unsigned char common_preempt_count;   offset:3;  size:1;  signed:0;
        field:int common_pid;      offset:4; size:4;     signed:1;

        field:unsigned long __probe_ip;    offset:8;   size:8;    signed:0;
        field:u64 hrtimer_sleeper;    offset:16;  size:8;     signed:0;
        field:u64 hrtimer_mode;   offset:24;     size:8;     signed:0;
```

---

[4] The syscall(2) man page summarizes calling conventions for different processors. An excerpt is in Section 14.13.4, perf-tools One-Liners.

```
print fmt: "(%lx) hrtimer_sleeper=0x%Lx hrtimer_mode=0x%Lx", REC->__probe_ip, REC-
>hrtimer_sleeper, REC->hrtimer_mode
```

Note that my custom hrtimer_sleeper and hrtimer_mode variable names are visible as fields that can be used with a filter. For example:

```
# echo 'hrtimer_mode != 1' > events/kprobes/brendan/filter
```

This will only trace do_nanosleep() calls where hrtimer_mode is not equal to 1.

14.6.5   kprobe Profiling

When kprobes are enabled, Ftrace counts their events. These counts can be printed in the kprobe_profile file. For example:

```
# cat /sys/kernel/debug/tracing/kprobe_profile
  p_blk_account_io_start_bcc_19454              1808         0
  p_blk_mq_start_request_bcc_19454               677         0
  p_blk_account_io_completion_bcc_19454          521        11
  p_kbd_event_1_bcc_1119                         632         0
```

The columns are: the probe name (its definition can be seen by printing the kprobe_events file), the hit count, and the miss-hits count (where the probe was hit but then an error was encountered and it wasn't recorded: it was missed).

While you can already get function counts using the function profiler (Section 14.3), I've found the kprobe profiler useful for checking the always-enabled kprobes used by monitoring software, in case some are firing too frequently and should be disabled (if possible).

14.7   uprobes

uprobes are user-level dynamic instrumentation, and were introduced in Chapter 4, Observability Tools, Section 4.3.7, uprobes. uprobes create uprobe events for tracers to use, which share tracefs output and control files with Ftrace.

This section covers uprobe event tracing and the Ftrace uprobe profiler.

14.7.1   Event Tracing

For uprobes the control file is uprobe_events, with the syntax documented in the Linux source under Documentation/trace/uprobetracer.rst [Dronamraju 20]. The synopsis is:

```
p[:[GRP/]EVENT] PATH:OFFSET [FETCHARGS] : Set a uprobe
r[:[GRP/]EVENT] PATH:OFFSET [FETCHARGS] : Set a return uprobe (uretprobe)
-:[GRP/]EVENT                           : Clear uprobe or uretprobe event
```

The syntax now requires a path and an offset for the uprobe. The kernel does not have symbol information for user-space software, so this offset must be determined and provided to the kernel using user-space tools.

The following example uses uprobes to instrument the readline() function from the bash(1) shell, starting with a lookup of the symbol offset:

```
# readelf -s /bin/bash | grep -w readline
   882: 00000000000b61e0   153 FUNC    GLOBAL DEFAULT   14 readline
# echo 'p:brendan /bin/bash:0xb61e0' >> uprobe_events
# echo 1 > events/uprobes/brendan/enable
# cat trace_pipe
          bash-3970  [000] d... 347549.225818: brendan: (0x55d0857b71e0)
          bash-4802  [000] d... 347552.666943: brendan: (0x560bcc1821e0)
          bash-4802  [000] d... 347552.799480: brendan: (0x560bcc1821e0)
^C
# echo 0 > events/uprobes/brendan/enable
# echo '-:brendan' >> uprobe_events
```

WARNING: If you mistakenly use a symbol offset that is midway through an instruction, you will corrupt the target process (and for shared instruction text, all processes that share it!). The example technique of using readelf(1) to find the symbol offset may not work if the target binary has been compiled as a position-independent executable (PIE) with address space layout randomization (ASLR). I do not recommend that you use this interface at all: switch to a higher-level tracer that takes care of symbol mappings for you (e.g., BCC or bpftrace).

14.7.2 Arguments and Return Values

These are similar to kprobes demonstrated in Section 14.6, kprobes. uprobe arguments and return values can be inspected by specifying them when the uprobe is created. The syntax is in uprobetracer.rst [Dronamraju 20].

14.7.3 Filters and Triggers

Filters and triggers can be used from the events/uprobes/... directory, as they were with kprobes (see Section 14.6, kprobes).

14.7.4 uprobe Profiling

When uprobes are enabled, Ftrace counts their events. These counts can be printed in the uprobe_profile file. For example:

```
# cat /sys/kernel/debug/tracing/uprobe_profile
  /bin/bash brendan                                              11
```

The columns are: the path, the probe name (its definition can be seen by printing the uprobe_events file), and the hit count.

14.8   Ftrace function_graph

The function_graph tracer prints the call graph for functions, revealing the flow of code. This chapter began with an example via funcgraph(8) from perf-tools. The following shows the Ftrace tracefs interface.

For reference, here is the original not-enabled state of the function graph tracer:

```
# cd /sys/kernel/debug/tracing
# cat set_graph_function
#### all functions enabled ####
# cat current_tracer
nop
```

No other tracer is currently in use.

14.8.1   Graph Tracing

The following uses the function_graph tracer on the do_nanosleep() function, to show its child function calls:

```
# echo do_nanosleep > set_graph_function
# echo function_graph > current_tracer
# cat trace_pipe
 1)    2.731 us    |  get_xsave_addr();
 1)                |  do_nanosleep() {
 1)                |    hrtimer_start_range_ns() {
 1)                |      lock_hrtimer_base.isra.0() {
 1)    0.297 us    |        _raw_spin_lock_irqsave();
 1)    0.843 us    |      }
 1)    0.276 us    |      ktime_get();
 1)    0.340 us    |      get_nohz_timer_target();
 1)    0.474 us    |      enqueue_hrtimer();
 1)    0.339 us    |      _raw_spin_unlock_irqrestore();
 1)    4.438 us    |    }
 1)                |    schedule() {
 1)                |      rcu_note_context_switch() {
[...]
 5) $ 1000383 us  |  } /* do_nanosleep */
^C
# echo nop > current_tracer
# echo > set_graph_function
```

The output shows the child calls and the code flow: do_nanosleep() called hrtimer_start_range_ns(), which called lock_hrtimer_base.isra.0(), and so on. The column on the left shows the CPU (in this output, mostly CPU 1) and the duration in functions, so that latency can be identified. High latencies include a character symbol to help draw your attention to them, in this output, a "$" next to a latency of 1000383 microseconds (1.0 seconds). The characters are [Rostedt 08]:

- **$**: Greater than 1 second
- **@**: Greater than 100 ms
- *****: Greater than 10 ms
- **#**: Greater than 1 ms
- **!**: Greater than 100 µs
- **+**: Greater than 10 µs

This example deliberately did not set a function filter (set_ftrace_filter), so that all child calls can be seen. This does, however, cost some overhead, inflating the reported durations. It is still generally useful for locating the origin of high latencies, which can dwarf the added overhead. When you want more accurate times for a given function, you can use a function filter to reduce the functions traced. For example, to only trace do_nanosleep():

```
# echo do_nanosleep > set_ftrace_filter
# cat trace_pipe
[...]
 7) $ 1000130 us  |  } /* do_nanosleep */
^C
```

I am tracing the same workload (sleep 1). After applying a filter, the reported duration of do_nanosleep() has dropped from 1000383 µs to 1000130 µs (for these example outputs), as it no longer includes the overhead of tracing all child functions.

These examples also used trace_pipe to watch the output live, but this is verbose, and it is more practical to redirect the trace file to an output file, as I demonstrated in Section 14.4, Ftrace Function Tracing.

14.8.2 Options

Options are available to change the output, which can be listed in the options directory:

```
# ls options/funcgraph-*
options/funcgraph-abstime   options/funcgraph-irqs      options/funcgraph-proc
options/funcgraph-cpu       options/funcgraph-overhead  options/funcgraph-tail
options/funcgraph-duration  options/funcgraph-overrun
```

These adjust the output and can include or exclude details, such as the CPU ID (funcgraph-cpu), process name (funcgraph-proc), function duration (funcgraph-duration), and delay markers (funcgraph-overhead).

14.9   Ftrace hwlat

The hardware latency detector (hwlat) is an example of a special-purpose tracer. It can detect when external hardware events perturb CPU performance: events that are otherwise invisible to the kernel and other tools. For example, system management interrupt (SMI) events and hypervisor perturbations (including those caused by noisy neighbors).

This works by running a code loop as an experiment with interrupts disabled, measuring the time taken for each iteration of the loop to run. This loop is executed on one CPU at a time and rotates through them. The slowest loop iteration for each CPU is printed, provided it exceeds a threshold (10 microseconds, which can be configured via the tracing_thresh file).

Here is an example:

```
# cd /sys/kernel/debug/tracing
# echo hwlat > current_tracer
# cat trace_pipe
          <...>-5820  [001] d... 354016.973699: #1     inner/outer(us): 2152/1933
ts:1578801212.559595228
          <...>-5820  [000] d... 354017.985568: #2     inner/outer(us):   19/26
ts:1578801213.571460991
          <...>-5820  [001] dn.. 354019.009489: #3     inner/outer(us): 1699/5894
ts:1578801214.595380588
          <...>-5820  [000] d... 354020.033575: #4     inner/outer(us):   43/49
ts:1578801215.619463259
          <...>-5820  [001] d... 354021.057566: #5     inner/outer(us):   18/45
ts:1578801216.643451721
          <...>-5820  [000] d... 354022.081503: #6     inner/outer(us):   18/38
ts:1578801217.667385514
^C
# echo nop > current_tracer
```

Many of these fields have been described in previous sections (see Section 14.4, Ftrace Function Tracing). What is interesting is after the timestamp: there is a sequence number (#1, ...), then "inner/outer(us)" numbers, and a final timestamp. The inner/outer numbers show the loop timing inside the loop (inner) and the code logic to wrap to the next loop iteration (outer). The first line shows an iteration that took 2,152 microseconds (inner) and 1,933 microseconds (outer). This by far exceeds the threshold of 10 microseconds, and is due to an external perturbation.

hwlat has parameters that can be configured: the loop runs for a period of time called the *width*, and runs one width experiment during a period of time called the *window*. The slowest iteration longer than a threshold (10 microseconds) during each width is logged. These parameters can be modified via files in /sys/kernel/debug/tracing/hwlat_detector: the width and window files, which use units of microseconds.

WARNING: I'd classify hwlat as a microbenchmark tool rather than an observability tool, because it performs an experiment that will itself perturb the system: it will make one CPU busy for the width duration, with interrupts disabled.

14.10   Ftrace Hist Triggers

Hist triggers is an advanced Ftrace capability added to Linux 4.7 by Tom Zanussi, which allows the creation of custom histograms on events. It is another form of statistical summary, allowing counts to be broken down by one or more components.

The overall usage for a single histogram is:

1. **echo 'hist:*expression*' > events/.../trigger**: Create a hist trigger.

2. **sleep *duration***: Allow histogram to populate.

3. **cat events/.../hist**: Print the histogram.

4. **echo '!hist:*expression*' > events/.../trigger**: Remove it.

The hist expression is of the format:

```
hist:keys=<field1[,field2,...]>[:values=<field1[,field2,...]>]
  [:sort=<field1[,field2,...]>][:size=#entries][:pause][:continue]
  [:clear][:name=histname1][:<handler>.<action>] [if <filter>]
```

The syntax is fully documented in the Linux source under Documentation/trace/histogram.rst, and the following are some examples [Zanussi 20].

14.10.1   Single Keys

The following uses hist triggers to count syscalls via the raw_syscalls:sys_enter tracepoint, and provides a histogram breakdown by process ID:

```
# cd /sys/kernel/debug/tracing
# echo 'hist:key=common_pid' > events/raw_syscalls/sys_enter/trigger
# sleep 10
# cat events/raw_syscalls/sys_enter/hist
# event histogram
#
# trigger info: hist:keys=common_pid.execname:vals=hitcount:sort=hitcount:size=2048
[active]
#

{ common_pid:        347 } hitcount:           1
{ common_pid:        345 } hitcount:           3
{ common_pid:        504 } hitcount:           8
{ common_pid:        494 } hitcount:          20
{ common_pid:        502 } hitcount:          30
{ common_pid:        344 } hitcount:          32
{ common_pid:        348 } hitcount:          36
{ common_pid:      32399 } hitcount:         136
{ common_pid:      32400 } hitcount:         138
```

```
{ common_pid:        32379 } hitcount:        177
{ common_pid:        32296 } hitcount:        187
{ common_pid:        32396 } hitcount:     882604

Totals:
    Hits: 883372
    Entries: 12
    Dropped: 0
# echo '!hist:key=common_pid' > events/raw_syscalls/sys_enter/trigger
```

The output shows that PID 32396 performed 882,604 syscalls while tracing, and listed the counts for the other PIDs. The final few lines show statistics: the number of writes to the hash (Hits), the entries in the hash (Entries), and how many writes were dropped if the entries exceeded the hash size (Dropped). If drops occur, you can increase the size of the hash when declaring it; it defaults to 2048.

14.10.2   Fields

The hash fields come from the format file for the event. For this example, the common_pid field was used:

```
# cat events/raw_syscalls/sys_enter/format
[...]
        field:int common_pid;         offset:4;   size:4;     signed:1;

        field:long id;   offset:8;  size:8;     signed:1;
        field:unsigned long args[6];      offset:16;    size:48;  signed:0;
```

You can use other fields as well. For this event, the id field is the syscall ID. Using it as the hash key:

```
# echo 'hist:key=id' > events/raw_syscalls/sys_enter/trigger
# cat events/raw_syscalls/sys_enter/hist
[...]
{ id:        14 } hitcount:        48
{ id:         1 } hitcount:     80362
{ id:         0 } hitcount:     80396
[...]
```

The histogram shows that the most frequent syscalls had IDs 0 and 1. On my system the syscall IDs are in this header file:

```
# more /usr/include/x86_64-linux-gnu/asm/unistd_64.h
[...]
#define __NR_read 0
```

```
#define __NR_write 1
[...]
```

This shows that 0 and 1 are for the read(2) and write(2) syscalls.

14.10.3 Modifiers

Since PID and syscall ID breakdowns are common, hist triggers supports modifiers that annotate the output: .execname for PIDs, and .syscall for syscall IDs. For example, adding the .execname modifier to the earlier example:

```
# echo 'hist:key=common_pid.execname' > events/raw_syscalls/sys_enter/trigger
[...]
{ common_pid: bash            [   32379] } hitcount:            166
{ common_pid: sshd            [   32296] } hitcount:            259
{ common_pid: dd              [   32396] } hitcount:         869024
[...]
```

The output now contains the process name followed by the PID in square brackets, instead of just the PID.

14.10.4 PID Filters

Based on the previous by-PID and by-syscall ID outputs, you may assume that the two are related and that the dd(1) command was performing the read(2) and write(2) syscalls. To measure this directly, you can create a histogram for the syscall ID and then use a filter to match on the PID:

```
# echo 'hist:key=id.syscall if common_pid==32396' > \
    events/raw_syscalls/sys_enter/trigger
# cat events/raw_syscalls/sys_enter/hist
# event histogram
#
# trigger info: hist:keys=id.syscall:vals=hitcount:sort=hitcount:size=2048 if common_
pid==32396 [active]
#

{ id: sys_write                   [  1] } hitcount:        106425
{ id: sys_read                    [  0] } hitcount:        106425

Totals:
    Hits: 212850
    Entries: 2
    Dropped: 0
```

The histogram now shows the syscalls for that one PID, and the .syscall modifier has included the syscall names. This confirms that dd(1) is calling read(2) and write(2). Another solution to this is to use multiple keys, as shown in the next section.

14.10.5 Multiple Keys

The following example includes the syscall ID as a *second key*:

```
# echo 'hist:key=common_pid.execname,id' > events/raw_syscalls/sys_enter/trigger
# sleep 10
# cat events/raw_syscalls/sys_enter/hist
# event histogram
#
# trigger info: hist:keys=common_pid.execname,id:vals=hitcount:sort=hitcount:size=2048
[active]
#
[...]
{ common_pid: sshd           [   14250], id:        23 } hitcount:          36
{ common_pid: bash           [   14261], id:        13 } hitcount:          42
{ common_pid: sshd           [   14250], id:        14 } hitcount:          72
{ common_pid: dd             [   14325], id:         0 } hitcount:     9195176
{ common_pid: dd             [   14325], id:         1 } hitcount:     9195176

Totals:
    Hits: 18391064
    Entries: 75
    Dropped: 0
    Dropped: 0
```

The output now shows the process name and PID, further broken down by the syscall ID. This output shows that dd PID 142325 was performing two syscalls with IDs 0 and 1. You can add the .syscall modifier to the second key to make it include the syscall names.

14.10.6 Stack Trace Keys

I frequently wish to know the code path that led to the event, and I suggested that Tom Zanussi add functionality for Ftrace to use an entire kernel stack trace as a key.

For example, counting the code paths that led to the block:block_rq_issue tracepoint:

```
# echo 'hist:key=stacktrace' > events/block/block_rq_issue/trigger
# sleep 10
# cat events/block/block_rq_issue/hist
[...]
```

```
{ stacktrace:
        nvme_queue_rq+0x16c/0x1d0
        __blk_mq_try_issue_directly+0x116/0x1c0
        blk_mq_request_issue_directly+0x4b/0xe0
        blk_mq_try_issue_list_directly+0x46/0xb0
        blk_mq_sched_insert_requests+0xae/0x100
        blk_mq_flush_plug_list+0x1e8/0x290
        blk_flush_plug_list+0xe3/0x110
        blk_finish_plug+0x26/0x34
        read_pages+0x86/0x1a0
        __do_page_cache_readahead+0x180/0x1a0
        ondemand_readahead+0x192/0x2d0
        page_cache_sync_readahead+0x78/0xc0
        generic_file_buffered_read+0x571/0xc00
        generic_file_read_iter+0xdc/0x140
        ext4_file_read_iter+0x4f/0x100
        new_sync_read+0x122/0x1b0
} hitcount:         266


Totals:
    Hits: 522
    Entries: 10
    Dropped: 0
```

I've truncated the output to only show the last, most frequent, stack trace. It shows that disk I/O was issued via the new_sync_read(), which called ext4_file_read_iter(), and so on.

14.10.7   Synthetic Events

This is where things start to get really weird (if they haven't already). A *synthetic event* can be created that is triggered by other events, and can combine their event arguments in custom ways. To access event arguments from prior events, they can be saved into a histogram and fetched by the later synthetic event.

This makes much more sense with a key use case: custom latency histograms. With synthetic events, a timestamp can be saved on one event and then retrieved on another so that the delta time can be calculated.

For example, the following uses a synthetic event named syscall_latency to calculate the latency of all syscalls, and present it as a histogram by syscall ID and name:

```
# cd /sys/kernel/debug/tracing
# echo 'syscall_latency u64 lat_us; long id' >> synthetic_events
# echo 'hist:keys=common_pid:ts0=common_timestamp.usecs' >> \
    events/raw_syscalls/sys_enter/trigger
```

```
# echo 'hist:keys=common_pid:lat_us=common_timestamp.usecs-$ts0:'\
    'onmatch(raw_syscalls.sys_enter).trace(syscall_latency,$lat_us,id)' >>\
    events/raw_syscalls/sys_exit/trigger
# echo 'hist:keys=lat_us,id.syscall:sort=lat_us' >> \
    events/synthetic/syscall_latency/trigger
# sleep 10
# cat events/synthetic/syscall_latency/hist
[...]
{ lat_us:    5779085, id: sys_epoll_wait             [232] } hitcount:          1
{ lat_us:    6232897, id: sys_poll                   [  7] } hitcount:          1
{ lat_us:    6233840, id: sys_poll                   [  7] } hitcount:          1
{ lat_us:    6233884, id: sys_futex                  [202] } hitcount:          1
{ lat_us:    7028672, id: sys_epoll_wait             [232] } hitcount:          1
{ lat_us:    9999049, id: sys_poll                   [  7] } hitcount:          1
{ lat_us:   10000097, id: sys_nanosleep              [ 35] } hitcount:          1
{ lat_us:   10001535, id: sys_wait4                  [ 61] } hitcount:          1
{ lat_us:   10002176, id: sys_select                 [ 23] } hitcount:          1
[...]
```

The output is truncated to show only the highest latencies. The histogram is counting pairs of latency (in microseconds) and syscall ID: this output shows that sys_nanosleep had one occurrence of 10000097 microsecond latency. This is likely showing the sleep 10 command used to set the recording duration.

The output is also very long because it is recording a key for every microsecond and syscall ID combination, and in practice I've exceeded the default hist size of 2048. You can increase the size by adding a :size=... operator to the hist declaration, or you can use the .log2 modifier to record the latency as a log2. This greatly reduces the number of hist entries, and still has sufficient resolution to analyze latency.

To disable and clean up this event, echo all the strings in reverse order with a "!" prefix.

In Table 14.4 I explain how this synthetic event works, with code snippets.

Table 14.4 **Synthetic event example explanation**

Description	Syntax
I'd like to create a synthetic event named syscall_latency with two arguments: lat_us and id.	`echo 'syscall_latency u64 lat_us; long id' >> synthetic_events`
When the sys_enter event occurs, record a histogram using common_pid (the current PID) as a key,	`echo 'hist:keys=common_pid: ... >> events/raw_syscalls/sys_enter/trigger`
and save the current time, in microseconds, into a histogram variable named ts0 that is associated with the histogram key (common_pid).	`ts0=common_timestamp.usecs`

Description	Syntax
On the sys_exit event, use common_pid as the histogram key and,	`echo 'hist:keys=common_pid: ... >> events/raw_syscalls/sys_exit/trigger`
calculate latency as now minus the start time saved in `ts0` by the prior event, and save it as a histogram variable named `lat_us`,	`lat_us=common_timestamp.usecs-$ts0`
compare the histogram keys of this event and the sys_enter event. If they match (the same `common_pid`), then `lat_us` has the right latency calculation (sys_enter to sys_exit for the same PID) so,	`onmatch(raw_syscalls.sys_enter)`
finally, trigger our synthetic event syscall_latency with `lat_us` and id as arguments.	`.trace(syscall_latency,$lat_us,id)`
Show this synthetic event as a histogram with its `lat_us` and id as fields.	`echo 'hist:keys=lat_us,id.syscall:sort=lat_us' >> events/synthetic/syscall_latency/trigger`

Ftrace histograms are implemented as a hash object (key/value store), and the earlier examples only used these hashes for output: showing syscall counts by PID and ID. With synthetic events, we're doing two extra things with these hashes: A) storing values that are not part of the output (timestamps) and B) in one event, fetching key/value pairs that were set by another event. We're also performing arithmetic: a minus operation. In a way, we're starting to write mini programs.

There is more to synthetic events, covered in the documentation [Zanussi 20]. I've provided feedback, directly or indirectly, to the Ftrace and BPF engineers for years, and from my perspective the evolution of Ftrace makes sense as it's solving the problems I've previously raised. I'd summarize the evolution as:

"Ftrace is great, but I need to use BPF for counts by PID and stack trace."

"Here you go, hist triggers."

"That's great, but I still need to use BPF to do custom latency calculations."

"Here you go, synthetic events."

"That's great, I'll check it out after I finish writing *BPF Performance Tools*."

"Seriously?"

Yes, I now do need to explore adopting synthetic events for some use cases. It's incredibly powerful, built into the kernel, and can be used via shell scripting alone. (And I did finish the BPF book, but then became busy with this one.)

14.11   trace-cmd

trace-cmd is an open-source Ftrace front end developed by Steven Rostedt and others [trace-cmd 20]. It supports subcommands and options for configuring the tracing system, a binary output format, and other features. For event sources it can use the Ftrace function and function_graph tracers, as well as tracepoints and already configured kprobes and uprobes.

For example, using trace-cmd to record the kernel function do_nanosleep() via the function tracer for ten seconds (using a dummy sleep(1) command):

```
# trace-cmd record -p function -l do_nanosleep sleep 10
  plugin 'function'
CPU0 data recorded at offset=0x4fe000
    0 bytes in size
CPU1 data recorded at offset=0x4fe000
    4096 bytes in size
# trace-cmd report
CPU 0 is empty
cpus=2
          sleep-21145 [001] 573259.213076: function:            do_nanosleep
      multipathd-348  [001] 573259.523759: function:            do_nanosleep
      multipathd-348  [001] 573260.523923: function:            do_nanosleep
      multipathd-348  [001] 573261.524022: function:            do_nanosleep
      multipathd-348  [001] 573262.524119: function:            do_nanosleep
[...]
```

The output begins with the sleep(1) invoked by trace-cmd (it configures tracing and then launches the provided command), and then various calls from multipathd PID 348. This example also shows that trace-cmd is more concise than the equivalent tracefs commands in /sys. It is also safer: many subcommands handle cleaning up tracing state when done.

trace-cmd can often be installed via a "trace-cmd" package, and if not, the source is available on the trace-cmd website [trace-cmd 20].

This section shows a selection of trace-cmd subcommands and tracing capabilities. Refer to the bundled trace-cmd documentation for all of its capabilities, and for the syntax used in the following examples.

14.11.1   Subcommands Overview

trace-cmd's capabilities are available by first specifying a subcommand, such as `trace-cmd record` for the record subcommand. A selection of subcommands from a recent trace-cmd version (2.8.3) are listed in Table 14.5.

Table 14.5   **trace-cmd selected subcommands**

Command	Description
record	Trace and record to a trace.dat file
report	Read the trace from the trace.dat file
stream	Trace and then print to stdout
list	List available tracing events
stat	Show the status of the kernel tracing subsystem
profile	Trace and generate a custom report showing kernel time and latencies
listen	Accept network requests for traces

Other subcommands include start, stop, restart, and clear for controlling tracing beyond a single invocation of record. Future versions of trace-cmd may add more subcommands; run trace-cmd with no arguments for the full list.

Each subcommand supports a variety of options. These can be listed with –h, for example, for the record subcommand:

```
# trace-cmd record -h

trace-cmd version 2.8.3

usage:
 trace-cmd record [-v][-e event [-f filter]][-p plugin][-F][-d][-D][-o file] \
          [-q][-s usecs][-O option ][-l func][-g func][-n func] \
          [-P pid][-N host:port][-t][-r prio][-b size][-B buf][command ...]
          [-m max][-C clock]
      -e run command with event enabled
      -f filter for previous -e event
      -R trigger for previous -e event
      -p run command with plugin enabled
      -F filter only on the given process
      -P trace the given pid like -F for the command
      -c also trace the children of -F (or -P if kernel supports it)
      -C set the trace clock
      -T do a stacktrace on all events
      -l filter function name
      -g set graph function
      -n do not trace function
[...]
```

The options have been truncated in this output, showing the first 12 out of 35 options. These first 12 include those most commonly used. Note that the term *plugin* (-p) refers to the Ftrace tracers, which include function, function_graph, and hwlat.

14.11.2   trace-cmd One-Liners

The following one-liners show different trace-cmd capabilities by example. The syntax for these is covered in their man pages.

Listing Events

List all tracing event sources and options:

```
trace-cmd list
```

List Ftrace tracers:

```
trace-cmd list -t
```

List event sources (tracepoints, kprobe events, and uprobe events):

```
trace-cmd list -e
```

List syscall tracepoints:

```
trace-cmd list -e syscalls:
```

Show the format file for a given tracepoint:

```
trace-cmd list -e syscalls:sys_enter_nanosleep -F
```

Function Tracing

Trace a kernel function system-wide:

```
trace-cmd record -p function -l function_name
```

Trace all kernel functions beginning with "tcp_", system-wide, until Ctrl-C:

```
trace-cmd record -p function -l 'tcp_*'
```

Trace all kernel functions beginning with "tcp_", system-wide, for 10 seconds:

```
trace-cmd record -p function -l 'tcp_*' sleep 10
```

Trace all kernel functions beginning with "vfs_" for the ls(1) command:

```
trace-cmd record -p function -l 'vfs_*' -F ls
```

Trace all kernel functions beginning with "vfs_" for bash(1) and its children:

```
trace-cmd record -p function -l 'vfs_*' -F -c bash
```

Trace all kernel functions beginning with "vfs_" for PID 21124

```
trace-cmd record -p function -l 'vfs_*' -P 21124
```

Function Graph Tracing

Trace a kernel function and its child calls, system-wide:

```
trace-cmd record -p function_graph -g function_name
```

Trace the kernel function do_nanosleep() and children, system-wide, for 10 seconds:

```
trace-cmd record -p function_graph -g do_nanosleep sleep 10
```

Event Tracing

Trace new processes via the sched:sched_process_exec tracepoint, until Ctrl-C:

```
trace-cmd record -e sched:sched_process_exec
```

Trace new processes via the sched:sched_process_exec (shorter version):

```
trace-cmd record -e sched_process_exec
```

Trace block I/O requests with kernel stack traces:

```
trace-cmd record -e block_rq_issue -T
```

Trace all block tracepoints until Ctrl-C:

```
trace-cmd record -e block
```

Trace a previously created kprobe named "brendan" for 10 seconds:

```
trace-cmd record -e probe:brendan sleep 10
```

Trace all syscalls for the ls(1) command:

```
trace-cmd record -e syscalls -F ls
```

Reporting

Print the contents of the trace.dat output file:

```
trace-cmd report
```

Print the contents of the trace.dat output file, CPU 0 only:

```
trace-cmd report --cpu 0
```

Other Capabilities

Trace events from the sched_switch plugin:

```
trace-cmd record -p sched_switch
```

Listen for tracing requests on TCP port 8081:

```
trace-cmd listen -p 8081
```

Connect to remote host for running a record subcommand:

```
trace-cmd record ... -N addr:port
```

14.11.3   trace-cmd vs. perf(1)

The style of trace-cmd subcommands may remind you of perf(1), covered in Chapter 13, and the two tools do have similar capabilities. Table 14.6 compares trace-cmd and perf(1).

Table 14.6   **perf(1) versus trace-cmd**

Attribute	perf(1)	trace-cmd
Binary output file	perf.data	trace.dat
Tracepoints	Yes	Yes
kprobes	Yes	Partial(1)
uprobes	Yes	Partial(1)
USDT	Yes	Partial(1)
PMCs	Yes	No
Timed sampling	Yes	No
function tracing	Partial(2)	Yes
function_graph tracing	Partial(2)	Yes
Network client/server	No	Yes
Output file overhead	Low	Very low
Front ends	Various	KernelShark
Source	In Linux tools/perf	git.kernel.org

- Partial(1): trace-cmd supports these events only if they have already been created via other means, and appear in /sys/kernel/debug/tracing/events.

- Partial(2): perf(1) supports these via the `ftrace` subcommand, although it is not fully integrated into perf(1) (it doesn't support perf.data, for example).

As an example of the similarity, the following traces the syscalls:sys_enter_read tracepoint system-wide for ten seconds and then lists the trace using perf(1):

```
# perf record -e syscalls:sys_enter_nanosleep -a sleep 10
# perf script
```

...and using trace-cmd:

```
# trace-cmd record -e syscalls:sys_enter_nanosleep sleep 10
# trace-cmd report
```

One advantage of trace-cmd is its better support for the function and function_graph tracers.

14.11.4   trace-cmd function_graph

The start of this section demonstrated the function tracer using trace-cmd. The following demonstrates the function_graph tracer for the same kernel function, do_nanosleep():

```
# trace-cmd record -p function_graph -g do_nanosleep sleep 10
  plugin 'function_graph'
CPU0 data recorded at offset=0x4fe000
    12288 bytes in size
CPU1 data recorded at offset=0x501000
    45056 bytes in size
# trace-cmd report | cut -c 66-

                 |  do_nanosleep() {
                 |    hrtimer_start_range_ns() {
                 |      lock_hrtimer_base.isra.0() {
  0.250 us       |        _raw_spin_lock_irqsave();
  0.688 us       |      }
  0.190 us       |      ktime_get();
  0.153 us       |      get_nohz_timer_target();
  [...]
```

For clarity in this example, I used cut(1) to isolate the function graph and timing columns. This truncated the typical tracing fields shown in the earlier function tracing example.

14.11.5   KernelShark

KernelShark is a visual user interface for trace-cmd output files, created by the creator of Ftrace, Steven Rostedt. Originally GTK, KernelShark has since been rewritten in Qt by Yordan Karadzhov, who maintains the project. KernelShark can be installed from a kernelshark package if available, or via the source links on its website [KernelShark 20]. Version 1.0 is the Qt version, and 0.99 and older are the GTK version.

As an example of using KernelShark, the following records all scheduler tracepoints and then visualizes them:

```
# trace-cmd record -e 'sched:*'
# kernelshark
```

KernelShark reads the default trace-cmd output file, trace.dat (you can specify a different file using -i). Figure 14.3 shows KernelShark visualizing this file.

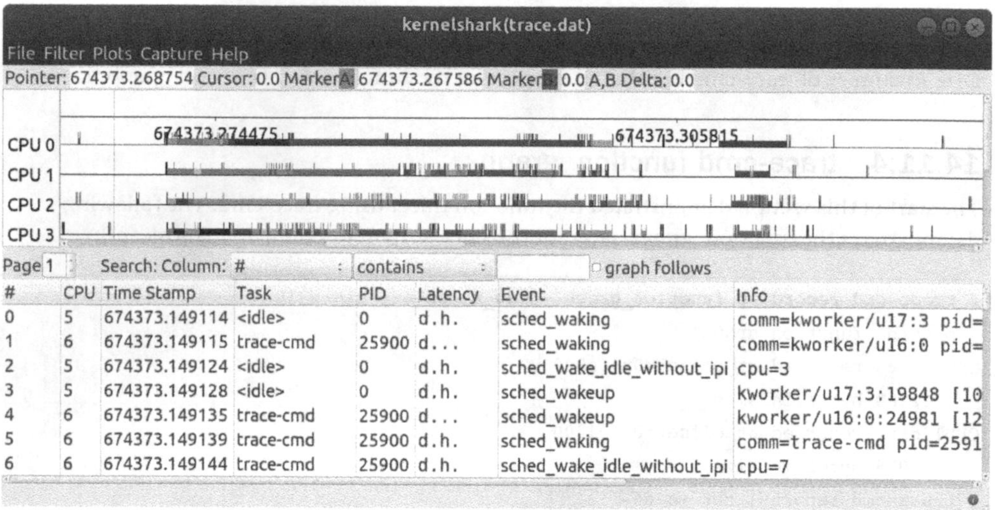

Figure 14.3　KernelShark

The top part of the screen shows a per-CPU timeline, with tasks colored differently. The bottom part is a table of events. KernelShark is interactive: a click and drag right will zoom to the selected time range, and a click and drag left will zoom out. Right-clicking events provides additional actions, such as setting up filters.

KernelShark can be used to identify performance issues caused by the interaction between different threads.

14.11.6　trace-cmd Documentation

For package installations, the trace-cmd documentation should be available as trace-cmd(1) and other man pages (e.g., trace-cmd-record(1)), which are also in the trace-cmd source under the Documentation directory. I also recommend watching a talk by the maintainer Steven Rostedt on Ftrace and trace-cmd, such as "Understanding the Linux Kernel (via ftrace)":

- Slides: https://www.slideshare.net/ennael/kernel-recipes-2017-understanding-the-linux-kernel-via-ftrace-steven-rostedt
- Video: https://www.youtube.com/watch?v=2ff-7UTg5rE

14.12   perf ftrace

The perf(1) utility, covered in Chapter 13, has an ftrace subcommand so that it can access the function and function_graph tracers.

For example, using the function tracer on the kernel do_nanosleep() function:

```
# perf ftrace -T do_nanosleep -a sleep 10
 0)   sleep-22821   |                  |  do_nanosleep() {
 1)   multipa-348   |                  |  do_nanosleep() {
 1)   multipa-348   | $ 1000068 us     |  }
 1)   multipa-348   |                  |  do_nanosleep() {
 1)   multipa-348   | $ 1000068 us     |  }
[...]
```

And using the function_graph tracer:

```
# perf ftrace -G do_nanosleep -a sleep 10
 1)   sleep-22828   |                  |  do_nanosleep() {
 1)   sleep-22828   | ==========>      |
 1)   sleep-22828   |                  |    smp_irq_work_interrupt() {
 1)   sleep-22828   |                  |      irq_enter() {
 1)   sleep-22828   |   0.258 us       |        rcu_irq_enter();
 1)   sleep-22828   |   0.800 us       |      }
 1)   sleep-22828   |                  |      __wake_up() {
 1)   sleep-22828   |                  |        __wake_up_common_lock() {
 1)   sleep-22828   |   0.491 us       |          _raw_spin_lock_irqsave();
[...]
```

The ftrace subcommand supports a few options including -p to match on a PID. This is a simple wrapper that does not integrate with other perf(1) capabilities: for example, it prints the trace output to stdout and does not use the perf.data file.

14.13   perf-tools

perf-tools is an open-source collection of Ftrace- and perf(1)-based advanced performance analysis tools developed by myself and installed by default on servers at Netflix [Gregg 20i]. I designed these tools to be easy to install (few dependencies) and simple to use: each should do one thing and do it well. The perf-tools themselves are mostly implemented as shell scripts that automate setting the tracefs /sys files.

For example, using execsnoop(8) to trace new processes:

```
# execsnoop
Tracing exec()s. Ctrl-C to end.
  PID   PPID ARGS
```

```
6684    6682 cat -v trace_pipe
6683    6679 gawk -v o=1 -v opt_name=0 -v name= -v opt_duration=0 [...]
6685   20997 man ls
6695    6685 pager
6691    6685 preconv -e UTF-8
6692    6685 tbl
6693    6685 nroff -mandoc -rLL=148n -rLT=148n -Tutf8
6698    6693 locale charmap
6699    6693 groff -mtty-char -Tutf8 -mandoc -rLL=148n -rLT=148n
6700    6699 troff -mtty-char -mandoc -rLL=148n -rLT=148n -Tutf8
6701    6699 grotty
[...]
```

This output begins by showing a cat(1) and gawk(1) command used by excesnoop(8) itself, followed by commands executed by a man ls. It can be used to debug issues of short-lived processes that can be invisible to other tools.

execsnoop(8) supports options including -t for timestamps and -h to summarize the command line usage. execsnoop(8) and all other tools also have a man page and an examples file.

14.13.1 Tool Coverage

Figure 14.4 shows the different perf-tools and the areas of a system they can observe.

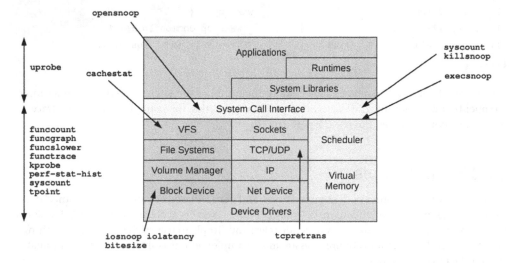

Figure 14.4   perf-tools

Many are single-purpose tools shown with a single arrow head; some are multi-purpose tools listed on the left with a double arrow to show their coverage.

14.13.2   Single-Purpose Tools

Single-purpose tools are shown with single arrow heads in Figure 14.4. Some were introduced in prior chapters.

The single-purpose tools such as execsnoop(8) do one job and do it well (Unix philosophy). This design includes making their default output concise and often sufficient, which helps aid learning. You can "just run execsnoop" without needing to learn any command line options, and get just enough output to solve your problem without unnecessary clutter. Options typically do exist for customization.

The single-purpose tools are described in Table 14.7.

Table 14.7   **Single-purpose perf-tools**

Tool	Uses	Description
bitesize(8)	perf	Summarize disk I/O size as a histogram
cachestat(8)	Ftrace	Show page cache hit/miss statistics
execsnoop(8)	Ftrace	Trace new processes (via execve(2)) with arguments
iolatency(8)	Ftrace	Summarize disk I/O latency as a histogram
iosnoop(8)	Ftrace	Trace disk I/O with details including latency
killsnoop(8)	Ftrace	Trace kill(2) signals showing process and signal details
opensnoop(8)	Ftrace	Trace open(2)-family syscalls showing filenames
tcpretrans(8)	Ftrace	Trace TCP retransmits, showing addresses and kernel state

execsnoop(8) was demonstrated earlier. As another example, iolatency(8) shows disk I/O latency as a histogram:

```
# iolatency
Tracing block I/O. Output every 1 seconds. Ctrl-C to end.

  >=(ms) .. <(ms)   : I/O     |Distribution                         |
       0 -> 1       : 731     |#####################################|
       1 -> 2       : 318     |#################                    |
       2 -> 4       : 160     |#########                            |

  >=(ms) .. <(ms)   : I/O     |Distribution                         |
       0 -> 1       : 2973    |#####################################|
       1 -> 2       : 497     |#######                              |
       2 -> 4       : 26      |#                                    |
       4 -> 8       : 3       |#                                    |
```

```
>=(ms) .. <(ms)   : I/O    |Distribution                             |
       0 -> 1     : 3130   |########################################|
       1 -> 2     : 177    |###                                      |
       2 -> 4     : 1      |#                                        |
^C
```

This output shows that I/O latency was typically low, between 0 and 1 milliseconds.

The way I implemented this helps to explain the need for extended BPF. iolatency(8) traces block I/O issue and completion tracepoints, reads all events in user-space, parses them, and post-processes them into these histograms using awk(1). Since disk I/O has a relatively low frequency on most servers, this approach was possible without onerous overhead. But the overhead would be prohibitive for more frequent events, such as network I/O or scheduling. Extended BPF solved this problem by allowing the histogram summary to be calculated in kernel space, and only the summary is passed to user space, greatly reducing overhead. Ftrace now supports some similar capabilities with hist triggers and synthetic events, described in Section 14.10, Ftrace Hist Triggers (I need to update iolatency(8) to make use of them).

I did develop a pre-BPF solution to custom histograms, and exposed it as the perf-stat-hist(8) multi-purpose tool.

14.13.3   Multi-Purpose Tools

The multi-purpose tools are listed and described in Figure 14.4. These support multiple event sources and can do many roles, similar to perf(1) and trace-cmd, although this also makes them complex to use.

Table 14.8   **Multi-purpose perf-tools**

Tool	Uses	Description
funccount(8)	Ftrace	Count kernel function calls
funcgraph(8)	Ftrace	Trace kernel functions showing child function code flow
functrace(8)	Ftrace	Trace kernel functions
funcslower(8)	Ftrace	Trace kernel functions slower than a threshold
kprobe(8)	Ftrace	Dynamic tracing of kernel functions
perf-stat-hist(8)	perf(1)	Custom power-of aggregations for tracepoint arguments
syscount(8)	perf(1)	Summarize syscalls
tpoint(8)	Ftrace	Trace tracepoints
uprobe(8)	Ftrace	Dynamic tracing of user-level functions

To aid usage of these tools you can collect and share one-liners. I have provided them in the next section, similar to my one-liner sections for perf(1) and trace-cmd.

14.13.4   perf-tools One-Liners

The following one-liners trace system-wide and until Ctrl-C is typed, unless otherwise specified. They are grouped into those that use Ftrace profiling, Ftrace tracers, and event tracing (tracepoints, kprobes, uprobes).

Ftrace Profilers

Count all kernel TCP functions:

```
funccount 'tcp_*'
```

Count all kernel VFS functions, printing the top 10 every 1 second:

```
funccount -t 10 -i 1 'vfs*'
```

Ftrace Tracers

Trace the kernel function do_nanosleep() and show all child calls:

```
funcgraph do_nanosleep
```

Trace the kernel function do_nanosleep() and show child calls up to 3 levels deep:

```
funcgraph -m 3 do_nanosleep
```

Count all kernel functions ending in "sleep" for PID 198:

```
functrace -p 198 '*sleep'
```

Trace vfs_read() calls slower than 10 ms:

```
funcslower vfs_read 10000
```

Event Tracing

Trace the do_sys_open() kernel function using a kprobe:

```
kprobe p:do_sys_open
```

Trace the return of do_sys_open() using a kretprobe, and print the return value:

```
kprobe 'r:do_sys_open $retval'
```

Trace the file mode argument of do_sys_open():

```
kprobe 'p:do_sys_open mode=$arg3:u16'
```

Trace the file mode argument of do_sys_open() (x86_64 specific):

```
kprobe 'p:do_sys_open mode=%dx:u16'
```

Trace the filename argument of do_sys_open() as a string:

```
kprobe 'p:do_sys_open filename=+0($arg2):string'
```

Trace the filename argument of do_sys_open() (x86_64 specific) as a string:

```
kprobe 'p:do_sys_open filename=+0(%si):string'
```

Trace do_sys_open() when the filename matches "*stat":

```
kprobe 'p:do_sys_open file=+0($arg2):string' 'file ~ "*stat"'
```

Trace tcp_retransmit_skb() with kernel stack traces:

```
kprobe -s p:tcp_retransmit_skb
```

List tracepoints:

```
tpoint -l
```

Trace disk I/O with kernel stack traces:

```
tpoint -s block:block_rq_issue
```

Trace user-level readline() calls in all "bash" executables:

```
uprobe p:bash:readline
```

Trace the return of readline() from "bash" and print its return value as a string:

```
uprobe 'r:bash:readline +0($retval):string'
```

Trace readline() entry from /bin/bash with its entry argument (x86_64) as a string:

```
uprobe 'p:/bin/bash:readline prompt=+0(%di):string'
```

Trace the libc gettimeofday() call for PID 1234 only:

```
uprobe -p 1234 p:libc:gettimeofday
```

Trace the return of fopen() only when it returns NULL (and using a "file" alias):

```
uprobe 'r:libc:fopen file=$retval' 'file == 0'
```

CPU Registers

Function argument aliases ($arg1, ..., $argN) is a newer Ftrace capability (Linux 4.20+). For older kernels (or processor architectures missing the aliases), you will need to use CPU register names instead, as introduced in Section 14.6.2, Arguments. These one-liners included some x86_64 registers (%di, %si, %dx) as examples. The calling conventions are documented in the syscall(2) man page:

```
$ man 2 syscall
[...]
      Arch/ABI      arg1  arg2  arg3  arg4  arg5  arg6  arg7  Notes

[...]
      sparc/32      o0    o1    o2    o3    o4    o5    -
      sparc/64      o0    o1    o2    o3    o4    o5    -
      tile          R00   R01   R02   R03   R04   R05   -
      x86-64        rdi   rsi   rdx   r10   r8    r9    -
      x32           rdi   rsi   rdx   r10   r8    r9    -
[...]
```

14.13.5 Example

As an example of using a tool, the following uses funccount(8) to count VFS calls (function names that match "vfs_*"):

```
# funccount 'vfs_*'
Tracing "vfs_*"... Ctrl-C to end.
^C
FUNC                            COUNT
vfs_fsync_range                    10
vfs_statfs                         10
vfs_readlink                       35
vfs_statx                         673
vfs_write                         782
vfs_statx_fd                      922
vfs_open                         1003
vfs_getattr                      1390
vfs_getattr_nosec                1390
vfs_read                         2604
```

This output shows that, during tracing, vfs_read() was called 2,604 times. I regularly use funccount(8) to determine which kernel functions are frequently called, and which are called at all. Since its overhead is relatively low, I can use it to check whether function call rates are low enough for more expensive tracing.

14.13.6 perf-tools vs. BCC/BPF

I originally developed perf-tools for the Netflix cloud when it was running Linux 3.2, which lacked extended BPF. Since then Netflix has moved to newer kernels, and I have rewritten many of these tools to use BPF. For example, both perf-tools and BCC have their own versions of funccount(8), execsnoop(8), opensnoop(8), and more.

BPF provides programmability and more powerful capabilities, and the BCC and bpftrace BPF front ends are covered in Chapter 15. However, there are some advantages of perf-tools[5]:

- **funccount(8)**: The perf-tools version uses Ftrace function profiling, which is much more efficient and less constrained than the current kprobe-based BPF version in BCC.

- **funcgraph(8)**: This tool does not exist in BCC, since it uses Ftrace function_graph tracing.

- **Hist Triggers**: This will power future perf-tools that should be more efficient than kprobe-based BPF versions.

- **Dependencies**: perf-tools remain useful for resource-constrained environments (e.g., embedded Linux) as they typically only require a shell and awk(1).

I also sometimes use perf-tools tools to cross-check and debug problems with BPF tools.[6]

14.13.7   Documentation

Tools typically have a usage message to summarize their syntax. For example:

```
# funccount -h
USAGE: funccount [-hT] [-i secs] [-d secs] [-t top] funcstring
                   -d seconds       # total duration of trace
                   -h               # this usage message
                   -i seconds       # interval summary
                   -t top           # show top num entries only
                   -T               # include timestamp (for -i)
   eg,
       funccount 'vfs*'         # trace all funcs that match "vfs*"
       funccount -d 5 'tcp*'    # trace "tcp*" funcs for 5 seconds
       funccount -t 10 'ext3*'  # show top 10 "ext3*" funcs
       funccount -i 1 'ext3*'   # summary every 1 second
       funccount -i 1 -d 5 'ext3*' # 5 x 1 second summaries
```

Every tool also has a man page and an examples file in the perf-tools repository (funccount_example.txt) that contains output examples with commentary.

14.14   Ftrace Documentation

Ftrace (and trace events) are well documented in the Linux source, under the Documentation/trace directory. This documentation is also online:

- https://www.kernel.org/doc/html/latest/trace/ftrace.html

- https://www.kernel.org/doc/html/latest/trace/kprobetrace.html

---

[5] I originally believed I would retire perf-tools when we finished BPF tracing, but have kept it alive for these reasons.

[6] I could repurpose a famous saying: A man with one tracer knows what events happened; a man with two tracers knows that one of them is broken, and searches lkml hoping for a patch.

- https://www.kernel.org/doc/html/latest/trace/uprobetracer.html

- https://www.kernel.org/doc/html/latest/trace/events.html

- https://www.kernel.org/doc/html/latest/trace/histogram.html

Resources for front ends are:

- **trace-cmd**: https://trace-cmd.org

- **perf ftrace**: In the Linux source: tools/perf/Documentation/perf-ftrace.txt

- **perf-tools**: https://github.com/brendangregg/perf-tools

14.15 References

[**Rostedt 08**] Rostedt, S., "ftrace - Function Tracer," *Linux documentation*, https://www.kernel.org/doc/html/latest/trace/ftrace.html, 2008+.

[**Matz 13**] Matz, M., Hubička, J., Jaeger, A., and Mitchell, M., "System V Application Binary Interface, AMD64 Architecture Processor Supplement, Draft Version 0.99.6," http://x86-64.org/documentation/abi.pdf, 2013.

[**Gregg 19f**] Gregg, B., "Two Kernel Mysteries and the Most Technical Talk I've Ever Seen," http://www.brendangregg.com/blog/2019-10-15/kernelrecipes-kernel-ftrace-internals.html, 2019.

[**Dronamraju 20**] Dronamraju, S., "Uprobe-tracer: Uprobe-based Event Tracing," *Linux documentation*, https://www.kernel.org/doc/html/latest/trace/uprobetracer.html, accessed 2020.

[**Gregg 20i**] Gregg, B., "Performance analysis tools based on Linux perf_events (aka perf) and ftrace," https://github.com/brendangregg/perf-tools, last updated 2020.

[**Hiramatsu 20**] Hiramatsu, M., "Kprobe-based Event Tracing," *Linux documentation*, https://www.kernel.org/doc/html/latest/trace/kprobetrace.html, accessed 2020.

[**KernelShark 20**] "KernelShark," https://www.kernelshark.org, accessed 2020.

[**trace-cmd 20**] "TRACE-CMD," https://trace-cmd.org, accessed 2020.

[**Ts'o 20**] Ts'o, T., Zefan, L., and Zanussi, T., "Event Tracing," *Linux documentation*, https://www.kernel.org/doc/html/latest/trace/events.html, accessed 2020.

[**Zanussi 20**] Zanussi, T., "Event Histograms," *Linux documentation*, https://www.kernel.org/doc/html/latest/trace/histogram.html, accessed 2020.

Chapter 15

BPF

This chapter describes the BCC and bpftrace tracing front ends for extended BPF. These front ends provide a collection of performance analysis tools, and these tools were used in previous chapters. The BPF technology was introduced in Chapter 3, Operating System, Section 3.4.4, Extended BPF. In summary, extended BPF is a kernel execution environment that can provide programmatic capabilities to tracers.

This chapter, along with Chapter 13, perf, and Chapter 14, Ftrace, are optional reading for those who wish to learn one or more system tracers in more detail.

Extended BPF tools can be used to answer questions such as:

- What is the latency of disk I/O, as a histogram?
- Is CPU scheduler latency high enough to cause problems?
- Arc applications suffering file system latency?
- What TCP sessions are occurring and with what durations?
- What code paths are blocking and for how long?

What makes BPF different from other tracers is that it is programmable. It allows user-defined programs to be executed on events, programs that can perform filtering, save and retrieve information, calculate latency, perform in-kernel aggregation and custom summaries, and more. While other tracers may require dumping all events to user space and post-processing them, BPF allows such processing to occur efficiently in kernel context. This makes it practical to create performance tools that would otherwise cost too much overhead for production use.

This chapter has a major section for each recommended front end. Key sections are:

- 15.1: BCC
    - 15.1.1: Installation
    - 15.1.2: Tool Coverage
    - 15.1.3: Single-Purpose Tools
    - 15.1.4: Multi-Purpose Tools
    - 15.1.5: One-Liners

- 15.2: bpftrace
  - 15.2.1: Installation
  - 15.2.2: Tools
  - 15.2.3: One-Liners
  - 15.2.4: Programming
  - 15.2.5: Reference

The differences between BCC and bpftrace may be obvious from their usage in prior chapters: BCC is suited for complex tools, and bpftrace is suited for ad hoc custom programs. Some tools are implemented in both, as shown in Figure 15.1.

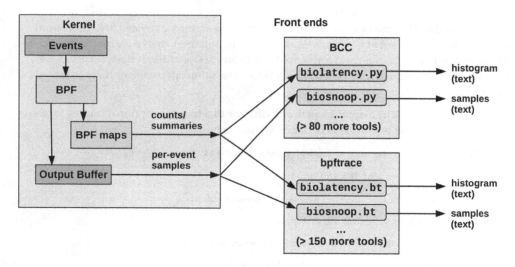

Figure 15.1   BPF tracing front ends

Specific differences between BCC and bpftrace are summarized in Table 15.1.

Table 15.1   **BCC versus bpftrace**

Characteristic	BCC	bpftrace
Number of tools by repository	>80 (bcc)	>30 (bpftrace) >120 (bpf-perf-tools-book)
Tool usage	Typically supports complex options (-h, -P PID, etc.) and arguments	Typically simple: no options, and zero or one argument
Tool documentation	Man pages, example files	Man pages, example files
Programming language	User-space: Python, Lua, C, or C++ Kernel-space: C	bpftrace
Programming difficulty	Difficult	Easy

Characteristic	BCC	bpftrace
Per-event output types	Anything	Text, JSON
Summary types	Anything	Counts, min, max, sum, avg, log2 histograms, linear histograms; by zero or more keys
Library support	Yes (e.g., Python import)	No
Average program length[1] (no comments)	228 lines	28 lines

Both BCC and bpftrace are in use at many companies including Facebook and Netflix. Netflix installs them by default on all cloud instances, and uses them for deeper analysis after cloud-wide monitoring and dashboards, specifically [Gregg 18e]:

- **BCC:** Canned tools are used at the command line to analyze storage I/O, network I/O, and process execution, when needed. Some BCC tools are automatically executed by a graphical performance dashboard system to provide data for scheduler and disk I/O latency heat maps, off-CPU flame graphs, and more. Also, a custom BCC tool is always running as a daemon (based on tcplife(8)) logging network events to cloud storage for flow analysis.

- **bpftrace:** Custom bpftrace tools are developed when needed to understand kernel and application pathologies.

The following sections explain BCC tools, bpftrace tools, and bpftrace programming.

15.1 BCC

The BPF Compiler Collection (or "bcc" after the project and package names) is an open-source project containing a large collection of advanced performance analysis tools, as well as a framework for building them. BCC was created by Brenden Blanco; I've helped with its development and created many of the tracing tools.

As an example of a BCC tool, biolatency(8) shows the distribution of disk I/O latency as power-of-two histograms, and can break it down by I/O flags:

```
# biolatency.py -mF
Tracing block device I/O... Hit Ctrl-C to end.
^C

flags = Priority-Metadata-Read
    msecs               : count    distribution
        0 -> 1          : 90       |****************************************|
```

---

[1] Based on the tools provided in the official repository and my BPF book repository.

```
flags = Write
     msecs                 : count    distribution
        0 -> 1             : 24       |****************************************|
        2 -> 3             : 0        |                                        |
        4 -> 7             : 8        |*************                           |

flags = ReadAhead-Read
     msecs                 : count    distribution
        0 -> 1             : 3031     |****************************************|
        2 -> 3             : 10       |                                        |
        4 -> 7             : 5        |                                        |
        8 -> 15            : 3        |                                        |
```

This output shows a bi-model write distribution, and many I/O with flags "ReadAhead-Read". This tool uses BPF to summarize the histograms in kernel space for efficiency, so the user-space component only needs to read the already-summarized histograms (the count columns) and print them.

These BCC tools typically have usage messages (-h), man pages, and examples files in the BCC repository:

>   https://github.com/iovisor/bcc

This section summarizes BCC and its single- and multi-purpose performance analysis tools.

15.1.1 Installation

Packages of BCC are available for many Linux distributions, including Ubuntu, Debian, RHEL, Fedora, and Amazon Linux, making installation trivial. Search for "bcc-tools" or "bpfcc-tools" or "bcc" (package maintainers have named it differently).

You can also build BCC from source. For the latest install and build instructions, check INSTALL.md in the BCC repository [Iovisor 20b]. The INSTALL.md also lists kernel configuration requirements (which include CONFIG_BPF=y, CONFIG_BPF_SYSCALL=y, CONFIG_BPF_EVENTS=y). BCC requires at least Linux 4.4 for some of the tools to work; for most of the tools, 4.9 or newer is required.

15.1.2 Tool Coverage

BCC tracing tools are pictured in Figure 15.2 (some are grouped using wildcards: e.g., java* is for all tools beginning with "java").

Many are single-purpose tools shown with a single arrow head; some are multi-purpose tools listed on the left with a double arrow to show their coverage.

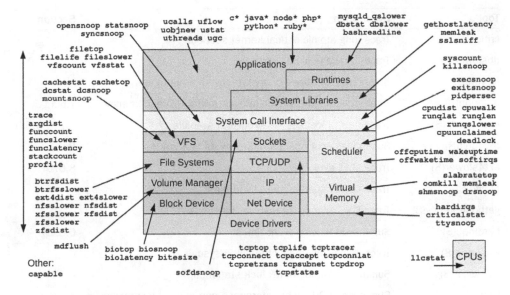

Figure 15.2   BCC tools

15.1.3   Single-Purpose Tools

I developed many of these according to the same "do one job and do it well" philosophy as those in perf-tools in Chapter 14. This design includes making their default output concise and often just sufficient. You can "just run biolatency" without needing to learn any command line options, and usually get just enough output to solve your problem without clutter. Options typically do exist for customization, such as biolatency(8) -F to breakdown by I/O flags, shown earlier.

A selection of single-purpose tools are described in Table 15.2, including their location in this book if present. See the BCC repository for the full list [Iovisor 20a].

Table 15.2   **Selected single-purpose BCC tools**

Tool	Description	Section
biolatency(8)	Summarize block I/O (disk I/O) latency as a histogram	9.6.6
biotop(8)	Summarize block I/O by process	9.6.8
biosnoop(8)	Trace block I/O with latency and other details	9.6.7
bitesize(8)	Summarize block I/O size as process histograms	-
btrfsdist(8)	Summarize btrfs operation latency as histograms	8.6.13
btrfsslower(8)	Trace slow btrfs operations	8.6.14
cpudist(8)	Summarize on- and off-CPU time per process as a histogram	6.6.15, 16.1.7
cpuunclaimed(8)	Show CPU that is unclaimed and idle despite demand	-

Tool	Description	Section
criticalstat(8)	Trace long atomic critical kernel sections	-
dbslower(8)	Trace database slow queries	-
dbstat(8)	Summarize database query latency as a histogram	-
drsnoop(8)	Trace direct memory reclaim events with PID and latency	7.5.11
execsnoop(8)	Trace new processes via execve(2) syscalls	1.7.3, 5.5.5
ext4dist(8)	Summarize ext4 operation latency as histograms	8.6.13
ext4slower(8)	Trace slow ext4 operations	8.6.14
filelife(8)	Trace the lifespan of short-lived files	-
gethostlatency(8)	Trace DNS latency via resolver functions	-
hardirqs(8)	Summarize hardirq event times	6.6.19
killsnoop(8)	Trace signals issued by the kill(2) syscall	-
klockstat(8)	Summarize kernel mutex lock statistics	-
llcstat(8)	Summarize CPU cache references and misses by process	-
memleak(8)	Show outstanding memory allocations	-
mysqld_qslower(8)	Trace MySQL slow queries	-
nfsdist(8)	Trace slow NFS operations	8.6.13
nfsslower(8)	Summarize NFS operation latency as histograms	8.6.14
offcputime(8)	Summarize off-CPU time by stack trace	5.5.3
offwaketime(8)	Summarize blocked time by off-CPU stack and waker stack	-
oomkill(8)	Trace the out-of-memory (OOM) killer	-
opensnoop(8)	Trace open(2)-family syscalls	8.6.10
profile(8)	Profile CPU usage using timed sampling of stack traces	5.5.2
runqlat(8)	Summarize run queue (scheduler) latency as a histogram	6.6.16
runqlen(8)	Summarize run queue length using timed sampling	6.6.17
runqslower(8)	Trace long run queue delays	-
syncsnoop(8)	Trace sync(2)-family syscalls	-
syscount(8)	Summarize syscall counts and latencies	5.5.6
tcplife(8)	Trace TCP sessions and summarize their lifespan	10.6.9
tcpretrans(8)	Trace TCP retransmits with details including kernel state	10.6.11
tcptop(8)	Summarize TCP send/recv throughput by host and PID	10.6.10
wakeuptime(8)	Summarize sleep to wakeup time by waker stack	-
xfsdist(8)	Summarize xfs operation latency as histograms	8.6.13

Tool	Description	Section
xfsslower(8)	Trace slow xfs operations	8.6.14
zfsdist(8)	Summarize zfs operation latency as histograms	8.6.13
zfsslower(8)	Trace slow zfs operations	8.6.14

For examples of these, see previous chapters as well as the *_example.txt files in the BCC repository (many of which I also wrote). For the tools not covered in this book, also see [Gregg 19].

15.1.4 Multi-Purpose Tools

The multi-purpose tools are listed on the left of Figure 15.2. These support multiple event sources and can perform many roles, similar to perf(1), although this also makes them complex to use. They are described in Table 15.3.

Table 15.3 **Multi-purpose perf-tools**

Tool	Description	Section
argdist(8)	Display function parameter values as a histogram or count	15.1.15
funccount(8)	Count kernel or user-level function calls	15.1.15
funcslower(8)	Trace slow kernel or user-level function calls	-
funclatency(8)	Summarize function latency as a histogram	-
stackcount(8)	Count stack traces that led to an event	15.1.15
trace(8)	Trace arbitrary functions with filters	15.1.15

To help you remember useful invocations, you can collect one-liners. I have provided some in the next section, similar to my one-liner sections for perf(1) and trace-cmd.

15.1.5 One-Liners

The following one-liners trace system-wide until Ctrl-C is typed, unless otherwise specified. They are grouped by tool.

funccount(8)

Count VFS kernel calls:

```
funcgraph 'vfs_*'
```

Count TCP kernel calls:

```
funccount 'tcp_*'
```

Count TCP send calls per second:

```
funccount -i 1 'tcp_send*'
```

Show the rate of block I/O events per second:

```
funccount -i 1 't:block:*'
```

Show the rate of libc getaddrinfo() (name resolution) per second:

```
funccount -i 1 c:getaddrinfo
```

stackcount(8)

Count stack traces that created block I/O:

```
stackcount t:block:block_rq_insert
```

Count stack traces that led to sending IP packets, with responsible PID:

```
stackcount -P ip_output
```

Count stack traces that led to the thread blocking and moving off-CPU:

```
stackcount t:sched:sched_switch
```

trace(8)

Trace the kernel do_sys_open() function with the filename:

```
trace 'do_sys_open "%s", arg2'
```

Trace the return of the kernel function do_sys_open() and print the return value:

```
trace 'r::do_sys_open "ret: %d", retval'
```

Trace the kernel function do_nanosleep() with mode and user-level stacks:

```
trace -U 'do_nanosleep "mode: %d", arg2'
```

Trace authentication requests via the pam library:

```
trace 'pam:pam_start "%s: %s", arg1, arg2'
```

argdist(8)

Summarize VFS reads by return value (size or error):

```
argdist -H 'r::vfs_read()'
```

Summarize libc read() by return value (size or error) for PID 1005:

```
argdist -p 1005 -H 'r:c:read()'
```

Count syscalls by syscall ID:

```
argdist.py -C 't:raw_syscalls:sys_enter():int:args->id'
```

Summarize the kernel function tcp_sendmsg() size argument using counts:

```
argdist -C 'p::tcp_sendmsg(struct sock *sk, struct msghdr *msg, size_t
size):u32:size'
```

Summarize tcp_sendmsg() size as a power-of-two histogram:

```
argdist -H 'p::tcp_sendmsg(struct sock *sk, struct msghdr *msg, size_t
size):u32:size'
```

Count the libc write() call for PID 181 by file descriptor:

```
argdist -p 181 -C 'p:c:write(int fd):int:fd'
```

Summarize reads by process where latency was >100 μs:

```
argdist -C 'r::__vfs_read():u32:$PID:$latency > 100000
```

15.1.6 Multi-Tool Example

As an example of using a multi-tool, the following shows the trace(8) tool tracing the kernel function do_sys_open(), and printing the second argument as a string:

```
# trace 'do_sys_open "%s", arg2'
PID     TID     COMM    FUNC         -
28887   28887   ls      do_sys_open  /etc/ld.so.cache
28887   28887   ls      do_sys_open  /lib/x86_64-linux-gnu/libselinux.so.1
28887   28887   ls      do_sys_open  /lib/x86_64-linux-gnu/libc.so.6
28887   28887   ls      do_sys_open  /lib/x86_64-linux-gnu/libpcre2-8.so.0
28887   28887   ls      do_sys_open  /lib/x86_64-linux-gnu/libdl.so.2
28887   28887   ls      do_sys_open  /lib/x86_64-linux-gnu/libpthread.so.0
28887   28887   ls      do_sys_open  /proc/filesystems
28887   28887   ls      do_sys_open  /usr/lib/locale/locale-archive
[...]
```

The trace syntax is inspired by printf(3), supporting a format string and arguments. In this case arg2, the second argument, was printed as a string because it contains the filename.

Both trace(8) and argdist(8) support syntax that allows many custom one-liners to be created. bpftrace, covered in the following sections, takes this further, providing a fully fledged language for writing one-line or multi-line programs.

15.1.7   BCC vs. bpftrace

The differences were summarized at the start of this chapter. BCC is suited for custom and complex tools, which support a variety of arguments, or use a variety of libraries. bpftrace is well suited for one-liners or short tools that accept no arguments, or a single-integer argument. BCC allows the BPF program at the heart of the tracing tool to be developed in C, enabling full control. This comes at the cost of complexity: BCC tools can take ten times as long to develop as bpftrace tools, and can have ten times as many lines of code. Since developing a tool typically requires multiple iterations, I've found that it saves time to first develop tools in bpftrace, which is quicker, and then port them to BCC if needed.

The difference between BCC and bpftrace is like the difference between C programming and shell scripting, where BCC is like C programming (some of it *is* C programming) and bpftrace is like shell scripting. In my daily work I use many pre-built C programs (top(1), vmstat(1), etc.) and develop custom one-off shell scripts. Likewise, I also use many pre-built BCC tools, and develop custom one-off bpftrace tools.

I have provided material in this book to support this usage: many chapters show the BCC tools you can use, and the later sections in this chapter show how you can develop custom bpftrace tools.

15.1.8   Documentation

Tools typically have a usage message to summarize their syntax. For example:

```
# funccount -h
usage: funccount [-h] [-p PID] [-i INTERVAL] [-d DURATION] [-T] [-r] [-D]
                 pattern


Count functions, tracepoints, and USDT probes


positional arguments:
  pattern               search expression for events


optional arguments:
  -h, --help            show this help message and exit
  -p PID, --pid PID     trace this PID only
  -i INTERVAL, --interval INTERVAL
                        summary interval, seconds
  -d DURATION, --duration DURATION
                        total duration of trace, seconds
  -T, --timestamp       include timestamp on output
  -r, --regexp          use regular expressions. Default is "*" wildcards
                        only.
  -D, --debug           print BPF program before starting (for debugging
                        purposes)
```

examples:

```
./funccount 'vfs_*'            # count kernel fns starting with "vfs"
./funccount -r '^vfs.*'        # same as above, using regular expressions
./funccount -Ti 5 'vfs_*'      # output every 5 seconds, with timestamps
./funccount -d 10 'vfs_*'      # trace for 10 seconds only
./funccount -p 185 'vfs_*'     # count vfs calls for PID 181 only
./funccount t:sched:sched_fork # count calls to the sched_fork tracepoint
./funccount -p 185 u:node:gc*  # count all GC USDT probes in node, PID 185
./funccount c:malloc           # count all malloc() calls in libc
./funccount go:os.*            # count all "os.*" calls in libgo
./funccount -p 185 go:os.*     # count all "os.*" calls in libgo, PID 185
./funccount ./test:read*       # count "read*" calls in the ./test binary
```

Every tool also has a man page (man/man8/funccount.8) and an examples file (examples/funccount_example.txt) in the bcc repository. The examples file contains output examples with commentary.

I have also created the following documentation in the BCC repository [Iovisor 20b]:

- Tutorial for end users: docs/tutorial.md

- Tutorial for BCC developers: docs/tutorial_bcc_python_developer.md

- Reference Guide: docs/reference_guide.md

Chapter 4 in my earlier book focuses on BCC [Gregg 19].

15.2 bpftrace

bpftrace is an open-source tracer built upon BPF and BCC, which provides not only a suite of performance analysis tools, but also a high-level language to help you develop new ones. The language has been designed to be simple and easy to learn. It is the awk(1) of tracing, and is based on awk(1). In awk(1), you write a program stanza to process an input line, and with bpftrace you write a program stanza to process an input event. bpftrace was created by Alastair Robertson, and I have become a major contributor.

As an example of bpftrace, the following one-liner shows the distribution of TCP receive message size by process name:

```
# bpftrace -e 'kr:tcp_recvmsg /retval >= 0/ { @recv_bytes[comm] = hist(retval); }'
Attaching 1 probe...
^C

@recv_bytes[sshd]:
[32, 64)            7 |@@@@@@@@@@@@@@@@@@@@@@@@@@@@@@@@@@@@@@@@@@@@@@@@@@@@@@@@@@|
[64, 128)           2 |@@@@@@@@@@@@@@                                          |
```

```
@recv_bytes[nodejs]:
[0]                 82 |@@@@@@@@@@@@@@@@@@@@@@@@@@@                              |
[1]                135 |@@@@@@@@@@@@@@@@@@@@@@@@@@@@@@@@@@@@@@@@@@@@@@@           |
[2, 4)             153 |@@@@@@@@@@@@@@@@@@@@@@@@@@@@@@@@@@@@@@@@@@@@@@@@@@@@@     |
[4, 8)              12 |@@@                                                     |
[8, 16)              6 |@                                                       |
[16, 32)            32 |@@@@@@@@@@                                              |
[32, 64)           158 |@@@@@@@@@@@@@@@@@@@@@@@@@@@@@@@@@@@@@@@@@@@@@@@@@@@@@@@@@@@|
[64, 128)          155 |@@@@@@@@@@@@@@@@@@@@@@@@@@@@@@@@@@@@@@@@@@@@@@@@@@@@@@@@@  |
[128, 256)          14 |@@@@                                                    |
```

This output shows nodejs processes that have a bi-modal receive size, with one mode roughly 0 to 4 bytes and another between 32 and 128 bytes.

Using a concise syntax, this bpftrace one-liner has used a kretprobe to instrument tcp_recvmsg(), filtered for when the return value is positive (to exclude negative error codes), and populated a BPF map object called @recv_bytes with a histogram of the return value, saved using the process name (comm) as a key. When Ctrl-C is typed and bpftrace receives the signal (SIGINT) it ends and automatically prints out BPF maps. This syntax is explained in more detail in the following sections.

As well as enabling you to code your own one-liners, bpftrace ships with many ready-to-run tools in its repository:

https://github.com/iovisor/bpftrace

This section summarizes bpftrace tools and the bpftrace programming language. This is based on my bpftrace material in [Gregg 19], which explores bpftrace in more depth.

15.2.1   Installation

Packages of bpftrace are available for many Linux distributions, including Ubuntu, making installation trivial. Search for packages named "bpftrace"; they exist for Ubuntu, Fedora, Gentoo, Debian, OpenSUSE, and CentOS. RHEL 8.2 has bpftrace as a Technology Preview.

Apart from packages, there are also Docker images of bpftrace, bpftrace binaries that require no dependencies other than glibc, and instructions for building bpftrace from source. For documentation on these options see INSTALL.md in the bpftrace repository [Iovisor 20a], which also lists kernel requirements (which include CONFIG_BPF=y, CONFIG_BPF_SYSCALL=y, CONFIG_BPF_EVENTS=y). bpftrace requires Linux 4.9 or newer.

15.2.2   Tools

bpftrace tracing tools are pictured in Figure 15.3.

The tools in the bpftrace repository are shown in black. For my prior book, I developed many more bpftrace tools and released them as open source in the bpf-perf-tools-book repository: they are shown in red/gray [Gregg 19g].

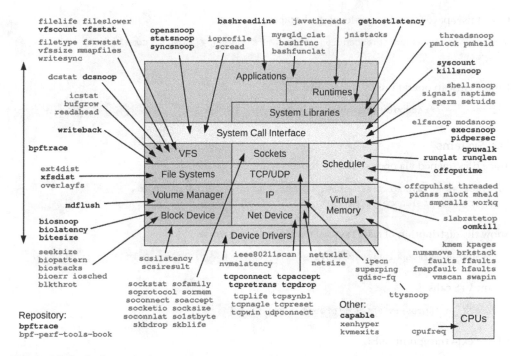

Figure 15.3 bpftrace tools

15.2.3 One-Liners

The following one-liners trace system-wide until Ctrl-C is typed, unless otherwise specified. Apart from their intrinsic usefulness, they can also serve as mini-examples of the bpftrace programming language. These are grouped by target. Longer lists of bpftrace one-liners can be found in each resource chapter.

CPUs

Trace new processes with arguments:

```
bpftrace -e 'tracepoint:syscalls:sys_enter_execve { join(args->argv); }'
```

Count syscalls by process:

```
bpftrace -e 'tracepoint:raw_syscalls:sys_enter { @[pid, comm] = count(); }'
```

Sample user-level stacks at 49 Hertz, for PID 189:

```
bpftrace -e 'profile:hz:49 /pid == 189/ { @[ustack] = count(); }'
```

Memory

Count process heap expansion (brk()) by code path:

```
bpftrace -e tracepoint:syscalls:sys_enter_brk { @[ustack, comm] = count(); }
```

Count user page faults by user-level stack trace:

```
bpftrace -e 'tracepoint:exceptions:page_fault_user { @[ustack, comm] =
    count(); }'
```

Count vmscan operations by tracepoint:

```
bpftrace -e 'tracepoint:vmscan:* { @[probe]++; }'
```

File Systems

Trace files opened via openat(2) with process name:

```
bpftrace -e 't:syscalls:sys_enter_openat { printf("%s %s\n", comm,
    str(args->filename)); }'
```

Show the distribution of read() syscall read bytes (and errors):

```
bpftrace -e 'tracepoint:syscalls:sys_exit_read { @ = hist(args->ret); }'
```

Count VFS calls:

```
bpftrace -e 'kprobe:vfs_* { @[probe] = count(); }'
```

Count ext4 tracepoint calls:

```
bpftrace -e 'tracepoint:ext4:* { @[probe] = count(); }'
```

Disk

Summarize block I/O size as a histogram:

```
bpftrace -e 't:block:block_rq_issue { @bytes = hist(args->bytes); }'
```

Count block I/O request user stack traces:

```
bpftrace -e 't:block:block_rq_issue { @[ustack] = count(); }'
```

Count block I/O type flags:

```
bpftrace -e 't:block:block_rq_issue { @[args->rwbs] = count(); }'
```

Networking

Count socket accept(2)s by PID and process name:

```
bpftrace -e 't:syscalls:sys_enter_accept* { @[pid, comm] = count(); }'
```

Count socket send/receive bytes by on-CPU PID and process name:

```
bpftrace -e 'kr:sock_sendmsg,kr:sock_recvmsg /retval > 0/ {
    @[pid, comm] = sum(retval); }'
```

TCP send bytes as a histogram:

```
bpftrace -e 'k:tcp_sendmsg { @send_bytes = hist(arg2); }'
```

TCP receive bytes as a histogram:

```
bpftrace -e 'kr:tcp_recvmsg /retval >= 0/ { @recv_bytes = hist(retval); }'
```

UDP send bytes as a histogram:

```
bpftrace -e 'k:udp_sendmsg { @send_bytes = hist(arg2); }'
```

Applications

Sum malloc() requested bytes by user stack trace (high overhead):

```
bpftrace -e 'u:/lib/x86_64-linux-gnu/libc-2.27.so:malloc { @[ustack(5)] =
    sum(arg0); }'
```

Trace kill() signals showing sender process name, target PID, and signal number:

```
bpftrace -e 't:syscalls:sys_enter_kill { printf("%s -> PID %d SIG %d\n",
    comm, args->pid, args->sig); }'
```

Kernel

Count system calls by syscall function:

```
bpftrace -e 'tracepoint:raw_syscalls:sys_enter {
    @[ksym(*(kaddr("sys_call_table") + args->id * 8))] = count(); }'
```

Count kernel function calls starting with "attach":

```
bpftrace -e 'kprobe:attach* { @[probe] = count(); }'
```

Frequency count the third argument to vfs_write() (the size):

```
bpftrace -e 'kprobe:vfs_write { @[arg2] = count(); }'
```

Time the kernel function vfs_read() and summarize as a histogram:

```
bpftrace -e 'k:vfs_read { @ts[tid] = nsecs; } kr:vfs_read /@ts[tid]/ {
    @ = hist(nsecs - @ts[tid]); delete(@ts[tid]); }'
```

Count context switch stack traces:

```
bpftrace -e 't:sched:sched_switch { @[kstack, ustack, comm] = count(); }'
```

Sample kernel-level stacks at 99 Hertz, excluding idle:

```
bpftrace -e 'profile:hz:99 /pid/ { @[kstack] = count(); }'
```

15.2.4 Programming

This section provides a short guide to using bpftrace and programming in the bpftrace language. The format of this section was inspired by the original paper for awk [Aho 78][Aho 88], which covered that language in six pages. The bpftrace language itself is inspired by both awk and C, and by tracers including DTrace and SystemTap.

The following is an example of bpftrace programming: It measures the time in the vfs_read() kernel function and prints the time, in microseconds, as a histogram.

```
#!/usr/local/bin/bpftrace

// this program times vfs_read()

kprobe:vfs_read
{
        @start[tid] = nsecs;
}

kretprobe:vfs_read
/@start[tid]/
{
        $duration_us = (nsecs - @start[tid]) / 1000;
        @us = hist($duration_us);
        delete(@start[tid]);
}
```

The following sections explain the components of this tool, and can be treated as a tutorial. Section 15.2.5, Reference, is a reference guide summary including probe types, tests, operators, variables, functions, and map types.

1. Usage

The command

```
bpftrace -e program
```

will execute the program, instrumenting any events that it defines. The program will run until Ctrl-C, or until it explicitly calls exit(). A bpftrace program run as a -e argument is termed a *one-liner*. Alternatively, the program can be saved to a file and executed using:

```
bpftrace file.bt
```

The .bt extension is not necessary, but is helpful for later identification. By placing an interpreter line at the top of the file[2]

---

[2]Some people prefer using #!/usr/bin/env bpftrace, so that bpftrace can be found from $PATH. However, env(1) comes with various problems, and its usage in other projects has been reverted.

```
#!/usr/local/bin/bpftrace
```

the file can be made executable (chmod a+x file.bt) and run like any other program:

```
./file.bt
```

bpftrace must be executed by the root user (super-user).[3] For some environments, the root shell may be used to execute the program directly, whereas other environments may have a preference for running privileged commands via sudo(1):

```
sudo ./file.bt
```

2. Program Structure

A bpftrace program is a series of probes with associated actions:

```
probes { actions }
probes { actions }
...
```

When the probes fire, the associated action is executed. An optional filter expression can be included before the action:

```
probes /filter/ { actions }
```

The action only fires if the filter expression is true. This resembles the awk(1) program structure:

```
/pattern/ { actions }
```

awk(1) programming is also similar to bpftrace programming: Multiple action blocks can be defined, and they may execute in any order, triggered when their pattern, or probe + filter expression, is true.

3. Comments

For bpftrace program files, single-line comments can be added with a "//" prefix:

```
// this is a comment
```

These comments will not be executed. Multi-line comments use the same format as those in C:

```
/*
 * This is a
 * multi-line comment.
 */
```

This syntax can also be used for partial-line comments (e.g., /* comment */).

---

[3] bpftrace checks for UID 0; a future update may check for specific privileges.

4. Probe Format

A probe begins with a probe type name and then a hierarchy of colon-delimited identifiers:

```
type:identifier1[:identifier2[...]]
```

The hierarchy is defined by the probe type. Consider these two examples:

```
kprobe:vfs_read
uprobe:/bin/bash:readline
```

The kprobe probe type instruments kernel function calls, and only needs one identifier: the kernel function name. The uprobe probe type instruments user-level function calls, and needs both the path to the binary and the function name.

Multiple probes can be specified with comma separators to execute the same actions. For example:

```
probe1,probe2,... { actions }
```

There are two special probe types that require no additional identifiers: BEGIN and END fire for the beginning and the end of the bpftrace program (just like awk(1)). For example, to print an informational message when tracing begins:

```
BEGIN { printf("Tracing. Hit Ctrl-C to end.\n"); }
```

To learn more about the probe types and their usage, see Section 15.2.5, Reference, under the heading 1. Probe Types.

5. Probe Wildcards

Some probe types accept wildcards. The probe

```
kprobe:vfs_*
```

will instrument all kprobes (kernel functions) that begin with "vfs_".

Instrumenting too many probes may cost unnecessary performance overhead. To avoid hitting this by accident, bpftrace has a tunable maximum number of probes it will enable, set via the BPFTRACE_MAX_PROBES environment variable (it currently defaults to 512[4]).

You can test your wildcards before using them by running `bpftrace -l` to list the matched probes:

```
# bpftrace -l 'kprobe:vfs_*'
kprobe:vfs_fallocate
kprobe:vfs_truncate
```

---

[4] More than 512 currently makes bpftrace slow to start up and shut down, as it instruments them one by one. Future kernel work is planned to batch probe instrumentation. At that point, this limit can be greatly increased, or even removed.

```
kprobe:vfs_open
kprobe:vfs_setpos
kprobe:vfs_llseek
[...]
bpftrace -l 'kprobe:vfs_*' | wc -l
56
```

This matched 56 probes. The probe name is in quotes to prevent unintended shell expansion.

6. Filters

Filters are Boolean expressions that gate whether an action is executed. The filter

```
/pid == 123/
```

will execute the action only if the pid built-in (process ID) is equal to 123.

If a test is not specified

```
/pid/
```

the filter will check that the contents are non-zero (/pid/ is the same as /pid != 0/). Filters can be combined with Boolean operators, such as logical AND (&&). For example:

```
/pid > 100 && pid < 1000/
```

This requires that both expressions evaluate to "true."

7. Actions

An action can be a single statement or multiple statements separated by semicolons:

```
{ action one; action two; action three }
```

The final statement may also have a semicolon appended. The statements are written in the bpftrace language, which is similar to the C language, and can manipulate variables and execute bpftrace function calls. For example, the action

```
{ $x = 42; printf("$x is %d", $x); }
```

sets a variable, $x, to 42, and then prints it using printf(). For a summary of other available function calls, see Section 15.2.5, Reference, under headings 4. Functions and 5. Map Functions.

8. Hello, World!

You should now understand the following basic program, which prints "Hello, World!" when bpftrace begins running:

```
# bpftrace -e 'BEGIN { printf("Hello, World!\n"); }'
Attaching 1 probe...
Hello, World!
^C
```

As a file, it could be formatted as:

```
#!/usr/local/bin/bpftrace

BEGIN
{
        printf("Hello, World!\n");
}
```

Spanning multiple lines with an indented action block is not necessary, but it improves readability.

9 Functions

In addition to `printf()` for printing formatted output, other built-in functions include:

- **exit()**: Exits bpftrace
- **str(char *)**: Returns a string from a pointer
- **system(format[, arguments ...])**: Runs a command at the shell

The action

```
printf("got: %llx %s\n", $x, str($x)); exit();
```

will print the $x variable as a hex integer, and then treat it as a NULL-terminated character array pointer (char *) and print it as a string, and then exit.

10 Variables

There are three variable types: built-ins, scratch, and maps.

Built-in variables are pre-defined and provided by bpftrace, and are usually read-only sources of information. They include `pid` for the process id, `comm` for the process name, `nsecs` for a time-stamp in nanoseconds, and `curtask` for the address of the current thread's task_struct.

Scratch variables can be used for temporary calculations and have the prefix "$". Their name and type is set on their first assignment. The statements:

```
$x = 1;
$y = "hello";
$z = (struct task_struct *)curtask;
```

declare $x as an integer, $y as a string, and $z as a pointer to a struct task_struct. These variables can only be used in the action block in which they were assigned. If variables are referenced without an assignment, bpftrace prints an error (which can help you catch typos).

Map variables use the BPF map storage object and have the prefix "@". They can be used for global storage, passing data between actions. The program:

```
probe1 { @a = 1; }
probe2 { $x = @a; }
```

assigns 1 to @a when probe1 fires, then assigns @a to $x when probe2 fires. If probe1 fired first and then probe2, $x would be set to 1; otherwise 0 (uninitialized).

A key can be provided with one or more elements, using maps as a hash table (an associative array). The statement

```
@start[tid] = nsecs;
```

is frequently used: the nsecs built-in is assigned to a map named @start and keyed on tid, the current thread ID. This allows threads to store custom timestamps that won't be overwritten by other threads.

```
@path[pid, $fd] = str(arg0);
```

is an example of a multi-key map, one using both the pid builtin and the $fd variable as keys.

11 Map Functions

Maps can be assigned to special functions. These functions store and print data in custom ways. The assignment

```
@x = count();
```

counts events, and when printed will print the count. This uses a per-CPU map, and @x becomes a special object of type count. The following statement also counts events:

```
@x++;
```

However, this uses a global CPU map, instead of a per-CPU map, to provide @x as an integer. This global integer type is sometimes necessary for some programs that require an integer and not a count, but bear in mind that there may be a small error margin due to concurrent updates.

The assignment

```
@y = sum($x);
```

sums the $x variable, and when printed will print the total. The assignment

```
@z = hist($x);
```

stores $x in a power-of-two histogram, and when printed will print bucket counts and an ASCII histogram.

Some map functions operate directly on a map. For example:

```
print(@x);
```

will print the @x map. This can be used, for example, to print map contents on an interval event. This is not used often because, for convenience, all maps are automatically printed when bpftrace terminates.[5]

Some map functions operate on a map key. For example:

```
delete(@start[tid]);
```

deletes the key-value pair from the @start map where the key is tid.

12. Timing vfs_read()

You have now learned the syntax needed to understand a more involved and practical example. This program, vfsread.bt, times the vfs_read kernel function and prints out a histogram of its duration in microseconds (us):

```
#!/usr/local/bin/bpftrace

// this program times vfs_read()

kprobe:vfs_read
{
        @start[tid] = nsecs;
}

kretprobe:vfs_read
/@start[tid]/
{
        $duration_us = (nsecs - @start[tid]) / 1000;
```

---

[5]There is also less overhead in printing maps when bpftrace terminates, as at runtime the maps are experiencing updates, which can slow down the map walk routine.

```
        @us = hist($duration_us);
        delete(@start[tid]);
}
```

This times the duration of the vfs_read() kernel function by instrumenting its start using a kprobe and storing a timestamp in a @start hash keyed on thread ID, and then instrumenting its end by using a kretprobe and calculating the delta as: now - start. A filter is used to ensure that the start time was recorded; otherwise, the delta calculation becomes bogus for vfs_read() calls that were in progress when tracing begins, as the end is seen but not the start (the delta would become: now - 0).

Sample output:

```
# bpftrace vfsread.bt
Attaching 2 probes...
^C

@us:
[0]                    23 |@                                                  |
[1]                   138 |@@@@@@@@@                                          |
[2, 4)                538 |@@@@@@@@@@@@@@@@@@@@@@@@@@@@@@@@@@@@@@@              |
[4, 8)                744 |@@@@@@@@@@@@@@@@@@@@@@@@@@@@@@@@@@@@@@@@@@@@@@@@@@@@@|
[8, 16)               641 |@@@@@@@@@@@@@@@@@@@@@@@@@@@@@@@@@@@@@@@@@@@@@        |
[16, 32)              122 |@@@@@@@@                                           |
[32, 64)               13 |                                                   |
[64, 128)              17 |@                                                  |
[128, 256)              2 |                                                   |
[256, 512)              0 |                                                   |
[512, 1K)               1 |                                                   |
```

The program ran until Ctrl-C was entered; then it printed this output and terminated. This histogram map was named "us" as a way to include units with the output, since the map name is printed out. By giving maps meaningful names like "bytes" and "latency_ns" you can annotate the output and make it self-explanatory.

This script can be customized as needed. Consider changing the hist() assignment line to:

```
@us[pid, comm] = hist($duration_us);
```

This stores one histogram per process ID and process name pair. With traditional system tools, like iostat(1) and vmstat(1), the output is fixed and cannot be easily customized. But with bpftrace, the metrics you see can be further broken down into parts and enhanced with metrics from other probes until you have the answers you need.

See Chapter 8, File Systems, Section 8.6.15, bpftrace, heading VFS Latency Tracing, for an extended example that breaks down vfs_read() latency by type: file system, socket, etc.

15.2.5   Reference

The following is a summary of the main components of bpftrace programming: probe types, flow control, variables, functions, and map functions.

1. Probe Types

Table 15.4 lists available probe types. Many of these also have a shortcut alias, which help create shorter one-liners.

Table 15.4   **bpftrace probe types**

Type	Shortcut	Description
tracepoint	t	Kernel static instrumentation points
usdt	U	User-level statically defined tracing
kprobe	k	Kernel dynamic function instrumentation
kretprobe	kr	Kernel dynamic function return instrumentation
kfunc	f	Kernel dynamic function instrumentation (BPF based)
kretfunc	fr	Kernel dynamic function return instrumentation (BPF based)
uprobe	u	User-level dynamic function instrumentation
uretprobe	ur	User-level dynamic function return instrumentation
software	s	Kernel software-based events
hardware	h	Hardware counter-based instrumentation
watchpoint	w	Memory watchpoint instrumentation
profile	p	Timed sampling across all CPUs
interval	i	Timed reporting (from one CPU)
BEGIN		Start of bpftrace
END		End of bpftrace

Most of these probe types are interfaces to existing kernel technologies. Chapter 4 explains how these technologies work: kprobes, uprobes, tracepoints, USDT, and PMCs (used by the hardware probe type). The kfunc/kretfunc probe type is a new low-overhead interface based on eBPF trampolines and BTF.

Some probes may fire frequently, such as for scheduler events, memory allocations, and network packets. To reduce overhead, try to solve your problems by using less-frequent events wherever possible. If you are unsure about probe frequency, you can measure it using bpftrace. For example, counting vfs_read() kprobe calls for one second only:

```
# bpftrace -e 'k:vfs_read { @ = count(); } interval:s:1 { exit(); }'
```

I chose a short duration to minimize the overhead cost, in case it was significant. What I would consider high or low frequency depends on your CPU speed, count, and headroom, and the cost of the probe instrumentation. As a rough guide for the computers of today, I would consider less than 100k kprobe or tracepoint events per second to be low frequency.

Probe Arguments

Each probe type provides different types of arguments for further context on events. For example, tracepoints provide the fields from the format file using their field names in an `args` data structure. For example, the following instruments the syscalls:sys_enter_read tracepoint and uses the `args->count` argument to record a histogram of the count argument (requested size):

```
bpftrace -e 'tracepoint:syscalls:sys_enter_read { @req_bytes = hist(args->count); }'
```

These fields can be listed from the format file in /sys or from bpftrace using -lv:

```
# bpftrace -lv 'tracepoint:syscalls:sys_enter_read'
tracepoint:syscalls:sys_enter_read
    int __syscall_nr;
    unsigned int fd;
    char * buf;
    size_t count;
```

See the online "bpftrace Reference Guide" for a description of each probe type and its arguments [Iovisor 20c].

2. Flow Control

There are three types of tests in bpftrace: filters, ternary operators, and if statements. These tests conditionally change the flow of the program based on Boolean expressions, which support those shown in Table 15.5.

Table 15.5   **bpftrace Boolean expressions**

Expression	Description
==	Equal to
!=	Not equal to
>	Greater than
<	Less than
>=	Greater than or equal to
<=	Less than or equal to
&&	And
||	Inclusive or

Expressions may be grouped using parentheses.

Filter

Introduced earlier, these gate whether an action is executed. Format:

```
probe /filter/ { action }
```

Boolean operators may be used. The filter /pid == 123/ only executes the action if the pid built-in equals 123.

Ternary Operators

A ternary operator is a three-element operator composed of a test and two outcomes. Format:

```
test ? true_statement : false_statement
```

As an example, you can use a ternary operator to find the absolute value of $x:

```
$abs = $x >= 0 ? $x : - $x;
```

If Statements

If statements have the following syntax:

```
if (test) { true_statements }
if (test) { true_statements } else { false_statements }
```

One use case is with programs that perform different actions on IPv4 than on IPv6. For example (for simplicity, this ignores families other than IPv4 and IPv6):

```
if ($inet_family == $AF_INET) {
    // IPv4
    ...
} else {
    // assume IPv6
    ...
}
```

else if statements are supported since bpftrace v0.10.0.[6]

Loops

bpftrace supports unrolled loops using unroll(). For Linux 5.3 and later kernels, while() loops are also supported[7]:

---

[6] Thanks Daniel Xu (PR#1211).

[7] Thanks Bas Smit for adding the bpftrace logic (PR#1066).

```
while (test) {
    statements
}
```

This uses the kernel BPF loop support added in Linux 5.3.

Operators

An earlier section listed Boolean operators for use in tests. bpftrace also supports the operators shown in Table 15.6.

Table 15.6 **bpftrace operators**

Operator	Description
=	Assignment
+, −, *, /	Addition, subtraction, multiplication, division (integers only)
++, −−	Auto-increment, auto-decrement
&, |, ^	Binary and, binary or, binary exclusive or
!	Logical not
<<, >>	Logical shift left, logical shift right
+=, −=, *=, /=, %=, &=, ^=, <<=, >>=	Compound operators

These operators were modeled after similar operators in the C programming language.

3. Variables

The built-in variables provided by bpftrace are usually for read-only access of information. Important built-in variables are listed in Table 15.7.

Table 15.7 **bpftrace selected built-in variables**

Built-in Variable	Type	Description
pid	integer	Process ID (kernel tgid)
tid	integer	Thread ID (kernel pid)
uid	integer	User ID
username	string	Username
nsecs	integer	Timestamp, in nanoseconds
elapsed	integer	Timestamp, in nanoseconds, since bpftrace initialization
cpu	integer	Processor ID

Built-in Variable	Type	Description
comm	string	Process name
kstack	string	Kernel stack trace
ustack	string	User-level stack trace
arg0, ..., argN	integer	Arguments to some probe types
args	struct	Arguments to some probe types
sarg0, ..., sargN	integer	Stack-based arguments to some probe types
retval	integer	Return value for some probe types
func	string	Name of the traced function
probe	string	Full name of the current probe
curtask	struct/integer	Kernel task_struct (either as a task_struct or an unsigned 64-bit integer, depending on the availability of type info)
cgroup	integer	Default cgroup v2 ID for the current process (for comparisons with cgroupid())
$1, ..., $N	int, char *	Positional parameters for the bpftrace program

All integers are currently uint64. These variables all refer to the currently running thread, probe, function, and CPU when the probe fires.

Various builtins have been demonstrated earlier in this chapter: retval, comm, tid, and nsecs. See the online "bpftrace Reference Guide" for the full and updated list of built-in variables [Iovisor 20c].

4. Functions

Table 15.8 lists selected built-in functions for various tasks. Some of these have been used in earlier examples, such as printf().

Table 15.8   bpftrace selected built-in functions

Function	Description
printf(char *fmt [, ...])	Prints formatted
time(char *fmt)	Prints formatted time
join(char *arr[])	Prints the array of strings, joined by a space character
str(char *s [, int len])	Returns the string from the pointer s, with an optional length limit
buf(void *d [, int length])	Returns a hexadecimal string version of the data pointer
strncmp(char *s1, char *s2, int length)	Compares two strings up to length characters

Function	Description
sizeof(expression)	Returns the size of the expression or data type
kstack([int limit])	Returns a kernel stack up to *limit* frames deep
ustack([int limit])	Returns a user stack up to *limit* frames deep
ksym(void *p)	Resolves the kernel address and returns the string symbol
usym(void *p)	Resolves the user-space address and returns the string symbol
kaddr(char *name)	Resolves the kernel symbol name to an address
uaddr(char *name)	Resolves the user-space symbol name to an address
reg(char *name)	Returns the value stored in the named register
ntop([int af,] int addr)	Returns a string representation of an IPv4/IPv6 address.
cgroupid(char *path)	Returns a cgroup ID for the given path (/sys/fs/cgroup/...)
system(char *fmt [, ...])	Executes a shell command
cat(char *filename)	Prints the contents of a file
signal(char[] sig | u32 sig)	Sends a signal to the current task (e.g., SIGTERM)
override(u64 rc)	Overrides a kprobe return value[8]
exit()	Exits bpftrace

Some of these functions are asynchronous: The kernel queues the event, and a short time later it is processed in user space. The asynchronous functions are printf(), time(), cat(), join(), and system(). The functions kstack(), ustack(), ksym(), and usym() record addresses synchronously, but do symbol translation asynchronously.

As an example, the following uses both the printf() and str() functions to show the filename of openat(2) syscalls:

```
# bpftrace -e 't:syscalls:sys_enter_open { printf("%s %s\n", comm,
    str(args->filename)); }'
Attaching 1 probe...
top /etc/ld.so.cache
top /lib/x86_64-linux-gnu/libprocps.so.7
top /lib/x86_64-linux-gnu/libtinfo.so.6
top /lib/x86_64-linux-gnu/libc.so.6
[...]
```

See the online "bpftrace Reference Guide" for the full and updated list of functions [Iovisor 20c].

---

[8] WARNING: Only use this if you know what you are doing: a small mistake could panic or corrupt the kernel.

5. Map Functions

Maps are special hash table storage objects from BPF that can be used for different purposes—for example, as hash tables to store key/value pairs or for statistical summaries. bpftrace provides built-in functions for map assignment and manipulation, mostly for supporting statistical summary maps. The most important map functions are listed in Table 15.9.

Table 15.9   **bpftrace selected map functions**

Function	Description
count()	Counts occurrences
sum(int n)	Sums the value
avg(int n)	Averages the value
min(int n)	Records the minimum value
max(int n)	Records the maximum value
stats(int n)	Returns the count, average, and total
hist(int n)	Prints a power-of-two histogram of values
lhist(int n, const int min, const int max, int step)	Prints a linear histogram of values
delete(@m[key])	Deletes the map key/value pair
print(@m [, top [, div]])	Prints the map, with optional limits and a divisor
clear(@m)	Deletes all keys from the map
zero(@m)	Sets all map values to zero

Some of these functions are asynchronous: The kernel queues the event, and a short time later it is processed in user space. The asynchronous actions are print(), clear(), and zero(). Bear this delay in mind when you are writing programs.

As another example of using a map function, the following uses lhist() to create a linear histogram of syscall read(2) sizes by process name, with a step size of one so that each file descriptor number can be seen independently:

```
# bpftrace -e 'tracepoint:syscalls:sys_enter_read {
    @fd[comm] = lhist(args->fd, 0, 100, 1); }'
Attaching 1 probe...
^C
[...]
@fd[sshd]:
[4, 5)               22 |                                        |
[5, 6)                0 |                                        |
[6, 7)                0 |                                        |
```

```
[7, 8)              0 |                                                              |
[8, 9)              0 |                                                              |
[9, 10)             0 |                                                              |
[10, 11)            0 |                                                              |
[11, 12)            0 |                                                              |
[12, 13)         7760 |@@@@@@@@@@@@@@@@@@@@@@@@@@@@@@@@@@@@@@@@@@@@@@@@@@@@@@@@@@@@@@@@|
```

The output shows that on this system sshd processes were typically reading from file descriptor 12. The output uses set notation, where "[" means >= and ")" means < (aka a bounded left-closed, right-open interval).

See the online "bpftrace Reference Guide" for the full and updated list of map functions [Iovisor 20c].

15.2.6 Documentation

There is more bpftrace in prior chapters of this book, in the following sections:

- Chapter 5, Applications, Section 5.5.7
- Chapter 6, CPUs, Section 6.6.20
- Chapter 7, Memory, Section 7.5.13
- Chapter 8, File Systems, Section 8.6.15
- Chapter 9, Disks, Section 9.6.11
- Chapter 10, Network, Section 10.6.12

There are also bpftrace examples in Chapter 4, Observability Tools, and Chapter 11, Cloud Computing.

In the bpftrace repository I have also created the following documentation:

- Reference Guide: docs/reference_guide.md [Iovisor 20c]
- Tutorial docs/tutorial_one_liners.md [Iovisor 20d]

For much more on bpftrace, please refer to my earlier book *BPF Performance Tools* [Gregg 19] where Chapter 5, bpftrace, explores the programming language with many examples, and later chapters provide more bpftrace programs for the analysis of different targets.

Note that some bpftrace capabilities described in [Gregg 19] as "planned" have since been added to bpftrace and are included in this chapter. They are: while() loops, else-if statements, signal(), override(), and watchpoint events. Other additions that have been added to bpftrace are the kfunc probe type, buf(), and sizeof(). Check the release notes in the bpftrace repository for future additions, although not many more are planned: bpftrace already has enough capabilities for the 120+ published bpftrace tools.

15.3 References

[Aho 78] Aho, A. V., Kernighan, B. W., and Weinberger, P. J., "Awk: A Pattern Scanning and Processing Language (Second Edition)," *Unix 7th Edition man pages*, 1978. Online at http://plan9.bell-labs.com/7thEdMan/index.html.

[Aho 88] Aho, A. V., Kernighan, B. W., and Weinberger, P. J., *The AWK Programming Language*, Addison Wesley, 1988.

[Gregg 18e] Gregg, B., "YOW! 2018 Cloud Performance Root Cause Analysis at Netflix," http://www.brendangregg.com/blog/2019-04-26/yow2018-cloud-performance-netflix.html, 2018.

[Gregg 19] Gregg, B., *BPF Performance Tools: Linux System and Application Observability*, Addison-Wesley, 2019.

[Gregg 19g] Gregg, B., "BPF Performance Tools (book): Tools," http://www.brendangregg.com/bpf-performance-tools-book.html#tools, 2019.

[Iovisor 20a] "bpftrace: High-level Tracing Language for Linux eBPF," https://github.com/iovisor/bpftrace, last updated 2020.

[Iovisor 20b] "BCC - Tools for BPF-based Linux IO Analysis, Networking, Monitoring, and More," https://github.com/iovisor/bcc, last updated 2020.

[Iovisor 20c] "bpftrace Reference Guide," https://github.com/iovisor/bpftrace/blob/master/docs/reference_guide.md, last updated 2020.

[Iovisor 20d] Gregg, B., et al., "The bpftrace One-Liner Tutorial," https://github.com/iovisor/bpftrace/blob/master/docs/tutorial_one_liners.md, last updated 2020.

Chapter 16

Case Study

This chapter is a systems performance case study: the story of a real-world performance issue, from initial report to final resolution. This particular issue occurred in a production cloud computing environment; I chose it as a routine example of systems performance analysis.

My intent in this chapter is not to introduce new technical content but to use storytelling to show how tools and methodologies may be applied in practice, in a real work environment. This should be especially useful for beginners who have yet to work on real-world systems performance issues, providing an over-the-shoulder view of how an expert approaches them, a commentary on what that expert might be thinking during the analysis, and why. This isn't necessarily documenting the best approach possible, but rather why one approach was taken.

16.1   An Unexplained Win

A microservice at Netflix was tested on a new container-based platform and was found to reduce request latency by a factor of three to four. While the container platform has many benefits, such a large gain was unexpected! This sounded too good to be true, and I was asked to investigate and explain how it happened.

For analysis I used a variety of tools, including those based on counters, static configuration, PMCs, software events, and tracing. All of these tool types played a role and provided clues that fit together. As this made for a broad tour of systems performance analysis, I used it as the opening story for my USENIX LISA 2019 talk on Systems Performance [Gregg 19h] and included it here as a case study.

16.1.1   Problem Statement

By speaking to the service team, I learned details of the microservice: It was a Java application for calculating customer recommendations, and was currently running on virtual machine instances in the AWS EC2 cloud. The microservice was composed of two components, and one of them was being tested on a new Netflix container platform called Titus, also running on AWS EC2. This component had a request latency of three to four seconds on the VM instances, which became one second on containers: three to four times faster!

The problem was to explain this performance difference. If it was simply due to the container move, the microservice can expect a permanent 3-4x win by moving. If it was due to some other factor, it would be worth understanding what it was and if it will be permanent. Perhaps it can also be applied elsewhere and to a greater degree.

What immediately came to mind was the benefit of running one component of a workload in isolation: it would be able to use the entire CPU caches without contention from the other component, improving cache hit ratios and thus performance. Another guess would be bursting on the container platform, where a container can use idle CPU resources from other containers.

16.1.2   Analysis Strategy

As traffic is handled by a load balancer (AWS ELB), it was possible to split the traffic between the VM and containers so that I could log in to both at the same time. This is an ideal situation for comparative analysis: I could run the same analysis command on both at the same time of day (same traffic mix and load) and compare the output immediately.

In this case I had access to the container host, not just the container, which allowed me to use any analysis tool and provided the permission for those tools to make any syscall. If I had had only container access, analysis would have been much more time-consuming due to limited observability sources and kernel permissions, requiring much more inference from limited metrics rather than direct measurement. Some performance issues are currently impractical to analyze from the container alone (see Chapter 11, Cloud Computing).

For methodologies, I planned to start with the 60-second checklist (Chapter 1, Introduction, Section 1.10.1, Linux Perf Analysis in 60s) and the USE method (Chapter 2, Methodologies, Section 2.5.9, The USE Method), and based on their clues perform drill-down analysis (Section 2.5.12, Drill-Down Analysis) and other methodologies.

I've included the commands I ran and their output in the following sections, using a "serverA#" prompt for the VM instance, and "serverB#" for the container host.

16.1.3   Statistics

I began by running uptime(1) to check the load average statistics. On both systems:

```
serverA# uptime
 22:07:23 up 15 days,  5:01,  1 user,   load average: 85.09, 89.25, 91.26


serverB# uptime
 22:06:24 up 91 days, 23:52,  1 user,   load average: 17.94, 16.92, 16.62
```

This showed that the load was roughly steady, getting a little lighter on the VM instance (85.09 compared to 91.26) and a little heavier on the container (17.94 compared to 16.62). I checked the trends to see whether the problem was increasing, decreasing, or steady: this is especially important in cloud environments that can automatically migrate load away from an unhealthy instance. More than once I've logged in to a problematic instance to find little activity, and a one-minute load average approaching zero.

The load averages also showed that the VM had much higher load than the container host (85.09 versus 17.94), although I would need statistics from other tools to understand what this meant. High load averages usually point to CPU demand, but can be I/O-related as well (see Chapter 6, CPUs, Section 6.6.1, uptime).

To explore CPU load, I turned to mpstat(1), beginning with system-wide averages. On the virtual machine:

```
serverA# mpstat 10
Linux 4.4.0-130-generic (...) 07/18/2019        _x86_64_    (48 CPU)

10:07:55 PM  CPU   %usr  %nice %sys %iowait  %irq %soft %steal %guest %gnice  %idle
10:08:05 PM  all  89.72   0.00 7.84    0.00  0.00  0.04   0.00   0.00   0.00   2.40
10:08:15 PM  all  88.60   0.00 9.18    0.00  0.00  0.05   0.00   0.00   0.00   2.17
10:08:25 PM  all  89.71   0.00 9.01    0.00  0.00  0.05   0.00   0.00   0.00   1.23
10:08:35 PM  all  89.55   0.00 8.11    0.00  0.00  0.06   0.00   0.00   0.00   2.28
10:08:45 PM  all  89.87   0.00 8.21    0.00  0.00  0.05   0.00   0.00   0.00   1.86
^C
Average:     all  89.49   0.00 8.47    0.00  0.00  0.05   0.00   0.00   0.00   1.99
```

And the container:

```
serverB# mpstat 10
Linux 4.19.26 (...) 07/18/2019          _x86_64_    (64 CPU)

09:56:11 PM CPU    %usr  %nice %sys %iowait  %irq %soft %steal %guest %gnice  %idle
09:56:21 PM  all  23.21   0.01 0.32    0.00  0.00  0.10   0.00   0.00   0.00  76.37
09:56:31 PM  all  20.21   0.00 0.38    0.00  0.00  0.08   0.00   0.00   0.00  79.33
09:56:41 PM  all  21.58   0.00 0.39    0.00  0.00  0.10   0.00   0.00   0.00  77.92
09:56:51 PM  all  21.57   0.01 0.39    0.02  0.00  0.09   0.00   0.00   0.00  77.93
09:57:01 PM  all  20.93   0.00 0.35    0.00  0.00  0.09   0.00   0.00   0.00  78.63
^C
Average:     all  21.50   0.00 0.36    0.00  0.00  0.09   0.00   0.00   0.00  78.04
```

mpstat(1) prints the number of CPUs as the first line. The output showed that the virtual machine had 48 CPUs, and the container host had 64. This helped me further interpret the load averages: if they were CPU-based, it would show that the VM instance was running well into CPU saturation, because the load averages were roughly double the CPU count, whereas the container host was under-utilized. The mpstat(1) metrics supported this hypothesis: the idle time on the VM was around 2%, whereas on the container host it was around 78%.

By examining the other mpstat(1) statistics, I identified other leads:

- CPU utilization (`%usr` + `%sys` + ...) showed that the VM was at 98% versus the container at 22%. These processors have two hyperthreads per CPU core, so crossing the 50% utilization mark typically means hyperthread core contention, degrading performance. The VM was well into this territory, whereas the container host might still be benefiting from only one busy hyperthread per core.

- The system time (`%sys`) on the VM was much higher: around 8% versus 0.38%. If the VM was running at CPU saturation, this extra `%sys` time might include kernel context switching code paths. Kernel tracing or profiling could confirm.

I continued the other commands on the 60-second checklist. vmstat(8) showed run queue lengths similar to the load averages, confirming that the load averages were CPU-based. iostat(1) showed little disk I/O, and sar(1) showed little network I/O. (Those outputs are not included here.) This confirmed that the VM was running at CPU saturation, causing runnable threads to wait their turn, whereas the container host was not. top(1) on the container host also showed that only one container was running.

These commands provided statistics for the USE method, which also identified the issue of CPU load.

Had I solved the issue? I'd found that the VM had a load average of 85 on a 48-CPU system, and that this load average was CPU-based. This meant that threads were waiting their turn roughly 77% of the time (85/48 – 1), and eliminating this time spent waiting would produce a roughly 4x speedup (1 / (1 – 0.77)). While this magnitude corresponded to the issue, I couldn't yet explain why the load average was higher: more analysis was necessary.

16.1.4 Configuration

Knowing that there was a CPU issue, I checked the configuration of the CPUs and their limits (static performance tuning: Sections 2.5.17 and 6.5.7). The processors themselves were different between the VMs and containers. Here is /proc/cpuinfo for the virtual machine:

```
serverA# cat /proc/cpuinfo
processor       : 47
vendor_id       : GenuineIntel
cpu family      : 6
model           : 85
model name      : Intel(R) Xeon(R) Platinum 8175M CPU @ 2.50GHz
stepping        : 4
microcode       : 0x200005e
cpu MHz         : 2499.998
cache size      : 33792 KB
physical id     : 0
siblings        : 48
core id         : 23
cpu cores       : 24
apicid          : 47
```

```
initial apicid  : 47
fpu             : yes
fpu_exception   : yes
cpuid level     : 13
wp              : yes
flags           : fpu vme de pse tsc msr pae mce cx8 apic sep mtrr pge mca cmov pat
pse36 clflush mmx fxsr sse sse2 ss ht syscall nx pdpe1gb rdtscp lm constant_tsc
arch_perfmon rep_good nopl xtopology nonstop_tsc aperfmperf eagerfpu pni pclmulqdq
monitor ssse3 fma cx16 pcid sse4_1 sse4_2 x2apic movbe popcnt tsc_deadline_timer aes
xsave avx f16c rdrand hypervisor lahf_lm abm 3dnowprefetch invpcid_single kaiser
fsgsbase tsc_adjust bmi1 hle avx2 smep bmi2 erms invpcid rtm mpx avx512f rdseed adx
smap clflushopt clwb avx512cd xsaveopt xsavec xgetbv1 ida arat
bugs            : cpu_meltdown spectre_v1 spectre_v2 spec_store_bypass
bogomips        : 4999.99
clflush size    : 64
cache_alignment : 64
address sizes   : 46 bits physical, 48 bits virtual
power management:
```

And the container:

```
serverB# cat /proc/cpuinfo
processor       : 63
vendor_id       : GenuineIntel
cpu family      : 6
model           : 79
model name      : Intel(R) Xeon(R) CPU E5-2686 v4 @ 2.30GHz
stepping        : 1
microcode       : 0xb000033
cpu MHz         : 1200.601
cache size      : 46080 KB
physical id     : 1
siblings        : 32
core id         : 15
cpu cores       : 16
apicid          : 95
initial apicid  : 95
fpu             : yes
fpu_exception   : yes
cpuid level     : 13
wp              : yes
flags           : fpu vme de pse tsc msr pae mce cx8 apic sep mtrr pge mca cmov pat
pse36 clflush mmx fxsr sse sse2 ht syscall nx pdpe1gb rdtscp lm constant_tsc arch_
perfmon rep_good nopl xtopology nonstop_tsc cpuid aperfmperf pni pclmulqdq monitor
est ssse3 fma cx16 pcid sse4_1 sse4_2 x2apic movbe popcnt tsc_deadline_timer aes
```

```
xsave avx f16c rdrand hypervisor lahf_lm abm 3dnowprefetch cpuid_fault
invpcid_single pti fsgsbase bmi1 hle avx2 smep bmi2 erms invpcid rtm rdseed adx
xsaveopt ida
bugs            : cpu_meltdown spectre_v1 spectre_v2 spec_store_bypass l1tf
bogomips        : 4662.22
clflush size    : 64
cache_alignment : 64
address sizes   : 46 bits physical, 48 bits virtual
power management:
```

The CPUs for the container host had a slightly slower base frequency (2.30 versus 2.50 GHz); however, they had a much larger last-level cache (45 versus 33 Mbytes). Depending on the workload, the larger cache size can make a significant difference to CPU performance. To investigate further, I needed to use PMCs.

16.1.5   PMCs

Performance monitoring counters (PMCs) can explain CPU cycle performance, and are available on certain instances in AWS EC2. I've published a toolkit for PMC analysis on the cloud [Gregg 20e], which includes pmcarch(8) (Section 6.6.11, pmcarch). pmcarch(8) shows the Intel "architectural set" of PMCs, which are the most basic set commonly available.

On the virtual machine:

```
serverA# ./pmcarch -p 4093 10
K_CYCLES   K_INSTR      IPC BR_RETIRED     BR_MISPRED    BMR% LLCREF       LLCMISS      LLC%
982412660  575706336   0.59 126424862460  2416880487    1.91 15724006692  10872315070  30.86
999621309  555043627   0.56 120449284756  2317302514    1.92 15378257714  11121882510  27.68
991146940  558145849   0.56 126350181501  2530383860    2.00 15965082710  11464682655  28.19
996314688  562276830   0.56 122215605985  2348638980    1.92 15558286345  10835594199  30.35
979890037  560268707   0.57 125609807909  2386085660    1.90 15828820588  11038597030  30.26
[...]
```

On the container instance:

```
serverB# ./pmcarch -p 1928219 10
K_CYCLES   K_INSTR      IPC BR_RETIRED    BR_MISPRED   BMR% LLCREF      LLCMISS     LLC%
147523816  222396364   1.51 46053921119   641813770    1.39 8880477235  968809014   89.09
156634810  229801807   1.47 48236123575   653064504    1.35 9186609260  1183858023  87.11
152783226  237001219   1.55 49344315621   692819230    1.40 9314992450  879494418   90.56
140787179  213570329   1.52 44518363978   631588112    1.42 8675999448  712318917   91.79
136822760  219706637   1.61 45129020910   651436401    1.44 8689831639  617678747   92.89
[...]
```

This showed instructions per cycle (IPC) of around 0.57 for the VM versus around 1.52 for the container: a 2.6x difference.

One reason for the lower IPC could be hyperthread contention, as the VM host was running at over 50% CPU utilization. The last column showed an additional reason: the last-level cache (LLC) hit ratio was only 30% for the VM, versus around 90% for the container. This would cause instructions on the VM to frequently stall on main memory access, driving down IPC and instruction throughput (performance).

The lower LLC hit ratio on the VM could be due to at least three factors:

- A smaller LLC size (33 versus 45 Mbytes).

- Running the full workload instead of a subcomponent (as mentioned in the Problem Statement); a subcomponent will likely cache better: fewer instructions and data.

- CPU saturation causing more context switching, and jumping between code paths (including user and kernel), increasing cache pressure.

The last factor could be investigated using tracing tools.

16.1.6 Software Events

To investigate context switches, I began with the perf(1) command to count the system-wide context switch rate. This uses a software event, which is similar to a hardware event (PMC) but implemented in software (see Chapter 4, Observability Tools, Figure 4.5, and Chapter 13, perf, Section 13.5, Software Events).

On the virtual machine:

```
serverA# perf stat -e cs -a -I 1000
#          time             counts unit events
       1.000411740       2,063,105      cs
       2.000977435       2,065,354      cs
       3.001537756       1,527,297      cs
       4.002028407         515,509      cs
       5.002538455       2,447,126      cs
       6.003114251       2,021,182      cs
       7.003665091       2,329,157      cs
       8.004093520       1,740,898      cs
       9.004533912       1,235,641      cs
      10.005106500       2,340,443      cs
^C    10.513632795       1,496,555      cs
```

This output showed a rate of around two million context switches per second. I then ran it on the container host, this time matching on the PID of the container application to exclude other possible containers (I did similar PID matching on the VM, and it did not noticeably change the previous results[1]):

---

[1] Then why don't I include the PID-matching output for the VM? I don't have it.

```
serverB# perf stat -e cs -p 1928219 -I 1000
#            time           counts unit events
       1.001931945          1,172    cs
       2.002664012          1,370    cs
       3.003441563          1,034    cs
       4.004140394          1,207    cs
       5.004947675          1,053    cs
       6.005605844            955    cs
       7.006311221            619    cs
       8.007082057          1,050    cs
       9.007716475          1,215    cs
      10.008415042          1,373    cs
^C     10.584617028           894    cs
```

This output showed a rate of only about one thousand context switches per second.

A high rate of context switches can put more pressure on the CPU caches, which are switching between different code paths, including the kernel code to manage the context switch, and possibly different processes.[2] To investigate context switches further, I used tracing tools.

16.1.7   Tracing

There are several BPF-based tracing tools for analyzing CPU usage and context switching further, including, from BCC: cpudist(8), cpuwalk(8), runqlen(8), runqlat(8), runqslower(8), cpuunclaimed(8), and more (see Figure 15.1).

cpudist(8) shows the on-CPU duration of threads. On the virtual machine:

```
serverA# cpudist -p 4093 10 1
Tracing on-CPU time... Hit Ctrl-C to end.

     usecs           : count     distribution
        0 -> 1       : 3618650   |****************************************|
        2 -> 3       : 2704935   |*****************************            |
        4 -> 7       : 421179    |****                                     |
        8 -> 15      : 99416     |*                                        |
       16 -> 31      : 16951     |                                         |
       32 -> 63      : 6355      |                                         |
       64 -> 127     : 3586      |                                         |
      128 -> 255     : 3400      |                                         |
      256 -> 511     : 4004      |                                         |
      512 -> 1023    : 4445      |                                         |
```

---

[2]For some processor and kernel configurations, context switching may also flush the L1 cache.

```
    1024 -> 2047       : 8173    |                                        |
    2048 -> 4095       : 9165    |                                        |
    4096 -> 8191       : 7194    |                                        |
    8192 -> 16383      : 11954   |                                        |
   16384 -> 32767      : 1426    |                                        |
   32768 -> 65535      : 967     |                                        |
   65536 -> 131071     : 338     |                                        |
  131072 -> 262143     : 93      |                                        |
  262144 -> 524287     : 28      |                                        |
  524288 -> 1048575    : 4       |                                        |
```

This output shows that the application typically spent very little time on-CPU, often less than 7 microseconds. Other tools (stackcount(8) of t:sched:sched_switch, and /proc/PID/status) showed that the application was usually leaving the CPU due to involuntary[3] context switches.

On the container host:

```
serverB# cpudist -p 1928219 10 1
Tracing on-CPU time... Hit Ctrl-C to end.

     usecs              : count    distribution
        0 -> 1          : 0        |                                        |
        2 -> 3          : 16       |                                        |
        4 -> 7          : 6        |                                        |
        8 -> 15         : 7        |                                        |
       16 -> 31         : 8        |                                        |
       32 -> 63         : 10       |                                        |
       64 -> 127        : 18       |                                        |
      128 -> 255        : 40       |                                        |
      256 -> 511        : 44       |                                        |
      512 -> 1023       : 156      |*                                       |
     1024 -> 2047       : 238      |**                                      |
     2048 -> 4095       : 4511     |****************************************|
     4096 -> 8191       : 277      |**                                      |
     8192 -> 16383      : 286      |**                                      |
    16384 -> 32767      : 77       |                                        |
    32768 -> 65535      : 63       |                                        |
    65536 -> 131071     : 44       |                                        |
   131072 -> 262143     : 9        |                                        |
   262144 -> 524287     : 14       |                                        |
   524288 -> 1048575    : 5        |                                        |
```

---

[3]/proc/PID/status calls them nonvoluntary_ctxt_switches.

Now the application was typically spending between 2 and 4 milliseconds on-CPU. Other tools showed that it was not interrupted much by involuntary context switches.

The involuntary context switches on the VM, and subsequent high rate of context switches seen earlier, caused performance problems. Causing the application to leave the CPU after often less than 10 microseconds also does not give the CPU caches much time to warm up to the current code paths.

16.1.8   Conclusion

I concluded that the reasons for the performance gain were:

- **No container neighbors:** The container host was idle except for the one container. This allowed the container to have the entire CPU caches all to itself, as well as to run without CPU contention. While this produced container-favorable results during the test, it is not the expected situation for long-term production use where neighboring containers will be the norm. The microservice may find that the 3-4x performance win vanishes when other tenants move in.

- **LLC size and workload difference:** The IPC was 2.6 times lower on the VM, which could explain 2.6x of this slowdown. One cause was likely hyperthread contention as the VM host was running at over 50% utilization (and had two hyperthreads per core). However, the main cause was likely the lower LLC hit ratio: 30% on the VM versus 90% on the container. This low LLC hit ratio had three probable reasons:

    □ A smaller LLC size on the VM: 33 Mbytes versus 45 Mbytes.

    □ A more complex workload on the VM: the full app, requiring more instruction text and data, versus the component run on the container.

    □ A high rate of context switches on the VM: around 2 million per second. These prevent threads from running on-CPU for long, interfering with cache warmup. The on-CPU durations were typically less than 10 µs on the VM compared to 2-4 ms on the container host.

- **CPU load difference:** A higher load was directed to the VM, driving the CPUs to saturation: a CPU-based load average of 85 on a 48-CPU system. This caused a rate of around 2 million context switches per second, and run queue latency as threads waited their turn. The run queue latency implied by the load averages showed the VM was running roughly 4x slower.

These issues explain the observed performance difference.

16.2   Additional Information

For more case studies in systems performance analysis, check the bug database (or ticketing system) at your company for previous performance-related issues, and the public bug databases for the applications and operating system you use. These issues often begin with a problem statement and finish with the final fix. Many bug database systems also include a timestamped comments history, which can be studied to see the progression of analysis, including hypotheses explored and wrong turns taken. Taking wrong turns, and identifying multiple contributing factors, is normal.

Some systems performance case studies are published from time to time, for example, as on my blog [Gregg 20j]. Technical journals with a focus on practice, such as *USENIX ;login:* [USENIX 20] and *ACM Queue* [ACM 20], also often use case studies as context when describing new technical solutions to problems.

16.3 References

[Gregg 19h] Gregg, B., "LISA2019 Linux Systems Performance," *USENIX LISA*, http://www.brendangregg.com/blog/2020-03-08/lisa2019-linux-systems-performance.html, 2019.

[ACM 20] "acmqueue," http://queue.acm.org, accessed 2020.

[Gregg 20e] Gregg, B., "PMC (Performance Monitoring Counter) Tools for the Cloud," https://github.com/brendangregg/pmc-cloud-tools, last updated 2020.

[Gregg 20j] "Brendan Gregg's Blog," http://www.brendangregg.com/blog, last updated 2020.

[USENIX 20] ";login: The USENIX Magazine," https://www.usenix.org/publications/login, accessed 2020.

Appendix A

USE Method: Linux

This appendix contains a checklist for Linux derived from the USE method [Gregg 13d]. This is a method for checking system health, and identifying common resource bottlenecks and errors, introduced in Chapter 2, Methodologies, Section 2.5.9, The USE Method. Later chapters (5, 6, 7, 9, 10) described it in specific contexts and introduced tools to support its use.

Performance tools are often enhanced, and new ones are developed, so you should treat this as a starting point that will need updates. New observability frameworks and tools can also be developed to specifically make following the USE method easier.

Physical Resources

Component	Type	Metric
CPU	Utilization	Per CPU: `mpstat -P ALL 1`, sum of CPU-consuming columns (`%usr`, `%nice`, `%sys`, `%irq`, `%soft`, `%guest`, `%gnice`) or inverse of idle columns (`%iowait`, `%steal`, `%idle`); `sar -P ALL`, sum of CPU-consuming columns (`%user`, `%nice`, `%system`) or inverse of idle columns (`%iowait`, `%steal`, `%idle`)
		System-wide: `vmstat 1`, us + sy; `sar -u`, `%user` + `%nice` + `%system`
		Per process: `top`, `%CPU`; `htop`, `CPU%`; `ps -o pcpu`; `pidstat 1`, `%CPU`
		Per kernel thread: `top`/`htop` (K to toggle), where VIRT == 0 (heuristic)
CPU	Saturation	System-wide: `vmstat 1`, r > CPU count[1]; `sar -q`, `runq-sz` > CPU count; `runqlat`; `runqlen`
		Per process: /proc/PID/schedstat 2nd field (sched_info.run_delay); getdelays.c, CPU[2]; `perf sched latency` (shows average and maximum delay per schedule)[3]

---

[1] The r column reports those threads that are waiting *and* threads that are running on-CPU. See the vmstat(1) description in Chapter 6, CPUs.

[2] Uses delay accounting; see Chapter 4, Observability Tools.

[3] There is also the sched:sched_process_wait tracepoint for perf(1); be careful about overheads when tracing, as scheduler events are frequent.

Component	Type	Metric
CPU	Errors	Machine Check Exceptions (MCEs) seen in dmesg or rasdaemon and ras-mc-ctl --summary; perf(1) if processor-specific error events (PMCs) are available; e.g., AMD64's "04Ah Single-bit ECC Errors Recorded by Scrubber"[4] (which can also be classified as a memory device error); ipmtool sel list; ipmitool sdr list
Memory capacity	Utilization	System-wide: free -m, Mem: (main memory), Swap: (virtual memory); vmstat 1, free (main memory), swap (virtual memory); sar -r, %memused; slabtop -s c for kmem slab usage Per process: top/htop, RES (resident main memory), VIRT (virtual memory), Mem for system-wide summary
Memory capacity	Saturation	System-wide: vmstat 1, si/so (swapping); sar -B, pgscank + pgscand (scanning); sar -W Per process: getdelays.c, SWAP2; 10th field (min_flt) from /proc/PID/stat for minor fault rate, or dynamic instrumentation[5]; dmesg | grep killed (OOM killer)
Memory capacity	Errors	dmesg for physical failures or rasdaemon and ras-mc-ctl --summary or edac-util; dmidecode may also show physical failures; ipmtool sel list; ipmitool sdr list; dynamic instrumentation, e.g., uretprobes for failed malloc()s (bpftrace)
Network interfaces	Utilization	ip -s link, RX/TX tput / max bandwidth; sar -n DEV, rx/tx kB/s / max bandwidth; /proc/net/dev, bytes RX/TX tput/max
Network interfaces	Saturation	nstat, TcpRetransSegs; sar -n EDEV, *drop/s, *fifo/s[6]; /proc/net/dev, RX/TX drop; dynamic instrumentation of other TCP/IP stack queueing (bpftrace)
Network interfaces	Errors	ip -s link, errors; sar -n EDEV all; /proc/net/dev, errs, drop6; extra counters may be under /sys/class/net/*/statistics/*error*; dynamic instrumentation of driver function returns
Storage device I/O	Utilization	System-wide: iostat -xz 1, %util; sar -d, %util; per process: iotop, biotop; /proc/PID/sched se.statistics.iowait_sum

---

[4] There aren't many error-related events in the recent Intel and AMD processor manuals.

[5] This can be used to show what is consuming memory and leading to saturation, by seeing what is causing minor faults. This should be available in htop(1) as MINFLT.

[6] Dropped packets are included as both saturation and error indicators, since they can occur due to both types of events.

Component	Type	Metric
Storage device I/O	Saturation	`iostat -xnz 1`, `avgqu-sz > 1`, or high `await`; `sar -d` same; perf(1) block tracepoints for queue length/latency; `biolatency`
Storage device I/O	Errors	`/sys/devices/` . . . `/ioerr_cnt`; `smartctl`; `bioerr`; dynamic/static instrumentation of I/O subsystem response codes[7]
Storage capacity	Utilization	Swap: `swapon -s`; `free`; /proc/meminfo `SwapFree`/`SwapTotal`; file systems: `df -h`
Storage capacity	Saturation	Not sure this one makes sense—once it's full, ENOSPC (although when close to full, performance may be degraded depending on the file system free block algorithm)
Storage capacity	File systems: errors	`strace` for ENOSPC; dynamic instrumentation for ENOSPC; /var/log/messages errs, depending on FS; application log errors
Storage controller	Utilization	`iostat -sxz 1`, sum devices and compare to known IOPS/tput limits per card
Storage controller	Saturation	See storage device saturation, . . .
Storage controller	Errors	See storage device errors, . . .
Network controller	Utilization	Infer from `ip -s link` (or `sar`, or /proc/net/dev) and known controller max tput for its interfaces
Network controller	Saturation	See network interfaces, saturation, . . .
Network controller	Errors	See network interfaces, errors, . . .
CPU interconnect	Utilization	`perf stat` with PMCs for CPU interconnect ports, tput/max
CPU interconnect	Saturation	`perf stat` with PMCs for stall cycles
CPU interconnect	Errors	`perf stat` with PMCs for whatever is available
Memory interconnect	Utilization	`perf stat` with PMCs for memory buses, tput/max; e.g. Intel uncore_imc/data_reads/,uncore_imc/data_writes/; or IPC less than, say, 0.2; PMCs may also have local versus remote counters
Memory interconnect	Saturation	`perf stat` with PMCs for stall cycles

---

[7] This includes tracing functions from different layers of the I/O subsystem: block device, SCSI, SATA, IDE... Some static probes are available (perf(1) scsi and block tracepoint events); otherwise, use dynamic tracing.

Component	Type	Metric
Memory interconnect	Errors	`perf stat` with PMCs for whatever is available; `dmidecode` might have something
I/O interconnect	Utilization	`perf stat` with PMCs for tput/max if available; inference via known tput from iostat/ip/ . . .
I/O interconnect	Saturation	`perf stat` with PMCs for stall cycles
I/O interconnect	Errors	`perf stat` with PMCs for whatever is available

General notes: `uptime` "load average" (or /proc/loadavg) wasn't included for CPU metrics since Linux load averages include tasks in the uninterruptible I/O state.

perf(1): is a powerful observability toolkit that reads PMCs and can also use dynamic and static instrumentation. Its interface is the perf(1) command. See Chapter 13, perf.

PMCs: Performance monitoring counters. See Chapter 6, CPUs, and their usage with perf(1).

I/O interconnect: This includes the CPU-to-I/O controller buses, the I/O controller(s), and device buses (e.g., PCIe).

Dynamic instrumentation: allows custom metrics to be developed. See Chapter 4, Observability Tools, and the examples in later chapters. Dynamic tracing tools for Linux include perf(1) (Chapter 13), Ftrace (Chapter 14), BCC and bpftrace (Chapter 15).

For any environment that imposes resource controls (e.g., cloud computing), check USE for each resource control. These may be encountered—and limit usage—before the hardware resource is fully utilized.

Software Resources

Component	Type	Metric
Kernel mutex	Utilization	With CONFIG_LOCK_STATS=y, /proc/lock_stat `holdtime-total / acquisitions` (also see `holdtime-min`, `holdtime-max`)[8]; dynamic instrumentation of lock functions or instructions (maybe)
Kernel mutex	Saturation	With CONFIG_LOCK_STATS=y, /proc/lock_stat `waittime-total / contentions` (also see `waittime-min`, `waittime-max`); dynamic instrumentation of lock functions, e.g., `mlock.bt` [Gregg 19]; spinning shows up with profiling `perf record -a -g -F 99` ...
Kernel mutex	Errors	Dynamic instrumentation (e.g., recursive mutex enter); other errors can cause kernel lockup/panic, debug with kdump/`crash`

---

[8] Kernel lock analysis used to be via lockmeter, which had an interface called lockstat.

Component	Type	Metric
User mutex	Utilization	`valgrind --tool=drd --exclusive-threshold=` ... (held time); dynamic instrumentation of lock-to-unlock function time[9]
User mutex	Saturation	`valgrind --tool=drd` to infer contention from held time; dynamic instrumentation of synchronization functions for wait time, e.g., `pmlock.bt`; profiling (perf(1)) user stacks for spins
User mutex	Errors	`valgrind --tool=drd` various errors; dynamic instrumentation of pthread_mutex_lock() for EAGAIN, EINVAL, EPERM, EDEADLK, ENOMEM, EOWNERDEAD, . . .
Task capacity	Utilization	`top/htop`, `Tasks` (current); `sysctl kernel.threads-max`, /proc/sys/kernel/threads-max (max)
Task capacity	Saturation	Threads blocking on memory allocation; at this point the page scanner should be running (`sar -B, pgscan*`), else examine using dynamic tracing
Task capacity	Errors	"can't fork()" errors; user-level threads: pthread_create() failures with EAGAIN, EINVAL, . . . ; kernel: dynamic tracing of kernel_thread() ENOMEM
File descriptors	Utilization	System-wide: `sar -v`, `file-nr` versus /proc/sys/fs/file-max; or just /proc/sys/fs/file-nr Per process: echo `/proc/PID/fd/* | wc -w` versus `ulimit -n`
File descriptors	Saturation	This one may not make sense
File descriptors	Errors	`strace` errno == EMFILE on syscalls returning file descriptors (e.g., open(2), accept(2), ...); `opensnoop -x`

A.1   References

[Gregg 13d]   Gregg, B., "USE Method: Linux Performance Checklist," http://www.brendangregg.com/USEmethod/use-linux.html, first published 2013.

---

[9] Since these functions can be very frequent, beware of the performance overhead of tracing every call: an application could slow by 2x or more.

Appendix B

sar Summary

This is a summary of options and metrics from the system activity reporter, sar(1). You can use this to jog your memory about which metrics are under which options. See the man page for the full list.

sar(1) is introduced in Chapter 4, Observability Tools, Section 4.4, and selected options are summarized in later chapters (6, 7, 8, 9, 10).

Option	Metrics	Description
-u -P ALL	**%user %nice %system %iowait %steal %idle**	Per-CPU utilization (-u optional)
-u	**%user %nice %system %iowait %steal %idle**	CPU utilization
-u ALL	... **%irq %soft** %guest %gnice	CPU utilization extended
-m CPU -P ALL	**MHz**	Per-CPU frequency
-q	**runq-sz** plist-sz ldavg-1 ldavg-5 ldavg-15 **blocked**	CPU run-queue size
-w	**proc/s cswch/s**	CPU scheduler events
-B	pgpgin/s pgpgout/s fault/s majflt/s pgfree/s **pgscank/s pgscand/s** pgsteal/s %vmeff	Paging statistics
-H	kbhugfree kbhugused %hugused	Huge pages
-r	kbmemfree **kbavail** kbmemused %memused kbbuffers kbcached kbcommit %commit kbactive kbinact kbdirty	Memory utilization
-S	kbswpfree kbswpused **%swpused** kbswpcad %swpcad	Swap utilization
-W	**pswpin/s pswpout/s**	Swapping statistics

Option	Metrics	Description
-v	dentunusd file-nr inode-nr pty-nr	Kernel tables
-d	**tps rkB/s wkB/s** areq-sz aqu-sz **await** svctm %util	Disk statistics
-n DEV	**rxpck/s txpck/s rxkB/s txkB/s** rxcmp/s txcmp/s rxmcst/s **%ifutil**	Network interface statistics
-n EDEV	**rxerr/s txerr/s coll/s rxdrop/s txdrop/s** txcarr/s rxfram/s rxfifo/s txfifo/s	Network interface errors
-n IP	irec/s fwddgm/s idel/s orq/s asmrq/s asmok/s fragok/s fragcrt/s	IP statistics
-n EIP	ihdrerr/s iadrerr/s iukwnpr/s idisc/s odisc/s onort/s asmf/s fragf/s	IP errors
-n TCP	**active/s passive/s iseg/s oseg/s**	TCP statistics
-n ETCP	atmptf/s estres/s **retrans/s** isegerr/s orsts/s	TCP errors
-n SOCK	totsck tcpsck udpsck rawsck ip-frag tcp-tw	Socket statistics

I have highlighted in bold the key metrics that I look for.

Some sar(1) options may require kernel features enabled (e.g., huge pages), and some metrics were added in later versions of sar(1) (version 12.0.6 is shown here).

Appendix C

bpftrace One-Liners

This appendix contains some handy bpftrace one-liners. Apart from being useful in themselves, they can help you learn bpftrace, one line at a time. Most of these were included in previous chapters. Many may not work right away: They may depend on the presence of certain tracepoints or functions, or on a specific kernel version or configuration.

See Chapter 15, Section 15.2, for an introduction to bpftrace.

CPUs

Trace new processes with arguments:

```
bpftrace -e 'tracepoint:syscalls:sys_enter_execve { join(args->argv); }'
```

Count syscalls by process:

```
bpftrace -e 'tracepoint:raw_syscalls:sys_enter { @[pid, comm] = count(); }'
```

Count syscalls by syscall probe name:

```
bpftrace -e 'tracepoint:syscalls:sys_enter_* { @[probe] = count(); }'
```

Sample running process names at 99 Hertz:

```
bpftrace -e 'profile:hz:99 { @[comm] = count(); }'
```

Sample user and kernel stacks at 49 Hertz, system wide, with the process name:

```
bpftrace -e 'profile:hz:49 { @[kstack, ustack, comm] = count(); }'
```

Sample user-level stacks at 49 Hertz, for PID 189:

```
bpftrace -e 'profile:hz:49 /pid == 189/ { @[ustack] = count(); }'
```

Sample user-level stacks 5 frames deep at 49 Hertz, for PID 189:

```
bpftrace -e 'profile:hz:49 /pid == 189/ { @[ustack(5)] = count(); }'
```

Sample user-level stacks at 49 Hertz, for processes named "mysqld":

```
bpftrace -e 'profile:hz:49 /comm == "mysqld"/ { @[ustack] = count(); }'
```

Count kernel CPU scheduler tracepoints:

```
bpftrace -e 'tracepont:sched:* { @[probe] = count(); }'
```

Count off-CPU kernel stacks for context switch events:

```
bpftrace -e 'tracepont:sched:sched_switch { @[kstack] = count(); }'
```

Count kernel function calls beginning with "vfs_":

```
bpftrace -e 'kprobe:vfs_* { @[func] = count(); }'
```

Trace new threads via pthread_create():

```
bpftrace -e 'u:/lib/x86_64-linux-gnu/libpthread-2.27.so:pthread_create {
    printf("%s by %s (%d)\n", probe, comm, pid); }'
```

Memory

Sum libc malloc() request bytes by user stack and process (high overhead):

```
bpftrace -e 'u:/lib/x86_64-linux-gnu/libc.so.6:malloc {
    @[ustack, comm] = sum(arg0); }'
```

Sum libc malloc() request bytes by user stack for PID 181 (high overhead):

```
bpftrace -e 'u:/lib/x86_64-linux-gnu/libc.so.6:malloc /pid == 181/ {
    @[ustack] = sum(arg0); }'
```

Show libc malloc() request bytes by user stack for PID 181 as a power-of-2 histogram (high overhead):

```
bpftrace -e 'u:/lib/x86_64-linux-gnu/libc.so.6:malloc /pid == 181/ {
    @[ustack] = hist(arg0); }'
```

Sum kernel kmem cache allocation bytes by kernel stack trace:

```
bpftrace -e 't:kmem:kmem_cache_alloc { @bytes[kstack] = sum(args->bytes_alloc); }'
```

Count process heap expansion (brk(2)) by code path:

```
bpftrace -e 'tracepoint:syscalls:sys_enter_brk { @[ustack, comm] = count(); }'
```

Count page faults by process:

```
bpftrace -e 'software:page-fault:1 { @[comm, pid] = count(); }'
```

Count user page faults by user-level stack trace:

```
bpftrace -e 't:exceptions:page_fault_user { @[ustack, comm] = count(); }'
```

Count vmscan operations by tracepoint:

```
bpftrace -e 'tracepoint:vmscan:* { @[probe]++; }'
```

Count swapins by process:

```
bpftrace -e 'kprobe:swap_readpage { @[comm, pid] = count(); }'
```

Count page migrations:

```
bpftrace -e 'tracepoint:migrate:mm_migrate_pages { @ = count(); }'
```

Trace compaction events:

```
bpftrace -e 't:compaction:mm_compaction_begin { time(); }'
```

List USDT probes in libc:

```
bpftrace -l 'usdt:/lib/x86_64-linux-gnu/libc.so.6:*'
```

List kernel kmem tracepoints:

```
bpftrace -l 't:kmem:*'
```

List all memory subsystem (mm) tracepoints:

```
bpftrace -l 't:*:mm_*'
```

File Systems

Trace files opened via openat(2) with process name:

```
bpftrace -e 't:syscalls:sys_enter_openat { printf("%s %s\n", comm,
    str(args->filename)); }'
```

Count read syscalls by syscall type:

```
bpftrace -e 'tracepoint:syscalls:sys_enter_*read* { @[probe] = count(); }'
```

Count write syscalls by syscall type:

```
bpftrace -e 'tracepoint:syscalls:sys_enter_*write* { @[probe] = count(); }'
```

Show the distribution of read() syscall request sizes:

```
bpftrace -e 'tracepoint:syscalls:sys_enter_read { @ = hist(args->count); }'
```

Show the distribution of read() syscall read bytes (and errors):

```
bpftrace -e 'tracepoint:syscalls:sys_exit_read { @ = hist(args->ret); }'
```

Count read() syscall errors by error code:

```
bpftrace -e 't:syscalls:sys_exit_read /args->ret < 0/ { @[- args->ret] = count(); }'
```

Count VFS calls:

```
bpftrace -e 'kprobe:vfs_* { @[probe] = count(); }'
```

Count VFS calls for PID 181:

```
bpftrace -e 'kprobe:vfs_* /pid == 181/ { @[probe] = count(); }'
```

Count ext4 tracepoints:

```
bpftrace -e 'tracepoint:ext4:* { @[probe] = count(); }'
```

Count xfs tracepoints:

```
bpftrace -e 'tracepoint:xfs:* { @[probe] = count(); }'
```

Count ext4 file reads by process name and user-level stack:

```
bpftrace -e 'kprobe:ext4_file_read_iter { @[ustack, comm] = count(); }'
```

Trace ZFS spa_sync() times:

```
bpftrace -e 'kprobe:spa_sync { time("%H:%M:%S ZFS spa_sync()\n"); }'
```

Count dcache references by process name and PID:

```
bpftrace -e 'kprobe:lookup_fast { @[comm, pid] = count(); }'
```

Disks

Count block I/O tracepoints events:

```
bpftrace -e 'tracepoint:block:* { @[probe] = count(); }'
```

Summarize block I/O size as a histogram:

```
bpftrace -e 't:block:block_rq_issue { @bytes = hist(args->bytes); }'
```

Count block I/O request user stack traces:

```
bpftrace -e 't:block:block_rq_issue { @[ustack] = count(); }'
```

Count block I/O type flags:

```
bpftrace -e 't:block:block_rq_issue { @[args->rwbs] = count(); }'
```

Trace block I/O errors with device and I/O type:

```
bpftrace -e 't:block:block_rq_complete /args->error/ {
    printf("dev %d type %s error %d\n", args->dev, args->rwbs, args->error); }'
```

Count SCSI opcodes:

```
bpftrace -e 't:scsi:scsi_dispatch_cmd_start { @opcode[args->opcode] =
    count(); }'
```

Count SCSI result codes:

```
bpftrace -e 't:scsi:scsi_dispatch_cmd_done { @result[args->result] = count(); }'
```

Count SCSI driver function calls:

```
bpftrace -e 'kprobe:scsi* { @[func] = count(); }'
```

Networking

Count socket accept(2)s by PID and process name:

```
bpftrace -e 't:syscalls:sys_enter_accept* { @[pid, comm] = count(); }'
```

Count socket connect(2)s by PID and process name:

```
bpftrace -e 't:syscalls:sys_enter_connect { @[pid, comm] = count(); }'
```

Count socket connect(2)s by user stack trace:

```
bpftrace -e 't:syscalls:sys_enter_connect { @[ustack, comm] = count(); }'
```

Count socket send/receives by direction, on-CPU PID, and process name:

```
bpftrace -e 'k:sock_sendmsg,k:sock_recvmsg { @[func, pid, comm] = count(); }'
```

Count socket send/receive bytes by on-CPU PID and process name:

```
bpftrace -e 'kr:sock_sendmsg,kr:sock_recvmsg /(int32)retval > 0/ { @[pid, comm] =
    sum((int32)retval); }'
```

Count TCP connects by on-CPU PID and process name:

```
bpftrace -e 'k:tcp_v*_connect { @[pid, comm] = count(); }'
```

Count TCP accepts by on-CPU PID and process name:

```
bpftrace -e 'k:inet_csk_accept { @[pid, comm] = count(); }'
```

Count TCP send/receives by on-CPU PID and process name:

```
bpftrace -e 'k:tcp_sendmsg,k:tcp_recvmsg { @[func, pid, comm] = count(); }'
```

TCP send bytes as a histogram:

```
bpftrace -e 'k:tcp_sendmsg { @send_bytes = hist(arg2); }'
```

TCP receive bytes as a histogram:

```
bpftrace -e 'kr:tcp_recvmsg /retval >= 0/ { @recv_bytes = hist(retval); }'
```

Count TCP retransmits by type and remote host (assumes IPv4):

```
bpftrace -e 't:tcp:tcp_retransmit_* { @[probe, ntop(2, args->saddr)] = count(); }'
```

Count all TCP functions (adds high overhead to TCP):

```
bpftrace -e 'k:tcp_* { @[func] = count(); }'
```

Count UDP send/receives by on-CPU PID and process name:

```
bpftrace -e 'k:udp*_sendmsg,k:udp*_recvmsg { @[func, pid, comm] = count(); }'
```

UDP send bytes as a histogram:

```
bpftrace -e 'k:udp_sendmsg { @send_bytes = hist(arg2); }'
```

UDP receive bytes as a histogram:

```
bpftrace -e 'kr:udp_recvmsg /retval >= 0/ { @recv_bytes = hist(retval); }'
```

Count transmit kernel stack traces:

```
bpftrace -e 't:net:net_dev_xmit { @[kstack] = count(); }'
```

Show receive CPU histogram for each device:

```
bpftrace -e 't:net:netif_receive_skb { @[str(args->name)] = lhist(cpu, 0, 128, 1); }'
```

Count ieee80211 layer functions (adds high overhead to packets):

```
bpftrace -e 'k:ieee80211_* { @[func] = count()'
```

Count all ixgbevf device driver functions (adds high overhead to ixgbevf):

```
bpftrace -e 'k:ixgbevf_* { @[func] = count(); }'
```

Count all iwl device driver tracepoints (adds high overhead to iwl):

```
bpftrace -e 't:iwlwifi:*,t:iwlwifi_io:* { @[probe] = count(); }'
```

Appendix D

Solutions to
Selected Exercises

The following are suggested solutions to selected exercises.[1]

Chapter 2—Methodology

Q. What is latency?

A. A measure of time, usually time waiting for something to be done. In the IT industry, the term may be used differently depending on context.

Chapter 3—Operating Systems

Q. List the reasons why a thread would leave the CPU.

A. Blocked on I/O, blocked on a lock, call to yield, expired time slice, preempted by another thread, device interrupt, exiting.

Chapter 6—CPUs

Q. Calculate the load average . . .

A. 34

Chapter 7—Memory

Q. Using Linux terminology, what is the difference between paging and swapping?

A. Paging is the movement of memory pages; swapping is the movement of pages to and from swap devices/files.

---

[1] If you manage a training course where students receive a copy of this text, contact either the publisher or myself for a full list of exercise solutions.

Q. Describe memory utilization and saturation.

A. For memory capacity, utilization is the amount that is in use and not available, measured against the total usable memory. This can be presented as a percentage, similar to file system capacity. Saturation is a measure of the demand for available memory beyond the size of memory, which usually invokes a kernel routine to free memory to satisfy this demand.

Chapter 8—File Systems

Q. What is the difference between logical I/O and physical I/O?

A. Logical I/O is to the file system interface; physical I/O is to the storage devices (disks).

Q. Explain how file system copy-on-write can improve performance.

A. Since random writes can be written to a new location, they can be grouped (by increasing I/O size) and written out sequentially. Both of these factors usually improve performance, depending on the storage device type.

Chapter 9—Disks

Q. Describe what happens when disks are overloaded with work, including the effect on application performance.

A. The disks run at a continual high utilization rate (up to 100%) with a high degree of saturation (queueing). Their I/O latency is increased due to the likelihood of queueing (which can be modeled). If the application is performing file system or disk I/O, the increased latency *may* hurt application performance, provided it is a synchronous I/O type: reads, or synchronous writes. It must also occur during a critical application code path, such as while a request is serviced, and not an asynchronous background task (which may only *indirectly* cause poor application performance). Usually back pressure from the increased I/O latency will keep the rate of I/O requests in check and not cause an unbounded increase in latency.

Chapter 11—Cloud Computing

Q. Describe physical system observability from an OS-virtualized guest.

A. Depending on the host kernel implementation, the guest can see high-level metrics of all physical resources, including CPUs and disks, and notice when they are utilized by other tenants. Metrics that leak user data should be blocked by the kernel. For example, utilization for a CPU may be observable (say, 50%), but not the process IDs and process names from other tenants that are causing it.

Appendix E

Systems Performance
Who's Who

It can be useful to know who created the technologies that we use. This is a list of who's who in the field of systems performance, based on the technologies in this book. This was inspired by the Unix who's who list in [Libes 89]. Apologies to those who are missing or misappropriated. If you wish to dig further into the people and history, see the chapter references and the names listed in the Linux source, both the Linux repository history and the MAINTAINERS file in the Linux source code. The Acknowledgments section of my BPF book [Gregg 19] also lists various technologies, in particular extended BPF, BCC, bpftrace, kprobes, and uprobes, and the people behind them.

John Allspaw: Capacity planning [Allspaw 08].

Gene M. Amdahl: Early work on computer scalability [Amdahl 67].

Jens Axboe: CFQ I/O Scheduler, fio, blktrace, io_uring.

Brenden Blanco: BCC.

Jeff Bonwick: Invented kernel slab allocation, co-invented user-level slab allocation, co-invented ZFS, kstat, first developed mpstat.

Daniel Borkmann: Co-creator and maintainer of extended BPF.

Roch Bourbonnais: Sun Microsystems systems performance expert.

Tim Bray: Authored the Bonnie disk I/O micro-benchmark, known for XML.

Bryan Cantrill: Co-created DTrace; Oracle ZFS Storage Appliance Analytics.

Rémy Card: Primary developer for the ext2 and ext3 file systems.

Nadia Yvette Chambers: Linux hugetlbfs.

Guillaume Chazarain: iotop(1) for Linux.

Adrian Cockcroft: Performance books [Cockcroft 95][Cockcroft 98], Virtual Adrian (SE Toolkit).

Tim Cook: nicstat(1) for Linux, and enhancements.

Alan Cox: Linux network stack performance.

Mathieu Desnoyers: Linux Trace Toolkit (LTTng), kernel tracepoints, main author of userspace RCU.

Frank Ch. Eigler: Lead developer for SystemTap.

Richard Elling: Static performance tuning methodology.

Julia Evans: Performance and debugging documentation and tools.

Kevin Robert Elz: DNLC.

Roger Faulkner: Wrote /proc for UNIX System V, thread implementation for Solaris, and the truss(1) system call tracer.

Thomas Gleixner: Various Linux kernel performance work including hrtimers.

Sebastian Godard: sysstat package for Linux, which contains numerous performance tools including iostat(1), mpstat(1), pidstat(1), nfsiostat(1), cifsiostat(1), and an enhanced version of sar(1), sadc(8), sadf(1) (see the metrics in Appendix B).

Sasha Goldshtein: BPF tools (argdist(8), trace(8), etc.), BCC contributions.

Brendan Gregg: nicstat(1), DTraceToolkit, ZFS L2ARC, BPF tools (execsnoop, biosnoop, ext4slower, tcptop, etc.), BCC/bpftrace contributions, USE method, heat maps (latency, utilization, subsecond-offset), flame graphs, flame scope , this book and previous ones [Gregg 11a][Gregg 19], other perf work.

Dr. Neil Gunther: Universal Scalability Law, ternary plots for CPU utilization, performance books [Gunther 97].

Jeffrey Hollingsworth: Dynamic instrumentation [Hollingsworth 94].

Van Jacobson: traceroute(8), pathchar, TCP/IP performance.

Raj Jain: Systems performance theory [Jain 91].

Jerry Jelinek: Solaris Zones.

Bill Joy: vmstat(1), BSD virtual memory work, TCP/IP performance, FFS.

Andi Kleen: Intel performance, numerous contributions to Linux.

Christoph Lameter: SLUB allocator.

William LeFebvre: Wrote the first version of top(1), inspiring many other tools.

David Levinthal: Intel processor performance expert.

John Levon: OProfile.

Mike Loukides: First book on Unix systems performance [Loukides 90], which either began or encouraged the tradition of resource-based analysis: CPU, memory, disk, network.

Robert Love: Linux kernel performance work, including for preemption.

Mary Marchini: libstapsdt: dynamic USDT for various languages.

Jim Mauro: Co-author of Solaris Performance and Tools [McDougall 06a], DTrace: Dynamic Tracing in Oracle Solaris, Mac OS X, and FreeBSD [Gregg 11].

Richard McDougall: Solaris microstate accounting, co-author of Solaris Performance and Tools [McDougall 06a].

Marshall Kirk McKusick: FFS, work on BSD.

Arnaldo Carvalho de Melo: Linux perf(1) maintainer.

Barton Miller: Dynamic instrumentation [Hollingsworth 94].

David S. Miller: Linux networking maintainer and SPARC maintainer. Numerous performance improvements, and support for extended BPF.

Cary Millsap: Method R.

Ingo Molnar: O(1) scheduler, completely fair scheduler, voluntary kernel preemption, ftrace, perf, and work on real-time preemption, mutexes, futexes, scheduler profiling, work queues.

Richard J. Moore: DProbes, kprobes.

Andrew Morton: fadvise, read-ahead.

Gian-Paolo D. Musumeci: *System Performance Tuning*, 2nd Ed. [Musumeci 02].

Mike Muuss: ping(8).

Shailabh Nagar: Delay accounting, taskstats.

Rich Pettit: SE Toolkit.

Nick Piggin: Linux scheduler domains.

Bill Pijewski: Solaris vfsstat(1M), ZFS I/O throttling.

Dennis Ritchie: Unix, and its original performance features: process priorities, swapping, buffer cache, etc.

Alastair Robertson: Created bpftrace.

Steven Rostedt: Ftrace, KernelShark, real-time Linux, adaptive spinning mutexes, Linux tracing support.

Rusty Russell: Original futexes, various Linux kernel work.

Michael Shapiro: Co-created DTrace.

Aleksey Shipilëv: Java performance expert.

Balbir Singh: Linux memory resource controller, delay accounting, taskstats, cgroupstats, CPU accounting.

Yonghong Song: BTF, and extended BPF and BCC work.

Alexei Starovoitov: Co-creator and maintainer of extended BPF.

Ken Thompson: Unix, and its original performance features: process priorities, swapping, buffer cache, etc.

Martin Thompson: Mechanical sympathy.

Linus Torvalds: The Linux kernel and numerous core components necessary for systems performance, Linux I/O scheduler, Git.

Arjan van de Ven: latencytop, PowerTOP, irqbalance, work on Linux scheduler profiling.

Nitsan Wakart: Java performance expert.

Tobias Waldekranz: ply (first high-level BPF tracer).

Dag Wieers: dstat.

Karim Yaghmour: LTT, push for tracing in Linux.

Jovi Zhangwei: ktap.

Tom Zanussi: Ftrace hist triggers.

Peter Zijlstra: Adaptive spinning mutex implementation, hardirq callbacks framework, other Linux performance work.

E.1   References

[**Amdahl 67**] Amdahl, G., "Validity of the Single Processor Approach to Achieving Large Scale Computing Capabilities," *AFIPS*, 1967.

[**Libes 89**] Libes, D., and Ressler, S., *Life with UNIX: A Guide for Everyone*, Prentice Hall, 1989.

[**Loukides 90**] Loukides, M., *System Performance Tuning*, O'Reilly, 1990.

[**Hollingsworth 94**] Hollingsworth, J., Miller, B., and Cargille, J., "Dynamic Program Instrumentation for Scalable Performance Tools," *Scalable High-Performance Computing Conference (SHPCC)*, May 1994.

[**Cockcroft 95**] Cockcroft, A., *Sun Performance and Tuning*, Prentice Hall, 1995.

[**Cockcroft 98**] Cockcroft, A., and Pettit, R., *Sun Performance and Tuning: Java and the Internet*, Prentice Hall, 1998.

[**Musumeci 02**] Musumeci, G. D., and Loukidas, M., *System Performance Tuning*, 2nd Edition, O'Reilly, 2002.

[**McDougall 06a**] McDougall, R., Mauro, J., and Gregg, B., *Solaris Performance and Tools: DTrace and MDB Techniques for Solaris 10 and OpenSolaris*, Prentice Hall, 2006.

[**Gunther 07**] Gunther, N., *Guerrilla Capacity Planning*, Springer, 2007.

[**Allspaw 08**] Allspaw, J., *The Art of Capacity Planning*, O'Reilly, 2008.

[**Gregg 11a**] Gregg, B., and Mauro, J., *DTrace: Dynamic Tracing in Oracle Solaris, Mac OS X and FreeBSD*, Prentice Hall, 2011.

[**Gregg 19**] Gregg, B., *BPF Performance Tools: Linux System and Application Observability*, Addison-Wesley, 2019.

Glossary

ABI Application binary interface.

ACK TCP acknowledgment.

adaptive mutex A mutex (mutual exclusion) synchronization lock type. See Chapter 5, Applications, Section 5.2.5, Concurrency and Parallelism.

address A memory location.

address space A virtual memory context. See Chapter 7, Memory.

AMD A processor vendor.

API Application programming interface.

application A program, typically user-level.

ARM A processor vendor.

ARP Address resolution protocol.

array A set of values. This is a data type for programming languages. Low-level languages typically store arrays in a contiguous range of memory, and value index refers to their offset.

ASIC Application-specific integrated circuit.

associative array A data type for programming languages where values are referenced by an arbitrary key or multiple keys.

AT&T The American Telephone and Telegraph Company, which included Bell Laboratories, where Unix was developed.

back end   Refers to data storage and infrastructure components. A web server is back-end software. See front end.

balanced system   A system without a bottleneck.

bandwidth   The frequency range for a communication channel, measured in Hertz. In computing, bandwidth is used to describe the maximum transfer rate for a communication channel. It is also frequently *misused* to describe the current throughput (which is wrong).

BCC   BPF compiler collection. BCC is a project that includes a BPF compiler framework, as well as many BPF performance tools. See Chapter 15.

benchmark   In computing, a benchmark is a tool that performs a workload experiment and measures its performance: the benchmark result. These are commonly used for evaluating the performance of different options.

BIOS   Basic Input/Output System: firmware used to initialize computer hardware and manage the booting process.

bottleneck   Something that limits performance.

BPF   Berkeley Packet Filter: a lightweight in-kernel technology from 1992 created to improve the performance of packet filtering. Since 2014 it has been extended to become a general-purpose execution environment (see eBPF).

BSD   Berkeley Software Distribution, a derivative of Unix.

buffer   A region of memory used for temporary data.

byte   A unit of digital data. This book follows the industry standard where one byte equals eight bits, where a bit is a zero or a one.

C   The C programming language.

cache hit   A request for data that can be returned from the contents of the cache.

cache miss   A request for data that was not found in the cache.

cache warmth   See Hot, Cold, and Warm Caches in Section 2.3.14, Caching, in Chapter 2, Methodologies.

CDN   Content delivery network.

client   A consumer of a network service, referring to either the client host or the client application.

command   A program executed at the shell.

concurrency   See Section 5.2.5, Concurrency and Parallelism, in Chapter 5, Applications.

contention   Competition for a resource.

core   An execution pipeline on a processor. These may be exposed on an OS as single CPUs, or via hyperthreads as multiple CPUs.

CPI   Cycles per instruction. See Chapter 6, CPUs.

CPU   Central processing unit. This term refers to the set of functional units that execute instructions, including the registers and arithmetic logic unit (ALU). It is now often used to refer to either the processor or a virtual CPU.

CPU cross call   A call by a CPU to request work from others on a multi-CPU system. Cross calls may be made for system-wide events such as CPU cache coherency calls. See Chapter 6, CPUs. Linux terms these "SMP calls."

CPU cycle   A unit of time based on the clock rate of the processor: for 2 GHz, each cycle is 0.5 ns. A cycle itself is an electrical signal, the rising or falling of voltage, used to trigger digital logic.

cross call   See CPU cross call.

CSV   The Comma Separated Values file type.

CTSS   Compatible Time-Sharing System, one of the first time-sharing systems.

daemon   A system program that continually runs to provide a service.

datagram   See segment.

debuginfo file   A symbol and debug information file, used by debuggers and profilers.

DEC   Digital Equipment Corporation.

disk   A physical storage device. Also see HDD and SSD.

disk controller   A component that manages directly attached disks, making them accessible to the system, either directly or mapped as virtual disks. Disk controllers may be built into the system main board, included as expansion cards, or built into storage arrays. They support one or more storage interface types (e.g., SCSI, SATA, SAS) and are also commonly called *host bus adaptors* (HBAs), along with the interface type, for example, *SAS HBA*.

DNS   Domain Name Service.

DRAM   Dynamic random-access memory, a type of volatile memory in common use as main memory.

duplex   Simultaneous bi-directional communication.

dynamic instrumentation   Dynamic instrumentation or dynamic tracing is a technology that can instrument any software event, including function calls and returns, by live modification of instruction text and the insertion of temporary tracing instructions.

dynamic tracing   This can refer to the software that implements dynamic instrumentation.

eBPF   Extended BPF (see BPF). The eBPF abbreviation originally described the extended BPF from 2014, which updated the register size, instruction set, added map storage, and limited kernel calls. By 2015, it was decided to call eBPF just BPF.

ECC   Error-correcting code. An algorithm for detecting errors and fixing some types of errors (usually single-bit errors).

ELF   Executable and Linkable Format: a common file format for executable programs.

errno   A variable containing the last error as a number following a standard (POSIX.1-2001).

Ethernet   A set of standards for networking at the physical and data link layers.

expander card   A physical device (card) connected to the system, usually to provide an additional I/O controller.

file descriptor   An identifier for a program to use in referencing an open file.

firmware   Embedded device software.

flame graph   A visualization for a set of stack traces. See Chapter 2, Methodologies.

FPGA   Field-programmable gate array. A reprogrammable integrated circuit used in computing to typically accelerate a specific operation.

frame   A message at the data link layer of the OSI networking model (see Section 10.2.3, Protocol Stack).

FreeBSD   An open source, Unix-like, operating system.

front end   Refers to end-user interface and presentation software. A web application is front-end software. See back end.

fsck   The file system check command is used to repair file systems after system failure, such as due to a power outage or kernel panic. This process can take hours.

Gbps   Gigabits per second.

GPU   Graphics processing unit. These can be used for other workloads as well, such as machine learning.

GUI   Graphical user interface.

HDD   Hard disk drive, a rotational magnetic storage device. See Chapter 9, Disks.

Hertz (Hz)   Cycles per second.

hit ratio   Often used to describe cache performance: the ratio of cache hits versus hits plus misses, usually expressed as a percentage. Higher is better.

host   A system connected to the network. Also called a network *node*.

HTTP   Hyper Text Transfer Protocol.

hyperthread   Intel's implementation of SMT. This is a technology for scaling CPUs, allowing the OS to create multiple virtual CPUs for one core and schedule work on them, which the processor attempts to process in parallel.

ICMP   Internet Control Message Protocol. Used by ping(1) (ICMP echo request/reply).

I/O   Input/output.

IO Visor   The Linux Foundation project that hosts the bcc and bpftrace repositories on GitHub, and facilitates collaboration among BPF developers at different companies.

IOPS   I/O operations per second, a measure of the rate of I/O.

Intel   A processor vendor.

instance   A virtual server. Cloud computing provides server instances.

IP   Internet Protocol. Main versions are IPv4 and IPv6. See Chapter 10, Network.

IPC   Either means: instructions per cycle, a low-level CPU performance metric, or inter-process communication, a means for processes to exchange data. Sockets are an inter-process communication mechanism.

IRIX   A Unix-derived operating system by Silicon Graphics, Inc. (SGI).

IRQ   Interrupt request, a hardware signal to the processor to request work. See Chapter 3, Operating Systems.

Kbytes   Kilobytes. The International System of Units (SI) defines a kilobyte as 1000 bytes, but in computing a kilobyte is typically 1024 bytes (which SI terms a kibibyte). Throughout this book, tools that report Kbytes are usually using the definition of 1024 (210) bytes.

kernel   The core program on a system that runs in privileged mode to manage resources and user-level processes.

kernel-land   Kernel software.

kernel-level   The processor privilege mode that kernel execution uses.

kernel-space   The address space of the kernel.

kprobes   A Linux kernel technology for kernel-level dynamic instrumentation.

latency   Time spent waiting. In computing performance it is often used to describe resource I/O time. Latency is important for performance analysis, because it is often the most effective measure of a performance issue. Where exactly it is measured can be ambiguous without further qualifiers. For example, "disk latency" could mean time spent waiting on a disk driver queue only or, from an application, it could mean the entire time waiting for disk I/O to complete, both queued and service time. Latency is limited by a lower bound, bandwidth by an upper bound.

local disks   Disks that are connected directly to the server and are managed by the server. These include disks inside the server case and those attached directly via a storage transport.

logical processor   Another name for a *virtual CPU*. See Chapter 6, CPUs.

LRU   Least recently used. See Section 2.3.14, Caching, in Chapter 2, Methodologies.

main board   The circuit board that houses the processors and system interconnect; also called the *system board*.

main memory   The primary memory storage of a system, usually implemented as DRAM.

major fault   A memory access fault that was serviced from storage devices (disks). See Chapter 3, Operating Systems.

malloc   Memory allocate. This usually refers to the function performing allocation.

Mbps   Megabits per second.

Mbytes   Megabytes. The International System of Units (SI) defines a megabyte as 1000000 bytes, but in computing a megabyte is typically 1048576 bytes (which SI terms a mebibyte). Throughout this book, tools that report Mbytes are usually using the definition of 1048576 (220) bytes.

memory   See main memory.

micro-benchmark   A benchmark for measuring single or simple operations.

minor fault   A memory access fault that was serviced from main memory. See Chapter 3, Operating Systems.

MMU   Memory management unit. This is responsible for presenting memory to a CPU and for performing virtual-to-physical address translation.

mutex   A mutual exclusion lock. They can become a source of performance bottlenecks, and are often investigated for performance problems. See Chapter 5, Applications.

mysqld   The daemon for the MySQL database.

NVMe   Non-Volatile Memory express: a PCIe bus specification for storage devices.

observability   The ability for a computing system to be observed. This includes the practice and tools used to analyze the state of computing systems.

off-CPU   This term refers to a thread that is not currently running on a CPU, and so is "off-CPU," due to either having blocked on I/O, a lock, a voluntary sleep, or other event.

on-CPU   This term refers to a thread that is currently running on a CPU.

operation rate   Operations per interval (e.g., operations per second), which may include non-I/O operations.

OS   Operating System. The collection of software including the kernel for managing resources and user-level processes.

packet   A network message at the network layer of the OSI networking model (see Section 10.2.3).

page   A chunk of memory managed by the kernel and processor. All memory used by the system is broken up into pages for reference and management. Typical page sizes include 4 Kbytes and 2 Mbytes (depending on the processor).

pagefault   A system trap that occurs when a program references a memory location where the virtual memory is not currently mapped to a physical backing page. This is a normal consequence of an on-demand allocation memory model.

pagein/pageout   Functions performed by an operating system (kernel) to move chunks of memory (pages) to and from external storage devices.

parallel   See Section 5.2.5, Concurrency and Parallelism, in Chapter 5, Applications.

PC   Program counter, a CPU register that points to the currently executing instruction.

PCID   Process-context ID, a processor/MMU feature to tag virtual address entries with the process ID to avoid flushing on context switches.

PCIe   Peripheral Component Interconnect Express: a bus standard commonly used for storage and network controllers.

PDP   Programmed Data Processor, a minicomputer series made by Digital Equipment Corporation (DEC).

PEBS   Precise event-based sampling (aka *processor* event-based sampling), an Intel processor technology for use with PMCs to provide more precise recording of CPU state during events.

Performance engineer   A technical staff member who works primarily on computer performance: planning, evaluations, analysis, and improvements. See Chapter 1, Introduction, Section 1.3, Activities.

PID   Process identifier. The operating system unique numeric identifier for a process.

PMCs   Performance Monitoring Counters: special hardware registers on the processor that can be programmed to instrument low-level CPU events: cycles, stall cycles, instructions, memory loads/stores, etc.

POSIX   Portable Operating System Interface, a family of related standards managed by the IEEE to define a Unix API. This includes a file system interface as used by applications, provided via system calls or system libraries built upon system calls.

process   A running instance of a program. Multi-tasked operating systems can execute multiple processes concurrently, and can run multiple instances of the same program as different processes. A process contains one or more threads for execution on CPUs.

processor ring   A protection mode for the CPU.

production   A term used in technology to describe the workload of real customer requests, and the environment that processes it. Many companies also have a "test" environment with synthetic workloads for testing things before production deployment.

profiling   A technique to collect data that characterizes the performance of a target. A common profiling technique is timed sampling (see sampling).

PSI   Linux pressure stall information, used for identifying performance issues caused by resources.

RCU   Read-copy-update: a Linux synchronization mechanism.

real-time workload   One that has fixed latency requirements, usually low latency.

registers   Small storage locations on a CPU, used directly from CPU instructions for data processing.

remote disks   Disks (including virtual disks) that are used by a server but are connected to a remote system.

RFC   Request For Comments: a public document by the Internet Engineering Task Force (IETF) to share networking standards and best practices. RFCs are used to define networking protocols: RFC 793 defines the TCP protocol.

RSS   Resident set size: a measure of main memory.

ROI   Return on investment, a business metric.

run queue   A CPU scheduler queue of tasks waiting their turn to run on a CPU. In reality the queue may be implemented as a tree structure, but the term run queue is still used.

RX   Receive (used in networking).

sampling   An observability method for understanding a target by taking a subset of measurements: a sample.

script   In computing, an executable program, usually short and in a high-level language.

SCSI   Small Computer System Interface. An interface standard for storage devices.

sector   A data unit size for storage devices, commonly 512 bytes or 4 Kbytes. See Chapter 9, Disks.

segment   A message at the transport layer of the OSI networking model (see Section 10.2.3, Protocol Stack).

server   In networking, a network host that provides a service for network clients, such as an HTTP or database server. The term *server* can also refer to a physical system.

shell   A command-line interpreter and scripting language.

SLA   Service level agreement.

SMP   Symmetric multiprocessing, a multiprocessor architecture where multiple similar CPUs share the same main memory.

SMT   Simultaneous multithreading, a processor feature to run multiple threads on cores. See hyperthread.

SNMP   Simple Network Management Protocol.

socket   A software abstraction representing a network endpoint for communication.

Solaris   A Unix-derived operating system originally developed by Sun Microsystems, it was known for scalability and reliability, and was popular in enterprise environments.

Since the acquisition of Sun by Oracle Corporation, it has been renamed Oracle Solaris.

SONET   Synchronous optical networking, a physical layer protocol for optical fibers.

SPARC   A processor architecture (from *s*calable *p*rocessor *arc*hitecture).

SRE   Site reliability engineer: a technical staff member focused on infrastructure and reliability. SREs work on performance as part of incident response, under short time constraints.

SSD   Solid-state drive, a storage device typically based on flash memory. See Chapter 9, Disks.

SSH   Secure Shell. An encrypted remote shell protocol.

stack   In the context of observability tools, stack is usually short for "stack trace."

stack frame   A data structure containing function state information, including the return address and function arguments.

stack trace   A call stack composed of multiple stack frames spanning the code path ancestry. These are often inspected as part of performance analysis, particularly CPU profiling.

static instrumentation/tracing   Instrumentation of software with precompiled probe points. See Chapter 4, Observability Tools.

storage array   A collection of disks housed in an enclosure, which can then be attached to a system. Storage arrays typically provide various features to improve disk reliability and performance.

struct   A structured object, usually from the C programming language.

SunOS   Sun Microsystems Operating System. This was later rebranded as Solaris.

SUT   System under test.

SVG   The Scalable Vector Graphs file format.

SYN   TCP synchronize.

syscall   See system call.

system call   The interface for processes to request privileged actions from the kernel. See Chapter 3, Operating Systems.

task   A Linux runnable entity, which may be a process, a thread from a multithreaded process, or a kernel thread. See Chapter 3, Operating Systems.

TCP   Transmission Control Protocol. Originally defined in RFC 793. See Chapter 10, Network.

TENEX   TEN-EXtended operating system, based on TOPS-10 for the PDP-10.

thread   A software abstraction for an instance of program execution, which can be scheduled to run on a CPU. The kernel has multiple threads, and a process contains one or more. See Chapter 3, Operating Systems.

throughput   For network communication devices, throughput commonly refers to the data transfer rate in either bits per second or bytes per second. Throughput may also refer to I/O completions per second (IOPS) when used with statistical analysis, especially for targets of study.

TLB   Translation Lookaside Buffer. A cache for memory translation on virtual memory systems, used by the MMU (see MMU).

TLS   Transport Layer Security: used to encrypt network requests.

TPU   Tensor processing unit. An AI accelerator ASIC for machine learning developed by Google, and named after TensorFlow (a software platform for machine learning).

tracepoints   A Linux kernel technology for providing static instrumentation.

tracer   A tracing tool. See tracing.

tracing   Event-based observability.

tunable   Short for tunable parameter.

TX   Transmit (used in networking).

UDP   User Datagram Protocol. Originally defined in RFC 768. See Chapter 10, Network.

uprobes   A Linux kernel technology for user-level dynamic instrumentation.

us   Microseconds. This should be abbreviated as µs; however, you will often see it as "us," especially in the output of ASCII-based performance tools. (Note that vmstat(8)'s output, included many times in this book, includes a us column, short for user time.)

µs   Microseconds. See "us."

USDT   User-land Statically Defined Tracing. This involves the placement of static instrumentation in application code by the programmer, at locations to provide useful probes.

user-land   This refers to user-level software and files, including executable programs in /usr/bin, /lib, etc.

user-level   The processor privilege mode that user-land execution uses. This is a lower privilege level than the kernel, and one that denies direct access to resources, forcing user-level software to request access to them via the kernel.

user-space   The address space of the user-level processes.

variable   A named storage object used by programming languages.

vCPU   A virtual CPU. Modern processors can expose multiple virtual CPUs per core (e.g., Intel Hyper-Threading).

VFS   Virtual file system. An abstraction used by the kernel to support different file system types.

virtual memory   An abstraction of main memory that supports multitasking and over-subscription.

VMS   Virtual Memory System, an operating system by DEC.

workload   This describes the requests for a system or resource.

x86   A processor architecture based on the Intel 8086.

ZFS   A combined file system and volume manager created by Sun Microsystems.

Index

G

Photo by Marvent/Shutterstock

VIDEO TRAINING FOR THE **IT PROFESSIONAL**

LEARN QUICKLY
Learn a new technology in just hours. Video training can teach more in less time, and material is generally easier to absorb and remember.

WATCH AND LEARN
Instructors demonstrate concepts so you see technology in action.

TEST YOURSELF
Our Complete Video Courses offer self-assessment quizzes throughout.

CONVENIENT
Most videos are streaming with an option to download lessons for offline viewing.

Learn more, browse our store, and watch free, sample lessons at
informit.com/video

Save 50%* off the list price of video courses with discount code **VIDBOB**

Photo by izusek/gettyimages

Register Your Product at informit.com/register

Access additional benefits and **save 35%** on your next purchase

- Automatically receive a coupon for 35% off your next purchase, valid for 30 days. Look for your code in your InformIT cart or the Manage Codes section of your account page.

- Download available product updates.

- Access bonus material if available.*

- Check the box to hear from us and receive exclusive offers on new editions and related products.

Registration benefits vary by product. Benefits will be listed on your account page under Registered Products.

InformIT.com—The Trusted Technology Learning Source

InformIT is the online home of information technology brands at Pearson, the world's foremost education company. At InformIT.com, you can:

- Shop our books, eBooks, software, and video training
- Take advantage of our special offers and promotions (informit.com/promotions)
- Sign up for special offers and content newsletter (informit.com/newsletters)
- Access thousands of free chapters and video lessons

Connect with InformIT—Visit informit.com/community

Addison-Wesley • Adobe Press • Cisco Press • Microsoft Press • Pearson IT Certification • Que • Sams • Peachpit Press

Ⓟ Pearson